Finance and accounting for busine

Bob Ryan

Finance and accounting for business

Second edition

SOUTH-WESTERN
CENGAGE Learning

Australia • Brazil • Japan • Korea • Mexico • Singapore • Spain • United Kingdom • United States

Finance and Accounting for Business
Bob Ryan

Publishing Director: John Yates

Publisher: Patrick Bond

Development Editor: Leandra Paoli

Content Project Editor: Jamina Ward

Manufacturing Manager: Helen Mason

Senior Production Controller: Maeve Healy

Marketing Manager: Anne-Marie Scoones

Typesetter: ICC Macmillan Inc.

Cover design: Adam Renvoize

Text design: Design Deluxe, Bath, UK

For product information and technology assistance, contact **emea.info@cengage.com.**

For permission to use material from this text or product, and for permission queries, email **clsuk.permissions@cengage.com**

British Library Cataloguing-in-Publication Data
A catalogue record for this book is available from the British Library.

ISBN: 978-1-84480-897-7

Cengage Learning EMEA
High Holborn House, 50-51 Bedford Row
London WC1R 4LR

Cengage Learning products are represented in Canada by Nelson Education Ltd.

For your lifelong learning solutions, visit **www.cengage.co.uk**

Purchase e-books or e-chapters at: **www.estore.bized.co.uk**

Printed by Seng Lee Press
1 2 3 4 5 6 7 8 9 10 – 10 09 08

Brief contents

Part 1   Introduction 1

1   The role of accounting and finance in business 3

Part 2   Financial accounting 31

2   Introduction to financial accounting 33

3   Building the accounts 54

4   Cash flow statements 81

5   Principles of financial accounting 101

6   Accounting for companies 139

7   The analysis of accounting information 174

Part 3   Management accounting and control 233

8   The principles of cost and revenue measurement 235

9   Cash forecasting, business planning and management control 280

10   Cost management and pricing 323

11   The management of working capital 359

Part 4   Finance and financial markets 391

12   Investment appraisal 393

13   The nature of the financial markets 434

14   Market measures of performance and value 471

Detailed contents

Preface xi
Walk-through tour xvi
Supplementary resources xviii
Acknowledgements xix

Part 1 Introduction 1

1 The role of accounting and finance in business 3

Introduction 3
The context and history of accounting and finance 4
Different types of business organisation 9
Business objectives and the decision-oriented approach 17
The purpose and characteristics of accounting information 19
The concept of income and the measurement of profit 24
The difference between financial and management accounting 25

Part 2 Financial accounting 31

2 Introduction to financial accounting 33

The first principles of financial accounting 34
Creating the balance sheet and income statement – a case exercise 43
The extended trial balance (ETB) 47
Two further principles 48
How to produce a set of simple accounts 49

3 Building the accounts 54

A case study in business start-up 55
Accounting for the second and subsequent years 61
Double-entry bookkeeping 66

4 Cash flow statements 81

Introduction 81
The measurement of cash flow 82
Preparing the cash flow statement 84
Laundering the accounts 92

5 Principles of financial accounting 101

Introduction 101
The principles of value creation and the matching principle 102
Accounting for real assets: depreciation and inventories 108
Extending your understanding of the principles of accounting 126

6 Accounting for companies 139

Introduction 139
The characteristics of limited companies 140
How limited companies are created 147
Group companies – acquisition and mergers 154
Becoming a public limited company 167

7 The analysis of accounting information 174

Introduction 174
The analysis of financial information 175
Financial analysis 184
Completing the narrative 210
Appendix to Chapter 7 218

Part 3 Management accounting and control 233

8 The principles of cost and revenue measurement 235

Introduction 235
Basic principles of costing 236
Costing for decisions: relevant costing 242
Cost behaviour and cost/volume/profit analysis 254
Marginal analysis 270

9 Cash forecasting, business planning and management control 280

Introduction 280
The business planning process 281
Business planning in practice 286
Budgeting methodologies and variance analysis 311

10 Cost management and pricing 323

Introduction 323
Cost management 324
Pricing 348

11   The management of working capital 359

Introduction   359
The role of working capital   360
Inventory management   364
Managing credit policy   373
Managing cash   381

Part 4   Finance and financial markets 391

12   Investment appraisal 393

Introduction   393
Matching cash flows over time   394
The net present value model   400
Other methods of investment appraisal   418

13   The nature of the financial markets 434

Introduction   434
Securities and the financial markets   435
The financial markets   435
The capital markets   442
The cost of capital   461

14   Market measures of performance and value 471

Introduction   471
Investor ratios   472
Valuing the firm   476
Measuring the performance of firms   483

Appendix Financial tables 490

Answers to selected review activities and end-of-chapter questions 493

Glossary 530

Bibliography 537

Index 539

11 The management of working capital 359

Introduction 360
The role of working capital 360
Inventory management 368
Managing cash cycle 373
Managing cash 377

Part 4 Finance and financial markets 391

17 Investment appraisal 393

Introduction 393
Earning cash flows over time 394
Investment appraisal methods 400
Other investment measures required 408

12 The nature of the financial markets 425

Introduction 426
Features and the financial markets 448
The financial markets 448
The price markets 448
The cost of capital 465

18 Market measures of performance and value 477

Introduction 477
Investor ratios 477
Market risk 479
Measuring the performance 484

Appendix: Annual tables 490
Answers to selected review activities and end-of-chapter questions 490
Glossary 530
Bibliography 537
Index 539

Preface

'I'm afraid you are going to need a heart transplant' was the news given to a very ill patient. The patient thought for a moment. 'That's OK', he replied, 'providing it's the heart of an accountant.' 'Why an accountant?' enquired the rather bemused surgeon. 'I want one that hasn't been used yet!' was the reply.

Jokes about accountants are commonplace and good fun too. However, accounting and its sister discipline, finance, are vital aspects of running any business enterprise, public body or indeed even the home. For the individual who is ambitious and wishes to make their mark in management these are 'need-to-know' subjects. In large companies, executive and non-executive directors and managers at all levels need to be intimately aware of the impact that their decisions are likely to have upon the reported performance of the business. Unfortunately, it is rarely sufficient to rely exclusively upon the advice of the professionals in the area. The bodies that regulate the conduct of accounting and other finance professionals rightly demand very high standards of integrity and competence. However, professional advice needs to be understood and on occasion challenged. In smaller organisations the manager often has to work through the financial implications of their actions themselves.

This book is for the reader who is willing to spend the time and energy required to master what for many are difficult subjects. The approach we have taken throughout this book is contextual. We explore the wider business and policy implications of the subject as well as their technical aspects. On the technical side we move out of the conventional approach to the subject and take a holistic approach to the understanding of accounting. The method we use has its genesis in the teaching of accounting that developed at the London School of Economics and the University of Manchester in the 1960s and 1970s. Using this method we sidestep the conventional double-entry approach and teach financial accounting from a systematic point of view. In the book you will find a brief explanation of the double-entry method of accounting but our principal approach follows an 'extended trial balance approach'. However, we explore the full range and power of this simple system showing how it can be adapted to deliver cash flow statements and even simple consolidated accounts.

In this second edition we have made a number of changes and improvements reflecting the fast-moving nature of our subject. The adoption of the International Financial Reporting Standards across Europe from 2005 has presented a number of challenges in writing a book like this. The focus of the new standards on the principles to be adopted is to be welcomed, but the changes in presentation of financial information introduced by the new standards vary from the odd to the bizarre. One wonders, for example, why the term 'fixed assets' should disappear to be replaced by 'non-current assets' and exactly what additional value this change offers. However, we hope that whilst not slavishly sacrificing clarity for compliance, our exposition of the new standards will give readers a reasonable understanding of the principles they have introduced. Following advice from our readers and long-suffering adopters we have made a number of changes which in turn have led to an extension of the material on management accounting. We have also developed the work in the area of finance to enhance compatibility with our *Corporate Finance and Valuation*.

This book will have its strongest appeal to students on non-specialist management programmes: MBA and diploma courses are our primary target. Also, students on undergraduate programmes in business and management will benefit greatly from the teaching approach we employ. The connections we make between accounting and finance and the range of other subjects students on these programmes normally undertake should help in the important task of integrating knowledge and understanding across the syllabus. Finally, this book is strongly recommended to the practising manager who simply wants to learn the subject without attending a formal course of study. There is enough here for you to achieve that aim and to put you into the position where you can develop more specialist expertise if you wish, or indeed just be able to talk to and question the specialists in a more informed and intelligent way.

To the student

First, here are some myths about accounting.

Myth 1: Accounting is boring

Monty Python certainly has much to answer for here. Accounting (and finance) is only boring in as far as business is boring. These subjects encapsulate the business problem: the accountant confronts the consequences of business decisions *close up and personal* as they say. Clever marketing and visionary strategy are very important in the search for competitive advantage. But neglect of the financial aspects of a business has one consequence. Failure. So, the reality rather than the myth is that if you find accounting and finance boring then you probably find business boring and if that's the case then perhaps a course in theology or early English poetry would be more to your taste.

Myth 2: Accounting and finance are mathematical

There is a tiny grain of truth in this if you think $2 + 2 = 4$ is mathematical. There are many astute and highly skilled accountants who could not solve a quadratic equation but they certainly know how to project a financial plan or unzip the meaning of a balance sheet. In this book we use a little mathematics to help you efficiently solve problems which would be impossible without its help. But it is only a little mathematics – the sort of maths they now teach in primary school and in most cases we also show you a non-mathematical 'work-around' which lets you see the point we are trying to make intuitively.

Myth 3: There is a lot to learn

In reality, for the average student of business at any level the key elements of the subject can be condensed into a book as short as this. This book contains about 90 per cent of all that you will ever need to know. In business 90 per cent is not enough – but it is a very good start. The remaining 10 per cent might come from a professional training course or by private study or, *in extremis,* by finding a good accountant or finance professional and asking appropriate questions.

Myth 4: It's all done by computers these days – accountants are obsolete

Indeed, the advent of computer-based accounting and information systems has increased the need for accountants to interpret the information produced.

In many respects, business faces too much information rather than too little. It is also often the case that the basis on which the information is produced within the entrails of the computer software is not what is expected. Throughout this book we will be encouraging you to make use of a spreadsheet program such as Excel. These programs are excellent tools but they can give you results you do not expect, often because of subtle differences between the way that their internal functions operate and the way that finance professionals normally expect. We will point out the major traps for the unwary as we proceed.

Myth 5: Accountants run business

For many years this was the case because there were few other opportunities for the young business manager or aspiring manager to gain a relevant education. The first MBA programmes were only launched in the UK in the early 1960s at the London and Manchester Business Schools. From being the most prestigious of programmes in business the MBA became the 'must-have' qualification of the 1980s and 1990s. Today US and UK universities are producing many more business graduates and MBAs, feeding the supply of qualified managers for industry and the public services. Professional accountancy is no longer the sure way to the top of the business ladder it once was.

'All I wanted in life was an MBA – until I discovered accounting'

How to use this book

This book adopts a narrative approach in that you will obtain most benefit by 'following the story'. What this means in practice is that we, like any good teacher, are trying to help you build your knowledge of the subject upon sound foundations. You will need some extras to make effective use of this book:

● Paper (lots of it) and something to write with to make copious notes.

● A good calculator with a scientific function. This means not just the usual '+' and '−' keys but also the ability to calculate the 'power' of a given number. Somewhere on the keyboard you should find a y^x key or similar. What is important is that the calculator has a good clear display and a well-laid-out keyboard that will fit your hand comfortably. The calculator function on most pocket organisers also has a 'scientific' capability.

- Access to a computer that runs an up-to-date version of Microsoft Excel. The spreadsheet in Star Office will also do the job perfectly well. A spreadsheet package is the computerisation of the accountant's 'spreadsheet paper' which was lined A3 paper ruled into columns across the page. The computerised version is much more versatile and remarkably easy to learn. For those who have not familiarised themselves with a spreadsheet we might suggest that you just switch it on and try to replicate the examples shown in the book.

- Web access. The World Wide Web, or the internet, is like the electric kettle. We wonder how we ever managed without it. Your most important resource on the web is the website for this book: **www.cengage.co.uk/ryan2**

That website includes remaining answers to the review activities and questions not found in the book. Other questions and further reading materials will be included on the website and are available for you to download. There is also a section where problems in the text are identified so that if you find something you really do not understand you can check the website and the answer may well be there.

For the teacher

This book is an introductory text in that it makes no demands on prior knowledge of the subject. This book is constructed over 14 chapters of roughly equal learning intensity. A full presentation of the subject matter can be covered in forty contact hours with approximately 80 self-study and assessment hours in support. It is possible to reduce the content of the course by the elimination of topics and in the support resources available we offer draft teaching plans for a range of postgraduate and undergraduate programmes. At undergraduate level this book could be used as a first text on degrees in business studies, management and related disciplines. It would also form a suitable book for service courses on degrees in engineering, sciences and medicine. Finally, the text is suitable for distance learning programmes at any of the above levels where the narrative style is important for the remote student.

Although we have tried to keep them to a minimum there are some mathematical models and equations at various points in the text. The most important ones are shown in display boxes. These are ones which, experience teaches us, students of the subject need to learn at some stage and are important in a number of different applications. Others of lesser importance but necessary for explanatory purposes are shown within the running text.

A support site is available at **www.cengage.co.uk/ryan2**
This contains password-protected resources for teachers adopting this text. These resources include a range of teaching materials including PowerPoint slides, spreadsheets from the text and answers to selected cases. Potential or actual adopters are also welcome to contact the author direct through the website link provided.

Sources, citations and further reading

Students at all levels approaching the subject for the first time find endless referencing a hindrance to effective learning. We handle this problem in the following way:

- Each chapter contains an annotated list of further reading.
- There is a short reference list of cited works at the end of the book.

● The website contains a downloadable 'advanced reading' resource which gives a list of readings from the academic and professional literature to support each chapter. This advanced reading resource can be used as a programme for masters-level courses and wherever possible we have endeavoured to ensure that all the readings cited are easily available. You will also find links to take you directly to websites mentioned in the book.

Walk-through tour

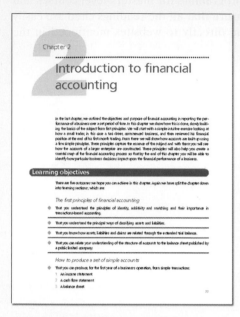

Introduction Brief overview of chapter with contextual comments linking to previous learning and concepts.

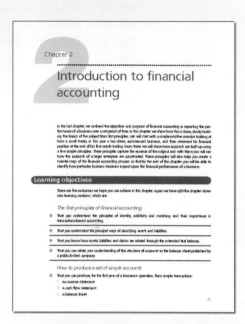

Learning objectives These are divided into sections and highlight the expected learning outcomes from each chapter. Success against these learning outcomes is assessed as the chapter proceeds.

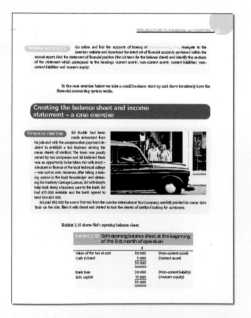

Financial realities These problems are fully explored in the text and provide a key component of the learning process.

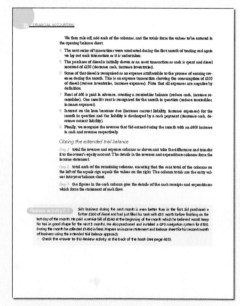

Review activities These short questions allow you to explore the learning you have just undertaken. They also include challenging issues which you may wish to use as the basis of discussion or further reading.

Exhibits These give a visual representation of key concepts or data. Look for 'Post-its' to guide you through the more complex analysis on spreadsheet exhibits.

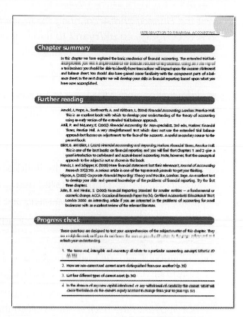

Progress check At the end of each chapter there are a dozen or more brief questions which are designed to test your knowledge of the content of the chapter. These are very useful for bringing the subject together and preparing you to undertake the more substantial questions that follow.

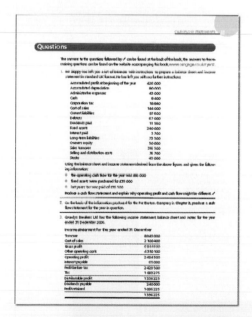

Questions The questions are designed to test your achievement of the learning objectives specified at the beginning of each chapter. Each question should take between 30 and 45 minutes to complete.

Case exercises These are much more substantial pieces of work which will allow you to explore, using current materials and data, the methods and concepts in the text.

Supplementary resources

Visit the *Finance and Accounting for Business* (second edition) accompanying website at **www.cengage.co.uk/ryan2** to find further teaching and learning material including:

For Students

- Information about the book to help guide you through using the text for your studies.
- Chapter overviews to give you an indication of the coverage of the book.
- Accounting definitions from the IEBM pocket dictionary to give you more detailed descriptions of some common terms in Accounting and Finance.
- Multiple choice questions to test your understanding of each chapter.
- Additional mini-cases with questions and answers to further your knowledge of specific topics.
- Answers to review and self-test exercises that do not appear in the back of the book so that you can check your knowledge as you work through the text.
- Reading lists/web references to guide you towards further study.

For Lecturers

A downloadable lecturers manual including:
- Answers to the more complex questions in the book for you to work through with your students.
- Some longer additional cases, plus questions and suggested answers/discussion points.
- PowerPoint slides containing useful diagrams and sections from the book.
- Teaching notes for each chapter.
- Additional multiple choice questions to distribute to your students as you work through your course.

Acknowledgements

It was my privilege to work at the University of Manchester in the 1970s with a group of outstanding scholars under the leadership of Professor Sir Bryan Carsberg. Many of the teaching methods used in this book have their roots in those happy years. My thanks to my colleagues for their generosity of spirit – many of the ideas in this book owe their origin to the free-ranging discussions we had about our subjects and how they should be taught.

Much of the content of this book has been developed through a range of short courses and management programmes at both graduate and undergraduate levels. In recent years my association with distance learning programmes operated by the University of London External Programmes and the Manchester Business School has brought me into contact with a wide diversity of students from different business, educational and cultural backgrounds. They have been an invaluable resource and inspiration as I have worked to develop a teaching method that works at all levels.

I owe a great debt to a team of peer reviewers selected by my publisher: Malcolm Anderson from Cardiff, University of Wales, Amanda Nayak from the University of Birmingham, Mary Taylor from the University of Hertfordshire and one other. Their comments and suggestions were very important in the development of this text. Other colleagues have also provided critical commentary on various chapters and in particular I would like to acknowledge the kindness of Angela Lorenz, Martin Bennett, Sue Davis, Margaret Greenwood, Jim Keane and Brian Miller. No book is ever completely free of mistakes. However, there would have been a lot more without them and the ones that are left – they are all mine!

Cengage has been brilliant: Pat Bond and Leandra Paoli have provided the editorial muscle, and an excellent production team led by Jamina Ward who put it all together. My thanks to them all. Grateful thanks are also due for the forensic skills of Michael Fitch who copyedited the manuscript, Rose James who worked on the second edition, Stephen York who proofread the book and to my agent Frances Kelly who negotiated the deal and then made sure I kept to it.

Finally a special mention to the person who makes it all worth doing. Alison.

1

Introduction

Chapter 1

The role of accounting and finance in business

Introduction

Accounting and finance lie at the heart of business. It is possible to survive, for a while at least, without an effective marketing plan, poor human resource management and indeed a poorly designed business strategy. However, if there are serious faults with the management and control of the business's financial systems, it will fail. On the positive side, good accounting and financial management helps keep the business under control; it also provides the owners, management and others with the information and the confidence to make the bold decisions and take the opportunities to help the enterprise grow. So for any student of business, accounting and finance are 'need to know' subjects. In this chapter we set the scene by exploring some of the basic ideas behind accounting and finance as well as some of the extensive history of the subject within its business context.

Learning objectives

The learning objectives in this chapter will provide the context for developing your understanding of accounting and finance.

The context and history of accounting and finance

- To give an overview of the role that accounting and finance play in business.

- To inform that overview with a wider understanding of the history and development of accounting and the financial markets.

Different types of business organisation

- That you can classify business firms by business type (distinguishing the four generic types of merchant, extractor, manufacturer and service), size and legal form.

- That you understand the concept of limited liability, and the rights and duties of the directors.

Business objectives and the decision-oriented approach

● That you understand the principal financial objectives of a firm from both a shareholder and a stakeholder perspective.

● That you understand the purpose of financial accounting information and the implications of the decision-oriented approach.

The purpose and characteristics of accounting information

● That you can describe the five quality criteria for accounting information and can rank them in order of precedence.

● That you understand the fundamental difference between financial and management accounting.

The context and history of accounting and finance

Accounting is concerned with the recording and provision of financial information to the individuals who run firms and to outsiders. We can classify these 'users' of accounting in the following way: the owners of the business (its shareholders), management, other employees, suppliers and customers, lenders and agencies of government such as the tax authorities and various regulatory bodies. Of these the most important have traditionally been those who provide the cash the firm requires for investment (its capital requirements) and for managing the peaks and troughs in its cash balances caused by trading (its working or 'operating' capital requirements). Finance is concerned with the process of raising capital from the financial markets and covers subjects such as the operation of the market for short- and long-term finance, sourcing the most appropriate form of capital, making good investment decisions within the firm and calculating the cost of the capital the firm employs.

The role of accounting

At its simplest level accounting is still about summarising and totalling up the financial values and transactions associated with a business or some other enterprise. However, accounting and the role of accountants has developed far beyond this simple idea. The modern accountant extracts meaning from a firm's financial data: partly to help control its activities, partly to determine what resources are available for future development and partly to satisfy the needs of a wide range of different groups who need financial information for their own purposes.

Accounting within firms has developed in two principal directions: first in fulfilling the information needs of external stakeholders and, second, in providing information to management to assist them in their decision-making and other activities. The externally oriented branch of the subject is called 'financial accounting' where statements of financial performance over a period of time are produced – the income statement (formerly the profit and loss account), the balance sheet and the cash flow statement. 'Management accounting' is concerned with producing internal information for the management of the firm. The range of information produced by management accountants is typically more diverse than that produced by financial accountants and will include: business plans, budgets and forecasts, control reports, costing statements, product prices and much more.

In the modern business firm the role of accounting has developed to fulfil a number of purposes.

Accounting and stewardship

Throughout history, the powerful and wealthy have needed to keep a record of what they had and what they were owed. The steward was a central figure in this process, keeping a record of all the assets and noting down the indebtedness of others to their master.

In today's business world, this stewardship function is still important. The accountant records the receipt and despatch of goods and the flows of cash in and out of the business, keeps records of financial assets and liabilities and provides statements of account summarising the financial position of the firm. Good stewardship, knowing where everything is, and keeping complete and accurate records of all business transactions is a legal requirement imposed on all firms and indeed on every citizen who is required to make a return to the Inland Revenue for tax purposes. This is yet another very good reason for learning some accounting!

Fundamentally, this reason for keeping account has changed little over the centuries. The ethical principles which govern the stewardship role are as relevant in an age of computerised accounting as they were when scribes scratched numbers on stone or papyrus: honesty and integrity, consistency of practice and diligence. Good accountants operate to the very highest ethical standards and inspire confidence and trust.

One consequence of the stewardship function is that the accountant has an important role maintaining the records or history of a business. In previous eras, such records would have been kept in books of account or ledgers. A **ledger** is another ancient term coming from the Middle English word for a large book and, indeed, it is only in the last twenty to thirty years that these large steel and leather-bound books have been superseded by computer-based accounting systems.

Accounting and control

Few people when starting a new business are ready for the pace with which things happen. Within days of making the start-up decision the business entrepreneur will find that cash starts to move in and out of the business: decisions snowball, taking a lease on an office, for example, creates liabilities for rent, rates, maintenance, service charges and so forth. Employing help in the office entails payments for office furniture, office supplies, computers, salary costs and tax payments. Now imagine what happens on a daily basis in the National Health Service or a large business like British Aerospace, Marks & Spencer or Rolls-Royce. A key management activity is simply one of keeping control, knowing what is happening and being able to adjust to changing circumstances. Accountants provide information to support management in this aspect of its work. They do this in a number of ways. One of the most important of which is to provide data that can be compared with predetermined plans and budgets. This requires the accountant to classify the raw financial data from the events of the business into a form where it is comparable with the plans and budgetary projections already made.

Accountants also serve the control function in another more subtle way. Accounting imposes a discipline on the business through its rules and procedures and these can become an important component of its control systems. The mere regularity with which the accounting procedures are applied and the requirement that all staff within the business comply with the accountant's request for accurate data in standard form, serves to impose a structure of accountability within the organisation which in turn helps management control the organisation.

Accounting and planning

The accountant as historian and information provider also has a pivotal role in the planning and budgeting process. As we will see later in this book, business planning and budgeting fulfils a number of functions, but most importantly it allows the managers of the business to summarise their expectations and beliefs about the future. The accountant provides the financial evidence required to justify those beliefs. The past is not a certain guide to the future, but in an uncertain world a good understanding of how business decisions have been made and turned out in the past, and a clear understanding of the current financial position of the firm, is the next best thing. Typically, the accountant will be able to generate future estimates of revenue (or, to use the accountant's term, turnover) and costs, and to produce summarised data in the form of projected statements of account and financial measures such as ratios and percentage changes from plan.

Accounting and information

Much of what has been said before can be bundled together into just one idea, namely that the accountant's role is to provide information for any individual or group that has a legitimate interest in the activities and performance of the business. We pull it out as a distinct role because information is somewhat different from the collection of data. Information is data which has value to the user and in this context information only has value if it is capable of being used to make decisions. When you think about it, data which cannot influence your future behaviour is valueless. Business decisions can have both a long-term and a short-term impact upon the organisation. Different users make different sorts of decisions which require relevant and timely financial information. Later in this chapter we will explore the implications of these varied information requirements for the accountant.

The origins and the role of the financial markets

Finance is concerned with the operation of the capital markets and with the financial investment decisions made by firms. As business firms exploited the advances of the scientific and industrial revolution in Europe during the sixteenth and seventeenth centuries they needed large amounts of capital funds to invest in machines and buildings. Their capital requirements soon outstripped the resources of the trading families of the time. Raising finance was achieved in one of two ways: first by borrowing from the banks of the time or, second, by inviting people with funds to invest to subscribe for shares in the newly established business firms.

The first banks had come into existence in the later part of the twelfth century lending funds and extending credit to travelling merchants at the important fairs held at that time in the Champagne region of France. Over the succeeding centuries the banks developed to meet the needs of this mercantile class and were reluctant to engage in financing the new firms of the industrial revolution. Manufacturing, unlike merchant trading, needs funds to be committed for long periods and so the predominant source of finance for industry was through private subscription for shares. However, once the shares were held the private investors also needed some way in which they could realise the value of their investment. This was achieved through the creation of a market for 'second-hand' shares. The buying and selling of shares in this secondary market establishes the price or open-market value for the shares concerned.

The market for short-term finance is now referred to as the money market and that for long-term finance is known as the capital market. In the modern capital economies these markets are regulated to ensure that firms can gain access to the funds they need at minimum cost and that they operate fairly in supplying capital resources to firms and indirectly in allocating the capital resources of the economy between competing users. Capitalism as a political and social system is above all else dependent upon the efficient operation of these markets. Nowadays this has global significance as the principal capital markets in individual countries have become more integrated and the free flow of funds across international borders has become a reality. We will return to the problem of capital market efficiency in Chapter 11.

FYI A number of traders in stocks and shares had established themselves buying and selling shares in companies at the Royal Exchange in Threadneedle Street in the City of London. The Royal Exchange was where merchants had gathered from the days of Queen Elizabeth I to trade their goods. In 1698 these traders (called jobbers) were evicted for rowdiness and established a club in Jonathan's Coffee House nearby. In 1748 Jonathan's was burnt down in the second fire of London and the informal market moved back to Threadneedle Street and in 1773 named itself the London Stock Exchange. It is also interesting to note that Lloyd's of London, the international insurance centre, takes its name from Lloyd's Coffee House.

A brief history of accounting

The origins of accounting are buried in antiquity. Clay tablets dating from 3300 BC show tax payments to the king being recorded by a scribe or accountant. Centuries later, there is further evidence of accountants at work in the Mesopotamian Valley and later in Greece and in Rome. In Mesopotamia for example, under the Code of Hammurabi (2285–2242 BC), merchants were required to quote the prices of goods under seal and as a result a careful system of recording transactions developed.

In Athens during the 5th century BC the local population appointed ten public auditors to monitor the public finances, and in Roman times the moneylenders kept careful records of their transactions. As cash was passed to them over the table (*the banca*) it would have been received on their left side and as a result the practice arose of recording the receipt on the left

Exhibit 1.1 Wall painting from the tomb of Chnemhotep (3300 BC) showing a scribe recording the King's account

and, as money was paid out, recording the payment on the right. This arrangement for recording transactions survived to become the basis for the concept of the 'debit' and 'credit' system in double-entry bookkeeping.

Most of the early accounting records were little more than listings of the assets owned by the individual concerned whether he was a merchant or a king. The penalties for pilferage were invariably severe and as a result the record keeping was meticulous. This system is what we now call a 'single-entry' system of account. The idea of double-entry recording, where each transaction was recorded twice, was known about in Roman times where it would have been common practice to compare the records of both parties in resolving disputes. In England, following the Norman Conquest, the payment of taxes on account to the king by the sheriffs was recorded on a pole with angled notches representing the amount. The pole was then split with one half going to the sheriff and the other being retained by the King's treasurer. At the date of final settlement the two halves would be matched up to verify the earlier payment.

Between the twelfth and fifteenth centuries two events occurred that led to the transformation of accounting. The first was the introduction into Europe of an Indian/Arabic number system that used a zero. Up until this time the European number system had been based on Roman numbers – but these numbers were difficult to manipulate arithmetically. An Italian mathematician called Leonardo Fibonacci introduced the idea of the zero into Europe and with it created a number system that could be readily applied to the recording of monetary values.

The second great event, as significant in its time as the development of the Internet in the last decade of the twentieth century, was the invention of the printing press. The printing press allowed books to be printed in large numbers. This allowed knowledge to be spread much more rapidly. It also rapidly expanded the demand for paper. As the mass production of paper was established it soon became possible for even the poorest business to use it to prepare its accounts.

Florence – the home of modern accounting

For the first time, scholars began to think about accounting in a systematic way. Florence, Genoa and Venice were the commercial hub of Europe from the thirteenth to the seventeenth centuries and it was here that a method of keeping account was developed which has largely survived intact until this day. Double-entry bookkeeping was a system devised to enable the merchants of Venice, Florence and Genoa to keep account of their business transactions with suppliers and customers. This method was popularised by a Franciscan friar and mathematician, Luca Pacioli, who in 1494 wrote and published *Summa de Arithmetica, Geometria, Proportioni et Proportionalita*. One section of that book contained his work on accounting, which still underpins accounting to this day. In Chapter 3 we describe the mechanics of the double-entry system still used by accountants today that has much in common with Pacioli's method.

Different types of business organisation

In this section we describe more fully what we mean by business and how different types of business organisations can be categorised. The word for a business organisation is 'firm' and firms come in many different shapes and sizes. We will also introduce the concept of **limited liability**, which describes the most common type of legal company.

We can categorise firms in three ways: by business type, size and legal form.

Business type

There is an almost infinite array of business opportunities open to any individual or firm. However, all business relies upon the ability to create surplus value or profit by trading over a period of time, although in practice these different opportunities fall into a small number of different business types or, as they are sometimes called, 'business models'. Each business type involves a different process for the creation of value.

Exhibit 1.2 Three categorisations of business enterprise

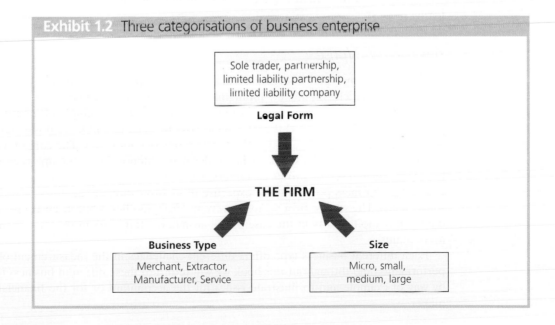

Merchant enterprise

A merchant enterprise is one where goods are bought and sold essentially unchanged. A retailer like Marks & Spencer plc buys goods from manufacturers and sells them through its high-street and out-of-town shopping centres. Some merchants operate purely as whole-salers, buying goods from suppliers and selling them on to retailers. The small corner shop is likely to buy most of its products for sale from the local 'cash and carry' – a colloquialism for a specialist wholesaler that deals in the types of product sold through small retail outlets. A merchant enterprise earns profit by purchasing goods in one market more cheaply than they can be sold in another.

An extractive enterprise

A firm engaged in mining or oil extraction, for example, uses the technical knowledge available to it to locate likely sites and if successful then deploys heavy machinery and other resources to recover the coal, oil or other resource it is interested in. Once it is in a position to extract the natural resource concerned the mining company can then exploit the reserves available to it, selling them on through specialist merchants called *brokers* to final users who may be either private consumers or manufacturers. The profit earned by the extractor is the difference between the revenues it earns and the costs of extraction, which may be heavily dominated by the cost of its capital equipment – the mine or oil well involved.

A manufacturing enterprise

Manufacturing involves purchasing raw materials and components and then, using capital equipment and machinery as well as technical know-how, converting those raw material inputs into finished goods and services. A company like Ford buys a wide range of materials and components from a number of different suppliers, it employs a wide variety of skilled engineers, designers and mechanics, and produces motor cars, vans and trucks which it sells through its network of distributors. Ford makes its profit by selling its vehicles at a price greater than the costs it both directly and indirectly incurs in its manufacturing processes.

A service enterprise

A service company exploits particular *real* assets at its disposal, which may be buildings, aeroplanes, ships, vehicles or, indeed, **intangible assets** such as the technical expertise of its staff, in order to provide a service to its customers. Airlines are an example of a business which provides a service (transport) through the use of the real assets at its disposal (aeroplanes). Virgin Atlantic is the airline within the Virgin group of companies. The core of its business is the use of owned and leased aeroplanes, flown and supported by its employees, who offer travel and related services to its customers. The international accountancy practice KPMG is a service business providing the expertise of its professionally qualified and other staff to its clients. The service firm makes its revenue from its clients but its costs are either predominantly capital costs in the case of the airline, or staff costs in the case of the firm of accountants.

Each different business type offers different challenges in the measurement of business performance and throughout this book we will return to these different business types both by way of example and to illustrate issues for the accountant or for the financial decision maker.

Review activity 1.1 Classify the following firms according to their principal business type: Monsoon plc, Rolls-Royce plc, British Airways plc, Manchester United plc. To what extent are these firms representative of a single business type, i.e. does Manchester United, for example, engage in manufacturing?

✓ Check the answer to this Review activity at the back of the book (see page 493).

Firm size

There has been much debate about what is small and what is large in business terms. It is easy to see that a company such as Virgin is large although in some respects it has many of the characteristics of a small business (it is currently headed by one person who effectively owns the enterprise). Some small firms although having few employees have an influence that reaches across different regions and different spheres of activity. To clarify matters we will follow the categorisation adopted by the European Union and the UK government.

The sole trader/single-owner-managed business (the micro-business)

These are the most common type of business organisation: they are enterprises set up by individuals with a small amount of capital with a short-term loan or overdraft from the bank. Typically, the owner runs the business with the help of his or her family and friends, and sometimes a small number of part- or full-time employees. This type of firm will have less than 10 employees, annual revenue and capital employed of less than £2 000 000. Small businesses like this include the independent corner shop, professional practices (lawyers, doctors, veterinary surgeons, etc.), public houses and so forth. The financial risk of this type of business falls on the owner who will, if the business fails, face full liability for its debts. The accounting requirements of such firms include: the creation of a business plan for obtaining finance, the keeping of full records of transactions for tax purposes, the preparation of an up-to-date cash account and the preparation of periodic statements of profit and loss and a balance sheet. With this type of business, the most important requirements for record keeping come from the tax authorities who can demand the production of information for the previous six years.

The small-owner-managed firm (the small business)

This type of firm will typically be run by a small group of people who also own the business. It is quite likely that such a firm will either be a professional partnership or a private limited company. Such firms are normally financed by their owners' capital supported by bank loans. Even though such a firm may have limited liability (a term we return to in detail in Chapter 5), banks invariably require **directors' guarantees**, which means that if the firm should fail the owner's risk losing all their assets and being rendered bankrupt. Small businesses encompass small manufacturing firms, professional partnerships, building firms and so forth. Firms such as this are defined by the European Union as having less than 50 employees, a maximum revenue and capital employed of less than €10 million. Their accounting requirements are similar to those of the micro-firm except that they will typically require more sophisticated systems for recording movements on customer and supplier accounts, a more comprehensive budgeting system and, if they have limited liability, the production of an annual financial report consisting of profit and loss account, balance sheet and cash flow statement as prescribed by the Companies Act (2006) in the UK or equivalent elsewhere.

The medium-sized firm

Medium-sized firms can have up to 250 employees and, following the definition laid down by the European Union, a maximum revenue of €50 million and capital employed of less than €27 million. Such firms may be family-owned but at this level it is common to see other shareholders involved who are not members of the family. Apart from the very largest professional practices, medium-sized firms invariably have limited liability and they may well be publicly quoted with a listing on the stock exchange. Such firms are likely to have well-developed management accounting systems providing budgetary, cost and pricing information to management and their financial accounting functions will be providing regular reports and a full financial statement at the end of each year for shareholders.

The large firm

The large firm category applies to any company which is too big to be deemed a small or medium sized enterprise (SME). They can range from domestic companies in the manufacturing and service sectors of the economy to large multinationals. Very few such companies are in private hands although a single very wealthy individual such as Bill Gates of Microsoft or Richard Branson of Virgin may effectively control the business. These companies are almost all public limited companies (plcs) and will be listed on the London Stock Exchange where their shares can be bought and sold. Their financial reporting requirements are more onerous than those of smaller firms and they will be expected to fully comply with the relevant accounting standards for the disclosure of information to the public as well as fulfil the requirements of membership of the Stock Exchange. You can find out more about accounting for these and smaller companies in Chapter 6. In Chapter 13 we will also discuss how such firms raise finance from the financial markets.

Exhibit 1.3	Classification by firm size			
Firm size	Maximum employees	Maximum annual revenue	Maximum capital employed	Typical business activities
Micro	10	€2 000 000	€2 000 000	Small retailers, professional practices
Small	50	€10 000 000	€10 000 000	Small manufacturers, professional partnerships and service companies
Medium	250	€50 000 000	€43 000 000	Professional practices, manufacturing and service firms in focused product areas
Large	unlimited	unlimited	unlimited	Firms in all sectors including multinationals

The legal form of firms

Sole traders

A sole trader who is self-employed acts as a private individual and is liable for all the debts that he or she incurs. Individuals who come together to form a business can do so in partnership, which in the absence of a formal agreement will be presumed in law to be an equal partnership. Partners have what is known as 'joint and several liability' for their business debts. So if one partner were to disappear with all the firm's assets, the remaining partners could be sued by the firm's creditors, i.e., all those individuals who were owed money. Sole traders and partnerships are only required to keep accounts for tax purposes. They may decide to keep accounts for their own personal use but they are not obliged to divulge that information publicly. This is an important reason why many individuals choose to run their business in this form.

Partnerships

Partnerships are a very common form of business arrangement, especially for professional practices such as accountants, lawyers, architects, doctors and dentists. Partnerships can employ other people and can register a business name. The advantage of a partnership over other types of business is that the individuals concerned can gain the benefits of working together, they can share the cost of premises and of employing staff, and they can build their business as a team. If a partner retires or leaves, he or she will be bought out by the remaining partners who will have to pay the full share of the value of the firm attributable to the individual concerned. The other most significant advantage of a partnership, especially for professional practices, is that each partner can build their own list of clients. This is important where clients expect to have a personal relationship with a specific partner.

A partnership can also be the most appropriate form of business where the requirements for capital are low and where the firm, by its nature, is unlikely to incur substantial liabilities to suppliers of goods and services during the normal course of business. The most significant source of risk for a partnership comes from professional negligence and a degree of protection against the cost of a successful claim against any of the partners can be achieved through professional indemnity insurance.

Limited-liability companies

Where capital requirements are high, or substantial liabilities are likely to be incurred then a firm can be registered as a limited liability company. Under UK company law, there are a number of variants of limited company.

- A private limited company (designated as 'Limited' or 'Ltd'), which is designed for firms where the founders wish to keep the ownership to a relatively small group of individuals.

Financial realities   On 20 December 1999 Richard Branson signed an agreement to sell a 49% stake of Virgin Atlantic to Singapore Airlines to form a unique global partnership. The cost of the transaction to Singapore Airlines was £600.25 million, which included a capital injection of £49 million and valued Virgin Atlantic at a minimum of £1.225 billion. The deal was finalised in 2000. Richard retains the controlling 51% stake in the airline.

Quoted from **www.virgin.com**

Virgin Atlantic is an example of a very large company that is controlled by one individual, Sir Richard Branson, but where another company also has a significant stake.

● A company limited by guarantee: this is a company which is not formally owned by share-holders but by 'members' who pay a small guarantee sum (usually £1 each). The guarantee signifies the limit of the member's liability to the company's debts. This type of company is not allowed to make a profit and is usually reserved for charities and other types of organisations who do not have a profit objective. In the UK railways, the track, signalling and stations are operated by a company limited by guarantee.

● A public limited company: this is a company where the owners' shares are openly traded on a stock exchange. These companies are registered on the 'list' of one or more exchanges around the world where the public can buy or sell their shares. There is a huge array of such companies ranging from the multinationals such as IBM and Pfizer to smaller nationally based companies.

Financial realities   Network Rail is responsible for the operation, maintenance and renewal of Britain's rail network – the tracks, signals, bridges, viaducts, level crossings and stations. Network Rail is a company limited by guarantee. It is a company without shareholders but which is run along commercial lines. Any operating surplus will be re-invested in the rail network. Network Rail has no shareholders (or share capital), but rather members.

Quoted from the Network Rail website **www.networkrail.co.uk**

A limited liability company (whether Ltd or plc) is characterised by the following:

● Limited liability: the liability of the members is limited to the extent of the nominal or face value of their shares in the company, or to the value of the guarantee in the case of a company limited by guarantee. In Chapter 4 we discuss the concept of limited liability more fully.

● Separate existence: a limited company is a distinct legal 'person' that can own property and enter into contracts in the same way as a private individual.

● Purpose: a limited company must have a specific purpose, which is defined in its 'articles' and 'memorandum' of association. This lays down the limits to its activities and the scope of legitimate action of its directors.

● Longevity: a limited company has an indefinite life that can only be terminated by its members or by the appointment of an 'official receiver' by the court if the company should default on its debts.

● Separation of ownership and control: formally the ownership of a company is vested in the hands of its shareholders or, in the case of a company limited by guarantee, its members. The owners then appoint 'directors' who formally owe their duty to the company and not the shareholders. The directors have a range of duties and responsibilities which impact upon the work of the accountant.

Limited-liability partnerships

The major disadvantage of a partnership is that each of the partners is responsible for the debts of the others. Partners have what is known in law as 'joint and several' liability for all the debts of the firm. Professional indemnity insurance can overcome much of this problem but in recent years the number of large claims that have been made against both legal and accounting firms in particular, but other professional partnerships as well, has made this form of business organisation perilous indeed for the individuals concerned. There has also been an issue of equity, particularly in the role of professional auditing firms and their relationship with their client companies. The shareholders of a client company are protected from the risks of the business by the existence of corporate limited liability (which we will consider more fully in the next section) whilst the partners of the firm that undertook the audit are exposed to unlimited liability. Claimants have therefore seen it as much more attractive to go after the audit firm rather than the company when fraud is perpetrated.

To surmount this problem the concept of a limited liability partnership has been introduced into UK law whereby the partners become agents of the firm rather than of one another and hence their liability is limited to the net assets of the firm. Limited liability partnerships can also acquire and dispose of assets as a firm rather than as a collective of individuals. To summarise using the words of the UK Department of Trade and Industry (Register, 2003):

- A limited liability partnership (LLP) is a body corporate, i.e. a separate legal entity distinct from its members. The LLP can own and hold property, employ people and enter into contractual obligations. Debts incurred are the debts of the LLP.

- An LLP has unlimited capacity which means that third parties need not be concerned about any restrictions on its activities.

- An LLP has members but no directors or shareholders. An LLP has no share capital and is not subject to the company law rules governing the maintenance of capital.

- The members of an LLP have limited liability (a point discussed further below). The LLP is liable for all its debts to the full extent of its assets.

- An LLP has complete flexibility as to the internal structure which it wishes to adopt: there are no requirements for board or general meetings or decision-making by resolution. An LLP does not have a memorandum or articles of association.

- As the members have limited liability, the protection of those dealing with an LLP requires that the LLP maintains accounting records, prepares and delivers audited annual accounts to the registrar of companies, and submits an annual return in a similar manner to companies.

The role of the directors of limited companies

Once a business is incorporated it becomes a separate legal person distinct from its shareholders or its directors. The directors are appointed by the shareholders to run the company. The directors must at all times act in the interest of the company to whom they owe their primary responsibility. The duties of the directors can be summarised as follows:

1. To operate the company in pursuit of its purpose. Whether a company is a small taxi business (see Chapter 2) or a large multinational enterprise the directors are required to pursue the aims of the business as specified within its memorandum and articles of association. They may be liable in law if they act in ways that may be viewed to be contrary to those aims. The directors, therefore, establish the policies and strategies that the company will follow in pursuit of its aims.

2. To report on the financial performance of the business. The directors are required each year to report to the company shareholders at a general meeting and to file a return to Companies House in the UK which is the government department operated by the Registrar of Companies. The report to the shareholders and the annual return must include the financial statements including a profit and loss account and balance sheet with supporting information in a form specified by the Companies Act (1985 and 2006). Other countries have very similar requirements for the public disclosure of information by companies.

3. To comply with the relevant law and regulations. A company, just like a private individual must comply with the law. The directors are responsible for all the actions of the company and can be held liable if, for example, they do not comply with the requirements of the Data Protection Act, the Health and Safety at Work Act, the Working Time Directives of the European Community and a range of other legislation covering employment, taxation and the sale and handling of goods.

4. To ensure that the business only trades whilst solvent. If the directors of a company knowingly continue trading whilst the company is insolvent then they will become fully liable for its debts and may be held criminally responsible by the courts. This could in some circumstances entail a prison sentence and indefinite removal of the power to act as directors in the future. A company is technically insolvent as soon as it is no longer able to settle its debts.

FYI Directors come together into what is known as the Board of Directors. The Board will normally consist of a Chairman or Chairwoman who runs the directors' meetings supported by a Company Secretary, a Managing Director (sometimes called the Chief Executive Officer or CEO) and a Financial Director. Some directors may be appointed who do not have any managerial responsibilities – these are the non-executive directors – who provide independent advice to the executive directors. The composition of boards and the role of directors are discussed more fully in Chapter 6.

The rights of shareholders

The shareholders technically own shares which mark the level of investment they have made in the company, and although they formally own the company they do not own the business conducted by the company. Shareholders have a right to any dividends that are declared by the directors, they can in the event of the winding up of the business take their share of any remaining assets left over when all of the outstanding debts are paid off, and they have a right to attend and vote at company meetings. However, they do not have the right to intervene in the management of the company. This separation of ownership and control has important implications which we will return to later in this chapter. We will consider the duties of directors and the rights of shareholders in more detail in Chapter 4.

FYI The concept of a company as an organisation, which could exist independently of its owners, has existed since Roman times. The word company comes from the Latin *cum panis,* which implies to share bread together. One of the earliest companies of the modern era was established in the reign of Elizabeth I and called the East India Company. The East India Company was important because it was one of the very first companies to invite its members to subscribe capital. The Queen granted a Royal Charter to a group of merchants in the City of London who wished to trade in the East Indies and later in India itself. In later years, the East India Company became hugely influential in the development of commerce and trade around the world and, indeed, it effectively ruled India for a period of time. The company was established with a Court of Directors and a General Court of Proprietors. The former operated the company, set its policies and goals and managed its affairs through a range of committees. From time to time the Directors would make report to the Court of Proprietors and when capital was required for a new venture they would open a 'subscription book' in which members of the Court could register their interest and the level of the investment they had made. The East India Company was one of the first chartered companies created by the sovereign. Later, the legal framework of law was established with the Joint Stock Companies Registration and Regulation Act 1844, whereby companies could be created by registration as well as by Act of Parliament or by the Crown. These 'joint stock companies' were the forerunner of the modern limited companies.

Business objectives and the decision-oriented approach

In this section we discuss the objectives of firms. Because firms are made up of people with a wide range of different interests it is not surprising that they will have interests which conflict with one another. Whilst being true at one level, the simple idea that a company exists to 'make a profit' or to 'make money' does not provide us with the insight that we need to understand the nature of accounting. We will now take a deeper look at this issue.

Understanding the financial objectives of firms

Legally the purpose of a company is defined in its Memorandum and Articles of Association. From a financial point of view, although it is never formally stated, the financial purpose of a company engaged in trade for profit is to maximise its own value. Traditionally, this has been interpreted to mean that a firm should maximise its profits available for distribution to its shareholders. In more modern terms this idea is generalised to one where the firm seeks to maximise its shareholders' value. There is another way of looking at the modern business firm and that is to regard it as subject to the interests of a variety of stakeholder groups of whom the shareholders are one. A **stakeholder** is anyone who has a financial or other interest in a particular business. The various stakeholder groups in a typical firm and their respective interests can be described as follows:

- The shareholders who will be interested in the distributable earnings of the firm from which any dividend to them can be paid. They will, therefore, be interested in the profit after all business costs including taxation and interest payments on borrowed capital have been discharged. This profit will give them a measure of their return on capital and what could be reinvested and/or distributed to them.

- Lenders of loan capital to the firm who will be interested in the profit before interest and tax and the ability of the firm to pay their interest at the due date and repay their capital.

- Management will have an interest in determining the success of their efforts in running the business over the period concerned. They will be interested in maximising their salary, bonuses and other perks like company cars.

- The employees at all levels who will be interested in the profit for the period as this measures the surplus earned by the firm on their labour and thus the maximum which management could distribute to them in terms of higher wages. The labour force may also be represented by a union which will become a separate stakeholder group in its own right.

- The suppliers and customers of the business will be interested in the financial strength of the business and its creditworthiness in the case of suppliers. Large customers will also be keen to measure the financial strength of the business in order to assure themselves of the supply of the goods or services offered – especially when stage or **prepayments** are involved.

- The taxation authorities who will be keen to establish the 'taxable profit' of the business which is the period's revenue less those costs which the business is allowed to deduct in deriving its taxable profit.

- Society at large also has an interest in the operation of firms. Society, through its legal system grants important protection to business by granting limited liability. The social *quid pro quo* is that companies comply with the regulations imposed by society and make a periodic disclosure of their financial affairs.

However, in seeking to maximise its value, on behalf of either its shareholders or its stakeholders more generally, a firm will be subject to a number of constraints. Those constraints include the availability of capital, labour and supplies. These are what we call resource constraints. It may also be constrained by a variety of regulatory constraints: these range from the conditions of a licence required to carry on the trade of selling alcohol for example, through to the standards required for an airworthiness certificate before an aeroplane can fly. In this book you will become familiar with a variety of accounting standards that specify the type of accounting information that can be produced.

The separation of ownership and control

It is often assumed that the role conflict between those who own firms (i.e., who want the firm to maximise the value of their stake in the business) and those who manage them (who want to maximise their own reward) will be detrimental to the pursuit of profit maximisation as an overriding objective. The significance of this separation of ownership and control and the potential problems it can cause were pointed out in an influential book by two American scholars, Adolf Berle and Gardiner Means, in 1932. Much of the modern economic theory of the firm is based upon this presupposition, and in particular **agency theory** is the study of the outcomes that can occur when one party to a relationship, the principal, has different objectives from the other, the agent. In the case of business firms, the principal is assumed to be the owner or shareholders and their agents are the directors. Economic (or agency) loss can occur because the agent acts in his or her own interest rather than that of the owner. There are two sources of this moral hazard that the principal faces:

- Information asymmetry: which simply means that given the agent necessarily knows more than the principal they will tend to use that knowledge to their own advantage.
- Adverse selection: which means that the agent will select opportunities that maximise their own remuneration and perks rather than those which maximise the value to the principal.

Agency theory leads to a number of predictions about the behaviour of agency relationships and the steps that must be taken to mitigate loss. These will involve the creation of risk-sharing contracts between the principal and the agent which specify the performance required of the agent, their remuneration and other forms of compensation, and the monitoring that will be imposed to ensure they do their job properly.

In reality, the agency problem between investors and directors is more illusory than real for the following reasons:

- The principal in the business relationship is the company rather than the shareholder and the directors set the priorities and goals for the business, not the shareholders.
- Because directors, in most firms, invariably own shares in their business they will benefit in the same way as the ordinary shareholders from the activities of the firm.

In small firms where the owner or owners leave the business entirely in the hands of an agent then the problems outlined above can occur. The theory is also useful when an independent agent is appointed by a company to undertake work on its behalf. For example, many firms appoint overseas agents to handle buying and selling their goods and services in a country where they have no knowledge of local conditions and practices. However, agency theory has been very influential in the United States and in the UK in establishing national policy with respect to the regulation of companies, though it is in this area that the theory seems most suspect. We will return to this issue in Chapter 6.

The purpose and characteristics of accounting information

Financial accounts are summarised statements of the performance of a business over a given period of time prepared for use by the external stakeholders of the business. The financial accountant makes comparisons between the revenue and costs incurred by a business in order to measure the surplus earned over that period. This surplus is what the accountant calls 'profit'. The estimation of accounting profit involves the following four stages:

1. Specifying the period over which the firm's profit will be measured. This is usually a year, but it may be a 3-month or 6-month period. This is termed the period of account.

2. Identifying to which period of account the revenues earned by the business should be attributed. This involves what accountants refer to as a 'revenue recognition concept', i.e., a set of principles for deciding, in any given case, into which period the revenue should be counted.

3. Matching the costs which can be fairly attributed to the effort involved in earning that revenue in the period concerned. The problem the accountant has to solve is how best to match the varying expenditure made by the business to the revenues it has earned. Expenditure on such things as plant, buildings and land may occur in years different from those in which they were used in the process of earning revenue. This problem is what accountants refer to as 'cost recognition'.

4. Finally, when the clearest and most logical matching has been achieved between revenues in a given period and the costs which can be fairly charged against those revenues then a figure for profit (accounting revenues minus accounting costs) can be calculated.

The accounting statement of matched costs against revenues is referred to as the 'income statement'. However, at any point in time certain expenditures and receipts will not have been matched to a given period. This list of unmatched balances forms the 'balance sheet' at a specific date.

The decision-oriented approach to accounting

The creation of a firm's profit and loss account and balance sheet is intended to provide a statement of the financial performance of the business over time in order to help the stakeholders of that firm make their own financial decisions.

This decision-oriented approach is fundamental because all of the other purposes to which accounting can be put, and as outlined at the beginning of this chapter, can be reduced to one of decision making. For example, it could be argued that accounts are prepared as part of the stewardship function of management, by ensuring that the managers of the company exercise their roles in ways that the principal stakeholders, the owners, or government expect. But the stewardship function of management involves decisions, namely has a particular individual, or part of the firm, managed its resources properly and in ways that were expected? If not, what remedial action can be taken to correct matters? These are all decisions so, arguably, the stewardship function of accounting is simply part of its wider purpose of supporting the decision-making needs of users.

In applying the decision-oriented approach it is necessary to:

1. Identify the user, whether they are a shareholder, manager, employees or any of the others mentioned above.

2. Ascertain the decision maker's financial objective: this could be, to give just two examples, to maximise the value of a shareholder's investment, or to increase the take-home pay in the case of an employee or manager.

3. Specify the decision: buy, hold or sell the company's shares as a shareholder, sell a product to the company concerned as a supplier for example.

4. Identify the information required to support the decision: projection of future distributable profits for the shareholder or projections of trading profit before salaries are charged for the employee.

5. Decide upon the most suitable form in which the information can be provided.

Although the above may appear like a statement of the obvious there are a number of problems with this decision-oriented approach:

- The decision-oriented approach can be so widely defined that it becomes a truism that the only value possessed by accounting information is that it supports someone's decision in some way or other. The trouble with truisms is that they rarely get us very far. To be effective a definition of the purpose of accounting must have limited applicability.

- Applying the approach to user groups entails identifying groups that have common information needs. The classification of groups outlined above hides important sub-groups: for example, owners of shares in companies range from institutional investors to those who own shares in their private capacity. Others hold shares for long-term capital growth and others for more immediate speculative purposes. Does it make sense to lump them together into a single category?

- The user group analysis ignores the fact that any given individual may fall within more than one category of user. A particular individual may be an employee of British Airways, for example, and also a shareholder in the company. She may also own shares in a bank that lends money to Virgin Atlantic (which competes with BA) and in another company that supplies it with machine parts. She is also a member of society and a taxpayer. This one individual straddles a number of different user groups. In such a situation her information requirements may well conflict with one another.

However, the decision-oriented approach has been very influential amongst accounting academics and accounting policy makers. Over the last twenty years, accounting policy makers have been searching for a conceptual framework for defining the nature of accounting information. The decision-oriented approach has been central in that search.

The nature of accounting information

Accounting information is data that has financial significance for users who need it for their own decision-making purposes. The crucial distinction between data and information is that information is any data which changes an individual's beliefs about the future. Because we make decisions upon the basis of our beliefs about the consequences of those decisions then information is necessarily data that can influence the outcomes of the decisions we wish to make.

The search for a conceptual framework for accounting has been a search for some set of overriding principles that would allow those that regulate the work of accountants to deduce a set of accounting standards specifying how financial information should be disclosed to users. Underlying this search has been the idea that there is a set of principles for judging whether accounting information will be useful to any given user or user group. In the end the UK's Accounting Standards Board (the ASB) produced a set of five quality criteria for testing the usefulness of accounting information and any standards regulating how it should be disclosed. These criteria are:

- materiality
- relevance

- reliability
- comparability
- understandability.

These are classified into 'threshold', 'primary' and 'secondary' as shown in Exhibit 1.4.

Exhibit 1.4	The three levels of information criteria		
Secondary criteria	Comparability		Understandability
Primary criteria	Relevance		Reliability
Threshold criteria		Materiality	

Materiality

Accounting information is only material if it is likely to have an impact upon the business decisions of the user who receives that information. **Materiality** is partly concerned with the size of the impact of the information upon the reported performance of the business. It is also partly concerned with the significance of the information in terms of any other transactions that might be involved and the legality of what is involved. It may also be the case that what is material at one level of a firm's consideration will not be material at another. A relatively low level manager may well worry about the outcome of a negotiation for a photocopier contract worth less than a £1000 a year, but at the level of the firm's financial reports this transaction would be insignificant, especially if the firm were so large that its published financial accounts are rounded to the nearest thousand pounds.

Materiality is referred to as a threshold quality in that none of the subsequent quality characteristics matter if the information is immaterial to the decisions of users.

Relevance

The more important of the two primary criteria is that accounting information should be relevant to the user's needs. This criterion of **relevance** is simply a restatement of the definition of information given above and clearly immaterial information fails the relevance test if it is so insignificant that it does not alter the beliefs of the decision maker. However, other information may well be irrelevant to the needs of a specific user. For example, knowledge that England won the World Cup in 1966 may be interesting but will have no significance to you when deciding whether or not to buy this book. Similarly, your decision to buy this book should not be influenced by the cost you incurred in travelling to the bookshop. As you are at the bookshop anyway what matters is whether this is a good book, how much cash you have to spend and whether this book is the best you can find in this subject area. The cost of travelling to the bookshop is irrelevant to your purchase even though it might be quite a substantial sum of money. This makes the important point that revenues and costs that have already occurred are almost certainly irrelevant when making decisions. Only information about your current choices and their future consequences are likely to be important to you in making a decision.

A further aspect of relevance is that accounting information should be timely. Clearly accurate and relevant information supplied too late to be useful to the decision maker is a waste of time and effort and may only serve to confuse the situation.

Reliability

For information to have **reliability** you must be confident that it has been produced in an unbiased way and is free from material error. If it is uncertain information, relating to future consequences based upon estimates and forecasts then you will want to be sure that it has been prepared in a reasonable way, making as few assumptions about what will happen as possible. The issues of bias and error can cause problems because one person's bias tends to be another person's reasonable assumption. Accountants, by and large, try to make prudent and cautious assumptions that tend to lead them to underestimate benefits and overstate costs. This is a form of bias which whilst reasonable in many situations can severely distort decision making in others.

Comparability

When information is produced relating to similar events it should be comparable. A measurement of profit for this year should be comparable to the same profit measure last year. Similarly, if profit is calculated for firm A then ideally it should be comparable, that is produced on the same basis, to that for firm B. In the former case, the principle of **comparability** is about ensuring consistency across time; in the second case it is ensuring consistency of practice. Generally, accountants find it easier to ensure that the same procedures are applied from one time to another, but have much greater difficulty in agreeing standards for the production of accounting information between different firms. This is an issue to which we will return in some detail in Chapter 5.

Understandability

Understandability is a relative term. The ASB, in its Statement of Principles for Financial Reporting (1995), suggests that accounting information should be understandable to the intended user. However, the ASB goes on to state that those who prepare information are entitled to assume that that the users have a 'reasonable knowledge of the business' and of

Financial realities   How much are you expected to know? This is what the accounting framework published by the International Accounting Standards Board says on the matter:

An essential quality of the information provided . . . is that it is readily understandable by users . . . users are assumed to have a reasonable knowledge of business and economic activities and accounting and a willingness to study the information with reasonable diligence. However, information about complex matters that should be included . . . because of its relevance to the economic decision making of users should not be excluded merely on the grounds that it may be too difficult for certain users to understand.

Framework for the Preparation and Presentation of Financial Statements, IASB, 1989 and subsequently adopted by the International Accounting Standards Committee (2001).

accounting and 'a willingness to study with reasonable diligence the information provided' (ASB Statement of Principles for Financial Reporting, 1999, para 3.25).

By the end of this book you will be able to understand most of the information which accountants produce. However, you will not be typical, and it is arguable the extent to which accounting reports for external users can ever be truly understandable to those who have not had some training in the subject. The more problematic issue is the extent to which the users of accounting information are able to put what they are given into context and that, as you will see in the following pages, is the real problem that most users face.

The trade-off between cost and relevance

In accounting we deal with a trade-off between cost and relevance. In order to make information more relevant to the needs of particular users the firm will incur higher costs. Low relevance or highly generalised data can be readily extracted from a firm's database and the cost of doing so is normally very low. The information produced will incur greater cost the more relevant the data become and the more refined and specific it is made to a particular user's decisions.

From the user's point of view, irrelevant data produce what we call misspecification error and the users will have to incur significant costs to correct that error. However, the more relevant the data become for their needs, the lower the misspecification cost they have to bear. As Exhibit 1.5 shows, there is a point at which their combined cost (the total cost) reaches a minimum – and that is the ideal point to be in terms of the effort made in making data relevant to the needs of users. The obvious conclusion is that the cost of producing perfect information will be unacceptably high to those who have to provide it. Accountants always have to make this balancing judgement: to what extent is it worth further refining the information produced? As the chapters of this book proceed you will be able to find out some of the answers yourself.

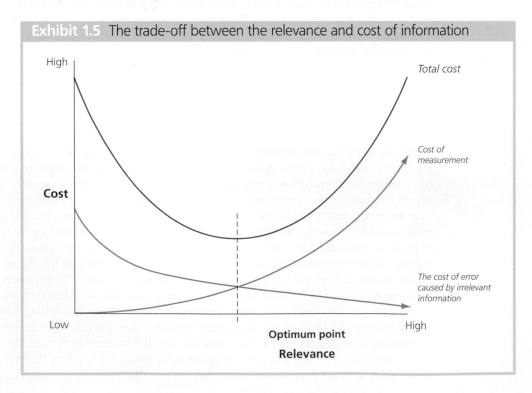

Exhibit 1.5 The trade-off between the relevance and cost of information

The concept of income and the measurement of profit

Financial accounting is primarily concerned with the problem of measuring the surplus value generated by a business over a given time period (normally a year). This surplus has traditionally been known by accountants as the 'profit' of the business. However, economists refer to the surplus generated by a business over time as 'income'. For accountants profit could be measured by taking the value flows into a business (its revenues) and deducting the value outflows (its costs). Economists, on the other hand, view income as the difference between a business's value at the end of a period minus its value at the beginning. The accounting or 'transactions' based approach to profit measurement and the economists' value-based approach to income measurement deliver the same answers if (and it's an important if) they can agree on the way that the business will be valued and what therefore counts as a revenue flow and as a cost.

To give an example: assume that an accountant and an economist agree that a business has £1 000 000 of net assets (i.e., assets less liabilities at the beginning of the year). It earns £500 000 of revenue and incurs £200 000 of costs. Let us also assume that the firm's assets do not wear out and that both the economist and accountant agree that the value of the business at the end of the year is £1 300 000. The accountant will do a very simple calculation to get to profit:

$$\text{Profit} = \text{total revenue} - \text{total cost}$$
$$= £500\ 000 - £200\ 000$$
$$= £300\ 000$$

He or she will also confidently assert that the value of the business at the end of the period will be £1 300 000 which is the opening value plus the profit accumulated in the year (i.e., value at the end of the year = value at the beginning plus profit retained in the business).

The economist will resort to a definition of income first proposed by John Hicks in his 1939 book *Capital and Value* that income is the difference between an individual's wealth at the beginning and the end of a period.

$$\text{Income} = \text{wealth at the end of the period} - \text{wealth at the beginning of the period}$$
$$= £1\ 300\ 000 - £1\ 000\ 000$$
$$= £300\ 000$$

However, in practice the accountant and the economist are rarely likely to agree. As we shall see later in this book the economist measures the value of the net assets of the business in terms of the future cash flows those net assets will generate over their expected lifetime converted to present value equivalents. The accountant will value them at either the cost they were originally purchased for or what is now termed their 'fair value', i.e., the amount they could be sold for between a willing buyer and a willing seller. So, in practice the measurement of profit or 'accounting income' is very unlikely to agree with the measurement of 'economic income' as the accountant will carry on reporting profit of £300 000 but the economist will report income at whatever level is determined by the revaluation of the net assets in question.

It may be difficult to see what the problem is here; after all accountants are not economists. Accountants get paid more for a start. However, the two principal accounting standard setting bodies in the world: the Federal Accounting Standards Board in the US and the International Accounting Standards Board (in the rest of the world) have been systematically downplaying the transactions approach and promoting the value-based approach to the measurement of profit. They have not been wholly successful, but one thing they have tried to do is to change

the term 'profit and loss account' to 'income statement'. The only problem is that within the income statement itself the word 'income' does not arise – the word profit is retained. One thing will become rapidly apparent to you as you study financial accounting – there is a confusion and indeed a profusion of terminology in the subject. As with religion (and accountants have been referred to as the high priests of business) – where clarity and mystery compete, mystery always wins – hands down.

The difference between financial and management accounting

The traditional distinction made between financial and management accounting is that financial accounting is about providing information for external users whilst management accounting is concerned about providing information for management. In reality this is not a particularly useful distinction because it is not strictly true.

Management accounting provides a wide range of internally used information much of which also contributes to the creation of the financial accounts. Financial accounts are also an important source of information to management. So, if the internal/external distinction isn't the real answer, what is? The answer is that management accounting uses different **matching principles** from financial accounting.

To illustrate the distinction between the matching principles employed by financial and management accountants consider a merchant business like that operated by Amazon.com. Amazon buys in stock from suppliers and sells that stock after a period of time to its customers. It may also, with certain lines, only buy the product in once it has a confirmed order. The inflow of stocks into the business, and their outflow to customers creates what accountants term cash flows. We show this simple business model in Exhibit 1.6.

The accountant, and presumably the merchant, will be interested to know how the cash receipts and the cash payments arising from the flow of stocks relate to one another, and there are a number of approaches to evaluating that relationship.

It might be that Amazon is interested in the surplus earned by the business from its sales of stocks over a set period of time (say a year of trading). The company's financial accountants would then attempt to identify which cash receipts from sales could be matched to the year in question (this will give the year's revenues) and then to match to those inflows all the costs which can fairly be attributed to the process of earning that revenue. Such costs will be the costs of the stock purchased as well as, perhaps, a range of other more general business costs incurred during the year. This process of matching financial flows to a given period is temporal matching, and the surplus created is called 'profit'.

Exhibit 1.6 The Amazon.com business model

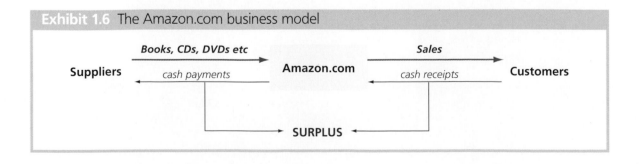

However, it is possible to create meaningful financial relationships using other matching bases. For example, the company may well be interested in the surplus earned by a given decision to sell a particular consignment of stock. The costs and revenues that can be uniquely attributed to that decision can be evaluated and the difference identified and measured. This is an example of what we would term 'decision matching' and **contribution** is the name we give to the surplus that results. In practice, decisions can have long- as well as short-term consequences. For example, the company may decide to invest in a distribution system for delivering orders to customers. The cash consequences of that decision may well be spread over many years. The measurement of the impact of that decision on the value of the firm will therefore need to be corrected for the different times at which they occur. The contribution of a long-run decision to the value of the firm is called its **net present value**.

Finally, Amazon might be interested in the cost or the surplus arising from the supply of just one unit of a particular stock line, taking into account a fair allocation of the costs of running the business as a whole to each of those particular units of stock. This would be an example of what we call 'allocation matching'.

Because managers are responsible for making business decisions and in assessing the results, management accounting is primarily concerned with decision and allocation matching whilst financial accounting is principally concerned with measuring the performances of the business over time.

Chapter summary

In this chapter we have explored some of the basic ideas and some of the history of accounting and finance. Accounting is a developing subject concerned with the provision of financial information for different users. But apart from that, accounting has many other roles within business firms. It is part of the process of maintaining control of a business and of keeping a check on its assets and liabilities. However, to gain a deeper understanding of the nature of accounting we have had to explore the different varieties of business firm in terms of their size, their purpose and their legal form.

The nature of information and the way it is used has also been a feature of this chapter. The principles which we have discussed are important in clarifying the purpose of accounting and the distinction between financial and management accounting.

These are all issues that we will return to as the chapters of this book and your understanding of the subject unfolds.

Further reading

Here is a brief selection of readings on the history of accounting and the financial markets:

Edwards, J.R. (1989) *A History of Financial Accounting*, London and New York: Routledge. This book is rather difficult to obtain now but well worth the effort of contacting your local library. It gives a comprehensive overview of accounting history from the ancient world to modern times.

Hennessy, E. (2001) *Coffee House to Cyber Market: 200 Years of the London Stock Exchange*, London: Ebury Press. This is a 'coffee-table book', full of pictures and anecdotes about the London Exchange.

Micklethwaite, J. and Woolridge, A. (2003) *The Company: A Short History of a Revolutionary Idea*, New York: Random House. This splendid little book traces the history of the company from 3000 BC to the present day.

Progress check

These questions are designed to test your comprehension of the subject matter of this chapter. They are straightforward, so if you do not know the answer we recommend that you return to the page referenced and refresh your understanding.

1. List four aspects of the role of accounting. (pp. 5–6)

2. Complete the following: Information is data which has .... (p. 6)

3. What distinguishes the money from the capital market? (p. 7)

4. What two events led to the transformation and spread of accounting between the 12th and 15th centuries? (p. 8)

5. Name four fundamental types of business operation. (p. 10)

6. Name three factors that distinguish firm size. (p. 12)

7. List five characteristics of a limited liability company (p. 14)

8. To whom are the directors of a company accountable? (p. 14)

9. What are the four principal duties of the directors of a company? (pp. 15–16)

10. List four stakeholder groups with an interest in the typical firm. (p. 17)

11. On what matching principle is financial accounting based? (p. 19)

12. Identify the five steps in the application of the decision-oriented approach to accounting. (pp. 19–20)

13. List the five quality criteria in the provision of accounting information. (pp. 20–21).

14. What are the two matching principles which characterise management accounting? (p. 25)

Questions

The answers to these questions can be found on the website accompanying this book **www.cengage.co.uk/ryan2.**

1. Consider the shareholder and the director user groups. Describe at least five ways in which their personal objectives might conflict. For each of the conflicts you have already described, how might the director use their position to ensure that it is their own objectives that are satisfied rather than those of the shareholders?

2. Obtain a copy of a quality daily newspaper and identify any article that refers to or discusses the financial problems of a named business firm. Using the World Wide Web as a source discover using a search engine such as Google or Yahoo! all that you can about the company concerned.

3. On a sheet of paper draw two columns. Head the left hand column 'financial accounting' and the right-hand column 'management accounting'. Using the two columns make comparative notes distinguishing between the two branches of accounting. Limit yourself to one page of paper.

4. Accounting developed in Europe in response to the needs of merchants. Discuss the extent to which the subject has had to change in response to the development of other types of business enterprise.

5. There are a number of different criteria for evaluating the quality of accounting information. Discuss the extent to which these add anything to our understanding of the nature of such information.

Case exercise

Most large companies have a website that contains 'investor information' such as the latest set of accounts and any other information relevant to shareholders. On the Internet locate the websites for the following companies using a suitable search engine such as Google or Yahoo!:

- Cobham
- IBM
- Marks & Spencer

- Merrill Lynch
- Rolls-Royce
- Royal Bank of Scotland.

Try to locate the overall company website and, starting from the homepage, navigate to the investor relations page (sometimes called 'financials'). Make a note of what you find in the way of financial accounts and for what year. You may find interim accounts – do not ignore these, as they are useful sources of updated information. Your most important find will be the most up-to-date set of final accounts. Once you have found those accounts:

1. Locate the main sections within the accounts: chairman's report, operating review, directors' report, auditor's report, profit and loss account/income statement, balance sheet, cash flow statement and notes to the accounts.

....

2. Identify the main business type and the size of the firm: by its turnover, and by its workforce.

....

3. Read the auditor's report: locate the phrase 'true and fair view'. Is this phrase qualified in any way?

Part 2

2
Financial accounting

Chapter 2

Introduction to financial accounting

In the last chapter, we outlined the objectives and purpose of financial accounting in reporting the performance of a business over a set period of time. In this chapter we show how this is done, slowly building the basics of the subject from first principles. We will start with a simple intuitive exercise looking at how a small trader, in this case a taxi driver, commenced business, and then reviewed his financial position at the end of his first month trading. From there we will show how accounts are built up using a few simple principles. These principles capture the essence of the subject and with them you will see how the accounts of a larger enterprise are constructed. These principles will also help you create a 'mental map' of the financial accounting process so that by the end of this chapter you will be able to identify how particular business decisions impact upon the financial performance of a business.

Learning objectives

There are five outcomes we hope you can achieve in this chapter. Again we have split the chapter down into 'learning sections', which are:

The first principles of financial accounting

- That you understand the principles of identity, additivity and matching and their importance in transactions-based accounting.

- That you understand the principal ways of classifying assets and liabilities.

- That you know how assets, liabilities and claims are related through the extended trial balance.

- That you can relate your understanding of the structure of accounts to the balance sheet published by a public limited company.

How to produce a set of simple accounts

- That you can produce, for the first year of a business's operation, from simple transactions:

  1. An income statement
  2. A cash flow statement
  3. A balance sheet

The first principles of financial accounting

In this section you will familiarise yourself with the basic principles upon which financial accounting is based.

The identity principle

If you buy a car, and borrow some money from the bank to help finance your purchase, then the value of the car will equal the bank borrowing plus the amount not covered by the loan. That amount is your own financial stake in the car. The car is an asset in that it is useful to you. You own the vehicle and, within the bounds of what is legal, you can use it any way you wish. From a financial point of view, the value of the asset you have acquired is equal to the cost of the bank loan and the remainder of its value which belongs to you. The value of the loan from the bank is the bank's claim on the value of the car and the balance which belongs to you is your claim as the owner.

If the car cost £10 000, and the loan was for £8000 then the following relationship is true:

$$\text{£10 000 (value of car)} = \text{£8000 (value of loan)} + \text{£2000 (value of your claim)}$$

This expresses a simple truism that the value of every asset, by definition, must equal the value of the financial claims on that asset. Similarly, if an individual or organisation owns a portfolio of assets, then the value of those assets must equal the value of the claims of third parties such as banks and other lenders plus the claim of the individual or business concerned.

In general terms, this idea gives rise to the simple business identity:

$$\text{Total asset value of the firm} = \text{Value of claims on those assets}$$

This balance between the value of a firm's assets and the claims upon those assets always holds true. Any net increase in the value of one side must be reflected in a corresponding increase in the other. We will expand this formal relationship later, but note for now that this relationship is fundamental in financial reporting and encapsulates what we term the identity principle.

The classification of assets

Our first step in understanding how accounts are prepared and what they mean is to understand the meaning of the terms 'asset' and 'claim'.

Assets are the valuable property of an individual or a business. The international body which regulates the way that financial accounts are produced, the International Accounting Standards Committee (IASC) – which is now called the International Accounting Standards Board (IASB), defines an asset as 'A resource controlled by the enterprise as a result of past events and from which future economic benefits are expected to flow' (IAS 16, IASC 1999) (Epstein 2006).

An asset may be held because of its intrinsic value: such assets enhance our quality of life. Other assets are held for their investment value, in that they can yield future cash flow. Some assets achieve both. Accountants have two ways of classifying assets: first as current or non-current, and secondly as tangible, intangible or monetary.

Non-current assets

Non-current assets used to be known as 'fixed assets'. However, the term 'fixed' did not fully capture the variety of assets that firms hold in order to create the operating capacity of the business concerned. For want of a better term, the International Accounting Standards Board (IASB) settled upon non-current assets to describe those assets that a business intends to hold for more than one year. Normally they are held in order to maintain or expand the operating capacity of a business which, in financial terms, means its ability to earn cash in future periods. Land and buildings, machines (referred to as 'plant') and equipment, and motor vehicles would all be classed as non-current assets. Exhibit 2.1 is an extract from the balance sheet of Cobham plc, a manufacturer of high technology systems in the aerospace industry. Note how this company has classified its non-current assets.

Cobham has distinguished between 'intangible assets', **tangible assets** in the form of property plant and equipment, investment properties, the share it owns of the assets and liabilities of joint ventures it has undertaken with other companies, and then some further assets which will not be turned into cash within twelve months. Trade and other receivables represent money receivable from customers who will pay some time beyond one year; derivative financial instruments are rather exotic financial securities owned by the company to help manage its interest rate and currency risk exposure, and deferred tax assets represent effective credits against future tax liabilities.

Current assets

Current assets are real, monetary and very occasionally intangible assets that have less than one year to run before they are converted into cash. Cash is also deemed to be a current asset. The most important current assets are inventories, receivables and cash.

Exhibit 2.1   Extract from the balance sheet of Cobham plc, 2006

£m	Note	2006	2005
Assets			
Non-current assets			
Intangible assets	12	482.6	528.1
Property, plant and equipment	14	187.6	202.8
Investment properties	15	6.4	4.0
Investments in joint ventures	16	15.7	14.7
Trade and other receivables	18	9.2	8.5
Derivative financial instruments	25	8.6	4.5
Deferred taxation assets	22	6.9	6.8
		717.0	769.4

Exhibit 2.2 The flow from raw materials, through work in progress to finished goods

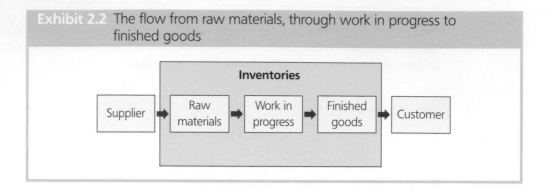

Inventories: this includes bought-in inventories which could in the case of a manufacturing company be raw materials and components; work in progress which is partly made products or partly completed services; and finished goods due for sale. For a manufacturer the production sequence is therefore as shown in Exhibit 2.2. In merchant businesses, the only stock held will be bought-in goods for resale. A firm's inventory is a real asset and as such we would expect its value to fluctuate with the changing levels of supply and demand for that type of asset. In Chapter 11 we will explore the valuation of inventory in more detail.

Receivables (traditionally known as 'debtors'): these are customer accounts due to be paid to the business in question. Most businesses sell their goods on credit. This means that when goods or services are delivered they are invoiced to the customer and the customer normally then has an agreed period to make payment. During this period their account is outstanding and, given that the amount owed is contractually certain, such balances represent monetary assets.

Cash and cash equivalents: cash is the most liquid asset of all and has its own special slot in the listing of current assets. It includes cash-in-hand, current account balances and short-term deposits held with banks. Long-term deposits or investments would be counted amongst the fixed assets.

In Exhibit 2.3 we show the balance sheet of Cobham plc giving the different current assets at the accounting year end. Note the layout of this statement of current assets with the least liquid asset (inventories) shown first, then descending to the most liquid asset of all (cash). Note also that the company has separately identified some other current assets which whilst

Exhibit 2.3 Extract from the balance sheet of Cobham plc, 2006

£m	Note	2006	2005
Current assets			
Inventories	17	160.2	167.2
Trade and other receivables	18	182.6	208.5
Corporation tax		3.2	2.1
Derivative financial instruments	25	7.0	1.7
Cash and cash equivalents	19	364.3	251.8
Assets classified as held for sale	33	–	18.1
		717.3	649.4

not of significant size compared with the total require separate disclosure. Corporation tax is where a tax has been overpaid or indeed prepaid and is therefore a benefit that can be claimed in the current year. Derivative financial instruments are again the rather exotic financial securities referred to under non-current assets but this time yielding cash returns within one year. Finally, assets classified for sale are those assets within a part of the business which is just due to be sold off. At the end of 2005, Cobham was just due to sell a subsidiary company called Wallop Defence Systems Ltd which had assets worth £18.1 million. In 2006 the sale had been completed, the cash received and thus the current asset had been fully disposed of.

The classification of claims

The claims against the assets of a business are of two types: the claim of the owner, which we term the owner's equity, and the claims of all others who are not the owner. These we refer to as the independent claims. In a business, the ownership claim is that of the group of individuals or other organisations who hold shares in the ownership of the business concerned. The sum total of their claim is the ownership claim of the business.

The owner's claim

When individuals set up a business they normally introduce some personal capital into their business. This forms the owner's initial claim on the assets of the business. Where there is a single owner operating as a sole trader this capital will be in the form of cash or other assets which will be taken over by the business at their current market value. Where there are a number of owners they will also donate capital to the business in the form of cash or other assets and will have in exchange an ownership share in that business. If there are no independent claims against the assets of the business then the following will be true:

$$\text{Total asset value of the firm} = \text{Value of capital introduced}$$

As the business develops the value of the assets of the firm will increase and, again assuming that there are no independent claims, the following will be true:

Exhibit 2.4 The relationship between the owner's claims and the total asset value of the firm where there are no independent claims

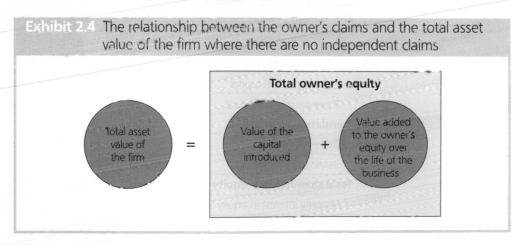

$$\text{Total asset value of the firm} = \text{Value of the capital introduced} + \text{Value added to the owner's equity over the life of the business}$$

Total owner's equity

Exhibit 2.8 Extract from the balance sheet of Cobham plc, 2006			
£m	Note	2006	2005
Non-current liabilities			
Borrowings	23	(132.2)	(151.6)
Trade and other payables	20	(7.8)	(7.8)
Derivative financial instruments	25	(2.5)	(2.0)
Deferred taxation liabilities	22	(25.6)	(8.8)
Provisions	21	(22.9)	(20.9)
Retirement benefit obligations	9	(29.6)	(81.0)
		(220.6)	(272.1)

Cobham accounts, that the tax authorities owe the company tax for an assessment (that will show up in receivables) and is owed tax by the company which will show up in receivables.

- *Provisions:* these are amounts that the company believes it may have to pay out in the next 12 months under headings such as warranties, or lose through such items as bad debts. In Cobham's case it is for possible losses on contracts and warranties on equipment supplied.

- *Derivative financial instruments:* in this case this is where the company owes money on purchases or sales of financial securities purchased not for investment but for managing interest rate and currency risk.

Typical non-current liabilities are as follows:

Borrowings: these are sometimes called loan stock, debentures or mortgages, and have maturities in excess of one year. Such loans are taken out to raise the often large sums of money needed to purchase fixed assets such as land, buildings, and plant and equipment. Note that interest payable on long-term loans, even though the loans are classed as non-current liabilities, will be short-term and included under 'other creditors'.

All the other headings apart from retirement obligations are the analogues of the current liabilities outlined above. Retirement benefit obligations occur when the company's pension fund is in deficit in that the fund's assets do not cover the future liabilities to pensions. Over the longer term the company must address the issue and pay sufficient funds into the scheme to remedy the shortfall.

Putting the balance sheet together

Now that we have surveyed the various elements of a balance sheet we can use the identity principle to show how it is constructed. Remembering for Cobham, as for any business, that the assets of the business will equal the claims upon those assets:

Non-current assets + Current assets = Current liabilities + Non-current liabilities + Owner's equity

Using the latest figures for Cobham this identity becomes:

$$£717.0 \text{ million} + £717.3 \text{ million} = £498.7 \text{ million} + £220.6 \text{ million} + £715.0 \text{ million}$$

We will use this identity relationship to create balance sheets and income statements: indeed this identity relationship is the basis of the double entry bookkeeping system described in the appendix at the end of the next chapter. The income statement focuses on the change in the owner's equity account bought about by process of operating and running the business for the year. The cash flow statement (which we explore in detail in the next chapter) focuses on how the cash of the business (shown within current assets) changed during the year.

Exhibit 2.9 shows the balance sheet for Cobham plc based upon the recommended layout under the International Financial Reporting Standards.

The Cobham balance sheet rearranges the identity relationship to highlight the owner's claim upon the business – and it is laid out in vertical format. Note also the accountants' practice of showing negatives with () rather than a minus sign which is easily lost in the printing process.

$$\text{Non-current assets} + \text{Current assets} - \text{Current liabilities} - \text{Non-current liabilities} = \text{Owner's equity}$$

$$£717.0 \text{ million} + £717.3 \text{ million} - £498.7 \text{ million} - £220.6 \text{ million} = £715.0 \text{ million}$$

The equals sign is where the balance is struck with the net assets of the business totalled to give the same value as the owner's equity at £715.0 million.

Irrespective of which regulatory body sets the standards to be used, every balance sheet will reflect the basic identity relationship. The US model, for example, uses a different ordering of the standard layout:

$$\text{Current assets} + \text{Non-current assets} = \text{Current liabilities} + \text{Non-current liabilities} + \text{Owner's equity}$$

The US layout does not highlight the owner's claim as clearly as the International Accounting Standards model but rather presents an 'entity' perspective highlighting all the claims on the business together.

Exhibit 2.9 2006 Balance sheet for Cobham plc

Consolidated balance sheet

As at 31 December 2006

£m	Note	2006	2005
Assets			
Non-current assets			
Intangible assets	12	482.6	528.1
Property, plant and equipment	14	187.6	202.8
Investment properties	15	6.4	4.0
Investments in joint ventures	16	15.7	14.7
Trade and other receivables	18	9.2	8.5
Derivative financial instruments	25	8.6	4.5
Deferred taxation assets	22	6.9	6.8
		717.0	769.4
Current assets			
Inventories	17	160.2	167.2
Trade and other receivables	18	182.6	208.5
Corporation tax		3.2	2.1
Derivative financial instruments	25	7.0	1.7
Cash and cash equivalents	19	364.3	251.8
Assets classified as held for sale	33	–	18.1
		717.3	649.4
Liabilities			
Current liabilities			
Borrowings	23	(231.2)	(276.9)
Trade and other payables	20	(182.6)	(174.2)
Derivative financial instruments	25	(1.8)	(3.5)
Corporation tax		(45.1)	(48.1)
Provisions	21	(38.0)	(42.7)
Liabilities classified as held for sale	33	–	(14.2)
		(498.7)	(559.6)
Non-current liabilities			
Borrowings	23	(132.2)	(151.6)
Trade and other payables	20	(7.8)	(7.8)
Derivative financial instruments	25	(2.5)	(2.0)
Deferred taxation liabilities	22	(25.6)	(8.8)
Provisions	21	(22.9)	(20.9)
Retirement benefit obligations	9	(29.6)	(81.0)
		(220.6)	(272.1)
Net assets		715.0	587.1
Capital and reserves			
Called-up share capital	26	28.3	28.1
Share premium account	27	94.2	87.5
Translation reserve	27	(8.9)	1.9
Other reserves	27	16.0	11.3
Retained earnings	27	585.3	456.8
Total shareholders' equity		714.9	585.6
Minority interest in equity		0.1	1.5
Total equity		715.0	587.1

Review activity 2.2 Go online and find the accounts of Boeing at www.boeing.com. Navigate to the investors website and download the latest set of financial accounts contained within the annual report. Find the statement of financial position (the US term for the balance sheet) and identify the sections of the statement which correspond to the headings 'current assets', 'non-current assets', 'current liabilities', 'non-current liabilities' and 'owner's equity'.

In the case exercise below we take a small business start-up and show intuitively how the financial accounting system works.

Creating the balance sheet and income statement – a case exercise

Financial realities Sid Buckle had been made redundant from his job and with the compensation payment decided to establish a taxi business serving the mean streets of Watford. The town was poorly served by taxi companies and Sid believed there was an opportunity to be taken. His wife, Beryl – a lecturer in finance at the local technical college – was not so sure. However, after taking a training course in the local 'knowledge' and obtaining his Hackney Carriage Licence, Sid with Beryl's help took along a business case to the bank. Sid had £15 000 available and the bank agreed to lend him £20 000.

Sid paid £30 000 for a new TX4 taxi from the London International Taxi Company, carefully printed his name 'Sid's Taxis' on the side, filled it with diesel and started to tour the streets of Watford looking for customers.

Exhibit 2.10 shows Sid's opening balance sheet.

Exhibit 2.10 Sid's opening balance sheet at the beginning of the first month of operation

	£	
Value of the taxi at cost	30 000	(Non-current asset)
Cash in hand	5 000	(Current asset)
	35 000	
Bank loan	20 000	(Non-current liability)
Sid's capital	15 000	(Owner's equity)
	35 000	

Note the following about this balance sheet:

1. The account is shown in 'vertical' format. That is, Sid's assets and the claims upon them are listed down the page. Where the statement is ruled off is where the 'equals' sign comes in the relationship of assets to claims. For Sid:

2. There is one other potential asset which we have not mentioned: the value of Sid's brand, 'Sid's Taxis'. Presumably, at the start of the business this brand would have zero value, but as the business develops this asset will become more valuable and could potentially be worth more than all the other assets combined.

3. The total value of the assets employed in the business is £35 000. As far as Sid is concerned, his claim is valued at the net value of all his business assets after the independent claim of the bank has been deducted. The net value of his ownership claim is £15 000.

The first month's financial statements

At the end of the first month of trading, Sid had taken £800 in fares, had spent £150 on diesel and had a full tank worth £45. His monthly interest payments to the bank were 0.5% of the outstanding loan. At the beginning of the month, he paid £60 for a six-month rental of a garage. He decided not to take any cash out of the business as his wife's earnings as a lecturer were more than enough to live on. When he totalled up what he had at the end of the month, he was able to put together a statement for his business as in Exhibit 2.11.

Notice what has happened. Sid has accumulated some assets: diesel in his tank, the right to use the garage for a further five months (this is an example of a prepayment) and some extra cash. Indeed, when he checked his bank account into which he had placed all his takings and made his expenditures he noted that his end-of-month balance had risen to £5490.

Exhibit 2.11 Sid's balance sheet at the end of the first month of operation

Total value of assets

Value of the taxi at cost	30 000	(Non-current asset)
Value of diesel in tank	45	(Current asset)
Five months' entitlement to garage	50	(Current asset)
Cash in hand	5 490	(Current asset)
	35 585	

Less independent claim

Bank loan	20 000	(Non-current liability)
	15 585	(Net assets employed)

Owner's equity

Sid's investment	15 000	(Owner's capital)
Net value added to Sid's claim	585	(Retained profit)
	15 585	(Owner's equity)

Exhibit 2.12 Sid's cash flow statement for the first month of trading

Opening cash balance		5000
Add cash from fares		800
		5800
Less:		
Diesel	150	
Garage rental	60	
Interest on bank loan	100	
		310
Closing cash balance		5490

We can readily deduce how this happy state of affairs had come about by taking the value of his cash receipts and deducting his cash payments during the month to give a simple cash flow statement.

However, when we check the increase in the value of Sid's owner's claim (£585) we note that this is not the same as the increase in his cash (£490). The reason is that whilst all his cash receipts were due to his efforts during the month, some of his cash payments were incurred in acquiring assets that were not fully used up during the month concerned. The diesel, for example, cost £150 but only £105 of this was used during the month, the rest being an asset available for use in the following month. Similarly, the garage rental was for six months but during the first month he only 'used up' one-sixth of this expenditure.

If you review this business start-up carefully, some issues might occur to you:

1. We have not accounted for Sid's time and effort, or for the knowledge of the roads of Watford which he presumably had when he started and which increased as the month went by. We have missed out both the value of, and the use of, a significant intangible asset. Sid.

2. Was his taxi still worth £30 000 at the end of the period? Has he not used up part of its value over the first month, and how much was that loss in value due to the use of the taxi and how much because a second-hand car is never worth the same as a new vehicle?

3. Has he built the value of his business because of his reputation as a safe and reliable taxi driver? In other words has the goodwill value of his business and the value of his company name increased?

Taken as it stands, Sid's taxi business has increased in net value to him by £585. That increase in Sid's net value is his accounting earnings or his profit for his first month of trading.

Exhibit 2.13 Sid's income statement for the first month of trading

Revenue (value adding activities)		
Fares		800
Less expenditures (value reducing activities)		
Cost of diesel used	105	
Proportion of garage rent	10	
Interest paid	100	
		215
		585

The three statements of account

Sid has produced three linked financial statements:

- A balance sheet showing the balance between the assets of the business and the claims on those assets.
- An income statement showing how the owner's equity has increased or decreased through the 'earning' activity of the business over the period of account.
- A cash flow statement showing how the cash balance of the business has changed over the period of account.

Two ways of measuring accounting income or profit

It is important to realise that profit can be measured in two ways:

1. In a direct valuation-based approach the difference in the net value of the business at the beginning of the period is compared with its net value at the end. To measure profit in this way we must be able to value all of the firm's assets and deduct the value of the independent claims against those assets. This means that we must employ an asset valuation principle which raises the question: do we value assets at their original cost of acquisition as we did in this example, or do we value them on some other basis such as their market value?

Financial realities   For Sid compare the balance sheet as it stood at the end of the month with the opening figures. We have reorganised the opening balance sheet in order to create a comparable layout. Note the value of the owner's claim: it has risen by £585 being the increase in the net value of the business. This gives the profit earned during the month.

Exhibit 2.14 **Sid's balance sheet at the start of his business and at the end of the first month of trading**

	1 month	opening
Total value of assets		
Value of the taxi at cost	30 000	30 000
Diesel in tank	45	
Five months entitlement to garage	50	
Cash in hand	5 490	5 000
	35 585	35 000
Less independent claim		
Bank loan	20 000	20 000
	15 585	15 000
Equals the owner's claim		
Sid's investment	15 000	15 000
Net value added to Sid's claim	585	0
	15 585	15 000

2. In a transactions-based approach we add together the revenues earned during the period and deduct the expenditures incurred in earning that revenue. If the market values of a firm's assets remain unchanged then the profit will equal the revenues earned less the costs incurred. To operationalise the transactions-based approach, the accountant needs some rules for recognising the revenue accruing during the period of account and for recognising the resultant costs in earning that revenue. If because of changes in the underlying market values of its assets the values of the firm's assets also change then it will have to reflect the new values in the statements of account. In the exercises that follow we will assume that the market values of the assets do not change and that the value they are carried at in successive balance sheets is their original or historic value.

The extended trial balance (ETB)

If we take the identity between assets and claims shown above and break it down further, we have the following relationship:

$$\text{Non-current assets} + \text{Current assets} = \text{Current liabilities} + \text{Non-current liabilities} + \text{Owner's equity}$$

We can develop this relationship further by subdividing the current assets into inventories, receivables and cash, and by separating out of the owner's equity the profit earned in the previous period of account, namely the revenue for the period less the matched expenses:

$$\text{Non current assets} + \text{Inventories} + \text{Receivables} + \text{Cash} = \text{Current liabilities} + \text{Non-current liabilities} + \text{Owner's equity} + \text{Revenue} - \text{Expenses}$$

This relationship between assets and claims contains nine items and is a variant of what accountants refer to as an 'extended trial balance' or 'ETB'. The reason for its name we will outline when we take a brief look at the double entry bookkeeping system at the end of the next chapter. It is important, so it is strongly recommended that you take the time to learn it. Your ultimate objective is to be able to see this balance between assets and claims in your mind's eye as a mental model of the way that the financial components of a business are organised.

For economy's sake we will use the following abbreviations when describing this equation:

$$\text{NCA} + \text{Inv} + \text{Rec} + \text{C} = \text{CL} + \text{NCL} + \text{OE} + \text{R} - \text{E}$$

In order to use this balance to construct balance sheets and income statements we need some simple rules. We also need a principle for deciding whether a transaction affects the revenue and expenditure of the business (in which case it is value-adding or -depleting from the owner's point of view) or whether it affects the balance sheet.

The identity principle again

Every transaction impacts upon the ETB twice so as to maintain the arithmetic balance between assets and claims. Therefore, any change in either side must be matched by either:

- a corresponding change on the other side of the equation or
- a contra entry on the same side where a positive change is matched by a negative change or vice versa.

Two further principles

As well as the identity principle, two further principles are required in order to produce accounts using the transactions approach to income measurement. The first principle allows us to decide whether a given transaction can be regarded as a revenue or an expense, and thus impact upon the profit for the year, or whether it should remain as an unmatched item and be left as an outstanding amount in the balance sheet. The second principle is more subtle in that we assume that the value added to the owner by way of profit is the sum of the value changes on all the transactions during the year.

The matching principle

The purpose of the matching principle is to ensure that value changes to the owner's equity are properly recognised in the accounting period in which they occur. Revenues are value-adding changes, and are recognised in a period of account if the effort involved in earning them took place during the time period concerned and the receipt of the money involved is reasonably certain. What that means is that the revenue should represent a sale transaction for which an order has been received and which has been discharged to the customer's satisfaction. Later on in this chapter we will explore this problem of revenue recognition more fully once you have understood how to use the principle to create an income statement.

Expenditures are value-depleting transactions that are recognised in the accounting period concerned if they can be directly attributed to the process of earning the revenue or, if they are more general business expenditures, be allocated on a time basis to the period of account. In Sid's case above, the cost of the diesel fuel is a direct expenditure, but the rental for the garage has to be allocated to the first month's period of account. Normally, expenditures are recognised if they are likely, as opposed to certain, as is the case when recognising revenues. This introduces a bias towards conservatism in the way that profit is calculated.

The additivity principle

No matter how assets are valued in the balance sheet, accountants assume that the value of the firm as a whole equals the sum of the values of its individual assets less its liabilities. This principle was first articulated by Frederick William Cronhelm in his book *Double Entry by Single* (1818), where he argued that the fundamental purpose of bookkeeping, as he called it, is to demonstrate the equilibrium of a set of accounts. Transactions, Cronhelm argued, served to either increase or decrease the account of the owner, increase or decrease liabilities, or increase or decrease assets. As we have done he used an algebraic approach to demonstrate that whatever happens to capital it will always be equal to the sum of its component parts, a principle he articulated as follows:

It is the primary axiom of the exact sciences, that the whole is equal to the sum of its parts; on this foundation rests the whole super structure of bookkeeping.

F. W. Cronhelm (1818, p. 4)

This principle is specifically referred to in the UK Companies Act (1985) as the non-aggregation principle which states that 'in determining the aggregate amount of any item the amount of each individual asset or liability that falls to be taken into account shall be determined separately' (para. 14, Companies Act, 1985). However, this all-pervasive principle can be challenged. Any business is more than the sum of its parts but rather a combination of various assets and liabilities put together in a way which creates value. Indeed, the whole process of adding value results from the successful combination of human ingenuity, physical resources and capital to create additional wealth. The additivity principle introduces a tendency to understate the value of the firm in the balance sheet as it ignores the way assets are linked together.

How to produce a set of simple accounts

In this section we will take the extended trial balance and use it to construct a simple set of accounts. Our first example will be to rework Sid's accounts described in the previous section. We will then tackle a more substantial problem where we will produce the accounts for the first year of a new business.

Using the extended trial balance

We will now use the extended trial balance to rework Sid's example. Our first step is to lay out the full extended trial balance across some paper or a spreadsheet as in Exhibit 2.15.

The first three transactions are:

1. The introduction of Sid's capital of £15 000. This will be shown as both an increase in owner's equity and cash of £15 000.

2. The loan is shown as an increase in the new business's non-current liabilities and a corresponding increase in cash.

3. The purchase of the taxi is shown slightly differently as it impacts on the asset side only, with a reduction in cash of £30 000 and an increase in non-current assets of the same amount.

Exhibit 2.15 The extended trial balance for the first year of trading

		NCA +	Inv +	Rec +	C =	CL +	NCL +	OE +	R −	E
(i)	Introduction of capital				15 000			15 000		
(ii)	Loan from bank				20 000		20 000			
(iii)	Purchase of taxi	30 000			−30 000					
	Opening balance sheet	30 000			5 000		20 000	15 000		
(iv)	Purchase of diesel		150		−150					
(v)	Diesel used in month		−105							105
(vi)	Rental for garage Rental charge to month			60 −10	−60					10
(vii)	Interest on loan Interest paid				−100	100 −100				100
(viii)	Cash from fares				800				800	
									800	215
	Profit for the period							585		585
	Closing balance sheet	30 000	45	50	5 490	0	20 000	15 585	800	800

The opening balance sheet

The transactions during the month

Closing off the account

We then rule off, add each of the columns, and the totals form the values to be entered in the opening balance sheet.

4. The next series of transactions were conducted during the first month of trading and again we lay out each transaction as it is undertaken.

5. The purchase of diesel is initially shown as an asset transaction as cash is spent and diesel received of £150 (decrease cash, increase inventories).

6. Some of that diesel is recognised as an expense attributable to the process of earning revenue during the month. This is an expense transaction showing the consumption of £105 of diesel (reduce inventories, increase expenses). Note that all expenses are negative by definition.

7. Rent of £60 is paid in advance, creating a receivables balance (reduce cash, increase receivables). One month's rent is recognised for the month in question (reduce receivables, increase expenses).

8. Interest on the loan becomes due (increase current liability, increase expenses) for the month in question and the liability is discharged by a cash payment (decrease cash, decrease current liability).

9. Finally, we recognise the revenue that Sid earned during the month with an £800 increase in cash and revenue respectively.

Closing the extended trial balance

Step 1: total the revenue and expense columns as shown and take the difference and transfer it to the owner's equity account. The details in the revenue and expenditure columns form the income statement.

Step 2: total each of the remaining columns, ensuring that the sum total of the columns on the left of the equals sign equals the values on the right. The column totals are the entry values into your balance sheet.

Step 3: the figures in the cash column give the details of the cash receipts and expenditures which form the statement of cash flow.

Review activity 2.3   Sid's business during the next month is even better than in the first. Sid purchased a further £200 of diesel and had just filled his tank with £35 worth before finishing on the last day of the month. He paid a service bill of £240 at the beginning of the month which he believed would keep his taxi in good shape for the next 3 months. He also purchased and installed a GPS navigation system for £560. During the month he collected £1450 in fares. Prepare an income statement and balance sheet for his second month of business using the extended trial balance approach.

✓ Check the answer to this Review activity at the back of the book (see page 493).

Chapter summary

In this chapter we have explored the basic mechanics of financial accounting. The extended trial balance provides you with a simple model of the financial structure of any business. Using Sid's start-up of a taxi business you should be able to identify how transactions will impact upon the income statement and balance sheet. You should also have gained some familiarity with the component parts of a balance sheet. In the next chapter we will develop your skills in financial reporting based upon what you have now accomplished.

Further reading

Arnold, J., Hope, A., Southworth, A. and Kirkham, L. (1994) *Financial Accounting*, London: Prentice Hall. This is an excellent book with which to develop your understanding of the theory of accounting using an early version of the extended trial balance approach.

Atrill, P. and McLaney, E. (2002) *Financial Accounting for Non-specialists*, 3rd edn, Harlow: Financial Times, Prentice Hall. A very straightforward text which does not use the extended trial balance approach but focuses on adjustments to the face of the accounts. A useful secondary source to the present book.

Elliot, B. and Elliot, J. (2001) *Financial Accounting and Reporting*, Harlow: Financial Times, Prentice Hall. This is one of the best books on financial reporting and you will find that Chapters 1 and 2 give a good introduction to cash-based and accrual-based accounting. Note, however, that the conceptual approach to the subject is not as shown in this book.

Francis, J. and Schipper, K. (1999) Have financial statements lost their relevance?, *Journal of Accounting Research* 37(2):319. A serious article in one of the top research journals to get you thinking.

Higson, A. (2002) *Corporate Financial Reporting: Theory and Practice*, London: Sage. An excellent text to develop your skills and general knowledge of the problems of financial reporting. Try the first three chapters.

John, B. and Healas, S. (2000) Financial Reporting Standard for smaller entities – a fundamental or cosmetic change, ACCA Occasional Research Paper No 30, Certified Accountants Educational Trust, London 2000. An interesting article if you are interested in the problems of accounting for small businesses with an excellent review of the relevant literature.

Progress check

These questions are designed to test your comprehension of the subject matter of this chapter. They are straightforward, so if you do not know the answer you should return to the page referenced and refresh your understanding.

1. The terms *real*, *intangible* and *monetary* all relate to a particular accounting concept. What is it? (p. 35)

2. How are non-current and current assets distinguished from one another? (p. 35)

3. List four different types of current asset. (p. 36)

4. In the absence of any new capital introduced, or any withdrawal of capital by the owner, what will cause the balance on the owner's equity account to change from year to year? (p. 37)

5. List three classes of current liability and two classes of non-current liability that will appear in the typical balance sheet. (pp. 39–40)

6. In what ways does a US balance sheet differ from that presented using the UK method of preparation? (p. 41)

7. State two different ways in which accounting income can be measured. (pp. 46–47)

8. Write out the headings of the full extended trial balance. (p. 47)

9. Why is the matching principle important when preparing an income statement and balance sheet? (p. 48)

10. What do you understand by Cronhelm's additivity principle and why does this principle tend to lead to the understatement of the net asset value of a company as shown in its balance sheet? (p. 48)

Questions

The answers to the questions followed by [✓] can be found at the back of the book, the answers to the remaining questions can be found on the website accompanying this book: **www.cengage.co.uk/ryan2**

1. On the extended trial balance show how the following transactions would be entered:
   (i) A purchase of fixed assets worth £500 000 from a supplier for payment in one month (show both the purchase transaction and its subsequent settlement).
   (ii) The depreciation of a fixed asset originally purchased for £800 000. The asset is four years old and one-tenth of its value is to be written off.
   (iii) A customer fails to settle an outstanding account of £2000 and you decide to write it off.
   (iv) Stock that was originally purchased for £80 000 has deteriorated in the stores and is now only worth £60 000.
   (v) Goods purchased for £50 000 are deemed unusable. The supplier has agreed to their return and will refund the purchase price in full. ✓

2. Ernie Buckle has a small business which at the end of the year had equipment of £60 000, inventories of £10 000, receivables of £18 000, current liabilities of £16 000, loans of £30 000 and subscribed capital of £30 500. At the beginning of the year his retained earnings reserve was £20 000 and during the year his retained earnings on his income account was £10 500.
   Required:
   (i) What is the missing value required to create Ernie's balance sheet?
   (ii) Draw up the balance sheet in the standard format required by the International Financial Reporting Standards. ✓

3. Continuing from question 2, at the end of the following year, Ernie's balance sheet showed equipment of £80 000, inventories of £12 000, receivables of £9000 and cash of £4500. His current

liabilities were £22 000. Neither his loan nor his subscribed capital changed during the year. How much profit did he make during the year?

4. The accounting year end was the 31 December. On 1 November Sid paid £2000 for a quarter year's rent in advance and £8000 on a vehicle lease, in advance. How much would be shown in his income statement for the year to 31 December in each case and how much in the balance sheet?

Case exercises

1. Locate and print out the latest published financial report from **www.Cobham.co.uk.**
    (i)   Compare the current- and prior-year figures in the balance sheet and income statement, noting the magnitude of changes and their significance to the company.
    (ii) Compare and contrast the figures in the current year's income statement and balance sheet with the figures for 2001 shown in the text.
    (iii) Using an information service such as FT.com or Reuters.com search for the most recent financial news about the company and in particular any items commenting upon the financial perfor- mance of the company for the year you have downloaded.

2. Locate and print out the most recent accounts of Marks & Spencer plc from the **www.marksandspencer.com** website for comparison with the accounts of Cobham plc. Place the balance sheets of the two companies side by side and, using the notes to the accounts, com- pare them.
    a. Are there entries in one balance sheet that are not in the other?
    b. Where is the manufacturing aspect of Cobham's business revealed in its balance sheet?
    c. Where is the merchant aspect of Marks & Spencer's business revealed in its balance sheet?
    d. What percentage of the total assets (fixed and current) of both companies are fixed and what is the likely reason for the differences between them?
    e. For both companies: what proportion of the cash inflows during the accounting year come from operating activities?

Chapter 3

Building the accounts

In this chapter we develop the techniques for preparing financial accounts. Using the extended trial balance method and a more sophisticated example we show how an income statement and balance sheet can be prepared. However, no book on accounting is complete without an introduction to double-entry bookkeeping. Although books of account are rarely kept manually, the terms and the structure of accounts used within the traditional system are still used within computer-based systems and the language of 'debits' and 'credits' is still spoken by accountants. For this reason we will reinterpret the exercises within the chapter using the double-entry bookkeeping system.

By the end of this chapter you will be able to produce the following financial statements:

● A balance sheet showing the value of a firm's assets and the claims on those assets at a specified point in time.

● An income statement showing how the value of the owner's claim on his or her business has increased or decreased between the start and the end of an accounting period.

Although you will not be in a position to produce the accounts of IBM or Microsoft by the end of this chapter, the principles discussed here will enable you to read such statements with understanding and, more importantly, you will also have a mental model of the accounting process. This model will allow you to understand the impact of business decisions and the transactions which result on the reported financial performance of the business concerned.

Learning objectives

There are three outcomes we hope you can achieve in this chapter. Again we have split the chapter down into 'learning sections', which are:

How to produce a set of accounts for a more substantial business

● That you can produce for a more substantial business, for the first year of operation:

1. An income statement
2. A balance sheet

Accounting for the second and subsequent years

● That you can produce an income statement and balance sheet for the second and subsequent years of a business's operation.

Understanding the double entry system

● That you can understand the double entry system, the meaning of the term 'books of account' and know your debits from your credits.

A case study in business start-up

We will now consider a more extended problem of a business starting up. This is a simple merchant business in that it buys stocks from suppliers, repackages the goods in a small production facility and then sells them on immediately. There is a single owner who is therefore entitled to the balance of the business's value after all the independent claimants have been settled. Our aim is to produce an income statement for the year and a balance sheet at the year-end. We will discuss a range of different ways that the balance sheet could be laid out. The example will also introduce a new problem, namely how to deal with capital expenditure on fixed assets.

The business commenced operation on 1 January. During the first year the owner:

1. Made a £20 000 personal investment.
2. Borrowed £35 000 from the bank as a long-term loan at 10 per cent per annum.
3. Purchased equipment for £28 000. It was decided to write off the equipment completely over four years.
4. Incurred £8000 rent of which £2000 was outstanding at the year-end.
5. Purchased £19 000 of stock on credit and during the year paid £18 000 for that stock, the balance being owed at the year-end.
6. Transferred £17 500 of that stock to production, all of which was sold during the year in question.
7. Sold the finished goods for £120 000, receiving £110 000 in cash by the year-end. It was discovered that of the outstanding £10 000, £2000 was a bad debt and irrecoverable.
8. Incurred £22 500 labour cost, of which £500 was unpaid at the year-end.
9. Incurred office overheads of £15 000 and marketing costs of £20 000 of which £5000 was unpaid at the year-end.
10. The interest was unpaid at the year-end.

Exhibit 3.1 shows the extended trial balance with each of these transaction summaries entered in the way we have described above. Note that in a real business there would be many more transactions than this. The sales, for example, would consist of numerous different sales transactions undertaken throughout the year and each recorded separately, some for credit, some for cash.

As you work through each transaction note the following points:

● We have shown the purchase of the equipment for £28 000 (line 3) and then shown a year's write-off assuming that the equipment loses value equally each year that it is held. This technique for writing down the value of an asset is known as straight-line depreciation. In the next chapter we will describe other methods of writing down assets.

Exhibit 3.1											
	NCA +	Inv +	Rec +	C	=	CL +	NCL +	OE	+ R	– E
1 Personal investment				20 000				20 000		
2 Borrowing				35 000			35 000			
3 Purchased equipment	28 000			–28 000						
Depreciation for year	–7 000									7 000
4 Incurred rent						8 000				8 000
Rent paid				–6 000		–6 000				
5 Inventory		19 000				19 000				
Payment to supplier				–18 000		–18 000				
6 Stock expensed		–17 500								17 500
7 Sale of goods			120 000						120 000	
Cash received from customers			–110 000	110 000						
Bad debt written off			–2 000							2 000
8 Labour cost incurred						22 500				22 500
Wages paid				–22 000		–22 000				
9 Office overheads incurred						15 000				15 000
Office overheads paid				–15 000		–15 000				
Marketing cost incurred						20 000				20 000
Marketing costs paid				–15 000		–15 000				
10 Interest charge for year						3 500				3 500
									120 000	95 500
Profit for the period								24 500		24 500
Balance sheet as at 31 December	21 000	1 500	8 000	61 000		12 000	35 000	44 500	120 000	120 000

- When we purchased inventory we have treated it as the acquisition of an asset and then subsequently expensed the inventory that has gone into production and been sold.
- Part of our outstanding receivables balance proved to be irrecoverable. In this eventuality the bad debt is written off as an expense in the year in question. It is incorrect to put this as a reduction in the sale figure of £120 000 as that will distort the value of what was sold during the year.

Constructing the balance sheet

As you can now see, the balance sheet is simply a listing of the assets and claims of the business outstanding at the end of a given accounting period. We will show three styles of layout. They all convey the same information but lay it out in a different way, emphasising different aspects of the accounting equation.

Horizontal format (traditional)

This is the traditional layout and is no longer used in the UK or the US but is still the basic pattern in some Far Eastern countries. This design emphasises the balance between assets and claims.

Exhibit 3.2

Balance sheet as at 31 December, year 1

Horizontal format

Non-current assets			Owner's equity	
Equipment		21 000	Capital introduced	20 000
Current assets			Accumulated profit	24 500
Stocks	1 500			44 500
Debtors	8 000		**Non-current liabilities**	35 000
Cash	61 000			
		70 500	**Current liabilities**	12 000
		91 500		91 500

You should be able to see quite easily how the total for each element of this balance sheet has been taken from the foot of each column of the accounting equation ignoring the last two columns (which are used to construct the profit and loss account). You should note that assets are laid out in descending order of liquidity with fixed assets at the top and cash at the bottom, and that sources of finance on the right are shown in decreasing order of priority. This format for the balance sheet was popular for many years but has been superseded in the UK and the US by vertical layouts, which are said to offer a clearer reading of the statement. The UK model follows the International Financial Reporting Standards.

Vertical format (UK/IFRS)

This format takes exactly the same data but rearranges the order of the headings in the extended trial balance to this:

$$\text{Non-current assets} + \text{Current assets} - \text{Current liabilities} - \text{Non-current liabilities} = \text{Owner's equity}$$

This equation emphasises the owner's claim. The claims of the suppliers and the bank are just shown as deductions from the value of the assets on the left, leaving a net asset figure which belongs to the owner whose claim is shown on the right. It is what we term a 'proprietary perspective' when reporting the financial position of the business. The vertical format takes this sequence and arranges the data down the page rather than across.

Vertical format (US)

This statement layout has marked differences from the UK format. In this case the first part of the statement shows the assets but in reverse order of liquidity. Cash is shown first and fixed or noncurrent assets last. The total assets are balanced against the sum of the claims, but in this case they are shown in ascending order with short-term liabilities first, long-term

Exhibit 3.3

Balance sheet as at 31 December, year 1

UK format

Non-current assets

Equipment		21 000

Current assets

Stocks	1 500	
Debtors	8 000	
Cash	61 000	
		70 500
Less current liabilities		−12 000
Less non-current liabilities		−35 000
Net assets		44 500

Owner's equity

Capital introduced		20 000
Retained earnings		24 500
Total equity		44 500

Exhibit 3.4

Balance sheet as at 31 December, year 1

US format

Assets

Cash	61 000
Accounts receivable	8 000
Inventories	1 500
Current assets	70 500
Noncurrent assets	21 000
Total assets	91 500

Liabilities and stock holders equity

Current liabilities	12 000
Long-term liabilities	35 000
Total liabilities	47 000
Capital introduced	20 000
Retained earnings	24 500
Total owner's equity	44 500
Total liabilities and stock holders equity	91 500

Exhibit 3.5

Income statement

for the year ended 31 December, Year 1

Turnover	**120 000**
Less cost of sales:	
Cost of goods sold	(17 500)
Labour	(22 500)
Depreciation	(7 000)
Gross profit	**73 000**
Less other operating costs	
Bad debts written off	(2 000)
Rent	(8 000)
Office overheads	(15 000)
Marketing costs	(20 000)
Operating profit	**28 000**
Net interest payable	(3 500)
Net profit retained	24 500

liabilities second and the owner's equity last. This arrangement is said to represent an entity or whole-business perspective where all the claimants are shown as having a stake in the total assets of the company.

Constructing the income statement

The income statement is drawn from the final two columns of the extended trial balance and shows the revenues and expenditures that can be matched to the period of account. With the income statement the issue is one of layout. Starting with the total revenue figure of £120 000 (accountants call this 'turnover') the first expenditure to be deducted is the cost of sales. Cost of sales is the direct production expenditures required to produce the goods that are sold in the current year. Here we have included the cost of the goods sold being the inventories expensed during the year, the cost of production labour and depreciation on plant and equipment used in production. This creates the gross profit figure which in this case is £73 000. From gross profit is deducted other operating expenses being the normal costs of running the business during the year. This leaves the **operating profit**, from which we subtract interest payable to get the net profit retained. Later we will refine this statement as we introduce further information into our examples.

Constructing the statement of cash flow

If we look at the cash column we can analyse the various cash receipts and expenditures into:

● cash flows due to operating the business (i.e., cash received from sales less cash expenditures on materials, labour, rent, overheads and marketing):

Exhibit 3.6

Cash received from sales		110 000
less cash expenditures:		
raw materials	18 000	
labour	22 000	
rent	6 000	
office overheads	15 000	
marketing	15 000	
		76 000
Net cash flow from operations		34 000

- cash received from the owner and from other sources of long-term finance
- cash spent on the acquisition of fixed assets.

The full cash flow statement is as follows:

Exhibit 3.7

Cash Flow Statement for the year ended 31 December Year 1

Net cash flow from operations		34 000
Interest paid		0
Acquisition of fixed assets		–28 000
Changes in financing the business		
Equity subscribed	20 000	
Loan	35 000	
		55 000
Net cash inflow during the year		61 000

Because of the application of the matching principle you will note significant differences between the statement of cash flow and the income statement. Compare, for example, the calculation of **operating cash flow** with the statement of operating profit and note the differences:

- The income statement recognises the full revenue earned during the period whilst the cash flow statement excludes the sales for which no cash has been received by the year-end.
- The income statement only recognises the goods used during the year as opposed to the cash payments to suppliers. Similarly the income statement is charged with the full year's expenditure on labour and marketing, the cash flow statement with only the cash paid in wages and the amounts actually paid to the supplier of marketing services.
- The income statement shows a depreciation charge representing the life of the fixed assets used during the year. Depreciation does not appear in the statement of cash flow.

Accounting for the second and subsequent years

Your study in the last section covered the basic principles of how to produce accounts. However, when a business commences, at the start of its life each column of the extended trial balance is empty. During the first year transactions are added and the first-year accounts come out at the end as you have seen. In the second and subsequent years the starting position is not zero so your next step is to learn how to prepare accounts where the transactions are added to an existing balance sheet which forms the 'opening position' for the business at the beginning of the year.

Preparing accounts for subsequent years

The procedure for preparing financial accounts in subsequent years is very similar to that shown in the previous section, except that the closing balance sheet for the preceding year becomes the opening balance sheet for the new year. Following the previous example, assume that the business carries on into the second year. The details for the transactions for the following year are as follows:

1. Additional plant was purchased for £16 000 cash.
2. Cash was received from all outstanding customer accounts.
3. All short-term liabilities outstanding at the beginning of the year were paid.
4. Rent of £8000 was paid.
5. New stock was purchased for £24 000 of which £2000 was unpaid at the end of the year.
6. The stock held at the beginning of the year was taken into production.
7. Further stock purchased for £22 500 was taken into production.
8. Labour costs – £22 500 incurred, £22 000 paid
9. Office overheads of £18 000 were paid in full.
10. Marketing expenditure of £25 000 was incurred of which £5000 was unpaid at the year-end.
11. Sales of £165 000 were made of which £5000 had not been received by the year-end.
12. Of that sales revenue a £10 000 prepayment had been received for work not due to be completed until the following financial year.
13. The interest was paid on the loan before the year-end.
14. Depreciation on the equipment was charged at 25 per cent of the original cost. A full year's depreciation was charged on the plant acquired.

The method of constructing the extended trial balance is as before. It is worth noting, however, that some of the early transactions in effect remove the balances for current assets and current liabilities in the opening balance sheet and either convert them into, or use up cash (2) and (3) or transfer them to the expenses column as costs for the year (6). The balance sheet and income statement are now prepared in the same way except that comparative figures for the previous year can now be added.

. To summarise, we proceed through the construction of the accounts step by step:

1. The first part of the analysis is to enter the closing balance sheet from the previous period as the opening balance sheet for the new period. Note that the opening balance sheet contains assets that are likely to be quickly converted into cash either directly, in the case of

Exhibit 3.8 Accounting equation for the second year of operation

	NCA	+ Inv	+ Rec	+ C	= CL	+ NCL	+ OE	+ R	− E
Opening balance sheet as at 1 January	21 000	1 500	8 000	61 000	12 000	35 000	44 500		
1 Additional plant purchase	16 000			−16 000					
2 Outstandings received			−8 000	8 000					
3 Outstandings paid				−12 000	−12 000				
4 Incurred rent					8 000				8 000
Rent paid				−8 000	−8 000				
5 Stock purchase		24 000			24 000				
Cash paid				−22 000	−22 000				
6 Opening stock to production		−1 500							1 500
7 Further stock to production		−22 500							22 500
8 Labour cost incurred					22 500				22 500
Wages paid				−22 000	−22 000				
9 Office overheads				−18 000					18 000
10 Marketing cost incurred					25 000				25 000
Marketing costs paid				−20 000	−20 000				
11 Sales			165 000					165 000	
Cash received from customers			−160 000	160 000					
12 Deferred revenue					10 000			−10 000	
13 Interest charge for the year					3 500				3 500
Interest paid				−3 500	−3 500				
14 Depreciation on existing plant	−7 000								7 000
Depreciation on new plant	−4 000								4 000
								155 000	112 000
Profit retained							43 000		43 000
Balance sheet as at 31 December	26 000	1 500	5 000	107 500	17 500	35 000	87 500	155 000	155 000

receivables, or via production in the case of inventories. Similarly, there are some current liabilities for outstanding wages, interest payable and supplies received but not paid for that will be settled early in the new accounting period.

2. The second stage of the analysis is, as in the first year, to enter each transaction into the extended trial balance making sure that those transactions which are increasing the net value of the firm such as sales are recognised as revenues, and those costs incurred in earning that revenue are also identified and treated as expenses.

3. Finally we calculate the net profit by deducting the expenses for the revenues and transfer the profit to the owner's equity account before ruling off the balance sheet and checking that the sum total of the assets equals the sum total of the claims.

Exhibits 3.9 and 3.10 are the resulting balance sheet and income statement.

Exhibit 3.9 Balance sheet at the 31 December, year 2

Balance sheet as at 31 December, year 2

UK/IFRS format

Non-current assets	Year 2	Year 1
Equipment	26 000	21 000
Current assets		
Inventories	1 500	1 500
Receivables	5 000	8 000
Cash	107 500	61 000
	114 000	70 500
Less current liabilities	−17 500	−12 000
Less non-current liabilities	−35 000	−35 000
Total net assets	87 500	44 500
Owner's equity		
Capital introduced	20 000	20 000
Accumulated profit	67 500	24 500
Total equity	87 500	44 500

Exhibit 3.10 Income statement for the year ended 31 December, year 2

	Year 2	Year 1
Turnover	155 000	120 000
Less cost of sales:		
Cost of goods sold	(24 000)	(17 500)
Labour	(22 500)	(22 500)
Depreciation	(11 000)	(7 000)
Gross profit	97 500	73 000
Less other operating costs:		
Bad debts written off	0	(2 000)
Rent	(8 000)	(8 000)
Office overheads	(18 000)	(15 000)
Marketing costs	(25 000)	(20 000)
Operating profit	46 500	28 000
Net interest payable	(3 500)	(3 500)
Profit before tax	43 000	24 500

You may discover that two numbers that should be the same are different, or your balance sheet doesn't balance, or the extended trial balance is a little out of sync. Perhaps in your year 2 balance sheet you discovered that the net assets of the business were £87 500 and the owner's equity £85 700. Before giving up and deciding that accounting is not for you, take the difference and divide by nine:

$$(87\ 500 - 85\ 700)/9 = 200$$

If you get an answer which is a round number, i.e., the difference is perfectly divisible by nine then you have what is called a transposition error. You have made the very common mistake of reversing two digits. You can also take the difference and divide by 2. You may then recognise the number as being on the wrong side of the account.

Other entries in the accounts

In the exercises we have considered so far, two important entries in the accounts have been ignored. First, profitable businesses invariably find themselves facing a tax liability and, second, the owners of the business may decide to appropriate a part of the profit as a dividend.

Charging the income statement for tax

Tax is charged to companies on their profits for the year. If a business is not established as a limited company the profit will be assessed as the income of the owner and will be taxed as such. If the business is in the form of a company then its profits will be charged with corporation tax. The taxation of business profits often bears little relationship to the accounting profit because certain expenditures may not be allowed as an expense and the write-down of assets for tax purposes may be different from the depreciation rate charged in the accounts. We will return to the problems of accounting for tax in more detail later, but for the moment assume that our new business discussed above is liable for tax at 25 per cent of profits payable nine months after the end of the accounting year. The final rows of the accounting equation would be revised as follows:

Exhibit 3.11

	NCA +	Inv +	Rec +	C	=	CL	+ NCL +	OE +	R	– E
									155 000	112 000
tax						10 750				10 750
Profit after tax, retained								32 250		32 250
Balance sheet as at 31 December	26 000	1 500	5 000	107 500		28 250	35 000	76 750	155 000	155 000

Note that the liability for tax assessed on the profits is deemed to be a short-term liability if the payment is required within the following accounting year. If for some reason the tax liability is not payable in the following accounting year but only some time after, it would be classed as a long-term liability. The resulting income statement is shown in Exhibit 3.12.

Showing dividends as a deduction from retained earnings

The profit after tax is known as the 'net profit' or more colloquially as the 'bottom line'. This figure represents the profit potentially available for distribution as a dividend to the owner.

Exhibit 3.12

Income statement

for the year ended 31 December, Year 2

	Year 2	Year 1
Turnover	155 000	**120 000**
Less cost of sales:		
Cost of goods sold	(24 000)	(17 500)
Labour	(22 500)	(22 500)
Depreciation	(11 000)	(7 000)
Gross profit	**97 500**	**73 000**
Less other operating costs:		
Bad debts written off	0	(2 000)
Rent	(8 000)	(8 000)
Office overheads	(18 000)	(15 000)
Marketing costs	(25 000)	(20 000)
Operating profit	**46 500**	**28 000**
Net interest payable	(3 500)	(3 500)
Profit before tax	**43 000**	**24 500**
Tax	10 750	0
Net profit attributable to shareholders	**32 250**	**24 500**

In practice the owner will make a choice about the proportion of the net profit he or she wishes to take as a dividend or leave as retained profit in the business. In the above example let us assume that the owner wishes to take a dividend payment of 5p per pound of subscribed capital. This dividend payment will be outstanding at the end of the year and the entry in the accounting equation will be as in Exhibit 3.12.

Since the implementation of the International Financial Reporting Standards, dividends are not shown as a deduction from distributable profit in the income statement but as a reduction in the retained earnings figure within the balance sheet. The resulting balance sheet is shown in Exhibit 3.13.

Exhibit 3.13

	FA +	St +	Db +	C	=	STL +	LTL +	OE +	R	–	E
									155 000		112 000
tax						10 750					10 750
dividend						1 000		(1 000)			
Profit after tax, retained								32 250			32 250
Balance sheet as at 31 December	26 000	1 500	5 000	107 500		29 250	35 000	75 750	155 000		155 000

Review activity 3.1 Taking the closing balance sheet from the example above prepare a balance sheet and income statement for the third year of trading incorporating the following transactions:

1. The owner purchased some land for £40 000 cash. This land would not be depreciated.
2. A customer went bankrupt and £1500 of the debtor balances at the beginning of the year had to be written off. The remaining customer accounts were received.
3. The owner settled all the outstanding short-term liabilities, recognised the deferred revenue and paid off £20 000 of the bank loan on 1 January.
4. The owner purchased new stock from suppliers for £30 000 and at the year-end stock count recorded raw materials originally purchased for £1800.
5. The finished goods produced were all sold for £175 000 of which £155 500 was received from customers by the year-end.
6. Labour costs incurred were £28 000 of which £25 500 were paid during the year.
7. Office overheads and rent were paid of £20 000 and £8000 respectively.
8. Marketing costs of £28 000 were incurred during the year which were paid in full along with a prepayment for the development of a new marketing campaign for the following year of £2000.
9. Interest was paid and depreciation charged on the existing fixed assets.
10. The liability for tax at 25% of accounting profits was assessed as due for payment the following year.
11. A dividend of 20p in the pound was declared but not paid at the year-end.
12. The owner withdrew an additional £25 000 from the capital account in cash.

Double-entry bookkeeping

So far in this book we have avoided the use of terms such as 'debit' and 'credit', 'journal', 'ledger' and so forth. In this section, our objective is to familiarise you with this 'language' of double-entry bookkeeping using the example of the start-up business described earlier in this chapter. Double-entry bookkeeping is not as straightforward as the techniques of account production discussed so far. However, the 'language' of double-entry bookkeeping is widely used by accountants. The terminology of double-entry also appears in most computerised accounting systems although internally those systems do not use the mechanics of the double-entry system.

You will remember that when we used the extended trial balance that every transaction was recorded twice. In essence the extended trial balance is a double-entry system: it is relatively easy at the end of each exercise to establish that the whole thing balanced. The traditional double-entry system allows much more systematic records of financial transactions to be kept and recorded in individual 'books of account'. Once the transactions for a period of time have been made the 'balances' on each of the books of account are taken out and the final accounts produced. Furthermore, the use of 'books of prime entry' allows the initial recording of transactions to be separated from the job of writing up accounts themselves.

Debits and credits

The easiest way to remember the idea of a debit and a credit is to remember the reality of the way that money lenders would give their customers cash and the way it was received. The Roman money lender would sit at one side of a table (the *banca*) and transfer money to his

Exhibit 3.14 The money lender and his client

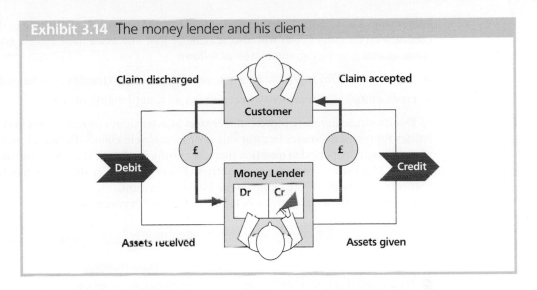

customer with his right-hand, naturally writing on the right hand-side of his slate the value of the cash paid out. A right-hand-side entry represented the value of an asset (in this case cash) given. When the cash was repaid the entry would naturally be put on the left-hand side (as that is where the money lender would most naturally pile the cash returned to him). The left-hand side represented the value of the asset received.

Now, note what happens if the money lender decides to keep a record of the cash received and paid by his customer. The customer's account will receive the cash on the left-hand side of that account and payments will be recorded on the right.

Note some other points as well: once the payment is recorded in the money lender's cash account on the right-hand side a corresponding entry appears in the left-hand side of the customer's account, and vice versa when the cash is repaid. As each transaction is recorded twice it is very easy to see that the sum of the left-hand balances in the customer's account in the money lender's books must equal the sum of the right-hand balances in his or her cash book and vice versa. The system is therefore self-balancing.

But why debit and credit? The words have Latin roots, meaning something owed (*debitum*) and trust (*creditum*). The customer received a cash sum which was owed to the money

Exhibit 3.15 The elements of the double-entry system

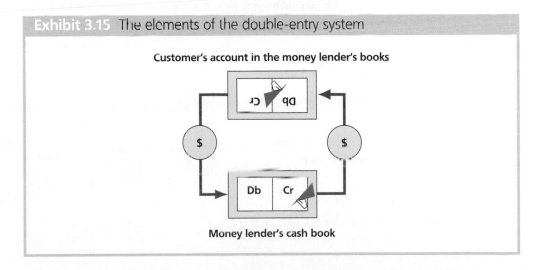

Customer's account in the money lender's books

Money lender's cash book

lender (thus a debit entry), the money lender in his turn entrusted the money to the customer (hence a credit entry). You will also remember that any asset must have a corresponding claim against it so we can summarise as follows:

- debit entries (Db) represent an asset received or a claim (liability) discharged
- credit entries (Cr) represent assets given or a claim (liability) incurred.

Debit entries therefore represent increases in asset values or reductions in claims. Credit entries represent decreases in asset values or increases in claims. Because revenue matched to the accounting period in question increases profit and hence the size of the owner's claim, revenue items are shown as credit entries. Expenditures, on the other hand, are profit-reducing and are therefore debits in the books of account.

Exhibit 3.16 shows the entries as far as the business is concerned.

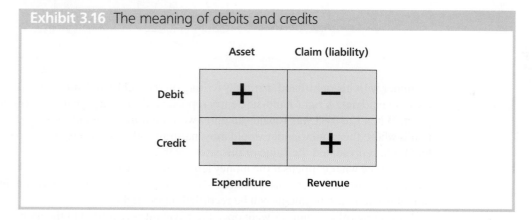

Exhibit 3.16 The meaning of debits and credits

If you still cannot remember your debits from your credits try remembering 'DC' as 'direct current' or 'District of Columbia', or whatever acronym works best for you.

The books of prime entry

In the days of the early merchants crossing Europe to the fairs of France, or those of Florence, buying and selling goods shipped in from around the Mediterranean, transactions were recorded in the **journal** as they were made and later written up in the books of account.

Financial realities

Luca makes and sells 6 jars of Old Spice to Paco for $20. He also receives cash of $50 owed by Antonio. Here are the journal entries:

Exhibit 3.17 Luca's journal

Paco's Account	Db	$20
To: Spice sales		$20
Sold to Paco, six jars of Old Spice		
Cash received	Db	$50
To: Antonio's Account		$50
Antonio's paid at last – the miserable vagrant		

Over the centuries and with the increasing volume of trade two specialised journals emerged: the sales day book and the purchases day book. The former recorded all of the sales made during the day analysed into columns by product type. The total sales of, for example, Old Spice would then be credited to the sales account (the equivalent of the revenue column in the balance sheet equation) and each customer's account would be debited with the individual sale made. Similarly with purchases, all purchases were entered into the day book and at the end of the day the totals were debited to either inventory or expenses, and each supplier's account was credited with the individual purchase made.

The ledgers

The books of account proper were maintained in four ledgers:

- Sales ledger: this ledger contained all of the individual customer accounts which when the balances on each account were totalled together gave the outstanding debtor balance at that point in time.
- Purchase ledger: similarly this ledger contained all the individual supplier accounts which when balanced and totalled gave the sum of trade creditors.
- Nominal ledger: this contained all of the other accounts except for the cash book.
- Cash book: most businesses maintain the cash book as a separate ledger.

In Exhibit 3.18 we show how these ledgers relate to the individual columns of the extended trial balance:

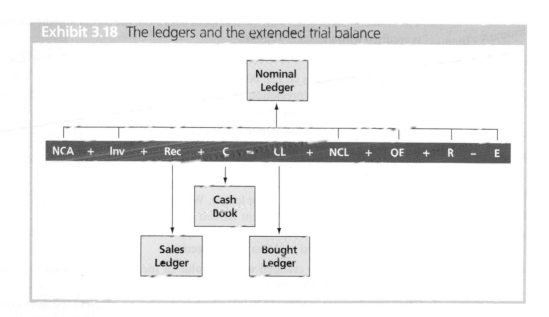

Exhibit 3.18 The ledgers and the extended trial balance

Entering transaction in the books of account

Putting the elements of learning so far together, it should be straightforward to see how accounts are constructed using the double-entry system. Returning to the start-up case exercise discussed earlier:

Customer's Account

Db		Cr	
7 Sales	120 000	7 Cash received	110 000
		7 Bad debt written off	2 000

Sales Account

Db		Cr	
		7 Sales to customers	120 000

Labour Cost

Db		Cr	
8 Staff wages	22 500		

Interest on Loan

Db		Cr	
10 Bank loan account	3 500		

Loan Account

Db		Cr	
		2 Borrowing	35 000
		10 Interest accrued	3 500

Owner's Capital Account

Db		Cr	
		1 Investment	20 000

Fixed Asset Account

Db		Cr	
3 Equipment	28 000		

Accumulated Depreciation

Db		Cr	
		3 Dep'n of equipment	7 000

Depreciation for the Year

Db		Cr	
3 Dep'n of equipment	7 000		

Cost of Goods Sold

Db		Cr	
6 Stock Account	17 500		

Bad Debts

Db		Cr	
7 Customer's account	2 000		

Office Overheads

Db		Cr	
9 Office overheads	15 000		

Marketing Expenditure		
Db		**Cr**
9 Marketing supplies	20 000	

Rent Account		
Db		**Cr**
4 Rent for the period	8 000	

Stock Account		
Db		**Cr**
5 Stock purchased	19 000	6 Cost of Good Sold	17 500

Striking a balance

At the end of the period of account the difference between the sum of the debits and the sum of the credits is entered as a balance carried forward and the two columns are totalled. This balance carried forward is then shown as the opening balance brought forward for the next period but on the opposite side. If we have a look at the cash account we can see the procedure for doing this:

Exhibit 3.20 Closing off the cash book

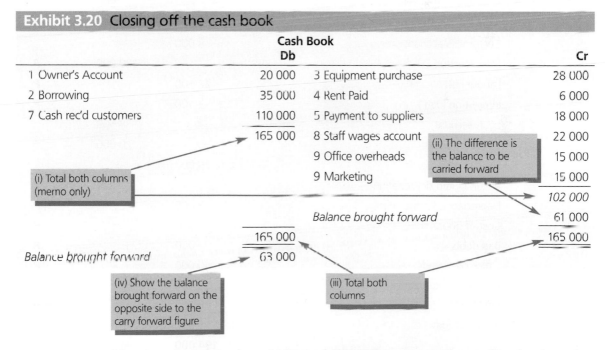

Note how the balance brought forward (£61 000) represents the surplus of cash receipts over expenditures during the period, and this would be the debit balance for the next period.

FYI   One point of confusion is that a cash balance in the favour of the firm is a debit balance but most people who get bank statements have always assumed that this would mean that they are in credit. The reason why a bank statement shows you 'in credit' is that the statement is your account in the bank's books. If you are in credit that means that the bank owes you money, i.e. you are, as far as it is concerned, a creditor.

Review activity 3.2 Take the balances on all of the other accounts in Exhibit 3.19 and list them in two columns: debit balances on the left-hand column, credit balances on the right-hand column.

Closing the accounts

This proceeds in two stages: first the accounts are proved by creating what is called a 'trial balance' (TB). This is a memorandum account only and functions simply to check that the double entries have been made consistently. Once the balances on each account have been calculated the brought-down figures are listed as you have already done in the review activity above. The result is like this:

Exhibit 3.21 The trial balance

Trial Balance	Db	Cr	
Cash book	61 000		
Landlord's account		2 000	
Trade suppliers		1 000	
Staff wages (payroll)		500	
Suppliers (marketing)		5 000	
Customer's account	8 000		
Sales revenue		120 000	P
Labour cost	22 500		P
Interest on loan	3 500		P
Loan account		38 500	
Owner's capital		20 000	
Fixed asset account	28 000		
Accumulated depreciation		7 000	
Depreciation for the year	7 000		P
Cost of goods sold	17 500		P
Bad debts	2 000		P
Office overheads	15 000		P
Marketing expenditure	20 000		P
Rent	8 000		P
Stock account	1 500		
	194 000	194 000	

When the two columns of the 'TB' are 'cast' they are equal to one another, thus proving the integrity of the double entries made during the year. Note that we have also marked some accounts 'P' – these are the accounts that contain revenue and expenditure that can be matched to the year in question. The second stage of closing the accounts is to transfer the balances on these accounts to a new account called 'income statement', the balance of which is in its turn transferred to a new account called 'earnings reserve'.

Exhibit 3.22 Closing off the 'revenue accounts' to the income statement account

Income statement

Db			Cr
Labour cost	22 500	Sales revenue	120 000
Interest on Loan	3 500		
Depreciation for the year	7 000		
Cost of goods sold	17 500		
Bad debts	2 000		
Office overheads	15 000		
Marketing expenditure	20 000		
Rent	8 000		
Balance to earnings reserve	24 500		
	120 000		120 000

Profit and loss reserve

Db		Cr
	Profit retained	24 500

Once a business starts to make profits the profit and loss reserve becomes a permanent part of the owner's capital in the nominal ledger. Once the revenue and expenditure accounts have been cleared from the books the trial balance reduces to this:

Exhibit 3.23 The final list of balances

Trial Balance	Db	Cr
Cash book	61 000	
Landlord's account		2 000
Trade suppliers		1 000
Staff wages (payroll)		500
Suppliers (marketing)		5 000
Customer's account	8 000	
Loan account		38 500
Owner's capital		20 000
Earnings reserve		24 500
Fixed asset account	28 000	
Accumulated depreciation		7 000
Stock account	1 500	
	98 500	98 500

This final 'sheet of balances' is of course the balance sheet at the year-end after rearrangement into an acceptable form and the profit and loss account above is the basis of the published profit statement. The only live balances now in the company's books of account are the

3. Describe three ways in which the income statement differs from the cash flow statement. (pp. 60–61)

....

4. When starting the accounts for a second or subsequent year what is the starting point? (p. 61)

....

5. What is deducted from turnover to get gross profit? (p. 63)

....

6. Following the implementation of the International Accounting Standards, dividends are not shown in the income statement. Where are they shown? (p. 65)

....

7. If an asset is received is it shown as a debit or a credit entry? (p. 67)

....

8. Is an expense a credit or a debit entry in the books of account? (p. 68)

....

9. What are the names of the four traditional ledgers of account? (p. 69)

....

10. What is the name of the summarised list of balances? (p. 74)

....

11. Give three reasons why double entry bookkeeping is not always reliable. (p. 76)

....

Questions

The answers to the questions followed by ✓ can be found at the back of the book, the answers to the remaining questions can be found on the website accompanying this book, **www.cengage.co.uk/ryan2**

1. On the extended trial balance show how the following transactions would be entered:
   (i) A purchase of fixed assets worth £500 000 from a supplier for payment in one month (show both the purchase transaction and its subsequent settlement).
   (ii) The depreciation of a fixed asset originally purchased for £800 000. The asset is four years old and one tenth of its value is to be written off.
   (iii) A customer fails to settle an outstanding account of £2000 and you decide to write it off.
   (iv) Stock that was originally purchased for £80 000 has deteriorated in the stores and is now only worth £60 000.
   (v) Goods purchased for £50 000 are deemed unusable. The supplier has agreed to their return and will refund the purchase price in full.

....

2. Mr Sloppy has left you a list of balances with instructions to prepare a balance sheet and income statement in standard UK format. He has left you with no further instructions.

Accumulated profit at beginning of the year	42 600
Accumulated depreciation	80 000
Administrative expenses	43 000
Cash	8 400
Corporation tax	18 840
Cost of sales	144 000
Current liabilities	97 600

Debtors	67 000
Dividends paid	11 560
Fixed assets	240 000
Interest paid	5 700
Long-term liabilities	73 500
Owner's equity	50 000
Sales turnover	316 500
Selling and distribution costs	76 700
Stocks	45 000

You are required:

(i) To produce a balance sheet and income statement as requested.

(ii) To explain how the figures in the income statement are related to those in the balance sheet. ✓

3. Far Eastern Limited commenced their year's operations with the balance sheet shown below:

	£
Non-current assets	86 000
Less depreciation	20 000
	66 000
Current assets:	
Inventories	13 000
Receivables	27 600
Cash	4 200
	44 800
Less: current liabilities	−37 600
Less: non-current liabilities	−50 000
	23 200
Equity capital	10 000
Profit retained	13 200
	23 200

During the year the business engaged in the following transactions:

- New plant was purchased for £8000 and depreciation provided at one tenth of the original cost of the firm's fixed assets.
- Sales of £176 000 were made, of which £16 000 were still outstanding at the end of the year. No bad debts were incurred in the year.
- Purchases of £65 000 were made during the year, and the outstanding payables were £31 200 at the end of the year. There was £8790 of stock on hand at the end of the year.
- Other expenses of £71 000 were incurred during the year
- A dividend of 15p per £1 share was declared and paid during the year.
- Corporation tax was provided at 40 per cent of net profit, excluding depreciation but including a writing down allowance of 25 per cent on fixed assets purchased during the year. No allowance was available against the company's other assets. The tax liability for the previous year had been calculated at £4100 and was paid during the current year.

You are required to:

Prepare an income statement and balance sheet for Far Eastern Ltd for the year.

Case exercises

1. Locate and print out the latest published financial report from **www.Cobham.co.uk**.

   Compare the current- and prior-year figures in the balance sheet and profit and loss account, noting the magnitude of changes and their significance to the company.

   Compare and contrast the figures in the current year's income statement and balance sheet with those for the previous year.

   Using an information service such as FT.com or Reuters.com search for the most recent financial news about the company and in particular any items commenting upon the financial performance of the company for the year you have downloaded.

2. Locate and print out the most recent accounts of Marks & Spencer plc from the **www.marksandspencer.com** website for comparison with the accounts of Cobham plc. Place the balance sheets and cash flow statements of the two companies side by side and, using the notes to the accounts, compare them.

   a. Are there entries in one balance sheet that are not in the other?

   b. Where is the manufacturing aspect of Cobham's business revealed in its balance sheet?

   c. Where is the merchant aspect of Marks & Spencer's business revealed in its balance sheet?

   d. What percentage of the total assets (non-current and current) of both companies are non-current and what is the likely reason for the differences between them?

   e. For both companies: what proportion of the cash inflows during the accounting year come from operating activities?

Chapter 4

Cash flow statements

Introduction

If you have followed the plot so far, you should be able to produce a simple income statement and balance sheet for a company. In so doing you have learned something of the principles of accounting and in particular the way in which revenues and costs are 'recognised' in a given period of account. In this chapter you will learn how to produce a cash flow statement.

Cash flow statements are regarded as the most reliable representations of a company's activities during a year. Unlike the income statement, they do not depend upon recognition principles in the measurement of revenue or costs: they record the cash received by a business and the cash paid out under a series of headings. Unless the company is acting fraudulently the cash flow statement should clearly show how much cash has been received and spent by the business. However, they do have their flaws. Cash flow statements do not show the flow of value in the form of commitments made (accounts receivable and payable, prepayments, deferred income and accrued revenues and costs). However, cash flow statements can provide a useful check on the integrity of the income statement.

In this short chapter, our task is to show how to produce a cash flow statement and how to interpret its significance as a check on the validity of the income statement produced with it. To achieve this learning goal we must imagine ourselves forward some years to a point where Sid is a multimillion pound business. This happy situation came about because of a chance encounter with Martin Pickle, the head of the Go All the Way Travel Group, who suggested he should get into the discount airline business. As a result Sid founded Sid's Squeezy Jet and much to the amazement of the long-suffering Beryl it took off.

Learning objectives

There are five outcomes you should achieve in this chapter. Split into three learning sections, their outcomes are as follows:

The measurement of cash flow

● That you can distinguish between the two different value flows in a business and how they relate.

● That you can identify the principal sources of a firm's cash flow.

The techniques of producing a cash flow statement

● That you can classify cash movements within a business into their principal headings within a cash flow statement and then produce a simple cash flow statement.

● That you can produce a cash flow statement from the income statement and balance sheet using the 'indirect' method.

Testing the income statement

● That you can make a comparison between the operating cash flow and operating profit for a business.

The measurement of cash flow[1]

Two financial flows dominate any business: the first and most important is its cash flow. The cash generation and expenditure of the firm determine the short-term success and the long-term survival of the business. The second flow is where revenues are recognised as chargeable to the year in question and accounting costs are matched to the process of earning that revenue and then allocated to different categories of account. These two flows, in so far as they impact upon the financial reports of the business, are shown in Exhibit 4.1.

These two flows have broad similarities but also some crucial differences, and it is easy to become confused between the two. The cash flow of the firm is reasonably straightforward: as operations generate surplus cash (the operating cash flow), interest and tax payments will be made and the remainder is free cash flow to equity (FCFE) before reinvestment. From that FCFE dividends are paid to investors and the balance retained for further reinvestment. From the analytical point of view, greater reliability can be placed upon the cash flow statement than the profit and loss account. It is difficult, but not impossible, to manipulate the reporting of cash flow figures. We will have a look at that scurrilous tendency later in this chapter.

The 'accounting' flow represents the creation of shareholder surplus over time which is accumulated in the owner's equity account. The closest analogue to operating cash flow within the income statement is EBITDA – earnings before interest, tax, depreciation and amortisation. This number is very important for reasons we will discuss later, but it is not reported: we have to calculate it directly from the income statement.

As we have described in earlier chapters, financial accountants employ various recognition rules for revenues and costs before arriving at EBITDA but there should, at steady state, be approximate parity between EBITDA and operating cash flow. Why this should be takes a moment's thought. If a firm's sales are constant and opening receivables, payables and accruals are likewise constant then the opening adjustments in measuring the profit of the business should be the same as the closing adjustments. As a result the firm's profit from its operations, but before it makes the large non-cash deductions for the use of its non-current assets in the form of depreciation and amortisation, should be the same as the net cash flow from its operation.

---

[1]This section is an edited version of material presented in Bob Ryan's (2005) *Corporate Finance and Valuation,* Cengage Learning, Chapter 10.

Exhibit 4.1 The two financial flows through the firm

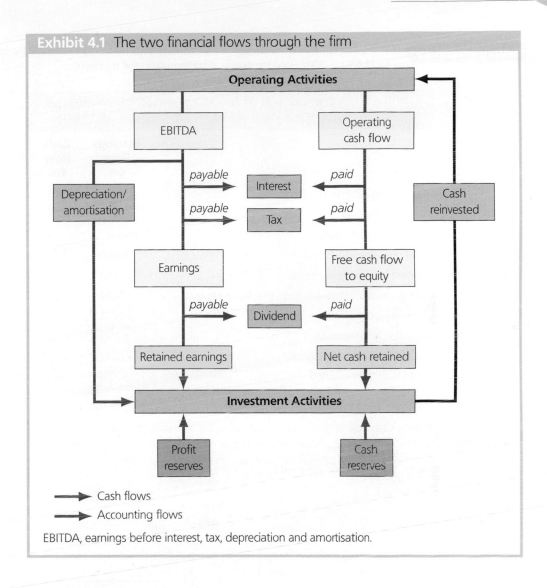

Cash flows

Accounting flows

EBITDA, earnings before interest, tax, depreciation and amortisation.

From EBITDA a substantial charge will be made for depreciation, amortisation and impairments representing the matching to the period in question and the consumption of the value represented by both real and purchased intangible assets (such as **goodwill** on acquisition, patents and licences). Further charges will then be made for interest and tax, but note the key distinction here is that what is charged is what is deemed to be payable and not necessarily what has been paid. This leads to an earnings figure which is a measure of smoothed income available for distribution to investors and out of which the directors may decide to declare (make payable) a dividend. What are then left are retained earnings which go to increase the capital account of the investors.

The accounting flow is a very limited interpretation of the extent to which shareholder value has been earned via the business transactions undertaken during a period of account. The cash flow shows the increase in the consumption power of the investor over the period of account irrespective of whether the cash is distributed directly or reinvested.

We now turn our attention to the preparation of the cash flow statement.

Financial realities   In the analysis below we show the reported earnings for Marks & Spencer plc for the year to 31 March 2007. Note the significant difference in the numbers.

Exhibit 4.2   A comparison of the income statement and cash flow statement for Marks & Spencer plc (2007)

	Earnings Flow £m	Cash Flow £m
Operating profit/cash flow		
continuing business	1045.9	1442.6
discontinued business	0.7	0.7
Total operating profit/cash flow	1046.6	1443.3
Interest received and receivable	33.8	13.2
Interest paid and payable and other financing costs	−173.4	−145
Tax paid and payable	−277.5	−150.8
Available for shareholders	629.5	1160.7
Equity dividends payable/paid	204.1	260.6
Profit/cash flow retained	425.4	900.1

The reported operating cash flow is considerably larger than the operating profit figure. The question we will have to answer is why should this be? Especially when we also notice that the firm's turnover increased by just over 10 per cent. When we add back the depreciation and amortisation in the accounts to the operating profit figure the gap between EBITDA and operating cash flow narrows:

	Earnings Flow £m	Cash Flow £m
Total operating profit	1046.6	1443.3
Add back depreciation/amortisation	282.7	
EBITDA/operating cash flow	1329.3	1443.3

These numbers are reasonably close together, but as we go down the two statements we note that the amount of cash retained is double the figure for retained profit. Clearly, we need to investigate quite why this has come about.

Preparing the cash flow statement

The simplest method for constructing a cash flow statement is to analyse the cash receipts and payments in the cash account (i.e., the cash column of the extended trial balance). For the external reader of accounts that is not possible, so we are forced to derive the statement indirectly.

If we take the extended trial balance described in earlier chapters:

$$NCA + Inv + Rec + Cash = CL + NCL + OE$$

Over the course of a year (or any other time period we choose) the change in the values on the left-hand side of the balance must equal the changes on the right. This gives us a 'difference relationship' or one that highlights the changes:

$$\Delta NCA + \Delta Inv + \Delta Rec + \Delta Cash = \Delta CL + \Delta NCL + \Delta OE$$

The delta symbol means 'the change in' the value concerned. We are interested in the change in cash flow over the year and so by rearrangement:

$$\Delta Cash = \Delta OE + \Delta CL + \Delta NCL - \Delta NCA + \Delta Inv + \Delta Rec$$

The changes in owner's equity, current liabilities and non-current liabilities we refer to as positive cash drivers, in that if they do impact upon cash then they affect it directly. An increase in a positive cash driver will, unless there is a counterbalancing change in any of the other balance sheet accounts, lead to a positive change in cash. This is not the case with the negative cash drivers in that if they impact upon the cash flows of the business it will lead to a decrease in cash.

Depending upon the jurisdiction, whether under IFRS or the US GAAP, the change in cash will be analysed into a number of subheadings. Using the IFRS headings we need to show the change in cash attributable to operations (operating cash flow), tax paid, investing and financing. The way our algorithm for generating a cash flow statement works is that we deconstruct each of the changes in the balance sheet into their relevant cash headings. This process of deconstructing the balance sheet has two very beneficial effects:

1. It allows us to create a cash flow statement without direct recourse to the cash transactions of the business, and
2. It allows us to see exactly what adjustments have been made in arriving at the published balance sheet and therefore, indirectly, the income statement.

Financial realities   Below are the accounts of Sid's Squeezy Jet plc. He has laid out the accounts under IFRS to show an entity view of his business. His profit and his cash flow have been steadily improving. Sid has taken substantial dividends, paid off his outstanding borrowing and is now preparing for his next big venture. However, one job is left to be done on the accounts and that is to prepare the cash flow statement for the year ended 31 December 2010.

▶

Exhibit 4.3 The accounts of Squeezy jet

Sid's Squeezy Jet

	2010 £m	2009 £m	2008 £m
Income statement			
Sales turnover	288	262	220
Cost of sales	143	133	104
Gross profit	145	129	116
Less other operating costs	36	27	24
Operating profit	109	102	92
Finance costs	0	2	2
Profit before tax	109	100	90
Income tax expense (at 30%)	33	30	27
Profit for the period	76	70	63

	2010 £m	2009 £m	2008 £m
Balance sheet			
Non-current assets			
Buildings, plant and aeroplanes	168	116	96
Current assets			
Inventories	3	4	2
Receivables	26	29	20
Cash	135	181	141
Total current assets	164	214	163
Total assets	332	330	258
Equity and liabilities			
Paid up share capital			
Ordinary shares (25p)	25	25	20
Other reserves	12	12	10
Retained earnings	218	170	120
Less dividends payable	−60	−28	−20
	158	142	100
Total equity	195	179	130

Current liabilities

Trade receivables	9	8	6
Deferred income and accrued expenses	19	17	14
Short-term debt	8	12	6
Tax payable	29	26	23
Dividends payable	60	28	20
Interest payable	0	2	2
Total current liabilities	125	93	71

Non-current liabilities

Loans	0	45	45
Provisions (deferred tax)	13	13	13
Total non-current liabilities	13	58	58

Total liabilities	138	151	129
Total equity and liabilities	332	330	259

Notes	2010	2009	2008
	£m	£m	£m
Fixed assets	280	200	160
Less accumulated depreciation	112	84	64
Net book value of fixed assets	168	116	96

The statement of cash flow

Step 1

Extract the balance sheet differences for each of the headings in the extended trial balance. After some practice this step is not strictly necessary, but it does allow us to check the numbers in the balance sheet:

Exhibit 4.4 An analysis of the principal balance sheet changes for Squeezy Jet

		Positive cash drivers			Negative cash drivers		
	Cash	OE	CL	LTL	NCA	Inv	Rec
2010	135	195	124	13	168	3	26
2009	181	179	93	58	116	4	29
Change =	−46	16	31	−45	52	−1	−3

If we total the change in the positive cash drivers we have £2 million and in the negative cash drivers we have £48 million giving the net change of £46 million on the cash account. All of the above numbers should be clearly identifiable within the balance sheet.

Generally, increases in the owner's equity, short-term liabilities and long-term liabilities bring about corresponding cash increases, whilst increases in fixed asset values, stocks or receivables reduce the cash of the firm. Changes in owner's equity, short-term liabilities and long-term liabilities are all directly associated with changes in the cash balances of the firm. However, changes in fixed assets, stocks and receivables are inversely associated with the cash balances of the firm.

If we review carefully the decrease of £46 million in this company's cash we see that the following occurred:

Exhibit 4.5 A summary of the cash impact following changes in the Squeezy Jet balance sheet

Balance sheet account	Effect on cash	Value change	Effect on cash
Owner's equity (OE)	Direct	Increase in OE by £16 million	Increase
Current liabilities (CL)	Direct	Increase in the short-term liabilities by £31 million	Increase
Non-current liabilities (NCL)	Direct	Decrease loan by £45 million	Decrease
Non-current assets (NCA)	Inverse	Increase of £52 million	Decrease
Inventories (Inv)	Inverse	Decrease in stockholding by £1 million	Increase
Receivables (Rec)	Inverse	Decrease in receivables by £3 million	Increase

Unfortunately, the differences shown on the right-hand side of the rearranged extended trial balance are not just cash figures but also include a variety of accruals, prepayments and, most importantly of all, depreciation – all of which were included originally in determining the profit for the business. We now have to go through a process of unravelling the non-cash entries on the right-hand side of this cash equation to create a 'clean' cash flow statement. We will proceed through this clean-up operation to produce a statement of cash flow which is laid out in a standard format showing separately:

Cash flows from operating activities:

● Net cash flow from operations (the cash-flow analogue of operating profit)

● Taxation

● Interest paid and received.

Cash flows from investing activities:

● Capital expenditures

● Capital disposals

● Acquisitions

● Interest received.

Cash flow from financing activities:

- Interest paid
- Dividends paid
- Issue or redemption of share capital
- New borrowing or borrowing repaid.

We will now introduce a simple spreadsheet method for adjusting the raw changes. Once we have been through the analysis we will explain the significance of the figures we have produced and in particular explain how we define operating cash flow.

Step 2

Create the working document shown in Exhibit 4.6 below. This document consists of a step-by-step analysis of the differences by following these rules:

(i)   Create a series of columns to include a delta column and then one for each principal heading in the final cash flow statement.

(ii)   Analyse the differences on the positive cash drivers and the differences on the negative cash drivers as separate exercises, ruling off and totalling each when you have finished.

(iii) Analyse the differences in the delta column and then extend the differences to the relevant analysis column without changing the sign. *This is very important.*

(iv)   Start with owner's equity and identify the changes to the retained profit reserve. This is partly retained profit and partly dividend payment. With the retained profit element layout the income statement from the operating profit figure downwards in the delta column – you need not include the subtotals.

(v)   Extend the elements of the income statement into the column that best matches the description of the item. Operating profit to operating cash flow (OCF), tax payable to tax and so on. Remember the dividend payments are a negative against retained earnings and should be copied to the 'Divs' column – remembering to keep the sign unchanged.

(vi)   Enter the differences on the other owner's equity accounts into the delta column and extend them across as shown.

(vii) Carefully calculate the differences on short-term liabilities, list them in the delta column and then post them across. Trade receivables and deferred income are related to operations; they affect the operating profit for the year and hence they are posted to operating cash flow. Note that one item under short-term liabilities relates to short-term debt. That should go in the ST column as shown. Do the same for changes in the long-term liabilities.

(viii) Once the positive cash drivers are complete simply add the delta and all the analysis columns, noting the total of each at the foot of each column.

(ix)   Repeat the process for the negative cash drivers. The only tricky one here is the non current asset account. The change in accumulated depreciation is, we assume in this case, the charge for the year. An increase in accumulated depreciation is a reduction in the non-current asset value in the balance sheet and hence a negative value. The depreciation for the year is posted to the operating cash flow column.

(x)   Once you have completed the negative cash drivers total them and then deduct the total of the negative cash driver columns from the total of the positive cash driver columns as shown.

You now have, in row form, the final cash flow statement.

2010 cash flow statement – working document

Exhibit 4.6 The Squeezy Jet cash flow master schedule

	Delta	OCF	Tax	Interest	CAPEX	Divs	Equity	ST debt	LT debt
Change in owner's equity									
Operating profit	109	109							
Interest payable	0			0					
Tax payable	−33		−33						
Profit for the period	76								
Movement on retained earnings									
Dividends payable	−60					−60			
New capital									
Share capital issued	0						0		
Share premium account	0						0		
	16								
Change in current liabilities									
Trade payables	1	1							
Deferred income and accrued expenses	2	2							
Short-term debt	−4							−4	
Tax payable	2		2						
Dividends payable	32					32			
Interest payable	−2			−2					
	31								
Change in non-current liabilities									
Loans	−45								−45
Deferred tax	0		0						
	−45								
Positive cash drivers	2	112	−31	−2	0	−28	0	−4	−45
Change in non-current assets									
Assets acquired	80				80				
Accumulated depreciation	−28	−28							
	52								
Change in current assets									
Inventories	−1	−1							
Receivables	−3	−3							
Negative cash drivers	48	−32	0	0	80	0	0	0	
Net cash flow	−46	144	−31	−2	−80	−28	0	−4	−45

Step 3

We can now finalise a cash flow statement for the year by taking the column totals and laying them out in a vertical format as follows:

Exhibit 4.7 The summarised cash flow statement for Squeezy Jet

Sid's Squeezy Jet cash flow statement

	£ million
Cash flow from operating activities	
Operating cash flow	143
Less taxation	−30
Cash inflow from operating activities	113
Cash flow from investing activities	
Capital expenditure	−80
	−80
Cash flow from financing activities	
Interest paid	−2
Short-term debt repaid	−4
Long-term debt repaid	−45
Equity dividends paid	−28
	−79
Net cash outflow from activities	−46
Opening net cash	181
Closing net cash	135

Reconciling operating cash flow and operating profit

In the above exercise we have analysed the cash changes in the balance sheet to calculate the overall cash change to the firm. We will now look at an important implication of what we have done so far. In the cash flow statement, shown in Exhibit 4.6, you will note that the operating profit is £109 million, whilst the operating cash flow in the statement above (Exhibit 4.7) is £143 million. How do we account for the difference?

The first difference we might note between operating profit and operating cash flow is that depreciation is charged as an expense in the former but does not appear in a statement of cash flow. We can correct for this as follows:

	£ million
Operating profit	109
Add back depreciation charge for the year	28
Operating profit before depreciation	137

The operating profit before depreciation and any other non-cash expenses such as amortisation and impairments is often referred to as 'Earnings before depreciation and amortisation' or EBITDA. Now the number is somewhat closer to the operating cash flow (later in this chapter we will explore how close the number should be). However, the second source of difference is that the revenues and expenditures shown in the income statement have been matched to the year, and some of the cash flow received during the year will be from outstanding receivables balances from sales in the previous year. Also, those cash flows will exclude sales for which cash has not been received from customers at the end of the year. If the outstanding receivables balances at the beginning of the year and the end of the year are the same then the revenue in the income statement will equal the cash received during the

The selling and marketing expenses and administrative expenses in the table above are further analysed in the table below:

| | 2007 | | | 2006 | | |
	Selling and marketing expenses £m	Administrative expenses £m	Total £m	Selling and marketing expenses £m	Administrative expenses £m	Total £m
Employee costs (see note 10A, Appendix to Chapter 7)	928.8	245.3	1 174.1	844.9	228.3	1 073.2
Occupancy costs	310.5	62.4	372.9	276.2	49.2	325.4
Repairs, renewals and maintenance of property	55.4	19.1	74.5	73.0	17.2	90.2
Depreciation and amortisation	264.4	18.3	282.7	243.5	30.5	274.0
Other costs	220.1	239.0	459.1	188.1	197.5	385.6
Operating expenses	1 779.2	584.1	2 363.3	1 625.7	522.7	2 148.4

For 2006 the charges for depreciation and amortisation were £282.7 million and the operating cash flow was £1442.6 million.

From 2006 to 2007 the growth in Marks and Spencer's turnover was 10.14 per cent and the cost gearing ratio in 2006 was:

$$G = \frac{1625.7 + 522.7 - 274.0}{4812.1 + 1625.7 + 522.7 - 274.0}$$

$$G = 0.2803$$

Our prediction of the COP ratio is therefore:

$$COP(predicted) = 1 + \frac{0.1014}{(1 - 0.2803)}$$

$$COP(predicted) = 1.14$$

What this suggests is that the actual COP should lie between 1 and this predicted figure. To see why consider the COP prediction as a prediction of the 2007 EBITDA growth based upon a 10.14 per cent increase in turnover and the upward cost gearing effect using the 2006 figure. If all of Marks & Spencer's costs were directly variable with turnover then EBITDA should correspondingly grow at 10.14 per cent. However, because some costs are fixed this tends to magnify the effect of revenue growth on EBITDA. In our case, an approximate value of 28.03 per cent for the proportion of fixed costs leads us to believe, on the basis of the 2006 cost gearing ratio that EBITDA should rise by 14 per cent.

If the cash flow of the firm did not rise at all during the year then the 10.14 per cent increase in revenue should mean that EBITDA is 1.14 times the magnitude of the cash flow or, put another way, would lead to a COP prediction of 1.14. If the cash flow increased exactly in line with revenue then we would expect the COP to remain where it is at 1. So our best prediction for Marks & Spencer is that the predicted value of the COP ratio should be between 1 and 1.14. As the company is a retailer we would expect the ratio to be close to one because most of the revenue is based on cash sales.

The actual COP ratio for Marks & Spencer plc is:

$$COP(actual) = \frac{\text{operating profit } + \text{ depreciation } + \text{ amortisation}}{\text{operating cash flow}}$$

$$COP(actual) = \frac{1045.9 + 274.0}{1442.6}$$

$$COP(actual) = 0.915$$

This suggests that Marks & Spencer plc has understated (either by accident or design) its income (at the level of EBITDA) compared with its cash generation by approximately 8.5 per cent. From a practical point of view this difference is small, but is a point we should bear in mind when trying to analyse these accounts in more detail.

The flow of cash in and out of Enron told a less spectacular story than its soaring revenue. In 1998, Enron actually had a negative cash flow of $59 million. . . . In 1999, Enron had a positive cash flow of $177 million – but that came from a rise in short term borrowing, while the net cash generated by operating activities fell by 25 per cent from 1998 levels. . . . Investors might have started to wonder if they had paid closer attention to these subtler measures of efficiency and profitability rather than to earnings, or to 'operating earnings'.

Fox 2003: pp. 175–176

The one important type of accounting misclassification that is not highlighted by the COP ratio is the claiming of capital receipts as income or, more problematically, the inappropriate capitalisation of costs. The problem with this type of misclassification error is that it impacts just as much upon the cash flow statement as upon the reported accounts. Although the financial statements are often opaque when it comes to this type of misclassification, there are some steps which can be taken to help identify the extent of the problem:

(i)   Check to see if there have been any changes in the accounting policies, particularly with respect to the recognition of revenues and expenditures and the rules for charging depreciation and amortisation.

(ii) Identify all acquisitions and disposals of fixed assets and intangible assets in the notes to the accounts. Details of such movements should be noted and reference to the capital expenditure can be checked with the various statements that precede the financial reports. If the case is sufficiently important or there is doubt concerning the reliability of the reported figures, details of acquired companies and the cost of acquisition can be obtained from the central registration authority for the acquired company.

Review activity 4.2   Calculate the COP ratio and the predicted COP for Sid's Squeezy Jet for the years 2009 and 2010.

The further reading section at the end of the chapter gives more information on reliability testing. The appendix to this chapter contains a summarised procedure for the pre-valuation correction of accounting data.

Chapter summary

In this chapter we have explained how to prepare a cash flow statement using a firm's published income statement and balance sheet. The method we have used focuses on the changes in each of the balance sheet items, analysing them into their correct headings for presentation in a standard cash flow statement. The cash flow statement also provides a check against the published income statement. It allows us to determine the degree to which the management or their accountants within a firm have been manipulating the earnings figures that they produce.

Further reading

There are few books specifically focused on cash flow reporting and analysis. These however may extend your understanding of the topic and how it can be used:

Fox, L. (2003) *Enron – the Rise and Fall,* Hoboken, NJ: John Wiley & Sons.
Mulford, C.W. and Comiskey, E.E. (2005) *Creative Cash Flow Reporting,* Hoboken, NJ: John Wiley and Sons.
Reider, R., and Heyler, R.B. (2003) *Managing Cash Flow: An Operational Focus,* Hoboken, NJ: John Wiley and Sons.

Progress check

Please refer to the page shown to check your answer.

1. What is the principal way that cash flow differs from income flow. (pp. 82–83)

2. What are the two methods of producing a cash flow statement? (pp. 84–85)

3. What does the term EBITDA mean? (p. 82)

4. Apart from depreciation and other non-cash movements relating to the firm's non-current assets, what other differences are there between operating cash flow and operating profit? (p. 83)

5. The change in the firm's cash for the year is equal to a series of changes in a firm's balance sheet. What are those changes? (p. 85)

6. Changes in owner's equity, current and non-current liabilities are referred to as? (p. 85)

7. Changes in non-current assets, inventories and receivables are referred to as? (p. 85)

8. An increase in non-current liabilities will either decrease or increase cash. Is this always true? (p. 88)

9. Increasing the depreciation charge for a business will either (a) increase cash, (b) decrease cash, or (c) have no impact on cash. Which is correct? (p. 91)

10. Cash flows arise from three principal sources: operating activities and financing activities. Which one is missing? (p. 91)

11. What is the value of the COP ratio when a firm is at steady state? (p. 93)

12. What is the formula for getting the range on the COP ratio when a company expands or contracts its revenues by a set amount? (p. 93)

Questions

The answers to the questions followed by ✓ can be found at the back of the book, the answers to the remaining questions can be found on the website accompanying this book, **www.cengage.co.uk/ryan2**.

1. Mr Sloppy has left you a list of balances with instructions to prepare a balance sheet and income statement in standard UK format. He has left you with no further instructions.

Accumulated profit at beginning of the year	426 000
Accumulated depreciation	80 000
Administrative expenses	43 000
Cash	8 400
Corporation tax	18 840
Cost of sales	144 000
Current liabilities	97 600
Debtors	67 000
Dividends paid	11 560
Fixed assets	240 000
Interest paid	5 700
Long-term liabilities	73 500
Owner's equity	50 000
Sales turnover	316 500
Selling and distribution costs	76 700
Stocks	45 000

Using the balance sheet and income statement derived from the above figures and given the following information:

- the operating cash flow for the year was £66 000
- fixed assets were purchased for £35 000
- last year's tax was paid of £16 500

Produce a cash flow statement and explain why operating profit and cash flow might be different. ✓

2. On the basis of the information produced for the Far Eastern Company in Chapter 3, produce a cash flow statement for the year in question.

3. Grundy's Breakers Ltd has the following income statement, balance sheet and notes for the year ended 31 December 2006.

Income statement for the year ended 31 December

Turnover	8 945 000
Cost of sales	2 100 400
Gross profit	6 844 600
Other operating costs	4 350 100
Operating profit	2 494 500
Interest payable	65 000
Profit before tax	2 429 500
Tax	1 093 275
Distributable profit	1 336 225
Dividends payable	240 000
Profit retained	1 096 225
	1 336 225

Balance sheet as at 31 December

Non current assets at cost		5 018 000
Accumulated depreciation		1 104 569
		3 913 431
Current assets		
Inventories	60 422	
Receivables	1 102 808	
Cash	99 747	
	1 262 977	
Less current liabilities	1 479 683	
		−216 706
		3 696 725
Less non-current liabilities		1 000 000
		2 696 725
Shareholder funds		
25p ordinary shares		500 000
Share premium account		354 500
Profit and loss reserve		1 842 225
		2 696 725

At the end of the first board meeting of the new financial year Mr Grundy, the company's chairman and principal shareholder, summarises the expectations and financial targets for the company:

1. The target increase in sales is 5 per cent.

2. The gross profit is unchanged over the year.

3. Other operating costs should be reduced by 2 per cent.

4. Half the loan of £1 million should be immediately repaid and an increase in the cost of borrowing to 7 per cent should be allowed for. Interest is provided for on the balance at the year-end.

5. Corporation tax rates are expected to rise to 50 per cent.

6. A new issue of 2 million 25p equity shares should be made early in the new year at an issue price of 50p.

7. The dividend per share should be raised to 15p per share, with 7.5p paid as an interim and the balance to be declared at the end of the year.

8. Planned capital investment should go ahead costing £2.2 million.

9. Depreciation should be provided at 10 per cent on the fixed asset net book value. Assets acquired during year are also depreciated at 10 per cent irrespective of their date of purchase.

10. Inventory values should be reduced to an average of 8 days of the year's cost of sales.

11. Debtors and trade creditors should be set at 40 days based on turnover and cost of sales respectively.

On the basis of the above information you are required to produce a short report for the next board meeting containing:

(i) A projected profit and loss account and balance sheet for the coming year

(ii) A projected statement of cash flow. ✓

4. Below are the accounts of Henry Engineering Ltd, a medium-sized enterprise in the systems development and fabrication business.

	2007 £m	2006 £m	2005 £m
Income statement			
Sales turnover	65.3	76.9	80.0
Cost of sales	43.1	55.0	51.0
Gross profit	22.2	21.8	29.0
less other operating costs	36.1	27.0	24.0
Operating profit	−13.9	−5.2	5.0
Finance costs	2.1	2.1	3.8
Profit before tax	−16.0	−7.3	1.2
Income tax expense (at 30%)	−4.8	−2.2	0.4
Profit for the period	−11.2	5.1	0.8

	2007 £m	2006 £m	2005 £m
Balance sheet			
Non-current assets			
Buildings, plant and machinery	37.0	92.0	54.0
Current assets			
Inventories	11.4	7.3	7.1
Receivables	32.7	19.2	15.6
Cash	7.2	−14.7	54.4
Total current assets	51.2	11.8	77.1
Total assets	88.2	103.8	131.1
Equity and liabilities			
Paid up share capital			
Ordinary shares (25p)	25.0	25.0	20.0
Other reserves	12.0	12.0	10.0
Retained earnings	11.6	22.8	32.9
less dividends payable	0.0	0.0	−5.0
	11.6	22.8	27.9
Total equity	48.6	59.8	57.9

	2007 £m	2006 £m	2005 £m
Current liabilities			
Trade creditors	2.6	3.2	3.1
Deferred income and accrued expenses	5.6	6.8	6.8
Tax payable	−2.1	0.3	5.7
Dividends payable	0.0	0.0	5.0
Interest payable	2.1	2.1	3.8
Total current liabilities	8.3	12.5	24.5
Non-current liabilities			
Loans	25.0	25.0	45.0
Provisions (deferred tax)	6.3	6.5	3.6
Total non-current liabilities	31.3	31.5	48.6
Total Liabilites	39.6	44.0	73.1
Total Equity and Liabilities	88.2	103.8	131.1

Notes	**2007 £m**	**2006 £m**	**2005 £m**
Fixed assets at start of year	170.0	220.0	190.0
additions	0.0	0.0	30.0
less disposals	−20.0	−50.0	0.0
	150.0	170.0	220.0
Depreciation at start of the year	128.0	136.0	114.0
less depreciation on disposals	−10	−25	0
depreciation charge for the year	15.0	17.0	22.0
less accumulated depreciation	133.0	128.0	136.0
Net book value of fixed assets	37.0	92.0	54.0

You are required to:

(i) Produce a cash flow statement for the years ended 28 February 2006 and 2007.

(ii) Comment on the difference between the cash generated by the business and its reported profits.

Chapter 5

Principles of financial accounting

Introduction

In the first four chapters we developed a simple procedure for producing a balance sheet and income statement for a small business. Using the accounting equation we demonstrated how different transactions could be analysed into those which transformed assets from one type into another, how liabilities were created and, most importantly, how value could be added to the owner. Three principles were necessary to operate the model: identity, matching and auditivity. In this chapter we build upon the ideas and techniques developed earlier: first by an examination of the matching principle in greater depth, focusing on the problems of accruals, depreciation and inventory valuation and, second, by reviewing in more detail how businesses create value. As we proceed we will also introduce some of the traditional terminology that professional accountants use and how business accounting systems operate in practice.

Learning objectives

There are seven outcomes you should achieve in this chapter. Split into three learning sections these outcomes are as follows.

The principles of value creation and the matching principle

- That you understand the principal ways that value is created in business, distinguishing, in particular, between the transactional and the transformational drivers of value.

- That you obtain a deeper understanding of the concept of matching through the practical application of the accruals principle.

Accounting for real assets: depreciation and inventories

- That you understand and can calculate appropriate depreciation charges using a range of different methods and know the various factors which influence the choice of method to use in practice.

- That you can measure the value of inventory using the FIFO, LIFO and average cost methods and know, in principle, the difference between marginal and absorption inventory valuation systems.

These we ... ...ndi- ... rious ... ansac- ...ase of ...is taxi, ...d of ac- ...a busi- ...sactional

...rers, for ex- ...heir real and ...its customers ...les of business ...ts own value in ...ation poses par- ...urces consumed ...in the eighteenth ...rces consumed in ...An internal trans- ...markets but is ex- ...used in a manufac- ...e fixed assets to the

...ions in the open-market ...the supply and demand ...se of a difference in the ...be prepared to pay for the ...Part of that value change ...e would count this as a cost ...of the transactions driver of ...asset has become relatively ...motor vehicles, their second- ...useful life expired. This addi- ...tants) will clearly influence the ...On the other hand, other assets ...of changes in the market supply ...ver of value.

The monetary driver of value

Finally, a firm's value will change if the purchasing power of money changes. In inflationary times, we would normally expect the purchasing power of a firm's cash balances and other monetary assets to fall. Likewise, if a firm holds money overseas then changes in the exchange rate will bring about changes in the value of its monetary assets held in its domestic currency. Managing a firm's monetary assets is the role of the treasury manager and most well-run firms attempt to minimise the value losses from this source by attempting to ensure that all monetary balances are kept at a minimum level commensurate with the efficient running of the business. Indeed, as we shall see later in this book, it is good business practice to ensure that all a firm's assets yield cash value as quickly and efficiently as possible. However, once a business holds a cash balance it should seek to get rid of it as quickly as possible, by investing it in assets that will generate more cash in the future or by returning it to its investors if no such opportunities exist.

Review activity 5.1

How would you classify these transactions in terms of the value driver involved?

1. A rise in the value of a firm's holding of land.
2. The sale of finished goods which cost £10 000 to produce for £12 000.
3. Some stock purchased for £18 000 was sold on for £24 000.
4. A fall in the value of the balance on a bank account denominated in euros.

Traditionally, accountants have only counted the impact of the transactions and transformational drivers of value when measuring how much a business has earned from its activities during a given accounting period. In practice it can be very difficult tracing how changing market prices and inflationary forces impact upon the value of the firm. Traditional accounting practice under the historical cost convention ignores their effect upon the firm and its value. Indeed, traditional accounting is sometimes known as 'transactions-based accounting' and the emphasis on 'earnings' in preparing statements of income emphasises the limited nature of what the accountant tries to measure. With periods of rapid inflation in the 1970s and 1980s the profession attempted to incorporate the impact of changes in the purchasing power of money in determining profit. More recently, attempts have been made to incorporate changes in the specific values of assets in company accounts. We will return to these issues later in this chapter, but, for the moment, we will assume that the only changes that matter are brought about by the transactions undertaken by a business.

The concept of accruals – matching in practice

In the last chapter we introduced the concept of matching in an intuitive way. In Sid's case we noted that some of his expenditure (the rent on his garage, for example) created benefits for him over more than one period of account. Accrual is the name given to the process of matching revenues and expenditures to the current period of account. The concept of accruals is reflected in two recognition principles: first, the process of recognising the revenue that can be fairly attributed to the period of account and, second, the process of recognising the expenditure that can be attributed to the process of earning that revenue. Indeed, so important is this notion of accruals that the method of producing income statements and balance sheets is also often referred to as 'accrual accounting'.

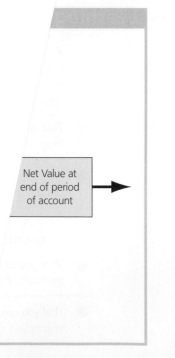

Net Value at end of period of account

Revenue recognition and the measurement of profit

The revenue that is credited to the income statement adopting the temporal matching principle is what we believe can be fairly attributed to the period of account. In general, we normally count revenue as arising in a particular accounting period if the effort in earning that revenue took place in that period and the receipt of the revenue is contractually certain. However, in any given business situation where goods or services are being produced and sold there are a number of points where the revenue could be deemed to arise.

In order to illustrate the problem of revenue recognition consider Exhibit 5.2 where we show the **operating cycle** of a service company or a company that makes products to order.

A company producing goods to order will start the production process or commence the service as soon as a confirmed order is received. However, at what stage would it be appropriate to say that the revenue accrues to the firm? At the point where an order agreement is entered into? At the point the service is completed or the point at which (if appropriate) the customer loses the right to return the goods supplied as faulty, or to the point at which the customer finally pays? Under International Accounting Standard 18 there are a number of tests for when revenue can be counted. Paraphrasing, these are:

1. Has ownership of the goods been transferred to the customer, or, in the case of a service, has the service been completed to the satisfaction of the customer by the balance sheet date?

2. Is it probable that the economic benefits of the transaction (usually the price paid by the customer) will flow to the business?

3. In the case of the sale of goods has the seller given up the control of the goods concerned?

4. Can the revenue be measured reliably?

5. Can the costs associated with the sale be reliably measured?

In the operating cycle diagram in Exhibit 5.2, the point at which the customer accepts the goods or service as complete is normally the point at which the supplier would be in a position to recognise the revenue and count it as part of the profit for the year. In some businesses it may be permissible to recognise the revenue in stages.

Exhibit 5.2 The operating cycle for a job manufacturer or service producer

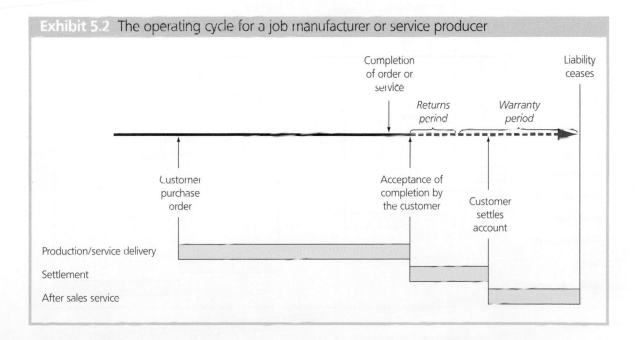

A university, for example, would conform to the pattern shown in Exhibit 5.2 for the payment of fees except that it normally asks for fees from a student when the student registers and enters the course. Where the fee is paid in advance a short-term liability is created which is reduced as the revenue is subsequently matched to the periods of account.

Financial realities You pay your fees to your university on 1 July for a twelve-month course commencing on 1 October. The university accounting year end is 31 July. When would the revenue be recognised?

Answer: Your fees would not be recognised as revenue in the year in which you paid them and would normally accrue to the following year. At the end of the year in which you paid your fees, you would appear as a 'current liability' in the university's books. We stress that this is not how your university really thinks of you but just reflects that in the year you have paid your fees will be regarded as **deferred revenue**.

Similarly, a construction company engaged on a major building project might agree with its client that it can receive stage payments when particular points in the building project are reached and certified by a surveyor.

In the case of a manufacturer producing goods for inventory which are eventually sold the recognition of revenue is more straightforward. Exhibit 5.3 shows the operating cycle of such a business. What this exhibit shows is a number of critical points in the process from purchasing raw materials or components to the end of the cycle where any warranty or service agreement on the final manufactured product ceases. In this situation the normal point of revenue recognition would be the point at which a customer accepts goods as being of satisfactory quality.

Exhibit 5.3 The operating cycle for a manufacturer

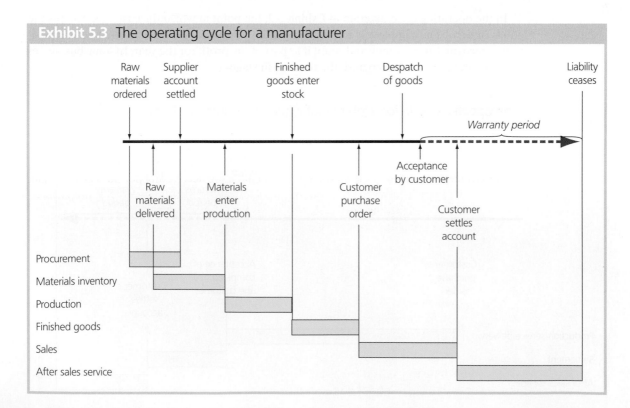

The process of revenue recognition creates two types of adjustments that have to be made to the accounts:

- **Deferred revenue** is revenue received in the current year which is attributable to the following year. This creates a deferred revenue item which will appear as a short-term liability in the balance sheet. It is a short-term liability because we have received cash from a customer that we have not yet recognised as revenue. The example of university fees paid in advance is a case of deferred revenue.

- **Accrued revenue** occurs where revenue attributable to the current year is not received until after the year-end and will be shown as part of the debtor balance in the balance sheet.

Expenditure recognition and the measurement of profit

In some respects, the recognition of expenditures is straightforward. Expenditures are matched to the period in question if they can be fairly attributed to the effort involved in earning the revenue recognised in that period. Some expenses may be directly related to the firm's sales activity such as the consumption of materials, or sales commission; others will be incurred in operating the business as a whole during the period concerned. Where a direct linkage of expenditure to sales cannot be made then the expenditure is normally made on a time apportionment basis. There are two levels at which this time apportionment will occur:

- by the accrual and prepayments of current expenditure
- by the depreciation or amortisation of capital expenditure.

FYI **'Amortisation'** is the term used for the process of writing off intangible assets as opposed to 'depreciation' which is the term for writing off real assets. In practice there is very little difference in the mechanics of writing off intangibles except that they rarely have a residual value and will therefore be written down to zero.

We will now examine both of these separately.

Accruals and prepayments of expenditures

Accruals occur when the cash paid in a particular period is less than the matched expenditure. The shortfall will be accrued and appear as a short-term liability in the balance sheet.

Prepayments occur when the amount actually paid in an accounting period is greater than the matched expenditure to be incurred. An amount will, therefore, appear as a prepayment and will appear as part of the receivables balance in the balance sheet.

Two examples using the accounting equation should make the matter clear:

- A company paid rates of £4000 per annum, quarterly in arrears. At the close of the accounts on 31 December the final quarter's rate bill had not been paid. This would represent an **accrued expense** at the year-end.

- It also paid rent on its head office of £80 000 per annum, a quarter in advance. The rent was paid for the first quarter of the new year on 31 December. At the start of the year it had been paid on 1 January. This would be deemed to be a prepayment.

One of the features of the manager's year in most organisations is when the accounting department formally requests all budget holders to let them know of any outstandings or prepayments. Now you know the reason why!

Exhibit 5.4

	NCA	Inv	Rec	C	=	CL	NCL	OC	R	–E
Rates paid in the year				–3 000						3 000
Accrued charge for unpaid rates						1 000				1 000
Rent paid in the year				–100 000						100 000
Prepaid rent		20 000								–20 000

Review activity 5.2 Indicate with a tick whether the following closing entries for an accounting year represent accrued revenue (AR), deferred revenue (DR), accrued expenditure (AE) or a prepayment (PP). The end of the accounting year is 31 December.

Exhibit 5.5

	AR	DR	AE	PP
1 A year's insurance paid on 1 June of £1800 at the end of the year half the bill will be deemed a ...				
2 Local taxes paid for the past year at the end of March for £24 000 at the end of the year £18 000 will be deemed to be ...				
3 Subscriptions for membership of a golf club for the calendar year £16 000 received from members in advance				
4 Agreed with a client that a building job was half completed Surveyor certifies half completion valued at £184 500				

Accounting for real assets: depreciation and inventories

In this section we explore the issues involved in accounting for real assets. In a firm's balance sheet its real assets are both fixed assets such as land, buildings, equipment and vehicles, and inventories which form part of its current assets. When accounting for fixed assets that are used over many different financial years the firm has to decide how the cost of those assets will be reflected in the annual income statement. This is the problem of **depreciation**. With inventories the accounting problem arises in valuing materials and components which are purchased and then transformed into **work-in-progress** and finished goods for sale.

Depreciation

Depreciation is the application of the temporal matching principle to capital expenditure. Large-scale capital expenditure may contribute to a business's productive capacity for many years. Depreciation is the process where the accountant attempts to match that expenditure in the fairest way possible to the years that the firm will receive the benefit from its use. International Accounting Standard No. 16 (IAS 16) regulates the recording of fixed assets in accounts:

The fundamental objective of depreciation is to reflect in operating profit the cost of the use of the tangible non-current asset (i.e., amount of economic benefit consumed) in the period.

Under traditional accounting practice depreciation is not designed to reflect the decline in the value of a tangible non-current asset but rather the consumption of its useful life. If the market value of an asset exactly mirrors the consumption of its useful life then the depreciated amount will equal its value. This would be purely coincidental. The purpose of depreciation is to match the cost of the capital expenditure involved to the revenue generated over its life. Following this principle, all tangible assets should be depreciated excluding land and buildings, unless the difference between the cost of the asset and its residual value is so small that any depreciation charge would be immaterial.

Financial realities   A new motor car costing £25 000 is expected to have a useful economic life of 250 000 miles. A motorist drives 10 000 miles in the first year and is surprised to discover that its second-hand value has dropped to £21 000. Would this be expected?

Given these figures we would expect the car to lose value over its life at the rate of 10p per mile, or £1000 in the first year. From the point of view of the consumption of the cost of the vehicle over its life the 'book value' of the asset should fall to £24 000. The market value of £21 000 may simply reflect that buyers in general prefer new vehicles to second-hand ones and are therefore not prepared to pay for the remaining 240 000 miles of useful life at the same price they would be prepared to pay for a new vehicle.

There are four issues that need to be considered when calculating the depreciation charge to be applied each year:

● the useful economic life of the asset
● the cost of the asset
● the asset's residual value
● the method of depreciation.

Economic life

Normally, the economic life of the asset is estimated from its expected physical capacity from the moment it is purchased by the firm to the point at which the cost of maintaining the asset is greater than the value it generates for the business. In the case of Sid's taxi, for example, he might decide that after 200 000 miles the cost of maintaining and repairing the vehicle would be greater than the value it produced for him. It may well be that the taxi, with suitable care, would carry on for another 200 000 miles after that, but as far as Sid is concerned its useful life is the time it takes for him to drive 200 000 miles. There is therefore a difference between the life over which a business can obtain benefit from an asset and its actual life. It is the former or economic life which should form the basis of the depreciation calculation. The calculation of economic life may also be conditioned by other factors such as the rate of technological obsolescence. Computers are an example of an asset whose economic life is constrained by the rate at which they become obsolete. As new software and operating systems become available, the physical machines become obsolete, not because they cease to operate physically nor indeed because a significant part of their potential life has elapsed, but simply because they can no longer run the most up-to-date software available.

FYI   The distinction between the economic and physical life of an asset can be reduced to a simple rule that an asset's life is governed by the time it takes for its value in use to the firm to drop below its replacement cost. Once that stage is reached, the firm should either replace or, if it is disengaging from that type of business, hold the asset until its value in use falls below its realisable or scrap value. At this point it should be scrapped. Of course, in practice making these judgements can be difficult and highly subjective.

Cost of the asset

The rules for calculating the cost of an asset are straightforward in principle but quite difficult to assess in practice. In principle, not only the acquisition cost but also all the other costs required to bring the new capital asset into operational use should be counted. So, for example, a cable laying company may have an engineer occupied primarily with maintaining and repairing cables. However, they are from time to time called to trenches where new cables are being laid. Their time spent in maintaining existing cables is an expense chargeable to the income statement, whilst the time spent working on the new cables is capitalised, i.e., it forms part of the capital cost of the new installation. Strictly, not only their wages but also a proportion of their annual holiday costs, the firm's contributions to their pension scheme, their travelling expenditures and all the other costs associated with their employment should also be split so that the capital cost of the new installation can be established.

FYI The WorldCom scandal in 2002 was mostly concerned with the inappropriate capitalisation of expenditures that should properly have been charged to the income statement. However, the question remains whether investors are really fooled by this type of accounting manipulation (see Chapter 13). The regulators certainly think so:

Judge approves SEC, WorldCom settlement

Extract from an article by Jon Swartz, *USA Today*, 26 November 2002

WorldCom and federal regulators Tuesday reached a partial settlement of civil fraud charges. WorldCom, whose MCI unit has 20 million customers, filed the largest bankruptcy in U.S. corporate history in July. The SEC in June charged WorldCom with fraud for misleading investors by misstating and hiding expenses. WorldCom has admitted to at least $9 billion in erroneous accounting that has plunged it into bankruptcy court. Four WorldCom executives have pleaded guilty to their roles in the scandal and are cooperating with prosecutors in exchange for possible leniency. Former WorldCom chief financial officer Scott Sullivan has pleaded innocent after being indicted in the scandal.

Residual value

'The residual value' is another term for the realisable or disposal value of an asset and is estimated at the commencement of an asset's life. The residual value will be the sale or scrap value of the asset less any costs incurred by the business in dismantling the asset concerned and any other transaction costs involved in its disposal. Residual values should be based on the prices ruling at the date of the asset's purchase. Normally all tangible assets, including land and buildings, should be depreciated; otherwise it would be possible for the residual value, if estimated at price levels at the anticipated date of disposal, to be greater than the purchase price of the asset concerned. Thus, a depreciation charge into the accounts would turn into an appreciation in value. For reasons we will discuss later, an inflationary holding gain such as this should not appear in the income statement.

The difference between the original cost of an asset and its residual value is termed the 'depreciable amount'.

Depreciation method

Broadly there are two methods of depreciation:

- straight-line depreciation
- reducing balance.

The first of these is the more popular but the latter, whilst more difficult to calculate, has certain accounting advantages that we will consider below.

Straight-line depreciation

With this method of depreciation the value of an asset is written off by a constant annual charge to the income statement. The formula for calculating the annual depreciation charge is:

$$\text{Annual depreciation} = (\text{original cost} - \text{residual value})/\text{useful economic life}$$

Financial realities   A £30 000 asset with an estimated residual value of £2000 would have an annual depreciation charge of £7000 if its useful life is expected to be four years. Exhibit 5.6 shows how the book value of the asset would be shown in the balance sheet in each year of its life.

Exhibit 5.6

Straight line depreciation (four years)	Initial investment	Year end 1	Year end 2	Year end 3	Year end 4
Cost of acquisition	30 000	30 000	30 000	30 000	30 000
Accumulated depreciation in balance sheet		7 000	14 000	21 000	28 000
Book value of equipment	30 000	23 000	16 000	9 000	2 000
Charge to income statement		7 000	7 000	7 000	7 000

The book value of the asset will show the characteristic straight-line pattern as the asset is progressively written down from £30 000 to £2000 over a four-year period:

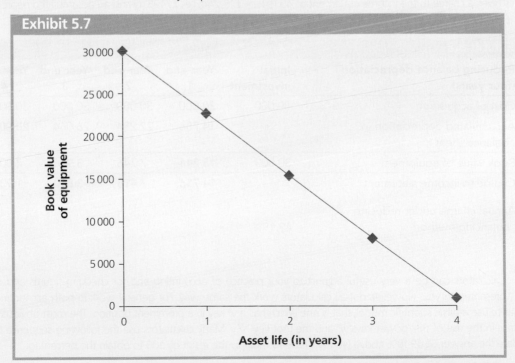

Exhibit 5.7

Reducing-balance depreciation

This method of depreciation is more complex in that what we are looking for is a constant percentage which, if applied to the preceding year's book value, will write the value of the asset down to its residual value by the end of its economic life.

In order to achieve this it is necessary to use the following formula:

$$\text{Annual depreciation charge } (d) = \left[1 - \sqrt[n]{\frac{\text{Residual value of the asset } (R)}{\text{The original cost of the asset } (C)}} \right] \times 100$$

where n = the economic life in years.

Financial realities

What is the percentage rate that would be required to write off an asset costing £30 000 to a residual value of £2000 over four years?

Answer:

Using the formula

$$d = \left(1 - \sqrt[4]{\frac{2000}{30\ 000}} \right) \times 100 = 49.19\%$$

At the end of year 1 the depreciation to be charged to the income statement would be 49.19 per cent × £30 000, i.e., £14 756 and the book value of the equipment would be £30 000 − £14 756 = £15 244. At the end of year 2, the same percentage rate is applied, not to the original cost but to the book value at the end of the previous year. This gives a charge to the income statement of 49.19% × £15 244, i.e., £7498, giving an accumulated depreciation of £14 756 + £7498 = £22 254 and a written-down value of £7746, and so on for years 3 and 4.

Exhibit 5.8

Reducing balance depreciation (four years)	Initial investment	Year end 1	Year end 2	Year end 3	Year end 4
Cost of acquisition	30 000	30 000	30 000	30 000	30 000
Accumulated depreciation in balance sheet		14 756	22 254	26 064	28 000
Book value of equipment	30 000	15 244	7 746	3 936	2 000
Charge to income statement		14 756	7 498	3 810	1 936
Annual charge under reducing balancing method	49.19%				

FYI Calculators can be a very useful adjunct to your practice of accounting and for checking figures and results presented to you. However, not all calculators work the same way. For general work in both accounting and finance use a basic scientific model, that is one which has a y^x key in a prominent position. The most obvious problem is in the use of the 'power keys' y^x and the root key $\sqrt[x]{y}$. Many calculators use the following sequence to calculate the answer of 49.19% above (you will have to multiply the result by 100 to obtain the percentage):

CLR 1 − 4 $\sqrt[x]{x}$ (2000 ÷ 30 000) =

If yours does not work it is probably because it is expecting the following:

CLR 1 - (2000 ÷ 30 000) $\sqrt[y]{}$ x 4 =

It is also good practice when using a calculator to check the output of the calculation to ensure that the number is of the order you are expecting. If not, re-do the calculation.

The reducing balance method gives a write-down of book values as shown in Exhibit 5.9.

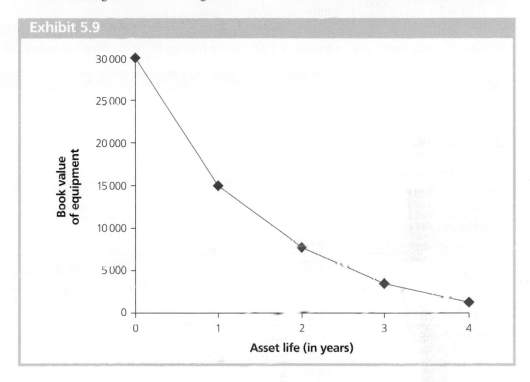

Exhibit 5.9

FYI Here is how the formula for reducing-balance depreciation is derived step by step:

The written down value (R_1) of the asset at the end of the first year will be:

$$R_1 = C \times (1 - d)$$

At the end of second year the written down value will be:

$$R_2 = R_1 \times (1 - d)$$
$$\therefore R_2 = (C \times (1 - d)) \times (1 - d)$$
$$\therefore R_2 = C \times (1 - d)^2$$

and by the same argument at the end of three years

$$R_3 = C \times (1 - d)^3$$

and at the end of n years the final residual value of the asset will be given by:

$$R = C \times (1 - d)^n$$

By rearrangement we come to the formula which in percentage terms is:

$$d = \left(1 - \sqrt[n]{\frac{R}{C}}\right) \times 100$$

Financial realities A firm acquired a fixed asset for £50 000 and planned to write the asset off over 10 years to a residual value of £5000. Show the book values and the annual write-off to the income statement using a depreciation charge on the reducing balance.

We calculate the percentage rate to use as follows:

$$d = \left(1 - \sqrt[n]{\frac{R}{C}}\right) \times 100$$

$$\therefore d = \left(1 - \sqrt[10]{\frac{5000}{50\,000}}\right) \times 100 = 20.5672\%$$

Applying this charge each year on the reducing balance the postings to the extended trial balance are as follows.

Exhibit 5.10

	FA	+ St	+ Db	+ C	=	STL	+ LTL	+ OC	+ R	–	E
Year 1 Capital investment	50 000										
1st year depreciation at 20.5672%	–10 284										10 284
Year 1 Book value	39 716										
2nd year depreciation at 20.5672%	–8 169										8 169
Year 2 Book value	31 548										
3rd year depreciation at 20.5672%	–6 489										6 489
Year 3 Book value	25 059										
4th year depreciation at 20.5672%	–5 154										5 154
Year 4 Book value	19 905										
5th year depreciation at 20.5672%	–4 094										4 094
Year 5 Book value	15 811										
6th year depreciation at 20.5672%	–3 252										3 252
Year 6 Book value	12 559										
7th year depreciation at 20.5672%	–2 583										2 583
Year 7 Book value	9 976										
8th year depreciation at 20.5672%	–2 052										2 052
Year 8 Book value	7 924										
9th year depreciation at 20.5672%	–1 630										1 630
Year 9 Book value	6 295										
10th year depreciation at 20.5672%	–1 295										1 295
Year 10 Book value	5 000										

As you can see, the formula has given us the correct percentage to reach our desired residual value, which is either magic or mathematics depending on your point of view. However, if you are magically inclined you still have to remember the spell, which in this case is the formula. Mathematicians can probably re-derive it every time they need to use it!

Sum of the year digits

The sum of the year digits method gives a different write-off pattern to either the straight-line or the reducing balance method of depreciation. To calculate the sum of the years take the series of years chosen from the expected life of the asset down to one and then add them together. So for 4 years we have:

$$4 + 3 + 2 + 1 = 10$$

and the first year's depreciation charge would be 4/10, the second 3/10 and so on. With the sum of the years method, the depreciation charge can be greatest at the start or, by reversing the sequence, at the end.

Financial realities An asset purchased for £30 000 reducing to £2000 residual value over four years. In case 1 we follow the conventional sequence, applying the greatest charge in the first year. In case 2, we reverse the sequence:

Exhibit 5.11

Case 1: Sum of the year digits (four years)	Initial investment	Year end 1	Year end 2	Year end 3	Year end 4
Cost of acquisition	30 000	30 000	30 000	30 000	30 000
Accumulated depreciation in balance sheet		11 200	19 600	25 200	28 000
Book value of equipment	30 000	18 800	10 400	4 800	2 000
Sum of years	10	4	3	2	1
Charge to income statement		11 200	8 400	5 600	2 800
Case 2: Reverse sum of the year digits (four years)	Initial investment	Year end 1	Year end 2	Year end 3	Year end 4
Cost of acquisition	30 000	30 000	30 000	30 000	30 000
Accumulated depreciation in balance sheet		2 800	8 400	16 800	28 000
Book value of equipment	30 000	27 200	21 600	13 200	2 000
Sum of years	10	1	2	3	4
Charge to income statement		2 800	5 600	8 400	11 200

If we look at the results graphically we can see the radically different write-off patterns for the two cases:

Exhibit 5.12

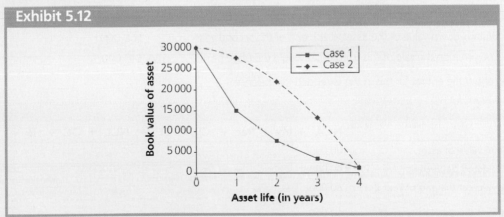

You may notice that the fall in book value is not so severe with the sum of the year digits (case 1) as with the reducing balance method. However, in certain circumstances the reverse method may give a pattern which is more appropriate than the other methods for the particular asset concerned.

A company owns an aeroplane which cost £1.8 million new. It wishes to write the aeroplane down to a residual value of £0.4 million over ten years. Show the different annual depreciation charges for the first year of operation using the straight-line, the reducing balance and the sum of the years' digits methods.

Choosing a depreciation method

The issue which a business must decide is which pattern of depreciation best reflects the consumption of the capital cost of the asset over its economic life. Where a capital asset is being used in production with a constant level of annual sales then the straight-line method will be most appropriate. However, where the sales are expected to be high initially and then decline, a reducing balance or sum of the year digits method, by making the heaviest charge against revenue in the early years, may be better. Conversely, where sales are expected to grow from a low initial position then the reverse sum of the year digits could be the most appropriate. However, in the end management must choose, but once the method has been selected it should be maintained consistently through the life of the asset.

Selling a non-current asset

When a fixed asset is sold both its original cost, and the depreciation accumulated against it should be eliminated from the balance sheet. The problem arises when the price at which the asset is sold is different from its written-down value in the balance sheet. We have shown, the gain or loss on the sale of a fixed asset is shown as an exceptional item in the income statement after the calculation of operating profit.

A company had a tangible non-current asset originally purchased for £100 000 which was being written off over four years to a residual value of £20 000. During the third year the asset was sold for £70 000. Show the accounting transactions for the third year.

At the beginning of the third year the written-down value of the asset would be:

Cost of asset	£100 000
Accumulated depreciation = $2/4 \times$ (£100 000 − £20 000)	£40 000
Written-down value of the asset at the end of the second year	£60 000
The profit on the sale of this fixed asset would therefore be	£10 000.

We can show the entries for this in the extended trial balance:

Exhibit 5.13

	NCA	+ Inv	+ Rec	+ C	= CL	+ NCL	+ OC	+ R	− E
Original value of asset	100 000								
Accumulated depreciation (year 2)	40 000								
Book value at the end of year 2	60 000								
1 Gain on the sale of the asset	10 000 ──────────────────────────────────→							10 000	
2 Realised value of the asset sold	70 000 ──────→ 70 000								
3 Sale proceeds			−70 000 ─→ 70 000						

Following through the three step process: once the sale is agreed the book value of the asset is revalued by the gain on the sale and because this gain is what is known as realised holding gain it can be treated as an exceptional item in the income statement (1). The sale value of the asset is then transferred to the purchaser's account creating a debtor balance (2) which will remain until the asset is paid for (3).

Keeping track of non-current assets

Although the straight-line method of depreciation is straightforward it does have one significant drawback in that each asset owned by a firm must be depreciated independently. The reason for this is that if assets with the same economic life are acquired at different times and simply 'pooled' there is a danger of over-depreciating an asset that has been fully written off. An asset register helps to get around this problem by logging the individual assets through their economic lives. Normally a register will contain the following information:

- The names of the assets concerned, classifying them into land and buildings, plant and equipment and any other subdivision required for the balance sheet (in the next chapter we discuss the disclosure requirements for non-current assets in more detail).
- Any identifying codes (this is necessary where firms have large numbers of individual fixed assets that need to be recorded).
- Date of acquisition and disposal.
- The original value of the asset acquired including any additional capitalised costs incurred in acquiring the asset concerned.
- The date and amount of any revaluation.
- Expected economic life.
- A year-by-year account of the depreciation charged and any additional impairment made during the asset to date (we discuss the concept of impairment later in this chapter)
- Proceeds on disposal, including dismantling and **transaction costs**.

Financial realities   A farmer purchased and depreciated assets as follows:

Year of purchase	Asset	Cost	Residual value	Life (years)
1998	Tractor	10 000	0	4
1999	Combine harvester	50 000	5000	5
2001	Silage tank	15 000	0	5
2002	Land Rover	16 000	4000	4

Construct an asset register for the years 1998 to 2004, showing the total asset cost, accumulated depreciation and charge to the income statement.

Exhibit 5.14

		1998	1999	2000	2001	2002	2003	2004	2005
Tractor	Asset cost	10 000	10 000	10 000	10 000				
	depreciation	2 500	2 500	2 500	2 500				
	accumulated depreciation	2 500	5 000	7 500	10 000				
	book value	7 500	5 000	2 500	0				
Combine	Asset cost		50 000	50 000	50 000	50 000	50 000		
Harvester	depreciation		9 000	9 000	9 000	9 000	9 000		
	accumulated depreciation		9 000	18 000	27 000	36 000	45 000		
	book value		41 000	32 000	23 000	14 000	5 000		
Silage	Asset cost				15 000	15 000	15 000	15 000	15 000
Tank	depreciation				3 000	3 000	3 000	3 000	3 000
	accumulated depreciation				3 000	6 000	9 000	12 000	15 000
	book value				12 000	9 000	6 000	3 000	0
Land	Asset cost					16 000	16 000	16 000	16 000
Rover	depreciation					3 000	3 000	3 000	3 000
	accumulated depreciation					3 000	6 000	9 000	12 000
	book value					13 000	10 000	7 000	4 000
	Asset cost	10 000	60 000	60 000	75 000	81 000	81 000	31 000	31 000
	accumulated depreciation	2 500	14 000	25 500	40 000	45 000	60 000	21 000	27 000
	book value	7 500	46 000	34 500	35 000	36 000	21 000	10 000	4 000
	depreciation	2 500	11 500	11 500	14 500	15 000	15 000	6 000	6 000

The pool of non-current assets

Unlike the straight-line and sum of the year digit methods the reducing balance method of depreciation is based upon the written-down value of the asset or assets concerned. Also, unlike the other methods it is impossible to write an asset off completely as the constant percentage rate applied to the prior year book value leaves a residual of value which approaches zero as the years go by. The use of a constant rate for writing of assets means that depreciation can be based on the pool of assets rather than individual items.

Financial realities The farmer decided to write off all her assets at a standard rate of 35 per cent per annum. Assets acquired during the year are fully depreciated irrespective of when they are purchased. Show the reducing balance depreciation charge for each year using the pooling method.

Year of purchase	Asset	Cost
1998	Tractor	10 000
1999	Combine harvester	50 000
2001	Silage tank	15 000
2002	Land Rover	16 000

First-in first-out (FIFO)

With this method, the charge for the value of inventory used during the year is based on the price levels of that acquired first. Items left at the end of the year will be valued for balance sheet purposes at the latest prices. This is termed first-in first-out or the FIFO method of inventory valuation.

With FIFO, the presupposition is that inventory items flow into production in the order in which they are purchased, i.e., the oldest items are used first. In most businesses where the physical deterioration of inventory is a problem, then good management of inventories should ensure that the oldest items are the first to be used. This does not necessarily imply that the valuation of inventory should follow this procedure, although in the majority of businesses FIFO is the preferred method.

In Exhibit 5.16 you can see how the FIFO method of inventory valuation is calculated.

Last-in first-out (LIFO)

The LIFO method is somewhat trickier to understand in that the latest items acquired are assumed to be the first taken into production and the older items retained in inventory. It is also important to calculate the value of inventory at each withdrawal stage (April and November in this case) and to carry forward the balance of stock at the oldest prices after each usage. It is not correct to add up all usages and apply them at the end of the year in a single exercise.

Average cost (AVCO)

With this method we calculate the average unit value of inventory at each stage and use this value to obtain the cost of goods sold and the remaining balance sheet value. The average unit cost of outstanding inventory is calculated at each stage both at the point of addition of new items and at the removal of inventory to manufacturing. So, for example, after the February purchase the average cost per unit is given as follows:

$$\text{Average cost per unit} = \frac{(\text{value of opening inventory } + \text{ value of February purchase})}{(\text{units of opening inventory } + \text{ units purchased})}$$

$$= (1950.00 + 2660.00)/(30 + 40)$$

$$= £65.86 \text{ per unit}$$

This value is then used to calculate the cost of the materials transferred to manufacturing and the value of items remaining in inventory.

Exhibit 5.18

AVCO method of inventory valuation

		units	unit cost	AVCO	Inv	CL	−E
				Affected columns in the extended trial balance			
01-Jan	Opening inventory	30	65.00	65.00	1950		
01-Feb	Purchases	40	66.50	66.50	2660	2660	
April	Transferred to sales	−40	65.86	65.86	−2634		2634
30-Apr	Inventory balances on the AVCO system	30	65.86	65.86	1976		
01-Nov	Purchases	30	70.00	70.00	2100	2100	
November	Transferred to sales	−50	67.93	67.93	−3396		3396
31-Dec	Closing inventory	10	67.93	67.93	680	Expense =	6030

In the example considered, the value of the purchased materials has risen. Under such a situation:

- when valuing the closing inventory,

    LIFO is lower than average cost is lower than FIFO

- when calculating the cost of inventory expensed during the period,

    FIFO is lower than average cost is lower than LIFO.

Other things being equal, reported profits will be higher using FIFO (because the expensed cost is lower) than is the case with LIFO during a period of rising prices. The average cost method lies somewhere between the two. Clearly a change in stock valuation policy could be used to change the level of reported profit in any given period and it is for this reason that accounting standards insist that such changes should be made explicit. If prices happen to be falling, then the logic of the above is reversed and profits will be understated using FIFO and overstated using LIFO.

To repeat a very important point: FIFO, LIFO and average cost are simply different ways of employing the matching principle. The choice of method determines exactly how much expense during the period should be matched to sales in the income statement (i.e., be 'expensed') and how much should be left as an unmatched balance (i.e., be 'inventoried'). Because all of these methods employ the original cost of acquiring the stock as the basis for calculating the charge to the income statement and the value to the balance sheet they will, if prices are changing, misrepresent the most up-to-date position. If prices are rising rapidly then FIFO tends to understate the cost of goods sold and LIFO overstate it. However, the move to more rigorous stock management policies, and an era of low inflation through the management of interest rates by the central banks, has reduced the impact of this problem on company accounts.

The cost of sales and the cost of goods sold

These are two expressions that are often confused. The cost of sales includes the cost of goods sold and all other costs which can be directly attributed to production and handling of goods for sale. These costs will include labour involved in production, manufacturing overheads (such as power, water, maintenance of production equipment) and depreciation. The cost of goods sold is the cost of materials and components transferred from inventories to sales (in the case of a merchant) or from finished inventory to sales (in the case of a manufacturer). The cost of goods sold is valued using any one of the valuation methods already discussed. Our calculation of the cost of goods sold charged to the income statement in the examples above has been done by valuing the individual transfers. Another way of doing it is by using the following formula:

$$\text{Cost of Goods sold} = \text{Opening inventories (FIFO, LIFO, AVCO)} + \text{Purchases} - \text{Closing inventories (FIFO, LIFO, AVCO)}$$

So, taking the AVCO example above, the cost of goods sold could be calculated as follows:

Cost of goods sold = Opening inventories (£1950)

    Plus

    Purchases during the year (£4760)

    Less

    Closing inventories (£576)

    = £6134

You may like to repeat the calculation of COGS (as accountants call it) for FIFO and LIFO.

The net realisable value rule

Under historic cost accounting practice, the overriding rule is that inventory should be valued at the lower of cost and net realisable value (the 'net realisable value rule'). This is an application of the 'reliability' principle described in Chapter 1 which leads accountants to make prudent judgements about the value that can be realised from a firm's assets. The concept of prudence is discussed in more detail later in this chapter.

For a merchant, who is just buying and selling without any conversion, it would be disastrous if a significant proportion of his or her inventory were valued at less than historical cost. This would mean, by definition, that in the accountant's judgement the stock involved could only be sold at a loss.

In manufacturing the application of the rule has to be qualified. Normally, a manufacturer will purchase a number of components that are assembled to form the finished product. When a component enters into a sub-assembly which has no external market except as scrap then one way of viewing the net realisable value rule is that the component values should be written down to their scrap value. This does not seem particularly sensible when in the normal course those components will carry on through production and become part of a finished product which is in due course sold. To deal with this, the accounting regulators define net realisable value as: 'the estimated selling price in the normal course of business less the estimated costs of completion and the estimated costs necessary to make the sale' (International Accounting Standard No. 2 (IAS 2), para 7).

The valuation of stock in a manufacturing firm

In a manufacturing firm, raw materials are bought in from suppliers, enter production as work-in-progress and when complete become finished goods ready for sale. At the end of the accounting year the problem arises as to how finished and part-finished inventory should be valued for balance sheet purposes. Clearly, finished goods should include the cost of all the bought-in materials and components required in their production. However, to what extent should they also include all the other costs of manufacture such as the necessary labour input, other direct production costs and indeed indirect overheads such as depreciation and general operating costs?

FYI We have introduced a costing term which we will define more fully in Chapter 8. For our purposes here we can define direct and indirect costs as follows:

Direct costs are those that can be directly attributed to the production of the stock concerned. Such costs will include:

- bought-in materials, components and services
- labour costs directly involved in the production of the finished goods
- energy and other utility costs such as water and fuel
- transport costs involved in the shipping of raw materials, and part-finished and finished goods
- plant and equipment costs directly attributable to the manufacture of the products concerned.

Indirect costs are those which cannot be directly attributed such as depreciation and other general expenditures concerned in running the business. As we shall see later in the book there are various techniques for allocating such costs to the production of individual products for accounting purposes.

There are two ways of valuing inventory in a manufacturing firm:

- By valuing the finished goods inventory solely in terms of its direct manufacturing cost. This is termed a marginal costing approach to inventory valuation.
- By valuing inventory in terms of its direct cost plus an allocation of the production overheads. This method is termed absorption costing, as indirect costs are absorbed into the cost of manufacturing inventory.

It is this second method which has now been accepted under International Accounting Standards as the method of choice. Finished goods inventory should:

comprise all costs of purchase, costs of conversion and other costs incurred in bringing inventories to their present location and condition . . . costs of conversion include a systematic allocation of fixed and variable production overheads.

(International Accounting Standard 2, para 10)

To explain how absorption costing works we will consider a situation where a manufacturer produces some finished goods during the year and finds that there are some left on hand. The procedure entails splitting the inventory column in two, distinguishing between raw materials (RMInv) and finished goods ready for sale (FGInv).

Financial realities   Diamond Gritters is a small business converting diamond dust and small irregular stones into diamond-coated papers used in a wide range of manufacturing applications. There was no raw material or finished goods on hand at the beginning of the year. During the year the company:

- purchased 5000 kilos of diamond grit at £240 per kilo
- incurred other direct production costs of £648 000
- charged depreciation on its production equipment of £59 000
- incurred other indirect production overheads of £1 245 000
- produced 8000 kilos of finished paper products for sale, of which 400 kilos were unsold at the end of the year. Raw materials inventory at the end of the year was 350 kilos of diamond grit.

The accounting equation entries for these transactions are as follows (the numbers relate to the explanations below):

Exhibit 5.19

	NCA	+	RMInv	+	FGInv	+	Rec	+ C	=	CL	+ NCL	+ OE	+ R	− E
1 Raw materials purchased			1 200 000							1 200 000				
2 Transfer of raw materials to production			−1 116 000		1 116 000									
3 Direct production costs incurred					648 000					648 000				
4 Depreciation on production equipment	−59 000				59 000									
5 Indirect production overheads allocated					1 245 000					1 245 000				
6 Cost of goods produced					3 068 000									
7 Cost of goods sold*					−2 914 600									2 914 600
8 Inventory valuation to balance sheet			84 000		153 400									

* Cost of goods sold = 7600/8000 × 3 068 000 = 2 914 600

Tracing through the entries one by one:

1. The raw materials purchases are shown as we have seen before, creating a current liability on the supplier's account (we have not shown the cash settlement in this exercise).
2. The raw materials are transferred to the finished goods account as one of the costs incurred in the creation of these new assets.
3. The purchase of the direct costs and the creation of the corresponding short-term liability is also added into the cost of creating the finished goods inventory.
4. The depreciation charge on the plant and equipment used in production is also charged to the cost of producing the finished inventory rather than being posted directly as expenditure for the year.
5. The indirect overheads to be charged to the production of these goods is then added, creating a corresponding current liability on the supplier's account.
6. The total cost of producing the diamond-coated papers is then totalled to give the 'cost of goods produced'.
7. The proportion of the cost of goods produced attributable to the goods sold is then transferred to the expenditure column in the profit for the year matched to the revenue earned in selling those goods.
8. The balance on hand at the end of the year will appear in the balance sheet as two entries under 'stocks' in current assets.

There is a big danger in all of this for some **creative accounting** in that supposing a business is operating well below its capacity then the indirect costs could be allocated across a smaller number of units. For example, if Diamond Gritters could normally produce 10 000 kilos of finished product rather than the 8000 units actually produced then allocating all of the depreciation and indirect costs to the production of those units will distort the value of the cost of goods sold in the income statement and the value of stock on hand at the end of the year. To avoid this under-recovery of overheads only a proportion of the indirect costs related to the normal capacity of the business can be charged:

Exhibit 5.20

	NCA +	RMInv +	FGInv +	Rec + C =	CL +	NCL + OE +	R −	E
1 Raw materials purchased		1 200 000			1 200 000			
2 Transfer of raw materials to production	−1 116 000	1 116 000						
3 Direct production costs incurred			648 000		648 000			
4 Depreciation on production equipment recovered in production (8000/10 000) unrecovered and expensed	−4/ 200 11 800		47 200					11 800
5 Indirect production overheads allocated recovered in production (8000/10 000) unrecovered and expensed			996 000		996 000 249 000			249 000
6 Cost of goods produced			2 807 200					
7 Cost of goods sold	−		2 666 840					2 666 840
8 Inventory valuation to balance sheet		84 000	140 360					

* Cost of goods sold = 7600/8000 × 2 807 200 = 2 666 840

Note what has happened. Only a proportion of the depreciation and the other indirect costs (8000/10 000) are included as part of the cost of producing the finished stock. The remainder is charged directly to the income statement. The finished goods on hand at the end of the year have a lower value in the balance sheet because they do not include the over-absorbed indirect costs. We have neatly closed a loophole whereby management could 'hide' the potential losses of under-capacity working by inflating the value of finished goods in the balance sheet.

Extending your understanding of the principles of accounting

In this section we extend your understanding of the principles of accounting which accountants understand implicitly but which are not always obvious to managers and other users of accounting information. We will round off this chapter with a look at how the problem of changing prices impacts upon the accounts and review the two different approaches that can be taken to the measurement of profit.

The principles of financial accounting

There are four traditional accounting concepts which have been incorporated into UK company law (Companies Act 1985). One of these, the accruals concept we have dealt with at length above.

Going concern

When producing accounts the normal assumption is that the business is operating as a going concern. What this means is that the accountant has no reason to believe that the business will cease to trade either as a deliberate choice of the owners or because of failure of its business. If the accountant is of the view that the business is not a going concern then the valuation of all the assets and liabilities will be restated on a realisations basis which is, as the term suggests, the sale value of the assets less the immediate discharge value of the liabilities.

Accruals

This is the specific application of the general matching principle which we have discussed earlier in this chapter. From the accruals concept arise the rules for recognising revenues and costs within a given period of account. It is the application of the accruals concept which produces the difference between a statement of cash flow and the income statement. However, it is the accruals concept which underpins the transactions basis for the determination of business income or profit. By using the accruals concept we can identify those transactions which add and those that subtract value to and from the business. As you may remember from Chapter 1, we can measure business income by taking the difference between two net values of the firm, one at the beginning of the period and one at the end. To follow this approach we need an asset valuation and capital maintenance concept which we will review later in this chapter.

The consistency concept

Financial accountants normally maintain the same practice in preparing accounts from one period to another. If a change in policy is made then the impact of that change would be fully disclosed in the notes to the accounts.

The prudence concept

It is normal accounting practice to fully recognise losses as soon as they become apparent but not to recognise revenues until they are certain. This naturally builds an inherent pessimism into the preparation of the accounting information. In more recent times the prudence concept has become known as the 'realisations principle' in that only gains that have been 'realised', i.e., have resulted in an open-market sale for cash or other assets, are recognised as income in the period. Unrealised gains (such as an increase in the value of Sid's taxi) would not be recognised until the value is realised through its sale. Potential losses are recognised immediately under the prudence concept.

Until recently this concept was given precedence over the other accounting concepts although arguably the 'going concern' concept mentioned above is just one aspect of the prudence approach to accounting. However, the concept has been so modified by changes in accounting practice and accounting standards that it is no longer mentioned under FRS 18 which just mentions two: accruals and going concern.

The recent history of the development of financial reporting has been one where different regulatory bodies, mainly in the United Kingdom and the United States, have attempted to establish principles which would govern the way company reports were produced. This was hindered for many years by a lack of what became known as a conceptual framework for accounting. In December 2000, the United Kingdom Accounting Standards Board (the ASB), a non-governmental regulatory agency, published Financial Reporting Standard 18 (FRS 18) which is designed to give clear guidance on the principles and bases which are to be used in the preparation of financial reports.

Value-based accounting

Traditionally accountants have recorded the values of assets in the balance sheet at their original cost of acquisition. This was known as the 'historical cost concept'. In our exercises above we have followed the historical cost principle in that we have not adjusted the values of fixed and current assets in the balance sheet to reflect changing market conditions. Once a fixed asset is purchased it will be maintained in the balance sheet at its original cost less its accumulated depreciation. The profit or loss as determined under the historical method is built up by the process of matching revenues to the period of account and then deducting the cost of the resources consumed priced at their original cost of acquisition. As Exhibit 5.1 makes clear there are important elements in the building of business value which are ignored by this approach. However, introducing value based accounting systems present two problems for the accountant:

1. The basis upon which the assets of the business will be revalued (the asset valuation problem).
2. The basis upon which the existing claims will be revalued. If we assume that the firm's independent claims (its long-term and short-term liabilities) are purely monetary claims then the only claim which needs to be revalued is the owner's capital claim (the capital maintenance problem).

Asset valuation

In principle there are two ways in which we could revalue the assets of a business:

- A transactions approach where changes in the value of a firm's assets are incorporated as soon as they occur by transferring changes in value to the owner's equity account.

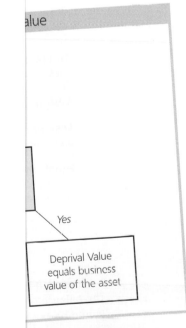

Financial realities More recently a new valuation approach has been advocated by the International Accounting Standards Committee which is based upon fair value. Fair value is defined as the amount for which an asset could be exchanged between knowledgeable willing parties in an arm's-length transaction (IAS 16, para 6). The key idea behind fair value is the idea that the owner of the business has to make a judgement about the price which the asset would achieve in an open-market transaction if it were sold for cash at the balance sheet date. Fair value is therefore what we have described as the realisable value of the asset in an open-market transaction.

However, whilst the use of current as opposed to historical values does increase the economic significance of the balance sheet to the owner it does remove the traceability of assets in the balance sheet. If historical values are used consistently then every asset figure in the balance sheet can be traced to its original purchase invoices within the primary records of the firm. So, in a rather subtle way, the argument between the use of historical values and current values is one between the stewardship objective of accounting and its economic relevance in supporting the decisions of users.

balance sheet is converted into cash or other liquid assets over its life. So, if Sid were to depreciate his taxi over (say) five years, then at the end of each month his profit, and hence the amount he could withdraw from the business, would be reduced by the monthly depreciation (which on a straight-line basis is a reduction in profit of £500 per month). If he withdraws his profit each month (less the depreciation charge) and does not invest the cash left in the business elsewhere the net result will be that at the end of the five years he will be back where he started with his original capital intact and his final balance sheet at the end of five years would look like this:

Exhibit 5.23

Opening valuation

Valuation basis	Acquisition	After five years
Total value of Assets		
Value of the taxi	30 000	30 000
Less accumulated depreciation	0	30 000
Net book value	30 000	0
Diesel in tank		45
Five months entitlement to garage		50
Cash in hand	5 000	34 905
	35 000	35 000
Less: non-current liability		
Bank loan	20 000	20 000
	15 000	15 000
Equals the Owner's Claim		
Sid's investment	15 000	15 000
Accumulated profits less withdrawals	0	0
	15 000	15 000
Cash withdrawal	0	0
	15 000	15 000

Indeed, if he sold off any remaining diesel in his tank and let his garage to another user for the balance of his tenancy at his current rent then his cash balance would be £35 000, which would be exactly where he started.

The depreciation charge has the purpose of maintaining his original capital intact. Historical-cost accounting therefore uses what is known as a nominal capital maintenance concept.

We also need to apply the 'lower of cost or net realisable value rule' for valuing stocks to ensure nominal capital maintenance. Supposing Sid's final tank had a sale value of £35 rather than £45, then the loss in stock value would be charged to his income statement and thus cut his level of withdrawal by £10.

However, Sid might not be happy at the prospect of just recovering his original capital at the end of five years. He might take the view that his original £15 000 has lost value because of inflation and he therefore would wish to retain sufficient profit to maintain the purchasing power of his original capital. If he did this he would be adopting what is known as 'proprietary capital maintenance'. Alternatively, if he wished to retain sufficient to ensure he stayed in business he would wish to retain sufficient profit so that he could purchase a new taxi of the same capability as the original. This is known as 'entity capital maintenance'.

In summary, therefore, the idea of capital maintenance is introduced to restrict the amount of profit which can be withdrawn to a level which is sustainable either in terms of ensuring that the owner's original capital is not inadvertently reduced, or in terms of ensuring that the owner's capital is maintained in general purchasing power terms or finally to a level which allows the owner to maintain the physical capability of the business by being able to fully replace its assets when they are exhausted by use. The key idea behind the concept of capital maintenance is to restrict the level of withdrawal to the point where the owner is as well-off at the end of the period of account as at the beginning. The difference arises in terms of what we mean by well-off!

Traditional versus value-based accounting

The debate as to whether assets should be revalued and some alternative capital maintenance to that employed under historical-cost accounting be used has proved inconclusive. The problem can be summarised with the following question: is it truly possible to value a business through its balance sheet or will the aggregation of values (no matter on what basis the individual assets are restated) always lead to something being missed?

As we shall see later in this book, the market values of firms whose equity is traded on stock exchanges is often substantially different from their balance sheet values even when those balance sheets are restated at current values. Part of the reason for this is that many assets which are of an intangible nature are not fully reflected in the balance sheet: the value of a company's name, the stock of know-how developed by its employees, the network of business contacts created over the company's life and so on. These intangibles can be more important to an assessment of a business's value than the value of its real assets. It is true that accountants have sought methods of valuing a business's goodwill and its know-how but the current regulations insist that where the value of such assets is recognised they are written off as quickly as possible. But even more than this the true value of an asset to a business is in how it is used. This is the 'sum of the parts' argument that we raised when we considered the additivity principle in the last chapter.

To summarise, one unwritten principle of accounting is that it will always miss something of value, and if that is the case, and a fair valuation of a firm through its balance sheet is impossible, why bother? Perhaps it would be better to concentrate on what the accountant can do well, and that is ensuring that all real and monetary assets of a business are effectively accounted for and that the surplus generated from its transacting is fully declared.

Chapter summary

In this chapter we have explored the issues and principles of financial reporting in some depth. We have looked at the problems of recognising revenues and costs and how to deal with accruals and prepayments before moving on to consider two substantial issues in traditional accounting: accounting for depreciation and for inventories. These problems have arisen because we are trying to reflect the process whereby firms add value to themselves by transforming assets through manufacturing rather than simply buying and selling them as merchants. We have also considered the impact of another important value driver on accounts whereby value is created or lost through the action of market forces. In the next chapter we will consolidate much of this learning as we go on to explore the issues raised by accounting for companies that have limited liability and are required to make full disclosure of their affairs in accordance with the accounting standards.

Further reading

Accounting Standards Board (1999) *Statement of Principles for Financial Reporting*, ASB Publications. A summary of this important document can be obtained from **www.frc.org.uk**.

Baxter, W. (1978) *Depreciation*, London: Sweet and Maxwell. A difficult book to track down but well worth the effort.

Davies, M., Paterson, R. and Wilson, A. (2001) *Ernst and Young's UK and International GAAP*, 7th edn, London: Butterworths Tolley. This is a blockbuster as well as being one of the heaviest books on accounting on the market. The opening chapters are good on the development of the framework of financial accounting.

Elliot, B. and Elliot, J. (2003) *Financial Accounting and Reporting*, Harlow: Financial Times, Prentice Hall. Chapters 2, 3 and 5 provide useful further reading for this chapter.

Progress check

Please refer to the page shown to check your answer.

1. Name the four principal drivers of company value. (p. 102)

2. List the five conditions for recognising the revenue accruing from a given sale. (p. 105)

3. How is an accrued expenditure shown in the income statement and in the balance sheet? (p. 108)

4. List the four issues that need to be considered when calculating the depreciation charge on an asset for the year. (p. 109)

5. If a fixed asset is sold for more than its book value how is the surplus on sale shown in the income statement? (p. 116)

6. What is the principal advantage in keeping a non-current asset register? (p. 117)

7. In a situation of rising prices for the purchase of inventory would you expect FIFO or LIFO to record the higher inventory value in the balance sheet at the year-end? (pp. 119–120)

8. In published accounts conforming to IAS 2 should inventory be valued on a marginal or an absorption basis? (p. 124)

9. Explain the difference between the cost of sales and the cost of goods sold. (p. 122)

10. What are the four accounting concepts mentioned in the Companies Act 1985? (pp. 126–127)

11. What are the two procedures by which a company can revalue its assets? (p. 127)

12. Define deprival value and fair value. (p. 129)

13. Name three capital maintenance concepts. (pp. 129–131)

Questions

The answers to the questions followed by ✓ can be found at the back of the book, the answers to the remaining questions can be found on the website accompanying this book (**www.cengage. co.uk/ryan2**).

1. A rare metal refiner had an inventory of 300 oz of platinum at 1 January with a book value of £310 per oz. During the year it purchased two further consignments of 1500 oz on 1 April at £324/oz and 1500 oz on 1 September at £380/oz. It used 1600 oz in production on 1 August and 1200 oz on 1 December. All platinum transferred to production was sold in its refined form by the year-end.

   You are required to:

   (i) Calculate the cost of goods sold at the year-end using the FIFO, LIFO and AVCO methods. You may assume that the opening book value is based upon the chosen valuation method.

   (ii) Calculate the value of the remaining inventory at the year-end.

   (iii) If the market price of platinum fell back to £305/oz at 31 December how would you adjust your values in (i) and (ii)?

2. A company has a non-current asset register that contains buildings, fixed plant and small equipment as follows:

Exhibit 5.24

Cost	Balance 31-Dec-02 £'000	Additions £'000	Disposals £'000	Balance 31-Dec-03 £'000
Buildings	2560	1800	0	4360
Plant	450	240	0	690
Equipment	288	132	24	396
Non-current at cost	3298	2172	24	5446

Accumulated depreciation	Balance 31-Dec-02 £'000	Depreciation for the year £'000	Disposals £'000	Balance 31-Dec-03 £'000
Buildings	1660			
Plant	338			
Equipment	144			
Depreciation	2142			

Buildings are depreciated on a straight-line basis over 20 years, plant on a reducing balance of 50 per cent per annum and equipment over 6 years straight-line. Some equipment had been disposed of which was in the sixth year of its life. The company places a nil value on the disposal of its assets at the end of their economic lives, which it believes fairly represents the net of any proceeds on sale less the disposal costs.

(i)   Calculate the depreciation charge for the year for each class of asset.

(ii) The balance on accumulated depreciation is to be shown in the balance sheet.

(iii) Outline the accounting steps you would take if (a) the value of the buildings were found on survey to be greater than the net book value as shown, (b) the value of the plant and equipment were found to be substantially overstated.   ✓

3. A company had a net profit before interest and tax of £450 000. You note the following:

- Interest received was £12 400.
- Interest paid on loans was £13 000.
- Depreciation had been charged of £25 000.
- Non-current assets had been purchased for £20 000 during the year that had a 50 per cent first-year writing-down allowance for tax purposes.
- The existing company non-current assets had been written down for tax purposes to £100 000. The company can offset a 10 per cent per annum writing-down allowance on this balance against its taxable profits.
- The company wishes to provide for corporation tax at a rate of 25 per cent per annum.

You are required to calculate the provision for corporation tax that should appear in the company's income statement.

4. Bernard had been operating a wholesale business for some years. His balance at 1 January was as follows:

Exhibit 5.25

Non-current assets at cost	240 000
Less accumulated depreciation	196 000
Net book value	44 000
Net current assets	
Inventories	65 000
Debtors	84 000
Cash	9 100
	158 100
Less current liabilities	−60 400
Borrowing from bank	−38 000
	103 700
Owner's equity	
Subscribed capital	50 000
Earnings reserve	53 700
	103 700

Within current liabilities you discover that there is a tax liability of £12 300 and a dividend payable to Bernard of £5000. During the year:

1. The tax and dividends were paid early in the New Year.

2. The business revenue was £270 000 and the receipts from customers was £330 000.

3. £140 000 was for inventory sold during the year. There was £38 000 of inventory at the end of the year.

4. Other operating expenditures charged to the year but excluding depreciation were £82 000. The trade payables at the year-end were £70 100.

5. Bernard had calculated depreciation of £28 000 on the basis of the assets owned at the beginning of the year.

6. He purchased a new van for £32 000 which he planned to write off over five years with a residual value of £7000.

7. He purchased a new inventory management system during the year costing £18 000 which he planned to write off completely over three years.

8. He had forgotten that he had sold a van during the course of the year purchased four years previously for £24 000. He had expected to sell the van after five years for £4000. The sale of the van realised £10 500.

9. Interest on the loan is charged at 8 per cent per annum. Like last year, this interest was fully paid during the year.

10. He wanted to provide for tax at 25 per cent of his net profit.

Bernard normally calculates depreciation on a straight line basis applying a full year's depreciation on acquisitions in the year of purchase. He is considering moving to a reducing balance method of writing down his assets and has suggested a rate of 30 per cent per annum.

On the basis of this information prepare a balance sheet, income statement and cash flow statement on the basis of the current method of depreciation. Bernard would also like an estimate of his current profit if he were to change to a reducing balance method of depreciation. ✓

Case exercise

Attached are the balance sheet entry and notes relating to the intangible and tangible assets within the group accounts of Marks & Spencer plc for the financial year ended 31 March 2007.

Balance sheet:

Exhibit 5.26

	Notes	As at 31 March 2007 £m	As at 1 April 2006 (restated) £m
Assets			
Non-current assets			
Intangible assets	13	194.1	163.5
Property, plant and equipment	14	4,044.5	3,575.8
Investment property	15	25.1	38.5

Notes to the financial statements

13. INTANGIBLE ASSETS

	Goodwill £m	Brands £m	Computer software £m	Computer software under development £m	Total £m
At 3 April 2005					
Cost or valuation	69.5	80.0	32.8	5.6	187.9
Accumulated amortisation	–	(2.7)	(19.8)	–	(22.5)
Net book value	69.5	77.3	13.0	5.6	165.4
Year ended 1 April 2006					
Opening net book value	69.5	77.3	13.0	5.6	165.4
Additions	–	–	0.2	10.7	10.9
Transfers	–	–	9.5	(9.5)	–
Disposals	–	–	–	(0.1)	(0.1)
Amortisation charge	–	(5.3)	(7.4)	–	(12.7)
Closing net book value	69.5	72.0	15.3	6.7	163.5
At 1 April 2006					
Cost or valuation	69.5	80.0	42.3	6.7	198.5
Accumulated amortisation	–	(8.0)	(27.0)	–	(35.0)
Net book value	69.5	72.0	15.3	6.7	163.5
Year ended 31 March 2007					
Opening net book value	69.5	72.0	15.3	6.7	163.5
Additions	–	–	0.3	46.2	46.5
Transfers	–	–	25.9	(25.9)	–
Disposals	–	–	(0.1)	(1.6)	(1.7)
Amortisation charge	–	(5.3)	(8.9)	–	(14.2)
Closing net book value	69.5	66.7	32.5	25.4	194.1
At 31 March 2007					
Cost or valuation	69.5	80.0	51.2	25.4	226.1
Accumulated amortisation	–	(13.3)	(18.7)	–	(32.0)
Net book value	69.5	66.7	32.5	25.4	194.1

Goodwill relates to the acquisition of 'per una', which was acquired in October 2004 and is not amortised, but tested annually for impairment with the recoverable amount being determined from value in use calculations. The key assumptions for the value in use calculations are those regarding the discount rate, growth rates and changes in income and costs.

The Group prepares discounted cash flow forecasts based on financial forecasts approved by management covering a three-year period, which takes account of both past performance and expectations for future market developments. Cash flows beyond this three-year period are extrapolated using a growth rate of 2.0%, which does not exceed the long-term average growth rate for retail businesses in the UK. Management estimates the discount rate using a pre-tax rate that reflects current market assessments of the time value of money and the risks specific to retail businesses. A pre-tax discount rate of 9.5% has been used.

Brands consist of the 'per una' brand which is being amortised on a straight-line basis over a period of 15 years.

14. PROPERTY, PLANT AND EQUIPMENT

	Land and buildings £m	Fixtures, fittings & equipment £m	Assets in the course of construction £m	Total £m
At 3 April 2005				
Cost	2,412.0	3,162.1	21.6	5,595.7
Accumulated depreciation	(82.7)	(1,926.8)	–	(2,009.5)
Net book value	2,329.3	1,235.3	21.6	3,586.2
Year ended 1 April 2006				
Opening net book value	2,329.3	1,235.3	21.6	3,586.2
Exchange difference	2.2	2.0	0.3	4.5
Additions[1]	34.7	251.8	40.3	326.8
Transfers	–	20.3	(20.3)	–
Disposals	(34.1)	(6.2)	–	(40.3)
Assets of discontinued operations	(11.4)	(21.0)	(1.4)	(33.8)
Depreciation charge[2]	(10.7)	(256.9)	–	(267.6)
Closing net book value	2,310.0	1,225.3	40.5	3,575.8
At 1 April 2006				
Cost	2,392.2	3,287.1	40.5	5,719.8
Accumulated depreciation	(82.2)	(2,061.8)	–	(2,144.0)
Net book value	2,310.0	1,225.3	40.5	3,575.8
Year ended 31 March 2007				
Opening net book value	2,310.0	1,225.3	40.5	3,575.8
Exchange difference	(2.7)	(1.6)	(0.2)	(4.5)
Additions[1]	63.9	578.7	103.3	745.9
Reclassification from investment proper	13.2	–	–	13.2
Transfers	8.8	27.3	(36.1)	–
Disposals	(6.4)	(10.7)	–	(17.1)
Depreciation charge[2]	(13.9)	(254.9)	–	(268.8)
Closing net book value	2,372.9	1,564.1	107.5	4,044.5
At 31 March 2007				
Cost	2,468.2	3,653.3	107.5	6,229.0
Accumulated depreciation	(95.3)	(2,089.2)	–	(2,184.5)
Net book value	2,372.9	1,564.1	107.5	4,044.5

[1]'Additions' includes £nil (last year £5.4m) in respect of the discontinued operation
[2]'Depreciation charge' includes £0.3m (last year £6.3m) in respect of the discontinued operation

The net book value above includes land and buildings of £43.7m (last year £44.9m) and equipment of £16.4m (last year £5.0m) where the Group is a lessee under a finance lease.

15. INVESTMENT PROPERTY

	2007 £m	2006 £m
Cost		
At start of year	38.6	38.6
Reclassification to property, plant and equipment	(13.3)	–
At end of year	25.3	38.6
Depreciation		
At start of year	0.1	–
Reclassification to property, plant and equipment	(0.1)	–
Depreciation charge	0.2	0.1
At end of year	0.2	0.1
Net book value	25.1	38.5

During the year, some investment properties have been transferred to property, plant and equipment (see note 14) as they are being converted into new trading space. These properties are excluded from the market value of investment properties below.

The investment properties were valued at £34.3m as at 31 March 2007 by qualified professional valuers working for CB Richard Ellis, Chartered Surveyors, acting in the capacity of External Valuers. Last year the investment properties were valued at £55.5m by qualified professional valuers working for DTZ Debenham Tie Leung, Chartered Surveyors, acting in the capacity of External Valuers.

All such valuers are Chartered Surveyors, being members of the Royal Institution of Chartered Surveyors (RICS). The properties were valued on the basis of Market Value. All valuations were carried out in accordance with the RICS Appraisal and Valuation Standards. As the investment properties are held at depreciated historical cost, this valuation has not been reflected in the carrying value of the assets.

The Group received rental income of £1.7m (last year £1.5m) in respect of these investment properties.

Using the information provided and any other information you can, reconcile the numbers in the balance sheet entry with those in the notes, checking that you understand the basis upon which they have been calculated. Write a brief report outlining the key features of these statements for a non-specialist reader.

Chapter 6

Accounting for companies

Introduction

By this stage you should have a good grasp of the method of preparing financial reports and have a good idea of the most significant issues with which accountants have to grapple. In Chapter 1 we introduced the idea of limited companies and traced their development from the early merchant trading businesses of the Elizabethan era, through the industrial revolution to the modern day. Accounting for companies opens up new areas of interest for us: how to account for equity financing through shares, the creation of reserves for different purposes, accounting for group companies and the requirements of the professional regulators and the Stock Exchange in setting standards for disclosure. In addition to this, limited liability companies have to operate in accordance with the Companies Acts in terms of their disclosure of information to the public. This introduces the requirement that accounts are audited so that the public and other stakeholders can have some assurance of the quality of the information they contain.

You may remember from Chapter 1 that there are two types of limited company: those that are limited by shares and those limited by guarantee. The former is overwhelmingly the most common type and is always used if the promoters of the company wish to run the company for personal profit. Companies limited by guarantee are technically not allowed to make profits for distribution to their owners but the surpluses must be used for the charitable or other purpose for which the business has been established. We will not explicitly consider the specific issues relating to such companies apart from saying that their disclosure requirements and liability to tax are in most respects identical to those for companies limited by shares.

In this chapter we will deal with all of these topics and also build upon the accounting skills you have already acquired both in producing but also in reading and interpreting accounting information. In the next chapter we will pursue the topic of interpretation in much more detail.

Learning objectives

The outcomes we seek to achieve in this chapter are as follows.

The characteristics of limited companies

● That you understand the nature of limited companies, and the reasons why they are created.

● That you are aware of the legal and other regulatory requirements placed upon companies and their management.

How limited companies are created

- That you know how companies are created and the role and importance of the shareholder.

- That you can perform the accounting transactions and create an opening balance sheet for a new limited company.

- That you understand the distinguishing features of the financial reports of a company compared with a sole trader or unincorporated partnership.

Group companies – acquisition and mergers

- That you can understand the meanings of the terms 'associated company' and 'subsidiary' and can undertake the accounting entries for the formation of a group.

- That you can consolidate the balance sheet and income statements for two companies to form a group and are aware of the distinctive features of a group financial report.

Becoming a public limited company

- That you have an understanding of how a public limited company is formed and the process it must go through to obtain a listing.

The characteristics of limited companies

Limited companies are created in order to protect their members from the risk to which a sole trader or unincorporated partnership is exposed. If a sole trader's business fails then the owner is liable for the financial commitments he or she has made. They will face bankruptcy and the consequential loss of their property. Their house and all other personal assets apart from a limited set of 'tools of their trade' can be sold to pay their creditors. Individuals in partnerships can be bankrupted if something goes wrong. In addition, they also face the jeopardy of 'joint and several liability' whereby all partners are liable for the debts of the whole company. So even if all the other partners were to disappear, the remaining partner would face the full claim in law.

Limited liability provides protection for businesses in that the company's creditors do not have an unlimited claim against the owners or the management, providing that the individuals concerned have not acted criminally by knowingly continuing to operate the business whilst it is insolvent. In the event of a company's failure the shareholders only risk the loss of the capital they have personally invested in the business.

The principal characteristics of limited companies are discussed in Chapter 1 but here are a few more points that are pertinent to accountants and financial managers more generally:

1. Under the Companies Act 1985, a business can be incorporated as either a private or a public limited company (the latter being designated as 'plc'). Private limited companies (designated as 'Ltd') cannot issue shares to the general public and their share capital is normally restricted to a small group of people such as a family or partners in a business who decide to incorporate.

2. The directors of a limited company are required to produce accounts and the type of information they are required to produce in the UK is dependent upon the company's size. Other countries have slightly different rules but most do not require small companies

to disclose as much information as that required of large firms. We will discuss the reporting requirements of limited companies in more detail below.

3. Limited company accounts must be 'audited' before being submitted to the Registrar of Companies and made public. An **auditor**, who is an independent professionally qualified person who has a licence to act in such a capacity, verifies that the published accounts are in accordance with accounting standards and company law, and present a *true and fair* view of the business.

4. Because a company is a separate legal person in law it will be liable for its own special tax – corporation tax. Because corporation tax rates are generally lower than personal tax rates many individuals regard establishing a limited company as a simple way of avoiding tax.

The legal framework regulating companies

In the UK, the law relating to companies and their management is contained in a number of Acts of Parliament. Other countries have their own legislation although the concept of limited liability is common throughout the market-based economies of the world. In the UK, the Department of Trade and Industry is headed by a government minister, the Secretary of State for Trade and Industry, and from time to time he or she will sponsor the passage of a new Companies Act through Parliament and into law. Company Law has slowly evolved since the first joint stock Companies Act of 1844, which required all businesses of more than twenty-five partners to be registered and incorporated (to become a company). The concept of Limited Liability was introduced by Act of Parliament in 1855 and from then on there has been a long sequence of Companies Acts that have modified and developed the law. Currently the basic Act is the 2006 Companies Act. The Companies Act covers the following:

- the process of incorporation and registration
- the issue and redemption of shares
- the preparation and disclosure of annual accounts and the annual report and their submission
- the duties and responsibilities of the directors
- the conduct of general meetings of the shareholders
- liquidation and winding up of a company.

In addition, companies must also comply with a wide range of other acts of parliament covering: taxation, health and safety at work, data protection, fair and unfair competition, disability and discrimination, and a wide variety of regulation and directives from the European Union concerning the conduct of trade and employment. In many of these areas the law prescribes penalties for non-compliance upon the directors, ranging from small fines for such things as the incorrect use of company stationery to criminal prosecution and imprisonment for breaches of the Health and Safety Act.

The reason for this legislation is that companies give business people important protection in that they limit the risk to which the individuals concerned are exposed. Through the sharing of ownership they also provide the means of raising large amounts of capital for investment and the development of the business. The action of companies can also have a huge impact on running the economy. The collapse of Enron, at one time one of the largest US oil and gas trading companies in the world with interests ranging from water to Internet trading, sent shock waves through the global financial markets, wiping many billions of dollars off the prices of equity shares. For all these reasons national governments both domestically and through international treaties attempt to regulate the conduct of companies.

The Annual Return and Accounts for a Limited Company © A.B.J. Price

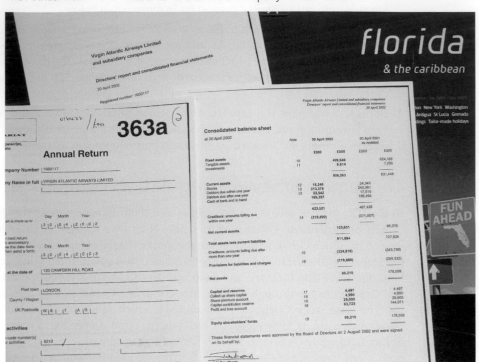

The duties of directors

Directors are individuals appointed by the shareholders who accept the responsibility of running the company. Their job is to set company goals and policies and to ensure that appropriate strategies are in place to achieve those goals. Some directors have executive roles which means that they have some general or functional management responsibility for which they are remunerated. Others are appointed to a non-executive role and their duty is to provide the executive directors with informed and impartial advice on the management of the business. Exhibit 6.1 shows the normal titles held by the directors of companies.

The directors of a company owe their primary duty to the company itself. What this means in practice is that within the terms of the constitution of the company as laid out in its memorandum and articles of association they are required to run the company in the collective interests of all the shareholders. Under proposals in the UK to change company law,

Exhibit 6.1

Executive Directors:	Non-executive Directors:
Managing Director (chief executive officer (CEO))	Chairman
Financial Director (chief financial officer (CFO))	Non-executive directors (one third of the total membership)
Marketing	
Human Resources (personnel)	**Other officers:**
Operations (production)	Company secretary
Research and Development	

directors would also have to recognise the role of the other stakeholder groups in the successful operation of the business.

The directors have certain responsibilities in the preparation of the financial accounts but they have an overriding duty to manage and safeguard the assets of the business. Furthermore, the directors have a duty to ensure that the company does not continue to trade if it is insolvent, that is when it is no longer in a position to meet its obligations and to pay its debts. This would only arise if the company had made such losses that it could no longer maintain its shareholder capital. As a result any further trading would put its creditors at risk.

Each year the directors are required to produce:

1. A directors' report: this document provides a range of information to supplement the financial accounts. Typical information found in the directors' report are: recommended dividends to be paid, material events which have occurred after the balance sheet date, a statement of the research and development (R&D) activities of the company, details of the directors and their interests in the company, details of the company's employment policies, and any political or charitable donations.

2. An income statement, balance sheet and cash flow for the company. These will necessarily be supported by extensive 'notes to the accounts' giving more detail on how the individual figures on the principal accounts have been derived. These notes are an invaluable source of information which in most company accounts will also include a five-year summary of the financial performance of the business.

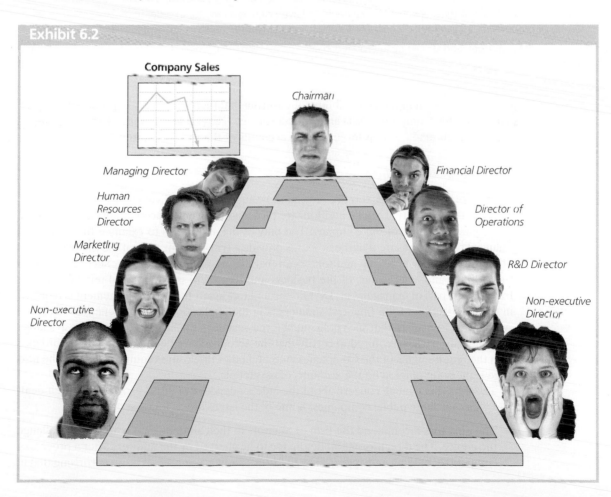

Exhibit 6.2

Exhibit 6.3

easyJet plc
Annual Report and Accounts 2006

Statement of Directors' Responsibilities

Company law requires the Directors to prepare financial statements for each financial year, which give a true and fair view of the state of affairs of the Company and Group and of the profit or loss for that period. In preparing those financial statements, the Directors are required to:

• select suitable accounting policies and then apply them consistently;
• make judgements and estimates that are reasonable and prudent;
• state whether applicable accounting standards have been followed, subject to any material departures disclosed and explained in the financial statements; and
• prepare the financial statements on the going concern basis unless it is inappropriate to presume that the Group will continue in business.

The Directors are responsible for keeping proper accounting records which disclose with reasonable accuracy at any time the financial position of the Company and the Group to enable them to ensure that the financial statements comply with the Companies Act 1985. The Directors have general responsibility for taking such steps as are reasonably open to them to safeguard the assets of the Group and to prevent and detect fraud and other irregularities.

Each of the persons who is a Director at the date of the approval of this report confirms that:

• so far as the Director is aware, there is no relevant audit information of which the Group's auditors are unaware; and
• the Director has taken all the steps that he/she ought to have taken as a Director in order to make himself/herself aware of any relevant audit information and to establish that the Group's auditors are aware of that information.

This confirmation is given and should be interpreted in accordance with the provisions of s.234ZA of the Companies Act 1985.

The directors have a responsibility for ensuring that their accounts are prepared in accordance with the Companies Acts and with all current accounting standards. Exhibit 6.3 shows the statement made by easyJet in its 2006 accounts of the responsibilities of its directors.

The role of the auditor

Each set of published company accounts must be audited by an individual or company licensed to act in that capacity. Usually auditors are professional firms of accountants and should be entirely independent of the company. The duty of the auditors is to examine the company's financial report to ensure that the accounts provide a **true and fair view** of the financial affairs of the business. By 'true' the auditors mean that the accounts accurately reflect the financial transactions and asset values of the business and that there is no material misstatement or fraud on the part of management. By 'fair' the auditors assert that where judgement is required in the preparation of the financial statements in the application of the 'Generally Accepted Accounting Principles' that such judgement is reasonable in the light of the evidence available. The auditors are also required to certify that the accounts have been prepared in accordance with the requirements of the Companies Acts and other disclosure requirements. On the next page is the audit opinion on the accounts of easyJet plc.

There has been much concern about the independence of auditors especially in their dealings with very large public companies. Some of the issues are as follows:

● The directors recommend the firm of auditors to their shareholders who rarely challenge the choice. The directors negotiate the fee to be charged by the auditors after a process of competitive bidding and appraisal by the firm's audit committee. It is not surprising that in

---

Exhibit 6.4

Opinion

In our opinion:

- the Group financial statements give a true and fair view, in accordance with IFRSs as adopted by the European Union, of the state of the Group's affairs as at 30 September 2006 and of its profit and cash flows for the year then ended;
- the parent company financial statements give a true and fair view, in accordance with IFRSs as adopted by the European Union as applied in accordance with the provisions of the Companies Act 1985, of the state of the parent company's affairs as at 30 September 2006 and cash flows for the year then ended;
- the financial statements and the part of the Directors' remuneration report to be audited have been properly prepared in accordance with the Companies Act 1985 and Article 4 of the IAS Regulation; and
- the information given in the Directors' report is consistent with the financial statements.

PricewaterhouseCoopers LLP
Chartered Accountants and Registered Auditors
St Albans, 13 November 2006

---

such situations the auditors feel beholden to management and are unwilling to challenge management's interpretation of events. It is not unusual for audit firms to acquire their work through their network of social and other relationships.

- The financial affairs of large companies can be exceedingly complex with many transactions which do not fall within the conventional accounting framework. It is impossible to check all the transactions that a firm undertakes and most audit firms employ a sample check system, often using relatively junior and unqualified staff to do some of the routine audit work. In such circumstances the subtleties of the transactions and the network of business relationships involved can be easily missed. Audit firms are often under great time pressure to complete an audit and move to the next job. All of these pressures mean that the auditors must rely on the statements made by the directors and senior management.

- Very large companies often feel constrained to appoint large multinational firms of auditors who have access to the staff necessary to complete the audit work locally and internationally when required. These firms often sell a wide range of other corporate services, including accountancy, management consultancy and taxation advice. It was not unusual for a firm of accountants to advise on the valuation of a company's intangible assets one day and return to audit the figures the next.

There have been many situations where the auditors have missed significant abuses including misstatement of accounts and even fraud. As a result there is pressure, principally in the UK and the US but in other countries as well, to prevent firms of accountants from both auditing and offering consultancy services to management at the same time.

Review activity 6.1   Here is a powerful criticism of auditors in the UK:

Hardly a week passes without revelations of some shortcomings in accounting and auditing. Enron, Global Crossing, Elan, Transtec, Versailles, Resort Hotels and Independent Insurance are just the latest. In each case, the companies concerned employed and remunerated accountants to massage their accounts. In accordance with carefully developed plans, large amounts of cash were siphoned off. Audit firms did not notice anything because in some cases, in their capacity as consultants, they created many of the transactions and opaque corporate structures. Auditors collected fat audit and consultancy fees and blamed everyone else for their own failures. Ordinary people lost their jobs, homes, investments, savings and pensions.

Accountancy firms enjoy a state-guaranteed monopoly of auditing. This provides the basis for selling consultancy and generates a double-digit growth in profits. Auditors are regulated by professional accountancy bodies who have no independence from the auditing industry. Audit firms are not required to publish any information about the conduct of an audit. No scandal has ever come to light because of audit firms or the professional accountancy bodies.

The practices of auditing firms encourage audit failures. Partners are given bonuses for selling consultancy services to audit clients. The prime concern of audit firms is to appease company directors. The same partners want to squeeze more productivity from the trainees doing company audits. They are expected to work evenings and weekends for free. Most find the work boring and resent the exploitation. More than 50 per cent admit to falsifying audit work.

The legal pressures for delivering good audits are weak. Auditors only owe a 'duty of care' to the company they audit, not to any individual shareholder, creditor or employee, no matter how negligent they are. In the wake of audit failures, most lawsuits are by one accountancy firm, acting as a receiver or liquidator, against another. Win or lose, they do very nicely out of it. Ordinary stakeholders rarely do.

Professor Prem Sikka, 'We are a nation of accountants', *Guardian*, 20 February 2002

Carefully read the article by Professor Prem Sikka. Identify those statements that are assertions of fact and those statements that are opinions. What evidence would you need to collect to verify his assertions of fact and on what basis would you decide whether his statements of opinion are reasonable in the light of the facts?

Corporate governance

Following a number of high-profile corporate scandals there has been a growing awareness of the importance of 'good conduct' on the part of directors in the way that they run their companies. After a series of reports a 'Combined Code of Practice' has been produced which specifies how companies should be 'governed' by the directors and the disclosures that they should make. Further readings on 'the Code' are given at the end of the chapter. The main elements of the code are:

1. The board of directors. The intention of the code is that boards should be properly constituted and that there is an adequate separation of responsibilities. In practice this means that the chairman and managing director (that is the director who has chief responsibility for the overall management of the business) should not be the same person. In addition the board should have at least a third of its membership as independent non-executive directors who can give impartial advice free from any business interest in the company. Under the Code, the directors are required to resubmit themselves for re-election by the shareholders every three years and also to establish formal procedures for setting their remuneration. Directors should not be involved in determining their own pay and terms of service.

2. Relationship with shareholders. The code lays down good practice for communications between the board and the shareholders and in particular that the annual general meeting of the company gives all shareholders a chance to effectively question the directors on the conduct of the company's business.

3. Accountability and audit. Apart from the production of the accounts as laid down in the Companies Acts the directors and the auditors are also required to provide a written explanation of their responsibilities in producing the financial reports. The directors must also confirm that the business is a going concern, giving any qualifications that they think appropriate.

4. Internal control. The directors are required to regularly check that they have effective systems of internal control covering the financial, operational and risk management of the business.

5. Audit committees. Apart from the necessity of having auditors, the code recommends that the company establishes an audit committee which includes at least three non-executive directors to oversee the audit and to ensure that the auditors are independent and objective in the exercise of their duty.

It is a requirement of the Stock Exchange that companies that are listed include a statement in their annual report explaining how it has applied the principles of the Code and produce a statement of their compliance with its requirements.

The pressure on public companies to be open and transparent in their dealings with shareholders and other stakeholders has become intense. However, it is not clear the extent to which such Statements and Codes have influenced the behaviour of directors for the better, nor is it clear that the existence of non-executive directors can deter unscrupulous boards.

Financial realities

Enron

In 2001 the largest corporate bankruptcy in US history occurred when the energy company Enron failed. Enron had commenced life as a small gas pipeline business in Houston, Texas. Over 15 years it transformed itself from a small Houston based natural gas company to a multi-billion-dollar, global enterprise trading oil, gas and other energy-related products. In the UK it acquired Wessex Water as well as a variety of interests in the North Sea. However, much of the growth was stimulated by 'aggressive accounting' practices such as:

- 'booking' all future income on contracts of up to 20 years' duration as revenue in the year in which the contract was signed,

- revaluing real assets to 'market values' (marking to market) and claiming the gains as income,

- hiding loss-making businesses or less valuable assets in 'special investment vehicles'. These special investment vehicles (SIVs) are small companies, set up and financed by the parent company for a limited purpose only. Under US accounting procedures, SIVs were not 'consolidated' into the parent company accounts if more than three per cent of the equity in the SIV is in independent hands. Enron acquired a network of over 4000 SIVs.

Enron had one of the world's most prestigious audit firms as well as non-executive directors on the board of the company who agreed these practices. Further readings on the Enron case are suggested at the end of the chapter.

How limited companies are created

If an individual or partnership wishes to incorporate their business there are normally two routes to doing this:

1. Establish and register a new limited liability company by preparing the necessary articles of incorporation: the articles and memorandum of association. These two documents will contain the names of the promoters, the proposed company name, its purpose and range of other information as required by the Companies Acts 1985, 1989 and 2006.

2. Buy a pre-registered company 'off the shelf' from a firm of solicitors or accountants. This company will have a name, a statement of general purpose and a standard set of articles and memorandum of association. Such companies can normally be purchased for a relatively small sum of money and once acquired a company meeting is arranged where the new shareholders (usually just two individuals holding one share each) vote on a change of name and such other modifications to the articles as are required to put the company in a form to begin trading.

Ordinary and preference shareholders

Limited companies can raise finance in the same way as private individuals through bank loans, leasing and hire-purchase agreements. In addition they can raise finance from their owners in exchange for shares in the company. There are two types of share which companies can issue:

● Ordinary shares: these are the most common type and are known generally as 'equity' shares. Ordinary shareholders have a right to the net assets of the business if it is wound up but after all prior claimants have been paid. The ordinary shareholders are also entitled to their share of any ordinary dividends that are declared by the directors.

● Preference shares: these shares carry an entitlement to a fixed percentage dividend which must be paid out of profits before any distribution to the ordinary shareholders is made. Like the payment of a dividend on ordinary shares, preference dividend payments are at the discretion of the directors. However, they are not allowed to make a dividend payment to ordinary shareholders and not the preference shareholders. Preference shares can be either 'cumulative' or 'non-cumulative'. With the former, if a preference dividend is not paid in one year it is held over until such time as it can be paid. With the latter, if a preference dividend is not paid then it is effectively lost as far as the preference shareholders are concerned.

 Shareholders do not have a share in the assets of the business. They have a share in the company that owns those assets. All the rights of ownership of those assets lie with the company.

The issue of ordinary shares

When new ordinary shares are issued there are two components to their value:

● **Nominal value**: this is a small value such as 25p, 50p or £1 at which the shares are denominated and carried in the balance sheet of the company.

● **Share premium**: this is the difference between the nominal value of the share and the payment potential subscribers are required to make in order to acquire the shares. The share premium account in the balance sheet of a limited company is what is known as a non-distributable reserve in that the balance on this account is unavailable for distribution back to the shareholders.

Exhibit 6.5 shows the capital account in the balance sheet of easyJet plc for the financial year ended 31 December 2006. Note that the company uses the term 'retained earnings' instead of 'profit reserve'.

Exhibit 6.5		
	2006	2005
	£000	£000
Shareholders' funds – equity		
Ordinary shares	**102.6**	100.1
Share premium	**591.4**	557.2
Retained earnings	**298.4**	206.0
Other reserves	**(9.5)**	0.1
	982.9	863.4

From the accounts of easyJet we learn that it has an **authorised share capital** of 500 million 25p shares. What this means is that the company can issue up to 500 million shares of which it has actually issued 391 676 000 of these 25p ordinary shares at different times during its life.

The authorised share capital is laid down in a company's memorandum and articles of association and is set high enough for any foreseeable needs it may have. However, if circumstances change, the members of the company (its shareholders) can approve an alteration to the authorised share capital. Usually, such authorisation may be required if a company has decided to 'go public' and seek a listing on a stock exchange or if it is contemplating the acquisition of another business.

Since the company was established, a number of new share issues have been made, each one at an issue price in excess of the nominal share value of 25p. These additional amounts have accumulated in the share premium account.

When new shares are issued part of the authorised share capital is 'called up' and the accounts will show in the notes to the balance sheet the amount of capital authorised and called up at the balance sheet date. Normally, when a company makes a share issue it requires the full value of the issue to be paid by the individual subscribers. However, sometimes the directors may choose to only call up part of what is due initially, with one or more 'calls' being made later.

Review activity 6.2
Obtain the most up-to-date set of accounts for Cobham plc (www.cobham.co.uk) or another company of your choice and identify the classes of shareholding in that company.
What is the company's authorised ordinary share capital?
What is the nominal share value?
How much of the ordinary share capital has been 'called up'?
Note that these values will change from year to year as the company issues or buys back share capital.

Starting up a limited company

Many sole traders and partnerships decide upon 'incorporation' for three principal reasons:

1. Tax savings – where the rate of corporation tax is generally lower than the rate of tax on personal income.

2. Risk protection – where the business involved is subject to exceptional risk which cannot be offset in other ways. Doctors, lawyers, accountants and similar professionals can face heavy liabilities for negligence in the conduct of their business. They can obtain protection through personal indemnity insurance and so, typically, they do not need the protection of limited liability. The owner of an import/export business or a manufacturer cannot insure against their business risk and the protection of limited liability is an important benefit.

3. Raising finance – private individuals are often limited in what they can raise to what they can beg or borrow from friends and the banks. As we shall see in Chapter 13, a limited company can raise finance through the equity market or through bond issues.

When a limited company comes into existence a new legal 'person' is created. The existing business has to be transferred to the new company with the agreement of the existing creditors, including suppliers, the bank and other lenders to the business, and where customers have service agreements they will also have to be notified. In addition, if there are existing employees their contracts of employment will have to be rewritten in favour of the new company. For a long-established business the administrative costs of incorporation can be large and well in excess of the legal costs of forming the company.

We will now return to a case we considered in previous chapters. Sid has done well, his business has prospered and he has now decided to set up a limited company.

Financial realities **Sid's Taxis goes limited**

Sid has been in business now for five years and his business has developed rapidly to include a fleet of taxis, a control centre, an office and a parking lot in Watford, and a team of highly qualified drivers and office workers. His balance sheet at the end of his fifth year of trading was as follows:

Exhibit 6.6

Balance sheet as at 31 December	year 5	year 4
Non-current Assets	1 250 000	985 000
Current Assets		
Inventories	9 800	12 500
Receivables	108 000	100 000
Cash in hand and at bank	22 600	125 500
	140 400	238 000
Less current liabilities	−123 400	−163 000
Less non-current liabilities	−12 000	−10 000
	1 255 000	1 050 000
Owner's equity	8 000	8 000
Profit reserve	1 247 000	1 042 000
	1 255 000	1 050 000

Sid has decided to convert his business into a company and buys one off the shelf which he renames DialaSid (Taxis) Ltd. The company is established with an authorised capital of 500 000 25p ordinary shares. He decides to transfer all of the assets and, with the agreement of his creditors, the current liabilities of his existing business to the new company in exchange for 150 000 shares each for himself and Beryl, his wife. A further 8000 shares are also to be issued to two of his employees, Jeff and Joan, who joined the firm during his first year of trading. They will get 4000 shares each fully paid. Both had a bonus due of £1000 which Sid had provided for in the year-end accounts and both have agreed that this should be used to part-finance the purchase of their shares. All of the shares will be issued at £3.25 per share to be paid for out of retained earnings including the balance of Joan's and Jeff's shares. The balance remaining on the existing retained profit account will remain in the business as a director's loan. Both Joan and Jeff agree to forgo their bonus in exchange for the shares in the new company. The bank has requested that its loan of £10 000 be repaid before incorporation.

The first task in setting up the new business is to make the closing adjustments to the year 5 balance sheet for Sid's Taxis. The first entry shows the repayment of the bank loan which will result in a reduction in cash. The second entry writes back the bonus provision to the retained profit account.

The next step is to construct the new balance sheet bringing down the assets and liabilities transferred. The owner's equity account now contains:

1. £77 000, being the nominal value of the 308 000 ordinary shares to which the four new shareholders have subscribed
2. £924 000, being the share premium of £3 per share on the 308 000 shares issued and counted as fully paid.

▶

The balance remaining on the old owner's equity account now becomes the directors' loan account.

Exhibit 6.7

	NCA +	Inv +	Rec +	C =	CL +	NCL +	OE
Sid's Taxis							
Year 5 Balance sheet	1 250 000	9 800	108 000	22 600	123 400	12 000	1 255 000
Repayment of bank loan				−10 000		−10 000	
Write back of bonus provision						−2 000	2 000
	1 250 000	9 800	108 000	12 600	123 400	0	1 257 000
DialaSid Ltd							
Assets and liabilities transferred	1 250 000	9 800	108 000	12 600	123 400		
Issue of new share capital							
Sid 150 000 shares @ 25p each							37 500
Beryl 150 000 shares @ 25p each							37 500
Jeff 4 000 shares @ 25p each							1 000
Joan 4 000 shares @ 25p each							1 000
Share premium 308 000 shares @ £3.00							924 000
Directors loan						256 000	
DialaSid Ltd – Opening Balance Sheet	1 250 000	9 800	108 000	12 600	123 400	256 000	1 001 000

DialaSid's Ltd opening balance sheet now looks like this:

Exhibit 6.8

DialaSid Ltd

Balance sheet as at 1 January	year 6 £
Non-current Assets	1 250 000
Current Assets	
stocks	9 800
debtors and prepayments	108 000
cash in hand and at bank	12 600
	130 400
Less current liabilities	−123 400
Less non-current liabilities	−256 000
	1 001 000
Owner's equity	
Ordinary 25p shares issued and fully paid	77 000
Share premium account	924 000
	1 001 000

Reserves

An important distinguishing feature of a set of company accounts is the detail which must be shown in the owner's equity account within the balance sheet. In the previous example we showed how the issued share capital and the share premium account are presented. However, there are a number of other 'reserves' which can appear under owner's equity.

A reserve is a fund, formally belonging to the owners of the business, which represents value retained in the business for some purpose or another. It is very important to realise that a reserve does not necessarily represent cash available to spend. A reserve is part of the equity investors' claim on the total assets of the business which includes fixed assets as well as current assets including cash.

The four principal types of reserve are:

- Profit reserve: this is the account to which profits and losses are accumulated during the life of the business. In principle, the directors of the company can put the value represented by this reserve to any number of uses:
  1. new capital investment within the business
  2. distribution to shareholders by way of a dividend
  3. conversion into shares for distribution to existing shareholders.

  It is against the balance on this account that a company is able to support losses. So if a business makes a loss in a year, that loss will be offset against this reserve. Dividends are paid out of this reserve.

- Share premium account: where a company issues shares for greater than their nominal value; the surplus is referred to as the 'share premium' and is shown as a reserve under owner's equity. The balance on the share premium account is not distributable back to the shareholders but may be used to write off the costs of forming the company, issuing fully paid bonus shares, and for a number of other costs incurred in financing the business as allowed under the Companies Acts.

- Revaluation reserve: if a company revalues its assets from time to time the surplus on revaluation must be added to this account. If an asset should be sold, the revaluation surpluses on this account are said to be 'realised' and can be transferred to the profit and loss account. Generally speaking, unrealised holding gains, that is the surplus created when assets are simply revalued rather than being sold, are not available for distribution. However, such gains can be used to create fully paid bonus shares for allotment to the shareholders of the company.

- Other reserves: a company can hold a range of other reserves under this heading. The most common are capital redemption reserves and merger reserves.

In order to protect the interests of creditors, companies are not allowed to distribute the value in their share capital and share premium account. Clearly, if the shareholders were to remove the value of their capital they would have to effectively liquidate a significant proportion of the firm's assets. This would leave the creditors exposed without sufficient assets left in the company to cover their claim on the business. For this reason the Companies Act 1985 does not allow the shareholders to withdraw their subscribed capital unless a 'share repurchase scheme' is authorised at a company meeting. In this case, a capital redemption reserve must be created, to which is transferred from the distributable reserves a sum equal to the capital repaid. The capital redemption reserve is included under the heading of 'other reserves' on the face of the balance sheet.

As you can see, of the different types of reserves that companies can create, only the profit and loss reserve is available for distribution. All the others must either be retained for a specific purpose or simply to maintain the capital of the business intact for the protection of creditors. However, nearly all of these reserves can be used to write off 'goodwill'. This is a topic we will return to later as we explore Sid's business adventures.

Provisions

Provisions are a cost charged to the profit and loss account and credited to 'provisions' under long-term liabilities in the balance sheet in anticipation of an expense which is expected to occur at some future time as a result of the current business activities. Deferred tax is an example where, perhaps, heavy current capital investment has reduced the company's tax bill in the current year at the expense of a higher liability in future years. The company will make a provision for this extra tax in its balance sheet.

Review activity 6.3 From the Cobham accounts identify the principal reserves and provisions held by the company, distinguishing between those that are distributable and those that are not. Work through the note to the Cobham accounts which details its reserves and identify the reasons for the movements on those reserves during the previous financial year.

Limited company accounts

A limited company is required to produce accounting information both for its shareholders and for submission in its annual return to the Registrar of Companies in the UK. Company law prescribes what a company is required to produce. In the UK the necessary documents are:

- directors' report
- auditor's report
- income statement
- balance sheet
- statement of total recognised gains and losses
- cash flow statement including a reconciliation of operating profit and operating cash flow
- notes to the accounts.

These documents have been supplemented by the recommendations of the International Accounting Standards Boards and the requirements of the Stock Exchange. A full company report will now include:

- a statement of the compliance with the combined code of practice on corporate governance
- a financial and operating review of the performance of the business over the previous year.

Now that we have an overview of the contents of a full set of public accounts, we will investigate the distinguishing features of the financial reports of limited companies by considering how DialaSid Ltd enters its new phase of growth.

Group companies – acquisition and mergers

The large majority of public company accounts are those of 'group companies' where one company has either merged with or acquired another. You will also see company accounts referring to 'joint ventures' and **associated companies**. These 'interests' in other companies can be formed in a number of ways. A company may make an offer to purchase the shares in another company (the 'target') from its existing shareholders in any one of the following ways:

1. Purchase for cash at an agreed value which is often a premium on the existing share price if the target company is publicly quoted.

2. Purchase for shares where the shareholders in the target company are offered shares in the acquiring company.

3. A mixture of shares, cash and sometimes other types of financial securities such as redeemable debentures or loan stock. We will discuss these different types of security in Chapter 11.

If a company acquires a controlling interest, which is normally taken to be more than 50 per cent of the target company shares, then the latter becomes a 'subsidiary' and a group is formed. If the parent company owns 100 per cent of the equity in a subsidiary then the latter is described as 'wholly owned'. Where the parent does have control but not a 100 per cent stake there will be some independent 'minority shareholders' remaining who will continue to be entitled to a portion of any profits earned and to their share of the net assets of the subsidiary company.

Where a company does not acquire a controlling interest but owns more than 20 per cent of the equity of another company, that latter company is termed an 'associate company'. The accounting procedures for dealing with subsidiaries as opposed to associate companies are quite different and, indeed, even with subsidiaries the procedure depends on whether a 'merger' or an 'acquisition' has occurred. However, whether merger or acquisition the accountant will undertake a process of **consolidation** showing the balance sheet, profit and loss and cash flow statement for the combined business.

Exhibit 6.9

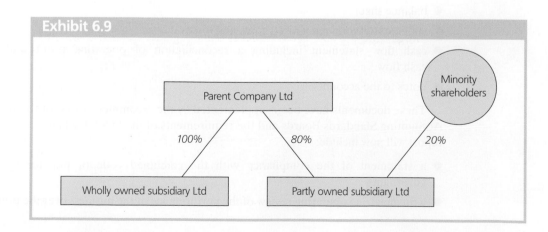

Financial realities Company law recognises three 'levels' of ownership of another firm. As Exhibit 6.10 shows, if a firm acquires less than 20 per cent of the equity of another company then that should be treated simply as an investment in the balance sheet.

Exhibit 6.10

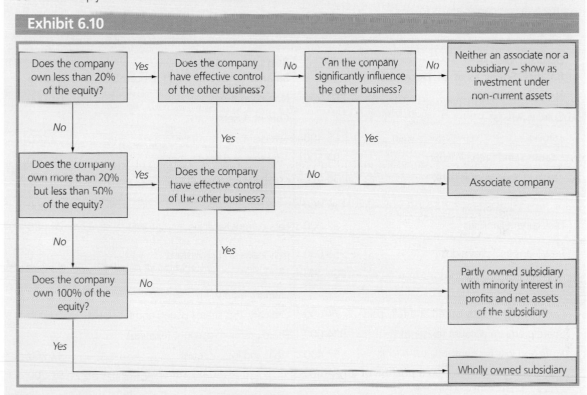

If more than 20 per cent but less than 50 per cent of the equity of another company is acquired then it will be classed as an 'associate company' in the balance sheet and more details of its performance will need to be shown in the published accounts. If more than 50 per cent of the other company's equity is acquired then it must be regarded as a 'subsidiary' and be fully consolidated, assuming either that a merger has taken place or a simple acquisition as outlined earlier.

Companies come together in one of two ways:

● Merger: this is where two companies come together to form a new business. Usually the two companies will be of approximately equal size and the equity investors in one of the firms will be offered shares in the other. With a merger, the consolidated accounts will be based upon the values shown in the individual company balance sheets. Normally, with merged business the new board of directors will consist of members of both of the merged companies.

● Acquisition: this is where one company 'takes over' the other business (which becomes a **subsidiary**) for its own ends. It may be so that it can gain control of a competitor, expand into a new product area, take over an important source of supply or acquire another firm that can be involved in the marketing and sale of its goods. The motivations for acquisition are numerous and many firms pursue a 'takeover strategy' aggressively as a means of growing the business.

Financial realities After his first year of trading Sid decides that he will launch the new financial year with a takeover of his old friend and rival's business Ron's Vans Ltd. Ron is very content because he is nearing retiring age and he has found it more difficult maintaining a very active business. The balance sheets of the two companies are as follows:

Exhibit 6.11

DialaSid Ltd Balance Sheet as at 31 December	year 6	Ron's Vans Ltd Balance Sheet as at 31 December	year 6
Non-current Assets	1 280 000	Non-current Assets	64 000
Current Assets		Current Assets	
stocks	5 400	stocks	2 000
debtors and prepayments	94 500	debtors and prepayments	18 600
cash in hand and at bank	36 500	cash in hand and at bank	600
	136 400		21 200
Less current liabilities	−92 000	Less current liabilities	−28 000
Less loans and provisions	−256 000	Less loans and provisions	−0
	1 068 400		57 200
Owner's equity		Owner's equity	
Ordinary 25p shares issued and fully paid	77 000	Ordinary 25p shares issued and fully paid	20 000
Share premium account (existing)	924 000	Share premium account (existing)	
Profit and loss account	67 400	Profit and loss account	37 200
	1 068 400		57 200

Ron and Sid agree, with the help of their accountants, that Ron's Vans Ltd is worth £100 000 and the fixed asset values as shown at their original cost represents their fair value. The excess is payment for the 'goodwill' that Ron has developed over the years.

Exhibit 6.12

	£
Agreed value of Ron Ltd	100 000
Net book value of assets acquired	57 200
Goodwill on acquisition	42 800

Sid is considering three options:

1. DialaSid Ltd will pay £100 000 in cash for 100 per cent of the equity in Ron's company. Sid will make a further loan to his company of £75 000 in order to support the purchase of the equity in Ron's Vans.
2. DialaSid Ltd will pay £100 000 in DialaSid Ltd shares at an agreed value of £4 per share.
3. DialaSid Ltd will pay £80 000 in cash for 80 per cent of the equity leaving the balance of Ron's Vans Ltd with Ron as a minority shareholder. In this case Sid will put £55 000 into his business as a short-term loan to finance the purchase.

Whichever course is chosen both DialaSid Ltd and Ron's Vans Ltd will still exist and will be required to produce their own balance sheet and accounts. In addition, DialaSid Ltd will be required to produce a 'consolidated' account showing the financial position, performance and cash flow of the two companies combined.

The detailed steps required to produce an opening consolidated balance sheet are as follows. We will then continue with Sid's case to show how the steps work in practice.

1. Lay out the extended trial balance but excluding for the moment the revenue and expenditure columns.

2. Using the parent company balance sheet proceed as follows:

   a. Open an 'investment in subsidiary' column (I Sub) alongside non-current assets in the extended trial balance.

   b. Enter the existing balance sheet values from the parent company in the extended trial balance.

   c. Record the financing transaction showing the purchase of the investment in the subsidiary for cash or for a corresponding issue of shares.

3. Create a new accounting equation for the consolidated balance sheet, renaming the 'investment in subsidiaries' column as 'goodwill on acquisition' (GW) and introducing (if the acquisition is for less than 100 per cent of the equity) a **minority interest** column as an addition to the owner's equity columns at the right-hand side.

4. Enter the values from the parent-company balance sheet in the new accounting equation (put the 'investment in subsidiary' value in the goodwill column).

5. Enter the values from the subsidiary balance sheet.

6. Transfer the balances in the owner's equity account of the subsidiary to (a) the goodwill column (GW) and (b) the minority interest (MI) column in the proportions acquired by the parent company and retained by the minority.

   Got that? If not, here is the first of Sid's options.

Acquisition for cash

In the first of the options to be considered, Sid plans to acquire all of Ron's business (by acquiring 100 per cent of his equity) for cash. This cash payment is the investment being made by DialaSid Ltd in Ron's Vans Ltd and, as we see, the amount paid is in excess of the value of the net assets acquired.

In this exercise we are using the extended trial balance as an easy way of showing the transactions involved. We have not included the revenue and expenses columns as these are not needed for this exercise. We have, however, expanded the owner equity column to show the ordinary share capital (OSC), the share premium account (SPA) and the accumulated profits and losses account (P&L).

The extended trial balance for DialaSid's balance sheet shows the modifications as follows:

1. a loan of £75 000 is introduced by Sid to finance the acquisition

2. a cash payment of £100 000 is made to acquire all the equity in Ron's Vans Ltd.

   The accounting equation for the consolidated balance sheet is then constructed, changing the (Inv) column to GW for 'goodwill on acquisition'.
   The steps are then as follows:

3. Bring down the values from the DialaSid balance sheet.

4. Enter the values from Ron's Vans Ltd balance sheet in the extended trial balance.

Exhibit 6.13 Option 1: Cash purchase of 100% of equity in Ron Ltd for £100 000											
									Owner's Equity		
	NCA +	ISub +	Inv +	Rec +	C	= CL +	NCL +	OSC +	SPA +	P&L	
DialaSid Ltd Balance Sheet pre acquisition	1 280 000		5 400	94 500	36 500	92 000	256 000	77 000	924 000	67 400	
Introduction of loan					75 000		75 000				
Investment in 100% of the equity in Ron's Vans Ltd		100 000			−100 000						
DialaSid Ltd Balance sheet as at 1 January year 7	1 280 000	100 000	5 400	94 500	11 500	92 000	331 000	77 000	924 000	67 400	

									Owner's Equity		
	NCA +	GW +	Inv +	Rec +	C	= CL +	NCL +	OSC +	SPA +	P&L	
DialaSid Ltd Consolidated Balance Sheet											
DialaSid's Balance Sheet	1 280 000	100 000	5 400	94 500	11 500	92 000	331 000	77 000	924 000	67 400	
Ron's Vans Ltd Balance Sheet	64 000		2 000	18 600	600	28 000		20 000		37 200	
Share capital acquired (100%)		−20 000						−20 000			
Preacquisition profits acquired (100%)		−37 200								−37 200	
Consolidated Balance Sheet as at 1 January year 7	1 344 000	42 800	7 400	113 100	12 100	120 000	331 000	77 000	924 000	67 400	

5. Show the purchase of 100 per cent of the equity capital of Ron's Vans Ltd as a deduction from the investment in the GW column and a corresponding deduction of the ordinary share capital account of £20 000.

6. Show the share of the pre-acquisition profits of Ron's Vans Ltd acquired. In this case it is a 100 per cent share, so show the purchase of the pre-acquisition profits as a deduction from the investment in the goodwill (GW) columns and a deduction of £37 200 in the profit and loss reserve.

7. Total the accounting equation and transfer to a balance sheet layout in whatever style is required. The parent-company consolidated balance sheets for DialaSid Ltd are shown in Exhibit 6.14.

Note that the owner's equity account in the consolidated balance sheet just shows the owner's equity for DialaSid Ltd. Sid has purchased a 100 per cent claim in the net assets of Ron's Vans Ltd worth £57 200 plus an extra £42 800 for Ron's good name, his brand and the loyalty of his customers. This purchase has been financed by an increase in Sid's borrowing.

Acquisition by the exchange of equity

If we consider option 2, which is an acquisition for shares, we follow the same procedure. This option involves issuing new shares at £4 each. In practice, if the company is not listed and its price is quoted on a stock exchange, a share-based acquisition would only be agreed after the shareholder in the target company had undertaken a professional valuation of the acquiring company. Ron, in this case, would have employed a firm of accountants, possibly aided by a quantity surveyor, to agree that DialaSid's shares were indeed worth what was being proposed.

The main difference between this and the previous case is in the creation of the parent company balance sheet. Clearly, Sid is not going to engage in a further loan but the new

Exhibit 6.14 Option 1: Parent company and consolidated balance sheets for DialaSid Ltd

DialaSid Ltd
Balance Sheet as at 1 January

	year 7
Non-current Assets	
Investment in Ron's Vans Ltd	1 280 000
Current Assets	100 000
stocks	
debtors and prepayments	5 400
cash in hand and at bank	94 500
	11 500
current liabilities	111 400
	−92 000
Less non-current liabilities	
	−331 000
Owner's equity	1 068 400
Ordinary 25p shares issued and fully paid	77 000
Share premium account	
Profit and loss account	924 000
	67 400
	1 068 400

DialaSid Ltd
Consolidated Balance Sheet as at 1 January

	year 7
Non-current Assets	
Goodwill on acquisitions	1 344 000
Current Assets	42 800
stocks	
debtors and prepayments	7 400
cash in hand and at bank	113 100
	12 100
current liabilities	132 600
	−120 000
Less non-current liabilities	
	−331 000
Owner's equity	1 068 400
Ordinary 25p shares issued and fully paid	77 000
Share premium account	
Profit and loss account	924 000
	67 400
	1 068 400

Exhibit 6.15 Option 2: Cash purchase of 100% equity in Ron Ltd for shares in DialaSid Ltd

	NCA	+ ISub	+ Inv	+ Rec	+ C	= CL	+ NCL	+ OSC	+ SPA	+ P&L
DialaSid Ltd Balance Sheet	1 280 000									
Shares issued to Ron's Vans Ltd		5 400	94 500	36 500	92 000	256 000	77 000		924 000	67 400
Acquisition of 100% of Ron's Vans Ltd		100 000					6 250		93 750	
DialaSid Ltd Balance Sheet as at 1 January year 7	1 280 000	100 000 5 400	94 500	36 500	92 000	256 000	83 250	1 017 750	67 400	

	NCA	+ GW	+ Inv	+ Rec	+ C	= CL	+ NCL	+ OSC	+ SPA	+ P&L
DialaSid Ltd Consolidated Balance Sheet								Owner's Equity		
DialaSid's Balance Sheet	1 280 000	100 000 5 400	94 500	36 500	92 000	256 000	83 250	1 017 750	67 400	
Ron's Vans Ltd Balance Sheet	64 000	2 000	18 600	600	28 000		20 000		37 200	
Share capital acquired (100%)		−20 000								
Preacquisition profits acquired (100%)		−37 200					−20 000			
Consolidated Balance Sheet as at January year 7	1 344 000	42 800 7 400	113 100	37 100	120 000	256 000	83 250	1 017 750	67 400	

interest' ... ion to recog- ... oduce ... of the ... y interest ... minority

P&L
67 400
67 400

		P&L	+ MI
	00	67 400	
		37 200	
			4 000
		−29 760	
		−7 440	7 440
	24 000	67 400	11 440

Review activity 6.4 Sid asks you to put together one further option. He introduces a loan of £25 000 and buys 90 per cent of the equity in Ron Ltd for £90 000, half in cash and half by shares valued at £4.00 per share. A merger reserve can still be created as 90 per cent or more of the equity has been acquired irrespective of whether it is acquired by cash or shares.

✓ Check the answer to this Review activity at the back of the book (see page 502).

Because the purchase is for cash no share premium or merger reserve arises and the resulting balance sheet is now:

Exhibit 6.18 Option 3: Parent company and consolidated balance sheets for DialaSid Ltd

DialaSid Ltd Balance Sheet as at 1 January	year 7	DialaSid Ltd Consolidated Balance Sheet as at 1 January	year 7
Non-current Assets	1 280 000	Non-current Assets	1 344 000
Investment in Ron's Vans Ltd	80 000	Goodwill on acquisitions	34 240
Current Assets		Current Assets	
inventories	5 400	inventories	7 400
receivables and prepayments	94 500	receivables and prepayments	113 100
cash in hand and at bank	11 500	cash in hand and at bank	12 100
	111 400		132 600
current liabilities	−147 000	current liabilities	−175 000
Less non-current liabilities	−256 000	Less non-current liabilities	−256 000
	1 068 400		1 079 840
Owner's equity		Owner's equity	
Ordinary 25p shares issued and fully paid	77 000	Ordinary 25p shares issued and fully paid	77 000
Share premium account	924 000	Share premium account	924 000
Profit and loss account	67 400	Profit and loss account	67 400
	1 068 400		1 068 400
		Minority interest	11 440
			1 079 480

Producing the consolidated accounts for a group

At the point that two companies come together, only a new balance sheet is created. However, from the point of acquisition the trading performance of the companies must be combined, creating a full set of consolidated accounts. It is important to remember, however, that the parent company and its subsidiaries continue to operate as independent businesses from the accounting point of view and will still need to prepare their own individual financial reports and financial returns for submission to the Registrar of Companies and for presentation to their respective shareholders.

There are two methods of producing consolidated or group accounts: the acquisitions method and the merger method. In this chapter we show the acquisitions method because that is the one most commonly found in practice. There is a note on the merger method later in the chapter.

The consolidated balance sheet

The process of creating the consolidated balance sheet is essentially as described before except that any inter-company transactions or loans must be eliminated. It is also necessary to determine whether there are any inventories or cash in transit between the two companies which have been recorded in one set of accounts but not in the other.

With these considerations in mind it is a fairly easy task to put the balance sheets together.

Financial realities   Sid and Ron eventually agreed to option 3 where DialaSid Ltd took 80 per cent of the equity in Ron's Vans Ltd. Both have traded successfully for twelve months with both businesses prospering under Sid's dynamic leadership. Their balance sheets at the end of the first year of trading are as follows:

Exhibit 6.19 DialaSid Ltd and Ron's Vans Ltd balance sheets, year 7

DialaSid Ltd Balance Sheet as at 31 December	year 7	Ron's Vans Ltd Balance Sheet as at 31 December	year 7
Non-current Assets	1 300 000	Non-current Assets	93 000
Investment in Ron's Vans Ltd	80 000		
Current Assets		Current Assets	
inventories	6 000	inventories	2 500
receivables and prepayments	94 000	receivables and prepayments	19 000
cash in hand and at bank	2 000	cash in hand and at bank	16 000
	102 000		37 500
Less current liabilities	−74 000	Less current liabilities	−30 000
Less non-current liabilities	−256 000	Less non-current liabilities	−10 000
	1 152 000		90 500
Owner's equity		Owner's equity	
Ordinary 25p shares issued and fully paid	77 000	Ordinary 25p shares issued and fully paid	20 000
Share premium account	924 000	Profit reserve	70 500
Profit reserve	151 000		90 500
	1 152 000		

During the year a short-term cash loan of £10 000 had been made by DialaSid Ltd to Ron's Vans Ltd and included in the receivables balance within its balance sheet. This loan was at zero interest.

The steps in producing a consolidated balance sheet are straightforward:

1. Lay out the two balance sheets across the extended trial balance.
2. Eliminate any inter-company transactions. In this case that entails reducing the outstanding debtors in DialaSid Ltd by £10 000 and reducing the long-term liability in Ron's Vans Ltd by £10 000.

Exhibit 6.20 DialaSid Ltd consolidation working sheets (balance sheets)

	NCA	+	GW	+	Inv	+	Rec	+	C	=	CL	+	NCL	+	OSC	+	SPA	+	P&L	+	MI
															Owner's Equity						
DialaSid Ltd Balance Sheet	1 300 000		80 000		6 000		94 000		2 000		74 000		256 000		77 000		924 000		151 000		
Ron's Vans Ltd Balance Sheet	93 000				2 500		19 000		16 000		30 000		10 000		20 000				70 500		
Elimination of inter-company loan							−10 000						−10 000								
DialaSid Ltd Consolidated Balance Sheet																					
acquisition of 80% of equity in Ron's Vans Ltd			−16 000												−16 000						
transfer of balance to minority interest																	−4 000				4 000
preacquisition profits attributable to DialaSid Ltd			−29 760																−29 760		
preacquisition profits attributable to minorities																			−7 440		7 440
postacquisition profit attributable to minorities																			−6 660		6 660
	1 393 000		34 240		8 500		103 000		18 000		104 000		256 000		77 000		924 000		177 640		18 100

3. Add back any dividends paid to either company shareholder to the profit reserve in the balance sheet.

4. Transfer that part of the ordinary share capital account and any pre-acquisition reserves in Ron's Vans Ltd attributable to DialaSid Ltd to the 'goodwill' column and the balance to the minority interest account.

5. There will now be a balance remaining on the profit reserve of Ron's Vans Ltd. In this case the share of this remaining balance belonging to the minority shareholders must be transferred to their minority interest account. We can calculate this as follows:

Exhibit 6.21 Calculating the consolidated balance on the profit reserve

Balance on Ron's Vans Ltd profit Reserve at 31 December, year 7	70 500
Less:	
Preacquisition profits attributable to DialaSid Ltd = 80% × £37 200 (from the opening balance sheet)	−29 760
Preacquisition profits belonging to the minority shareholder = £37 200 − £29 760	−7 440
Post acquisition profits on reserve	33 300
Less: Attributable to minorities (20% × £33 300)	−6 660
Post acquisition profits attributable to DialaSid Ltd	26 640
Add DialaSid's profit reserve	151 000
Consolidated profit reserve	177 640

In summary, the profit reserve in the consolidated balance sheet consists of two parts: first, the profit reserve of the parent company, DialaSid Ltd, and, second, the part of the accumulated post-acquisition profits which belongs to DialaSid Ltd by virtue of its 80 per cent stake in Ron's Vans Ltd.

The consolidated balance sheet will be as follows:

Exhibit 6.22 DialaSid Ltd consolidated balance sheet

DialaSid Ltd Consolidated Balance Sheet as at 31 December	year 7
Non-current Assets	1 393 000
Goodwill on acquisitions	34 240
Current Assets	
inventories	8 500
receivables and prepayments	103 000
cash in hand and at bank	18 000
	129 500
Less current liabilities	−104 000
Less non-current liabilities	−256 000
	1 196 740
Owner's equity	
Ordinary 25p shares issued and fully paid	77 000
Share premium account	924 000
Profit reserve	177 640
	1 178 640
Minority interest	18 100
	1 196 740

The consolidated income statement

The creation of a consolidated income statement is relatively straightforward and goes through the following steps:

1. Any dividend paid by the subsidiary to the parent company is ignored in the consolidated income statement. So if a dividend has been paid the amount received by the parent company should be eliminated along with the payment of the whole dividend paid by the subsidiary including any paid to the minority shareholders. Obviously the payment of a dividend by a subsidiary to its parent is a transfer payment between them and is not income to the group as a whole.

2. All items in the income statement of the parent company and its subsidiaries are added together to create an overall statement of income. This is done even when the subsidiaries are not wholly owned.

3. If there are any minority interests in one or other of the subsidiaries then the share of the profit must be shown as a minority interest. This element must be separately shown before the profit available for distribution to investors.

Financial realities DialaSid Ltd and Ron's Vans Ltd produced the following income statements at the end of the financial year 31 December, year 7. As you can see, both companies have performed well.

Exhibit 6.23 DialaSid Ltd and Ron's Vans Ltd income statements year 7

DialaSid Ltd — Income statement for the year ended 31 December, year 7		Ron's Vans Ltd — Income statement for the year ended 31 December, year 7	
Sales Turnover	382 000	Sales Turnover	187 000
less cost of sales	163 000	less cost of sales	87 000
Gross profit	219 000	Gross profit	100 000
Other operating expenditures	88 225	Other operating expenditures	40 700
Operating profit	130 775	Operating profit	59 300
Interest payable	12 800	Interest payable	0
Profit on ordinary activities before taxation	117 975	Profit on ordinary activities before taxation	59 300
Taxation	30 000	Taxation	14 000
Profit retained	87 975	Profit retained	45 300
Earnings per share	29	Earnings per share	57

1. Add together the income statements of the parent with that of its subsidiary down to the line 'profits after taxation'.
2. Deduct the part of the subsidiary's profit due to the minority interest. In this case the minority interest is 20 per cent of the profits of Ron's Vans Ltd, i.e., £9060. This equals £2400 of dividend paid to the minority shareholders (20 per cent × £12 000) and £6660 added to their reserve in the balance sheet.

Exhibit 6.24 DialaSid Ltd consolidation working sheets (profit and loss)

DialaSid Ltd
Consolidated income statement for the year ended 31 Dec. 20x7

	DialaSid Ltd	Ron's Vans Ltd	Consolidated
Sales turnover	382 000	187 000	569 000
less cost of sales	163 000	87 000	250 000
Gross profit	219 000	100 000	319 000
Other operating expenditures	88 225	40 700	128 925
Operating profit	130 775	59 300	190 075
Interest payable	−12 800	0	−12 800
Profit on ordinary activities before taxation	117 975	59 300	177 275
Taxation	30 000	14 000	44 000
Profit after taxation	87 975	45 300	133 275
Less minority interest		20 per cent	9 060
Profit retained			124 215

3. Produce the consolidated income statement. This statement shows the income and expenditures of the group as a whole and shows the distribution of its surplus to the minority shareholders and to the parent-company shareholders.

Exhibit 6.25   DialaSid Ltd consolidated income statement

DialaSid Ltd
Consolidated income statement for the year ended 31 December, year 7

Sales turnover	569 000
less cost of sales	250 000
Gross profit	319 000
Other operating expenditures	128 925
Operating profit	190 075
Interest payable	12 800
Profit on ordinary activities before taxation	177 275
Taxation	44 000
Profit after taxation	133 275
Less minority interest	9 060
Profit for the financial year	124 215

Becoming a public limited company

A company may reach a stage where it needs greater access to capital than can be provided by friends and family. At this stage it may decide that becoming a 'public limited company' is worth the cost in order for the business to move on to its next stage of development.

In Chapter 1 we discussed how the stock market emerged from the coffee houses of the City of London. However, the modern stock market is just one part of a wider network of markets making up the international capital and money markets. The broad distinction between the two is that the money market is the market for short-term finance where firms, individuals, institutions and government can borrow or lend money for relatively short periods of time and always for durations of less than one year. The capital market is the market for longer-term finance and it divides into two:

- The primary capital market: this is the market for new funds. This is the market where private individuals and financial institutions subscribe to new capital issues by companies. So a company wishing to issue shares publicly would be participating in this market.

- The secondary capital market: this is the market where investors can buy and sell shares using the services of a number of 'market makers', i.e., individuals and firms licensed to trade shares on the exchange itself.

Within each stock exchange there may be different listings available. In the London Stock Exchange a company can seek listing on either of the following:

1. The main market for UK equities. This market has approximately 1800 UK and 450 overseas companies listed. The performance of this market is reported through a number of

indices that will be discussed in Chapter 13. The most important are the Financial Times index of the top 100 companies (FTSE 100), and the more broadly based FTSE 250, 350 and All Share indices. When commentators talk about 'the stock market' they are normally referring to this market. The main market also contains two 'sub-groups':

- the 'techMARK', which is a grouping of approximately 235 high-technology companies across a range of different industries
- the techMARK mediscience, which combines together approximately 50 companies in the healthcare sciences.

2. The Alternative Investment Market (AIM), which is designed for small growing companies who do not want the expense of a full listing on the main index. Approximately 700 UK and overseas companies are quoted on the AIM. Generally the requirements in terms of capitalisation are not as onerous as those of the main market.

Applying and being accepted for a listing entails certain obligations upon companies, particularly where they look for a listing on the main market. Normally they must meet a minimum size requirement in terms of their capitalisation, they must have been actively trading for a number of years and at least 25 per cent of the equity shares must be in public hands.

There are a number of steps that a company must go through to become a public listed company.

- The company must reregister as a public limited company, changing its status from 'Ltd' to 'plc'. This entails a resolution of its members in a general meeting and then an application to the Company Registrar.

- The company must apply for a 'listing' from the UK Listing Agency (UKLA), which is part of the Financial Services Authority (FSA). The FSA is a government agency which regulates the conduct of all financial services in the UK. The UKLA requires that a company meets certain requirements concerning the length of time it has been trading, its minimum capital requirements (which currently is set at a minimum of £700 000), its solvency (i.e., the amount of working capital it has available), and its independence from the control of others. Once having passed the UKLA's requirements the company will be placed on an 'official list'.

- Once having satisfied the requirements of the UKLA, the company must then apply to the London Stock Exchange to be admitted to trading. The guidance issued by the London Stock Exchange identifies the following criteria that a company should meet:

  1. The company should have a record of successful management with a broad customer base and range of products.

  2. The company should be able to demonstrate a consistent and growing performance in terms of profit and revenue.

  3. The company should have a carefully worked out and practical business plan. We discuss the issues around business planning in Chapter 9.

  4. The quality and experience of the directors and management team. The make-up of the board is most significant and it should contain people who are experienced in the business, some of whom fulfil a non-executive role and can offer the executive directors independent advice on the operation of the business.

  5. The company should comply with the 'Combined Code' for the governance of companies (see above).

6. The company's ownership should be clear and open so that potential investors can be assured that the company is not effectively under the control of some individual or organisation of which they are unaware.

Most companies who seek listing and permission to trade will want to raise equity capital. As part of this process, a company will need to publish a prospectus which details its future plans and provides cash and profit projections forecasting its likely trading performance. The prospectus will also include details of the price at which the company will commence trading.

The process of becoming a public limited company, obtaining a listing and then floating a new issue is an expensive process and the directors of a company need to be sure that this is the right way forward for the business. This process will mean that the company can have access to large capital sums for expansion. By and large, the public visibility and independence of such companies inspires confidence on the part of creditors and lenders. However, the directors do run the risk of losing control in three ways:

1. The directors' freedom of action is much more highly regulated and they will need approval of their shareholders for any significant acquisitions and disposals.

2. The company will be more susceptible to 'hostile takeovers' where another company makes a bid for control of the business to the shareholders over the heads of the directors.

3. If a company reaches the stage where it is regarded as an appropriate investment by the institutions who run pension funds, mutual funds and similar financial products based upon equities, it will find that the 'fund managers' begin to make demands upon the business in terms of its earnings growth which are hard to sustain.

Chapter summary

In this chapter you have taken a significant step forward in enhancing your understanding of the financial accounts of limited companies. We have explored the system of law and regulation which governs the way limited companies, their directors and auditors should behave. This degree of regulation is justified by the fact that limited companies offer protection to their owners from the risk of bankruptcy in the event of business failure. This is a necessary requirement for ensuring that productive, wealth-creating businesses can obtain the capital they need for expansion and development. However, this limitation of liability comes at a cost. The cost is openness in the financial affairs of limited companies so that creditors can make themselves aware of the potential risk they face in dealing with a particular company. From the accounting perspective we have explored the unique characteristics of limited company accounts: the construction of the owner's equity account with its share capital and reserves, the formation of group companies and the regulation of accounting disclosure. We have presented the minimum that we believe you need to know in order to have an intelligent understanding of the financial accounts and this lays the groundwork for our work in interpreting the information which published accounts reveal. We explore this in the next chapter of the book.

Further reading

Alexander, D. and Britton, A. (1996) *Financial Reporting,* London: International Thomson Business Press. A good authoritative book covering a wide range of policy and regulatory issues.

Elliot, B. and Elliot, J. (2002) *Financial Accounting and Reporting,* Harlow: Financial Times, Prentice Hall. Chapters 7 and 8 start a more in-depth treatment of the topics covered in this chapter.

Fusaro, P.C. and Miller, R.M. (2002) *What went wrong at Enron,* New Jersey: John Wiley and Co. An excellent account of the accounting fiasco that was Enron.

KPMG (1998) *The Companies Act 1985 and 1989,* London: Accounting Books. This is a useful reference for anything to do with the Companies Acts. Heavy-going but invaluable when you need it.

Underdown, B. and Taylor, P. (1985) *Accounting Theory and Policy Making,* Oxford: Butterworth-Heinemann. This is a superb, clearly written book that, whilst nearly twenty years old, is still relevant and worth reading.

Progress check

Please refer to the page shown to check your answers.

1. What does the term 'limited liability' mean? (p. 140)

2. Identify three issues raised by limited company status that are relevant to accountants. (p. 140)

3. Name the two types of director on the board of a company. (p. 142)

4. What is the key statement of opinion that appears in an auditor's report? (pp. 144–145)

5. What distinguishes an ordinary from a preference shareholder? (p. 148)

6. What is the purpose of a 'share premium account'? (p. 148)

7. Name three types of reserve which will be shown in the typical limited company balance sheet and state whether each reserve you name is potentially distributable to the shareholders. (p. 152)

8. List the documents that company law in the UK requires to be published in the financial report. (p. 153)

9. What is the difference between an associated company and a subsidiary? (pp. 154–155)

10. List two ways in which an interest in another company may be acquired. (p. 155)

11. What does the term 'goodwill on acquisition' mean? (p. 158)

12. If a company acquires less than 100 per cent of the equity of another company what is the name given to the shareholders that remain in the acquired subsidiary? (p. 161)

13. When producing a consolidated balance sheet what items should be eliminated? (pp. 163–165)

14. When producing a consolidated income statement what item found in the subsidiary company income statement should be ignored? (pp. 165–166)

15. List the criteria that a limited company should meet before it can obtain a listing on the London Stock Exchange. (p. 168)

Questions

The answers to the questions followed by ✓ can be found at the back of the book, the answers to the remaining questions can be found at the website accompanying this book **(www.cengage.co.uk/ryan2)**.

1. There are three stages through which a limited company can progress:

   1. private limited company
   2. public limited company
   3. listed company.

   Outline the main requirements for the formation of each of these different types of company and discuss the advantages and disadvantages of each from the viewpoint of the owners.

2. Outline the difference between an associated company and a subsidiary and describe the principal changes you would expect to see between the accounts of a company which does not have any other interests and a company which has (a) an associate and (b) a subsidiary.

3. The regulation of company reporting has produced a number of different financial reporting standards. What problem do such standards seek to address, to what extent are they successful and what are the advantages and disadvantages of this method of regulation?

4. What do you understand by the term 'corporate governance' and what are the principal requirements of the 'Combined Code of Practice'?

5. Arthur Belling formed a limited company on 1 January with an authorised share capital of 500 000 shares. On 1 January the company issued 120 000 25p ordinary shares to Belling, his wife and his brother. Each subscribed £1 for the shares. At the end of the first year of trading the company had made a profit of £60 000 after interest and tax. Belling declared a dividend of 20 pence per share.

You are required to:

(i) Show the owner's equity account in the balance sheet of the company at the end of the year.

(ii) Write a brief note for the directors, outlining the uses to which the reserves that have been created can be put. ✓

6. Knitpika Ltd was formed on 1 April by the issue of 600 000 25p shares. The new company acquired the assets and liabilities from the owner of Knotalot and Co., a family business owned by the promoters of Knitpika Ltd. The bank has agreed that a £350 000 unsecured loan can be transferred to the new company subject to a provision of a directors' guarantee.

The assets acquired at their balance sheet values were:

Freehold land and buildings	£850 000
Other fixed assets	£154 000
Stocks	£18 000
Debtors less than one year old	£43 000
Debtors more than one year old	£10 000
Short-term liabilities	£165 000
Unsecured bank loan	£350 000
Cash in hand	£25 000

You are required to:

(i) Prepare the opening balance sheet of Knitpika Ltd as at 1 April assuming that the purchase of the shares in Knitpika Ltd was paid out of the retained earnings of Knotalot.

(ii) Prepare the balance sheet assuming that the owners decide to inject sufficient funds to pay off the bank loan and leave £10 000 of cash for working capital purposes. Half would be by way of a directors' loan and half by equity. ✓

7. Below are the balance sheets and income statements of Parent Ltd and Daughter Ltd. Parent had acquired 70 per cent of the equity of Daughter Ltd for cash two years previously. The profit reserve of Daughter Ltd at the date of acquisition had stood at £18 000.

Exhibit 6.26

Parent Ltd Balance Sheet as at 31 December		Daughter Ltd Balance Sheet as at 31 December	
Non-current Assets	200 000	Non-current Assets	100 000
Investment in Daughter Ltd	70 000		
Current assets:		Current assets:	
Inventories	80 000	Inventories	25 000
Receivables	45 000	Receivables	10 000
Cash	3 000	Cash	8 000
	128 000		43 000
Less current liabilities	−80 000	Less current liabilities	25 000
Less non-current liabilities	−40 000	Loan from Parent Ltd	−10 000
	278 000		108 000
Owners Equity		Owners Equity	
Share capital	45 000	Share capital	10 000
Share premium account	90 000	Share premium account	60 000
Profit reserve	143 000	Profit reserve less dividend paid of 1000	38 000
	278 000		108 000

Parent Ltd Income statement For the year ended 31 December		Daughter Ltd Income statement For the year ended 31 December	
Sales turnover	100 000	Sales turnover	51 750
Cost of sales	20 000	Cost of sales	10 000
Gross profit	80 000	Gross profit	41 750
Other operating costs	39 700	Other operating costs	28 000
Operating profit	40 300	Operating profit	13 750
Add dividend from Daughter Ltd	700	Corporation tax	2 750
Profit before interest and tax	41 000	Profit available for distribution	11 000
less interest payable	1 000		
	40 000		
Corporation tax	7 860		
Profit available for distribution	32 140		

You are required to produce a consolidated income statement and balance sheet for Parent (Group) Ltd. ✓

Chapter 7

The analysis of accounting information

Introduction

In this chapter we describe a general approach and method for the interpretation of accounting information. This methodology proceeds through a number of stages designed to maximise your chance of identifying the important issues that the chosen company is facing and the most likely financial implications for the business. However, a common mistake when considering the financial performance of firms is to immediately open the accounts. We recommend that you avoid that temptation and follow a process of research on your company beforehand. This prior research will allow you to construct a framework of analytical questions that you can then use as the basis of your analysis.

In this chapter we discuss a range of financial techniques including ratio analysis and discuss their limitations. Financial techniques only provide partial answers to our questions but supported by careful research they do allow us to 'read between the lines of the accounts'. In this chapter, we will use as our case example a famous retail company that went through a period of difficult trading in the late 1990s. Marks & Spencer, having been celebrated as a great British success story, had suddenly fallen out of favour with the stock market and its customers. In the late 1990s Marks & Spencer opened a financial services business offering credit card services, loans, pension products, insurance and other such products to its customers. One issue of concern is the extent to which the company has been successful in developing this side of its business. However, in recent years it has reclaimed its position as the UK's premier clothes retailer.

FYI There are a number of investor ratios whose significance cannot be fully understood until we have explored the workings of the capital markets in Chapter 14.

Our analysis of these accounts will also give you the opportunity to build upon the knowledge gained in the previous six chapters and in particular to provide an understanding of how limited company accounts are presented.

An abridged version of Marks & Spencer's accounts for the financial year ended 31 March 2007 is appended to this chapter. You can get a full copy of these accounts from their website: **www2.marksandspencer.com/thecompany/**

Learning objectives

The learning outcomes which we hope you will achieve by studying this topic are:

The analysis of financial information

- Using a range of critical techniques upon the company under analysis, be able to construct a set of financial issues for detailed investigation.

- Be familiar with the layout of the financial statements of public limited companies.

Financial analysis

- Apply the techniques of (a) difference analysis, (b) margin analysis and (c) ratio analysis to elicit useful information from a set of company accounts.

- Be able to calculate and assess a number of ratios measuring the performance, efficiency, risk and liquidity of a business.

Completing the narrative

- Be able to construct an evidence-based financial narrative of a company's performance, efficiency, risk and liquidity using the tools and techniques discussed.

- Be able to categorise the main methods of accounting manipulation.

- Be able to identify when a company is in serious financial distress and has a high risk of imminent failure.

The analysis of financial information

This book advocates a top-down approach to the analysis of accounting information. What this means is that we commence with the most general level of business issues and proceed, refining our understanding as we go. This approach offers a number of important benefits:

- Our analysis will be directed towards satisfying either our own or our clients' decision requirements.
- The principal issues and concerns about a business are explored in a wider context before we plunge into the murky depths of the accounting information.
- We should have a clearer idea of the likely deficiencies of standard published accounting information for the business we are investigating.
- We will have thought about other relevant information, which we can seek out and read prior to our analysis of the accounts.

● Finally, our accounting analysis will be led by the issues we are interested in resolving rather than being used as a tool to discover those issues (this does not mean that new issues will not emerge from our analysis, but where they do the context in which they have arisen should be much clearer).

The key steps are as shown in Exhibit 7.1.

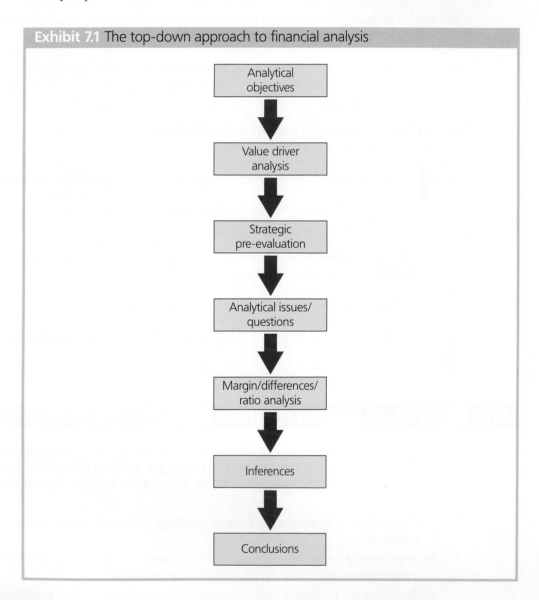

Exhibit 7.1 The top-down approach to financial analysis

Analytical objectives

Value driver analysis

Strategic pre-evaluation

Analytical issues/ questions

Margin/differences/ ratio analysis

Inferences

Conclusions

Financial realities It is often claimed that some business people can understand the full implications of a set of accounts within moments of opening them. The only way this can happen is where the individual concerned has such a thorough understanding of the background business issues that they know exactly what they are looking for. This is very rare and rather dangerous in practice – there is no hidden secret to understanding accounts apart from a willingness to undertake a careful reading and analysis of the information presented. Skill in reading accounts improves with practice; it is never a quick process.

The analytical objectives

The first step in accounts analysis is to ask and answer the questions: who are we undertaking the analysis for, and what do they want to know?

It is possible to analyse the accounts from an individual's perspective or, more generally, from the point of view of a stakeholder group. Such groups, as we discussed in Chapter 1, may be shareholders, fund managers, creditors, lenders, managers, employees, society and so forth. The point to remember is that different groups are likely to want some information that is common to all and some that is group-specific. To understand the significance of this issue, consider the likely decision-making requirements and information requirements of the most important stakeholder groups (Exhibit 7.2).

Other things being equal, shareholders, fund managers and management compensated through equity will seek to minimise costs and maximise revenue: and the workforce and their negotiating bodies are likely to want to maximise the labour element of cost. There is, potentially, a conflict of objectives between these groups. In choosing the most appropriate information to gather the financial analyst must be quite clear whose interest they are serving and the purpose of the analytical exercise to be undertaken.

This is not an exhaustive analysis of the likely decisions and information requirements of each stakeholder group. However, for the purposes of our analysis of Marks & Spencer plc, we will assume that we are analysing the accounts from a shareholder perspective. Marks & Spencer is a public limited company and we will be interested to know:

- Is the company performing in line with what we would expect and what is its growth potential over the foreseeable future?
- Is the company operating as efficiently as it might or is there room for improvement?

Exhibit 7.2

Stakeholder group	Presumed objectives	Likely decisions	Information requirements
Shareholders	Maximise shareholder value	Buy/sell or hold shares	Forecasts of earnings and growth
Fund managers	Maximise fund values	Buy/sell or hold	As shareholders plus compliance information relevant to the management of the fund
Lenders	Minimise default risk	Debt foreclosure	Profit before interest and tax/ liquidity/capital gearing and interest cover
Non-management employees	Maximise earned income	Employment/wage bargaining	Sales growth and gross margins Liquidity and ability to pay
Management	Maximise compensation function	Strategic and operational business decisions	As with non-managerial employees but also compensation packages and personal performance measures
Suppliers	Minimise settlement period and default risk	Contract engagement/debt recovery procedure	Gross margins/liquidity/creditor ages/gearing
Customers	Minimise default risk	Buy or not buy	Short-term liquidity/long-term measures of performance
Revenue service	Recovery of tax liability	Level of tax liability	Taxable profit

- Are the earnings of the company at significant risk and, if so, what are the worst and best outcomes that could be achieved?
- Is the company generally solvent and, if so, is the liquidity of the company sufficiently robust to sustain future growth or will it be forced to raise new funds from the capital market?

These four issues of performance, efficiency, risk and liquidity – PERL – arise sufficiently often to provide a general framework of analysis. We will use this PERL framework later in the chapter. In Chapter 14 we will develop the work done in this chapter to show how a company's equity can be valued. Our work on valuation will be informed by the outcome of our analysis in this chapter.

Value driver analysis

Once the objectives of the analysis are clear, the next step is to identify the type of business or businesses in which a firm is engaged and the predominant ways in which it creates value. In Chapter 1 we discussed four generic business types: merchant, manufacturer, extractive and service. In Chapter 2 we developed those ideas and discussed how businesses create value. However, businesses can be categorised in many ways: Exhibit 7.3 offers a useful typology:

Exhibit 7.3 Six basic types of business		
Business type	**Value driver**	**Example**
Merchant	Product price differentials	Marks & Spencer plc
Service (R)	Service company based on the exploitation of real assets	DialaSid Ltd
Service (I)	Service company based on the exploitation of intangible, often knowledge-based assets	KPMG
Manufacturing	Company based on the exploitation of both real and intangible assets, transforming bought-in goods and services	Cobham plc
Extractive	Business concerned with the exploitation of natural resources through the use of real assets	British Gas
Banking	Differentials in price of money and deposit creation	HSBC

Clearly, any large business will have many different sources of value creation. What we are interested in here is: what is the principal motor for the creation of value in a business? A hotel, for example, employs people and depends upon their knowledge and talent. However, the principal driver of its value is how it exploits its real assets, the hotels themselves, to create value. When measuring the performance and efficiency of such businesses, a knowledge of its value drivers can help point to particular financial ratios.

Review activity 7.1 What types of real and intangible assets are likely to be important in Marks & Spencer plc? How are they used by the company in creating value?

The strategic pre-evaluation of the company

Once you are clear about who your client is and the type of business you are seeking to analyse, the next step is to consider the economic environment and the market and other strategic issues it faces. There are a number of tools that you can use to help you in this: competitive analysis (economics), strengths, weakness, opportunities, threats (SWOT) (strategy) and political, economic, social and technological (PEST) (strategy) are just three examples.

Good sources of relevant information about a company's affairs can be found as follows:

1. The chairman's foreword, the business review and the directors' report which is presented in the first part of the published financial report.
2. The company's own website
3. The World Wide Web where you will find organisations who can provide you with company news and analysis such as Reuters.com, Bloomberg.com, FT.com, ThomsonFN.com, Yahoo finance and Hemscott.com.
4. The Bank of England and other central bank websites which provide general information about the economy and also some sector by sector reports.
5. The BBC, CNN and other news media websites, all of which have archives that can be searched.
6. Companies House in the UK can provide copies of documents lodged by companies plus a variety of other useful information.

Some of these sources charge to download data.

The economic context

Companies, as part of the wider economy, both contribute to and are affected by the prevailing economic conditions. A significant influence upon the performance of retailers, for example, is the general level of economic activity and the level of inflation in the economy.

1. The growth in the gross domestic product (GDP) in the economy is the primary indicator of economic activity. It measures the output of goods and services within the domestic economy but ignores inflows and outflows abroad. The Bank of England, in the UK, publishes a quarterly report which gives the historical growth in GDP and projections for the immediate future. This growth in GDP is measured in current-day prices ignoring the effect of inflation. In reviewing the performance of a company we will need to compare it with what we would expect if its sales revenue and profitability had kept pace with general economic growth and with inflation.
2. Inflation is the general increase in the prices of a wide 'basket' of goods and services across the economy. In constructing the retail price index, which is the principal measure of inflation, government statisticians attempt to replicate the buying pattern of people across the economy. Again, the Bank of England provides an inflation summary and forecast which can be compared with the GDP growth estimates to give the nominal growth in GDP including the effect of changing prices.

Exhibit 7.4 shows two very useful charts produced by the Bank of England which give both GDP growth and inflation including projections with the levels of risk shown by the 'fan' part of the chart. These data provide a very useful tool for measuring our expectation of the improvements a company should have made during the period concerned.

We would expect any company to achieve this level of growth to keep pace with the general rate of increase in the economy.

Two questions are raised about Marks & Spencer plc by this analysis of the growth of the economy:

- Has the company continued to improve its performance following the steep decline in turnover and profitability between 2000 and 2003?
- If the company has improved its performance, has this been won through increased turnover or by cutting costs?

Exhibit 7.4 GDP and inflation projections (courtesy of the Bank of England)

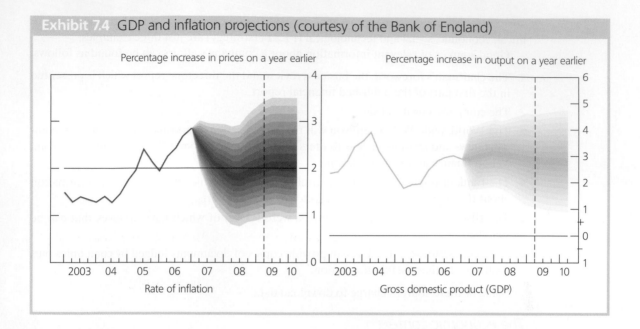

Percentage increase in prices on a year earlier

Rate of inflation

Percentage increase in output on a year earlier

Gross domestic product (GDP)

Financial realities During the financial year ended 31 March 2007 the average growth in GDP, taking the midpoint date at the end of May, was 2.8 per cent (real). The corresponding average rise in the rate of inflation was also 2.8 per cent. The combined rate of growth expressed in nominal terms is given by the following formula (this formula is explained in more detail in Chapter 13):

$$1 + \boxed{\begin{array}{c}\text{Nominal rate of}\\\text{growth of GDP}\end{array}} = \left(1 + \boxed{\begin{array}{c}\text{Real rate}\\\text{of growth of}\\\text{GDP}\end{array}}\right) \times \left(1 + \boxed{\begin{array}{c}\text{Inflation}\\\text{rate}\end{array}}\right)$$

therefore:

$$\boxed{\begin{array}{c}\text{Nominal rate of}\\\text{growth of GDP}\end{array}} = \left(1 + \boxed{\begin{array}{c}\text{Real rate}\\\text{of growth of}\\\text{GDP}\end{array}}\right) \times \left(1 + \boxed{\begin{array}{c}\text{Inflation}\\\text{rate}\end{array}}\right) - 1$$

Substituting the rates expressed as decimals rather than percentages:
Nominal rate = (1.028) × (1.028) − 1 = 0.05678 ≡ 5.68 per cent

A number of economic variables will also impact upon business firms such as changes in interest rates, taxation and exchange rates:

1. *Interest rates* Interest rates are set by the Bank of England and rate changes have both direct and indirect effects upon a firm's performance. First and most directly they influence the company's cost of borrowing and, because of the interdependencies we will explore in Chapter 12, will influence the rates of return required by its equity investors. Indirectly, changes in interest rates impact upon consumer spending in the shops: high rates of interest mean a high cost of credit which will tend to reduce spending and vice versa. Also, the higher the level of interest rates the higher the exchange rate between the domestic and overseas currencies. This will tend to cut the cost of imported goods but increase the cost of exports.

2. *Taxation* Changes in personal taxation (income tax) influence the disposable income people have to spend. Changes in corporation tax affect the amount of profit a firm can make available for distribution and retention for further investment. Other taxes such as value-added tax (VAT) and excise duty directly influence consumer spending. How a particular tax change will affect a given company is dependent upon a number of factors: how it is targeted, whether it causes a redistribution from one sector of the population to another, and the ability of the company to offset the tax against liabilities elsewhere in the business. As far as the financial accounts are concerned the most obvious impact of tax is in the deduction for corporation tax in the income statement and provisions for deferred taxation in the balance sheet. More subtle effects occur in revenues, expenditures and capital investment caused by changes in other taxes.

3. *Exchange rates* The exchange rate measures the rate of conversion between the domestic currency (sterling in the UK) and the currency of a given overseas country. A high exchange rate means that UK goods are expensive in the foreign country involved and overseas goods and services are relatively cheap in the UK. A high exchange rate will favour companies that import a large proportion of their raw materials and components but will make UK company exports more expensive and thus more difficult to sell. The reverse is true if the domestic currency falls in value.

Inflation, interest rates, taxes and exchange rates are to a degree dependent upon one another and their impact upon a given firm's performance will depend upon the exposure of its costs and revenues to changes in these factors. For a company such as M&S (Marks & Spencer) relatively high exchange rates should give it a cost advantage as much of its stock for sale is imported. A company like Marks & Spencer is susceptible to changes in interest rates and other factors influencing consumer spending. However, the effect may not be quite what is expected. Marks & Spencer's positioning as a high quality but low price supplier may attract customers who are turning away from the more expensive brands because of adverse movements in interest rates.

Our economic analysis might suggest that with continual tightening of interest rates consumer spending may be under some pressure, especially for luxury goods and 'big-ticket' items. However, the company has an extensive offering in the food and everyday clothing markets which may mean that it can resist some of the negative pressure against consumer spending in the wider economy.

Strategic analysis

Understanding the strategic issues faced by a firm entails analysis of its market position, any competitive advantage it may have and the threats to which it is exposed. There are a wide range of methods which can assist in analysing a company's strategic position. One of the most fundamental is to undertake a review of its strengths, weaknesses, opportunities and threats (SWOT): SWOT analysis allows a free-ranging review of the internal and external factors which determine business success. It also allows the analyst to form a judgement about the appropriate balance of a firm's costs. Here are some useful tips in conducting SWOT analysis:

1. Identify points under each heading as precisely as possible, noting supporting evidence and references. Avoid general statements – they are difficult to justify with evidence and are too easily contradicted. Such statements are best reserved for the end of the exercise when conclusions can be arrived at and supported.

2. For each strength identify its mirror weakness: large cash holdings, for example, would be counted as strength, but historic under-investment would be a weakness. Similarly, where you identify a weakness, look for a corresponding strength.

3. Where you identify a threat look for a corresponding opportunity and vice versa. Threats entail exposure to risk and you might wish to review how a company is managing risk (remember that the company's corporate governance statements may include some reference to internal control and the management of risk). Attempt to link each threat with weaknesses to gauge the firm's exposure to the risk that threat represents. Similarly, review the strengths that a business possesses and how it can use them to capitalise on its opportunities.

4. Once your review is complete, seek to make linkages between individual points under each of the four headings. If you can identify a common theme around the four corners of the SWOT this usually points to a strategic issue facing the business.

5. Against each of the headings identify the principal impact of the points you have identified on the revenue, costs, asset values, liabilities and cash flow of the firm.

Your SWOT analysis can form a template against which various ratios can be judged – we will pick up on this point later in this chapter.

PEST analysis focuses on the political, economic, social and technological forces that impact upon a specific business. The PEST analysis will be informed by your study of the economic environment and in particular the economic forecasts of bodies such as the Bank of England and the Confederation of British Industry. PEST, like SWOT, requires you to think clearly about the principal issues facing the firm under each of its headings.

Review activity 7.2 Consider the following extract from the May 2007 Bank of England Inflation Report. The Inflation Report gives detailed forecasts used by the Bank's monetary policy committee in setting interest rates. The MPC is mandated to maintain inflation at a target rate of 2 per cent. What would be the likely implications of the forecasts contained within this statement for a large retailer of clothes, furnishing and food, such as Marks & Spencer plc?

Overview

In the United Kingdom, solid growth in GDP has been maintained. Credit and broad money growth remained rapid. Household spending has been volatile but the underlying trend appears firm. Business investment gathered pace. The world economy continued to expand briskly. Under the assumption that bank rate follows market yields, the committee's central projection is for output growth to stay near its average over the past decade. CPI inflation reached 3.1 per cent in March. Regular pay growth remained subdued, though oil prices rebounded. The margin of spare capacity in firms appears to be relatively limited and businesses seem to have become more confident in their ability to raise prices. In the central projection, CPI inflation drops back, dipping a little below the 2 per cent target before picking up to settle around the target in the medium term. The risks to growth are balanced, while those to inflation are weighted to the upside in the medium term.

Domestic demand

The pattern of household spending was erratic through 2006 and that appears to have continued into early 2007. Smoothing through this volatility, underlying consumption growth has been near to its average over the past 20 years. Looking forward, household spending should be supported by a recovery in real take-home pay, helping to offset the drag from the increase in interest rates since last August. Government spending has been a significant contributor to overall demand growth in recent years and that was maintained through 2006. According to the spending plans set out in the budget, the public sector's contribution to nominal demand growth is set to decline over the next few years.

Bank of England Inflation Report May 2007, available at www.bankofengland.co.uk/publications/inflationreport/index.htm

Exhibit 7.5 SWOT analysis with cost implications

Cost of maintaining capability:
- Capacity and technology
- Market power (brands etc.)
- Product base
- Human resources (training)
- Networks and relationships

'Catch-up' costs of:
- Reinstatement or renewal of asset base
- Investment in information systems
- Business network repair and development
- Staff development, redeployment

Strengths:
- Specific points where the company has clear advantages over its competitors

Weaknesses:
- Often the converse of strengths
- Look for specific problem areas where the company could be vulnerable to competitive attack

INTERNAL

INTERNAL

Opportunities:
- Opportunities in terms of procurement, manufacturing, R&D, new markets etc.
- Often the converse of threats
- Again look for specific points taking care to define the opportunity and the constraints upon its exploitation

Threats:
- Often the converse of opportunities
- Threats and corresponding weaknesses can lead to undue risk exposure
- Make threats specific and attempt to measure their likely impact upon the business

EXTERNAL

EXTERNAL

Investment in:
- New technology and R&D
- Market and brand development
- Staff development
- Capital equipment

Avoidance costs:
- Costs of market intelligence
- Insurance costs
- 'Hedging' strategies
- Internal control and internal and external monitoring and audit

GDP to be 5.68 per cent. The turnover in 2006 was £7797.7. The turnover corrected for GDP growth is:

$$2006 \text{ turnover (GDP corrected)} = £7797.7 \times 1.0568 = £8240.5$$

8. Repeat steps (3) and (4) above on the difference between the actual 2007 figures and the preceding-year figures as corrected for the nominal increase in GDP.

In Exhibit 7.6 we have proceeded through this analysis step by step. Now review those differences and see to what extent they inform the questions you have set up about this business. When testing the differences look for the most significant changes. You may also wish to calculate each or at least some of the changes, as percentages of the preceding-year or preceding-year-corrected figures to make sure that you are clear about the significance of each change.

As we review this list of changes we note that the company has increased its turnover, gross profit and operating profit. Operating profit has increased from £850.1 million to £1045.9 million (a 23 per cent increase). This has fed through to an increase to the bottom line figure (profit attributable to shareholders) taking it from a 2006 profit of £523.1 million to a profit of £659.9 million in 2007. When we review the details of the changes in operating performance we discover:

- Turnover has increased at a significantly faster rate than inflation and GDP growth. Turnover growth was 10 per cent, which implies that there has been a real increase in the volume of goods sold as opposed to simply charging customers more for the same level of sales.

- The operating profits have risen by 23 per cent and distributable profit by 26 per cent. Our attention should now focus on exactly how that increase in profitability has come about. The first point that we note is that although turnover has increased by 10 per cent, gross profit has increased by 12 per cent, operating profit by 23 per cent and distributable profit by 27 per cent. The most significant improvement lies between the gross profit and the operating profit levels and this is due to an effect we will discuss later under the heading of 'operating leverage'.

Review activity 7.3

Conduct a simple analysis of the differences from the group balance sheet and cash flow statement. What are the principle differences in the balance sheet? Are those differences explicable in terms of what you have noted from your analysis of the differences in the income statement?

Margin analysis

This simple step should help support the information you have extracted from the difference analysis. Taking the income statement extract the profit margins. These are all shown as percentages in Exhibit 7.7:

- gross profit/sales turnover (gross profit margin)
- operating profit/sales turnover (operating profit margin)
- profit before tax/sales turnover
- distributable profit/sales turnover (net profit margin)
- retained profit/sales turnover.

Exhibit 7.6 Analysis of the differences in the income statement

Step (i) - Extract from latest income statement current year and prior year figures

Step (ii) - Add in figures from notes for cost of sales, gross profit and other operating costs

Step (iii) - Take the difference between the 2007 and 2006

Step (iv) - If the change will increase profits put an 'f', if it tends to decrease profit put an 'a'. 'f' = favourable; 'a' = adverse.

Step (v) - Inflate the 2006 figure by multiplying each number by 1.03. This adds 3.00% to the original value

Step (vii) - Correct the 2006 figures for the 5.68% increase in nominal GDP.

Step (iii) as repeated - take the difference between the 2006 corrected figures and the 2007 values

	2006 £m	2007 £m	difference £m		2006 inflated £m	2007 £m	difference £m		2006 nom. GDP £m	2007 £m	difference £m	
Turnover	7 797.7	8 588.1	790.4	f	8 031.5	8 588.1	556.5	f	8 240.5	8 588.1	347.6	f
Cost of sales	(4 812.1)	(5 246.9)	434.8	a	(4 956.5)	(5 246.9)	290.4	a	(5 085.3)	(5 246.9)	161.6	a
Gross profit	**2 985.6**	**3 341.2**	**355.6**	**f**	**3 075.2**	**3 341.2**	**266.0**	**f**	**3 155.1**	**3 341.2**	**186.1**	**f**
Employee costs (see note 1CA)	1 073.2	1 174.1	100.9	a	1 105.4	1 174.1	68.7	a	1 134.1	1 174.1	40.0	a
Occupancy costs	325.4	372.9	47.5	a	335.2	372.9	37.7	a	343.9	372.9	29.0	a
Repairs, renewals and maintenance of fixed assets	90.2	74.5	15.7	f	92.9	74.5	18.4	f	95.3	74.5	20.8	f
Depreciation	274.0	282.7	8.7	a	282.2	282.7	0.5	a	289.6	282.7	6.9	f
Other costs	385.6	459.1	73.5	a	397.2	459.1	61.9	a	407.5	459.1	51.6	a
Total net operating expenses	(2 148.4)	(2 363.3)	214.9	a	(2 212.9)	(2 363.3)	150.4	a	(2 270.4)	(2 363.3)	92.9	f
Other operating income	8.6	66.1	47.5	f	19.2	66.1	46.9	f	19.7	66.1	46.9	f
Profit/(loss) on property disposals	(5.7)	1.9	7.6	f	(5.9)	1.9	7.8	f	(6.0)	1.9	7.9	f
Operating profit	**850.1**	**1 045.9**	**195.8**	**f**	**875.5**	**1 045.9**	**170.3**	**f**	**898.4**	**1 045.9**	**147.5**	**f**
Finance income	30.5	33.8	3.3	f								
Finance costs	(134.9)	(112.6)	22.3	f								
Exceptional finance costs	–	(30.4)	30.4	a								
Net interest income	(104.4)	(109.2)	4.8	a								
Profit/(loss) on ordinary activities before taxation	**745.7**	**936.7**	**191.0**	**f**								
Income tax expense	(225.1)	(277.5)	52.4	a								
Profit/(loss) on ordinary activities after taxation	**520.6**	**659.2**	**138.6**	**f**								
Profit from discontinued operations	2.5	0.7	1.8	a								
Profit/(loss) attributable to shareholders	**523.1**	**659.9**	**136.8**	**f**								
Dividends	(204.1)	(260.6)	56.5	a								
Retained profit/(loss) for the period	**319.0**	**399.3**	**80.3**	**f**								
Earnings per share	**31.3p**	**39.1p**	**7.8p**	**f**								
Diluted earnings per share	**31.0p**	**38.5p**	**7.5p**	**f**								
Adjusted earnings per share	**31.4p**	**40.4p**	**9.0p**	**f**								
Diluted adjusted earnings per share	**31.1p**	**39.8p**	**8.7p**	**f**								
Dividend per share	**12.3p**	**15.5p**	**3.2p**	**f**								

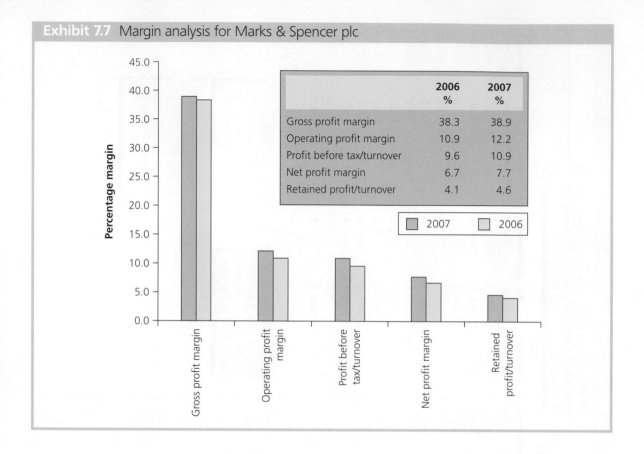

Exhibit 7.7 Margin analysis for Marks & Spencer plc

	2006 %	2007 %
Gross profit margin	38.3	38.9
Operating profit margin	10.9	12.2
Profit before tax/turnover	9.6	10.9
Net profit margin	6.7	7.7
Retained profit/turnover	4.1	4.6

These margin ratios give a clue as to the financial structure of the business and its exposure to business risk. Many companies have strong margins at the gross profit level but much narrower operating margins, as is the case with Marks & Spencer plc. Some other companies have relatively low gross margins but relatively low other operating costs (see Exhibit 7.8). This can be caused by a number of factors, but clearly a business with low margins at the operating level is particularly exposed to the fluctuations in fortunes which afflict all companies from time to time.

In looking for a cost-saving strategy, for example, a manufacturer will be forced to look at the cost of materials and components as this is where the bulk of the cost is incurred. The merchant or retailer will typically find the fall-off in costs distributed across all of its operating expenditures including its cost of goods for sale. The service-sector firm will, however, be forced to target its other operating costs as the cost of goods sold is likely to be a much smaller proportion of the firm's total expenditure.

Financial ratios

There are two classes of financial ratio:

● Accounting ratios drawn from the financial reports and using other published physical measures as necessary to assist in the analysis of the accounts. This book recommends a particular framework for classifying these ratios which classifies them as measuring:

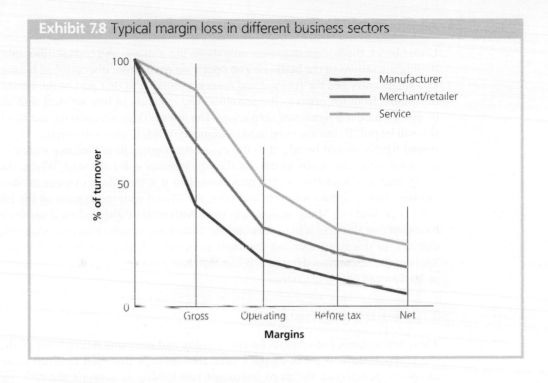

Exhibit 7.8 Typical margin loss in different business sectors

performance (P), efficiency (E), risk (R) and liquidity (L). The PERL acronym is useful for remembering this classification.

● Investment ratios which measure the performance of the firm against the quoted market price of its equity. These ratios only apply to firms that have a market listing. We will defer our discussion of these ratios until Chapter 14 where they will be assessed in the context of the value of the firm.

A ratio, like any arithmetic fraction, consists of a numerator and a denominator and may be expressed as a percentage, as a simple proportion, or in terms of some other scalar value such as number of days or months. We will come across each type. When constructing financial ratios the numerator will always be a financial value drawn from one or other of the principal statements of account. The denominator may be a financial value or it may be some other physical measure such as the number of passenger flights, the number of employees or the square metres of floor space. However, when considering the usefulness of a given ratio there are a number of tests that can be applied:

1. Are the numerator and denominator related to one another and what is the significance of the relationship?

2. Are the measurement bases of the numerator and denominator consistent?

3. How do we judge the significance of the ratio values derived for the firm?

   ● Do the ratios selected measure performance in a way that reflects the value drivers for a business of this type?

   ● Is there enough information to calculate the ratios needed, or must we look elsewhere?

   ● Given the questions posed are there ratios that will help specifically in dealing with the problems identified?

Dealing with discontinued business

Under IAS 1, the income statement only shows the turnover and costs attributable to the continuing operations of the business. The operating profit from discontinued business is shown as a single entry and the revenue and costs attributable to that part of the business are only obtainable from the notes to the accounts. The question of how we deal with discontinued business where it is significant then arises. The answer depends upon the use to which the ratios will be put. If they are to be used to examine trends in past performance then the discontinued figures should be added to the equivalent figures in the income statement to give a revenues, costs and profit figures for the whole business for the year. Where the ratios are being used as a basis for forward projection then it is important to focus on the continuing business and to ignore revenues and costs associated with those parts of the business that have been sold off. Many analysts will work with ratios expressed on a variety of different bases but our aim here is to understand the underlying structure and message that each ratio delivers. In this respect we are fortunate in our choice of company, in that with Marks & Spencer the discontinued business is less than half a per cent in 2006 and almost non-existent in 2007 so can be safely ignored.

The PERL framework

There are a number of schemes for categorising and analysing ratios. Some of these, such as the DuPont Method, focus on the formal relationships that exist between ratios. From an analytical perspective the more important relationship is between the ratio measures we choose and the underlying analytical framework we have already developed. Some ratios focus upon the performance of the business; they tell us the extent to which the organisation is able to create benefit for its investors from its strengths. Other ratios focus on the relative efficiency or inefficiency of the business; these ratios tell us the extent to which the business is able to overcome its weaknesses. A third set of ratios reveal a business's capacity to exploit new opportunities by focusing on its liquidity whilst the final group give an insight into its exposure to risk, or in terms of the SWOT analysis conducted earlier – its threats. The PERL framework allows the astute analyst to begin the process of linking the strategic position of the firm and the decisions made by its management to the financial outcomes reported in the accounts.

Measuring performance

The focus in measuring performance (P) is on the income statement and the measures of profit disclosed within.

Broadly, the performance of a business is measured by the efficiency by which we convert various financial inputs such as capital employed or sales turnover into our ultimate measure of financial performance – profit. There are other less direct measures of efficiency, which we will look at later.

There are four key ratios for measuring financial performance.

Margin ratio

This ratio was discussed under the margin analysis above. It measures the proportion of sales being 'captured' by the firm as profit. It can be calculated at any of the profit levels chosen. The general formula is

(gross, operating, net) margin = profit / sales turnover × 100

At any given level the cost to sales ratio will be the difference between the margin and 100 per cent:

$$\text{Cost/sales ratio} = (1 - \text{margin}) \times 100$$

For Marks & Spencer we can calculate the operating margin and the corresponding cost to sales ratio as follows:

	2006%	2007%
Operating profit margin %	10.9	12.2
Operating cost to sales ratio %	89.1	87.8

The operating cost to sales ratios are given by:

Operating cost to sales (2006) = $(1 - 0.109) \times 100 = 89.1$ per cent

Operating cost to sales (2007) = $(1 - 0.122) \times 100 = 87.8$ per cent

Return on total capital employed

The return on capital employed (ROCE) ratio is the principal return measure that can be derived from the accounts. It measures the return of profit on all of the capital invested in the business including long-term loans, preference capital and equity. The equity figure included is all the balances on the owner's account including the profit and loss reserve, share premium account and other reserves. Normally this ratio is calculated by comparing the profit before interest and tax with the total capital employed.

Return on capital employed = $\dfrac{\text{Profit before interest and tax}}{\text{Total equity capital + long-term borrowing}} \times 100$

It can be calculated net of tax (ROCE (net)) as follows:

ROCE (net) = $\dfrac{\text{Profit before interest and tax − tax}}{\text{Total equity capital + long-term borrowing}} \times 100$

Which is correct? To a certain extent it doesn't matter providing that you are consistent when making comparisons between years or with other companies. We will use the gross version and calculate proceeding as follows:

1. Identify the long-term borrowing of the company from the balance sheet. The borrowing classed as 'non-current' is shown as £1133.8 million in 2006 and £1234.5 million in 2007
2. Add the borrowing to the balance of the owner's equity account in the balance sheet to obtain the relevant capital employed figures (in £ million) of:

Capital employed (2006) = 1203.7 + 1133.8 = 2337.5

Capital employed (2007) = 1648.2 + 1234.5 = 2882.7

3. Identify the profit before interest and tax from the income statement:

Profit before interest and tax (2006) = 850.1

Profit before interest and tax (2007) = 1045.9

...CE), which we

...ed assets including

...nt

...ent

...apital employed in the

...ify below:

...urrent   Owner's
...lities   +   equity

...less current liabilities as net cur-
...s and owners' equity as total cap-

= Total capital employed

...apital employed then the net current
...main in balance. With a given level of
...greater than the return on capital em-
...a 23 per cent current return on its fixed
...on its total capital. It is achieving this by
...aging its net current assets. We will see

...it is difficult to imagine that in 2003 the
...prime target for an acquisition. This disas-
...of bad management, as described in the

New management and an aggressive turnaround policy coupled with a hostile takeover bid in 2004 brought new focus to the business.

Return on total assets

Return on total assets (ROTA) is a popular ratio regarded by many as an important driver of return on equity (ROE). You will remember that equity is what is left after all the payables – loans and other independent claims on the business – have been deducted from the value of the assets of the business. However, it is sometimes valuable to remove the sources of finance from the denominator of the ratio and include only the value of the assets of the business. To measure the raw return on assets we should be similarly consistent and eliminate the return to the suppliers of finance from the numerator of the ratio. ROTA is therefore:

$$\text{Return on total assets} = \frac{\text{Profit before interest and tax}}{\text{Fixed assets} + \text{current assets}} \times 100$$

...., the denomina-
value (the firm's
..n. Second, when
providers, it is im-
..e method we have
..of the ratio. This is
..pital employed from

..employed, reflecting
..e of the financial year.
..or capital employed is

..cent

..ote where an average is
..for simplicity, as we shall

(before or after corporation
..e or after minority interests.
..of Marks & Spencer we have
..sheet after minority interests.

..olders
..ies) $\times$ 100

..r cent

..er cent

..cognise that the figure for the eq-
..d upon it by the stock market. This

..of return it earns on its equity capital
..sumption that there is no change in the

..o measures the return that the company
..nally be taken to be the total fixed assets
..ir net book value as shown in the balance

For Marks & Spencer the ratio for the two years is as follows:

$$\text{ROTA (2006)} = 850.1/5258.9 \times 100 = 16.16 \text{ per cent}$$
$$\text{ROTA (2007)} = 1045.9/5381.0 \times 100 = 19.44 \text{ per cent}$$

This ratio tells the same story as the return on fixed capital employed in that Marks & Spencer has improved its return. The message is not as focused as the return on fixed capital employed, because a substantial part of current assets included in this ratio (receivables) do not generate a return for the business. Generally, the various return ratios discussed above will follow a similar trend unless there is some structural change in the business by perhaps significantly altering the proportion of fixed assets to total assets, the proportion of borrowed funds to shareholder funds or the working capital policy of the firm.

Measuring efficiency

Less direct efficiency (E) measures can give us some important clues as to how a business is performing. We will consider efficiency at three levels:

1. the efficiency of the firm in controlling its costs (cost efficiency ratios)
2. the efficiency with which the business converts resources into sales (conversion ratios)
3. the efficiency with which the company uses its working capital (working capital ratios).

Cost efficiency

The cost efficiency of a firm is measured relative to the revenue it earns. If we expect the operating cost of the firm to be directly related to output we can predict what the current year's operating costs should be on the basis of the previous year. The cost efficiency ratio (CER) is therefore the ratio of actual cost to predicted cost.

Exhibit 7.9 takes us through the calculations of the cost efficiency ratios at the gross and the operating cost levels. From note 3 to the Marks & Spencer plc accounts we find the turnover for 2007 compared with 2006 and calculate the ratio of one to the other. Taking the actual cost of sales first, we multiply the 2006 figure by the ratio we have just calculated to obtain a predicted cost of sales for 2007:

$$\text{Predicted cost of sales (2007)} = \text{actual cost of sales (2006)} \times \frac{\text{turnover (2007)}}{\text{turnover (2006)}}$$
$$= (4812.1) \times 1.1014 = (5299.9)$$

Exhibit 7.9

	2007 £(m)	2006 £(m)
Turnover	8 588.1	7 797.7
Ratio of 2007 turnover to 2006	1.1014	
Cost of sales (2006)		(4 812.1)
Cost of sales (2007) - predicted	(5 299.9)	
Cost of sales (2007) - actual	(5 246.9)	
Direct cost efficiency ratio = actual cost of sales/predicted	0.99	
Net operating expenses (2006)		(2 148.4)
Net operating expenses (2007) - predicted	(2 366.2)	
Net operating expenses (2007) - actual	(2 363.3)	
Operating cost efficiency ratio = actual net operating costs/predicted	1.00	

		2007	2006
		5 235	4 601
		64 074	57 687
		2 396	2 325
		850	732
		3 316	2 959
		–	2 006
		75 871	70 310

Exhibit 7.12

			Trade receivables	Trade payables	Inventory
Sales turnover (£m)	2006	7 797.7	42.0		
	2007	8 588.1	67.9		
Cost of sales (£m)	2006	4 812.1			
	2007	5 246.9		242.6	374.3
Receivables age (days)	2006			259.7	416.3
	2007		2		
Payables age (days)	2006		3		
	2007				
	2006			18	
Inventory holding period (days)	2007			18	
	2006				28
	2007				29

turnover, cost of sales and relevant working capital items. We then show the ages using the formulae above.

These ratios reveal that Marks & Spencer is essentially a cash business with a receivables period of just one day. It settles its suppliers' accounts at an average of 18 days and holds approximately 29 days of inventory in its stores and its warehouses. In the director's report a lower figures is presented:

Trade creditor days for Marks & Spencer plc for the year ended 31 March 2007 were 14.7 days, or 9.8 working days (last year 13.1 days, or 8.8 working days), based on the ratio of company trade creditors at the end of the year to the amounts invoiced during the year by trade creditors.

The difference is that the company has access to the underlying purchases figures which are part of the cost of sales but are not separately disclosed. The figures in the director's report are subject to audit and are reliable. We can use this to isolate the purchases component of the cost of sales:

$$\text{Purchases on credit} = \frac{\text{Trade payables}}{\text{Payables age}} \times 365$$

$$= 259.7/14.7 \times 365 = \text{£}6448.3 \text{ million}$$

This gives us a problem which we will need to resolve through further investigation. Using the company's trade creditors figure and its stated payables age of 14.7 days we come up with a purchases figure which is greater than the company's cost of sales. There are three possible reasons for this mismatch:

- The payables period in the director's report is incorrectly stated
- The cost of sales given in the income statement is understated
- The figure for trade payables in the balance sheet includes other items than accounts payable for purchases.

Unfortunately, the accounting information provided by the company does not give us any clue as to which of these is the correct explanation.

ek, the equivalent average year 46,989).

elative labour efficiency of labour cost figures for the d with its turnover:

.31 was generated in sales in

of full-time equivalent (FTE) nany part-time staff within its ployed, we learn that in 2006, ployed (continued and discon-

7
5

of these ratios. There has been a he revenue generated per pound clined. This may be because the s:

006) = 1073.2/46 989 = £22 839

2007) = 1174.1/52 670 = £22 292

acy with which the company converts se ratios are measured in days to en-hat is the time from the moment the

We will explore the significance of these working capital efficiency ratios for the liquidity of the business later in this chapter.

Measuring risk

There are a number of different types of risk (R) which management (and other stakeholders) might consider important. Different risks, impact upon the firm in different ways. In Exhibit 7.13 we show the risk hierarchy.

Business risk is the overall variability in the firm's economic earnings and hence its return from all sources.

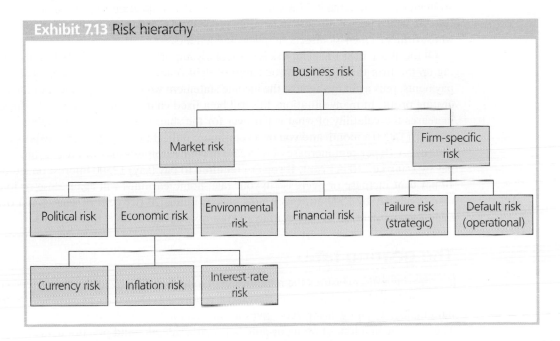

Exhibit 7.13 Risk hierarchy

Business risk is decomposed into two separate sources of risk:

● Market risk, which is variability in the firm's economic earnings caused by market-wide factors such as the environment, and the firm's economic and political context. All firms are susceptible in different degrees to this type of risk and in Chapter 13 we will show how it can be measured.

● Firm-specific risk: this is variability in the firm's economic earnings caused by internal factors which, as we shall see in Chapter 13, can be eliminated from a portfolio of investments by diversification. Such internal factors include a firm's relative success in dealing with its competitive environment, the quality or otherwise of its management, and its ability to cope with technological and other changes. This type of risk we split into two headings: strategic and operational. Strategic risk originates from the choices made by management about the long-term goals of the business and the means of achieving those goals. Weakness at this level opens the firm to the risk of progressive failure which could end in the liquidation of the firm by the shareholders, default on borrowing and receivership or acquisition by another firm. Operational risk comes from a number of sources: short-term market failure in terms of the firm's sales and hence its revenues, cost failure or some regulatory or legal shock to the firm that puts it in risk of immediate default. One key source of operational risk is created by overtrading. This is where a firm expands its business more quickly than its financial resources will allow. We consider this more fully when we look at the operating cycle of the business. Operational risk creates a potential for default whereby a firm no longer has the capacity to pay its creditors and, more specifically, its lenders. Default usually means that the company will be forced into bankruptcy or some other arrangement with its creditors.

Do note however that the risk relationships shown in Exhibit 7.13 are not absolute. There is a degree of interaction between risk at given levels. Currency risk is normally taken to be a market-wide phenomenon but it will impact upon both the revenue and costs of the firm (and hence default risk) and at the strategic level if the firm does not come up with the long-term strategies for managing it. However, there is another important reason for stressing this distinction which we will discuss in later chapters: market risk principally affects shareholders, whilst firm-specific risk affects suppliers and lenders.

Of the above risks financial risk is particularly important. Financial risk is induced by gearing up the firm through the introduction of debt finance. Debt, with its associated interest payments, puts a charge against the income statement which is independent of the firm's operating profit. In many situations this will be a fixed charge. The presence of a fixed charge increases the volatility of what is left over for the shareholders as distributable earnings. If you earn £5000 a month and you own your house outright then you are not exposed to financial risk. A 10 per cent increase or decrease in your earnings raises or lowers your take-home pay by £500, i.e., 10 per cent. If you are required to pay (say) £2500 interest on a mortgage a 10 per cent increase or decrease in your take-home earnings will again raise or lower your take home pay by £500 but this is now plus or minus 20 per cent of what is left over. This additional percentage in the volatility of your residual earnings is financial risk.

The gearing ratio

The gearing ratio measures the relationship of long-term borrowing to the owners' equity invested in the business. Sometimes the ratio is reported as long-term borrowing over total capital employed. The gearing ratio gives an indication of a firm's exposure to financial risk. There has been a long-running dispute between academics and practitioners about whether altering gearing has any affect on the value of the firm and we will return to this issue in Chapter 13. However, high levels of gearing do expose the firm to both financial and default risk. With debt financing the firm is under a contractual liability to repay capital and interest to the lender at the due date. If the firm is a limited company and is unable to pay, the lender can force the company into liquidation by appointing a receiver to run the company on the debt holders' behalf before either selling the business as a going concern or selling off the assets. If a sole trader or unincorporated partnership cannot pay its debts then the owners or partners face bankruptcy.

The gearing ratio for Marks & Spencer is:

$$\text{Gearing ratio} = \frac{\text{Long-term borrowing}}{\text{Owner's equity}}$$

Or

$$\text{Gearing ratio} = \frac{\text{Long-term borrowing}}{\text{Total capital employed}} \times 100$$

where total capital employed is equal to long-term borrowing plus owner's equity.

The second version of the ratio is preferable as it has a range from zero to 100 per cent, whilst the former version has a range of zero to infinity, which is difficult to interpret and to make valid comparisons between firms.

For Marks & Spencer we can exploit our calculation of capital employed earlier in the chapter:

Capital employed (2006) = 1203.7 + 1133.8 = 2337.5

Capital employed (2007) = 1648.2 + 1234.5 = 2882.7

to give the gearing ratios for the two years as follows:

Gearing (2006) = 1133.8/2337.5 × 100 = 48.50 per cent

Gearing (2007) = 1234.5/2882.7 × 100 = 42.82 per cent

This represents a modest decrease in gearing, mostly brought about because the company's increasing profitability is increasing the value of the owner's equity in the balance sheet at a faster rate than the company's increase in borrowing.

Interest cover and interest gearing

Interest cover measures the number of times profit before interest and tax 'covers' the interest payment. Interest gearing measures a firm's exposure to default through non-payment of interest to debt holders. It is simply the ratio of interest paid and/or payable to the firm's profit before interest and tax. Clearly, this ratio must be less that one. Given the absence of a requirement to repay capital in the near future, interest gearing gives a better indication of a firm's real exposure to financial risk than capital gearing taken from the balance sheet.

Exhibit 7.14

	2007 £m	2006 £m
Profit on ordinary activities before taxation	936.7	745.7
Add back finance costs (interest paid and payable)	143.0	134.9
Profit before interest payable	1 079.7	880.6
Interest cover (profit before interest/interest)	7.55	6.53
Interest gearing (1/interest cover)	13.2%	15.3%

Cost or operational gearing

Cost gearing is the proportion of fixed to total operating costs in the income statement. The higher the level of fixed costs in a firm's cost structure, the more vulnerable that firm is to fluctuations in profitability. If a firm, for example, has a 100 per cent cost gearing that would imply that any variation in turnover would immediately impact upon the operating profit of the business. This ratio is valuable when attempting to assess the exposure to business risk that a firm faces as a result of its internal cost flexibility.

In the operating profit statement for Marks & Spencer we count the cost of sales and the employee costs as variable, the remainder as fixed (Exhibit 7.15):

Operating cash flow to maturing obligations

This liquidity ratio has been used in a number of studies to test the likelihood of company failure. It measures the ratio of operating cash flow to what are sometimes referred to as 'maturing obligations' or, as you now know them, short-term liabilities. Clearly, the first call on a company's cash is to pay off the obligations that are currently falling due (hence the term maturing). The larger this ratio the greater will be the surplus liquidity generated by the firm.

The operating cash flow figures are highlighted in a company's cash flow statement and its short-term liabilities in the balance sheet. For Marks & Spencer, this ratio stands at:

$$\text{Operating cash flow to maturing obligations (2006)} = 1197.5/2017 \times 100$$
$$= 59.37 \text{ per cent}$$
$$\text{Operating cash flow to maturing obligations (2007)} = 1443.3/1606.2 \times 100$$
$$= 74.55 \text{ per cent}$$

This ratio was shown to be in excess of 15 per cent for successful firms and −5 per cent or less for failing firms, within five years of eventual collapse. Clearly Marks & Spencer is not in that unhappy state, and indeed the ratio has shown a significant improvement over the last twelve months.

Operating cycle analysis

When we considered the working capital efficiency ratios for Marks & Spencer we noted that on average the company takes 14 days to pay its suppliers, holds its inventory for an average of 29 days and receives cash from its customers within three days.

This means that for 17 days (32 − 15) on average the company is without cash to pay its suppliers. To what extent is this a problem? It would appear that the company is somewhat 'cash-dry' for ten days, in that it is having to finance its inventory holding out of its own cash resources. This would become a problem if the company were to rapidly expand its sales because the expansion would make the company less and less 'liquid', drawing cash from its cash account to pay its creditors ahead of the cash inflow from customers. However, it is not quite as bad as it seems because the volume of cash arriving from customers at day 32 is larger than the volume of cash being paid to suppliers. So as this operating cycle is being continuously repeated we should extend the supplier payment period for comparison purposes by the

Exhibit 7.19 Operating cash cycle for a retailer (quotations to nearest day)

studies is that the
ing failure and another not. The Beaver failure ra
the firm's ability to meet its obligations in the form of outstanding debt. It can al
preted as the maximum interest rate liability that could be sustained on the current borrowing from its operating cash flow.

ratio of the company's turnover to its credit purchases. Using the cost of sales as a close approximation to this figure:

Corrected creditor age $= 14.7 \times 8588.1/5246.9 = 24$ days

In straightforward terms what this correction means is that for a given volume of sales, the receipts from customers are sufficient to cover 24 days of payments to suppliers for purchases. The comparison of 32 days to 24 days is much more favourable but suggests that the company still has some work to do in getting its stock holding period down. This difference in days means that the company has to finance two days of its cost of sales out of its own resources, i.e.:

Short-term liquidity requirement $= 2/365 \times 5246.9 = £28.75$ million

Review activity 7.7 Calculate the operating cycle analysis for Marks & Spencer plc for 2006 and estimate the reduction in its liquidity requirement from 2006 to 2007.

✓ **Check the answer to this Review activity at the back of the book (see page 507)**

Assessing the significance of the accounting ratios

On their own, or indeed taken from one year to the next, it is difficult to interpret the significance of particular ratios for a business. There are broadly three ways that ratios can be used. They can be compared with some standard, compared over time or compared with other similar companies.

Standard analysis

With this approach the chosen ratio is compared with some 'ideal value' that is either theoretically deduced or can be inferred from the firm's own budgets and business planning documents. For reasons we have discussed above a norm for the current asset ratio is one. However, the more usual standards are ones that have been created by the firm as it sets up its business plans and budgets incorporating the targets that management is seeking to achieve.

Time series analysis

This is where ratios are collected over a sequence of accounting periods and compared. Five years is often regarded as a minimum time period with ten to twelve years being necessary to extrapolate trend figures. Reviewing ratios over time allows trends and turning points in the fortunes of the business to be determined. This type of approach is most suited to the risk and failure ratios, although it is important to note any structural changes which have occurred with the firm over the time period in question. Substantial acquisitions, disposals or mergers can invalidate the significance of any time series analysis.

Cross-sectional analysis

With this approach, ratios are collected from different companies that have comparable businesses to the one being investigated or from a single company that is regarded as a market leader. In some industries it is relatively straightforward to find a comparator that is meaning-ful. In Marks & Spencer's situation it would be difficult to find another UK company which had a similar business range, size and form of capitalisation with which to make comparison. Cross-sectional analysis using both financial and non-financial measures for comparison is re-ferred to as 'benchmarking'. In benchmarking the comparators can be either *in-industry* where comparison is being made of business performance in products or markets, or *out-industry* where comparison is being sought with what is deemed to be best business practice.

Review activity 7.8 Recalculate as many of the above ratios as you can but using the firm's continuing operations from the income statement rather than the total figures as used in the examples above. To what extent does this alter your perception of the performance of the business?

Completing the narrative

Our analysis of the market context in which Marks & Spencer operates and the financial in-formation that they have provided has led us to a position where we can come to a number of conclusions about the business. However, before doing so it is worth pausing to consider the limitations of the type of financial exercise that we have undertaken.

Limitations of ratios

Ratios, like any other financial technique, need to be interpreted with care. There will be a number of potential biases and inaccuracies in the underlying data, as well as alternative methods for calculating the ratios themselves that can cause difficulty. Here are some of the most obvious pitfalls.

1. Underlying accounting principles

Any ratio is necessarily dependent not only on the accuracy of the financial data on which it is based but also on the fairness with which the financial data represents the underlying economic reality. There are many stages on the journey from the fundamental transactions upon which the economics of a business are built to the final audited financial report used in our analysis. This journey involves collecting, categorising and manipulating figures and each stage involves the applications of both rules and judgement as various accounting principles are applied. As we have seen in the earlier chapters of this book, even the application of the matching principle to the recognition of revenues and costs is open to a variety of interpretations. This problem is particularly acute when making comparisons between earnings figures between organisations and attempting to value businesses using earnings-based investment ratios.

2. Timing problems

Many businesses such as Marks & Spencer are subject to heavy seasonality in their patterns of sales. A retailer, for example, might expect their heaviest selling season in November and December and if the company has a year-end on 31 December it would be likely to show low levels of stocks, high cash balances and increased receivables and payables. Marks & Spencer has a 31 March year-end which avoids the problem. Large construction businesses may have large contracts that produce sudden and dramatic changes to their reported figures, whilst com-panies that buy and let property often collect their rents on quarter days. For any particular company it is worth enquiring whether the nature or seasonality of its trade may have a distorting effect on the accounts it publishes and, therefore, any ratios that you may produce.

3. Fraudulent manipulation and window dressing

High-profile cases such as Enron and WorldCom have led many to question the underlying truthfulness of accounting numbers. Distortion can arise from two sources: the fraudulent misappropriation of company funds or assets and the use of 'creative' accounting practices to present financial reports that favour a view that management is trying to put across. The surest way to detect the latter is through very careful reading of the accounts and the rigorous search for the explanation of year-on-year differences that are not explained by changes in economic or market conditions. Such window dressing boils down to a very simple set of strategies:

- accelerating revenue by recognising payments received before they have been earned
- decelerating revenue by ignoring income in the current financial year
- accelerating expenditures by the over-rapid depreciation of assets or amortisation of goodwill, or treating capital expenditures as current charges to the income statement
- decelerating expenditures by counting them as capital expenditure in the balance sheet rather than charges to the income statement
- hiding unprofitable assets by selling them and leasing them back or by transferring them to associate companies or joint ventures which are not fully consolidated but are under the effective control of the parent company
- overstating the value of assets by the aggressive use of the 'mark to market' principle where assets are revalued to their current open market value
- increasing liabilities by the recognition of provisions for future events that are not fully justified
- ignoring future liabilities and not making full provision for future losses.

There is a useful technique for deciding whether there is systematic misstatement in the income statement. Take the current year operating profit and add back depreciation and amortisation. This figure should then be divided by the operating cash flow from the cash flow statement. This ratio should be approximately one and significant variance year on year would require investigation.

For Marks & Spencer the figures are:

$$(\text{Operating profit} + \text{depreciation})/\text{operating cash flow}$$
$$(2006) = (850.1 + 274)/1183.6 = 0.95$$
$$(2007) = (1045.9 + 282.7)/1442.6 = 0.92$$

Both of these values are less than one, suggesting that the company is either reducing its earnings below what they should be or accelerating cash flow. However, the ratio will only be one if the company is at steady state — neither expanding nor contracting its sales. If it is expanding then we would normally expect the ratio to be greater than one with an addition of up to twice the percentage increase in turnover. This multiple of two is a useful rule of thumb — it may in practice be more, it may be less.

For Marks & Spencer the increase of 10 per cent in its revenue over the year leads to a maximum ratio of 1.2. We should see the actual ratio therefore between 1.0 (where the company has increased its operating cash flow in line with the increase in business) and 1.2 (where the company has not been able to increase its cash flow growth in line with its sale revenue). For a retailer selling for cash the ratio is likely to be close to one. At 0.92 Marks & Spencer is

Exhibit 7.20 Marks & Spencer plc — reconciliation of operating profit and operating cash ratio

	2007	2006
	£m	£m
Operating profit	**1 045.9**	850.1
Increase in inventories	**(42.8)**	(42.2)
Decrease/(increase) in receivables	**12.5**	(4.1)
Payments to acquire leasehold properties	**(13.5)**	(38.0)
Increase in payables	**136.6**	128.0
Exceptional operating cash outflow (see note 29F)	**(4.2)**	(14.6)
Depreciation and amortisation	**282.7**	274.0
Share-based payments	**27.3**	24.7
(Profit)/loss on property disposals	**(1.9)**	5.7
Cash generated from operations – continuing	**1 442.6**	1 183.6

a little lower than we would expect, but much of the difference can be explained by movements in its working capital.

4. The impact of price changes

If the balance sheet has been maintained at historic cost rather than fair value any balance sheet components within a ratio are likely to be understated because of the impact of price changes on the business. The most significant impact is likely to be on balance sheet-based return measures such as return on capital employed, return on fixed capital employed and return on fixed assets. It is possible to make rough and ready correction to the balance sheet figures by adjusting the values in the balance sheet to reflect changing prices. However, these adjustments will only be approximations at best.

Constructing the narrative

Once you have completed your analysis, focusing on ratios that address the issues you have identified, your next task is to make the necessary inferences about the performance, efficiency, risk and liquidity of the business and to attempt to answer the questions you have posed. It may well be that some of the ratios provide their own answer: in the case of Marks & Spencer, for example, the liquidity ratios are deteriorating and this suggests it is largely down to the continuing capital investment programme and the repayment of debt falling due in the current year. Other ratios such as those measuring performance need to be compared with other businesses comparable with Marks & Spencer: Next plc is the leading contender. For this you will need to find other information sources. Other ratios such as those that are indicative of financial distress need to be measured over at least five years of back data or possibly longer. Some ratios such as gearing and payout may actually be irrelevant to the performance of the business, for reasons we discuss in Chapters 13 and 14.

However, whichever way you decide to proceed, the analysis you have conducted so far should allow you to construct a coherent narrative about the business you have investigated. We will defer our comments on Marks & Spencer until Chapter 14 when we can place them in the context of our study of the capital markets and the company's performance in those markets.

Chapter summary

This brings you to the end of your study of financial accounting. If you have grasped all that you have read – very well done. You now have a conceptual model of the financial reporting system, you can construct simple accounts from the basic transactions and you can predict the consequences of your business decisions on the financial accounts. Furthermore, you have the tools and the methods to deconstruct the accounting information and arrive at inferences about the finances of the business concerned based upon evidence. You now have more financial knowledge than the large majority of business managers. If you have not grasped it all, you are probably being honest and this is the stage where re-reading the last five chapters will pay dividends.

Here is a summary of the PERL framework showing the ratios (by their acronyms) covered in this chapter. This is not an exhaustive list of ratios that can be used, but it is a formidable toolkit for unpicking accounts.

Exhibit 7.21

PERFORMANCE	EFFICIENCY
ROCE	CER
ROE	FAT
RFCE	LAT
ROTA	LPR
MARGINS (Gross, Operating, Net)	Debtor age
	Creditor age
	Stock turnover (days)
RISK	**LIQUIDITY**
GEARING	CAR
INTEREST COVER	Acid test
INTEREST GEARING	Cash exhaustion ratio
COST (OPERATIONAL GEARING)	Operating cash flow to
BEAVER FAILURE RATIO	maturing obligations

Review activity 7.9   In the PERL framework above spell out the acronyms without reference to the text.

Further reading

Parker, R.H. (1999) *Understanding Company Financial Statements*, London. Penguin. This book is an absolute classic and continues to inform many years after its first publication. Very good on the interpretation of accounting information.

Penman, S. (2000) *Financial Statement Analysis and Security Valuation*, Singapore: McGraw-Hill. This is the book the academic community is talking about. Impenetrable in places but some excellent material on the estimation of earnings quality and similar matters.

Rice, A. (2002) *Accounts Demystified: How to Understand Financial Accounting and Analysis*, London: Prentice Hall. A useful supplement to this book if you want to get an alternative perspective to help you come to terms with the subject.

Schilt, H. (2002) *Financial Shenanigans: How to Detect Accounting Gimmicks and Fraud in Financial*

Exhibit 7.22

Income statement	2001	2000
Sales revenue	100	96
less cost of goods sold	40	39
Operating profit	60	57
less other expenses	20	20
Profit before interest and tax	40	37
Interest payable	10	10
Profit before tax	30	27
less corporation tax	12	11
Net profit after tax	18	16
Dividends to ordinary shareholders	6	5
Profit retained	12	11

Balance sheet	2001	2000
Fixed assets	300	300
less accumulated depreciation	100	90
Net fixed assets	200	210
Current assets		
Inventories	10	8
Receivables	10	11
Cash	5	6
	25	25
Less: Current liabilities	15	13
Net current assets	10	12
	210	198
Less Non-current liabilities	90	90
Net assets	120	108
Ordinary share capital	50	50
Share premium account	20	20
Retained profits	50	38
Capital employed	120	108

Exhibit 7.23

Balance sheet		Year +1
Fixed assets	2500	2944
Accum depreciation	1000	1294
	1500	1650
Inventories	104	115
Receivables	208	301
Cash	0	−32
	313	384
Creditors	52	57
	260	327
	1760	1977
Long-term borrowing	880	988
	880	988
Owners capital	100	100
Profit reserves	780	888
	880	988

Income statement		Year +1
Revenue	2500	2750
cost of good sold	1250	1375
Gross profit	1250	1375
Administrative expenses	400	440
Depreciation	250	294
	650	734
Earnings before interest and tax	600	641
interest paid	88	99
	512	542
Tax at 50%	256	271
Net profit for distribution	256	271
Dividends	154	163
Profit retained	102	108
	256	271

Exhibit 7.24

Interest rate	8%	Net profit margin	15%
Gearing (debt to total capital)	0.25	FAT ratio	75%
25p ordinary shares issued at	0.75	Creditor age	1 month
Current asset ratio	4.75	Debtor age	1.5 months
Retention ratio (distributable profit/retained profit)	0.8	Cash	30 000
Tax rate	25%	Gross profit margin	40%

Income statement

Sales revenue

Cost of sales _____

Gross profit

Operating costs _____

Operating profit

Interest payable

Profit before tax

Tax _____

Distributable profit

less dividends _____

Earnings per share   30p

Balance sheet

Non-current assets

Current assets

  inventories

  receivables

  cash _____

Current liabilities _____

Long term borrowings   150 000

Owners quity:

  Ordinary share capital   100 000

  Share premium account

  Profit and loss reserve _____

Case exercises

1. Using the most up to date accounts for Marks & Spencer plc found at **www.marksandspencer. co.uk** update all of the analysis in this chapter amending the conclusions along with your revised judgements about the firm's performance, efficiency, risk and liquidity.

   ....

2. Select any firm that has a public listing on an international stock exchange. For your chosen company you should obtain accounting data for the last financial year.

   You are required to undertake a full financial appraisal of the performance of the business over the year, based upon a comprehensive analysis of the company. Your written report should contain:

   (i) A statement of the principal stakeholder group for whom you will be undertaking the analysis and their likely information needs

   (ii) An analysis of the strategic issues facing the company and their likely financial implications for the firm during the year under analysis.

   (iii) An analysis of the firm's current financial position and its ability to meet the challenges posed by the issues you have identified.

Appendix to Chapter 7

Marks and Spencer plc
Consolidated income statement

	52 weeks ended 31 March 2007 £m	52 weeks ended 1 April 2006 £m
Revenue – continuing operations	**8 588.1**	7 797.7
Operating profit – continuing operations	**1 045.9**	850.1
Finance income	**33.8**	30.5
Finance costs	**(143.0)**	(134.9)
Analysed between:		
Before exceptional finance costs	**(112.6)**	(134.9)
Exceptional finance costs	**(30.4)**	—
Profit on ordinary activities before taxation – continuing operations	**936.7**	745.7
Analysed between:		
Before property disposals and exceptional items	**965.2**	751.4
Profit/(loss) on property disposals	**1.9**	(5.7)
Exceptional finance costs	**(30.4)**	—
Income tax expense	**(277.5)**	(225.1)
Profit on ordinary activities after taxation – continuing operations	**659.2**	520.6
Profit from discontinued operation	**0.7**	2.5
Profit for the year attributable to shareholders	**659.9**	523.1
Basic earnings per share	**39.1p**	31.4p
Diluted earnings per share	**38.5p**	31.1p
Basic earnings per share from continuing operations	**39.1p**	31.3p
Diluted earnings per share from continuing operations	**38.5p**	31.0p
Non-GAAP measure:		
Adjusted profit before taxation (£m)	**965.2**	751.4
Adjusted basic earnings per share from continuing operations	**40.4p**	31.4p
Adjusted diluted earnings per share from continuing operations	**39.8p**	31.1p

Consolidated statement of recognised income and expense

	52 weeks ended 31 March 2007 £m	52 weeks ended 1 April 2006 £m
Profit for the year attributable to shareholders	**659.9**	523.1
Foreign currency translation differences	**(14.0)**	11.1
Actuarial losses on retirement benefit deficit	**(8.6)**	(169.3)
Cash flow and net investment hedges		
— losses deferred in equity	**(7.4)**	(3.1)
— recycled and reported in net profit	**10.7**	(1.4)
— amount recognised in inventories	**2.1**	(3.8)
Tax on items taken directly to equity	**24.5**	80.7
Net gains/(losses) not recognised in the income statement	**7.3**	(85.8)
Total recognised income and expense for the year	**667.2**	437.3
Prior year adjustment	**48.4**	
Total recognised income and expense since last annual report	**715.6**	

Consolidated balance sheet

	As at 31 March 2007 £m	As at 1 April 2006 (restated) £m
ASSETS		
Non-current assets		
Intangible assets	**194.1**	163.5
Property, plant and equipment	**4 044.5**	3 575.8
Investment property	**25.1**	38.5
Investment in joint venture	**9.3**	9.0
Other financial assets	**3.0**	3.3
Trade and other receivables	**247.0**	242.8
Deferred tax assets	**11.6**	83.9
	4 534.6	4 116.8

(Continued)

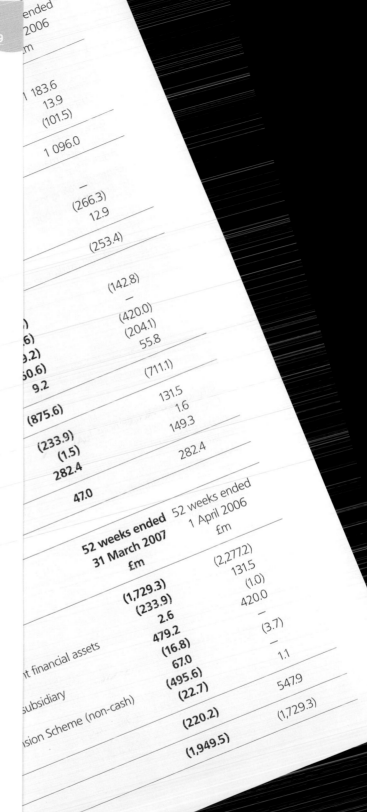

3. EXPENSE ANALYSIS

	2007 £m	2006 £m
Revenue	8 588.1	7 797.7
Cost of sales	(5 246.9)	(4 812.1)
Gross profit	3 341.2	2 985.6
Selling and marketing expenses	(1 779.2)	(1 625.7)
Administrative expenses	(584.1)	(522.7)
Other operating income	66.1	18.6
Profit/(loss) on property disposals	1.9	(5.7)
Operating profit	1 045.9	850.1

The selling and marketing expenses and administrative expenses in the table above are further analysed in the table below:

	2007			2006		
	Selling and marketing expenses £m	Administrative expenses £m	Total £m	Selling and marketing expenses £m	Administrative expenses £m	Total £m
Employee costs (see note 10A)	928.8	245.3	1 174.1	844.9	228.3	1 073.2
Occupancy costs	310.5	62.4	372.9	276.2	49.2	325.4
Repairs, renewals and maintenance of property	55.4	19.1	74.5	73.0	17.2	90.2
Depreciation and amortization	264.4	18.3	282.7	243.5	30.5	274.0
Other costs	220.1	239.0	459.1	188.1	197.5	385.6
Operating expenses	1 779.2	584.1	2 363.3	1 625.7	522.7	2 148.4

4. PROFIT BEFORE TAXATION

	2007 £m	2006 £m
The following items have been included in arriving at profit before taxation:		
Depreciation of property, plant, and equipment		
— Owned assets	266.8	259.2
— Under finance leases	1.7	2.1
Amortisation of intangibles	14.2	12.7
(Profit)/loss on property disposals	(1.9)	5.7
Operating lease rentals payable		
— Property	143.4	127.1
— Fixtures, fittings and equipment	7.2	8.5
Exceptional finance costs (see note 5)	30.4	—

5. FINANCE COSTS/INCOME

	2007 £m	2006 £m
Finance costs:		
Interest payable on bank borrowings	4.1	4.2
Amortisation of issue costs of bank loans	1.5	2.3
Interest payable on syndicated bank facility	6.8	7.7
Interest payable on medium term notes	77.5	96.2
Interest payable on securitised loan notes	19.0	20.3
Interest payable on finance leases	2.2	2.3
Dividend on non-equity B shares	0.2	2.3
Unwinding of discount on Partnership liability to the Marks & Spencer UK Pension Scheme	1.3	—
	112.6	135.3
Less: amounts included in profit from discontinued operation	—	(0.4)
Before exceptional finance costs	112.6	134.9
Exceptional finance costs[1]	30.4	—
Finance costs	143.0	134.9
Finance income:		
Bank and other interest receivable	13.0	13.4
Pension finance income (net) (see note 11C)	20.8	17.5
Fair value hedges[2]	—	0.2
	33.8	31.1
Less: amounts included in profit from discontinued operation	—	(0.6)
Finance income	33.8	30.5
Net finance costs[3]	109.2	104.4

7. DISCONTINUED OPERATION

On 31 March 2006, the Group announced the sale of Kings Super Markets Inc to a US investor group for $61.5m excluding cash in the business at the date of disposal. The disposal of the business was completed on 28 April 2006.

A. Profit from discontinued operations

	2007 £m	2006 £m
Revenue	13.0	228.2
Cost of sales	(8.2)	(144.7)
Gross profit	4.8	83.5
Net operating expenses	(4.5)	(80.5)
Net interest receivable	—	0.2
Profit before taxation	0.3	3.2
Taxation on results	—	(0.7)
Profit after taxation	0.3	2.5
Gain on disposal of subsidiary net assets	0.4	—
Taxation	—	—
Net gain on disposal	0.4	—
Profit from discontinued operation	0.7	2.5

13. INTANGIBLE ASSETS

	Goodwill £m	Brands £m	Computer software £m	Computer software under development £m	Total £m
At 3 April 2005					
Cost or valuation	69.5	80.0	32.8	5.6	187.9
Accumulated amortisation	—	(2.7)	(19.8)	—	(22.5)
Net book value	69.5	77.3	13.0	5.6	165.4

(Continued)

	Goodwill £m	Brands £m	Computer software £m	Computer software under development £m	Total £m
Year ended 1 April 2006					
Opening net book value	69.5	77.3	13.0	5.6	165.4
Additions	—	—	0.2	10.7	10.9
Transfers	—	—	9.5	(9.5)	—
Disposals	—	—	—	(0.1)	(0.1)
Amortisation charge	—	(5.3)	(7.4)	—	(12.7)
Closing net book value	69.5	72.0	15.3	6.7	163.5
At 1 April 2006					
Cost or valuation	69.5	80.0	42.3	6.7	198.5
Accumulated amortisation	—	(8.0)	(27.0)	—	(35.0)
Net book value	69.5	72.0	15.3	6.7	163.5
Year ended 31 March 2007					
Opening net book value	69.5	72.0	15.3	6.7	163.5
Additions	—	—	0.3	46.2	46.5
Transfers	—	—	25.9	(25.9)	—
Disposals	—	—	(0.1)	(1.6)	(1.7)
Amortisation charge	—	(5.3)	(8.9)	—	(14.2)
Closing net book value	69.5	66.7	32.5	25.4	194.1
At 31 March 2007					
Cost or valuation	69.5	80.0	51.2	25.4	226.1
Accumulated amortisation	—	(13.3)	(18.7)	—	(32.0)
Net book value	69.5	66.7	32.5	25.4	194.1

Goodwill relates to the acquisition of 'per una', which was acquired in October 2004 and is not amortised, but tested annually for impairment with the recoverable amount being determined from value in use calculations. The key assumptions for the value in use calculations are those regarding the discount rate, growth rates and changes in income and costs. The Group prepares discounted cash flow forecasts based on financial forecasts approved by management covering a three-year period, which takes account of both past performance and expectations for future market developments. Cash flows beyond this three-year period are extrapolated using a growth rate of 2.0%, which does not exceed the long-term average growth rate for retail businesses in the UK. Management estimates the discount rate using a pre-tax rate that reflects current market assessments of the time value of money and the risks specific to retail businesses. A pre-tax discount rate of 9.5% has been used. Brands consist of the 'per una' brand which is being amortised on a straight-line basis over a period of 15 years.

14. PROPERTY, PLANT AND EQUIPMENT

	Land and buildings £m	Fixtures, fittings & equipment £m	Assets in the course of construction £m	Total £m
At 3 April 2005				
Cost	2 412.0	3 162.1	21.6	5 595.7
Accumulated depreciation	(82.7)	(1 926.8)	–	(2 009.5)
Net book value	2 329.3	1 235.3	21.6	3 586.2
Year ended 1 April 2006				
Opening net book value	2 329.3	1 235.3	21.6	3 586.2
Exchange difference	2.2	2.0	0.3	4.5
Additions[1]	34.7	251.8	40.3	326.8
Transfers	–	20.3	(20.3)	–
Disposals	(34.1)	(6.2)	–	(40.3)
Assets of discontinued operations	(11.4)	(21.0)	(1.4)	(33.8)
Depreciation charge[2]	(10.7)	(256.9)	–	(267.6)
Closing net book value	2 310.0	1 225.3	40.5	3 575.8
At 1 April 2006				
Cost	2 392.2	3 287.1	40.5	5 719.8
Accumulated depreciation	(82.2)	(2 061.8)	–	(2 144.0)
Net book value	2 310.0	1 225.3	40.5	3 575.8
Year ended 31 March 2007				
Opening net book value	**2 310.0**	**1 225.3**	**40.5**	**3 575.8**
Exchange difference	**(2.7)**	**(1.6)**	**(0.2)**	**(4.5)**
Additions[1]	**63.9**	**578.7**	**103.3**	**745.9**
Reclassification from investment property (see note 15)	**13.2**	**–**	**–**	**13.2**
Transfers	**8.8**	**27.3**	**(36.1)**	**–**
Disposals	**(6.4)**	**(10.7)**	**–**	**(17.1)**
Depreciation charge[2]	**(13.9)**	**(254.9)**	**–**	**(268.8)**
Closing net book value	**2 372.9**	**1 564.1**	**107.5**	**4 044.5**
At 31 March 2007				
Cost	**2 468.2**	**3 653.3**	**107.5**	**6 229.0**
Accumulated depreciation	**(95.3)**	**(2 089.2)**	**–**	**(2 184.5)**
Net book value	**2 372.9**	**1 564.1**	**107.5**	**4 044.5**

[1] Additions' includes £nil (last year £5.4m) in respect of the discontinued operation (see note 7).
[2] Depreciation charge' includes £0.3m (last year £6.3m) in respect of the discontinued operation (see note 7).

The net book value above includes land and buildings of £43.7m (last year £44.9m) and equipment of £16.4m (last year £5.0m) where the Group is a lessee under a finance lease.

18. TRADE AND OTHER RECEIVABLES

	2007 £m	2006 £m
Non-current		
Other receivables	1.4	5.3
Prepaid leasehold premiums	242.8	235.8
Other prepayments and accrued income	2.8	1.7
	247.0	242.8
Current		
Trade receivables	69.0	45.2
Less: Provision for impairment of receivables	(1.1)	(3.2)
Trade receivables – net	67.9	42.0
Other receivables	51.9	27.4
Prepaid pension contributions	—	57.7
Prepaid leasehold premiums	7.6	7.6
Other prepayments and accrued income	69.3	75.8
	196.7	210.5

20. TRADE AND OTHER PAYABLES

	2007 £m	2006 £m
Current		
Trade payables	259.7	242.6
Other payables	327.8	196.6
Social security and other taxes	49.6	40.7
Pension contributions payable	40.3	—
Accruals and deferred income	366.5	387.9
	1 043.9	867.8
Non-current		
Accruals and deferred income	87.6	74.8

26. SHARE CAPITAL

	Shares	2007 £m	Shares	2006 £m
Authorised ordinary shares of 25p each	3 200 000 000	800.0	3 200 000 000	800.0
Allotted, called up and fully paid ordinary shares of 25p each:				
At start of year	1 682 437 014	420.6	1 658 095 142	414.5
Shares issued on exercise of share options	17 336 086	4.3	24 341 872	6.1
At end of year	1 699 773 100	424.9	1 682 437 014	420.6

Issue of new shares

17,336,086 (last year 24,341,872) ordinary shares having a nominal value of £4.3m (last year £6.1m) were allotted during the year under the terms of the Company's schemes which are described in note 12. The aggregate consideration received was £44.9m (last year £61.8m).

29. ANALYSIS OF CASH FLOWS GIVEN IN THE CASH FLOW STATEMENT

	52 weeks ended 31 March 2007 £m	52 weeks ended 1 April 2006 £m
A Cash flows from operating activities – continuing		
Profit on ordinary activities after taxation	659.2	520.6
Income tax expense	277.5	225.1
Interest payable and similar charges	143.0	134.9
Interest receivable	(33.8)	(30.5)
Operating profit	1 045.9	850.1
Increase in inventories	(42.8)	(42.2)
Decrease/(increase) in receivables	12.5	(4.1)
Payments to acquire leasehold properties	(13.5)	(38.0)
Increase in payables	136.6	128.0
Exceptional operating cash outflow (see note 29F)	(4.2)	(14.6)
Depreciation and amortisation	282.7	274.0
Share-based payments	27.3	24.7
(Profit)/loss on property disposals	(1.9)	5.7
Cash generated from operations – continuing	1 442.6	1 183.6
B Cash flows from operating activities – discontinued		
Profit on ordinary activities after taxation	0.7	2.5
Profit on sale of business	(0.4)	—
Income tax expense	—	0.7
Net interest receivable	—	(0.2)

(Continued)

B Cash flows from operating activities –discontinued	52 weeks ended 31 March 2007 £m	52 weeks ended 1 April 2006 £m
Operating profit	0.3	3.0
Decrease in working capital	0.1	3.5
Depreciation and amortisation	0.3	6.3
Loss on property disposals	—	1.1
Cash generated from operations – discontinued[1]	0.7	13.9
C Capital expenditure and financial investment		
Purchase of property, plant and equipment	(666.9)	(298.5)
Proceeds from sale of property, plant and equipment	2.9	45.1
Purchase of intangible fixed assets	(46.5)	(10.9)
Sale/(purchase) of non-current financial assets	0.3	(3.0)
(Purchase)/sale of current financial assets	(2.6)	1.0
	(712.8)	(266.3)
D Other debt financing		
Cash inflow/(outflow) from borrowings	21.6	(144.6)
Drawdown/(repayment) of syndicated bank facility	296.4	(200.0)
Redemption of securitised loan notes	(319.6)	(3.1)
Redemption of medium term notes	(818.2)	(58.3)
Issue of medium term notes	397.5	—
Decrease in obligations under finance leases	(2.2)	(3.0)
Redemption of B shares	(54.7)	(11.0)
	(479.2)	(420.0)
E Other equity financing		
Shares issued on exercise of employee share options	44.9	61.8
Purchase of own shares held by employee trust	(18.4)	(6.0)
Purchase of call option for Company's shares	(17.3)	—
	9.2	55.8
F Exceptional operating cash flows		
UK restructuring costs	(2.8)	(7.0)
Closure of Lifestore	(0.7)	(6.7)
Closure of European operations	(0.7)	(0.7)
Defence costs	—	(0.2)
	(4.2)	(14.6)

[1] The discontinued operation relates to Kings Super Markets Inc. There was a cash outflow of £nil (last year £5.2m) in relation to investing activities, £nil inflow (last year £0.1m) in relation to financing activities and £nil outflow (last year £0.6m) for taxation.

Additions to property, plant and equipment during the year amounting to £13.6m (last year £1.3m) were financed by new finance leases.

30. ANALYSIS OF NET DEBT

A. Reconciliation of movement in net debt

	At 1 April 2006 £m	Cash flow £m	Discontinued operations £m	Fair value movement on derivatives £m	Exchange and other non-cash movements £m	At 31 March 2007 £m
Net cash:						
Bank loans (see note 21)	(90.0)	(366.1)	—	—	—	(456.1)
Less: amounts treated as financing (see below)	5.0	318.0	—	—	—	323.0
	(85.0)	(48.1)	—	—	—	(133.1)
Cash and cash equivalents (see note 19)	367.4	(180.9)	(4.9)	—	(1.5)	180.1
Net cash per cash flow statement	282.4	(229.0)	(4.9)	—	(1.5)	47.0
Current financial assets (see note 17)	67.7	2.6	(18.8)	—	(0.6)	50.9
Debt financing:						
Bank loans, overdrafts and commercial paper treated as financing (see above)	(5.0)	(21.6)	—	—	—	(26.6)
Syndicated bank facility (see note 21)	—	(296.4)	—	—	—	(296.4)
Securitised loan notes (see note 21)	(310.8)	319.6	—	—	(8.8)	—
Medium term notes (see note 21)	(1 656.7)	420.7	—	67.0	1.8	(1 167.2)
Finance lease liabilities (see note 21)	(52.2)	2.2	2.0	—	(13.6)	(61.6)
Non-equity B Shares (see note 21)	(54.7)	54.7	—	—	—	—
Partnership liability to the Marks & Spencer UK Pension Scheme (see note 22)	—	—	—	—	(495.6)	(495.6)
Debt financing	(2 079.4)	479.2	2.0	67.0	(516.2)	(2 047.4)
Net debt	(1 729.3)	252.8	(21.7)	67.0	(518.3)	(1 949.5)

(Continued)

B. Reconciliation of net debt to balance sheet

	2007 £m	2006 £m
Balance sheet and related notes		
Cash and cash equivalents	180.1	362.6
Current financial assets (see note 17)	50.9	48.8
Bank loans, overdrafts and commercial paper (see note 21)	(159.7)	(90.0)
Syndicated bank facility (see note 21)	(296.9)	—
Medium term notes (see note 21)	(1 177.3)	(1 680.0)
Securitised loan notes (see note 21)	—	(311.7)
Finance lease liabilities (see note 21)	(61.6)	(50.2)
Non-equity B shares (see note 21)	—	(54.7)
Partnership liability to the Marks & Spencer UK Pension Scheme (see note 22)	—	(496.9)
	(1 961.4)	(1 775.2)
Financial assets included within assets of discontinued operation	—	21.7
Interest payable included within related borrowing	11.9	24.2
Total net debt	(1 949.5)	(1 729.3)

Part 3

Management accounting and control

Cost behaviour and cost/volume/profit analysis

● To distinguish between variable, fixed and other types of cost and revenue patterns.

● To be able to estimate a cost to output relationship on the basis of historical data.

● To be able to construct a flexible budget to include both linear and non-linear cost and revenue patterns.

● To create a breakeven graph over a relevant range of output.

Marginal analysis

● To understand the concept of marginal cost and marginal revenue and how to identify the output level that generates maximum profit for the firm.

Basic principles of costing

The role of management accounting is to produce information which will assist managers in their work. Management is a diverse function and there are many different activities which managers undertake. In practice, given this diversity of activity, it is easier to define management accounting in terms of the principles under which it operates rather than in terms of the decisions that managers are likely to make. Management accounting uses two matching principles which distinguish it from financial accounting:

● *Decision matching:* this is concerned with measuring the cost and revenue changes to a firm as a whole as a result of a specific decision that has been made or is being considered.

● *Allocation matching:* this is where the accountant attempts to match costs and revenues to the various productive activities which a firm undertakes or to different departments or divisions within the firm.

In this chapter we will explore both of these matching concepts. However, before we do so we will consider some important costing concepts.

Cost objects

A cost object is literally anything we wish to cost. So, for example, Virgin Atlantic may wish to cost a flight to Orlando. In that case, a flight to Orlando is the cost object. The company may wish to cost the operation of a Boeing 747-400 for a year's flying. A year's flying of such an aeroplane would therefore be the cost object. It may, at the other end of the spectrum, wish to cost the provision of a particular in-flight meal. Then that meal would be the cost object. The idea of a cost object is very general but very important because once defined we can then decide which costs are directly attributable to the given cost object and which are not.

Direct costs

Any cost which can be directly attributed to a cost object is termed a **direct cost**. To be a direct cost, a particular cost must pass the following tests:

1. Would the cost be incurred if the cost object did not exist or is the cost shared with other cost objects?
2. Is the cost measurable?

If the answer is 'no' to the first question and 'yes' to the second then the cost is almost certainly a direct cost. The word which is used to describe the process of attaching a direct cost to a cost object is 'attribution'. Direct costs are those costs which can be directly attributed to a given cost object and would not be incurred if the cost object did not exist.

Exhibit 8.1

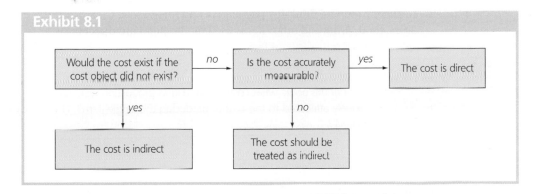

A Boeing 747 carries 216 840 litres of aviation fuel on take-off, which at a cost of 90p per litre prices a full load at £195 156

Boeing 747 on take-off

So, flying a Boeing 747-400 from London (Gatwick) to Orlando the following costs would be direct costs of a return flight:

1. Airport landing and holding charges. These are direct costs because the airline is required to pay a landing and holding charge to the airport authority every time it lands an aeroplane.

2. Fuel. Each time an aeroplane flies it carries a payload of fuel which has a fixed volume that it must carry to give it a margin of safety in case of diversion and a variable volume which is dependent upon the expected flight distance and flying conditions. It is this variable component of fuel which is the direct cost.

3. Stopover expenses for aircrew. If the aeroplane is not in a position to return immediately with the same crew then their expenses of stopover would be a direct cost of the flight.

4. In-flight food and drink for passengers and flight crew. Clearly, all the in-flight consumables, food, drink and other items used on the flight are direct costs.

Review activity 8.1   Consider this book: what costs incurred in its production were direct costs and could be uniquely attributed to the cost of producing this single item? (Use the two tests above to check.)

Indirect costs

An **indirect cost** is any cost which cannot be directly attributed to the cost object concerned. Such costs are ones which do not meet the direct cost criteria above and therefore must be allocated on some basis such as the number of labour hours involved in production, the square metres of floor space occupied by the factory or the number of particular activities conducted by an engineer. We will discuss the principal methods of allocation of indirect costs later in this chapter. However, it is important to remember that all allocation procedures are to a certain extent arbitrary.

The cost hierarchy

The cost structures of firms depend upon the type of business involved. Costs are normally classified as production, operational or strategic (business) costs. Production costs are the direct costs of manufacturing the goods or services concerned. Operational costs are the direct costs of running the operational facility, whether it be a factory or an office, on a day-to-day basis, whilst strategic- or business-level costs are those concerned with running the whole business. The **cost hierarchy** of these three levels is dependent upon the type of business. Heavy manufacturing of consumer goods and vehicles tends to be weighted towards high concentrations of direct production costs in their cost structure. Service firms with heavy investment in offices or other buildings tend to be weighted towards more strategic costs. Every firm has its own cost structure depending upon its value creation processes, its markets, its internal structure and management as well as a wide range of network issues such as the way it distributes its products and the deals it can put together with its suppliers.

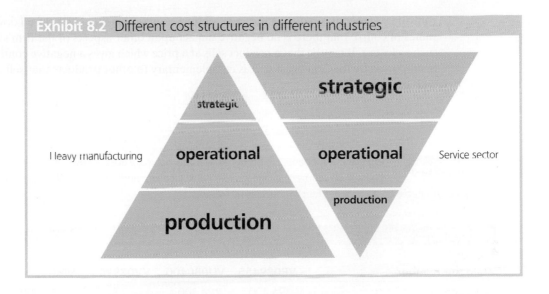

Exhibit 8.2 Different cost structures in different industries

Revenue attribution and allocation

Generally management accountants speak about **cost objects** because their primary concern is with costing different aspects of the business's activities. However, the concept of 'direct' and 'indirect' can also be applied to revenue. Direct revenue is that revenue which can be directly attributed to the revenue object concerned. Indirect revenue is that which can only be allocated.

Financial realities   The university receives undergraduate tuition fees of £1100 per annum from each student and a per capita grant from the funding council of £1600. It also receives a block grant of £6 500 000 for teaching from the funding council.

In this case, assuming that the student is the 'revenue object' then the direct revenue is £2700 as this income passes the tests above applied to revenue rather than costs. The £6 500 000 is a block grant and although loosely tied to the admissions targets must be allocated if the university wished to calculate a 'revenue per student' figure. In this case a fairly straightforward allocation would be to divide the block grant by the total number of students registered. However, because in practice certain subjects are classed as 'laboratory' subjects in that they require expensive equipment, then a more complex method of allocation may be chosen.

Contribution and contribution margin analysis

'Contribution' is a term used to describe the surplus made by any product, department or division of a firm that is a contribution to the overall profitability of the business. Contribution is therefore the difference between the revenue and the direct costs which can be matched to a particular 'revenue' or 'cost' object. **Contribution margin** is the name given to the ratio of contribution to sales revenue attributable to a given revenue or cost object:

Contribution margin ratio = contribution/sales revenue × 100

Contribution is the surplus that the firm should seek to maximise if it wishes to maximise profits and, generally speaking, if a given product, activity or part of a firm is making a negative contribution then it is reducing the value of the business and should be closed down. This assumes of course that there is no negative impact upon other aspects of the firm's business by such a closure. It may be that a product sells at a price which gives a negative contribution but is supported by the firm because it is complementary to other products that sell at a considerable surplus.

Financial realities   Aggretti Components plc produces four mechanical valves for the oil refining industry in a separate department within its mechanical components division. The sales revenue and direct costs attributable to each of the four products is as follows:

Exhibit 8.3

Product Catalogue number	VP089455	VU080400	VV089900	VM080411
Sales revenue	396 400	724 300	832 560	750 900
Direct costs				
materials and components	−178 380	−144 860	−374 652	−262 815
labour	−237 840	−507 010	−333 024	−225 270
other direct production costs	−39 640	−36 215	−33 302	−90 108

Other costs of £85 600 are directly attributable to this department but cannot be directly attributed to any one of the four products.

The calculation of each product's contribution and its contribution margin ratio is straightforward. In Exhibit 8.4 we show the product contribution for each valve, the totals for the department (with the average product contribution), and the departmental contribution when the departmental costs of £85 600 are deducted.

Exhibit 8.4

Product Catalogue number	VP089455	VU080400	VV089900	VM080411	Total
Sales revenue	396 400	724 300	832 560	750 900	2 704 160
Direct costs					
materials and components	−178 380	−144 860	−374 652	−262 815	−960 707
labour	−237 840	−507 010	−333 024	−225 270	−1 303 144
other direct production costs	−39 640	−36 215	−33 302	−90 108	−199 265
Product contribution	−59 460	36 215	91 582	172 707	241 044
Product contribution margins (%)	−15	5	11	23	8.91

	Total
Total product contribution	241 044
Less departmental overheads	−85 600
Departmental contribution	155 444
Departmental contribution margin (%)	5.75

Note that the first product has a negative contribution margin. Removing this item from production should increase the value of the firm. To test this, recalculate the analysis but exclude product VP089455:

Exhibit 8.5

Product Catalogue number	VU080400	VV089900	VM080411	Total
Sales revenue	724 300	832 560	750 900	2 307 760
Direct costs				
materials and components	–144 860	–374 652	–262 815	–782 327
labour	–507 010	–333 024	–225 270	–1 065 304
other direct production costs	–36 215	–33 302	–90 108	–159 625
Product contribution	36 215	91 582	172 707	300 504
Product contribution margins (%)	5	11	23	13.02

Total product contribution	300 504
Less departmental overheads	–85 600
Departmental contribution	214 904
Departmental contribution margin (%)	9.31

As you can see, this closure decision has transformed the contribution made by the department as a whole to the firm, boosting the average product contribution from 8.91 per cent to 13.02 per cent and the department's contribution margin from 5.75 per cent to 9.31 per cent. The closure strategy has certainly transformed this department's fortunes but there may be unforeseen consequences if the elimination of this product damages the firm's overall market position or its reputation for carrying a full product line.

Review activity 8.2 Before recommending discontinuing valve VU080400 from the product line what alternative strategies would be open to management which, if successful, could increase the departmental contribution above that shown following the closure strategy?

✓ Check the answer to this Review activity at the back of the book (see page 509).

The measurement of contribution and contribution margin for individual product lines and then for departments and divisions of the business as a whole, is a very powerful means for identifying areas which are adding value to the business and those which are not. The general rule is that any area of activity which generates a negative contribution should be discontinued but care must be exercised first to ensure that there is no unforeseen damage to the firm's other business and second that there is no possibility of the area concerned earning a positive contribution in the future.

Accountability centres

Firms often classify their activities, or indeed their departments and divisions into various kinds of **accountability centres**: 'revenue centres', 'cost centres, 'contribution centres' or 'profit centres'. A centre is a unit of accountability. So a revenue centre is any part of the firm to which a significant component of its revenues can be attributed. A production department making valves at our aviation firm, or the food aisles at a Marks & Spencer's store could each be classified as a revenue centre. Normally, if a part of a business is designated as a revenue centre it will also have costs that can be directly attributed to it and as a result it will almost certainly be a contribution centre as well. Some parts of the business may have costs that can be directly attributed to them but they do not earn revenues directly. Such parts of the firm are known as 'cost centres'. Service departments such as finance or general marketing would be classified as cost centres in most firms. Finally, a firm may have a substantial department or division that has a high degree of operational and business autonomy. In such cases it may decide to nominate that part of the business as a 'profit centre'.

The point about this classification is to devolve accountability to the management of the centres concerned.

Exhibit 8.6

Centre Type	Accountability	Examples	
Revenue	Direct revenue only	Sales force	Most costs (salaries, office costs etc) will be fixed and will be very small in relation to the revenue earned
Cost	Direct cost only	Service function such as finance, marketing, research and development	Significant proportion of directly attributable cost but no direct revenue
Contribution	Direct revenue and costs only	Production or sales unit such as a department within a general store, or a production line within a factory	Direct costs and revenues can be attributed but are usually too small to be regarded as an autonomous business unit
Profit	Direct and indirect revenues and costs	Department or division with a reasonable degree of autonomy in terms of policy and management	Both revenues and costs may be allocated as well as those that are directly attributed

We will return to the issue of accountability centres in the next chapter when we turn our attention to budgeting and the problems of management control.

Costing for decisions: relevant costing

Decisions are a particular type of cost object and the concept of direct costing is just as applicable to costing decisions as it is to costing the flight of a jumbo jet or the production of valves at Aggretti Components plc. In this chapter we will consider decisions which only have a short-term impact upon the value of the individual or firm. The issue of how the principles discussed here are applied to decisions with longer-term implications is dealt with in Chapter 12. The principles that underpin decision costing are as follows.

The rationality principle

Decision makers, whether they be firms, committees or individuals, have objectives. That is, they have some implicit criteria for choosing between the alternatives that are open to them. We assume that in making their decisions individuals and firms seek to maximise the value of their firm. In doing this we also assume that when they make their choices they are:

- capable of ranking the choices in front of them in terms of the objectives they have set themselves and
- they are consistent in their ranking of the alternatives.

This is known as the **rationality principle**.

Financial realities   You are deciding whether to purchase a small car and are faced with three choices: Ford Fiesta, Volkswagen Polo and Fiat Punto. If you said that you preferred the Fiesta to the Polo and the Polo to the Fiat you would be inconsistent if you also said that you preferred the Punto to the Fiesta. We assume that as a decision maker you are consistent, but can you see reasons why someone might appear to be inconsistent in their rankings?

The answer is that cars like many other things in life have many different attributes against which we can rank their value (in the widest sense) to us, such as colour, performance, comfort and price. Strictly, the assumption of consistency only applies to a single attribute (such as price). So if you preferred the Ford Fiesta to the VW Polo to the Fiat Punto on the basis of price you would be inconsistent if you then said you preferred the Fiat Punto to the VW Polo on the same grounds. In practice, decision makers often have different and conflicting objectives which lead them to make what appear to be inconsistent choices.

Review activity 8.3   Think of any decision you have made recently (choice of university or college for example) – how did you apply the rationality principle in the choice you made? To what extent did other factors such as social or peer pressure interfere with your decision making?

The bygones principle

The **bygones principle** concerns the fact that decisions are made at a specific point in time. At that point in time the only thing that should matter to the decision maker is the future consequences that result from a particular decision. What is past is past and all costs incurred by the firm prior to the decision point will be indirect with respect to that decision. It is one of the toughest lessons in finance that 'bygones are bygones'. From a financial point of view, if expenditures are made prior to the point of making a decision then those costs will have been incurred no matter what decision is made. Those prior costs are known as 'sunk costs' and should not influence the choice between alternative courses of action.

The opportunity forgone principle

When costing any particular course of action from the opportunities available we measure the cost to the decision maker compared with that of undertaking the next best alternative. This idea flows directly from the rationality principle that the cost of any course of action is assessed on the basis that a decision maker will always pursue the best course of action open to them in terms of maximising their own personal value. Direct decision costs are therefore known as **opportunity costs**.

The cash difference principle

Taking these principles together, the direct cost attributable to any decision is the difference in the value of the decision maker on the assumption that a given course of action is chosen rather than the next best alternative available. This can be summarised as follows:

Opportunity cost equals the net cash loss to the decision maker as a direct result of taking a given course of action compared with the next best alternative.

If a decision does not cause any cash change to the decision maker then no opportunity cost is incurred. In the business context the management accountant's task is to isolate the cash changes to the firm which result as a necessary consequence of the decision concerned, compared with the next best alternative.

Financial realities   A manager decides to give up her job which earns a salary of £36 000 for a year to undertake a one-year MBA degree. The course fees are £8000 and she estimates her living costs to be £25 000. What is the cost of undertaking the MBA degree?

Answer: The manager's next best alternative to doing the MBA degree is staying at work for the year. This is one 'opportunity' she forgoes by doing the MBA. The other opportunity she forgoes is the ability to spend £8000 on the next best thing she would like to spend that sum of money on! The overall cost of doing the degree will therefore be £8000 + £36 000, i.e. £44 000. But what about the £25 000 – is that not part of the cost of doing the degree? The answer is 'no', the cost of living must be found whichever alternative is pursued, whether she stays at work or takes the MBA.

Taking the case of the potential MBA student we can draw up a statement (Exhibit 8.7) showing her net cash position if she takes the degree compared with the next best alternative (NBA) open to her. If she takes the MBA her salary is zero, but it is £36 000 if she stays in work and forgoes the opportunity to study for the degree. The difference of –£36 000 is directly attributable to the decision to take the MBA. The fee is only paid if she takes the MBA and is not paid otherwise. Finally, the living expenses are a net cash outflow to her whatever she does, and so the cash change as far as this decision is concerned is zero.

Exhibit 8.7

	MBA	NBA	Cash change
Salary	0	36 000	–36 000
Fees	–8 000	0	–8 000
Living expenses	–25 000	–25 000	0
Opportunity cost =			–44 000

Estimating opportunity costs in practice

When estimating the opportunity cost associated with a decision it is necessary to:

1. Identify the choices open to the decision maker.
2. Identify which resources such as materials, labour and fixed capital plant will be used up if a given choice is exercised.
3. Ascertain whether the resources to be consumed are held by the decision maker or not.
4. Decide the opportunity cost of each resource in relation to the economic value the decision maker places upon them.
5. Sum the opportunity costs of the resources consumed and which can be unambiguously matched to the decision. This will give the total opportunity cost of the decision concerned.

Of these steps, (4) is the one which in practice causes the most difficulty. In the following case exercise, we analyse the basic elements of opportunity costing at the operational level with some implications at the production level of decision-making.

In order to explore the issues involved in costing for decisions and some of the logic of opportunity costs here is a practical example taken from the building industry. We have simplified the issues somewhat but this example is very typical of those in many areas of industry and commerce.

Financial realities   Pegg Ltd is a small building firm which undertakes projects for schools and other local government agencies and has found it difficult to get work in recent months. Pegg's management is considering the terms of a small construction project for a private client. Although Pegg does not normally engage in this type of building work the firm does have the capacity to complete the contract without any additional capital investment. The building could be completed in four weeks and the client is prepared to pay a cash price upon completion of £60 000. The construction project will involve the following.

Labour: 1500 unskilled hours will be required. Men and women capable of doing this work can be hired on subcontract at a rate of £15 per labour hour. In addition, four skilled tradespeople will be required:

● a carpenter, who has been served with an immediate redundancy notice, but by mutual consent this could be delayed until the end of the project. A compensation package of £8000 had been agreed but if the project does proceed a revised figure of £8400 will be paid;

● an electrician, who could be redeployed from other work on which he is currently engaged, which would have to be subcontracted at a cost of £1100;

● a plasterer/bricklayer, who would have been on stand-by duties for the month, on full pay, as no other work is available;

● a plumber, who for many years they have hired out for plumbing work to a number of firms locally. The annual contribution earned by this plumber to the firm is estimated to be £36 000 for the current financial year after his salary costs have been taken into account.

Each tradesperson is paid £24 000 per annum (gross) inclusive of taxes and National Insurance, except for the plumber who is paid £30 000.

Materials: the following materials will be required to fulfil this contract:

● 200 tons of concrete mix which Pegg currently holds in stock. The mix was purchased some time previously at £36 per ton, but the contract upon which it was to be used had fallen through. Due to the short shelf life of the mix, Pegg was considering disposing of the mix to another company at £18 per ton net;

▶

- 100 cubic metres of timber had been ordered, on contract, at a purchase price of £55 per cubic metre, although it is now only due for delivery. This type of timber is used on a number of different jobs within the firm. Since ordering, its purchase price has risen to £64 per cubic metre;

- Other materials will have to be purchased at a net cost of £6700.

Stocks are valued by the firm's accountants at the lower of cost and net realisable value.

Plant and equipment: one excavator was due to be sold for £18 000 but can be held for the life of the project. However, the renegotiated price for delivery one month late will be £17 000. The original purchase price of the excavator was £90 000. The other necessary equipment can be hired at a cost of £5500 for the duration of the project. Pegg normally charges 10 per cent of the original cost of equipment as a depreciation charge in its accounts.

Other information: to date design costs have been spent on preparing for the new project. Pegg normally allocates part of its fixed overheads to projects. In this case Pegg's accountants have decided to allocate £12 000 to this project. Prior to the date of the decision Pegg had spent an estimated £2500 on estimating the job and negotiating with the customer. The managing director has also estimated that because the client is a friend and a member of his golf club that he will incur an extra £1600 of entertainment expenses if the project proceeds.

1 Identify the decision choices available

Pegg Ltd faces two alternatives, as shown in Exhibit 8.8. If we have a complete description of the decision problem then the rational choice for Pegg is governed by the relative magnitudes of the payoffs associated with the construction project. However, before proceeding Pegg would in practice consider whether other alternatives exist:

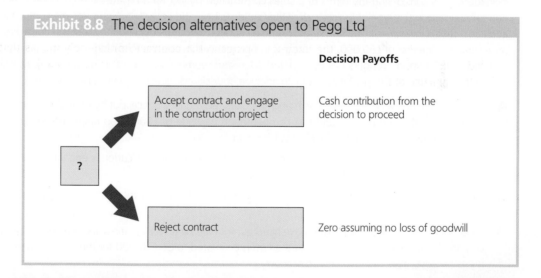

Exhibit 8.8 The decision alternatives open to Pegg Ltd

- Could an improvement be gained in the proposed contract by further, but perhaps risky, negotiations with the customer? If so, this would offer a third choice to Pegg that would have to be evaluated.

- Could the contract be assigned to someone else (a subcontractor), minimising perhaps the risks associated with this business for Pegg?

- Would acceptance of this contract lead to further business from the customer that would be more in line with Pegg's existing activities? Conversely, would rejection of this contract lead to an expensive loss of goodwill on the part of the customer?

Exhibit 8.9

Production-level costs	Operational-level costs	Business-level (strategic) costs
Materials and components likely to be procured externally	Design and development costs	Changes in costs of product marketing/advertising
Materials and components only available from other departments within the firm	Changes to operational costs attributable to the opportunity (plant, equipment, floor space)	Changes in financial costs
Energy costs and other utilities (water, waste disposal, etc.)	Changes in production support costs and procurement	Changes in costs of general management and administration
Production labour directly attributable to the opportunity concerned	Changes in production management costs	
Managerial resource at the production level (supervisory management)	Changes in quality management procedures	
Distribution and product insurance costs		

2 Identify the resources to be consumed

In the Pegg case, the decision to engage the contract immediately means that a range of resources will be used up as a result. In practice, when looking for the costs which will be incurred in any particular activity, review the cost hierarchy discussed earlier and attempt to identify those costs which are associated with the specific decision and are likely to be incurred if a given option is chosen. A listing of typical decision costs within each level of the cost hierarchy is shown in Exhibit 8.9.

3 Ascertain ownership of the resource

This step is necessary to determine whether the resources are owned by the business or must be procured from the external market. Generally, if a resource is not owned, then the cost of acquiring it will be the open-market price plus the associated costs of transport (if necessary) and all other transaction costs necessarily incurred in bringing the item concerned into a state of readiness for production. If a resource is not owned and is not available on the open market then the unavailability of that resource will mean that the particular course of action being pursued by the firm is not feasible.

4 Determine the opportunity cost of the resources consumed

In this case exercise, assuming that the facts as given above fully reflect the problem faced by Pegg's management, it is possible to identify the consequential change in cash which will occur if they decide to go ahead.

In this type of exercise it is important to be rigorous and to stick carefully to the principles that underpin this type of analysis. We will go through the analysis of cost step by step, drawing out the general lessons as we go. The cash consequences to Pegg Ltd are analysed in Exhibit 8.10, to which the following notes relate.

Exhibit 8.10 Decision-matched costs for Pegg

Pegg Ltd
Cash flow differences

Cash lost through using this resource on this contract

Cash loss to firm if contract not accepted

		Accept contract	Next Best Alternative	Difference
Unskilled labour	1500 × £15 =	−22 500	0	−22 500
Skilled trades				
Carpenter (redundancy pay)		−8 400	−8 000	−400
Carpenter (salary)	£24 000/12 =	−2 000	0	−2 000
Electrician (salary)	£24 000/12 =	−2 000	−2 000	0
Electrician (subcontract costs)		−1 100	0	−1 100
Plasterer/bricklayer (salary)		−2 000	−2 000	0
Plumber (contribution before salary)	£36 000/12 + £30 000/12 =		5 500	−5 500
Plumber (salary)	£30 000/12 =	−2 500	−2 500	0
Direct labour cost				**−31 500**
Materials				
Concrete (original purchase)	200 × £36 =	−7 200	−7 200	0
Concrete (sale opportunity lost)	200 × £18 =	0	3 600	−3 600
Timber (original purchase contractually committed)	100 × £55 =	−5 500	−5 500	0
Timber (cash cost of replacement to stock)	100 × £64 =	−6 400	0	−6 400
Other material		−6 700	0	−6 700
Direct material cost				**−16 700**
Plant and equipment				
Sale of excavator		17 000	18 000	−1 000
One month's depreciation on excavator excluded				
Other equipment		−5 500	0	−5 500
Direct plant and equipment costs				**−6 500**
Fixed overheads		−12 000	−12 000	0
Estimation and contracting costs		−2 500	−2 500	0
Entertainment costs		−1 600	0	−1 600
Decision direct cost				**−56 300**

This is the contribution earned by the plumber if he is kept on his original work

Depreciation is invariably irrelevant in a decision making context

Fixed costs and past costs are irrelevant in a decision making context

Unskilled labour will cost the firm £22 500 (1500 hours at £15 per hour). During the course of the project (or very shortly afterwards) Pegg's bank account should show a payment to the unskilled labour totalling £22 500. This figure represents the direct cash loss attributable to the use of direct labour on this project.

The carpenter was due to be made redundant. If we show the redundancy payment in the event that the contract goes ahead and on the basis that it does not, the difference is £400 which is part of the cost attributable to this opportunity. However, in addition Pegg Ltd will pay an additional salary payment that it would not otherwise have incurred of £2000 for the extra month worked. The electrician will be paid a salary irrespective of whether the project proceeds or not. The only cash difference between the decision to proceed and the decision not to is associated with the subcontracting cost of £1100. The plasterer/bricklayer would have been idle for the month in any event, so no cash change follows from the decision to proceed with the project.

Finally, we must consider the case of the plumber. This raises an important issue of principle. The plumber is already employed on other work which brings in a cash contribution to the firm of £36 000 per annum. Note, however, that this is the cash contribution after his salary cost has been deducted. In the absence of this contract, his salary would be a direct cost of the other work he does for the firm. Presumably, if that other work had not been available he too would have been made redundant. However, this new opportunity means that his time and hence his salary cost is redeployable and it is therefore not a direct cost of the other work (remember the definition of a direct cost). The contribution of the other work to the firm must be assessed before his salary cost is charged, which is as in Exhibit 8.11. The next line of the analysis reinforces the point because the plumber's salary will be the same irrespective of whichever work he is required to do.

Exhibit 8.11

Contribution after salary cost	3000
Add back salary cost	2500
Contribution of alternative work	5500

The materials costs raise issues that are more complicated: in the case of the concrete mix, the decision to proceed with the project entails the loss of the opportunity to sell the concrete. As result, proceeding means that £3600 (£18 per ton × 200) will be forgone. The original purchase price of £36 per ton (£7200 in total) is the same whichever course of action the company follows. With the timber, the decision to proceed with the project implies that the stock will be replaced, as a number of other uses exist within the firm. As a result of its use, the replacement cost will be £6400, i.e. there will be a cash flow out of the firm of £6400 which will have arisen as a direct result of accepting the project. The original contract price is irrelevant as the contract has already been entered into and the commitment to pay the £55 per cubic yard already made. The figure of £5500 will be paid for that timber irrespective of whether or not the contract proceeds. The remaining materials must be purchased at their full cost (which is their actual cash outflow to suppliers) of £6700.

The use of the excavator means that its sale must be delayed by one month, as a result of which the immediate sale price of £18 000 will be forgone and £17 000 received instead. The cash change resulting from the decision is therefore £1000. Note, however, that the depreciation charge is excluded as it does not represent a value change to the firm but is simply an internal transfer between the profit and loss account and the balance sheet. The other plant and equipment costs clearly give rise to an immediate value change to the firm.

The allocation of fixed overheads is an arbitrary allocation of expenditures associated with the decision to found and maintain the whole business and the means of production. The magnitude of the firm's overall overhead expenditure will remain unchanged by the decision to proceed with the project. The design costs have already been incurred prior to the time at which the decision has been made. At the point at which the decision is made the expenditure of £2500 has been made, irrespective of whether Pegg decides to proceed with the project or not. The design costs are what we have referred to before as 'sunk costs'. The sum of £1600 for additional entertainment will only be incurred if the decision to proceed goes ahead; this expenditure is, therefore, an opportunity cost associated with this decision.

5 Summary of the opportunity costs of the decision to proceed

The consequences of this decision-matching exercise are analysed in Exhibit 8.10. In that exhibit, the cash flows which will occur to Pegg as a whole if the contract is undertaken on the one hand or not undertaken on the other are analysed, and the difference recorded. It is this difference between the two alternatives available to the company that are the decision-matched or opportunity costs associated with this decision. Remember these are different terms describing the cost which can be directly attributed to the decision concerned measured as the difference in the overall value of the firm if it accepts the contract compared with the next best alternative. If we have done our sums correctly Pegg Ltd should be able to record a cash outflow from the firm as a direct result of the decision to proceed with this contract of £56 300. If the firm earns revenue of £60 000 from this contract a net cash contribution of £3700 will be made to all the other costs of running the firm. Given that a positive cash contribution is better than zero cash contribution (the consequence of not proceeding), it would be worthwhile for Pegg to proceed.

You will discover that some sources and in particular the Chartered Institute of Management Accountants suggest that an opportunity cost only arises when a sacrifice is involved which cannot be measured directly in cash terms. They would argue that the £56 300 above contains only one opportunity cost: the contribution lost of £5500 on the plumber's alternative work. The balance is what they term the **relevant cost** of the decision. However, the view that most economists take is that an opportunity cost arises whenever a resource such as labour, materials or capital equipment is used up. Even if these resources are freely available and can be purchased on an open market, that open market price will represent the value of the sacrifice made by the firm when deciding to use those resources.

Optimising contribution with a single resource in short supply

In order to develop the opportunity cost concept in more detail we will consider the situation where a company produces a range of products all using the same resources but where one of the resources involved is in limited supply. Our job is to allocate that resource across the alternative products so that the cash contribution of the firm is maximised. To explain we will work through an example of a company that is constrained in what it can produce by a lack of the necessary labour.

Financial realities Athens Ltd makes just four products using only labour and materials. We assume that the firm can produce fractions of units if necessary, that it wishes to maximise its contribution overall and that the labour and materials are direct costs.

Exhibit 8.12

	alpha	beta	gamma	delta
Sales price	44	62	40	82
Labour hours per unit (£20 per labour hour)	0.75	1	0.5	1.5
Materials cost per unit	20	25	20	40
Maximum demand (units)	400	300	250	1000

In Exhibit 8.12 we show the necessary production information. We are also told that the firm has a limit of 650 labour hours which cannot be relaxed in the short run. The question is what products should it manufacture, given the shortage of labour time. If we calculate the total labour required to meet the maximum demand for each product we would need to divide the demand in each case by the labour hours required to produce each unit and then sum to obtain the total:

Total labour required = 400 × 0.75 + 300 × 1 + 250 × 0.5 + 1000 × 1.5
= 2225 labour hours

The answer to the problem of which products to manufacture and how much to produce would be easy if there were no constraint on demand. The firm would identify the product which gave the maximum contribution per unit and produce all it could using the available labour. However, there is a limit to how much of each product can be sold and in this situation the best solution is found by maximising the contribution per unit of scarce resource (labour in this case) employed in production. Proceeding step by step:

Exhibit 8.13

	alpha	beta	gamma	delta
Sales price	44	62	40	82
Labour cost per unit	−15	−20	−10	−30
Materials cost per unit	−20	−25	−20	−40
Contribution per unit	9	17	10	12

1. Prepare a table of contribution per unit for each of the four products (Exhibit 8.13). Note, however, that ranking the products in order of priority for production according to their contributions per unit will not give the best result. To achieve this we need to adapt the ratio to take account of each product's utilisation of the scarce resource concerned.

2. Rank the products according to the contribution of each per unit of scarce resource:

Exhibit 8.14

	alpha	beta	gamma	delta
contribution per labour hour	12	17	20	8

Exhibit 8.15

	alpha	beta	gamma	delta
contribution per labour hour	12	17	20	8
ranking	3	2	1	4
demand taken up	300	300	250	0
labour hours per unit (Exhibit 8.12)	0.75	1.0	0.5	1.5
labour hours used	225	300	125	0

Note how the ranking has changed. Gamma is the best in that even though it has a relatively low contribution per unit, it also has the lowest rate of labour utilisation.

Contribution per labour hour (gamma) = 10/0.5 = £20

3. Allocate the 650 labour hours to each product, working from the best down to the worst in terms of the ranking (Exhibit 8.15)

Note how we have done this: we have produced as much gamma as we can (that uses $250 \times 0.5 = 125$ labour hours), followed by beta (which uses 300 labour hours), followed by alpha. We could produce 400 units of alpha but because we only have 225 hours of labour left we are limited to:

Production of alpha = labour hours available/labour utilisation per unit

= 225/0.75

= 300 units

4. We now have an optimum production plan:

Exhibit 8.16

	alpha	beta	gamma	delta
Amount produced and sold	300	300	250	0
Sales revenue	13 200	18 600	10 000	0
Labour cost	−4 500	−6 000	−2 500	0
Materials cost	−6 000	−7 500	−5 000	0
Product contribution	2 700	5 100	2 500	0

The total contribution earned by the firm from this production plan is £10 300.

Now, no matter how you try to reconfigure the utilisation of labour you will not be able to devise a plan with a greater level of contribution overall. Our analysis also reveals something else.

The opportunity cost of labour

Labour time in this case is limited, just as in the case with the plumber in Pegg Ltd discussed earlier. What would be the cost of taking an hour of labour time out of production and putting it to use on something different? If we recast the production plan but with just 649

Exhibit 8.17

	alpha	beta	gamma	delta
Amount produced and sold	298.67	300	250	0
Sales revenue	13 141.33	18 600	10 000	0
Labour cost	−4 480.00	−6 000	−2 500	0
Materials cost	−5 973.33	−7 500	−5 000	0
Product contribution	2 688.00	5 100	2 500	0

labour hours available rather than 650 hours then the number of hours available for alpha production will fall from 225 to 224 hours. As a result the number of units of alpha that can be produced and sold will fall to:

$$\text{Production of alpha} = \text{labour hours available/labour utilisation per unit}$$
$$= 224/0.75$$
$$= 298\tfrac{2}{3}\ \text{units}$$

(Note: this is allowed because the firm can make fractional units)

The revised plan has a product contribution overall of £10 288 – a difference of £12 per unit from the original plan. So the cash contribution lost by the firm as a result of the decision to redeploy one labour hour is £12. Note, however, that this is the cash lost after the cost of the labour hour has been deducted so the overall cash loss to the firm will be:

$$\text{Total cost of redeployment} = \text{contribution loss before labour cost}$$
$$= £20 + £12 = £32$$

So the total opportunity cost of labour is £32. Another way of thinking about this issue is to work out how much it would be worth to the firm if it could hire just one extra labour hour. In this case the firm would be able to produce 301⅓ units. Because alpha earns a contribution of £9 per unit the firm would earn an extra £12 in contribution from one extra labour hour. In calculating that extra contribution we have included a labour cost at a rate of £20 per hour so it would be worthwhile for the firm to pay up to £32 per labour hour to gain extra staff time.

The total opportunity cost can be seen as containing two elements:

- the open-market price of the scarce resource if the labour were freely available (£20 in the above example)
- the scarcity premium being the change in the total contribution from production if one extra unit were made available (£12 in the above example).

This information is invaluable to a firm. First, it reveals the full cost of redeploying labour internally. Second, it reveals the maximum amount a firm would be prepared to pay above the current labour rate to hire new staff on short-term contract. Third, it suggests that an overtime rate of anything up to £32 per labour would be worthwhile.

FYI In practice this type of exercise is limited by the assumptions made in setting up the problem. However, the logic of the analysis is still sound in that to measure the full cost of using a scarce resource it is important to look at what is lost and that is measured in terms of lost contribution.

Make-or-buy decisions

We can bring together the costing concepts we have developed so far to throw light on an important type of decision that many firms face. Is it better for a firm to make a component to be used in its manufacturing or to buy the product in from an external supplier? Decisions of this type present mutually exclusive alternatives either of which can have a significant impact upon the firm. The simple rule for deciding whether to 'make' or to 'buy' is to choose that alternative which minimises the opportunity costs of production.

Financial realities Athens Ltd requires a component called an Omicron on its production of the Zeta. The direct cost of producing each Zeta is £60 per unit excluding labour time of two hours per unit. The labour rate is £20 per hour but as we have already noted the labour is fully deployed on other production. The purchase price of each Omicron from a component manufacturer is £110 per unit.

Exhibit 8.18

	Make	Buy
Direct cost	£60	£110
Labour cost = 2 × £32	64	0
Opportunity cost	£124	£110

Note that we have included the full opportunity cost of using the resources necessary to produce each Omicron. The labour cost for the 'make decision' has been included at its full value of £32 to include the contribution lost if this labour is redeployed. In this case, the 'buy' decision is the one that produces the lowest cost.

In reality, buy-or-make decisions will involve a number of other factors: buying a component requires establishing and maintaining a relationship with the supplier, the cost of arranging the purchase contracts and ensuring delivery when required. Making a component often involves hidden 'internal' management costs and the redeployment of a wide range of different resources such as factory space, design time and product testing. The full opportunity cost of all these 'hidden' resources may be very high, especially if the firm is under a number of different capacity constraints.

Cost behaviour and cost/volume/profit analysis

In many situations a firm will not be making a decision about whether to go ahead with a contract or not, as in Pegg's case above, but rather will be choosing the most appropriate level of output at which to produce. These are some typical output decisions:

- The quantity of oil to produce at a refinery.
- The number of copies of a book to print as a batch.
- The number of flights per day to Orlando during the holiday season.
- The number of loaves baked daily in a bakery.

Some direct production costs will vary with the level of output chosen and these are known as **variable costs**. 'Fixed cost' is the general term given to all other costs which do not vary with the level of output. In this section we will explore the different patterns of cost behaviour and how accountants have traditionally analysed the impact on a business of choosing different output levels.

Cost variation

Variable costs are those that are expected to change directly with output level. However, many costs exhibit different degrees of variability: some may have 'step changes' at set levels of outputs and others may be curved. Taking variable costs first, a graph of such a cost against output level would be of this type:

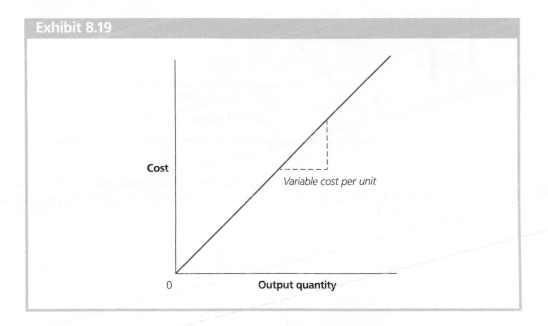

Exhibit 8.19

At zero output the cost will be zero. As output rises the cost rises in direct proportion to the volume produced.

A printer charges a publisher a variable charge of £1.80 per copy of a new booklet. The publisher would like to know the variable cost of production to any level up to 5000 copies. Our first step is to produce a chart of the variable cost against the number of copies produced (see Exhibit 8.20). These data can then be shown on a cost output graph as shown in Exhibit 8.21.

Exhibit 8.20

Copies produced (output)	0	1000	2000	3000	4000	5000
Variable cost per copy	0	1800	3600	5400	7200	9000

The variable cost per unit is the direct cost, which is £1.80 per unit.

Exhibit 8.21

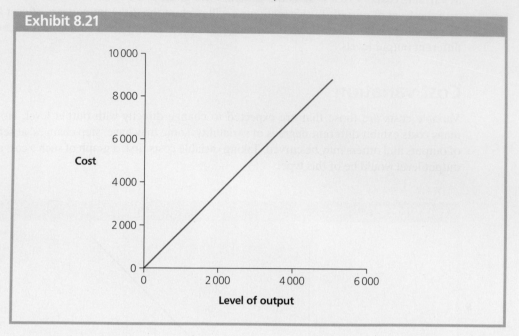

Other costs may be direct costs of the print run as a whole but are indirect costs at the level of the individual book. These other costs are fixed with respect to output and have a typical graph as follows:

Exhibit 8.22

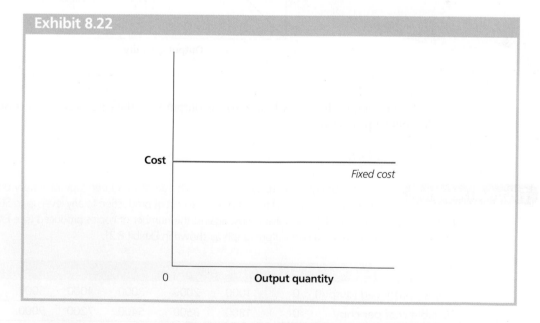

In practice there are many different patterns of cost variation that will be observed in practice. In Exhibit 8.24 we show eight different cost patterns.

Financial realities The printer also charges a fixed cost per print run of £8000. Show the graph of this cost. The graph for this is as shown:

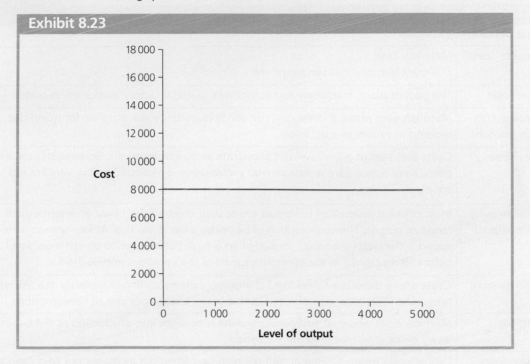

Exhibit 8.23

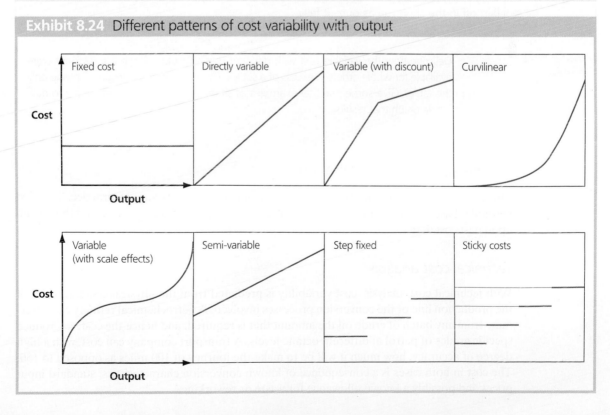

Exhibit 8.24 Different patterns of cost variability with output

Typically we find that the following production level costs fall into these different categories:

Exhibit 8.25

Cost pattern	Examples
Variable cost	Materials cost Energy (electricity, gas consumption)
Fixed cost	The cost of plant, machinery and equipment. General factory and/or office costs.
Variable cost with discount	Materials cost where a lower cost per unit is quoted, by the supplier, for quantities ordered in excess of a set level.
Curvilinear	Costs that start at a low level but accelerate as output increases. Some materials are particularly scarce (rare metals such as palladium and platinum) and in very limited supply.
Variable (with scale effects)	Most physical production processes are at their most efficient over an intermediate range of output. The consumption of petrol by a car is like this. At low speeds (where speed is the output variable) consumption is high but reduces to an optimum level before rising rapidly as the maximum speed of the vehicle is approached.
Semi-variable	Costs where there is a linked fixed charge (so-called standing charges for the use of telephone lines is an example) and then a usage charge per unit of consumption.
Step fixed	Machine costs where an additional machine is brought into production as the capacity levels on existing machines are exceeded.
Sticky costs	Labour costs where additional staff are recruited as output increases but who cannot be laid off in the short run as output falls.

Review activity 8.4   Describe how the variable cost with discount graph would change if a discount were available for whole orders in excess of a set level (rather than the discount applying only to the excess as stated in the table). Give some practical examples of situations where discounts apply to bulk orders and sketch the cost/usage graph that results.

Estimating cost variability

There are two ways that accountants use to estimate how costs vary in practice. The first method is based upon the fundamental characteristics of the process involved and the second upon past cost data.

Technical cost analysis

With technical cost analysis, cost variability is predicted from the physical characteristics of the production line or the conversion processes involved. A petrochemical refinery can determine from any batch of crude oil the amount that is required, and hence the cost, to produce specific grades of petrol at different octane levels. A transport company can cost, with a high degree of accuracy, how much it will be to make the journey of 100 miles as opposed to 150. The cost in both cases is a consequence of known conversion characteristics, standard input prices and possibly a known allowance for waste or reworking.

Review activity 8.5 Carefully cost a day's journey to a major city. Your analysis should include the fares for the journey or the exact costs of using a car, the costs of extras such as newspapers, cups of coffee, meals out. How much of the cost can you predict accurately and how much do you need to estimate? To what extent could you use prior experience in determining the costs?

Statistical cost estimation

Statistical cost estimation is based upon the idea that actual cost data when plotted against output levels achieved in the past can allow us to estimate the way that cost and output are related for current purposes.

If total cost is assumed to be made up of a fixed cost and a variable cost only, the cost/output relationship should look like this:

Exhibit 8.26

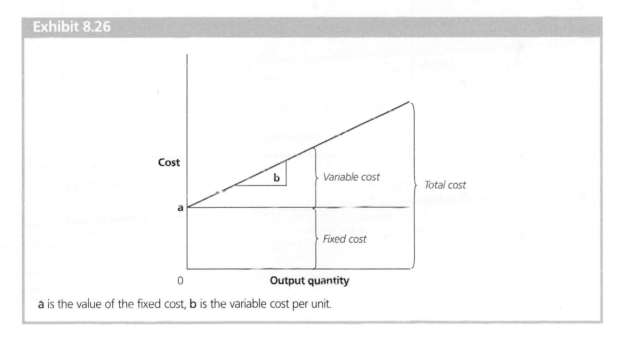

a is the value of the fixed cost, b is the variable cost per unit.

Financial realities An airline company recorded the following costs against the number of flights made available for its charter business to the Far East.

Exhibit 8.27

Month	Flights (output)	Cost
1	10	835 000
2	13	940 000
3	11	1 075 000
4	6	480 000
5	9	680 000
6	11	875 000

Plotting cost against output gives the following scattergram:

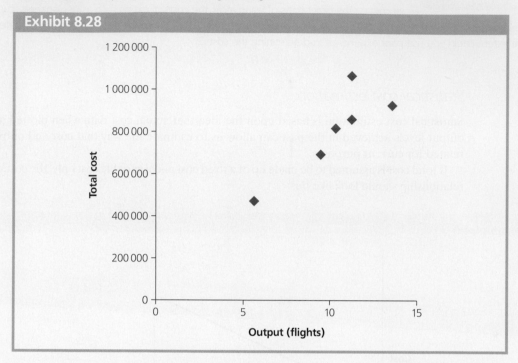

Exhibit 8.28

As you can see the data in the diagram do not represent exactly what we would expect. The costs appear to show a positive relationship but the value of the fixed costs and the variable costs are not clear. Linear regression is a statistical technique that allows us to 'estimate' the line of best fit through the data points. Linear regression solves for the value of a and b using the following two formulae:

$$\Sigma y = an + b\Sigma x$$
$$\Sigma xy = a\Sigma x + b\Sigma x^2$$

where Σ means 'the sum of', y is the variable on the upright axis (cost in this case), x is the horizontal variable (output) and n is the number of data points (6 in this case).

The data above were incorporated into Excel as follows and two columns added, giving the product of x and y, and the value of x^2:

Exhibit 8.29

Month	Cost (y)	Flights (x)	(xy)	x^2
1	835 000	10	8 350 000	100
2	940 000	13	12 220 000	169
3	1 075 000	11	11 825 000	121
4	480 000	6	2 880 000	36
5	680 000	9	6 120 000	81
6	875 000	11	9 625 000	121
Sum =	4 885 000	60	51 020 000	628

The column totals are entered into the two linear regression equations:

$$4\,885\,000 = 6a + 60b \tag{1}$$
$$51\,020\,000 = 60a + 628b \tag{2}$$

These two simultaneous equations can be solved by multiplying the first equation throughout by 10 (which makes the coefficient of a the same in both equations) to give equation.

$$48\,850\,000 = 60a + 600b \tag{3}$$

This equation is identical mathematically to (1) except that it has been scaled up tenfold.

We then deduct equation (3) from equation (2) to give an equation (4) containing b as the only unknown, which can then be solved:

$$51\,020\,000 = 60a + 628b \tag{2}$$
$$48\,850\,000 = 60a + 600b \tag{3}$$
$$\overline{\quad 2\,170\,000 = \quad 0 \ + \ 28b} \tag{4}$$

Solving equation (4) for b we get:

$$b = 2\,170\,000/28$$

so that

$$b = 77\,500$$

and by substituting this value into equation (1):

$$4\,885\,000 = 6a + 60 \times 77\,500$$

or

$$a = 39\,167$$

Putting these results into English, the analysis reveals that our best estimate of the fixed cost of flying this charter service is £39 167 per month and the variable cost per unit (per flight in this case) is £77 500. Graphically we can now show this result as:

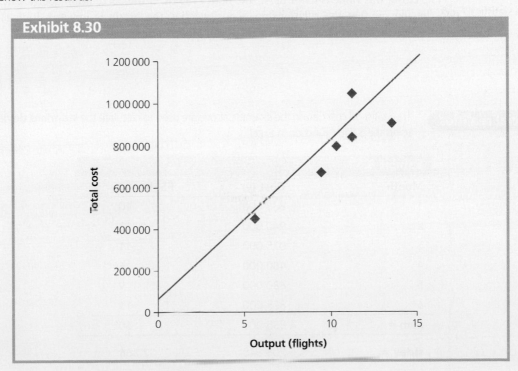

Exhibit 8.30

The results of statistical cost data can be used to predict the cost at any planned output level. So if, for example, this airline business planned to fly 14 flights in month 7, its expected cost would be:

Total cost = £39 167 + 14 × £77 500
           = £1 124 167

Unfortunately, real data rarely fall neatly on a straight line. Statistical cost estimation provides a method of estimating the best value of a (the value of the fixed cost) and b (the variable cost per unit) from past cost information.

Statistical cost data must always be interpreted with care:

1. How many data points do we have? Are there sufficient past data for a reliable relationship to be estimated?

2. How good is the data fit? One way of checking this is by calculating the **correlation coefficient** (see the example below). The closer the correlation coefficient is to +1 the better for a cost relationship such as the one we have drawn above.

3. Has the data been collected over widely different time periods? If so the data may have to be brought to current price levels by adjusting for past price inflation.

Measuring the goodness of fit

The correlation coefficient is used to test the goodness of fit for statistical data. It can be calculated easily from the regression data using the formula:

Correlation = b × standard deviation (x)/standard deviation (y)

The closer this value is to +1 or −1, the better the fit. If the correlation coefficient is positive that means that the relationship is positive (i.e. the graph is upward-sloping) and if negative it means that the relationship is negative with a downward-sloping graph.

Financial realities   The statistical cost data in the example above are used to calculate the **standard deviation** using the STDEV function in Excel.

Exhibit 8.31

Month	Cost (y)	Flights (x)
1	835 000	10
2	940 000	13
3	1 075 000	11
4	480 000	6
5	680 000	9
6	875 000	11
Sum =	4 885 000	60
stdev =	208 648	2.366

Substituting these values into the formula above we obtain:

Correlation coefficient = 77 500 × 2.366/208 648
= 0.879

For most practical purposes a correlation coefficient of 0.879 would be regarded as very good, although a variety of further tests, beyond the scope of this book, may be required to measure how confident we can be in the results obtained from this cost study.

Note: the method of calculation of the standard deviation is shown in the Glossary.

Revenue variation

The total revenue (or 'revenue' for short) which arises from selling any good or service is given by the relationship:

Revenue = quantity sold × price per unit

So, if a garage sells 50 000 litres of unleaded petrol at 79p per litre its revenue will be:

Revenue = 50 000 × 79p = £39 500

This looks transparently easy: the more we sell, the more we get. Unfortunately that is not always true. Indeed, it is possible to sell more and for the total revenue earned by the firm to actually fall. It all depends upon the demand for the product concerned and the amount that the market will purchase for a given price. The simplest assumption is that the price of the product concerned will remain constant no matter how much the firm produces. In such a situation the price/demand relationship faced by the firm (where demand is the amount of the firm's products or services purchased) will be flat as shown in the left-hand diagram in Exhibit 8.32.

The resulting total revenue line will be upward-sloping. If the quantity sold is zero, the total revenue is zero and as more is sold so the revenue rises in proportion. The slope of the revenue line will be the selling price which is constant along its length.

In practice few firms can achieve a constant price no matter how much they sell. Normally they will find that the market price they can achieve is inversely related to their level of output. This is an outcome of the economic law of demand that states that the lower the price

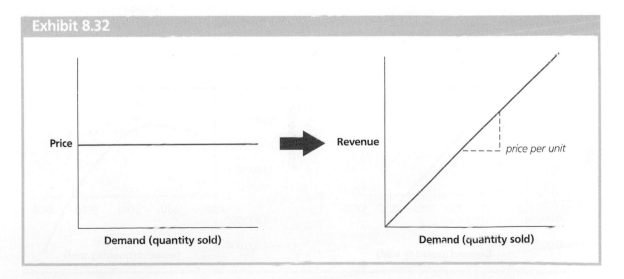

Exhibit 8.32

Exhibit 8.33 The relationship between total revenue and price

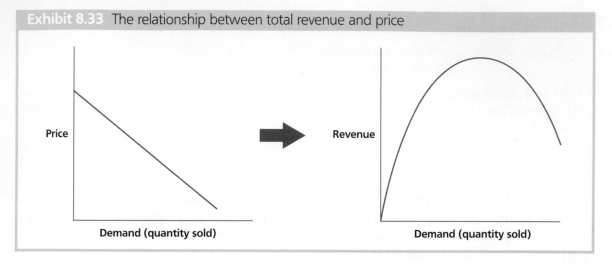

the greater the demand will be for a given product. The simplest relationship between price and demand is shown in Exhibit 8.33 where price falls in direct proportion to the increase in quantity demanded.

We will now demonstrate the truth of this rather odd and counterintuitive result.

Financial realities
A national motor distributor currently sells through its dealerships 600 per month of its series 3, 2.2 litre model at the list price of £24 500 on the road. The marketing director believes that for every reduction in price of £1500 a further 200 sales could be made. She would like to examine the impact of decreases in selling price on the revenue from the sale of this model of car. Her price, sales and revenue will be as follows:

Exhibit 8.34

Price	24 500	23 000	21 500	20 000	18 500	17 000	15 500	14 000	12 500
Demand	600	800	1 000	1 200	1 400	1 600	1 800	2 000	2 200
Total revenue	14 700 000	18 400 000	21 500 000	24 000 000	25 900 000	27 200 000	27 900 000	28 000 000	27 500 000

These data when extended further and shown graphically produce:

Exhibit 8.35

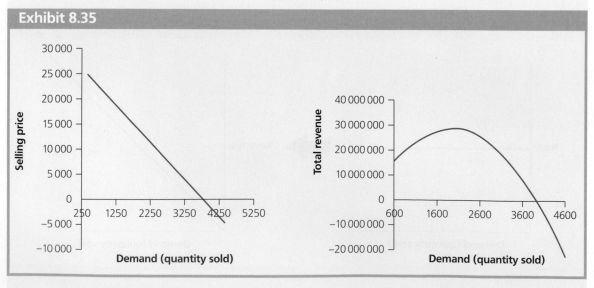

Note how any reduction in price brings a corresponding increase in revenue down to a sale price per vehicle of £14 000. Beyond that point, sales revenue will begin to fall. Can you see what would happen if the company were to increase its current price? The outcome would be a decrease in total revenue.

In practice it is difficult to estimate the true demand curve for any product. Market researchers use test marketing studies in order to see how demand is influenced by different selling price for a product in different outlets. Other methods seek to measure consumer preferences for given products compared with others using 'panels' and 'focus groups'.

Cost/volume/profit analysis

Cost/volume/profit analysis or 'breakeven analysis', as it is traditionally known, is a technique for matching costs and revenues together in order to identify the output level at which production goes into profit. It is important to remember that graphs of costs and revenues varying with different levels of output are what we refer to as analytical functions. In other words, they give an instantaneous description of the cost, revenue and surplus that we can expect at any given level of output. They are not designed to show how costs vary over time.

FYI In many cost and management accounting techniques the word 'profit' is used in a general sense to mean 'surplus' which could be either contribution (being the difference between direct revenues and direct costs) or profit (being the difference in the revenues and costs over a period of time). This can create confusion, so we will endeavour to point out those situations where what is being measured is actually contribution.

Cost/volume/profit analysis is normally conducted over a **relevant range** of output. The relevant range of output is usually that range through which we expect our assumptions about cost and revenue variability to hold and where extreme scale effects are unlikely to impact upon the cost of production or the revenues that can be won.

In the old days, accountants were very adept at drawing **breakeven** graphs using a ruler and pencil. Today, a spreadsheet package will do a much more effective job. However, the principles of the technique are as follows:

1. Draw up a graph of total cost at a range of different output levels. It is important when drawing such a graph to make sure:

   - that any critical points (i.e. steps) are properly included
   - costs are added together to get a total cost line, fixed costs first proceeding to the most variable last.

Financial realities A publisher faces charges of £1.80 per copy and £8000 per print run from an independent company that prints books on its behalf. The 'net price' of each copy of the book produced for the publisher is £3.50. He would like to know the contribution he can expect from any size of print run up to a maximum of 10 000 copies.

The steps involved in drawing up the breakeven chart are as shown in Exhibit 8.36.

The result for this publisher is shown in Exhibit 8.37. Note that when drawing in the variable cost it is added on top of the fixed cost. At a print run of zero, the variable cost is zero and the total cost will be:

Total cost (0 units) = fixed cost (£8000) + variable cost (0) = £8000
Total cost (10 000 units) = fixed cost (£8000) + variable cost (£18 000)
= £26 000

The revenue line is superimposed. Note again that at zero output the revenue will also be zero. However, the maximum print run will produce a revenue of £35 000. The straight line need only be drawn between these two points. Finally, the contribution line must run from a loss of £8000 at zero output to a figure of £9000 at the maximum print run of 10 000.

Exhibit 8.36 Steps in producing a cost/volume/profit (breakeven) graph

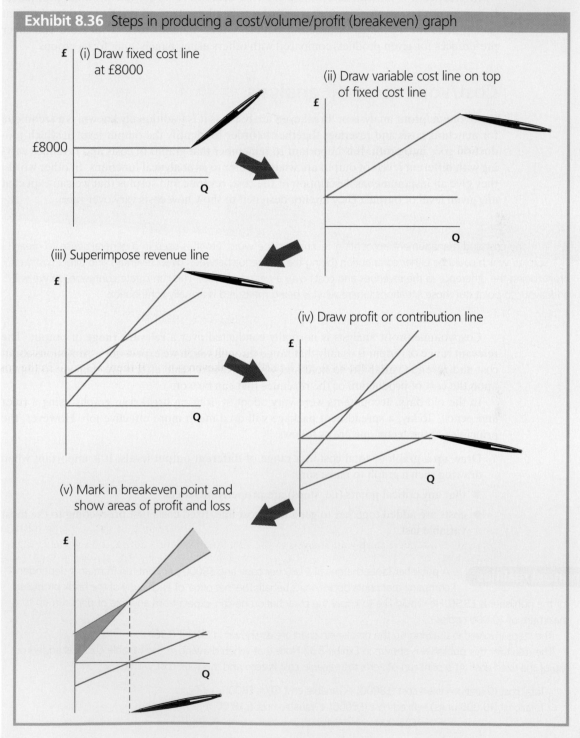

Exhibit 8.37 The finished breakeven graph

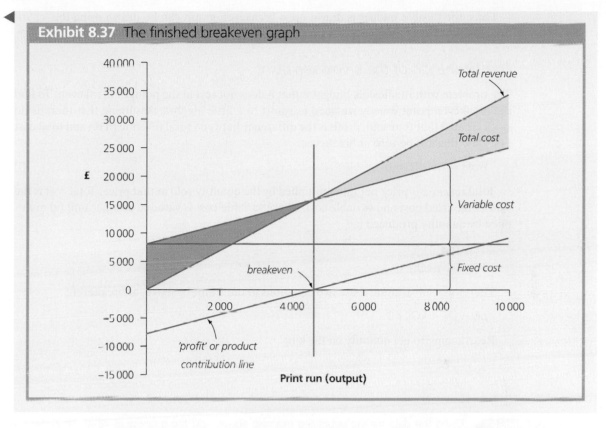

2. Add a revenue line over the corresponding range of output, noting the points where the revenue line crosses the total cost line (the breakeven point). If there are steps in the cost and revenue functions there may be multiple breakeven points.

3. Take the difference between the revenue and total cost curves (the 'profit') and superimpose the profit line on your graph.

4. Note onto your graph the relevant range of output and the ranges over which profit and loss will be incurred.

Creating a flexible budget

The break-even chart is a useful presentation tool and is easily understood. However, for formal analytical purposes the accountant will usually create a **flexible budget** on a spreadsheet. A flexible budget is simply an analysis of the revenues and costs across the relevant range of output. For the publisher example, a flexible budget will look like this (incrementing output in steps of 1000 units):

Exhibit 8.38

Size of print run	0	1 000	2 000	3 000	4 000	5 000	6 000	7 000	8 000	9 000	10 000
Revenue	0	3 500	7 000	10 500	14 000	17 500	21 000	24 500	28 000	31 500	35 000
Variable cost	0	1 800	3 600	5 400	7 200	9 000	10 800	12 600	14 400	16 200	18 000
Fixed cost	8 000	8 000	8 000	8 000	8 000	8 000	8 000	8 000	8 000	8 000	8 000
Total cost	8 000	9 800	11 600	13 400	15 200	17 000	18 800	20 600	22 400	24 200	26 000
Contribution	–8 000	–6 300	–4 600	–2 900	–1 200	500	2 200	3 900	5 600	7 300	9 000

Once the flexible budget is drawn up, a breakeven graph can be drawn using the 'chart' function in your spreadsheet package.

Formal analysis of the breakeven point

The problem with the flexible budget is that it does not reveal the point of breakeven. To find the breakeven point exactly we need to resort to a little algebra. Assuming that there is no stock created that is unsold, profit is the difference between total revenue (TR) and total cost (TC) and this will be zero at breakeven:

$$\text{Profit} = \text{TR} - \text{TC} = 0 \tag{1}$$

Total revenue is price per unit multiplied by the quantity sold at that price. Total cost is the sum of the fixed cost and variable cost, where variable cost is variable cost per unit (v) multiplied by quantity produced (Q).

$$\text{TR} = pQ$$
$$\text{TC} = \text{FC} + vQ$$

Therefore, substituting these two equations in the formula above, at breakeven:

$$pQ - [\text{FC} + vQ] = 0$$

Rearranging to get quantity on the left:

$$Q = \frac{\text{FC}}{p - v}$$

Financial realities Using the data for the publishing example above, find the quantity at which breakeven occurs.

Because the price per unit (p) is £3.50 and the variable cost per unit (v) is £1.80 the answer is:

$$Q = \frac{8000}{3.5 - 1.80} = 4706 \text{ units}$$

More generally we can use the profit formula (i) above to calculate the quantity required to produce any level of profit (Pr):

$$\text{Pr} = \text{TR} - \text{TC}$$

Therefore:

$$\text{Pr} = pQ - [\text{FC} + vQ]$$

Rearranging, the output quantity is shown to be equal to the fixed cost plus the desired profit, all divided by the difference between the price per unit and the variable cost per unit:

$$Q = \frac{\text{FC} + \text{Pr}}{p - v}$$

Financial realities The publisher wished to make a profit of £4000. What print run would be required to achieve this?

$$Q = \frac{8000 + 4000}{3.5 - 1.8} = 7059 \text{ units}$$

This formula can be restated in terms of contribution. The sum of the fixed costs and profit is equal to the total contribution. The difference between the price per unit and the variable cost per unit is the contribution per unit. As a result the required quantity of output can be restated as:

Quantity = contribution required/contribution per unit

Financial realities

The publisher required a total contribution of £17 000. The contribution per unit was £1.70. Therefore:

$Q = $ £17 000/1.7 = 10 000 units

Problems with cost/volume/profit analysis

Breakeven analysis is a straightforward technique that focuses a business's attention on its performance at different levels of output. However, it does have some limitations.

Stepped cost and revenue functions

In most situations a firm will be able to obtain and offer discounts on goods it both buys and sells. This will introduce steps into the functions which may make production profitable at one level, but possibly loss-making at a higher level. Steps can also occur if capacity has to be expanded in 'jumps' rather than continuously. Once a machine, a member of staff or a building meets capacity then new investment must be made, creating further fixed costs, to expand the levels of production which can be achieved. It is possible to 'model' these cost and revenue steps and use the resulting analysis to identify ranges of output that are profitable rather than those that are not. However, the point to note about the introduction of steps is that it can create a problem of multiple breakeven points with zones of loss making at intermediate levels of production.

Certainty

It is assumed that the cost and revenue functions can be predicted across the whole range of output. This is unlikely to be the case. Most production systems become less reliable in operation the closer they are forced to work to capacity. There are advanced modelling techniques that can be used to incorporate such uncertainty into the breakeven analysis.

Multiple products

Cost/volume/profit analysis is only meaningful if the fixed costs in the analysis are direct costs of the production activity itself. If a business makes just one product then all of its costs will be direct with respect to the production of that product. Where a firm has many products there will be some firm-level costs that are not attributable to a single product line. In that case, the cost/volume/profit analysis can only be used to measure the contribution to the fixed costs of the firm from the product line concerned. It is meaningless to allocate the firm's indirect costs to each product line on some arbitrary basis as the breakeven point will as a result be arbitrary. In the next chapter we will explore the issue of cost allocation and the problems it creates for business decision-making.

Non-linear cost and revenue functions

As we have discussed earlier in this chapter, the assumption of a linear revenue function ignores the fact that in most situations a firm will face a downward-sloping demand curve.

This will give rise to a revenue curve which has the shape of an inverted parabola with a maximum value and a part where revenues rise with increasing output level and a part where they fall. We now turn to how we deal with this particular problem.

Marginal analysis

The concept of marginality is very important in accounting and finance. The **marginal revenue** or the **marginal cost** is the increase in revenue or cost which occurs if output increases by just one unit. Now, remember the typical revenue function that arises if we have a downward-sloping demand curve? At the origin of the curve, i.e. near zero output, adding an extra unit of output will increase the revenue dramatically. However, as we 'climb up' the curve the extra revenue obtained from an additional unit of output will get smaller until the point is reached, when, at the top of the curve, the additional revenue from one extra unit of output equals zero. From that point on, the revenue will decrease with each extra unit produced (Exhibit 8.39).

The very simple intuition here is that at the maximum value of the revenue curve the marginal revenue will be zero.

If we take the revenue curve as shown and add a total-cost line we can create a curve for the profit that is achieved at any level of output. Note how the profit curve is the difference between the total revenue and total cost, and that it rises to a peak before falling away and eventually turning into a loss. As with the marginal revenue, the point of maximum profit will be the point at which the slope of the profit curve equals zero. Therefore, when the marginal profit is equal to zero that is the point of maximum profit (Exhibit 8.40).

Because profit equals total revenue less total cost it is reasonable to assume that marginal profit equals marginal revenue less marginal cost. It follows therefore that when marginal profit is zero, the total profit from production is maximised or, to put it another way, marginal

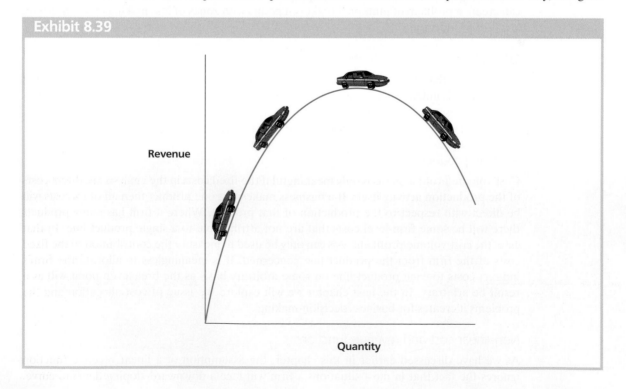

Exhibit 8.39

Exhibit 8 40

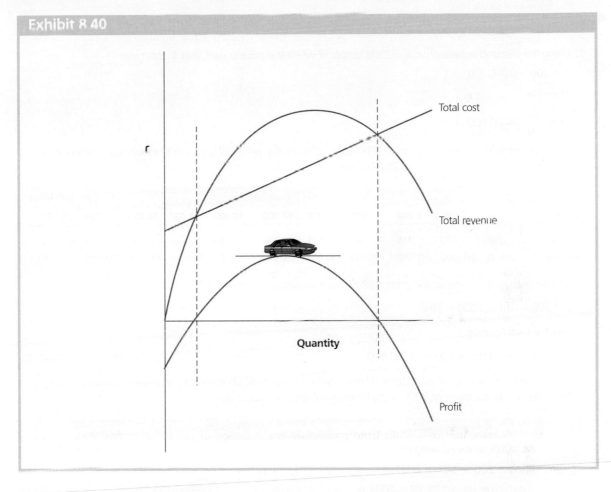

revenue less marginal cost also equals zero when profit is at a maximum. To restate, at maximum profit:

Marginal revenue − marginal cost = 0

or

Marginal revenue = marginal cost

This is known as the **marginality rule**. The marginality rule tells us the level of output which will generate the maximum profit for the firm. It is that level of output at which marginal revenue equals marginal cost.

Using a spreadsheet and the 'chart function' it is possible to identify the output level at which marginal revenue equals marginal cost.

Financial realities   A company faces a demand curve for its product that suggests that the price it can obtain falls with the level of output (Q) it produces. The price per unit (p) is estimated to be:

$p = 200 - 0.01Q$

Its fixed cost of production is £650 000 and its variable cost per unit is £10 throughout all levels of output.

To solve this proceed through the following steps:

1. Using the demand equation work out the output at which the price equals zero. In this case:

$$p = 200 - 0.01Q = 0$$

Therefore

$$Q = \frac{200}{0.01} = 20\,000 \text{ units}$$

2. On a spreadsheet at intervals of (say) 2000 units, calculate the price per unit and total revenue starting at zero output and proceeding through to 20 000 units:

Exhibit 8.41

output	0	2 000	4 000	6 000	8 000	10 000	12 000	14 000	16 000	18 000	20 000
price	200	180	160	140	120	100	80	60	40	20	0
revenue	0	360 000	640 000	840 000	960 000	100 000	960 000	840 000	640 000	360 000	0

At zero output, for example, the price is £200 and the revenue is zero. At 2000 units the price will be:

$$p = 200 - 0.01 \times 2000 = £180$$

and the total revenue:

Total revenue = £180 × 2000 = £360 000

3. At each level of output calculate the additional revenue that would be earned by increasing the level of output by 1 unit. So, for example, at 2000 units the marginal revenue would be:

Exhibit 8.42

At 2001 units of output

Price = 200 − 0.01 × 2001 =	£179.99	
Total revenue = 179.99 × 2001 =		£360 159.99
At 2000 units of output		
Price = 200 − 0.01 × 2000 =	£180.00	
Total revenue = 180.00 × 2000 =		£360 000.00
Marginal revenue		£159.99

4. Repeat for costs:

Exhibit 8.43

At 2001 units of output

Total cost = £650 000 + £10 × 2001 =	£670 010.00
At 2000 units of output	
Total cost = £650 000 + £10 × 2000 =	£670 000.00
Marginal cost	£10.00

Note that the marginal cost is £10, which is the same as the variable cost. This will always be the case when dealing with a straight-line total cost function as the slope of the line (the marginal cost) will be the same along its length.

5. Complete the analysis for all output levels (the calculation of the numbers can be done by the use of formulas in the spreadsheet):

Exhibit 8.44

output	0	2 000	4 000	6 000	8 000	10 000	12 000	14 000	16 000	18 000	20 000
price	200	180	160	140	120	100	80	60	40	20	0
total revenue	0	360 000	640 000	840 000	960 000	1 000 000	960 000	840 000	640 000	360 000	0
marginal revenue	199.99	159.99	119.99	79.99	39.99	−0.01	−40.01	−80.01	−120.01	−160.01	−200.01
total cost	650 000	670 000	690 000	710 000	730 000	750 000	770 000	790 000	810 000	830 000	850 000
marginal cost	10	10	10	10	10	10	10	10	10	10	10

Construct a chart of the marginal revenue and marginal cost rows in the table against output.

Exhibit 8.45

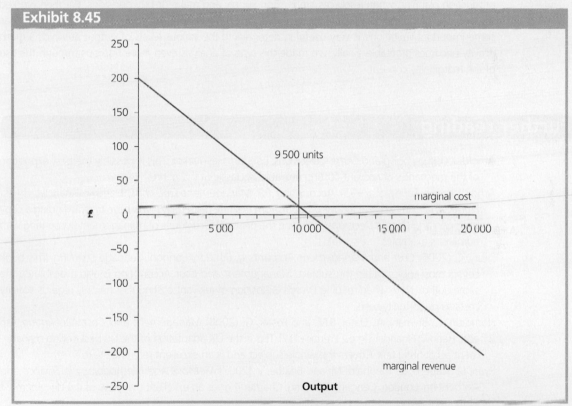

The graph shows the cross-over point where marginal cost equals marginal revenue as 9500 units. At this point the total profit is as follows:

Exhibit 8.46

At 9500 units of output

Price = 200 − 0.01 × 9500 =	£105.00
Total revenue = 105 × 9500 =	£997 500.00
Total cost = £650 000 + 10 × 9500 =	£745 000.00
Total profit	£252 500.00

You may wish to re-do the calculation at 9499 and 9501 units of output to satisfy yourself that the total profit is less than the £252 500 shown above.

Chapter summary

In this first chapter devoted to management accounting we have discussed the concept of revenue and particularly cost, noting the difference between 'direct' and 'indirect' revenues and costs. The concept of a direct cost is different from that of a variable cost. A direct cost is measured relative to a particular cost object, whilst with a variable cost the cost is measured relative to output level. We then proceeded to a discussion of relevant costs for decisions. The notion of relevant cost is very close to the economist's opportunity cost concept although we define it in terms of what is measurable, specifically the cash change resulting from the choice to pursue one course of action rather than the next best alternative available. When measuring costs in this way we noted that some costs are always likely to be irrelevant in a decision-making context: non-cash costs, sunk costs and fixed costs. The concept of decision matching is useful for a range of different management decisions. We have explored the problems of production planning when resources are in short supply and make-or-buy decisions. We then worked through one of the most traditional cost accounting techniques: breakeven analysis, which whilst it has some important limitations, is very useful in determining the various levels of output at which a given activity becomes profitable. Finally, we made this type of analysis even more rigorous through the use of the marginality concept.

Further reading

Arnold, J. (1973) *Pricing and Output Decisions*, London: Haymarket. This is possibly the best exposition of the mechanics of relevant costing available. A classic of the genre.

Arnold, J. and Turley, S. (1995) *Accounting for Management Decisions*, Harlow: Financial Times/ Prentice Hall. An excellent follow-on book from this one (especially if you have trouble finding a copy of *Pricing and Output Decisions*), covering the principal techniques of management accounting with numerous examples.

Drury, C. (2006) *Cost and Management Accounting*, 6th edn, London: Cengage Learning. This book covers most topics within the subject. *Management and Cost Accounting* is also available by the same author. Note when reading Drury's exposition of relevant costing that he only regards scarcity costs as opportunity costs.

Horngren, C., Bhimani, A., Datar, S.M. and Foster, G. (2008) *Management and Cost Accounting*, 4th edn, Harlow: Financial Times: Prentice Hall. This is the UK adaptation of the US best-selling management accounting text. Covers the whole subject and is an excellent reference text.

Ryan, B., Scapens, B., Theobald, M. and Beattie, V. (2002) *Methods and Methodology in Finance and Accounting*, London: Cengage Learning. Chapter 4 gives an excellent overview of the development of thought in management accounting.

Progress check

Please refer to the page shown to check your answers.

1. Define a 'direct cost' and say how it differs from an indirect cost. (p. 237)

....

2. If attribution is the process of matching direct cost to cost objects what is the name of the process of matching 'indirect costs'? (p. 238)

....

3. Define the terms 'contribution' and 'contribution margin'. (p. 239)

4. List the four principles that support decision costing. (pp 242–244)

5. Define the term 'opportunity cost'. (p. 244)

6. What rule is used for ranking different products that use a common scarce resource? (p. 251)

7. In the make-or-buy decision what costs should management compare when considering the two alternatives? (p. 254)

8. Define a 'variable cost' and say how this cost concept is different from the concept of a direct cost. (p. 255)

9. List eight different cost patterns. (p. 258)

10. There are two approaches to estimating costs in practice. What are they? (pp. 258–262)

11. What statistic is used to measure the 'goodness of fit'? (p. 262)

12. If a demand curve slopes downwards for a product, sketch the total revenue curve that will result. (p. 264)

13. The point at which total revenue equals total cost is known as what? (pp. 265–267)

14. List four problems with the use of cost/volume/profit analysis. (pp. 269–270)

15. Define the terms 'marginal revenue' and 'marginal cost'. (p. 270)

16. At optimum profit what is the relationship between marginal cost and marginal revenue? (p. 271)

Questions

The answers to the questions followed by ✓ can be found at the back of the book, the answers to the remaining questions can be found on the website accompanying this book, **www.cengage.co.uk/ryan2**.

1. Financial accounting and management accounting differ in their purpose and in the techniques employed. What in your view are the principal differences between these two branches of accounting?

2. The Imperial Navy of Tierra del Fuego has requested tenders for the supply of three hunter–seeker missiles and has asked English Aerospace to tender. Essentially, these missiles have three parts as shown in Exhibit 8.47 (copyright of the INTF). Part A is designed to make a very large bang and generally frighten the enemy into submission. Part C is the engine that is designed to make the thing go and part B is the bit that joins part A to part C.

Brian, the project manager, is trying to price the bid with the help of Alf (who is technically in charge of the stores) and Molly Quelle who has been drafted in from R&D to provide scientific advice. This high-powered team starts work.

'Let's start from the beginning. They want one hundred of these things and we have six months to deliver. Can we do that?', asks Brian.

'Well', says Molly with a sharp intake of breath. 'We could if we could get the warheads.'

'Let's keep this non-technical', says Brian sharply. 'Any ideas, Alf?'

Alf was not noted for his ideas but for once he had a surprise for Brian. 'Down in the yard I have just the thing. One hundred and fifty warheads, in pristine condition which might fit, with some persuasion.'

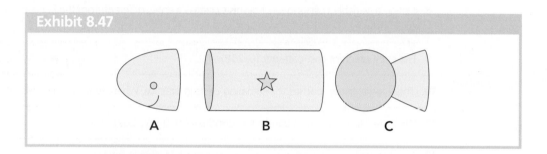

Exhibit 8.47

'Pristine?', queries Brian. Molly also looks doubtful. 'What are they doing in the yard?', she asks. Alf looks smug: 'You remember that deal signed by HMG: one real warhead for ten fakes – these are the fakes! I kept them all and chucked a tarpaulin over them to keep them dry.'

Brian soaked up this news. 'So, what you're suggesting is that we use these old warheads for this contract. You must be nuts!'

'Come on', said Alf, looking slightly hurt. 'They are never going to use them in anger, so why should we bother? And in any event, do we really want the Tierra del Fuego Navy firing off a warhead made in Britain which could potentially kill someone?'

'OK, let's assume for the sake of argument that we use these warheads. Can we put them at zero cost as far as we are concerned? Presumably, because they are scrap they have no value to us.'

'No, I don't think so', interjected Molly, 'we must assume their cost to be what we originally paid for them.'

'Let's look at the figures', said Brian, thumbing through the computer printout on his desk. 'These warheads originally cost us a hundred and fifty dollars each.'

'Yes', said Alf, 'but I doubt whether we would get a third of that for them as scrap. Shouldn't we cost them at what they would be if they were purchased new?'

'Good point', exclaimed Brian. 'Perhaps we should. Let's leave them at that then. Now let's look at the motors. We have lots of these in stock. They're a standard item. We would have to modify them to fit the configuration of the warhead but I think we could do that for about 10 dollars per missile. The accounts show that these originally cost just three hundred dollars each. But I do remember that the suppliers had put through a 10 per cent price rise for any new stock.'

'Yes', interrupted Molly, 'but we ought to use the original price, as they are already in stock.'

But Alf looked doubtful. 'Shouldn't we cost them at what we could get if we sold them? These motors have a high price on the black market where I bet we could sell them for four hundred dollars each.'

'Don't be daft', retorted Brian. 'Everything in this factory would command a high price on the black market!'

Alf did not look convinced. 'All right then, how are you going to cost the bodies? We have got no idea how much they will be, we have never used them before.'

'Oh, don't worry', said Brian. 'We will be able to pick these up at the Farnborough bring-and-buy sale. A hundred dollars each – I saw some last week and they're always there.'

Advise Brian on the appropriate cost for the parts.

3. Alfred Cookers Ltd is considering a contract to produce for a kitchen fitting company a special range (a type of oven) that is an adaptation of a model Alfred had recently discontinued. The contract is for fifty units to be produced and installed by Alfred over twelve months although company management believes that this business will not be repeated as it has already advanced orders for a new range for the next big selling season from this kitchen company and from others. The production of this special range, which the company has called the Fuego, could start immediately, although it is estimated that it will affect its other business, as the installation engineers who do the installations are particularly busy. Alfred's management believes that if it goes ahead with the production of the 50 Fuegos they will lose 50 sales of their current planned production because of the scarcity of trained installation engineers who are all currently fully occupied. A machine installed from their existing catalogue generates a net cash contribution to Alfred of £1200 (after installation costs) and takes the heating engineer 2 days to install at an average labour cost (they are paid on a day rate) of £150 per day. There is a great shortage of trained installation engineers and Alfred, like most oven manufacturers, has had great trouble recruiting suitably qualified staff.

Reviewing the cost of producing the 50 Fuegos the project team at Alfred notes that it has spent 10 person-days so far working on this contract and preparing the specifications. Each person-day is charged at £280 including a 100 per cent mark-up on direct labour cost to cover overheads.

The materials to produce 40 of the Fuegos are already in stock and cost originally £1750 per unit. Their current buying-in price would be £1950 but a decision had already been made to return the iron casings to the foundry for recasting at an agreed price of £100 per unit returned net of transport costs. Internal parts purchased for £500 per unit were to be salvaged at a net cost of £50 per unit saving parts for the new models costing £350 per unit.

A significant problem with the Fuego is that it would have to be hand built and would require the equivalent of one engineer a year to build the 50 units required by this contract. Each engineer employed at the firm earns an average annual salary (including employer's pension and national insurance contribution) of £24 000 per annum. Because of the firm's heavy investment in computer-aided design, they had planned to lay off one of the engineers in six months' time although the plant manager had no idea what they were going to do with the spare man for that six months. The redundancy pay would be three months' salary and the planned redundancy could be deferred until this special contract had been completed. The engineer concerned was quite happy because the kitchen company taking the order are keen to take him on as a maintenance engineer.

The firm normally costs £1500 of overheads into each machine produced. There would be no additional plant requirements, although some old tools which have been fully depreciated and have a carrying value of £1 in the accounts will be retained. Their current scrap value is £4000 which would fall to £2500 after another year's use. The kitchen company has been negotiating a price (ex-factory) of £2800 per unit. Alfred's financial director is of the opinion that this is too low, in fact he says it is derisory given their normal trade price of £4200 when they were in production. What should Alfred do? ✓

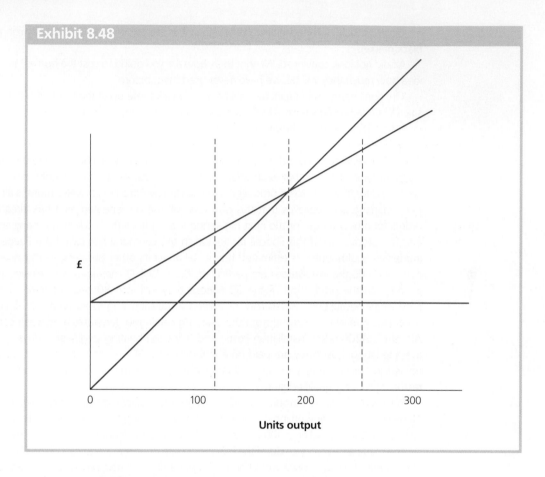

Exhibit 8.48

£

0   100   200   300

Units output

4. Using the breakeven graph above:

   Mark on the graph the following:

   (i) the output at which the point of breakeven occurs

   (ii) the total revenue line

   (iii) fixed cost

   (iv) variable cost

   (v) relevant range of output

   (vi) a profit line.

5. A company wishes to create a flexible budget from zero output to 100 000 units in 10 000 unit intervals. The costs are as follows:

   ● variable production costs of £25 per unit

   ● plant costs of £60 000 up to and including output levels of 40 000 units, £350 000 thereafter up to and including 100 000 units

   ● fixed cost of £550 000

   ● revenue of £45 per unit.

You are required to:

(i) Prepare a flexible budget at 10 000-unit intervals but also showing profit at 40 001 units.

(ii) Using the charting facility in your spreadsheet program or by drawing by hand produce a breakeven graph including a profit line, clearly showing the step in the costs of this production process.

(iii) Identify the point(s) of breakeven.

(iv) Calculate the marginal cost at 40 000 units of output.

(v) If current plant capacity is fully used but the further investment in plant costs is not undertaken what is the best possible profit level? ✓

---

6. The fixed cost of production are £100 000 and the variable costs £20 per unit. The sales revenue is £35 per unit sold.

(i) Calculate the required output level to achieve breakeven.

(ii) Calculate the required output to earn a profit of £60 000. ✓

---

7. The fixed costs of production are £30 000 and the variable costs £20 per unit. The sales price per unit is estimated to be £200 less 20p per unit sold.

(i) Calculate the output that maximises total revenue by drawing a marginal revenue curve and identifying when it passes through zero.

(ii) Calculate the optimum profit level.

Chapter 9

Cash forecasting, business planning and management control

Battle plans rarely survive the first encounter with the enemy. (Anon.)

Introduction

This chapter forms a bridge between your studies of financial accounting in Chapters 1–7 and the practical problems of management accounting within the firm. In this chapter, we discuss the role of business planning in establishing and running a business and the basic process for constructing a business plan. This description of the business planning process is designed to help you bring together the various components of a business idea and construct a working proposal that can be used to raise finance or, just as important, to organise and control a business. From the accounting point of view, the main output of the business planning process is the creation of a financial plan for a number of years into the future. At the centre of that financial plan is the cash flow forecast. That forecast is designed to capture within a statement the financial consequences of the firm's current strategic plans, taking into account both how it expects to earn its money and how it intends to spend it. We will demonstrate how such a cash flow forecast can be prepared.

Business planning is not just about business start-ups. Many firms use it as an ongoing discipline by creating a 'master plan' which is regularly reviewed and updated. This process enables senior management to construct and agree 'budgets' with the other employees of the organisation. In this chapter we will explain the different ways that budgets can be created, agreed and monitored as the business proceeds through its financial year. We also address the human and organisational issues in budgeting and in particular consider the problems of gaining compliance and enhancing motivation towards the firm's goals throughout the organisation. Finally, we will turn our attention to the techniques of variance analysis and control where management extracts the differences between budgeted and actual performance and acts to correct significant variations between what was expected and what was achieved.

Learning objectives

In this chapter we cover a range of learning objectives over three headings:

The business planning process

- To understand the business planning process and the role of the financial plan.

- To know the structure and purpose of the principal components of a financial plan.

Business planning in practice

- To be able to identify the most appropriate planning period for a firm.

- Using the principal financial policy variables to be able to project a cash flow statement and summary financial figures for a whole business or part of a business.

Budgeting methodologies and variance analysis

- To understand and be able to advise on the most appropriate budgeting methodology for a firm and be aware of the multiple purposes that budgeting fulfils.

- To be able to prepare and understand the significance of a range of revenue and cost variance measures.

The business planning process

Business planning is vital whenever a proposal is put forward for funding internally to a board of directors or externally, in the case of a start-up, to banks, venture capitalists or, in the case of a public flotation, through a prospectus. Existing businesses can make use of the planning approach as a basis for the long-term management control of the firm. It is important to construct a business plan whenever:

- a new business is to be formed and capital is required
- a new investment project is being proposed and a maximum capital need must be specified
- a new product line or project is being proposed
- a company 'floats' its shares on the stock exchange.

A business plan consists of a number of integrated elements covering the product or business proposal, the objectives that the company or proposer wishes to achieve, the strategy for delivering those objectives, and a range of marketing and organisational issues that flow from the strategy described. All of this will then be summarised into a financial plan that lays out the implications of the proposal in terms of cash flow, financial requirements, projected financial statements and a range of planning ratios and financial performance targets. Later in this chapter we will discuss in more detail how these component parts are put together. However, it is important to note that what matters for a business is not so much the plan itself but the process of creating it. Good business planning allows managers or entrepreneurs, in the case of new business ventures, to work through the implications of what they are proposing and to minimise the impact of the law of unintended consequences which we define as follows:

Unintended consequences are inversely related to the number of questions asked about any intended course of action.

This is why most banks, finance houses, venture capitalists and indeed the stock exchange insist that firms seeking finance or flotation on the exchange have in place effective business planning processes.

The overall process of business planning described in this chapter is sometimes referred to as 'corporate planning'. John Argenti in his book *Practical Corporate Planning* (1980) reserves the use of the term 'business planning' for the more restricted product-level-type planning where operational details are resolved and short-term financial forecasts are made. However, 'business planning' is now taken to mean the overall planning of a new or existing business.

The structure of the business plan

A full business plan is a comprehensive document consisting of a series of interlinked statements. At the highest level of analysis the business plan will be driven by the vision of those who are putting it forward. That vision motivates what the individuals concerned are trying to achieve, but to be effective it must be developed into a coherent set of strategic plans which describe how that vision will be achieved.

In Exhibit 9.1 we lay out the sequence of documents that are likely to be created for a business plan. In any given business context, variations on this basic structure may well suggest themselves. However, this outline contains all the basic elements required for an overall planning document for a business proposal or an ongoing business.

The executive summary

In practice, most business proposals are not read fully by the decision makers concerned. Impression and intuition are often relied upon and any formal analysis of the proposal concerned is used to rationalise the decision after it has been made. In this context, the executive summary becomes a very important device in the hands of the advocate of a new business proposal. Good executive summaries should be short and cover three points:

1. the facts of the proposal, outlining the nature of the product or service and indicating the scale and timing of the financial investment entailed
2. the benefits which will accrue to the organisation making the investment decision and, in some cases, to the individual making the decision
3. the success factors by which the investment can be judged.

The strategic summary

The strategic summary within a business plan should include: a statement of overall purpose or intention (the mission), the *objectives* which the project or business is attempting to realise

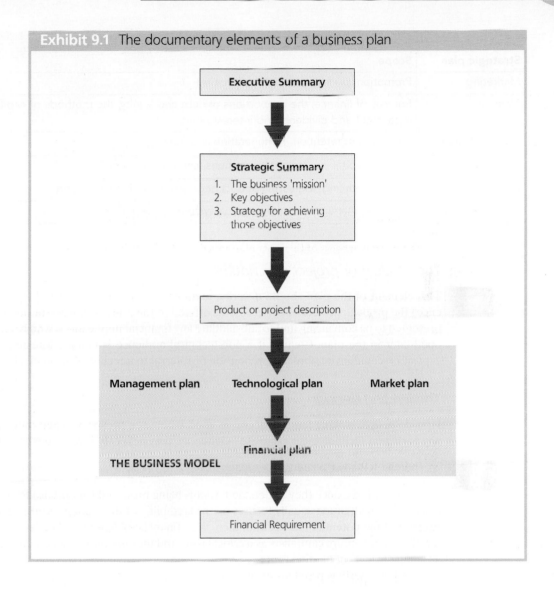

Exhibit 9.1 The documentary elements of a business plan

and the method which will be employed to realise those objectives (the strategy). Strategic statements can be decomposed into a number of 'strategic plans' covering the key aspects of the business.

In assessing a strategy lending institutions will pose a series of questions;

1. Is the strategic intention behind the business proposal ethical and legal?

2. Is the strategy logically consistent? A minimum cost strategy will be difficult to achieve alongside aspirations to become a high-quality producer.

3. Is the strategy likely to yield competitive success given the known state of the market and the regulatory environment?

4. How much risk will the lender face, is their some form of downside protection in the event of failure (e.g. significant real assets which may be realised in the event of problems)?

5. Is the strategy simple and direct in its purpose of achieving the business mission?

Exhibit 9.2	
Strategic plan	**Scope**
Marketing	Promotion, pricing, product, positioning
Finance	Sources of finance, the proportions of debt and equity, the methods of capital repayment and dividend and interest policy
Human Resources	Recruitment, retention, remuneration and training
Production	Design, capital investment, operations, and quality control
Procurement	Product sourcing, logistics, contract negotiation, and stockholding
Organisational	Structure, management, information systems, governance

The product or project description

This element of the plan should describe to an appropriate level of detail (given the audience) the product, project or service being offered to the market. Sufficient detail should be presented to be convincing and to substantiate any financial implications which may be developed later in the plan. Clearly, if a non-technical audience is being addressed a technical exposition could invite non-comprehension or referral to a technical specialist for advice.

The lending decision

How do people making lending decisions choose between prospects when they do not have any particular technological expertise? Generally, they order their priorities as follows:

human > market > financial > organisational > technical

In other words, once they understand what is being proposed (in outline) from the executive brief then attention usually focuses on the credibility of the team presenting the case, the strength of the potential market and, then, their financial obligations. The level of finance is rarely seen by venture capitalists as a critical issue and they are more concerned with ensuring an adequate level of funding for the needs of the project. Unplanned second-wave financing is regarded as a serious problem for any business or project using the venture capital market.

The business model

When producing a business plan, it is important to articulate the *business model* underpinning the revenue generation and consequential expenditures that will be incurred by the firm. As we showed in Exhibit 9.1, the development of a coherent business model relies upon the successful application of a number of different business ideas and techniques. The business model consists of three parts, leading to the four plans outlined in Exhibit 9.1.

1. The revenue model, which describes how the new business will win revenue. It will answer questions such as what is the product, what is the unique selling proposition (USP), what is the size of the market and what are the future prospects for developing market position and share? The new business proposal will also have to explain how the venture will be able to open new markets and create the networks of relationships which enhance the chances of success. For an existing business, the revenue model will be based upon an understanding of the company's competitive position, its product portfolio, the market

opportunities that exist, and rigorous market research exploring the potential of the business in exploiting those opportunities.

2. The expenditure model, which describes the necessary expenditures required to achieve the revenue goals specified by the revenue model. The expenditure model will reflect the technology and expertise available to the proposer; it will also be dependent upon the way that the business organises itself and upon its ability to create effective relationships with suppliers and other stakeholders. It is very tempting in practice to devote much more time to the implications of the expenditure model than to the correct specification and rationalisation of the revenue model. However, it is the revenue model that ultimately drives the business.

3. The financing model, which describes how the firm will raise its finance (equity/debt), how it will serve that finance through interest payments or dividends and how it will repay that finance. The link between this model and the revenue and expenditure models is the calculation of the firm's maximum financial need. The maximum financial need is governed by the magnitude and timing of the cash flows generated by the firm and the firm's existing resources. Methods of raising finance will be discussed more fully in Chapter 13.

In Exhibit 9.3 we show how these three components of the business model link together and depend upon the internal constraints and external opportunities that the business confronts.

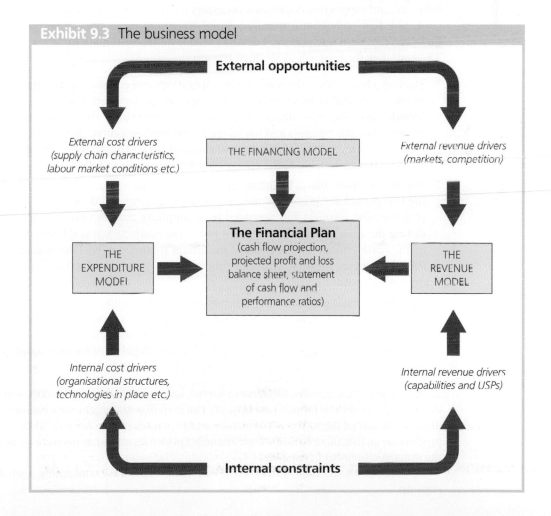

Exhibit 9.3 The business model

Business planning in practice

In this section we will focus on the financial aspects of the business planning process. The financial plan consists of the following:

- a detailed forecast of cash flow over the short term
- projected profit and loss accounts and balance sheets
- projected summary cash flow statements
- relevant ratios.

We will use as an example a case of a new start-up rather than an existing business. This covers all of the phases of business start-up as well as continuing operations.

Preparing a cash flow forecast

The core of any financial planning exercise is the cash flow forecast. From the cash flow forecast it is a straightforward step to project future balance sheets, income statements and summary cash flow statements. The method is simple; the difficult part is collecting all the evidence and supporting documents necessary for the exercise to commence.

A cash flow statement is usually a month-by-month projection of cash inflows and outflows broken down into sufficient detail to enable all the subsidiary forecasts to be prepared. The cash flow forecast will cover three phases:

1. Start-up phase: this is the phase before operations can commence. It is the period during which the capital transactions of the business are undertaken. These capital transactions include acquiring new finance (via equity or borrowing), the investment in the fixed resources of the business and the hiring of the key personnel. At the end of the start-up phase it is common to 'capitalise' all of the start-up costs excluding any expenditures that are directly attributable to the operations of the business to follow.

2. Pre-profit phase: this is the phase of early operations where business commences. During this period the growth of the cash flow to the firm will depend on the credit terms that the new business has arranged with suppliers and its first customers. Normally, during the early part of the pre-profit phase the business will reach and pass the bottom of the 'cash trough' or the point of maximum financial need. The end of this phase is normally set as the first year-end following the point at which a firm comes to full operating profit.

3. Operating profit phase: during this period the firm will be making an operating profit but not a full profit, usually because of the interest costs of servicing its debt. This phase may last for some years as the company progressively develops its market position and operating capacity to the point that it is capable of earning a full bottom-line profit.

A cash flow projection is, therefore, a literal statement of when cash will flow in and out of the business, month by month, year by year. The cash flow statement for a business plan is the direct analogue of the statement of income and expenditure that any individual or family will produce to enable them to assess their spending priorities and what needs to be done to keep the domestic finances in balance.

To describe the methods involved we will work with a case concerning a small business start-up.

A case exercise in preparing a cash flow projection

In this exercise, we will build a cash flow projection for a high-tech 'spin-out' company from a UK university that wished to secure finance through a small-business start-up loan and private equity subscribed by the owner and his family.

The case notes are as shown on page 288. Read them carefully and then proceed to the analysis of the cash flow implications for this business.

Our challenge is to produce a cash flow projection over the first six months of trading, which, given his 3 months' start-up, will be until the end of June, year 1.

This section features an extensive case study in new start-up drawn from a real-world example. Only the names and numbers have been changed to protect the innocent. When learning from a case it is important, after the initial briefing to spend some time working on understanding the case itself. Naturally, a case study is an abstraction and you will gain the most from it if you begin to fill in the details yourself. Here are some practical steps:

- familiarise yourself with the details as specified in the case 'write-up'
- if possible, familiarise yourself with the technology being proposed (in this case a ground positioning system for navigation (see **www.garmin.co.uk** for more details of these instruments)
- if possible, get some understanding of the type of market in which the business will be operating. Magazines such as *Boat Owner* or *Yachting Monthly* make a good starting point in this case.

This case study was based on real events. However, the technology and market have developed rapidly, so in your researches try to find out what developments are currently under way in this market.

GPS as part of the navigator's equipment (© A.B.J. Price)

Financial realities Peter Plant

Peter Plant has taken out a series of patents securing the technology on his new GPS (see the press release in Exhibit 9.4) in the UK, Europe and the US. He is in discussion with a local venture capitalist over funding, and has secured agreement in principle from a national chain of ship chandlers giving them exclusive rights to sell the standard model. The chandlers believe that they can sell 2200 units per annum of the standard model through their own catalogues at a price of £225 per unit. A large component of their sales would be made during the first three months of the year and at the Southampton Boat Show in September. The remainder would be sold equally throughout the year. The chandler would expect a 30 per cent margin on the agreed recommended retail price (RRP), a full replacement guarantee and 60 days' credit.

Exhibit 9.4 Press Release

Peter Plant, a Southborne University academic, has spent two years refining and developing a handheld position finder that could transform navigation at sea. The new Plant GPS uses diffraction interferometry to overcome the positioning error in standard satellite Ground Position Systems. The small handheld device can locate a ship's position to within 6 metres at sea level with 99 per cent accuracy. This is close enough for pilotage of craft in constrained waters. Two models of the instrument will be available: a standard 12v rechargeable battery model with a 200-hour usage rating and an advanced model rechargeable through a solar photaic cell, which can recharge the battery in daylight under full cloud cover.

The new models will be available from January. Tackles Chandlery will be selling the standard model for £225. Both the standard and the advanced model will be demonstrated at the London and Southampton boat shows this year.

Plant believes that he can sell 600 units per annum of an advanced unit through mail order and on his own stand at the London and Southampton boat shows at a price of £275. Plant has negotiated a merchant contract with two credit card companies who pay one month after sale, deducting 4 per cent commission from the sale value. He expects all of his own sales of the advanced model to be via credit card transactions.

Plant expects sales to increase by 5 per cent in the second and third years and that cost inflation of 3 per cent per annum could be passed into sales prices with the chandler and for the more advanced model without losing sales to competitors.

His sales projections for the first full year of trading are as shown below:

	Jan	Feb	Mar	Apr	May	June	July	Aug	Sep	Oct	Nov	Dec
Chandler	500	500	500	50	50	50	50	50	300	50	50	50
Plant	200	20	20	20	20	20	20	20	200	20	20	20

Expenditures

Plant's material and component costs are expected to be 35 per cent of the final selling price to the customer, including the cost of packaging and the printing of the instruction manual.

Plant would need to invest in a 'stock float' of £10 000 to be purchased in the month before trading commences and he has negotiated 30 days' credit with his materials and component suppliers. Both the standard and advanced models have a very high reliability after soak testing and only one in 300 is likely to require complete replacement. This level of replacement could be achieved within Plant's planned labour capacity.

Plant's partner has helped in the development of the product and would work in the new business as marketing manager. Four other employees would be necessary: three in production and one as an office manager and secretary. The production salaries, including a small fixed salary for Plant and his partner are as follows:

Production employees:	One senior production technician	£24 000 per annum
	Two production assistants	£14 400 per annum
Office manager		£18 000 per annum
Plant and partner	each	£12 000 per annum

Plant has managed to recruit a senior production technician and one production assistant who will also help set up the office until the office manager and second production assistant can commence on 1 January.

Plant is well advanced in discussion with the landlords of a new science park attached to his old university. He has an option on a 25-year lease for a 200 square metre production unit, ready partitioned into work and office space, at a rent of £150 per square metre per annum including maintenance and common services. The rent would be payable a quarter in advance but through his university contacts he has negotiated a three-month 'rent holiday' allowing him to occupy the premises from 1st October to set up production. The business rates (local government taxes) would be £4800 per annum, payable from October and quarterly in arrears.

The indirect costs of running the business, all payable in the month they are incurred, would be: instruments and consumables £1400 per month (payable from the month that production starts), electricity and heating £600 per month and office costs £1200 per month (including mailing and telephone). Plant expects to produce enough each month to meet his expected monthly demand and, during the slack parts of the year, divert attention to product and business development. Ongoing advertisement in *Boat Owner* and *Yachting World* is expected to cost £1400 per month and the pitch for his stand at the boat shows is £1100 payable each January and September subsequently.

The capital equipment would cost £180 000 including final fitting out of the premises, and some initial start-up expenditure including design costs and the purchase and fitting of an exhibition stand would cost a further £18 000. These costs would be paid equally over the first three months. The equipment would have a useful life of five years and he plans to write off his initial start-up costs over three years.

Finance

Plant and his partner have £150 000 of equity that they can put into their new business. The venture capital division of Plant's bank is impressed by his proposal and is prepared to extend a start-up loan bearing interest payable at 0.5 per cent per month. Based on his estimate of maximum financial need Plant agrees to borrow £150 000. Plant is to establish a limited company with an authorised share capital of 500 000 £1 ordinary shares. He expects to pay start-up fees of £3000 and an annual accounting and audit charge of £1000 paid in February after each succeeding financial year-end. The first business planning exercise is to project a cash flow statement for the start-up period and the first six months of trading to show the maximum financial need of the business.

Step 1: Construct the revenue model

From the detail in Financial realities, Plant has two sources of revenue: sales of the standard model via the chandler and own sales of the advanced model, both commencing in January. Plant has produced a sales projection, which we assume he has researched thoroughly. The difficulty arises in that the resulting cash inflows will only be received one month after his sales of the advanced model and two months (60 days) after the sales made by the chandler have commenced. Exhibit 9.5 is a monthly analysis of Plant's revenues.

This is not his cash flow from sales, however. In the table, sales by Tackles Chandlery are shown at their catalogue price less their margin. This net figure is relevant to Plant in calculating

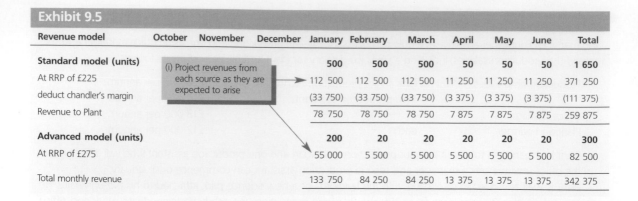

Exhibit 9.5

Revenue model	October	November	December	January	February	March	April	May	June	Total
Standard model (units)			(i) Project revenues from each source as they are expected to arise	500	500	500	50	50	50	1 650
At RRP of £225				112 500	112 500	112 500	11 250	11 250	11 250	371 250
deduct chandler's margin				(33 750)	(33 750)	(33 750)	(3 375)	(3 375)	(3 375)	(111 375)
Revenue to Plant				78 750	78 750	78 750	7 875	7 875	7 875	259 875
Advanced model (units)				200	20	20	20	20	20	300
At RRP of £275				55 000	5 500	5 500	5 500	5 500	5 500	82 500
Total monthly revenue				133 750	84 250	84 250	13 375	13 375	13 375	342 375

Review activity 9.1 Reproduce the spreadsheet of Exhibit 9.5 on Excel or some other software package. Extend the revenue model to twelve months and 'cast' a twelve-monthly revenue total. Repeat this for two further years except in the second year raise the level of sales revenue by 5 per cent. Assume that this is an increase in the volume of sales and not the price per unit sold.

The answer is available for download from our website (details are in the Preface).

his turnover as that is deemed his revenue for accounting purposes. The sales he makes on his own account are shown before credit card commission is deducted, as that is part of his cost of sales. However, because the chandler is only expected to pay 2 months later, and he only receives cash on his own sales one month in arrears we see a 'lag' effect in his cash flow.

Negotiating the credit period for sales and purchases can often be crucial from a financial point of view during a start-up phase of a new business. Customers who demand a period to pay that is longer than the average time the business has to pay its own operating costs force the new enterprise to rely on its own capital resources to finance any expansion in the volume of trade. In such a situation any rapid expansion in the volume of trade will draw liquid resources from the new firm's balance sheet into outstanding debtor balances. It is very easy for an unplanned expansion of a new business to drive it into insolvency.

Therefore, taking care to make sure that we have accounted for the correct credit period:

- two months (60 days) for the sales by Tackles Chandlery
- one month for sales of the advanced unit.

The projection of cash inflows for sales is as follows.

Exhibit 9.6

Cash inflow	October	November	December	January	February	March	April	May	June	Total
Cash flow to Plant (chandler)			(ii) Project cash inflows but note the time lags to payment			78 750	78 750	78 750	7 875	244 125
Cash flow to Plant (own sales)					55 000	5 500	5 500	5 500	5 500	77 000
Total sales cash inflow			(iii) Cast the total cash inflow		55 000	84 250	84 250	84 250	13 375	321 125

Review activity 9.2   Recast the cash flow projections above, assuming that the chandler:

- agrees to pay within one month
- takes three months rather than two to pay.

Step 2: Construct the operating expenditure model

The operating model contains the cost of sales and all other running expenditure for this new business. We lay out the model in the 'layered' format of the income statement account, showing operating cash flow analysed into:

- direct production costs
- indirect production costs
- other indirect operating costs (see Exhibit 9.7).

Any finance house such as a bank or venture capitalist may wish to see a projection of cash flow including all other finance charges before its own interest is deducted. That is the case with this exercise where initially interest will be charged on the outstanding balance.

Note that we have shown the totals of the operating costs and the start up costs separately as these are shown separately within the financing model. Plant wants to regard his costs during this initial three months as part of his capital expenditure and not part of his first year's trading.

Spreadsheet software such as Excel is an excellent tool when business planning but there is little that tests the logic of what you have done programmed into the software. You will be warned if you try to create 'circular referencing' when constructing formulas. The most usual problems are:

- forgetting to extend the (=sum) formula when new columns or rows are added
- referencing cells in formulas and functions and forgetting to change them after revising or adding in new formulas or data
- not being aware of the way a particular function performs. This is a particular problem with some of the financial functions.

To avoid some of these problems: use functions sparingly. When making changes ensure that all formulas have been correctly updated. When 'cross-casting numbers' take column casts and check that the row tasks agree with the row casts. When linking spreadsheets take a printout and check one to the other to satisfy yourself that it is doing what it is supposed to do. Finally, manually test your spreadsheet with a calculator!

Step 3: Combine the revenue and expenditure models and calculate total cash flow position

We are now in a position to summarise the projections, combining the revenue and operating expenditure models, adding in the capital expenditure and start-up costs to produce a summary statement of cash flow as in Exhibit 9.8. In this summary statement, we avoid unnecessary detail, focusing on the principal cost headings. The final lines of the summary show the cumulative cash flow without and with interest payments.

The ex-interest cash flow gives the maximum financial need if further equity could be found to finance this project. It is calculated by adding the relevant month's net cash flow

Exhibit 9.7

Cash outflow	October	November	December	January	February	March	April	May	June	Total
Direct selling expenditures		(iv) Based on 4% of Plant's sales (note incidence matches receipt of cash from credit card company)			(2 200)	(220)	(220)	(220)	(220)	(3 080)
Credit card commission (own sales)	0				(2 200)	(220)	(220)	(220)	(220)	(3 080)
Direct production costs										
Materials										
Stock float				(10 000)						(10 000)
Cost of goods sold					(58 625)	(41 300)	(41 300)	(5 863)	(5 863)	(152 950)
Cost of replacements		(vi) Take as 1/300 of the cost of goods sold			(195)	(138)	(138)	(20)	(20)	(510)
	0		0	(10 000)	(58 820)	(41 438)	(41 438)	(5 882)	(5 882)	(163 460)
Indirect production expenditures										
Labour										
Senior technician	(2 000)	(2 000)	(2 000)	(2 000)	(2 000)	(2 000)	(2 000)	(2 000)	(2 000)	(12 000)
Production Assistant	(1 200)	(1 200)	(1 200)	(1 200)	(1 200)	(1 200)	(1 200)	(1 200)	(1 200)	(7 200)
Production Assistant				(1 200)	(1 200)	(1 200)	(1 200)	(1 200)	(1 200)	(7 200)
Instruments and consumables				(1 400)	(1 400)	(1 400)	(1 400)	(1 400)	(1 400)	(8 400)
	(3 200)	(3 200)	(3 200)	(5 800)	(5 800)	(5 800)	(5 800)	(5 800)	(5 800)	(34 800)
Other indirect operating expenditures										
Salaries										
Office manager				(1 500)	(1 500)	(1 500)	(1 500)	(1 500)	(1 500)	(9 000)
Plant and partner	(2 000)	(2 000)	(2 000)	(2 000)	(2 000)	(2 000)	(2 000)	(2 000)	(2 000)	(12 000)
	(2 000)	(2 000)	(2 000)	(3 500)	(3 500)	(3 500)	(3 500)	(3 500)	(3 500)	(21 000)
General overheads										
Electricity and heating	(600)	(600)	(600)	(600)	(600)	(600)	(600)	(600)	(600)	(3 600)
Office cost	(1 200)	(1 200)	(1 200)	(1 200)	(1 200)	(1 200)	(1 200)	(1 200)	(1 200)	(7 200)
	(1 800)	(1 800)	(1 800)	(1 800)	(1 800)	(1 800)	(1 800)	(1 800)	(1 800)	(10 800)
Marketing costs										
Initial	(6 000)	(6 000)	(6 000)							
Advertising				(1 400)	(1 400)	(1 400)	(1 400)	(1 400)	(1 400)	(8 400)
Boat show pitch				(1 100)						(1 100)
	(6 000)	(6 000)	(6 000)	(2 500)	(1 400)	(1 400)	(1 400)	(1 400)	(1 400)	(9 500)
Property costs										
Lease rental				(7 500)			(7 500)			(15 000)
Local rates			(1 200)			(1 200)			(1 200)	(2 400)
	0	0	(1 200)	(7 500)	0	(1 200)	(7 500)	0	(1 200)	(17 400)
Legal, accounting and audit (3 000)										
Total operating cash flows (ongoing)				(31 100)	(73 520)	(55 358)	(61 658)	(18 602)	(19 802)	(260 040)
Start-up costs	(16 000)	(13 000)	(14 200)							

Annotation: (v) One-off stock purchase in December

Annotation: (vii) Split labour into production and other operating expenses

Exhibit 9.8

CASH INFLOW	October	November	December	January	February	March	April	May	June	Total
Cash flow to Plant (chandler)						78 750	78 750	78 750	7 875	244 125
Cash flow to Plant (own sales)					55 000	5 500	5 500	5 500	5 500	77 000
Total sales cash inflow					55 000	84 250	84 250	84 250	13 375	321 125
CASH OUTFLOW										
Operating cash flows										
Direct selling costs					(2 200)	(220)	(220)	(220)	(220)	(3 080)
Direct production costs				(10 000)	(58 820)	(41 438)	(41 438)	(5 882)	(5 882)	(163 460)
Indirect production costs				(5 800)	(5 800)	(5 800)	(5 800)	(5 800)	(5 800)	(34 800)
Indirect operating costs				(15 300)	(6 700)	(7 900)	(14 200)	(6 700)	(7 900)	(58 700)
Total operating costs				(31 100)	(73 520)	(55 358)	(61 658)	(18 602)	(19 802)	(260 040)
Total operating cash flow				(31 100)	(18 520)	28 892	22 592	65 648	(6 427)	61 085
CAPITAL EXPENDITURES										
Start up costs	(16 000)	(13 000)	(14 200)							(43 200)
Capital equipment	(60 000)	(60 000)	(60 000)							(180 000)
Total capital expenditures	**(76 000)**	**(73 000)**	**(74 200)**							**(223 200)**
FINANCING										
Issue of equity	150 000									150 000
Total financing receipts	**150 000**									**150 000**
Projected monthly cash flow	74 000	(73 000)	(74 200)	(31 100)	(18 520)	28 892	22 592	65 648	(6 427)	(12 115)
Interest charge			(366)	(523)	(619)	(477)	(367)	(40)	(73)	(2 464)
Total monthly cash flow	**74 000**	**(73 000)**	**(74 566)**	**(31 623)**	**(19 139)**	**28 415**	**22 226**	**65 608**	**(6 500)**	**(14 579)**
Cumulative cash flow (ex int)	74 000	1 000	(73 200)	(104 300)	(122 820)	(93 928)	(71 336)	(5 688)	(12 115)	
Cumulative cash flow (cum int)	74 000	1 000	(73 566)	(105 189)	**(124 328)**	(95 913)	(73 687)	(8 080)	(14 579)	

(revenue less all expenditures) to the previous month's accumulated total. So, for example in January:

Exhibit 9.9

	£
December cumulative cash flow (ex-int.)	(73 200)
Add: January monthly cash flow (ex-int.)	(31 100)
January cumulative cash flow (ex-int.)	(104 300)

The cum-interest cumulative cash flow is slightly less straightforward. To calculate it, we added the monthly cash flow to the previous month's cumulative cash flow and calculate interest on the total, adding this in to the calculation of the current cumulative total.

'Ex-interest' and 'cum-interest' are terms used within the finance professions to mean that a statement is being made or quotation given assuming that any interest payment has just been made (ex-) or is just about to be made (cum-). This terminology arises in the stock markets as well, where shares are quoted 'ex-div' or 'cum-div'. In the former the share is priced on the basis that the latest dividend has just been paid and the latter on the assumption that it will be paid shortly.

So, for example, January's cum-interest cash flow is calculated as follows:

Exhibit 9.10

	£
December cumulative cash flow (cum-int)	(73 566)
Add: January monthly cash flow (ex-int.)	(31 100)
	(104 666)
Add interest at 0.5% = 0.005 × (104 666)	(523)
January cumulative cash flow (cum-int.)	(105 189)

In practice, it is difficult to judge how much to borrow. In this exercise, if all went to plan his maximum borrowing need would be £124 328 (see Exhibit 9.8). However, if he gets it wrong and requires more he would need what is known as 'second-wave' financing. This is very difficult to obtain as obviously his original plan will have lost credibility and any further plans he produces will be regarded far less favourably than the first. Here are some strategies Plant might pursue:

- borrow the £124 328 and hope for the best
- borrow an additional amount to cover contingencies and bear the additional interest charges
- negotiate a further funding 'call-down'. Borrow what is needed for start-up plus an additional amount for contingency, which will only be requested if required later.

This final strategy will work well providing that the commitment to provide further funds is secure before the project commences. In this case, Plant has decided to borrow £150 000, which is more than sufficient to cover his maximum financial need.

Exhibit 9.11

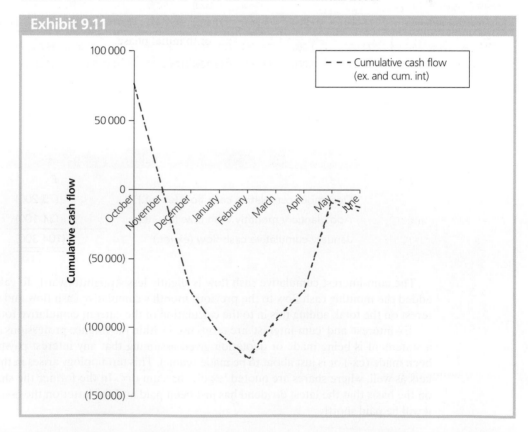

Review activity 9.3   Adjust your cash flow projection assuming that Plant can negotiate payment from the chandler in 30 days rather than 60. What difference does this make to the magnitude and timing of his maximum financial need?

A key issue for Plant is the timing of this financial requirement. As you can see from the projections both the cum- and ex-interest cumulative cash flows reach their maximum deficit in February. In this case the impact of the interest payments is relatively tiny during the first six months.

Note from this exercise that we have achieved two things: first we have identified the maximum financial need of the business of £124 328 and we have created a summary cash flow statement showing the cash flow over the first nine months of the business. Now we turn our attention to the projection of the financial statements.

Projecting the financial statements

In producing Plant's business plan, we need to create a balance sheet at 31 December (i.e. at the end of the start-up period) and at the end of each of the subsequent five years accompanied by income statement and cash flow statements. In practice there are two ways of proceeding:

1. Project five years of monthly cash flows taking annual 'slices' to obtain each of the five-year financial statements.

2. Prepare an initial cash flow on a monthly basis with a summary set of financial reports at the end of the start-up period followed by a projection of summary statements.

Although the first approach is perfectly feasible given the power of modern spreadsheets, the second approach is usually more than sufficient for most presentation purposes.

In the Plant case study we have identified a three-month preproduction phase, where all expenditures are capitalised, and a six-month initial phase.

In this exercise we show how to prepare the financial statements after the first six months of operations. A full set of projects over five years is available for download from the website.

Plant's cash flow statement for the first three months whilst he sets up his business will be as follows (based upon a borrowing of £150 000):

Exhibit 9.12

	October	November	December	Total
Capital Expenditures				
Start-up costs	(16 000)	(13 000)	(14 200)	(43 200)
Capital equipment	(60 000)	(60 000)	(60 000)	(180 000)
Total capital expenditures	(76 000)	(73 000)	(74 200)	(223 200)
Financing				
Issue of equity	150 000			150 000
Loan	150 000			150 000
Total financing receipts	300 000			300 000
Interest payable	(750)	(750)	(750)	(2 250)
Total monthly cash flow	**223 250**	**(73 750)**	**(74 950)**	**74 550**
Cumulative cash flow (cum int)	223 250	149 500	74 550	

Note how we have separated it into 'layers'. There are no operating cash flows as yet; however, there has been significant capital expenditure financed by Plant's equity and loan. There is now a monthly interest payment of £750 per month, being 0.5 per cent per month on £150 000. Plant has decided that he wants all of his start-up costs to be capitalised so these interest payments must also be added into the start-up costs of the business. This is common business practice as the interest payments, like the other start-up costs, are costs incurred in getting ready to commence production rather than the ongoing costs of production and operations. The fixed assets at 1 January are therefore:

Exhibit 9.13

Capital equipment	180 000
Start-up costs	43 200
Interest payable	2 250
	225 450

We also note that we have an outstanding creditor (shown as a current liability), as Plant has purchased inventory of £10 000 which is unpaid as at 31 December. His opening balance sheet will look like this:

Exhibit 9.14

Opening Balance Sheet

as at 1 January year 1	£
Non-current Assets	225 450
Current Assets	
Inventories	10 000
Receivables	0
Cash in hand	74 550
	84 550
Less current liability	−10 000
Less non-current liability	150 000
	150 000
Owner's Equity	150 000
Profit and loss reserve	0
	150 000

Over the subsequent six months, if all goes to plan, Plant will earn operating cash flows and his resulting cash flow projection will be as follows:

Exhibit 9.15

	January	February	March	April	May	June	Total
CASH INFLOW							
Cash flow to Plant (chandler)			78 750	78 750	78 750	7 875	244 125
Cash flow to Plant (own sales)		55 000	5 500	5 500	5 500	5 500	77 000
Total sales cash inflow		55 000	84 250	84 250	84 250	13 375	321 125
CASH OUTFLOW							
Operating cash flows							
Direct selling costs		(2 200)	(220)	(220)	(220)	(220)	(3 080)
Direct production costs	(10 000)	(58 820)	(41 438)	(41 438)	(5 882)	(5 882)	(163 460)
Indirect production costs	(5 800)	(5 800)	(5 800)	(5 800)	(5 800)	(5 800)	(34 800)
Indirect operating costs	(15 300)	(6 700)	(7 900)	(14 200)	(6 700)	(7 900)	(58 700)
Total operating costs	(31 100)	(73 520)	(55 358)	(61 658)	(18 602)	(19 802)	(260 040)
Total operating cash flow	**(31 100)**	**(18 520)**	**28 892**	**22 592**	**65 648**	**(6 427)**	**61 085**
Capital Expenditures							
Start-up costs							
Capital equipment							
Total capital expenditures							
Financing							
Issue of equity							
Loan							
Total financing receipts							
Interest payable	(750)	(750)	(750)	(750)	(750)	(750)	(4 500)
Total monthly cash flow	(31 850)	(19 270)	28 142	21 842	64 898	(7 177)	56 585
Cumulative cash flow (cum int)	42 700	23 430	51 572	73 414	138 312	131 135	

Note how this has changed in the light of the financing agreement to borrow £150 000 at a set monthly rate of interest. The overall statement of cash flow for the first six months of operations is:

Exhibit 9.16

Cash flow statement
as at 30 June year 1

	£
Cash flow from operations	61 085
less cost of financing	4 500
Net cash flow for period	56 585

The end-of-period income statement and balance sheet is created by calculating the outstanding balances at the end of June. These outstanding balances will include outstanding debtor and creditor balances from sales and purchases and all the capital expenditure items not written off. Here is an analysis of the outstanding items for Plant on his operating account:

Exhibit 9.17

	Total	Outstanding
CASH INFLOW		
Cash flow to Plant (chandler)	244 125	15 750
Cash flow to Plant (own sales)	77 000	5 500
Total sales cash inflow	321 125	21 250
CASH OUTFLOW		
Operating cash flows		
Direct selling cost	(3 080)	(220)
Direct production costs	(163 460)	(5 882)
Indirect production costs	(34 800)	0
Indirect operating costs	(58 700)	0
Total operating costs	(260 040)	(6 102)
Total operating cash flow	61 085	

If you review the original revenue and cost models you should be able to see how these outstandings have arisen. The cash flow to Plant lags sales by two months in the case of those made by the chandler and one month in the case of his own sales. Therefore, at 30 June his outstanding receipts from the chandler are £15 750, being £7875 of revenue from each of May and June. He also has £5500 of his own sales outstanding. On the cost side he has credit card commission of £220 due to be paid on his own credit card sales during the previous month as well as payments for goods purchased in June.

The only other items which we need to note before extending an income statement and balance sheet column is the planned write-off of capital equipment and start-up costs.

We can use the spreadsheet approach to analyse the balance sheet and income statement account. In Exhibit 9.18 we show that the opening balance sheet is altered by the cash receipts and payments, and the outstanding balances outlined above, to give the closing figures at the end of the six-month period.

The first column contains the opening balance sheet. We have entered asset values as positives and all the claims as negatives. The next column shows the change in the cash flow of the business over the six months of £56 585. The third outstanding shows the adjustment to

Exhibit 9.18

	Opening Balance Sheet	Total Cash Flow	Outstanding	Income Statement	Closing Balance Sheet
CASH INFLOW					
Cash flow to Plant (chandler)		244 125	15 750	259 875	15 750
Cash flow to Plant (own sales)		77 000	5 500	82 500	5 500
Total sales		321 125		342 375	
CASH OUTFLOW					
Operating cash flows					
Direct selling costs		(3 080)	(220)	(3 300)	(220)
Direct production costs	(10 000)	(163 460)	(5 882)	(159 342)	(5 882)
Indirect production costs		(34 800)	0	(34 800)	0
Indirect operating costs		(58 700)	0	(58 700)	0
Total operating costs		(260 040)		(256 142)	
Operating Cash Flow/Profit		61 085		86 233	
Stocks	10 000				10 000
Capital Expenditures					
Start-up costs	45 450			(7 575)	37 875
Capital equipment	180 000			(18 000)	162 000
Financing					
Issue of equity	(150 000)				(150 000)
Loan	(150 000)				(150 000)
Total financing receipts					
Interest payable		(4 500)		(4 500)	
Profit for period				56 158	(56 158)
Cash flow	74 550	56 585			131 135

the income statement for:

Outstanding receivables (Tackles Chandlery) – 2 months	£15 750
Own sales (from credit card company) – 1 month	5 500
Outstanding credit card commission	2 200
Outstanding production costs	5 882

The fourth column shows the income statement that results including adjustments for depreciation. The fifth column shows the outstandings on each row that form the basis of the balance sheet.

Another approach to creating the statements of account is to use the extended trial balance method.

Exhibit 9.19

	NCA +	Inv +	Rec +	C =	CL +	NCL +	OE +	R −	E
Opening balance sheet (1 January Year 1)	225 450	10 000	0	74 550	10 000	150 000	150 000		
Revenues									
cash flow from chandler				244 125				244 125	
cash flow from Plant				77 000				77 000	
chandler's sales outstanding			15 750					15 750	
Plant's sales outstanding			5 500					5 500	
Operating expenses									
direct selling costs				(3 080)					3 080
direct production costs				(163 460)	(10 000)				153 460
indirect production costs				(34 800)					34 800
indirect operating costs				(58 700)					58 700
direct selling costs outstanding					220				220
direct production costs outstanding					5 882				5 882
Depreciation on capital equipment	(18 000)								18 000
Operating revenues less costs								342 375	274 142
Other expenditures									
start-up costs written off	(7 575)								7 575
interest paid				(4 500)					4 500
Net profit							56 158	342 375	286 217
Closing balance sheet (30 June Year 1)	199 875	10 000	21 250	131 135	6 102	150 000	206 158	342 375	342 375

From this statement it is an easy job to extract an income statement and balance sheet in standard form:

Exhibit 9.20

Balance Sheet as at 30 June year 1	£		Income Statement for the 6 months ended 30 June year 1	£
Non-current Assets	199 875			
			Sales revenue	342 375
Current Assets			less cost of sales	215 442
Inventories	10 000		Gross profit	126 933
Receivables	21 250		less other operating costs	58 700
Cash in hand	131 135		Operating profit	68 233
	162 385		Start-up costs written off	(7 575)
Less current liability	−6 102		Interest payable	4 500
Less non-current liability	−150 000		Net profit retained	56 158
	206 158			
Owner's Equity	150 000			
Profit and loss reserve	56 158			
	206 158			

Review activity 9.4 Extend the cash flow analysis for the full year and project the year-end summary cash flow, income statement and balance sheet at 31 December.

Once the financial models are set up it is a straightforward task to project forward the cash flow figures over any planning period that is necessary. For most business start-ups a five-year projection is usually sufficient for most funding purposes. For some projects the planning period may be much longer. Indeed, the Eurotunnel business plan constructed in 1985 included projections for the first 50 years of operations.

Appraising a business plan

The process of business planning and, particularly, financial planning is important in defining funding requirements, establishing the priorities for a business and setting the parameters for the annual budgeting process as the business becomes established. The appraisal of a business plan consists of the following four stages:

1. ensuring that all the necessary components, as described earlier in the chapter, are in place

2. ensuring that the plans are internally consistent, i.e. conclusions from one plan are translated into others

Exhibit 9.21 Cash flow profile of typical start-ups

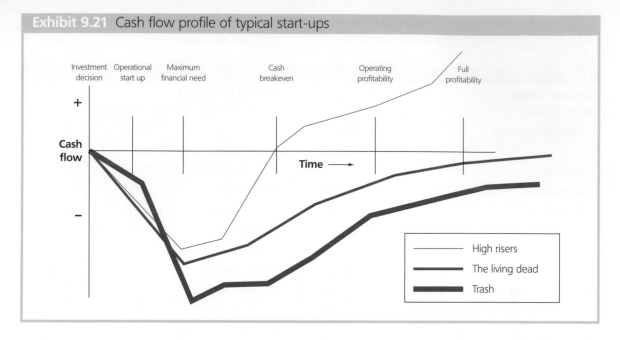

3. testing the assumptions within each plan and providing revised plans under different assumptions

4. evaluating the conclusions of the plan, i.e. whether the plan fits within the total portfolio of other activities or lending, whether it promises performance at a level which justifies investment within it.

Exhibit 9.21 shows the cash flow profiles of the three classes of start-up faced by the typical venture capitalist. Some start-ups do not turn out to be viable: the business fails to reach operating profitability and its capital is exhausted. These are the projects where the financial gamble has failed and the objective is to close as quickly as possible with minimum losses. Out of every ten start-ups as many as three can be like this. The intermediate category is the 'living dead', that is businesses that do not realise their promise. With these the venture capitalist will attempt to inject management expertise to help boost the business but, if that fails, to get out in the medium term – recovering as much as they can of their original investment often leaving the owners seeking new finance or the prospect of closure. Out of ten start-ups four or five will be in this category. Finally, there are the star performers or 'high-risers' that produce super rates of return and come to full and sustainable profitability well ahead of the original plan. These businesses help finance the losses elsewhere and offer significant capital gains when the venture capitalist exits either by a stock exchange flotation, takeover or management buyout. Out of ten start-ups, only two or three will be in this category.

In appraisal, a critical stage is in the testing of assumptions. Assumptions fall into a hierarchy which can be classified as follows:

- *assumptions of capability* – these specify the opportunities which the business would be capable of following given the range of skills and technologies which it has at its disposal

- *assumptions of state* – these are assumptions about future values, the type of market, the market share which can be gathered at a particular price, yields on new processes, labour productivity in the future and so on

- *assumptions of fact* – these are assumptions about current conditions: market prices, demand, competitor products, current process yields, tax regimes and rates, etc. In this context, what may appear to be hard data from sample surveys still generate assumptions of fact concerning the population from which those data are drawn.

Review activity 9.5 Review the business case for Plant above. List all the assumptions that have been made in the exercise and work through those that you believe could be resolved before start-up.

A business plan which is shown to have deficiencies at any of the above levels will lose credibility in the eyes of whoever is appraising its viability. Clearly, assumptions of fact should be replaced by actual evidence if it can be found although data rarely come free of some implicit assumptions in their measurement or in their classification. Even judgements of competitor prices rely upon assumptions about the comparability of their products with the one(s) specified in the business plan and the other customer support which might be provided. Assumptions of state should be backed by evidence from properly conducted trials, pilot plant experiments or market research as the case may be. In studies on corporate failure, the absence of market research, for example, has been shown as a prime mistake by management and one which sows the seeds of weakness within any business. Assumptions of capability are generated to a certain extent by the plan itself and will be critical in the funding decision. But, the assumption of capability in delivering the business as planned may still be insufficient to gain a lender's support if the project does not promise high enough returns or does not fit within the lender's perception of what is appropriate business to be engaged in.

When a venture capitalist looks at potential business or one that is seeking new finance they have certain key ratios that they believe are critical in assessing the financial prospects of the business. In a survey of all members of the Venture Capital Association in the UK the following were identified as the most popular ratios when appraising projects:

- cash flow/total debt (the Beaver failure ratio)
- interest coverage (ratio of profit before interest and tax to interest payable)
- receivables age (receivables to credit sales ($\times$ 365))
- cash flow/sales
- acid test ratio
- debt/equity ratio (gearing).

In Chapter 7 we described how these ratios are calculated.

Business planning for the continuing business

Business planning for the continuing business is very similar to that undertaken for the new start-up. Many businesses construct a business plan over a five-year time horizon (a 'quinquennial' planning cycle) and revise their plans on an annual basis taking into account relevant outcomes as they occur. As Argenti and many other management writers have pointed out, a five-year business plan will have different phases:

- Phase A (budget time horizon). This is the immediate future where on the basis of past business decisions and commitments the consequences are known with a reasonable degree of certainty. Given a good degree of predictability in the market, budgets can be established and allocated to centres of activity within the business. This time period is usually around one full seasonal cycle for most businesses, i.e. one year.

- Phase B (business planning horizon). On the basis of what is known about the business and its current market conditions this is the period over which future forecasts can be made with a reasonable degree of confidence. This is the time horizon over which significant capital plans can be established. This time period is usually from one to five years but may be shorter in very volatile industries (such as fashion goods and computer systems) or longer in industries providing staple goods and services (transport, foodstuffs, etc.)

- Phase C (strategic planning horizon). This far into the future the firm is setting its long-term aspirations in terms of its market and its own internal capabilities. This is the time horizon over which major capital investments currently undertaken will bear fruit. Few small or medium-sized businesses are in a position to put down strategic plans of greater than ten years. Some large firms involved in capital-intensive industries such as Eurotunnel or the pharmaceutical industries (where it can take ten to fifteen years to bring new products to market) may well be planning over this timescale.

In the short run firms who create and maintain a business planning process can use the results to create their short-term budgets. This is the issue to which we will now turn.

The role of budgeting in the firm

Budgeting is an activity we all engage in some time or other – often because we have discovered that our cash outgoings have exceeded our cash income for some reason. Cash, having many of the attributes of water, flows away with amazing rapidity and, as one sage put it, life is a cash-flow problem.

The motivations for budgeting by individuals and firms are also surprisingly similar. Most individuals feel motivated to budget for some very simple reasons:

- in order to plan expenditures so that they remain within the bounds of what is available to spend

- in order to motivate themselves to earn more or to keep to or cut expenditures

- to help minimise uncertainty about their financial future. Individuals often find the urge to produce a budget when times are hard and they are concerned about where the money is coming from or going to

- to keep control of their financial affairs

- to help forecast the financial future so that large spending decisions can be made and financed to best effect.

Companies find themselves in exactly the same situation as the individual who is trying to manage his or her own personal affairs, except that the sums of money involved are usually much larger. We can identify six important purposes for budgeting in firms:

- as a method of planning the use of the firm's resources in the light of potential market opportunities

- as a regular and systematic vehicle for the firm's forecasting activities (although these forecasts, allied with the planning aspect of budgeting, are likely to be self-fulfilling)

- as a means of controlling the activities of various groups within the firm

- as a means of motivating individuals within the firm to achieve the performance levels agreed and set for them

- as a means of communicating the wishes and aspirations of senior management to other interest groups within the firm
- as a means of resolving conflicts of interest between the various groups within the firm.

This idea of planning, motivating, controlling and forecasting is significant in business organisations. Much of what is done in budgeting is self-evident and quite straightforward – the ability to project a statement of cash income and expenditure, the ability to summarise that information and, then, the hard part, check back later to see how well actual performance agrees with the budget. However, the subtleties of budgeting lie in the processes that firms adopt in order to set budgets and the effect that they have upon the behaviour of the individuals who run the budgetary centres within the firm.

The role of budgeting within different firms will differ, depending upon the organisational needs of each. Each company will have different practices and procedures depending upon its own organisational characteristics. Therefore, very few general rules can be laid down concerning the practice of budgeting. Budgeting is not a simple technical skill which can be divorced from the context in which it is carried out.

In this section we will briefly discuss the six reasons for budgeting outlined above.

Budgeting and planning

At each of the different levels within the firm, management faces the need to plan the resources under its control. Senior management, with its primary concern with strategic decision-making will wish to ensure that the firm achieves its long-term targets. This will entail:

Review activity 9.6 Construct a personal (or family) budget for yourself over the next month. Plan on the basis of cash inflows (wages or salary, grants, etc.) and cash outflows under different expenditure headings (food, clothing, drink, entertainment, etc.). Regard any permanent savings as 'expenditure' to a deposit or other long-term savings account. Keep a record of all the cash receipts and expenditure you make during the month and then, at the end of the month, answer the following questions:

1. What aim did you set yourself when drawing up your budget (making a cash surplus, breaking even, reducing your overdraft, etc.)?
2. What information did you use to make your plans?
3. How carefully did you have to time your cash payments in order to avoid running into deficit?
4. Can you allocate causes to the differences between your planned and actual figures?
5. Can you reconcile the figure on your bank statement and credit card bills with your summary of actual receipts and payments?
6. How did you motivate yourself to keep within your budget?

- planning the long-term aggregate cash resources of the firm
- planning the deployment of physical resources to meet new market opportunities
- planning to increase the welfare of the firm's various stakeholder groups.

The planning activity of lower levels of management will be determined by the degree of discretion which particular managers have over the types of decision they can make. However, the success of the budgeting exercise is largely dependent upon the degree of involvement of all levels of management in the planning process. A desirable feature of any budgeting system is the degree of consensus which it promotes throughout all levels of the firm. Unless all levels of management are involved in the planning process the formal budgets will be seen, by those who are not involved in their preparation, as a simple extension of senior management's authority. In the long run, imposed budgets are less effective than budgets agreed through negotiation and consensus.

Financial realities One of the pressing and less welcome tasks faced by many departmental managers is to prepare or revise a staffing budget. This is usually required for negotiating the overall expenditure budgets, which in most cost centres in firms and public-sector organisations are separated into 'pay' and 'non-pay'. A staff budget shows monthly salary costs over the next twelve months. Here are some of the issues that staffing budgets create:

● Staff costs will include salary (gross paid), employer's national insurance contributions, and employer's contribution to a pension scheme (these are called 'on-costs').

● For salaried staff on a 'scale' there will be 'incremental drift' as salaries are raised by the scale increment each year. Occasionally, the increment may only be awarded if performance is judged to have been satisfactory or better. Projected cost of living increases should also be included.

● Where increases are awarded they can be 'consolidated' into salary, which means they are included in future years, or they can be non-consolidated, which means that they are a 'one-off payment'.

Tom's department has four employees. Tom's salary is £32 000 and he is at the top of a 20-point incremental salary scale. The employees have each been highly rated in their annual review and as a result will get the £450 (current scale) annual increment paid in September. A 3 per cent cost-of-living award has been negotiated by the union and is payable in two equal instalments in April and October. Arthur has received a one-off merit award (non-consolidated) of £600 payable at the end of January. On-costs add 18 per cent to salary. Sally has resigned and is serving three months' notice until the end of February. Her replacement has been advertised for but is unlikely to take up the post until 1 June. It is expected that the replacement will be appointed at scale point 5. The members of Tom's department are paid as follows:

Exhibit 9.22		
	Scale point	Salary
Tom	20	32 000
Arthur	14	29 300
Pete	8	26 600
Alison	8	26 600
Sally	5	25 250

Tom's staffing budget would be as shown in Exhibit 9.23. The steps followed in producing it were:

1. The full annual cost at each staff member's current position on the scale is calculated.

2. The monthly amount is projected for all staff (including AN Other), adding one twelfth of the annual increment to each salary from September onwards.

3. Each monthly salary payment is raised by 1.5 per cent from April through to September and by 3 per cent from October onwards.

4. The additional flat-rate payment is added to Arthur's salary in January.

5. The projection for Sally is deleted from March forward and included for AN Other from January to June inclusive.

▶

Exhibit 9.23

	Scale	Salary	on-costs	total	Jan	Feb	March	April	May	June	July	Aug	Sept	Oct	Nov	Dec	TOTAL
Tom	20	32 000	5760	37 760	3148	3148	3148	3196	3196	3196	3196	3196	3234	3281	3281	3281	38 501
Arthur	14	29 300	5274	34 588	3482	2882	2832	2926	2926	2926	2926	2926	2964	3007	3007	3007	35 861
Pete	8	26 600	4788	31 376	2616	2616	2616	2656	2656	2656	2656	2656	2694	2733	2733	2733	32 021
Al son	8	26 600	4788	31 375	2616	2616	2616	2656	2656	2656	2656	2656	2694	2733	2733	2733	32 021
Sally	5	25 250	4545	29 800	2483	2483											4 967
AN Other	5	25 250	4545	29 800							2521	2521	2559	2556	2596	2596	15 389
					14 347	13 747	11 263	11 432	11 432	11 432	13 953	13 953	14 143	14 352	14 352	14 352	158 759

Budgeting and forecasting

The planning aspect of the budgeting process is concerned with extending management's control over as many decision variables as possible. However, a number of decision variables will be outside of management's control at any point in time. Two possible reasons why this may be are:

● The variables may not be under the firm's direct control. Examples are: government interest rate policy, the future demand for the company's product (although this can be controlled to a limited extent through the firm's marketing activity), the level of inflation, nationally agreed wage claims affecting the company's labour force, exchange rate movements, the impact of new technology and so on.

● The variables concerned are not expected to arise for a considerable period of time (the eventual sales level of a novel product still in the early stages of development).

In the first case, management will have to make forecasts or rely upon the forecasts of others when drawing up its budgets. Where management has some control over the variables in question the process of forecasting merges into that of planning and the forecasts management make tend to become self-fulfilling. This is most pronounced where there is only a short time difference between the budgeting process and the impact of the variables in question.

Budgeting as a method of organisation control

Firm budgets are a very important instrument of managerial control. Once plans have been agreed and implemented, the need will arise to compare them with actual results as they occur. Differences (or variances) between actual and budgeted figures will guide management in:

● identifying areas where performance has been better or worse than anticipated and deciding what (if any) corrective action is appropriate

● rewarding those individuals who have performed better than expected and taking remedial actions where necessary with those who have failed to come up to expectations

● deciding the necessary revisions to future plans and targets in the light of current actual results.

An important technique of short-term control is called 'management by exception'. This technique entails identifying differences between actual and budgeted figures (variance analysis) and where these differences exceed certain preset bounds management will attempt to assign causes and take corrective action if appropriate. We look at variance analysis in more detail later in this chapter.

Budgets and motivation

The idea of controlling performance through a firm's reward system is closely related to an understanding of how financial and non-financial rewards and punishments can motivate individuals. One of the most useful spin-offs from the budgeting procedure is its use for relating staff performance to motivation. A number of theories have been put forward to explain what motivates individuals to perform tasks to a specific standard. Some of these theories are needs-based, suggesting that people are motivated to satisfy needs ranging from having the necessary income to support their chosen lifestyle to gaining esteem for a job well done. Other theories argue that individuals are motivated by an inbuilt sense of equity and fairness in their relationship with others. However, what is interesting about most of these theories of human motivation is that financial rewards are only part of the equation for most individuals. Setting worthwhile and understandable goals and rewarding achievement by recognising the worth of the individual are just as important.

Budgets and organisational structure

In highly bureaucratic organisations with formal 'line' management systems the budgeting system will reflect the hierarchy of management within the firm. For example, a traditional budgeting system will reflect the lines of management seniority and accountability.

At each stage going down through the organisation, the various budgets, reflecting the operating and tactical planning decisions made within the firm (sales, purchases, production, cash, labour, marketing, etc.) are derived from the 'master budget'. The master budget is expressed in terms of the company's financial statements: budgeted income statement, balance sheet and cashflow. In a system such as shown in Exhibit 9.24 the budgeting procedure is designed to reflect the aspirations of senior management and also reflect their performance.

In less formal organisations, the budgeting system should support the informal lines of communication within the firm and the shared nature of authority common in such organisations. The highly centralised authority associated with the formal, bureaucratic firm has high 'compliance' costs associated with enforcing senior management's will throughout the business. In such organisations senior management will have to spend considerable time ensuring that its wishes are properly complied with and that the firm's control systems are working effectively. In the less formal organisation these compliance costs may be lower, but management must work much harder to integrate the overall activities of the various differentiated aspects of the firm.

Exhibit 9.24 The budget structure in a functionally organised business

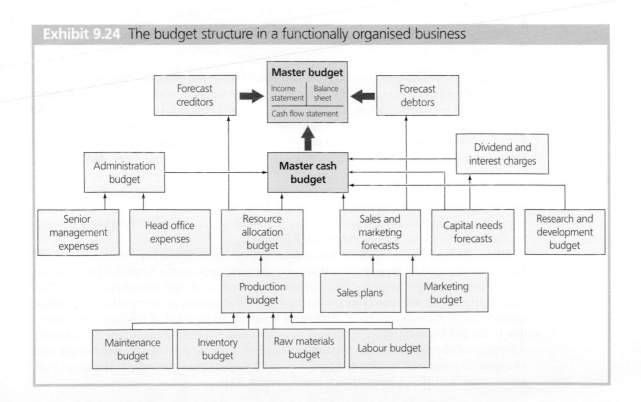

Budgeting and conflict resolution

In Chapter 1 we described a firm as a collection of different stakeholder groups. The budgeting system can provide an important means for resolving the conflicts of interest which arise and producing the consensus necessary for the effective operation of the firm. A number of ways in which budgeting can help to resolve conflicts between various groups are as follows:

- By providing a mechanism for negotiation (both overt and covert) between different groups within the firm. Overt negotiation is normally conducted in the formal committees and other meetings set up to settle the budgets for the coming period. On the other hand, covert negotiation can occur in many different ways. For example, if a particular group within the firm (say a research and development department) realised that it was likely to underspend in a particular financial year then we would expect a large amount of 'catch-up' spending as the financial year comes to a close. Often this spending is not about making necessary expenditures for the good of the firm but rather to inform senior management that its budget should not be cut in future years.

- By the planned creation of slack within the system so that incompatible aims can be satisfied without destructive internal competition between the various interest groups. Indeed, at any point in time a large proportion of a firm's planned surplus will be devoted to allowing groups with incompatible aims to exist side by side.

- By directing the attention of the organisation at different times to different aims. For example, within a production group one month's budget may be aimed toward enhancing the quality of materials produced. Another month's budget, on the other hand, could well be orientated toward cutting costs. Thus the budgeting system can, sequentially, focus attention upon two different aspects of production performance which are in conflict.

Budgetary slack

We have distinguished between budgets and forecasts when discussing business planning. For the perfectly efficient firm, that is a firm able to maximise its economic performance under all conditions and over all timescales, the projections of its financial performance will be the same as its forecast of what it is potentially able to achieve given its capabilities and resources. In the real world, firms recognise that they may not be able to achieve what they forecast and for this reason set projections which incorporate varying degrees of **budgetary slack**. Leaving some budgetary slack is necessary, recognising the fact that perfectly efficient working is an impossible target. However, in large organisations, there can be powerful tendencies by lower-level managers to build in more slack than is desirable. Even in those organisations where budgets and plans are imposed, lower-level managers can always find ways of subverting the budgetary system to create the slack required.

Oliver Williamson, an eminent US academic who has explored the behaviour of firms and their management using **transaction cost economics** argues that managers gain position in their firms through the size of their 'empires': the more staff they control the more important their position and power in the hierarchy. This all serves to create what Williamson refers to as 'organisational bloat'. This bloat leads to the creation of misalignment costs – that is, the hidden costs incurred because the organisation is not optimally structured to take advantage of the markets and opportunities open to it. These costs are the deadweight that an organisation carries and the principal source of waste. The uncontrolled creation of budgetary slack is a prime source of such misalignment costs.

Budgeting methodologies and variance analysis

Over the years different methodologies have arisen for the creation of annual budgets. These can be summarised as follows.

Planned budgeting

These are derived from a rolling business plan as described above. The business plan specifies the target outcomes in terms of overall profitability and cash flow but will also set various performance targets. The problem for senior management is to negotiate, with divisional and departmental heads, responsibilities for achieving targets within the plan. The benefit of such a system is that budgets are created around a coherent strategy as formulated within the business plan. The downside is that unless more junior levels of management were involved in the original planning process they might not 'buy in' to what is being proposed.

Incremental budgeting

This is the traditional mode of budgeting where senior management adjust the next annual budget in terms of the previous year's outcomes 'plus or minus' a bit depending on what they believe to be achievable. Different levels of management within the firm will spend considerable effort attempting to gain the full benefits of the increase or to minimise their exposure to any cuts. Such systems are a recipe for a firm which does not have strong aspirations to change or a public-sector body that is adjusting its spending plans as new funding is announced by central government.

Zero-based budgeting

With **zero-based budgeting (ZBB)**, budgets are assumed to be zero at the beginning of each planning period and departments and divisions are required to justify their next year's activities from a nil base. Each budget unit within the firm is required to produce its plans for the next twelve months and prepare a bid for resources against those plans. In the 1980s and 1990s the UK government was keen to promote ZBB in local authorities to see if public services could be provided more cheaply by contract suppliers rather than through existing departments. Likewise many firms that have adopted the method use it to test whether departments or divisions can be justified or whether it makes more economic sense to 'buy' the goods or service from a third-party supplier. As a result, ZBB is now often treated with suspicion by labour unions and it is rarely used consistently by firms because of the disruption that it can cause to work relationships.

There are many other budgeting systems that have been tried but most firms in recent years have tended towards the planned budgeting system described above.

Management by exception and variance analysis

Once budgets are in place and the business is under way the differences between budget and actual will start to emerge. The differences are termed 'budgetary variances' and the process of collecting and acting upon exceptional variances is termed 'management by exception'.

Many budgeted figures such as budget sales revenue, budgeted materials usage and budgeted labour hours involve a price per unit component and a quantity component. Budgeted materials cost is budgeted unit cost for the material concerned multiplied by the budget usage. Budgeted labour usage is budgeted wage rate (the price component) multiplied by budgeted labour hours (the quantity component).

In practice budgets are often built using **standard costing**, from standard costs and quantities such as 'standard cost per unit', 'standard labour rate', 'standard material usage' and so on. A 'standard' is a planned cost per unit, usage or rate based upon what would be reasonably expected given the physical specification of the product, current price lists of bought-in items and current catalogue prices for goods to be sold. Management accountants often refer to costs or prices at the unit level as 'standards' and reserve the term 'budget' for aggregated figures such as total sales revenue or total cost.

Revenue variances

The variance between budgeted sales revenue and actual sales revenue for example is going to be given by:

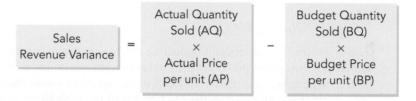

Exhibit 9.25 shows the difference between the actual revenue and the budgeted revenue as two rectangular areas superimposed on one another (remember the area of a rectangle equals its height times its breadth).

The difference between the actual sales revenue and the budget sales revenue is given by the area of the border. The price variance is given by the area of the price variance rectangle:

Price variance = [AP – BP] × AQ

and the sales volume variance:

Volume variance = [AQ – BQ] × BP

Exhibit 9.25 From gross variance to price and volume variances

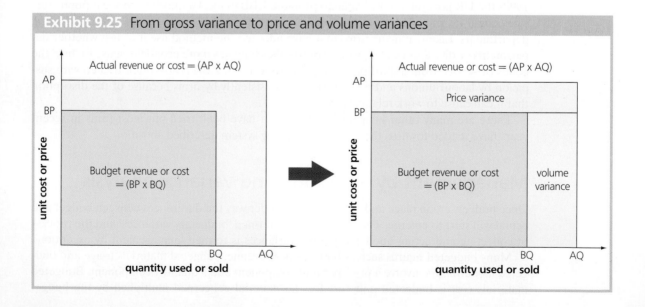

Financial realities BMW sold 650 series 3.30 sports convertibles for an average price of £31 750 each in May. It had budgeted to sell 625 vehicles for £33 355 during that month.

Its actual sales revenue, budget sales revenue and sales variance were as follows:

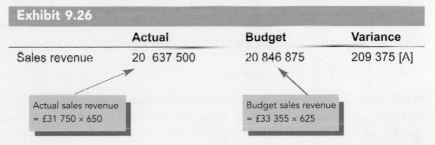

Exhibit 9.26

	Actual	Budget	Variance
Sales revenue	20 637 500	20 846 875	209 375 [A]

Actual sales revenue = £31 750 × 650

Budget sales revenue = £33 355 × 625

The overall or 'gross' sales revenue variance is −£209 375 or, to use the convention suggested in Chapter 7, is simply labelled [A] for adverse. This variance is just 1 per cent of the budget. We can split this adverse variance down into its two constituent parts using the formulas shown earlier:

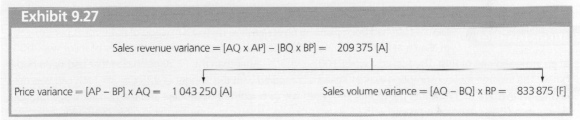

Exhibit 9.27

Sales revenue variance = [AQ × AP] − [BQ × BP] = 209 375 [A]

Price variance = [AP − BP] × AQ = 1 043 250 [A]

Sales volume variance = [AQ − BQ] × BP = 833 875 [F]

- an adverse price variance of £1 043 250 as a result of the lower-than-expected selling price (presumably due to discounts offered at the dealership)
- a favourable sales volume (or quantity sold) variance of £833 875 because more vehicles were sold in the month than anticipated.

The calculations are shown in detail in Exhibit 9.27.

The net of the price and the sales volume variance add back to the adverse gross sales variance of £209 375.

Interpreting the sales revenue variances

In the BMW example the adverse price variance has almost certainly been brought about by discounting in the dealerships but this has not been overcome by the increase in sales. The automatic response might be to argue that discounting should not occur. However, another explanation of the variance may be that the original budgeted sales volume was too optimistic given the list price, or the list price consists of a margin to allow for some discounting by the dealers, or it may simply have been a less favourable selling period during this particular month than in previous years. All the **variance analysis** does at this level is to focus attention on the possible source of the problem rather than definitively pinpointing 'blame'.

Direct cost variances

The technique of splitting an overall variance into its constituent parts is the same for direct cost variances as for the sales revenue variances discussed above. So, for example, total labour cost is the product of the wage rate per hour and the number of hours worked. Returning to

Exhibit 9.26, the 'actual price' would in the case of labour be the actual wage rate per hour and the 'actual quantity' would be the actual labour usage in hours. Similarly, for materials, we would have an actual cost per unit and a budget (or standard) cost per unit. We would also have an actual materials usage and a budgeted materials usage. In the example below we have actual and budgeted sales revenues and labour, material and variable overheads costs. Our first task is to split out the 'price' effect and the 'volume' effect using the method described above and demonstrated by another example from DialaSid Ltd below.

Efficiency and activity variances

When reviewing the volume (quantity or usage) variances under each of the cost headings it should be apparent that part of the reason for the differences observed is because the actual number of miles charged to customers was different from that originally budgeted. We can measure the impact of the change in output level by revising the original budget for fuel, driver wages and variable overheads to take account of the larger number of metered miles charged to customers. This revised budget is called a 'flexible' or sometimes a 'flexed' 'budget'.

DialaSid Ltd had been planning on an average metered mileage of 4000 miles per taxi-cab in March at a standard rate of 90p per mile. In fact the average number of miles was 4100 at an increased rate of 94p. The fuel cost was £3.00 per gallon rather than the £2.70 per gallon that had been budgeted. The average fuel consumption was 210 gallons compared with the budget of 225 gallons. Each cab was driven for an average of 320 hours per month compared with a budget of 300 hours and the budget wage rate for drivers was £6.40 per hour compared with £6.50 actually paid. Variable maintenance and other overheads averaged £25.80 per month with an average of four cleaning and maintenance checks per week. Based on the previous year's figures 4.2 checks had been planned at an average cost of £27 per check. These maintenance costs are assumed to be directly variable with mileage.

Here is a statement of the actual and budget figures for fare revenue (sales), petrol costs (materials), driver wage rates and variable overheads:

Exhibit 9.28

Sid's Taxis Ltd
Taxi Cab Analysis – March

	Actual Price	Actual Quantity	Actual Total	Budget Price	Budget Quantity	Budget Total	Total Variance	Price/cost Variance	Quantity/ Usage Variance
	1	2	3	4	5	6	7	8	9
			$= 1 \times 2$			$= 4 \times 5$	$= 3 - 6$	$= (1 - 4)$ $\times 2$	$= (2 - 5)$ $\times 4$
Sales revenue									
Total Fares per Cab	0.94	4100	3854	0.9	4000	3600	254 [F]	164 [F]	90 [F]
Cab Costs									
Fuel	3	210	630	2.7	225	607.5	22.5 [A]	63 [A]	40.5 [F]
Driver wages	6.5	320	2080	6.4	300	1920	160 [A]	32 [A]	128 [A]
Variable overheads	25.8	4	103.2	27	4.2	113.4	10.2 [F]	4.8 [F]	5.4 [F]
Contribution per cab			1040.8			959.1	81.7 [F]	73.8 [F]	7.9 [F]

Note how the variances under each heading have been designated as [F] for favourable or [A] for adverse. Favourable variances are those that will lead to an increase in contribution, and adverse variances to a decrease. If you net off the favourable and the adverse variances under each heading you will see that they agree with the contribution variance on the bottom row. Note also that each variance has been split into its component 'price' element and its component 'volume' element using the formulas shown earlier in this section.

Financial realities The flexed budget for Sid's Taxis during the month of March was as follows:

Exhibit 9.29

Sid's Taxis Ltd
Taxi Cab Analysis   March

	Budget Quantity	Actual Quantity	Flexed Budget	Budget Price	Activity Variance	Efficiency Variance	Quantity Variance
	5	2	10	4	$= (10 - 5) \times 4$	$= (2 - 10) \times 4$	
Sales revenue							
Total Fares per Cab	4000	4100	4100	0.9			
Cab Costs							
Fuel	225	210	230.6	2.7	15.12 [A]	55.62 [F]	40.5 [F]
Driver wages	300	320	307.5	6.4	48 [A]	80 [A]	128 [A]
Variable overheads	4.2	4	4.3	27	2.7 [A]	8.1 [F]	5.4 [F]

The flexed budget for fuel usage, for example, is as follows:

$$\text{Flexed Usage (quantity)} = \text{Budget Usage/quantity} \times \frac{\text{Actual Output Level}}{\text{Budget Output Level}}$$

Using this formula we would have expected the budgeted usage of fuel to have been 230.6 gallons, assuming the actual level of metered miles, and that fuel is directly variable with output level:

Flexed usage $= 225 \times 4100/4000 = 230.6$ gallons

The difference between the original budget and the flexed budget is the variance in fuel used because the level of output or 'activity' is different from that which formed the basis of the original budget. Thus the 'activity variance' is given by:

Activity variance $= (230.6 - 225) \times 2.7 = £15.12$ [A]

Note it is an adverse variance because the usage was more than originally budgeted. Because the activity variance is part of the original usage or quantity variance it is 'priced' at the budgeted price per unit, which in this case is £2.70 per gallon of fuel.

The difference between the actual usage and the flexed budget is caused by more or less efficiency in the use of fuel:

$$\text{Efficiency variance} = (210 - 230.6) \times 2.7 = £55.62 \text{ [F]}$$

This indicates that the drivers were considerably more efficient in their usage of fuel than anticipated when the budget was originally established for the year. Note also that the sum of the activity and the efficiency variance net off to the quantity variance.

Interpreting the direct cost variances

Actual costs will differ from budgeted costs for a number of reasons:

1. Variations in the level of overall output will bring about equivalent variations in the usage of the resource represented by the cost item concerned. The activity variance is normally attributed to the management level that is responsible for the levels of output and sales achieved rather than to the managers responsible for production.

2. Variations in the efficiency with which different resources are used in production. In Sid's case, for example, there were considerable efficiency savings in the use of fuel and in the maintenance of the taxis. However, it appears that the drivers have been less efficient in the use of their time. Of course there may be many reasons why this has come about. It may be that drivers have been parked up for a greater proportion of their time using less fuel overall (and with less maintenance requirements on their vehicles) but at the expense of their labour time. However, it is not necessarily the case that efficiency variances are directly attributable to the manager 'doing the driving'. All the variance analysis does is suggest where problems may lie and point to where management should investigate rather than uniquely attributing blame.

In general, once the variances of actual from budget have been established a *management report* for the period will be produced and some procedure applied to determine whether the variances are material. There will always be minor variations from budget due to random effects: a driver may go sick or a maintenance repair take much longer than expected. Management will need to establish acceptable ranges within which managers will not be called to account. Sometimes these ranges are set using percentages of the budgeted figures. Sometimes they will be set using historical data and statistical evidence of the random variation collected and break-points established.

Other levels of variance analysis

More sophisticated variance analysis procedures are employed by some firms. It is not uncommon for variance analysis to include the over- or under-recovery of indirect costs to production. We do not cover this topic in this book although the problems of overhead analysis are discussed in the next chapter. The end-of-chapter readings will give you further guidance if you wish to pursue this topic.

Chapter summary

In this chapter we have summarised the main issues and methods in generating business plans. We emphasised the central importance of the business model and the specification of the cash flows that are likely to arise from it. Our discussion of financial planning focused on the forecasting of cash flows and the creation of summary cash flow statements, profit and loss and balance sheets. As well as discussing the approach to appraising business plans we also showed how many firms use them as the basis for establishing budgets within the context of an integrated planning and budgeting system. After reviewing the different methods and issues relating to budgeting we have then spent some time discussing how variances between actual and budget figures can be analysed. In the next chapter we will move on to discuss the related issues of cost management.

Further reading

Argenti, J. (1980) *Practical Corporate Planning*, London: Unwin. This is a classic in the management literature and well worth the effort to track it down. Argenti tries to force a distinction between corporate and business planning which you should bear in mind when reading his book alongside this chapter.

Drury, C. (1992) *Standard Costing*, London: Cengage Learning. This tiny book goes through the mechanics of variance analysis – readable and short.

Emmanuel, C. and Otley, D. (1997) *Readings in Accounting for Management Control*, London: Cengage Learning. An excellent book of readings, but from the perspective of this chapter we recommend number 12 as giving a useful overview of the budgeting process.

Gupta, U. (2000) *Done Deals: Venture Capitalists Tell Their Stories*, Boston: Harvard Business School Press. An interesting book from the US, in which venture capitalists, mostly from the high-tech end of the business, tell their story.

Hay, M. and Peters, J. (1999) *The Venture Capital Handbook: Strategies for Successful Private Equity Investment*, Harlow: Financial Times Prentice Hall.

Stutley, R. (2002) T*he Definitive Business Plan*, Harlow: Financial Times Prentice Hall. This is a useful practical guide to business planning which extends some of the ideas presented in this chapter. It also gives good practical advice on how to make a submission.

Progress check

1. Identify four situations in which business planning would be an important exercise. (p. 281)

2. The executive summary of a business plan should consist of three component parts. What are they? (p. 282)

3. What are the six components of a strategic plan? (p. 283)

4. A business model consists of three interdependent sections. What are they? (pp. 284–285)

5. What would you expect to see in a financial plan? (p. 286)

6. How does a sales revenue projection differ from a statement of cash inflows? (p. 286)

7. List the four steps in appraising a business plan. (pp. 301–302)

8. List the six accounting ratios favoured by venture capitalists when appraising a business proposal. (p. 303)

9. Identify the six purposes of budgeting outlined in the chapter. (pp. 304–305)

10. How does 'budgetary slack' and 'organisational bloat' arise? (p. 310)

11. Write out the formulas for gross, price, quantity, activity and efficiency variances. (pp. 312–316)

12. What is a flexible budget? (pp. 314–315)

Questions

The answers to the questions followed by ✓ can be found at the back of the book, the answers to the remaining questions can be found on the website accompanying this book, **www.cengage.co.uk/ryan2.**

1. A retail business is projecting January sales figures of £30 000. Over the last six months sales have been increasing at a rate of 0.5 per cent per month. Sales are likely to remain constant in January and February following the Christmas period but to then start growing again at a rate of 0.25 per cent per month until November in which month and in December sales are expected to rise to 1 per cent. Half of sales are for cash and half are on credit. Customers settle on average one month after the point of sale.

You are required:

(i) to project sales revenue for the next twelve months

(ii) to project a statement of cash inflow for the next twelve months

(iii) to explain the difference in the twelve month total figures for both projections.   ✓

2. Below is a table of cash flow projections from a business plan. Assume:

- constant monthly sales and costs in each year
- customers obtain 2 months' credit and suppliers one month's
- administrative costs and property costs carry no accruals or prepayments
- stock holdings are held constant
- capital equipment is depreciated straight-line over 10 years

Exhibit 9.30

	year 1	year 2	year 3
Revenues	904 500	1 265 900	1 548 000
Operating costs	701 400	949 425	1 269 360
Administrative costs	35 800	85 000	90 345
Property costs	48 000	48 000	48 000
Initial stock purchase	28 800		
Capital equipment	450 000	105 000	
Equity	400 000		
Withdrawals	30 000	60 000	80 000

You are required to:

(i) produce a projected income statement for this company each year

(ii) summarise the expected performance, liquidity and risk of the business

(iii) outline the steps which a small or medium-sized enterprise should undertake to create a business plan for the launch of a new product which is expected to expand and to contribute to 40 per cent of future revenue and profitability over five years.   ✓

....

3. You are assisting a small start-up enterprise which has produced the projection of cash flow for its first year of trading (see Exhibit 9.31).

Sales are planned to commence immediately in January but customers are likely to require a two-month credit period. Suppliers are likely to extend just one month. Capital equipment write off can be assumed over five years with straight-line depreciation and a 10 per cent residual value. The bank is being approached to provide start up finance with a maximum borrowing facility of £100 000. Interest is assumed to be charged on a monthly basis. Interest can be earned on positive cash balances.

You are required to:

(i) produce a balance sheet, income statement and cash flow statement for the first year of trading
    (12 marks)

(ii) calculate gross and net profit margin ratios, the current asset ratio and acid test ratio
    (6 marks)

(iii) outline any other information that you would need to produce a comprehensive business plan.
    (7 marks)

....

4. Your company is considering creating an integrated financial planning and corporate budgeting system in order to increase the coherence between policy formation and operational control. Discuss the advantages and disadvantages of such a system and the problems of effectively integrating the two systems.

....

Exhibit 9.31

Johnson

Statement of Cash Flow – year 1

	Jan	Feb	Mar	Apr	May	Jun	Jul	Aug	Sep	Oct	Nov	Dec	TOTAL
Trading Account													
Sales			40 000	42 000	44 100	46 305	48 620	51 051	53 604	56 284	59 098	62 053	503 116
less:													
Initial Stock Purchase		(8 000)											(8 000)
Costs of materials		(28 000)	(29 400)	(30 870)	(32 414)	(34 034)	(35 736)	(37 523)	(39 399)	(41 369)	(43 437)	(45 609)	(397 790)
Salary Costs	(1 200)	(1 200)	(1 200)	(1 200)	(1 200)	(1 200)	(1 200)	(1 200)	(1 200)	(1 200)	(1 200)	(1 200)	(14 400)
Office Costs	(250)	(250)	(250)	(250)	(250)	(250)	(250)	(250)	(250)	(250)	(250)	(250)	(3 000)
Initial Marketing	(10 000)												(10 000)
Advertising Costs	(1 500)	(1 500)	(1 500)	(1 500)	(1 500)	(1 500)	(1 500)	(1 500)	(1 500)	(1 500)	(1 500)	(1 500)	(18 000)
Rent	(1 700)			(1 700)			(1 700)			(1 700)			(6 800)
Rates			(1 500)			(1500)			(1 500)			(1 500)	(6 000)
Trading Monthly Cash Flow	(14 650)	(38 950)	6 150	6 480	8 737	7 821	8 234	10 579	9 755	10 265	12 711	11 994	39 126
Capital Account													
Capital Equipment	(30 000)												(30 000)
Capital Input	20 000												20 000
Capital Withdrawals				(2 000)			(2 000)			(2 000)			(6 000)
Monthly ex int Cash Flow	(24 650)	(38 950)	6 150	4 480	8 737	7 821	6 234	10 579	9 755	8 265	12 711	11 994	23 126
Interest	(197)	(510)	(465)	(433)	(367)	(307)	(260)	(177)	(100)	(35)	66	163	(2 623)
Net monthly cash flow	(24 847)	(39 460)	5 685	4 047	8 370	7 514	5 975	10 401	9 655	8 230	12 777	12 157	20 502
Cumulative Cash Flow	(24 847)	(64 308)	(58 623)	(54 576)	(46 206)	(38 692)	(32 718)	(22 316)	(12 662)	(4 432)	8 346	20 502	20 502

5. The budgeted and actual sales revenue and labour costs for a particular process are as follows:

Exhibit 9.32

Sales revenue:

Actual price per unit	£65.00
Budgeted price per unit	£60.00
Actual quantity produced (tons)	12 000
Budgeted quantity produced (tons)	15 000

Labour costs:

Actual labour rate per hour	£10.50
Budgeted labour rate per hour	£12.00
Actual labour hours employed in production	8 400
Budgeted labour hours employed in production	8 200

Calculate the labour wage rate, the labour usage, the labour efficiency and the labour efficiency variances.

6. Exhibit 9.33 is a production cost report for three handheld navigation units:

Exhibit 9.33

Product	xp199	xs200	xx880
Sales Revenue			
Sales (actual)	10 450	19 680	12 450
Sales (budget)	10 500	19 000	13 500
Sales price per unit (actual)	220	180	230
Sales price per unit (budget)	220	200	220
Direct cost			
Labour hours (actual)	2 718	4 010	3 380
Labour hours (budget)	2 625	3 800	3 375
Labour rate (actual)	18.5	18.1	17.7
Labour rate (budget)	18	18	18
Materials cost per unit (actual)	56	48	59
Materials cost per unit (budget)	55	45	60

You are required to:

(i) produce a variance analysis, showing total, volume and price variances for each revenue and cost heading and for contribution overall

(ii) analyse the labour usage variance into activity and efficiency effects

(iii) outline the practical issues in using this type of analysis for the control of production departments. ✓

7. Using the information in Exhibit 9.34 extract as much information as you can for a management report.

Exhibit 9.34

	Actual		Budget	
	Quantity	Price (Cost per unit)	Quantity	Price (Cost per unit)
Sales and production level	18 000 units	£28.00	17 000 units	£30.00
Material A	27 000 kg	£14.00	23 000 kg	£13.00
Material B	32 000 kg	£13.00	28 000 kg	£8.00
Labour – semiskilled	2 000 hours	£12.00	2 100 hours	£10.00
Labour – skilled	600 hours	£8.00	550 hours	£8.00
Overheads (variable)		£2.00		£1.50
Overheads (fixed)		£16.00		£15.00
(allocated on semiskilled hours)		(per hour)		(per hour)

Case exercises

1. Create a business plan to seek funding from a charitable institution or from your employing firm to undertake a business course. Here are some choices:

- funding to support an undergraduate degree or professional qualification
- a diploma or masters programme in business (DipBA or MBA)
- a senior management development programme at a top US or European business school.

In developing your plan you should seek information about the charity or, in the case of your firm, from the personnel or human resources department as to their requirements. How would you modify the above planning structure for such an exercise?

....

2. Put together an outline business plan for one of the following:

(i)   setting up a small restaurant

(ii) opening a hair salon

(iii) establishing a management or technical consultancy business.

Outline the issues you would consider in developing such a plan and the type of evidence you would need to collect.

Chapter 10

Cost management and pricing

Introduction

In this chapter we look at the problems of cost measurement and control within management accounting and in particular at the issues of cost and resource allocation. We describe the traditional resource-based systems of cost allocation using a variety of cost drivers and applied to firms with service and cross-functional departments. The conceptual issues with cost allocation are then explored and a range of managerial interpretations offered as to why rational competitive firms engage in what from an economic perspective is irrational costing practice. From this, we explore some of the more modern methods of cost and resource allocation using output and activity measures. The techniques of activity-based costing are then explored with worked examples of the processes involved. A theme that is developed here is the analysis of generic cost drivers and the role of cost minimisation strategies in the development of quality and economy in the use of scarce resources. Finally, the chapter discusses the issue of cost-based and economic-based pricing systems.

Learning objectives

In this chapter the learning outcomes are distributed across two sections:

Cost management

- To be able to recognise the principal drivers of cost in organisations and to separate them into those that add value and those that do not.

- To understand the purpose of cost allocation and be able to define the meaning of the term 'full cost'.

- To be able to allocate cost with both single and multiple cost objects.

- To understand how indirect costs can be 'drawn down' to the unit level of production.

- To understand the differences and the relative advantages and disadvantages between resource- and activity-based cost management methods.

- To be able to understand the limitations of cost allocation methods and why they can lead to the mis-allocation of resources.

Pricing

- To understand the difference between market-based and cost-based pricing systems.

- To be able to describe market-based pricing systems and their appropriateness for different situations.

- To understand how full-cost product prices are built up using 'cost plus' and 'rate of return' pricing methods.

- To understand the intuition behind target costing and how it is used to drive down costs.

Cost management

In Chapter 8 we introduced the concept of direct and indirect cost. A direct cost is any cost that we can uniquely attribute to a given cost object and an indirect cost is any other cost that cannot be directly attributed but which has to be allocated to the cost object. 'Contribution' is the term we gave to the difference between directly attributable cost and directly attributable revenue. The first issue we address in this chapter is the basis upon which we can allocate indirect costs to specific cost objects and the rationale for doing so. Our second issue for discussion concerns the pricing of products and the different pricing approaches adopted by firms in practice. Pricing is one of the most difficult tasks faced by management: overpricing will lead to a loss of potential sales and possibly a fall in revenue, underpricing has the opposite effect. Product pricing methods fall into two broad categories: market-based and cost-based. We will describe the situation where each is relevant and the dangers and pitfalls of adopting the wrong approach. Finally, although we talk about 'products' and 'manufacturing' in this chapter nearly all the ideas and methods we discuss can be applied to service firms as well.

The impact of cost upon the firm

Costs are incurred whenever a firm decides to purchase any of the resources it needs for production. As we noted in Chapter 8, costs fall into a hierarchy: strategic or business-level costs being those required to create and sustain the business as a going concern, operational-level costs being those required to sustain the capacity of the business to conduct its day-to-day operations, and production-level costs being those required to produce and deliver the product or service concerned. However, there is a deeper level of analysis that suggests that costs arise along two different vectors or dimensions within the firm:

- The organisational or structural vector: these are all the costs required to maintain the business as an organisation. In general, it is possible for virtually any good or service to be produced by independent contractors in an open market. Adam Smith in his *Wealth of Nations* described how the 'invisible hand of the market' can bring about the production of complex goods without the need for any overall coordination. However, organising production through firms, where the costs of contracting in open markets is replaced by the costs of managing the firm, can sometimes be a more cost-effective method of production.

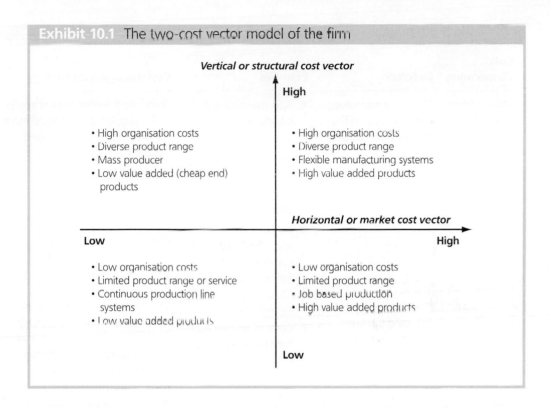

Exhibit 10.1 The two-cost vector model of the firm

Therefore, the costs of managing – the firm or business 'overheads' – are incurred by the decision to produce or provide a service within a firm rather than through open-market transacting.

● The market or process vector: these are the costs that are incurred by the firm in taking a supply of raw materials or any other input service through production and out to the customer as a finished product. These costs form part of the value which is added to the product.

Exhibit 10.1 shows the typical types of products and production systems which dominate in each quadrant. The vertical or structural cost vector arises because of the way the firm organises itself. Large firms with many functional levels and complex and interconnected internal systems of communication and control will have relatively high levels of 'vertical cost'. It is this vector that creates what we refer to as 'business overheads', and generally these costs add little value to the customer but are incurred because of the way that the firm has chosen to organise itself. We also notice a tendency for firms to expand this type of cost as the business environment becomes more complex; the introduction of new regulations, for example, will often result in new levels of management, and indeed whole departments are created to ensure compliance. Rarely do such costs disappear when the regulation disappears or is superseded, and this tendency is what is sometimes referred to as 'organisational bloat'.

The horizontal or market cost vector is that vector along which process or production costs are incurred in the manufacture and delivery of the service concerned. It is along this vector of cost that management will usually attempt to make savings. However, in practice it is along this dimension that incurring cost adds value to a firm's products and for which, in the end, its customers will reward the firm by paying higher prices for better-produced, higher-quality goods.

Exhibit 10.2

Cost Classification	Definition	Examples	Cost management strategy
Value adding (horizontal)	Costs that add value to the product in the hands of the customer	● Raw materials and components ● The direct costs of transforming inputs into finished goods ● Direct marketing and sales costs ● Costs of machinery and other fixed resources necessary for production	These are the core costs of production which would be incurred no matter how the production was organised – whether through an open market or through firm based manufacturing. The objective of the firm is to maximise the efficiency of the conversion of these costs, deriving the best value for the customer at the lowest input cost.
Change costs: (vertical)	Costs incurred in changing the fixed means of production	● Retooling costs ● Costs of relocation of fixed plant, equipment or personnel	Seek all means to eliminate these costs. These costs are incurred because the firm has organised itself in a way which is not optimal for the type of production concerned. Retooling, for example, arises because a firm was producing something else and needs to change over to the new product.
Logistic costs: (vertical/ horizontal)	Costs incurred as a result of moving raw materials, work in progress or finished goods from one location to another	● Transport costs ● Costs of procurement ● Distribution and distribution management	These costs should be reduced to zero although some transport costs are intrinsic to the creation of the product or service and are therefore 'value adding' to the customer.
Control costs: (vertical)	Cost incurred in ensuring that a product or service is in accord with its design and customer requirements	● Quality control costs ● Organisation overheads ● Management costs of control	The firm should seek to minimise these costs commensurate with ensuring that the product is of the quality specified. Quality costs are incurred in ensuring that the product is without defects and is in accordance with its design requirements. Competitive markets do not reward firms for bearing these costs.
Service costs: (horizontal)	Costs of providing after sales service and warranties	● After sales service agreements ● Cost of guarantees ● Cost of technical support	Generally these costs add value to the product in the hands of the customer. As with other value adding costs the firm should seek to maximise the value derived at the best price.

This idea of vertical and horizontal structure allows us to think about costs in a different way and to focus on how to manage them effectively.

Review activity 10.1   Here are five costs. How would you classify them using the cost classification scheme outlined above?

- A firm buys products from a 'spin out' company with which it has a long-term contract. There are alternative sources of supply locally at cheaper prices. How would you classify the cost of purchase of the goods concerned?
- A firm makes components at its Manchester division and then transfers them to its Chester plant for final production. How would you classify the internal transport cost?
- A car manufacturer has a car body pressing plant which it needs to switch over to the production of a new model. How would you classify the changeover cost?
- A company runs an after-sales and warranty division. How would you classify the cost of running that division?
- A firm has a customer complaints department. How would you classify the cost of operating that department?

✓ Check the answer to this Review activity at the back of the book (see page 515).

As Exhibit 10.2 shows, there are certain types of cost that the market will not reward the firm for bearing. The Japanese-inspired drive towards 'lean' and 'agile' manufacturing systems where firms seek to drive down the level of their logistic and change costs to zero is an example of cost management being used as a primary tool for winning competitive advantage. Process re-engineering is another related approach that focuses on the job of driving down all vertical costs, and in particular the costs of control.

Lean manufacturing

Lean manufacturing (LM) and more recently *agile* manufacturing methods have been driven principally by the search for the maximum cost-efficiency in production. Companies such as Canon and Toyota in Japan pioneered the approach, although many western companies have adopted lean manufacturing successfully, which suggests that there are no cultural barriers to its implementation.

LM is now recognised as an approach to managing business of all types. It originated in the 1950s at Toyota. Taiichi Ohno (1912–1990), their then head of production, has been described as *'the most ferocious foe of waste in human history'*.

Lean manufacturing emphasises the elimination of waste effort from the production process by 'grinding out' costs which do not add value to a product. Of these costs 'change' and 'logistic' costs are by far the most important. Change costs are incurred when a firm changes its fixed resources such as machinery from one type of production to another. For example, Ford used to take three working days to change a highly specialised body pressing machine from one type of car production to another. Six unions and up to thirty people were involved in the change process. At Nissan, using a small team of six, they finally organised their systems to the point that the changeover took less than five minutes. As change costs are driven down, smaller and smaller batch sizes become viable and thus the lean manufacturer is able to shift production from one model to another at very high speed. Logistic costs are incurred when a firm moves its resources from one place to another – ordering materials, removing stock from inventory, transporting partly finished goods are all examples of such costs. By seeking to minimise these costs the firm becomes a highly flexible and agile manufacturer able to respond to any demands that the market may place upon it.

One of the paradoxes of lean manufacturing is that the pursuit of the elimination of cost and waste in production actually leads to higher-quality products rather than lower. The traditional view was that product quality was expensive and had to be purchased for a high price. Most of us think of the very expensive Rolls-Royce as a high-quality car – what BMW has demonstrated is that the same standards of production can be achieved at much lower cost through LM. The Japanese first discovered that total cost falls as the firm moves to the point of zero defects. They also discovered that the focused search for waste and its elimination led them inexorably towards defect-free production.

The virtual firm

The virtual firm was an idea that became popular during the 'dot.com' boom in the late 1990s. A virtual firm is conceived of as one where there is little formal management structure (the vertical dimension) and all the different steps in the production process are conducted by independent contractors. The model for this was the Japanese firms like Toyota which built large networks of supplier and distributor relationships in what was termed a 'keiretsu'. The keiretsu firms were largely independent contractors. Many of the dot.com start-up companies attempted to replicate this model of the networked firm by creating very small and flexible central management systems with suppliers, production (where undertaken) and distributors coordinated by systems using the World Wide Web.

The purpose of cost allocation

With cost allocation the accountant attempts to identify cost 'causalities' which link particular cost objects (products, cost centres, production departments) to elements of indirect cost within the indirect cost pool of the firm. The reasons for doing this can be summarised as follows.

Estimating full cost

Managers often need to estimate the total value of the firm's resources devoted to producing a given product or service, running a department or managing any other cost centre within the firm. By 'full cost' they mean that cost which if consistently matched by the revenues earned over the longer run will produce a situation of breakeven for the business.

Accountability

Firms invariably hold managers responsible for any direct costs that they incur through their cost centres. However, senior management may also wish to set performance targets which include a loading for the indirect cost of the operations concerned. Managerially, this is known as 'performance delegation' where senior managers (whose decisions created the indirect cost base of the firm) require that more junior managers in charge of operations or production activities are held accountable for performance against these additional costs.

Pricing

Many firms attempt to set prices that cover the 'full cost' of producing the product or service concerned. We will consider pricing in some detail later in the chapter but it is worth noting that full costs can form the basis for establishing prices in those situations where the customer will only reimburse cost plus a mark-up percentage and in those situations where the manufacturer must set a price in the absence of reliable demand information.

Rationing

Senior management may wish to limit the consumption of central resources by divisions and departments within the firm. If the senior management of the firm want to minimise the cost of labour then one way of achieving this is by requiring cost centre managers to 'recover' indirect costs charged as an addition to the basic labour rates.

Decision making

Managers often want to know the full sacrifice of resources that will result from a given business decision. The full cost, including allocated central costs, is often believed to give a clearer view of what is being sacrificed in terms of the 'hidden' resources devoted to a particular product rather than the incremental costs associated with the decision. What this means is that managers believe that the full cost measures the cost of using scarce central resources on the particular product or service concerned.

Cost allocation for product costing also recognises that level of output (the quantity of supply) is not the only determinant of price and hence total revenue in the market. Other factors such as product quality, assured delivery dates and after-sales service are all factors in determining the price which customers will pay. The costs of achieving these product attributes are rarely fully reflected in the direct costs of production but are 'lost' within the general expenditures of the firm.

However, allocation matching presents many problems to the accountant in that it conflicts with the logic of relevant or opportunity costs as outlined in Chapter 8. We will return to these issues after having discussed the methods of cost allocation.

Building a cost allocation model

Most business firms attempt to allocate costs in some way or other to units of production, cost centres such as production departments or divisions or to service functions such as the marketing department or research and development. In Chapter 8 our discussion focused on the distinction between direct and indirect costs and the importance of the concept of the 'cost object'. In this section we describe in general terms how these concepts can be applied in creating a 'cost allocation model' (CAM) for allocating firm-wide costs to individual cost objects.

Here is a six-step procedure for building a cost allocation model:

1. Identify the cost object. As outlined in Chapter 8, a cost object is simply anything that you wish to cost. It may be a single item of production, the cost of operating a production line, the cost of a specific project or the cost of running a division. The key point about this stage is to make sure that the cost object is precisely defined.

2. Decide upon the costing methodology. Indirect costs can be allocated to cost objects on different bases all of which will give a different answer. We may wish to allocate on the basis of some key resource consumed (such as labour time in production), or on a variety of resources consumed, or by some measure of activity. We will discuss the various possibilities with some examples later.

3. Identify the depth of the allocation. Decide how far you want to go in allocating the firm's overall costs to the given cost object. In costing a single item of production do you intend to allocate a part of the firm's overall costs (including its business-level costs) incurred or just allocate indirect costs to a certain level (perhaps production-level costs only)?

4. Identify the cost pools. Decide for the given cost object the most appropriate indirect cost pools. That is, cost categories that have clear boundaries to which the firm's indirect expenditure can be unambiguously attributed. If the cost pool were to be defined as the cost object then those expenditures would be direct costs with respect to that cost pool. A firm may have many different cost pools but may only choose to allocate costs from certain cost pools to individual cost objects.

5. Define the cost drivers. A cost driver is the allocation formula which is used to take some portion of the costs collected in any given indirect cost pool and attach them to the cost object concerned. Each cost pool will have its own cost driver and the cost driver will be defined according to the type of indirect costing methodology we wish to employ.

6. Allocate costs from all cost pools relevant to the cost object concerned to the cost object to obtain a measure of full cost.

Exhibit 10.3

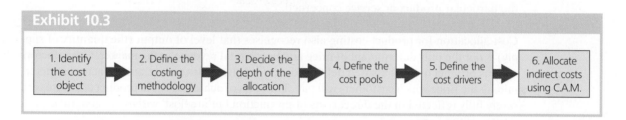

We will now see how the principles of this system were applied by a small building firm.

Cost allocation for a single-product/service business

If we take a simple firm such as a small building firm we can see how cost allocation works where one type of product is produced or activity undertaken. In such a business, the task is to identify the direct cost of the product or job and then choose some system for allocating the indirect costs of running the business to each product or job to obtain a 'full cost'. The following is a case study of a building firm operating as a limited company in the home improvement business.

Financial realities   ## Wallie Wilts (Builder) Ltd

This is a simplified version of a real case. The builder concerned used a variety of cost estimation techniques including third-party estimation services to get the direct job cost. What follows is a typical issue for many firms and not just those in the construction industry where it is necessary to 'price in' the business overheads and to take a reasonable profit from the job.

Wallie runs a small but successful family building firm which he and his wife carefully manage. He is working on an estimate for a new job to build a house extension. Wallie has access to a number of estimating services which allow him to price individual parts of the job. However, he much prefers to build his costs in the same way he does his extensions – from the ground up.

After lengthy discussions with the client and the client's architect he produced a statement of the direct costs he will incur. He estimates that it will be an eight-week job with one week for contingency. All of the labour for the job is hired on subcontract and Wallie also works full time on each job he undertakes. His yard is alongside his house and he has an office extension built on to the side of the property. His reputation has been built on the quality of his work and the fact that he personally sees each job through from start to completion. Here is the job costing which he has worked out covering the direct costs of construction through its five stages (see Exhibit 10.4):

1. ground works to oversite
2. shell construction to wall plate
3. roof and glazed oak screen to one elevation
4. interior trades
5. site clearance.

Exhibit 10.4   Wallie Wilts's cost schedule

Wallie Wilts (Builders) Ltd	Quote	03/8
Job Costing	File reference	03/RYA/2
	Target start date	12/05/03
40 metre^2 extension to Yellowshrub Cottage	Completion	18/07/03

		£	£
Groundworks to oversite			
Equipment hire		560	
Readymix (9 cubic metres)		450	
Landfill disposal		350	
Shuttering		120	
Subcontract Labour (1 week) – Rich and Tom		600	
	Groundworks total		2 080
Materials			
Stone for facings, sills and coins	20 cubic metres	2000	
Thermal bricks for walls	3 pallets	1200	
Fibre linings		430	
Ceiling joists	2 × 6 metre RSJs	430	
Cement and sand		290	
Windows (quote to supply)		930	
Oak Doors + door furniture		1800	
Other materials		1900	
Door casing		120	
		9100	
Subcontract Labour (3 weeks) – two men		1800	
	Shell total		10 900
Roof and glazed oak screen			
Roof contractor at quote		4900	
Oak screen at quote		5600	
	Roofing and screen total		10 500
Interior Trades (subcontract)			
Electrician		1000	
Plasterer		500	
Interior joinery		1600	
Interior decoration		500	
Plumber		800	
	Interior trades total		4 400
Site clearance and reinstatement			
Labour			400
Direct job cost			28 280

Wallie has long experience in this type of business and he is confident of his estimates of all the costs that can be directly attributed to this job. However, he also expects to incur in this trading year £42 300 of costs in running the business as a whole as shown below.

Exhibit 10.5

Office costs		
Jane's salary		14 000
Office equipment (depreciation)		2 700
Share of rates, heat and light		3 400
Accounting and tax		2 100
Office consumables		2 400
	Total office costs	24 600
Yard		
Equipment, lorry and van (depreciation)	8 500	
Small tools	2 400	
Misc materials stock	1 000	
Van and lorry running costs	3 300	
Property maintenance	2 500	
	Total yard costs	17 700
Total business overhead		42 300

Notice that none of the costs shown in Exhibit 10.5 are directly attributable to any specific job but are attributable to the job of running the business overall. His long-running practice has been to charge to each job a share of this overhead on the basis of the number of weeks each job takes compared with the total number of weeks of his time available in the year. He would like to see what difference it would make to his costs if he allocated his office costs and yard costs on a different basis.

Going through the costing stages:

1. Define the cost object: in this case the cost object is this contract to build the extension.
2. Define the costing methodology. Our initial methodology is based upon the allocation of both office and yard costs on a time basis to each extension built.
3. Decide on the depth of allocation. Wallie wishes to allocate a share of all his yard (operating) and office (business) costs to each job he undertakes.
4. Define the indirect cost pools. Under the methodology specified in (1) there is only one indirect cost pool, namely the total of indirect costs incurred in running the office and the yard.
5. Define the cost driver(s). In this case Wallie has decided to allocate the cost in both cost pools according to the number of weeks of his time each job takes. His indirect 'cost driver' is therefore job duration and the total number of cost driver units attributable to the indirect cost pool is 45, i.e. the number of weeks he can work during the year.
6. Allocate indirect costs using the cost allocation model defined in (1) to (5). The formula for doing this is as shown below.

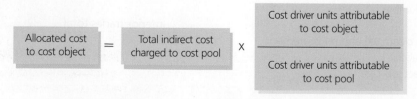

Given that Wallie limits himself to a 45-week working year and this job is expected to take 9 weeks we can allocate a portion of the £42 300 indirect cost as follows:

Allocated cost to Job = £42 300 × 9/45

= £8460

Exhibit 10.6

	£
Direct job cost	28 280
Indirect costs	
Allocated overheads	8 460
Total job cost	36 740
Agreed price at 40 × £1100/m²	44 000
Profit	7 260

Now consider what would happen if we adopted an alternative costing methodology assuming:

- Office costs are allocated on the basis of the number of individual jobs undertaken during the year. Wallie thinks that this is the more appropriate measure because each job, irrespective of its size, takes the same amount of time in the office to (a) set up the estimates, (b) prepare letters, (c) organise supplies and (d) arrange subcontractors. During the year Wallie expects to start and complete eight jobs.
- Yard costs are to be allocated on the same basis as currently.
- We now have two cost pools and two associated cost drivers.
- The yard cost pool, which will attract all the indirect costs charged to that aspect of Wallie's business and they will be charged on the basis of Wallie's time spent on each job.
- The office cost pool, where the cost driver units are number of jobs undertaken during the year. Note that this is a measure of activity (jobs done) rather than resource used up (Wallie's time on the job).

Using the allocation formula shown above and on the basis of eight jobs being completed in the year Wallie's revised cost summary is as follows:

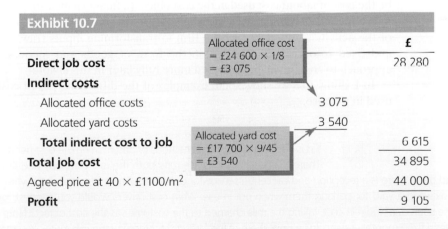

Exhibit 10.7

		£
Allocated office cost = £24 600 × 1/8 = £3 075		
Direct job cost		28 280
Indirect costs		
Allocated office costs	3 075	
Allocated yard costs	3 540	
Total indirect cost to job		6 615
Total job cost		34 895
Agreed price at 40 × £1100/m²		44 000
Profit		9 105

Allocated yard cost = £17 700 × 9/45 = £3 540

So on the basis of the revised costing methodology we now have a profit of £9105 compared with a profit of £7260! Not bad going – just short of £2000 profit increase just by changing the system of allocating costs. This presents us with the first and most obvious problem of cost allocation: the result of any costing exercise will depend upon the method employed.

A note on stock valuation

'Absorption costing' is the name given to valuation of finished inventory stocks using full-cost allocation methods. 'Marginal costing' for inventory purposes is where finished inventories are valued only in accordance with the direct costs involved in their production. Although variations in allocation method can make individual products appear more or less profitable across the whole product portfolio changes in the way that indirect costs are charged should not affect the level of overall profitability.

Cost driver analysis

The concept of the cost driver is relatively new in management accounting. It is the idea that although indirect costs are by definition not directly attributable to specific cost objects they may exhibit 'traceability'. For example, in the Wallie Wilts case we identified two indirect cost drivers:

1. The number of jobs that Wallie could undertake during the course of a year. The office is primarily devoted to the administration of the business, and to a certain extent the more jobs Wallie undertakes the greater is the utilisation of this resource. If, for example, he took on 45 jobs of one week's duration each, rather than the eight planned, then the office would have to undertake five times the level of activity. There is, therefore, a reasonable degree of traceability between the effort applied in the office and the allocation of cost to each job.

2. The time spent on each job. Given that the time spent on each job is a reasonable approximation of the effort involved it is reasonable to use this in allocating the cost of running the yard. Again it is straightforward to see the element of traceability in the choice of the cost driver for this element of the firm's total overhead.

In practice cost drivers can be identified that are either financially or non-financially based: they can be related to the consumption of direct resources by the cost object or they can be related to some measure of its activity. **Traditional overhead costing methods** favour cost allocation based upon the resources used by the cost object. Two such cost drivers could be the cost of labour cost used in the cost object (a financial measure) or machine hours used in production (a non-financial measure). More modern cost methods favour some measure of the activities undertaken by the firm in transforming inputs (raw materials, labour time and fixed resources) into output in the form of goods and services. This activity-based approach to costing will be discussed more fully later in this chapter.

In Exhibit 10.8 we show some examples of the different types of cost driver that can be used in practice.

Review activity 10.2 Sid is deciding upon some methods of determining the cost per mile of his taxi service. There is a head office which runs both the taxi company and Ron's Vans Ltd. In that head office there is a reception and call centre service for customers. There is a workshop which maintains the fleet of taxis and a yard for parking them when not in use. What cost drivers would you suggest for allocating each of these sources of indirect cost, taking the mile charged to the customer as the cost object? Note that each driver receives a fixed monthly salary plus a small share of the fares as recorded on the cab meter. You may assume that fares are strictly charged by the mile or part of a mile driven.

Exhibit 10.8 Different types of cost driver

	Resource	Activity
Financial	• direct labour cost • direct materials cost	• value of goods sold • total fees charged
Non-financial	• direct labour time • floor area used • machine hours	• number of purchase orders made • number of quality inspections

The criteria for choosing a cost driver can be summarised as follows:

Traceability

Can some attribute of the cost object be traced to the indirect cost to be allocated? For example, in the production of motor cars considerable cost is incurred in ordering materials and components from suppliers. The number of orders made would be a cost driver where the effort involved in ordering supplies could be used to allocate the cost of operating the purchasing department's costs to each car produced.

Rationing

Where a resource is in short supply using a measure of that resource can be an effective cost driver. As we have seen above, in such a shortage situation, the cost driver can be a useful accounting approximation to the opportunity costs of the scarce resource concerned.

Incentive

Where management wishes to set particular constraints in the use of a given resource, or to set particular targets in undertaking a particular type of activity, then using that resource or activity as the cost driver can be used as part of the incentive system for rewarding more junior-level management.

Multi-objective/multi-driver analysis

In the Wallic Wilts case the firm is a single business company but we used two cost drivers to distribute its indirect costs to each job. Other firms produce different products simultaneously and often as a continuous process rather than on the job-by-job basis that characterised Wallie's business. The principles for allocating costs in this situation is straightforward and use the approach described above except that there will be multiple cost objects, as shown in Exhibit 10.9.

Cost allocation with more than one cost object

In the following example we discuss a case where more than one cost object exists and there is more than one source of indirect cost. The cost drivers chosen were those used by the company concerned.

Exhibit 10.9 Single rate analysis

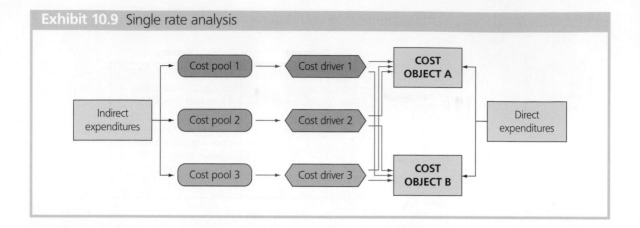

Financial realities   The Bristol and Wells (Newspapers) Ltd is a small, long-established business producing four weekly newspapers and three magazines that are sold throughout the Avon and Somerset region. The company operates two editorial offices, one in Bristol and the other in Chippenham, but uses a common layout, printing and distribution facility at Bath Road, Bristol. Head-office costs are charged to each title and to the printing works on a headcount basis. Print and production costs are charged to each editorial office on a page make-up basis. Because the direct costs of producing each newspaper or magazine are very small and difficult to measure management has regarded these as an indirect cost of production. This form of cost analysis had been routinely prepared by the company accountant but this year he has been asked to identify the profitability of the newspaper business and the periodicals business individually, and as a separate exercise the profitability of the Bristol and Chippenham offices. Some title-specific direct costs are incurred by each editorial office.

The following are the steps that the firm's accountant goes through to estimate the budgeted full weekly cost of each title and the budgeted full cost per copy.

Step 1: Define the cost objects

Three levels of cost analysis present themselves in this case: first, the cost of operating each editorial office; second, the cost of operating the print and production facility; and third, the title cost. Each of these three cost objects can be costed on a time basis or on an output basis.

The definition of the most appropriate cost objects for analysis can allow a business to identify cost centres. The concept of a cost centre was introduced in Chapter 8 and it is an organisational point of accountability. In this case the business regarded the head office, the production facility and each of the editorial offices as cost centres. Each title was regarded as a cost object but was not regarded as a cost centre in its own right.

Step 2: Define the costing methodology

In this case we define three levels of analysis:

- the production facility which can be analysed as a cost object in its own right. All of the costs of the production and distribution facility are to be allocated to the two editorial offices
- the editorial offices which are revenue centres and which can be analysed as revenue and cost objects in their own right
- the individual titles which will carry the editorial-office cost burden in proportion to their sales.

Newspapers – what is the cost? (© A.B.J. Price)

This is not an unusual approach but does unfortunately mix up the different ways in allocating costs.

Step 3: All business and production costs to be absorbed into each unit produced

Step 4: Define the cost pools

Exhibit 10.10 is a cost structure diagram showing how the costs are collected and 'drawn down' to the different levels of the cost analysis. The company operates three cost pools:

- a central expenses cost pool where all head-office expenses are collected
- a production and distribution cost pool where these costs are collected
- an editorial cost pool where the costs of operating the Bristol and Chippenham editorial offices are collected.

Step 5: Define the cost drivers

The cost drivers for this analysis are straightforward and are reasonably simple to measure in practice:

- central expenses on a headcount employed basis
- production costs on an average page count basis
- editorial costs on a sales volume basis.

Exhibit 10.10 Cost structure diagram for Bristol and Wells (Newspapers) Ltd

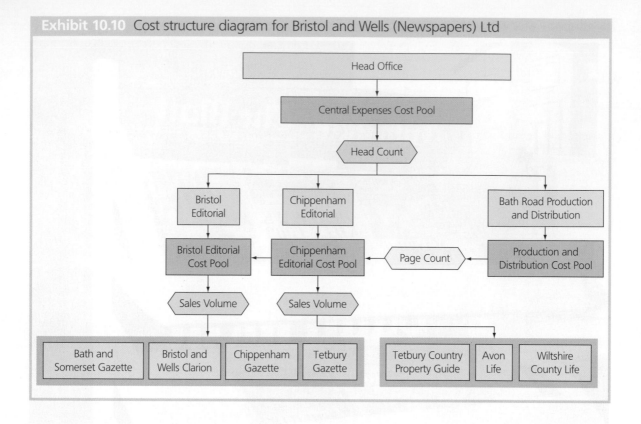

Step 6: Allocate costs using the chosen cost allocation model

Below are the basic data relating to each title with a projected annual revenue from each attributable to sales and advertising. The annual direct costs incurred against each title by the respective editorial office are also shown. The budgeted expenditure by head office, including all non-operating items such as interest payments and taxes, is set at £780 000.

The analysis in Exhibit 10.11 shows budgeted figures for the coming twelve months:

- direct cost attributable to each cost centre: each title, the two editorial offices and the production unit
- the weekly sales of each title which are estimated to be 10 per cent less than the weekly production to account for returns
- the weekly production figures for each title (number of copies produced)
- the average page count (APC) per issue, of which there are 52 each year
- the headcount in full-time-equivalent staff
- the direct sales and advertising revenue attributable to each title.

Our first task is to allocate the central office costs to the editorial offices and the Bath Road production facility. In Exhibit 10.12 we show how this has been achieved. The cost diagram shows the drawdown of costs. First, the head-office cost pool is allocated to the two editorial offices and the production facility using headcount as the cost driver. This creates the head-office cost burden at each of the three cost centres. However, the total production and distribution costs incurred at Bath Road and shown as the production and distribution cost pool must be redistributed to the two editorial offices using average page count as the cost driver. Each

Exhibit 10.11

Bristol and Wells (newspapers) Ltd

APC = average page count	Direct Costs	Weekly Sales	Weekly Production	APC	Head Count	Direct Revenue Sales	Advertising
Bristol Editorial	607 200						
Newspapers							
Bath and Somerset Chronicle	12 100	22 000	24 200	36	8	343 200	390 000
Bristol and Wells Clarion	6 800	12 400	13 640	22	6	193 440	435 000
				58			
Periodicals							
Avon Life	17 600	1 800	1 980	85	8	280 800	154 000
				85	22		
Chippenham Editorial	514 080						
Newspapers							
Chippenham Gazette	5 300	9 500	10 450	18	4	148 200	268 000
Tetbury Gazette	4 400	8 000	8 800	20	5	124 800	48 000
				38			
Periodicals							
Tetbury Country Property Guide	19 800	2 500	2 750	66	5	390 000	95 000
Wiltshire Country Life	9 700	2 200	2 420	90	4	343 200	138 000
				156	18		
Bath Road Production	388 000				20		

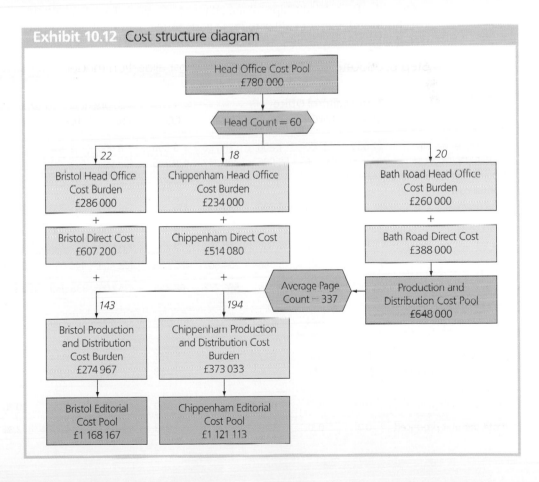

Exhibit 10.12 Cost structure diagram

Exhibit 10.13

Head Office Cost Allocation	Bristol Editorial	Chippenham Editorial	Bath Road Production	Total
Head Count	*22*	*18*	*20*	*60*
Allocated Head Office Cost	286 000	234 000	260 000	780 000
Bath Road Cost Burden				
Bath Road Direct Costs			388 000	
Bath Road Share of Head Office Costs			260 000	
Total Production Cost			648 000	
Editorial Office Cost Burden				
Average page count	143	194		337
Direct Editorial Office Cost	607 200	514 080		1 121 280
Allocated Production Cost	274 967	373 033		648 000
Allocated Head Office Cost	286 000	234 000		520 000
Total Editorial Office Cost	1 168 167	1 121 113		2 289 280

editorial office then has a production and distribution cost burden, which together with the direct costs incurred in running the editorial offices and the allocated head-office cost creates the two editorial cost pools. Exhibit 10.13 shows the spreadsheet calculations.

Once the Bristol and Chippenham editorial cost pools have been established it is then a straightforward matter to allocate these costs to the individual titles on the basis of the expected sales volume (Exhibit 10.14).

Exhibit 10.14

Titles	Bristol Editorial Office				Chippenham Editorial Office				
	B&SC	BWC	AL	Total	CG	TG	TCPG	WCL	Total
Sales (copies per title)	22 000	12 400	1 800	36 200	9 500	8 000	2 500	2 200	22 200
Allocated indirect cost	709 936	400 146	58 086	1 168 167	479 755	404 005	126 251	111 101	1 121 113
Income and expenditure account by title									
Annual cost									
Sales revenue	733 200	628 440	434 800	1 796 440	416 200	172 800	485 000	481 200	1 555 200
Direct costs	12 100	6 800	17 600	36 500	5 300	4 400	19 800	9 700	39 200
Indirect cost	709 936	400 146	58 086	1 168 167	479 755	404 005	126 251	111 101	1 121 113
Total cost	722 036	406 946	75 686	1 204 667	485 055	408 405	146 051	120 801	1 160 313
Profit	11 164	221 494	359 114	591 773	−68 855	−235 605	338 949	360 399	394 887
Unit analysis									
Sales revenue per unit produced	0.58	0.89	4.22		0.77	0.38	3.39	3.82	
Direct costs	0.01	0.01	0.17		0.01	0.01	0.14	0.08	
Allocated editorial office cost burden	0.56	0.56	0.56		0.88	0.88	0.88	0.88	
Cost per unit produced	0.57	0.57	0.74		0.89	0.89	1.02	0.96	
Profit per unit produced	0.01	0.31	3.49		−0.13	−0.51	2.37	2.86	

From this table there appears to be a considerable disparity between the performance of each title. The high-volume newspapers appear to do badly on the basis of each copy produced, whereas the magazines do very well. The magazines have a much higher cover price but they do not appear to attract as much advertising as the newspapers. The obvious problem with this cost allocation system is that it is distributing a substantial component of cost on a page count basis, which means that the magazines carry a relatively smaller production and editorial office charge, even given their larger number of pages per copy.

Review activity 10.3   Devise a cost allocation system where head-office indirect costs are not charged to the production facility but are allocated to each editorial office (i) on the basis of staff employed and (ii) on the basis of projected sales revenue. The cost of each copy sold is then to be charged with a production and distribution overhead based upon the number of pages printed and an editorial and management overhead based upon the number of copies sold. What difference would this make to the reported profitability of each unit produced?

Economists versus accountants

In Chapter 8 we described the 'marginality rule' which, you may remember, states that profit is optimised for a firm when its marginal revenue equals its marginal cost of production. In other words, a firm should expand its level of production to the point where one extra unit of output incurs an increase in cost to the firm overall which is just equal to the increase in revenue that can be obtained. An alternative description of this rule is that a firm should increase the level of its output to the point where the change in the contribution earned exactly equals zero. It is an easy step to then make the assertion that when we are looking for the optimum level of output we should focus on the contribution gained and ignore any fixed or indirect costs. If we do count them in we can, to use an economist's term, misallocate resources. Here is an example of what we mean on a grand scale.

Financial realities   ### The story of Farmer Jo

The story of Farmer Jo illustrates the problems of using cost allocation to make production decisions. Farmer Jo, so the story goes, had sown wheat, barley, potatoes and beans on his farm and everything was proceeding well. That is, until his accountant turned up. The accountant wanted to know how much he spent running and maintaining his farmhouse and outbuildings. Farmer Jo replied, '£7800', after thinking about the problem for a while. 'Well', said the accountant, 'what we need to do is to work out the profitability of each of your crops after deducting a fair overhead for running the farm.' The accountant went on to suggest that the overheads should be charged according to the number of hours Farmer Jo spent looking after his crops each year. 'After all', he said, 'you have got to live to work, so it's only right when assessing the viability of your crops that we charge them with the cost of the house.' The accountant took away Farmer Jo's estimate of the net cash contribution he would make from each crop and promised to let him know what profit he could expect from each crop.

Exhibit 10.15

	Wheat	Barley	Potatoes	Beans
Contribution (£)	4000	4200	1000	1800
Labour hours	185	250	165	150

A week later, Farmer Jo received the following statement from his accountant which told him that potato growing was not profitable, and enclosed with this statement and a note of the accountant's fee was a letter advising Farmer Jo to discontinue potato farming forthwith.

Exhibit 10.16 Farmer Jo – profitability analysis

	Wheat	Barley	Potatoes	Beans
Contribution (£)	4000	4200	1000	1800
Allocated Overhead	1924	2600	1716	1560
Profit/Loss	2076	1600	−716	240

Farmer Jo had no idea how his accountant had prepared this statement but the method is simple:

Allocated overhead (wheat)

$$= \text{total farm overheads} \times \frac{\text{hours spent in wheat production}}{\text{total hours spent farming crops}}$$

$$= \pounds7800 \times 185/750$$
$$= \pounds1924$$

and so on for the other crops.

Farmer Jo, trusting his professional adviser absolutely, ploughed up his potato crop.

Two weeks later, he receives another visit from his accountant, who asks again to see his books. 'Ah', says the accountant, 'I suspect that beans are not truly profitable and don't pay their way. Let me do some further figures.' A week later Farmer Jo is ploughing up his beans. Note this time that the same amount of overhead (£7800) must be apportioned over a reduced set of crops and it is too late in the season to seed the ploughed-up potato field with wheat or barley.

Exhibit 10.17

	Wheat	Barley	Potatoes	Beans
Contribution (£)	4000	4200	X	1800
Allocated Overhead	2467	3333		2000
Profit/Loss	1533	867		−200

Exhibit 10.18

	Wheat	Barley	Potatoes	Beans
Contribution (£)	4000	4200	X	X
Allocated Overhead	3317	4483		
Profit/Loss	683	−283		

And a week later he is ploughing up his barley following yet another visit from his accountant:

Exhibit 10.19

	Wheat	Barley	Potatoes	Beans
Contribution (£)	4000	✗	✗	✗
Allocated Overhead	7800			
Profit/Loss	−3800			

And a week after that he is out of business.

Amusing as this exercise may appear it does bear careful reflection. The allocation of overheads on the basis of labour hours bears no relationship to the ability of each crop to earn a cash contribution for the farmer. Furthermore, because Farmer Jo has no alternative use for his land at this late stage in the season, ploughing up his fields is depriving him of contribution that he would otherwise have been able to earn. This would appear to be game, set and match to the economists. Making production decisions on the basis of fully allocated costs has only led him to disaster. Only if he had been able to substitute alternative crops would it have been worthwhile looking at the relative performance of each crop and, in that case, given that his time is the binding constraint, it would have been sensible to rank the alternatives according to contribution per labour hour ratio.

Exhibit 10.20

	Wheat	Barley	Potatoes	Beans
Contribution (£)	4000	4200	1000	1800
Labour hours	185	250	165	150
Contribution per labour hour	21.62	16.80	6.06	12.00

This ratio gives the ranking of the products in terms of their efficiency in converting labour hours into contribution. So, if we are in a situation where we need to make the most efficient use of labour that we can, then we should substitute potato for wheat production and beans for barley – indeed, if Farmer Jo can he should switch his entire farm to wheat production.

However, you may notice that the accounting approach of allocating overheads gives us the same ranking as using the contribution to labour hours ratio.

Exhibit 10.21

	Rank	Contribution per labour hour	Profit
Wheat	1st	21.62	2076
Barley	2nd	16.80	1600
Beans	3rd	12.00	240
Potatoes	4th	6.06	−716

Because accountants regularly use allocation systems such as that described for Farmer Jo it is important to know how to use the information effectively.

● Profitability measures using full costs which include allocated overheads should not be used for production decisions. A product is financially sustainable if it is making a positive contribution to the firm.

● Where a firm can substitute its scarce resources from one activity to another then product profitability measures using those scarce resources as cost drivers in overhead allocation can indicate which area of production to expand and which to contract.

● Where more profitable alternatives are available that make more efficient use of a firm's scarce resources then a full cost profitability measure does reveal which product to cut back.

Many firms, and notably the majority of Japanese manufacturers, use simple systems of indirect cost allocation using labour time as the cost driver. They have not been impressed by the more sophisticated cost driver analyses that form the basis of **activity-based costing**. They have recognised that cost allocation helps create a bias against the consumption of scarce labour time and, in the case of the Japanese, helped support the drive towards 'lean' manufacturing described earlier in the chapter.

An explanation of why overhead allocation is good for firms

Some scholars have argued that the real reason why cost allocation methods are so prevalent although they appear to contradict the axioms of economically rational behaviour on the part of firms is that they offer a method of rationing scarce resources and cost management. It is argued that firms that do not have some form of central cost allocation mechanism will find that the operating parts of the firm will make ever-increasing demands upon the scarce resources of the firm: its central management time, its capital and its pool of available labour. The problem of rationing scarce common resources is known in game theory as 'the problem of the commons'. The problem of the commons demonstrates a situation where individuals will continue to exploit a fixed common resource even though the welfare of all users of that resource are diminished by the actions of the individual.

Consider a stretch of common land held by the members of a village. The villagers have the right to graze their sheep on the common land and it can satisfactorily support 100 sheep which will return a net profit at market of £10 each. However, if an extra animal is put on the land it will be overgrazed and the net profit of the sheep will be reduced at market to £9.90 each. Each additional sheep over the 100 sustainable by the land will reduce the net profit by 10p per head.

The additional sheep (number 101) will yield £9.90 to the farmer but the net profit of all the commoners falls by the sum of profits with 101 sheep less the sum of profit at the land's capacity:

Profit to all with 100 sheep grazing the land = £1000.00
Profit to all with 101 sheep grazing the land =   £999.90

If a commoner introduces yet another sheep the net profit will fall to £9.80, giving a loss to the whole community of 40p overall – four times as much as with the first sheep.

This problem presents a conflict between the individual who will wish to keep adding sheep to the common whilst there is any profit to be made and the sum of the commoners

Exhibit 10.22

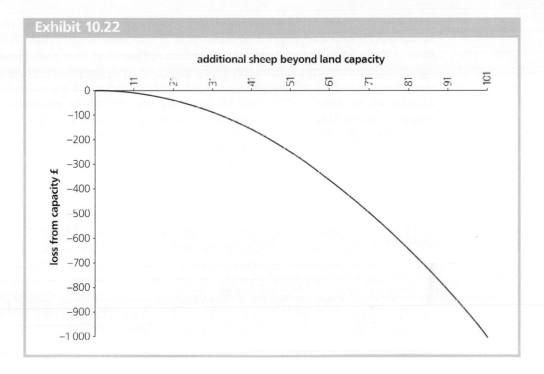

who are losing value overall. Indeed, if there are no constraints on the rights of the common-ers to keep adding sheep then the land will be quickly grazed to exhaustion and no one will earn any profit. Exhibit 10.22 shows the loss to the village as the land is exhausted.

There are two ways that this problem of overgrazing can be controlled:

● by the head of the village controlling the use of the land by force, or
● by the head of the village charging a rent for the use of the land such that the available supply of land just matches the demand at the price set.

Both methods have their advocates but the advantage of charging a rent is that in practice those villagers who are able to earn the best profit from the use of the land will be most likely to be able to afford to pay while the rest will have to give up sheep and take up say weaving instead.

The connection between this simple example and the problem of cost allocation was pointed out by Jerold Zimmerman in an important article (see the end of chapter for the reference). A firm which has common resources will find that they will be over-consumed by its departmental managers unless there is some mechanism for rationing the supply of those resources. The conditions for this to occur are as follows:

● The common resources can potentially add value to the product of the departments. This will almost certainly be the case where those resources include central management exper-tise, marketing, research and development and personnel functions, which in many firms are centrally rather than departmentally organised.
● These common resources represent a binding constraint upon the capacity of the firm to meet its various markets.
● Departmental managers can call upon those resources without cost.
● Departmental managers are compensated for their performance against profit targets where profit is calculated after charging indirect costs.

As with the problems of the commons senior management has essentially two strategies for preventing over-consumption of centrally held resources: it can ration their supply by *diktat* or it can set a price on those resources which will just clear their available supply at full capacity. Zimmerman argues that cost allocation is effectively the process where senior managers charge departmental managers a rent for the resources which are in short supply. In a situation where there is a tendency for operating departments to over-utilise central resources firms which ration those resources through cost allocation are likely to perform better than those that do not.

This argument is quite persuasive in that it gives a positive reason why firms that do operate cost allocation are more likely to be successful in rationing the use of central resources than those who do not.

Review activity 10.4   The marketing department of a company is housed within the company head office. Direct costs of £250 000 can be traced directly to the department, and of these £210 000 are salary costs. The building costs £620 000 a year for rent, maintenance and services. The company head office has a staff salary budget of £2 000 000 and has 1200 square metres of floor space. The marketing department uses 400 square metres of space. The objective of this exercise is to allocate the indirect cost for the building as a whole to the marketing department, which is, for the purposes of this analysis, the cost object. Two cost drivers can be chosen; calculate the indirect charge to the marketing department using each.

Activity-based costing

Activity-based costing or ABC is a variant of traditional indirect cost allocation in which the costing system does not focus on the resources used but on the activities undertaken by the firm in producing its products. Following the work of the Harvard corporate strategist Michael Porter, the originators of ABC identified the activities that a firm undertakes as either 'primary' or 'secondary'. Costs fall into three categories:

● Directly traceable costs: these are activity costs which can be directly attributed to the creation of the product concerned. They are normally the costs incurred in undertaking the primary activities involved in production: buying in components and raw materials, engaging in physically transforming those resources (operations), distributing them to customers, engaging in marketing and sales and providing after-sales service.

● Indirectly traceable costs: these are costs of the various support activities that can be traced to products through the design of appropriate cost drivers. Examples of indirectly traceable costs are those that are, for example, shared by production such as salaried labour and management time, shared plant costs, and the fixed costs of supplying utilities such as water and electricity.

● Untraceable costs: these are business-level costs which although important in running the business cannot be traced to particular products. The costs of running the head-office systems are an example of a cost which may be untraceable to an individual aspect of production. In ABC these are normally left out of the cost allocation exercise.

Exhibit 10.23 shows Porter's value chain; the idea behind ABC is to trace into products or services the activities undertaken in all steps in the process of manufacture. The idea behind the value chain model is that value is created (or lost) at a variety of stages during the 'business processes' that a firm undertakes. Firms can create value by superior logistics, operations, distribution, marketing or service (the so-called primary activities) and indirectly

Exhibit 10.23 Porter's value chain

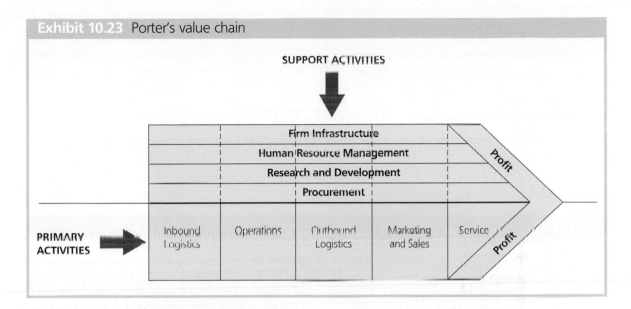

by building effective and efficient support operations such as procurement, research and development, human resource management and even financial management.

The methodology for tracing costs into products is similar to that described in the six-step process for cost allocation. The principal difference lies in identifying and categorising the different activities undertaken and how they fit together to create the value chain which takes raw materials or components at one end and converts them into products that satisfy the customers' needs at the other. The focus of the analysis in ABC is therefore on activities rather than the consumption of resources and activity-based cost drivers are designed to reveal the relative effort expended by the firm across its range of different products.

Activity-based costing is an exhaustive technique that is designed to overcome the objections to traditional cost allocation. However, it is a form of cost allocation where indirect costs are traced to the activities undertaken in the process of creating products rather than the resources consumed. It is not always understood that 'activities' are fundamentally undertaken by people and that ABC is a system for breaking down the total labour time of the business into its constituent parts. There has been much criticism that ABC is expensive to implement and it is undoubtedly true that analysing all of the activities undertaken by a firm into meaningful categories is an expensive process. An effective ABC system will help a firm to identify where 'bottlenecks' are occurring and focal points for managing indirect cost expenditure.

Review activity 10.5   Wallie Wilts conducted an analysis of the work undertaken in the office. These are some of the activities that he identified:

- ordering supplies for customer contracts
- ordering office supplies
- checking deliveries against orders
- raising building contracts
- arranging visits from the building inspectors to construction sites

- arranging subcontractors
- making supplier and subcontractor payments
- invoicing and receiving stage payments
- preparing and filing insurance claims
- preparing and settling value-added tax returns.

Where in Porter's value chain would you place each of these activities and how would you suggest that they could be measured in practice?

Pricing

Product pricing is one of the most difficult areas for business to get right. Any mispricing will have a direct impact upon the profitability of the firm. Underpricing will lead to a firm losing profit and producing and selling more than it should do if it were operating at the ideal level. Overpricing will again mean that the firm will be losing profit, as sales that it should be making are lost because the price is too high. Getting the price right is key therefore to making sure that the resources of the firm are efficiently used and converted into profit in the most effective way possible.

There are two broad approaches to pricing:

- market-based methods that set prices according to market conditions and what the customer is willing to pay, and
- cost-based methods that set prices according to what it costs the firm to produce the item concerned plus a mark-up.

For a firm producing in a perfectly competitive market, these two methods amount to the same thing. In all other market types different prices will arise using the two methods.

The nature of perfect competition

A perfectly competitive market is one characterised by a very large number of buyers and sellers of a common product. There are no transaction costs in buying and selling, no taxes and every firm can see what its competitors are doing. In this ideal market type no firm can survive if it sells at anything different from the current market price as dictated by the market demand curve. Because there are so many buyers and sellers no firm can alter the market price by increasing or decreasing its output level.

Product markets of this type are rare with perhaps agricultural goods being the commonest example. In such a market the firm has to take the ruling market price as given. The degree of competitiveness also ensures that all abnormal profits are competed away so if a perfectly efficient firm knows its costs it can determine the price at which it can sell. However, this type of market is an extreme case and most manufacturing and service firms face markets that do not conform to this ideal and, indeed, many firms may be able to create such a high degree of competitive advantage that they become monopolies. Once a firm creates some distinguishing feature that sets its product off against the market then the demand curve that the firm faces will no longer be flat, as shown in Exhibit 10.24, but will take on the familiar downward-sloping demand curve in accordance with the law of demand described in Chapter 8.

Exhibit 10.24 Demand curves under perfect competition

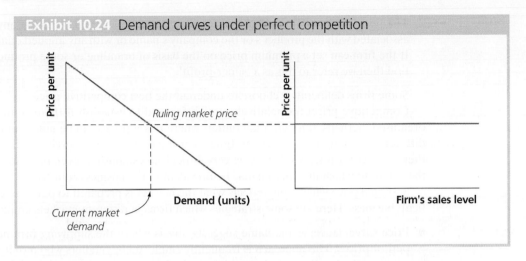

Market-based pricing

In all real markets it is the customer who ultimately determines the price that they are prepared to pay for the product on offer. The base price or price below which the firm should not supply is its opportunity or marginal cost of production.

It should then be able to identify two further price levels:

1. The competitive price at which its competitors are selling an equivalent product or service. If the firm sets its price at this level then it will earn what we term the 'normal profit' given its costs of production.

Exhibit 10.25 The components of price

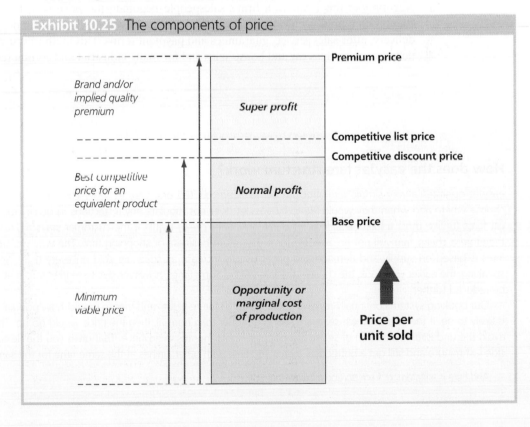

2. The premium price it could obtain for the product concerned including any brand value associated with the product's or the company's name or with any implied quality premium. If the firm can set a premium price on the basis of branding or some product differentiation then we refer to this as a 'super-profit'.

Some firms deliberately choose to undercut the best competitive price.

Competitive prices are relatively straightforward to establish if there is an open market organised, perhaps, through retail outlets where ticket prices can be noted and compared in different locations and at different times. For industrial or commercial products or services then competitor price levels may be very difficult to establish as even price lists do not show the extent to which discounting may be prevalent in the business concerned.

Setting a price which fully reflects what the market is prepared to pay is an extremely difficult business. Here are some strategies which firms in different markets employ:

- Price surveillance: as the name suggests, this is where the supplying firm monitors competitor prices. This approach is frequently employed by retailers who monitor competitor prices in the locality and where price sensitivity can be crucial (petrol retailers and supermarkets are good examples).

- Price matching: companies who are willing to match any price (usually within a defined region) for an identical product or service. An example is the retailer John Lewis Partnership. These companies are effectively using their customers as their market researchers!

- Test marketing: different prices are charged in different locations that have similar market characteristics (population size, spending power and social class) and the demand is matched against the price to see if there is a discernible relationship. Large retailers such as Tesco and Sainsbury's use these techniques.

- Negotiation: this is where a firm's salespeople negotiate the price with the customer or client. Often price is only one factor in the negotiation which will also include discussion of delivery, after-sales service, guarantees and payment terms. This method is used for 'large-ticket' items such as car and house sales and for many industrial and commercial products.

Review activity 10.6   Here is a statement by easyJet about how they set their fares.

How does the easyJet fare structure work?

easyJet operates a very simple fare structure. All fares are quoted one way to allow customers the flexibility to choose where and when they would like to fly. easyJet does not stipulate any restrictions to qualify for the cheapest fares (unlike most traditional airlines who will only offer cheap flights if the customer stays a Saturday night, therefore a cheap fare will not be available for a day-return business or shopping trip). The way we structure our fares is based on supply and demand and prices usually increase as seats are sold on every flight. So, generally speaking, the earlier you book, the cheaper the fare will be. Sometimes, however, due to market forces our fares may be reduced further.

Our booking system continually reviews bookings for all future flights and tries to predict how popular each flight is likely to be. If the rate at which seats are selling is higher than normal, then the price would go up. This way we avoid the undesirable situation of selling out popular flights months in advance. That gives you the flexibility to decide last minute and still get a better deal than if you flew with other airlines at the same time for the same journey.

And here is a statement from BA about its low-fare policy:

Are low fares making British Airways a low cost carrier?

We are restructuring our UK domestic and shorthaul business to provide a competitive response to the no-frills carriers. Under our new fare structure we offer you greater choice and flexibility. With the removal of Saturday night stay and advance purchase restrictions, we are now offering new lower year round air tickets on flights within the UK and Europe. This means that on these routes you can now choose between tickets which are non-changeable & non refundable or flexible fares which offer you more choice to suit your travel needs.

We are not becoming a no frills airline but will compete profitably and intelligently alongside them by adopting what they do well – online bookings, high aircraft utilisation and simple affordable pricing. We will mix it with what we do well – providing a great network and schedule with frequent flights from convenient & central airports, as well as delivering world class customer service (our new pricing structure still entitles every passenger to our full onboard product).

Using the diagram in Exhibit 10.25 locate where easyJet and BA are positioning themselves in terms of pricing. What information would these two companies need to collect on a routine basis to set their prices?

Cost-based pricing

There are a number of cost-based pricing approaches. The two most popular are cost-plus pricing and target rate of return pricing. Both methods try to ensure that a given profit target is achieved if the firm operates at budgeted output.

Cost-plus pricing

Cost-plus pricing is a popular pricing technique used widely in both manufacturing and the service sector. The mechanics of the method are simple in that a set percentage is added to the full cost of producing the given product or service.

$$\text{Price} = \text{Full cost} + \frac{\text{Mark-up}}{(\%)} \times \text{Full cost}$$

In principle, with cost-plus pricing we expect to see a 'layered' statement of total unit cost including direct costs of production, a charge for production overheads and a general overhead recovery.

The price analysis for this product is shown in Exhibit 10.26.

Financial realities   Elco Ltd, a subsidiary of a large UK energy company makes and soak-charges batteries for the storage of domestic electricity produced using photovoltaic cells. These batteries are sold to customers of the 'sunshine programme' of the parent company. The direct costs include the component and electrolyte cost (£220 per unit), the metered cost of the soak charge (£18), labour cost at 4 hours per unit on an hourly labour rate of £20 per hour and other direct expenses of £15.50 per unit. Production overheads are based on a machine-time charge related to two hours' usage of equipment carrying production overheads of £270 000 including supervision costs, plant costs and depreciation. The budgeted machine utilisation is 4000 hours per annum. General company overheads are charged to sales at a rate of £6 per pound of direct labour. The total capital investment in the battery plant is £12.40 million and the budgeted sales for the coming year are 8400 units. The company attempts to recover a 40 per cent mark-up on total cost or a 15 per cent rate of return on the total capital employed, whichever is the greater. How much will the company charge per battery?

Exhibit 10.26

Elco Ltd

Battery Price Analysis

	Cost Plus £	ROR target £
Direct costs		
component costs	220.00	220.00
metered power	18.00	18.00
labour cost	80.00	80.00
other direct expenses	15.50	15.50
	333.50	333.50
Production overheads		
machine time	135.00	135.00
General overhead recovery		
labour cost recovery	480.00	480.00
Total cost	948.50	948.50
Mark-up (40%)	379.40	
Target rate of return		221.43
Price to supply	1327.90	169.93

You will note that the company has counted labour as a direct cost although strictly it does not comply with the criteria for a direct cost described in Chapter 8. Labour in this company is paid an annual wage which is averaged over all technical employees and allocated as a standard hourly rate. However, many companies do regard their standard hourly pay rate as a direct cost.

To these costs is then added a fixed percentage 'margin'. On average, if the firm operates at its budget capacity, this margin should translate into the operating profit margin of the firm. If the firm operates beyond its budgeted capacity then there will be an 'over-recovery' of the firm's overheads and the resulting profit margin will be correspondingly greater than the standard mark-up rate. If, on the other hand, the firm operates below its budget capacity then there will be an under-recovery of overheads and the firms overall profit margin will be less than the standard mark-up rate. However, as we will see below, there may be other more important factors that come into play when firms attempt to operate at or beyond their physical capacity.

In practice standard mark-up rates are rarely achieved. Usually the firm will find itself having to offer some form of discount, especially in situations where it is under capacity and unable to achieve its targeted volumes of sales. However, it is also possible for a firm to charge a mark-up on its full cost and still make a loss.

The problems of using cost-plus pricing is that it is almost impossible to get the best price for the firm using this method, and because the opportunity cost of production is ignored it is quite possible to produce and sell at an economic loss.

In Exhibit 10.27 we show some possibilities of what can go wrong. The centre chart shows the accounting breakdown of cost, building to the price the firm wishes to set on a cost-plus basis. The two other charts show the potential contribution if the best price is achieved after deducting the opportunity cost of production. The chart to the left assumes that there are no capacity constraints that will inflate the opportunity cost of production. This tends to be the situation when business is in recession and the best market prices that can be obtained are

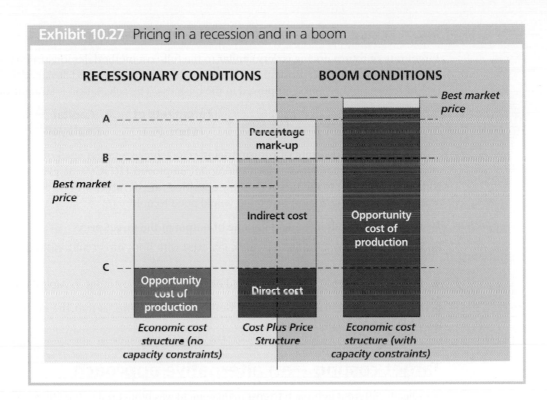

Exhibit 10.27 Pricing in a recession and in a boom

lower than normal. The chart to the right shows the situation where there is a binding constraint on production and an increased opportunity cost arises as a result.

Full-cost pricing in a recession

In a business recession there will be surplus capacity in the industry and a tendency for firms to be in a situation of oversupply. This causes downward pressure on prices. However, because firms are under capacity the opportunity cost of production (see Chapter 8) will tend to fall towards the direct cost of buying in the necessary resources. The firm that sticks doggedly to its full-cost pricing strategy will attempt to charge price (Λ) and as a result its sales and volumes will plummet. In such a situation, the firm either chooses to weather the recessionary storm or it cuts its prices. This will achieve some level of contribution to the firm's burden of indirect cost, which is better than the alternative of sticking with its full price and making no contribution at all!

Full-cost pricing in a boom

When a business finds itself at the top of its business cycle and under capacity constraints it will find that the opportunity cost of production can expand rapidly as the firm is forced into redeploying resources internally to meet the pressures of customer demand. In this situation the opportunity cost can rapidly expand beyond the level of the indirect charge used in full-cost pricing and indeed beyond the fully marked-up price. Indeed, it is quite common for firms to find themselves charging a full-cost price but making a net cash loss on the products they are selling.

This important analysis suggests that when firms are operating at full capacity, cost-plus pricing will tend to understate the true cost of production and indeed lead to activity which whilst appearing to be profitable in an accounting sense is bleeding cash from the business.

Target or rate of return pricing

Target rate of return pricing is very similar to the full-cost method demonstrated above except that instead of a standard profit margin based on cost, a rate is charged designed to earn a fixed rate of return on the capital employed in the business. The calculation is straightforward:

$$\text{Price} = \text{Full cost} + \frac{\text{Target rate of}}{\text{return (\%)}} \times \frac{\text{Capital}}{\text{employed}}$$

The aim with target rate of return pricing is to achieve a target level of return on sales as measured by the company's return on capital employed (ROCE). If everything about the company works out to the target then the specified rate of return will be achieved. However, here are some of the assumptions that would need to hold:

- The company sells its budget volume of output at the target price.
- The company's operating margin is achieved with both direct and indirect costs meeting target.
- The company is not forced to expand or contract its investment in capital equipment.

The most problematic of these, as we have noted before, is that the customers are prepared to accept the price set.

Target costing – an alternative approach

A radically different approach to cost management was pioneered in the 1980s and 1990s at the major Japanese manufacturers. Target costing is a cost management philosophy which takes as its starting point the price that the customer is prepared to pay. At the Citizen Watch Company:

> Cost plus pricing was rarely used . . . Occasionally Citizen would bring out a watch or movement for which there was no direct competitor . . . the selling price was determined using a 'to be accepted' market price . . . by market studies and analysis that consisted of an evaluation of the attractiveness of the product and a comparison with other watches . . . (Cooper, 1994)

Citizen's focus on the price the market would accept is a key concept in target costing. At Olympus, Cooper also notes that once the distinctive features of a new product were identified and 'price points . . . determined from the competitive analysis and technology review . . .' a target cost could be established. As a result, the cost-plus equation shown above is turned on its head:

$$\frac{\text{Target}}{\text{cost}} = \frac{\text{Target}}{\text{price}} - \frac{\text{Margin}}{\text{(\%)}} \times \frac{\text{Target}}{\text{price}}$$

So, cost, not price, is the dependent variable and once the price is set, the expected margin-determined target cost can be set. This is the firm's total, fully allocated cost of production and once established it is expected that the firm will focus on achieving it. The first and most important lesson is that the objective of management is now clearly set – to get costs down to the target. Target costing forces management to seek ways of 'engineering the cost out' of new products, of forcing better deals with suppliers and of refining manufacturing systems to eliminate waste and reworking. As we shall see in the next chapter, this approach to cost management is complemented by a range of other operational strategies – most particularly in the development of 'Just-in-Time' manufacturing systems.

Chapter summary

In this chapter we have focused on the twin pillars of financial management strategy: cost management and pricing. In the area of cost management we have explored the traditional systems for costing products and services and pointed out the dangers and the advantages of using conventional cost allocation. The Farmer Jo problem highlighted the dangers of using fully absorbed costs as a tool in production and resource allocation decision-making. However, we also showed that such costing strategies can lead to the correct ordering of production priorities when the cost driver represents a resource that is in short supply. In this situation, fully allocated costs indicate the relative but not the absolute profitability of different products. We then turned our attention to activity-based costing which presents an alternative approach to the allocation of indirect costs. Finally, we reviewed the two basic methods of pricing products: the first based upon market prices, the second upon costs. We argued that market-based pricing is likely to be more effective in competitive markets than the cost-based approach, especially when allied with target costing.

Further reading

Atkinson, A.A., Kaplan, R. S., Matsumura, E.M. and Young, S.M. (2007) *Management Accounting*, 3rd ed., Upper Saddle River, NJ: Prentice-Hall. The best modern treatment of the subject which will take you on from the introduction provided by this book. An excellent treatment of costing and performance measurement methods.

Glad, E. and Becker, H. (1996) *Activity Based Costing and Management*, Chichester: Wiley. A great 'how to do it' book which is mercifully slim in volume on what is, for most managers, a less than interesting topic.

Johnson, H.T. and Kaplan, R.S. (1987) *Relevance Lost – The Rise and Fall of Management Accounting*, Boston: Harvard Business School Press. Occasionally a book comes along that turns the subject on its head. This is one of them. In this book the authors mercilessly dissect the problems of management accounting and how then to put them right. Unfortunately, some say the cure was worse than the complaint.

Ryan, B. (1995) *Strategic Accounting for Management*, London: Cengage. An interesting book which provides a deeper level of analysis than many of the topics covered in this book. Of particular note is the work on the theory of costs in Chapter 4.

Zimmerman, J. (1979) The Costs and Benefits of Cost Allocation, *The Accounting Review*, 54.

Progress check

1. What distinguishes direct and indirect costs? (p. 324)

2. List five different cost classifications, separating them into vertical and horizontal costs. (p. 326)

3. Give five reasons for cost allocation in practice. (pp. 328–329)

4. List the six steps involved in the creation of a cost allocation model. (pp. 329–330)

5. What do you understand by the terms 'cost pool' and 'cost driver'? (p. 330)

6. List four categories of cost driver. (p. 335)

7. If there are three cost pools how many cost drivers would you expect to find? (p. 336)

8. On what basis would economists argue that production output decisions be made? (p. 341)

9. Under what circumstances will ranking products by profitability be consistent with ranking them by contribution per unit of scarce resource? (p. 344)

10. What is the implication of the 'problem of the commons' for cost allocation in practice? (p. 345)

11. Upon what model of the firm is activity-based costing constructed? (p. 346)

12. Identify four strategies for identifying the best market price for a product. (p. 350)

13. How does cost-plus pricing differ from target rate of return pricing? (p. 352)

14. Give two benefits of target costing. (p. 354)

Questions

The answers to the questions followed by ✓ can be found at the back of the book, the answers to the remaining questions can be found on the website accompanying this book, **www.cengage.co.uk/ ryan2**.

1. You are given the following information concerning a particular product.
   - The direct cost of production is £16.80 per unit.
   - Each unit requires 0.5 labour hours and 0.1 machine hours in production.
   - The total annual indirect costs attributable to the factory are £6 400 000. During the year, 150 000 labour hours and 40 000 machine hours were employed in the factory.
   - The company has a target rate of return on capital employed of 15 per cent per annum. The capital employed in the factory is £4 620 000.
   - The factory's products are all physically similar to one another, although they have varying amounts of labour and machine inputs.

   You are required to:

   (i) Calculate the price which will give the target rate of return when applied to the total cost per unit produced on the basis of labour hours and machine hours.

   (ii) Calculate the price on the assumption that management would prefer the indirect charge to be absorbed on the basis of labour time and the capital employed in the factory on the basis of the product's usage of capital equipment.

   (iii) Discuss the relative merits of the allocation bases you have used and comment upon the reasonableness of cost-based pricing procedures.   ✓

2. Your company has received a request to tender for a contract to produce 100 components as a trial run for a larger order, which may follow.

In assessing this tender you know the number of inputs that will be required, some of which the firm has available in its current inventories and some of which will have to be purchased from suppliers. In particular, one sub-assembly in the component concerned is fabricated within another division of your firm. The production process required to manufacture this sub-assembly is long and difficult and there have been many production delays over the last 12 months. Demand for that sub-assembly from customers is very high and the company currently enjoys substantial profit margins on all its sales. In addition, you also discover that the necessary labour skills required to produce the components are currently fully deployed elsewhere within the firm. The skills require expensive and extensive training and are not available in the labour market. Withdrawing labour from current production in order to manufacture these components would entail a loss of full-cost profit on the existing work.

In discussion with marketing, you are informed that the marketing and sales team responsible for this area of trade has been nurturing this client for the previous 18 months. Over that period, substantial expense has been incurred in securing the invitation to tender. The marketing department see it is a very high priority that the firm respond positively to this tender. In assessing the price to bid, you also note that the firm has a policy of adding a 200 per cent mark-up to labour costs in order to recover fixed overheads. The firm also has a practice of pricing at full cost plus 20 per cent. In the view of the marketing department, such a full-cost price is likely to be much more than the customer would be prepared to pay, even for short-run production.

Your final round of discussions with the project development team lead you to believe that there is considerable uncertainty as to whether the firm has sufficient capability to be able to produce 100 components without a large number of rejects. Indeed, the firm's quality assurance manager is adamant that no greater than 75 per cent success is likely during the production stage.

Taking all this into account you are required to recommend a costing strategy for this contract which reflects the uncertainties attached to it and the full economic cost of production. Your report should provide a critical analysis of the available costing methodologies available to you.

3. The direct cost of producing a play at the Bell Theatre in Cold Ashton is £80 000 for a two-week run of one evening performance daily (except Sundays) and an additional matinee performance on Wednesday and Saturday. The direct costs are typical of productions at the Bell. The indirect costs of running the theatre are £1 890 000 per annum for which an Arts Council grant of £350 000 and other bequests amounting to £163 000 are budgeted in the current year. The theatre seats 676 and 60 per cent of seats or more are expected to be sold at all seating levels apart from the boxes. Seat prices are £12 for the upper circle (150 seats), £18 for the circle (220 seats) and £22 for the stalls (270 seats). There are 36 box seats currently priced at £55 each, although occupancy has been 50 per cent. Each showing generates a contribution of around £1000 for merchandise, drinks and programmes. Management believes that any increase in seat prices will bring about a fall in overall sales by 10 per cent. However, they have considered a cut of 10 per cent in the ticket price for this production which they believe will increase occupancy of the upper circle seats by 20 per cent and the circle by 10 per cent. Occupancy in the boxes and the stalls would remain unchanged. The trustees are not so sure and would like to see some justification. Currently the theatre is open for an average of 40 weeks of performance.

On the basis of the above information you are required to produce a report for the theatre trustees commenting upon the pricing of this production in particular and the pricing of tickets more generally. ✓

4. Your company is considering changing its costing policy from one which is placed upon the allocation of overheads using labour cost as the resource driver to one based upon a wider range of activities routinely undertaken during production. Discuss the implications of this move, outlining any theoretical or practical difficulties which you can foresee and the potential benefits which may follow.

5. Sid's Taxis Ltd has 55 cars in its fleet and there are an average of 16 hirings per day. On average each car covers an actual and a metered mileage of 63 000 miles and 48 000 miles respectively. The standard charge per hiring is £2.20, on to which a mileage rate is added. Each driver's base pay is £5000 per annum and they earn a bonus of 5p per metered mile. Each driver works an average of 2300 hours per annum and each car is on the road for 5500 hours for an average of 300 days per annum. The direct cost of fuel is 85p per litre and each cab averages 5 miles per litre. The annual road tax and insurance is £800 and each cab typically costs £18 000 new, has a road life of 150 000 miles when it is sold at auction for £5000. On average the cabs are two years old. Sid has a garage and parking lot which cost £255 000 per annum to run including the direct costs of servicing and maintaining the vehicles. The head office costs are £650 000 per annum. Sid would like to know the rate he should charge per mile.

You are required to:

(i) Calculate the metered charge per mile that will recover full cost and earn a profit margin of 15 per cent.

(ii) Calculate the metered charge per mile that will recover 15 per cent of the capital invested in the cab fleet.

(iii) Calculate the target cost that must be met if a mileage rate of 80p is set with a 15 per cent mark-up on cost.

(iv) Comment upon the assumptions you have made in your analysis.

Case exercise

This project is designed to help you recover the cost of this book at least.

For the organisation you currently work for, or study at, you are required to find a cost saving for the business which meets the following criteria:

● is measurable in cash terms, having the direct effect of increasing the annual cash flow of the organisation

● will not result in redundancy of existing staff nor involve significant redeployment of duties or change of location

● will not entail any cash investment

● will not reduce the efficiency of the business's overall operation

● will not reduce the quality of the product or service to the customer.

You are required to:

(i) Prepare a report containing your proposal which should be fully justified with appropriate evidence.

(ii) Analyse the extent to which your proposal could lead to an increase in the quality of your organisation's overall operations.

Chapter 11

The management of working capital

Introduction

In this chapter we draw together a number of issues and learning points from previous chapters as we introduce the topic of working or 'operating' capital management. Our first concern will be to consider the role of working capital within the firm and how companies gear the asset side of their balance sheet to optimise the levels of the two types of capital in the business. We then turn our attention to the problem of managing inventories to ensure that the firm's commitment to stock holding is kept to a minimum. Similarly we discuss the problems of managing credit and in particular the difficulties firms have in controlling their receivable accounts. Finally, we turn our attention to cash and discuss the extent to which it can be in a firm's interest to build significant cash balances and how to manage the treasury function of the firm. Working capital management is a central concern in most businesses and even for small firms this area of financial management and control can be the most difficult. One route that some firms have pursued is to install resource management systems. We will explore the development of these systems and the facilities that one leading software system offers.

Learning objectives

The learning objectives for this chapter are as follows:

The role of working capital

- To understand the role of working capital in the firm.

- To be able to trace the flows of working capital through the accounts of the business.

- To be able to identify whether a working capital management policy is 'aggressive', 'neutral' or 'defensive'.

Inventory management

- To be able to calculate an economic order quantity and reorder level for a given stock line.

- To understand how the process of cost minimisation described in Chapter 8 is required to create a Just-in-Time inventory management system.

- To have an outline understanding of the role of MRP, MRP2 and enterprise resource planning software.

Managing credit policy

- To be aware of the importance of managing credit for the ongoing liquidity of the firm.

- To be able to conduct a credit risk assessment.

- To be able to measure the benefits of reducing average debtor ages.

- To understand the strategies for minimising the costs and risks of late payment.

Managing cash

- To understand the principal reasons why firms should hold reserves of cash.

- To be aware of the role of the short-term financial markets and the role of the treasury manager.

- To be able to estimate the maximum holding of cash using the Baumol model.

The role of working capital

Working capital consists of inventories, accounts receivable (debtors) and cash on the asset side of the balance sheet less accounts payable on the claims side. One of the undesirable side-effects of studying accounting is that it is too easy to see the different parts of working capital as distinct categories which need to be managed in different ways. In reality the working capital of a business is a dynamic system where financial resources are being continuously transformed from one type of asset to another in what is known as the 'operating cycle' of the business. Working capital management is the process of ensuring that all aspects of this system operate efficiently: inventories are maintained at the minimum level necessary to meet the needs of production and of customers; receivables and payables are settled promptly and bad debts are minimised; and, finally, cash is put to use quickly within the business or is returned to investors.

To understand how the operating cycles of the business work we will return for a moment to the extended trial balance as described in the first chapters of this book. In Exhibit 11.1 we have expanded the equation to include three types of inventories: raw materials, work in progress and finished goods. This typology of inventories is most relevant to a manufacturer but is also found to a lesser extent in other industries where conversion of real assets forms part of the value creating process. If we trace through the steps of the typical sequence of transactions we can build a picture of the problems of working capital management:

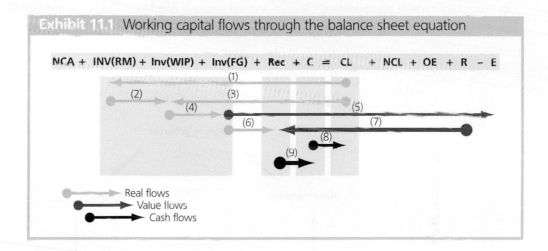

Exhibit 11.1 Working capital flows through the balance sheet equation

$$NCA + INV(RM) + Inv(WIP) + Inv(FG) + Rec + C = CL + NCL + OE + R - E$$

Real flows
Value flows
Cash flows

Stage (1) The firm purchases raw materials and components from suppliers, creating both an inventory of raw materials and a current liability.

Stage (2) The raw materials are taken from inventory and passed into production. Whilst in production the materials in the process of being manufactured into the finished product are classed as 'work in progress'.

Stage (3) Other services (such as energy and other utilities) may be bought in from suppliers to support the conversion process.

Stage (4) Once manufacturing is complete the final products are transferred to finished goods inventory.

Stage (5) Once the goods are sold the value of the inputs into the creation of the finished inventories are 'expensed' as a charge to the income statement for the year.

Stage (6) Upon sale the finished goods are transferred to the customer.

Stage (7) The sale value is transferred from 'revenue' in the income statement to the customer's account to create an outstanding receivables balance or 'account receivable'.

Stage (8) The current liability for the raw materials, components and other inputs into the production process is discharged by a payment of cash to the supplier.

Stage (9) The whole process is completed when the customer settles their account, paying the firm in cash.

There are a number of observations that we can make about this process. First, there are three sets of 'flows' in operation: a flow of real goods and services from suppliers to inventory to production and ultimately to the customer; value flows as the value added and realised in the eventual sale is captured in the income statement; and finally cash flows as the claims of suppliers and the indebtedness of customers are discharged by cash payments and receipts. The second point to note is that the real flows and value flows follow in a set sequence, However, the cash payments and receipts can arise at any stage in the sequence and not necessarily in the order shown.

Using the same approach as in Exhibit 11.1 add:

- the capital cycle of equity and debt finance and the payment of interest, dividends and capital
- the capital investment cycle in terms of the acquisition of capital plant, its write-off and eventual disposal.

Exhibit 11.2 The operating cycle of a business

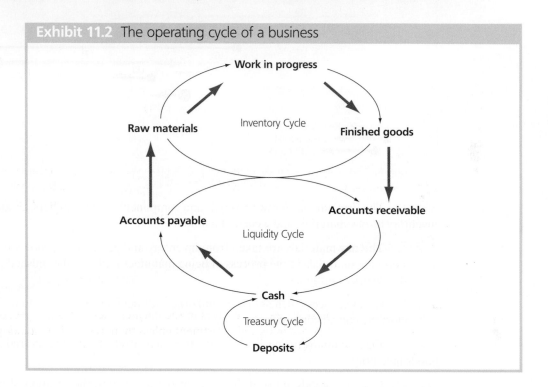

The operating cycle of the business shown in Exhibit 11.2 therefore consists of two subsidiary cycles: the inventory cycle which is concerned with the flow of inventories in, through and out of the business and a liquidity cycle which is concerned with the receipt and payment of cash from customers and to suppliers. Finally, the cash cycle also has a subordinate cycle which is termed the 'treasury cycle' where the short-term liquid resources of the business are actively managed to ensure that maximum return is realised on temporary cash balances. In subsequent sections of this chapter we consider how these three cycles are managed.

Working capital in the balance sheet

The operating cycle of the business is where value is created from the non-monetary assets of the business and cash and other monetary assets are generated. However, different businesses have different policies with respect to the management of their working capital which is partly a matter of choice and partly a consequence of the financial characteristics of the business in which the firm is engaged. The key ratio for measuring working capital and its prominence in the balance sheet is the current asset ratio. The current asset ratio is simply the sum of the current assets divided by the current liabilities

Exhibit 11.3

Policy	Current Asset Ratio	Returns	Implications
Aggressive	Less than 0.9	ROCE > ROFCE	Business is 'over-invested' with short-term creditor balances financing capital expenditure
Neutral	0.9–1.1	ROCE ~ ROFCE	Business is 'fully invested' with long-term capital (debt plus equity) wholly employed in financing fixed assets
Defensive	Greater than 1.1	ROCE < ROFCE	Business is 'underinvested' with excess current assets. This excess may be caused by a cash mountain, overinvestment in stock or a very loose credit policy

In a balance sheet where the capital employed in the business is fully invested in non-current and other long-term assets, the working capital will be zero and the current asset ratio will be at its 'neutral value' of one. An aggressive policy with respect to the management of working capital is where the current asset ratio is maintained at a value less than one. This has the effect of increasing the return on capital employed (ROCE) relative to the return on fixed capital employed (ROFCE). A defensive policy would be one where the net current asset ratio is held at a value greater than unity. With a defensive policy the return on capital employed will be necessarily lower than the return on fixed capital employed.

The working cycle has a critical role to play in the internal financing of capital investment. The presence of substantial equity reserves in the balance sheet does not necessarily mean that a firm is able to engage in capital investment unless there is sufficient liquidity within the business to finance the acquisitions. If the firm is fully invested already, that is all available cash has already been used or is required to sustain the operations of the business, then it will be forced to seek external finance from the capital markets (see Chapter 14).

Review activity 11.2   Review the current asset, return on fixed capital employed and return on capital employed ratios for the following companies (Exhibit 11.4). To what extent would you classify them as following neutral, aggressive or defensive working capital management policies?

Exhibit 11.4

	CAR	ROCE	ROFCE
BP plc	0.97	11.11%	11.00%
Cobham plc	1.54	19.40%	23.87%
easyJet plc	2.01	8.78%	12.60%
Marks & Spencer plc	2.15	6.14%	9.79%
Sainsbury's plc	0.79	10.10%	8.44%
Tesco plc	0.43	15.90%	11.50%

Inventory management

The costs of holding inventory consist of two important elements: the cost of the stock item and the cost incurred in ordering the item from the supplier, or, if it is finished goods, the cost of setting up a production run within the firm's own manufacturing process. For raw materials the cost is the price negotiated with the supplier for a given product or component of the required quality and service potential. The buyer will normally seek to achieve the lowest bought-in price although a number of other factors may well be important factors in agreeing the product price:

● After-sales service and product support. This is not usually a problem when buying paper-clips. However, when purchasing sub-assemblies such as gearboxes for cars or seats for aeroplanes the support of the original equipment manufacturer (OEM) can be an important factor in determining an acceptable price for the items concerned.

● Delivery: as well as agreeing different lead times for the supply of the goods or services concerned, most suppliers can offer a variety of delivery options that can be integrated with their customers' material handling systems.

● Packaging: for many products the nature of the packaging can be an important factor in the serviceability of the product or component concerned. Packaging is not just a box but is also a storage and protection system. Increasingly many firms insist that packaging, whilst fulfilling its necessary function, is also easily disposed of, or better, can be recovered by the supplier, recycled and reused.

It is a common misconception that only manufacturing firms are concerned with inventory management. All companies carry stock of some sort or other: for a few firms this may be limited to a cupboard full of office supplies, for another it could be a holding tank of aviation fuel. It is generally the case that only manufacturing firms have a full operating cycle running from raw materials through work in progress to finished goods. However, many predominantly service firms are also engaged in manufacturing to a certain extent. The hotel kitchen is an example of a process system which goes through all the stages from raw material to finished product. The only difference is usually one of scale – many of the principles of running an efficient factory are the same as those of running a good kitchen.

Managing inventory levels

Two types of cost affect the level of inventory that it is desirable for a firm to hold. The first type increase with the average levels of inventory held and the second type decrease. Whatever inventory management system a firm employs it needs to understand the underlying financial realities:

● The more inventories a firm holds on average, the less frequently it will have to reorder stock. However, it will bear two significant direct costs: the opportunity cost of the capital invested in inventory and the cost of the space, human resources, physical handling systems and security that are required to keep the stock in a fit condition for use or, in the case of finished goods, for sale. Both of these costs tend to increase with the greater the average inventory level held.

● The greater the average inventory levels the less frequently the firm will be required to re-order stock from suppliers. Many of the activities involved in the ordering process involve fixed costs. The costs of setting up an order for one box of paper-clips are generally the same as setting up an order for two hundred. These fixed transactions costs, associated with ordering new supplies, will be smaller the larger the reorder quantity and consequently the fewer the orders that are placed.

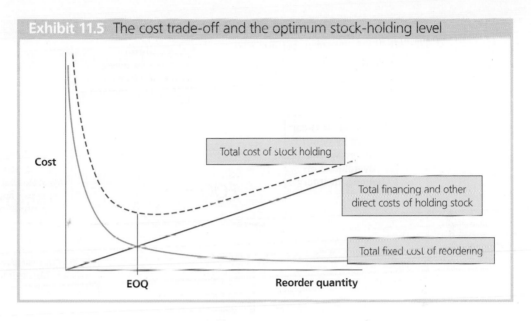

Exhibit 11.5 The cost trade-off and the optimum stock-holding level

Cost

Total cost of stock holding

Total financing and other direct costs of holding stock

Total fixed cost of reordering

EOQ

Reorder quantity

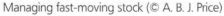

The net effect of these two contradictory cost patterns is shown in Exhibit 11.5 which also shows the total overall cost of holding stock given different reorder quantities and the optimum position of minimum cost which defines the **economic order quantity** (EOQ).

Therefore we have two different types of cost to trade off: a range of direct costs which increase with increasing levels of inventory held, and a range of order-specific transaction costs which will be a diminishing cost burden the less frequently orders for supplies are placed over a given period of time. This leads to the obvious conclusion that there should be an optimal

Managing fast-moving stock (© A. B. J. Price)

Exhibit 11.6 The economic order quantity

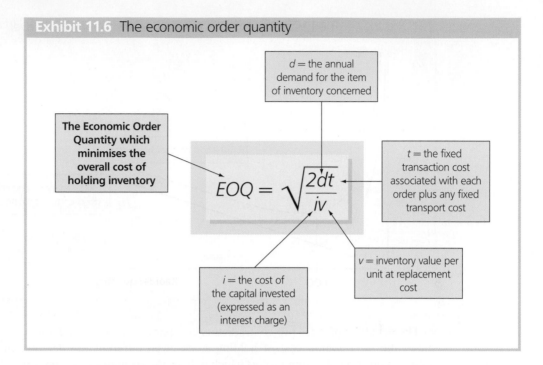

The Economic Order Quantity which minimises the overall cost of holding inventory

d = the annual demand for the item of inventory concerned

t = the fixed transaction cost associated with each order plus any fixed transport cost

$$EOQ = \sqrt{\frac{2dt}{iv}}$$

i = the cost of the capital invested (expressed as an interest charge)

v = inventory value per unit at replacement cost

reorder quantity which represents the best trade-off between these two types of cost. Some swift mathematics delivers the answer. Exhibit 11.6 gives the formula for the most economic order quantity that a firm should place for a given line of stock.

This formula is very straightforward to use. We have expressed the demand in the equation (d), and therefore the interest rate charge for the working capital tied up in inventory (i) as annual figures. Figures for any time period can be used. To give an example let us take the fast lane to Watford to see how Sid uses this formula to optimise the replenishment of his fuel stocks.

Financial realities DialaSid has a private refuelling facility for the firm's taxi fleet. The cost per litre to the holding tank is 110p. There is a fixed delivery and reorder charge of £150. Sid's annual demand to service his fleet is 650 000 litres. His cost of capital is 8 per cent per annum. What is the optimum reorder quantity to minimise his average cost of holding fuel?

Entering the information into the EOQ formula above:

$$EOQ = \sqrt{\frac{2 \times 650\ 000 \times 150}{0.08 \times 1.10}}$$

$$= 47\ 073 \text{ litres}$$

Note the assumptions in this analysis:

- the demand for fuel is known with certainty over the next twelve months
- the price of the fuel delivered does not change
- the fixed cost of reorder does not change, and
- DialaSid's cost of capital does not alter (we discuss this in more detail in Chapter 13).

Finally, there is a technical but nonetheless important assumption embedded in the maths which generated this formula, and that is that the cost functions are smooth and continuous. The formula does not work if there is a fixed quantity discount involved.

Having established an economic order quantity, the second step in inventory management requires the establishment of a **reorder level**. This is the point where a reorder for new supplies is triggered and it is a function of two variables:

1. The lead time for delivery: this is the total time from the point that stock is ordered to the point that it is available for use by the customer. The lead time demand is the expected stock usage over the delivery period and any trigger point for a new order must leave sufficient in stock to cover requirements during this period.

2. A **buffer stock**: over and above the lead time demand, an extra level of stock must be set aside to cover both fluctuations in demand and delays in delivery.

If we put these two items together we can specify the reorder level as in Exhibit 11.7 and if the system works as it should, then the process of ordering, delivery, stock depletion and so on should produce a pattern of stock holding as shown in Exhibit 11.8.

In the DialaSId example we have expressed the buffer stock as the number of days' supply of fuel required to cover delays. It may be that there is an element of uncertainty in the level of demand, in which case the buffer can be adjusted to eliminate the likelihood of a stockout

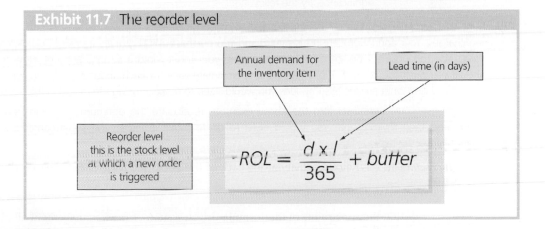

Exhibit 11.7 The reorder level

Annual demand for the inventory item

Lead time (in days)

Reorder level this is the stock level at which a new order is triggered

$$ROL = \frac{d \times l}{365} + buffer$$

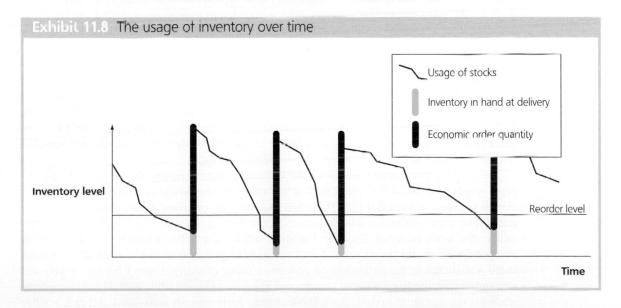

Exhibit 11.8 The usage of inventory over time

Usage of stocks

Inventory in hand at delivery

Economic order quantity

Inventory level

Reorder level

Time

Financial realities   DialaSid's supplier usually delivers fuel for the taxi fleet within five working days of a telephone order for more fuel. However, there could be up to a two day delay particularly if the order was placed after 12am Saturday. At what reorder level should Sid place a new order?

$$\text{ROL} = \frac{650\ 000 \times 4}{365} + \frac{650\ 000 \times 2}{365}$$

$$= 10\ 684\ \text{litres}$$

So, once the holding tanks fall below this level, Sid or one of his colleagues needs to get on the telephone to order a new delivery.

or reduce its likelihood to any set level of confidence. The readings at the end of the chapter will assist you if you wish to tackle the statistics necessary for this degree of fine-tuning of the buffer level.

Review activity 11.3   In order to demonstrate the practical usefulness of this model and understand its significance, try the following:

(i) Your fixed costs of going to the local supermarket to collect groceries is approximately £2 in petrol and car parking charges. Your annual grocery bill is £9000 and you purchase 4500 grocery items of approximately equal value. You can obtain 4 per cent per annum putting your money into a savings account. How many items should you purchase on each trip, what is the approximate value of each shopping bill, and how frequently should you go? What are the assumptions you would need to make in using the model in this situation?

(ii) Superimpose your own costs into the above example, recalculate the optimum shopping frequency and spend and then review what you would need to do to make going to the supermarket once a week financially worthwhile.

✓ Check the answer to this Review activity at the back of the book (see page 517).

Within the constraints of this formula-driven system of stock management all can work well especially for the bulk ordering of inventories used on a continuous basis. However, the formula for the economic order quantity gives a useful clue as to how management can set about reducing stocks. Supposing Sid was able to negotiate a lower fixed delivery charge. Exhibit 11.9 is a graph of EOQ against different levels of fixed charge for DialaSid's deliveries of fuel.

Note how the economic order quantity drops towards zero as the fixed delivery charge is reduced. What this means is that if Sid could persuade his supplier to deliver for nothing he could get the tanker along every time he wanted to fill one of his taxis. In practice this would be most unlikely to happen, but imagine that this is the car plant at BMW or Ford ordering high-value gearboxes or drive transmissions from a component supplier. It would be very much in their interests to drive down the fixed cost of reordering and to request their supplier to deliver on demand.

Internally within a firm the logic of the economic order quantity also prevails. If the finished goods warehouse is deemed to be a 'customer' of the production line then they face a similar problem to DialaSid Ltd. There is a fixed cost of 'ordering' finished goods from production because production has to change over and set up the relevant systems to make and deliver the items required. Each item of stock will have a 'value' which is the sum of all its component costs and the direct and indirect costs of production. For a given level of costs there will therefore be an associated economic order quantity. From Chapter 10 you will remember that the fixed costs of changeover are a non-value-adding cost. It may be worthwhile for management to drive down those change costs towards zero – and, if it can, smaller

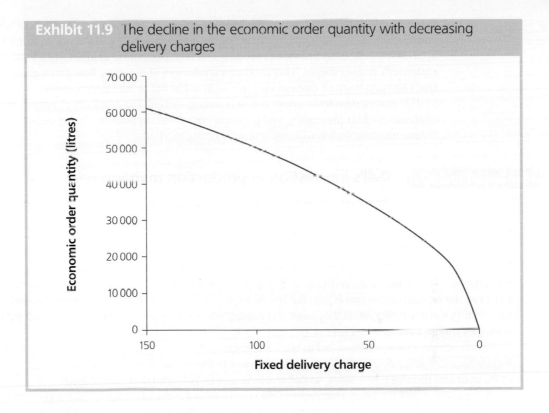

Exhibit 11.9 The decline in the economic order quantity with decreasing delivery charges

Just-in-time management

The use of the economic order quantity model and the 'optimising' approach to stock management can lead to a 'production push' mentality in the management of inventories and the design of manufacturing systems. If a particular economic order quantity is dictated by the costs of setting up new orders then warehouses will be built to accommodate that stock. Incentives will then be in place to push stocks through production and to get them into finished goods as quickly as possible. An alternative approach first developed by weapons manufacturers during the Second World War, but later refined by the major Japanese automotive and electronics firms, exploits 'demand-pull' inventory management alongside production systems dedicated to driving down change and logistic costs as described in the last chapter. The **just-in-time** (JIT) system of inventory control relies upon the accurate matching of supply with demand at each stage of the manufacturing process.

In principle, with a fully functioning JIT system, when the customer places an order with the firm, this then results in a product request being passed to the final stage of the manufacturing system which then calls a unit forward from the intermediate stages and so on back down the line until an order is despatched to the supplier for immediate fulfilment. In job-based manufacturing the lot size is reduced to the single product request. In continuous manufacturing pull from production is matched consistently with average levels of final demand.

JIT raises a number of issues for the accounting system: every item produced has a discrete job card which is passed down through the production line setting up the order sequence. This card, originally known as the **kanban** in Japanese firms then comes back up the line as the item

and smaller economic order quantities will result until the point is achieved at which production produces solely on demand. This type of stock management opens up new strategic possibilities for the firm, and it is to this topic that we now turn.

is produced. With complex systems, paper cards have been replaced by workplace terminals connected to a resource management system. For accountants, JIT tends to force a job-costing approach where each individual product can take on unique characteristics according to the customer's requirements. This produces challenges in creating flow through costing systems that can keep track of costs as they are incurred in the production process.

JIT places demands upon the accounting system for 'real-time' actual costs, and for continuous order processing and payment systems as supplies are being delivered much more frequently than with traditional manufacturing methods.

Financial reality   ## Dell's innovation in production management

Take apart a PC and you will probably find it is only made up of 23 different parts. Understanding this is the key to manufacturing PCs quickly. But none is quicker than Dell Computer which can deliver a PC to a customer in three short days, from the time an order is put in to the time the PC arrives at the customer's place. Its competitors take about three weeks to do the same. However, when a manufacturer is shipping thousands of PCs daily, even 23 parts in one PC can add up to hundreds of thousands. This is the challenge Dell Computer faces every day. Its direct selling model and its quick delivery has enabled it to snare 13 per cent of the market share, turning it into the world's number one PC vendor. The secret of Dell's success is: build according to demand. Customers can order PCs in any configuration they want and pay accordingly whereas its competitors only sell the configurations they choose to build.

Good inventory management as well as quick and smooth information flow from the order-taking process to the factory floor. Dell keeps only four days of stock compared to 24 days for Compaq. This is critical today as the price of PC chips and parts fall by the week, so Dell is able to save on parts and drive prices down.

Each customer gets a specially built system unique to him. For the manufacturer, there is no inventory, no warehousing and no finished goods to worry about. The challenge is that carrying inventory stifles innovation. If there's no inventory, there is no liability associated with product transition. If you build to order, then you can always use the latest technology and flow that to the customer. This business model applies to other industries too. If you don't have inventory on the shelves or in the warehouse, newer technology reaches the customer faster.

Speed, information and direct connection to all parties, be they customers or sales, are the critical elements. Speed is all about how quickly a customer order is processed and transformed into a product. Within minutes, the process should take over. This includes knowing what components are needed, collecting and getting them ready, building the PC within an hour or two and then dealing with the logistics to ship the product. Information is critical. From the engineering point of view, it is knowing what configurations can be built, what the different permutations for a PC system are and how much customisation there should be. The challenge here is to ensure that all the correct components, for a desktop PC for example, are fitted correctly. Then the other parts like the mouse pad and printer cartridge must be properly packed for shipment. This is a challenge for freighting. Lastly, direct connection allows a company to talk to a customer, understanding his needs and working with him to get products out quickly.

An edited article extracted from Computertimes Online edition, 3 October 2001

Robert Kaplan, a Harvard academic who has been at the forefront of modern developments in management accounting, once described at a lecture at the London School of Economics how the JIT approach as used by companies such as Nissan and Toyota drove down work-in-progress and the total cost of production whilst boosting product quality. In the JIT system each worker in the production system is empowered to stop the line if a faulty part-assembled product is delivered to his or her stage of the manufacturing process. This is a powerful incentive for the workforce to get the job done correctly the first time and to drive down reworking to zero. This saves time and the cost of reworking and correcting faults. Rework raises the levels of work-in-progress on the production line, and in Japanese manufacturing work-in-progress is regarded as a source of waste.

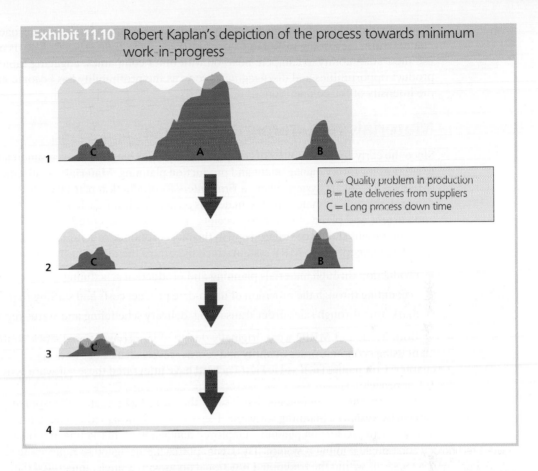

Exhibit 11.10 Robert Kaplan's depiction of the process towards minimum work-in-progress

A = Quality problem in production
B = Late deliveries from suppliers
C = Long process down time

Kaplan gave this powerful description of the Japanese approach. Work-in-progress is like a flowing river. A fault or bottleneck in the production system, such as a quality fault, is like a rock (A) sticking out of the water, and once it is discovered all of the effort of the workforce goes into digging out the rock. Once it has been removed, the water level (i.e. the amount of work-in-progess) is lowered until another rock appears (B), this time perhaps a problem with late deliveries from suppliers, at which point the rock clearing starts again. This is repeated, perhaps through a problem with long process down times (C), until there are no more rocks, at which point the level of the river has been reduced to the absolute minimum.

A number of factors are required to make a JIT system work:

1. Excellent manufacturing systems with high quality designed into the product rather than enforced through checking. Any part of the chain of production can stop the line if a part-assembled product is found to have a fault. The aim of management is to 'grind out the faults and delays in the system'.

2. Excellent relationships with suppliers who will provide components on demand and of the required quality.

3. A workforce committed to the 'quality' ideal.

An extension of the JIT system into management has led many firms to develop 'lean' or 'agile' manufacturing systems where changeover times from one production line to another are minimised, work-in-progress is held purely at the level required to sustain the line and no more, and where changing customer requirements or demand can be followed by a swift response from the firm. Indeed, lean manufacturing with its emphasis on rapid changeover times, customer-led operations and high quality has become a strategic approach. The lean manufacturer, according to Robin Cooper in *When Lean Enterprises Collide,* is one who can use their adaptability to compete head-on with other companies, engaging rapidly with new product opportunities and disengaging as soon as the profitability has become exhausted by the intensity of the competition.

Materials requirement planning

Since the early 1970s a number of computerised systems have become commercially available to support inventory management and production planning. **Materials requirement planning** (MRP) is a software system where a firm enters its production plans with forecasts of future demand, the 'bill' of materials (the materials requirement for each unit of eventual product) and current and planned inventory receipts. The system then produces a schedule of when particular items should be ordered and in the most economic order quantities. MRP2 is a further development of the MRP system which integrates the different functions of the firm:

- production through materials planning and production scheduling
- accounting through the provision of up-to-date product costs and staffing requirements
- marketing through sales order transacting, delivery scheduling and status reports.

Both MRP and MRP2 were originally designed in a conventional stock control environment using economic order quantity and reorder level calculations as described earlier in this chapter. Companies such as Hewlett Packard have integrated these software systems with the JIT approach.

More recent developments have seen the introduction and widespread adoption of **enterprise resource planning** software. This software is designed to give a total organisation solution with production planning, employee management, marketing and finance integrated within a single computer system. The ERP approach is designed to replace the multiple database systems within the traditional functional areas with a single, integrated database called a 'data warehouse'. The planning systems that are designed to exploit this data environment are constructed upon a definition of a firm's business processes that is a map of all the activities that are undertaken from the point that raw materials or components are procured through to its final delivery to the customer. This conception of the firm as a series of horizontal processes is derived from Porter's value chain model outlined in the last chapter. ERP systems have been implemented by many large firms globally, but like all systems they do present problems:

- Because ERP is based upon a single data warehouse concept much hangs upon the effectiveness of the data structures employed. Once a computer database has been defined it is not easy to make changes to the way that data are stored. The multiple database systems within the traditional functions did mean that if one were lost the firm could still function and possibly repair its data quickly. With a single system the reliability and integrity of the database is absolutely essential.

- Because of the technical complexities of the ERP systems the working assumptions upon which they are based are only known to a few technical managers within the firm.

- They embed a way of doing things within a firm's information and reporting systems. This can reduce the ability of the firm to introduce new systems and procedures.

- The hidden cost of such systems is the creation and maintenance of the extensive databases which they employ. Such systems also have a tendency towards 'data profligacy', generating huge amounts of reports whose meaning is often not clear to the end-users.

- ERP systems can be very expensive to install with figures of between $2 million to $350 million being quoted by users.

Nevertheless, ERP and similar approaches to the computerisation of business processes can offer significant advantages to management. The management of complex production systems using Just-in-Time methods would be impossible without sophisticated inventory management systems linking the firm to its suppliers as well as providing a wide variety of internal reports. Here follows an example of leading-edge computerised developments in stock management.

Review activity 11.4   Read the following article from *Business Wire*. What does the article claim are the benefits of the Inventory Visualisation System and what might be the disadvantages for Metaldyne of giving its suppliers access to this level of detail about its production processes?

Metaldyne Chooses QAD for Vendor-Managed Inventory; QAD Supply Visualization Helps Reduce Inventory Holdings and Speed Replenishment of Critical Materials

(An edited extract from an article in *Business Wire*, 18 June, 2003)

A designer and supplier of metal-based components, assemblies and modules for the automotive industry, Metaldyne has begun using QAD Supply Visualization to give its suppliers a secure, real-time view into its inventory, so that they can monitor and replenish stock automatically. The manufacturer also will begin testing QAD Kanban Visualization this month as part of its efforts to better synchronize suppliers' deliveries and customers' needs and minimize inventory holdings, for more efficient, cost-effective operations.

'Supply chain efficiency is crucial to manufacturers' ability to thrive in the fast-paced real-world business environment, and QAD Supply Visualization is helping Metaldyne achieve lean manufacturing standards', said Pamela Lopker, QAD president and chairman of the board.

QAD Supply Visualization extracts data from multiple ERP systems and stores it securely on a hosted exchange where authorized suppliers can access the data and initiate a message that triggers the replenishment process. Metaldyne's first installation of QAD Supply Visualization already has reduced raw material inventory by 20 percent and slashed inventory carrying costs.

Metaldyne is testing QAD Kanban Visualization, a module designed to complement Supply Visualization with specific features for management of inventory produced through kanban methods. The status and quantity of kanbans are represented graphically so that suppliers can see when stock needs replenishing and print kanban cards immediately, instead of waiting for Metaldyne to send a copy. QAD Kanban Visualization will alert Metaldyne managers and suppliers to relevant inventory changes via their preferred device, whether phone, email or mobile device, so that they can respond quickly and ensure efficient replenishment.

Managing credit policy

One of the most common causes of failure amongst small to medium-sized enterprises is lack of effective credit management. There are three principal tools of credit management. First, setting a clear **credit policy** with respect to customers and ensuring that payments are collected on or before the due date. Second, negotiating favourable payment terms with suppliers. Third, keeping good and up-to-date client accounts. Small businesses are particularly vulnerable to the problems caused by late payment especially with large corporate customers who can use their market position to dictate their own payment terms. Many large firms use their small-firm suppliers as a bank – taking, what is in effect, an interest-free overdraft.

The first step in building a sound credit policy is to put in place an effective process of **credit risk** assessment.

● Have there been any recent county court judgments against the business concerned for non-payment of debts?

● Have there been any resignations from the company's board of directors in the immediate past that do not appear to have reasonable explanation?

● Has the company filed its accounts and annual report on time?

● Has a major customer or trading partner been made bankrupt or gone into liquidation within the last twelve months?

● If the accounts are published do they appear sound, noting in particular the liquidity and risk ratios discussed in Chapter 7?

● Can the customer requesting credit supply bank references or references from other suppliers?

In addition, the latest credit risk assessment can be obtained from a high-quality **credit rating** agency. One of the longest established and most highly regarded is Dunn and Bradstreet. These agencies analyse the accounts published by companies and monitor listings of county court judgments, bankruptcy petitions and a variety of other sources to produce a credit rating. Dunn and Bradstreet provides detailed risk assessments on companies under the headings of:

● credit risk assessment, measuring the likelihood of a company defaulting on its debts

● an assessment of the business's payment performance from its published data

● a comparative risk assessment, comparing the target company with others in the industry.

Exhibit 11.11 shows a sample assessment from Dunn and Bradstreet.

Setting credit policy

To a large extent, the credit terms a supplier can negotiate with its customers are dependent upon a number of factors: the nature of the product being sold, the relative sizes of the two firms, the duration of the relationship between them, the availability of alternative supply, and standard practice within the industry. If the supply is for a high-priced product built to the customer's specification then the supplier is more likely to be able to negotiate good terms of trade. It is common for many large companies to grant 'preferred supplier' status to other businesses that supply key goods or services. Preferred supplier status usually means that the buying company will offer favourable terms of trade but with very strict price agreements (which may include a clause specifying that the price should fall by a set percentage each year against a programme of cost improvement agreed between the two parties).

In deciding what length of credit period to offer a supplying firm will need to bear in mind that the risk of default increases with the length of time over which credit is taken. Similarly, the risk of default also increases if a business is not proactive in recovering its outstanding debts and allows accounts to remain outstanding beyond the agreed credit period.

Measuring the benefits of reducing average debtor age

Reducing the length of time sales accounts are outstanding produces two effects on the firm's cash flow:

● It provides a cash stimulus as payment is received earlier than previously for the current month's sales. Because prior sales are still being converted into cash according to the previously agreed credit policy this means that there will be a 'double flow' at the end of the new credit period.

● It will produce a cash flow difference in subsequent months equal to the rate of growth in sales.

Exhibit 11.11 A sample credit assessment by Dunn and Bradstreet

D&B Sample Co Ltd
11th Floor, Centre City Tower
7 Hill St
Birmingham
West Midlands B5 4UN
UK

Tel number:	0121-631-2323
Fax number:	0121 631 3268

D-U-N-S®:	21-456-7885
CRO registration number:	434567
VAT Number:	
Line of Business:	Laptop personal computer distributors

Date of latest accounts available: 14-11-2000

D&B Risk Rating	****Lower than average risk
D&B credit limit recommendation	£3600
Payment Performance	*****6 to 15 days late
Trading opinion	Proceed with transaction but monitor closely with tracker
How does its D&B Risk Rating compare with other businesses in the same industry?	*****Worse than average for this industry
Year this business started	1993
Are there any significant legal proceedings/events against this business?	A County Court Judgment was registered against this business on 16/02/1999
How large is this business? Sales Number of employees	***** £312 066 25 Employees
Who are the directors/proprietors?	Mrs Joan Culloden: Managing Director Miss Julie Whittaker: Director, Company Secretary
Who owns the business?	D&B Sample Holdings PLC
Financial figures	Year 2000 1999 1998 Turnover £312 066 £307 962 £277 387 Profit £65 180 £56 766 £50 679 Net worth £59 289 £55 533 £61 484 Current ratio 2.0 1.6 1.7
Bank details Name Sort code	Barclays Bank PLC P.O. Box 279 20 98-57

The spreadsheet in Exhibit 11.12 shows an example of a company whose sales are increasing on a monthly basis and that offers a three-month credit period to customers. It is seeking to negotiate a reduction in the agreed terms to two months with immediate effect. If it is successful the change in policy will have an impact on its cash flow from customer accounts. The company is currently at month 'zero', the month where it decides to change its credit policy. In month zero it receives the cash from sales three months previously and likewise in the first month after the change. It is in the second month that the impact of the change will be apparent as it receives its cash from the month immediately prior to the change and from the month of the change as well. From that month forward, the company will find that its cash flow is increased (or decreased) by the rate of growth in its sales.

Exhibit 11.12

Month	−3	−2	−1	0	1	2	3	4	5
Sales	97 000	98 000	99 000	100 000	101 000	102 000	103 000	104 000	105 000
Cash received (existing terms)				97 000	98 000	99 000	100 000	101 000	102 000
Debtors receivable (revised terms)				97 000	98 000	199 000	101 000	102 000	103 000
change to cash flow				0	0	100 000	1 000	1 000	1 000

Review activity 11.5 Using the above example see what would happen to the monthly cash flows if:

(i) the credit terms were extended to 4 months rather than 3 months

(ii) sales had been decreasing by £1000 per month with the sales at month 0 of £100 000.

✓ Check the answer to this Review activity at the back of the book (see page 517).

Late payment

In order to combat the problems of late payment of debts the UK and more recently the European Union have introduced legislation to allow firms to claim 'statutory interest' on outstanding accounts. In 1998, the UK government allowed small firms, that is businesses with less than 50 employees to claim interest on any outstanding account that was overdue by more than 30 days. From August 2002, the UK government came into line with the EC directive on combating late payment in commercial transactions, giving all firms, irrespective of their size, the option to claim interest on late payment. The late payment legislation gave four areas of protection:

1. the right to charge interest on overdue accounts at a rate which is set at a specified percentage above the Bank of England base rate

2. the right to recover reasonable debt collection costs

3. the right to have any onerous terms in a contract for supply set aside by the courts

4. the right for a small or medium-sized enterprise to be represented in court by a 'representative body' that will act on its behalf.

The main problem with the legislation is that many small firms would be very reluctant to exercise their rights and possibly alienate their customers. However, setting an expectation into a sale agreement that late payment will automatically trigger the interest charge may help to ensure prompt payment. Here are some other methods of reducing the problems of late payment.

Persuasion

Undoubtedly the most effective way of recovering debts quickly is by following a rigorous process of following up outstanding accounts. The stages that should be followed are:

1. Only offer credit after having made a careful risk assessment of the customer's credit-worthiness. There is always some risk in offering credit, but by knowing the level of risk involved steps can be taken to minimise it.

2. Make sure before the sale is completed, on any quotations or estimates, that the customer understands the terms of trade you are offering and when payment is expected. Failing a signed acceptance of a quotation or estimate, the customer should be willing to sign an agreement to the credit terms.

3. Ensure that the goods or services supplied are accepted and that invoices are carefully prepared, minimising the customer's potential grounds for non-payment because of disagreement over the invoice.

4. As soon as the credit period has expired contact the customer with a reminder letter, followed a few days later by a telephone or faxed request for payment.

5. After a reasonable period formally request payment without delay stipulating a date by which payment should be received.

6. If payment is still not forthcoming this is the stage at which a telephone call or letter requesting payment with the threat of legal action for non-payment should be made.

7. If still the customer does not pay, refer the debt (if small) to a debt collection agency or send a solicitor's letter; if the debt is large commence legal proceedings for recovery

In Exhibit 11.13 we show the typical sequence of dealing with a bad debt that has been given a 30-day credit period but has failed to pay by the due date.

Exhibit 11.13 From start to finish with a case of non-payment

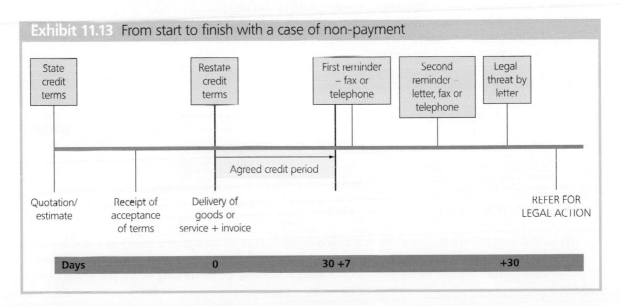

Discounts

Many companies offer a discount on the agreed sale price if payment is received within a set period. Discounting rarely makes sense in competitive markets where the supplier has little room for manoeuvre in setting the price of the product or service concerned. Discounts also set an expectation on a customer's part that the price can be reduced and this can lead to more intense negotiations to reduce the price during future sale negotiations. There is the added complication that a customer may well pay late and still take the discount knowing that the supplier, especially if it is a small firm, will be very unlikely to jeopardise a business relationship by pursuing what could be a modest sum of money.

The cost of discount is the firm's cost of capital, a topic that we discuss in more detail in the next two chapters. In essence it can be regarded as the effective rate of return that the firm would have to offer to its investors in order for them to recapitalise the firm in its current gearing ratio.

Discounts on agreed prices for early payment, even for modest percentages, can have big implications on a firm's overall performance. In essence, a discount enables the future cash flow from the customer to be brought forward in time. The cost of the discount in terms of the lower price paid by the customer must be compared with the savings in the cost of finance to the firm of having access to its cash earlier than expected.

Financial realities   A firm has sales outstanding of £100 000. Its normal credit terms are 3 months but it is considering offering a two and a half per cent discount for payment within 1 month. The firm's weighted average cost of capital is 8 per cent per annum.

Step 1 Calculate the equivalent monthly cost of capital

$$\text{Monthly rate} = \sqrt[12]{(1 + \text{annual rate})} - 1$$

So, if the annual rate is 8 per cent, the rate the company should use on a monthly basis is 0.6434 per cent:

$$i_m = \sqrt[12]{1.08} - 1$$
$$= 0.006434 \equiv 0.6434\%$$

Step 2 Calculate the present value which if invested at 0.6434 per cent per month would accumulate to £100 000 after 3 months. This gives £98 094.

Step 3 In the same way, calculate the present value of £97 500 receivable in 1 month. This is the account outstanding less the discount of 2.5 per cent.

Exhibit 11.14

	0	1	2	3
expected recovery of debt				100 000
present value at 8 per cent	98 094			
discounted if paid within 30 days		97 500		
present value at 8 per cent	96 877			
Value loss through discounting	1 218			

Note that even taking into account the cost of finance this level of discount gives a value loss to the firm of £1218. Indeed, by trial and error or using the 'goal-seek' function in your spreadsheet package, the maximum discount that compensates for the extra two months delay in receiving the outstanding debt is just 1.3 per cent.

Factoring debts

Some of the major banks such as HSBC and the Royal Bank of Scotland, as well as a number of other finance companies, offer **debt factoring** services. The process works as follows: when an invoice is raised by the client company all proceeds from that invoice are paid by the customer to the factor. The factor pays (usually) 80 per cent of the face value of an invoice to the client immediately and the balance less interest and charges when the account is finally settled by the customer. Unless there is an arrangement to the contrary, the supplier is still responsible for the management of their customer accounts and for chasing overdue payments. The overall process is outlined in Exhibit 11.15.

Factoring services by the banks can be an expensive source of trade finance; however, the supplier is assured of immediate payment of 80 per cent of the debt and the balance (less their charges) when the customer finally pays. The factor's interest runs from the point that cash is transferred to the client's account until the point that the customer pays. Naturally, factors are careful about the type of business that they accept – they will usually only accept what are referred to as 'clean and unencumbered' debts against invoices that are not in dispute and where the customer offers a very low risk of default. Firms offering factoring services can also offer a sales ledger service whereby they take over the process of keeping record of the client's customer accounts and of chasing payment if necessary.

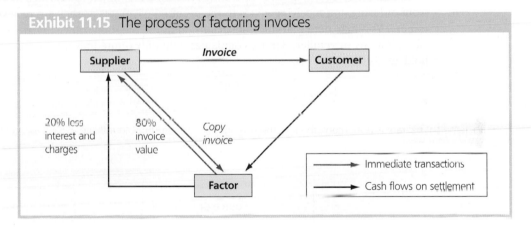

Exhibit 11.15 The process of factoring invoices

DialaSid has been providing a daily taxi service for children attending a small private school. Sid had personally agreed a 30-day credit period and the school had paid regularly and on time, though nothing had been put in writing. There had been some recent changes on the school's management committee and the headmistress and bursar had left in a hurry. Until these changes Sid had been paid regularly by the due date and he had reciprocated with the odd half-case of Bollinger (Gran Cuvée) for the headmistress and the bursar. Since the changeover, his invoices were regularly challenged, often after five or six weeks of chasing the outstanding payment, and his latest invoices are two months overdue. Each invoice is worth approximately £800. What are the options open to him in this case?

Receivables management and overtrading

In Chapter 7 we introduced the concept of the operating cycle and how a company may find itself without cash from its sales to pay its suppliers when their accounts fall due for payment. As you may remember, it is possible to estimate the various ages from the financial

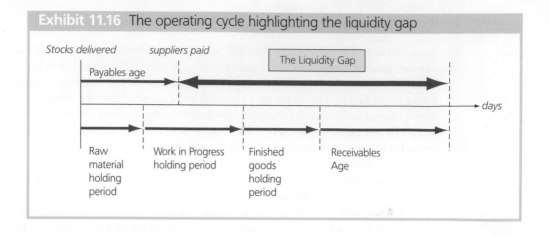

Exhibit 11.16 The operating cycle highlighting the liquidity gap

accounts using the various 'age ratios' for creditors (stated in the directors' report), debtors and the speed with which various items of stock are 'turned over' during the normal course of business.

In Exhibit 11.16 we show the operating cycle for a manufacturer through its various stages from ordering and receiving goods to the eventual payments as they are received from customers. You may note that this is an extension of the diagram shown in Chapter 7 for a service company or retailer. Service companies hold only limited inventories and retailers only hold goods for sale.

Financial realities   Cobham's data for its various ages from its 2006 accounts are as shown below:

Exhibit 11.17

Age ratio	Source or calculation	Ages (days)
Payables age	Directors' report	46
Inventory turnover	$= \dfrac{\text{Raw inventory}}{\text{Cost of sales}} \times 365$	82
Receivables age	$= \dfrac{\text{Trade receivables}}{\text{Sales}} \times 365$	53

To what extent does the adverse liquidity gap present a problem for a company like Cobham plc? It would appear that the business has to wait 89 days to receive its cash from its customers after the date at which it has paid its suppliers. If the company were to expand its sales then its business would become less liquid. However, the ratios as they stand do not tell the full story. If, for example, the company has a high gross profit margin it can survive for much longer than a company on a slim margin.

When a company has an adverse liquidity gap, as shown for Cobham, expanding sales can have adverse consequences if there are insufficient cash resources available to finance the new business. This is a phenomenon known as **overtrading**. The indicators of a company's exposure to overtrading are as follows:

● an adverse liquidity gap which suggests that any expansion of trade will increase outstanding liabilities at a faster pace than cash is received from customer accounts

● a low gross margin business

● low cash reserves with a short cash exhaustion ratio

● limited access to further funds from either shareholders or other sources of finance.

The normal symptom of distress for a business that is overtrading is an inability to pay its suppliers as they fall due, followed by forced redundancies of staff.

Review activity 11.7 Obtain the latest accounts for Tesco the supermarket chain from www.tesco.com. Determine whether the company has an adverse or favourable credit gap.

Managing cash

Treasury management is the term that is applied to the management of a firm's monetary assets. Treasury managers are specialists employed by many large firms to ensure that the cash resources of the business are used to best effect. It is one of the paradoxes of business that a firm should seek to maximise the cash value of the enterprise, but once they have cash in hand to put it to use as quickly as possible.

Cash is not just notes and coins but includes deposits with banks and other financial institutions (sometimes called 'near cash'). Deposits will normally be interest-bearing; this means that the bank will return interest on the cash deposited at either a variable or a fixed rate. Cash can be put on 'immediate call', 'overnight deposit' or 'term call'. A three-month call account would mean that a firm depositing cash would have to give three months' (90 days') notice to the bank of its intention to withdraw. The longer the call, the higher the interest rate that the bank will generally offer.

Firms hold cash in liquid form for three reasons: it may be that they expect to make payments in the short term to creditors, lenders or investors; it may be that they are attempting to guard against a sudden and unexpected call on their cash or it may be that they wish to hold a reserve of cash so that they can make rapid investments or acquisitions. These three reasons are described by monetary economists as the liquidity, precautionary and speculative motives for holding cash. However, in terms of the management of a firm's cash resources we can be more specific about the reasons why it may wish to build its cash reserves above that strictly required to service its immediate trading needs:

1. For capital investment in return-generating assets including capital plant, equipment, land and intangibles. This is the preferred choice providing the chosen investments add value to the equity investors. We discuss the methods for dealing with such long-run decisions in the next chapter.

2. For investment in working capital to exploit its existing productive capacity to its best advantage or to support new capital investment. This may well involve financing an expansion

in trade as discussed earlier in this chapter. This is worthwhile providing the short-term investment offers a net cash contribution to the firm.

3. To hold a reserve of cash to protect against unforeseen variability in the demand for cash. This is the precautionary motive but does not imply that the cash is simply held in a safe or stuffed under the managing director's mattress. Precautionary holdings of cash should be held on deposit at varying terms depending upon the perceived liquidity risk that the firm faces.

4. Distribute the cash back to the investors by repaying capital loans, share buy-backs or dividend payments. This is the option of last resort once all the firm's opportunities to put the cash to use have been exhausted.

We can summarise this by stating that the objectives of effective cash management are threefold: to ensure that cash holdings are held at a minimum commensurate with the needs of the business, to ensure that any cash surpluses are deposited at the best interest rate possible (and where money is borrowed it is at the most competitive borrowing rate given its term) and, finally, to ensure that the exposure of the business to monetary risk is minimised.

The problem of changing price levels

In earlier chapters of this book we have described the phenomenon of inflation. Inflation is the general tendency for prices of goods and services to rise within the economy. The converse of this is that if the prices of goods and services are rising the purchasing power of a set sum of money will decline over time. Thus a modest amount of inflation in the economy stimulates spending and encourages businesses to invest now rather than later. **Deflation** is the reverse, where the value of goods and services is falling and the value of money is consequently rising. This is a phenomenon which has afflicted Japan and to a lesser extent Hong Kong during the 1990s and the early years of this century. Deflation creates an incentive for consumers to delay spending and firms to delay investment. The UK and the European Union have set inflation targets (currently 2.5 per cent in the UK) which the Bank of England and the European Central Bank are required to meet through their management of interest rates. Modest inflation is generally regarded as desirable; deflation is the economic evil to be avoided. Inflation is one of the reasons why treasury managers place such great emphasis on putting money to work as soon as it has been earned. Under deflationary conditions treasury managers might do the opposite and hold back on spending in the hope of falling prices.

Financial realities   ### The risk of deflation in 2003

In an environment where inflation is already low, excess capacity plus inadequate demand equals a big risk of deflation. Given that the 1930s have left an indelible mark on the conduct of US economic policy ever since, it is hardly surprising that Greenspan, Head of the US Federal Reserve, was worried.

As Japan showed, once inflation turns negative, the real cost of borrowing rises because interest rates cannot fall below zero. In those circumstances, the real value of debt increases, consumers stop spending in anticipation of even lower prices and companies go bust because the cost of labour falls far less quickly than prices, thereby leading to big falls in profitability. Even when prices were falling at 15 per cent a year in the depression, wages – for those lucky enough to be employed – were still going up.

Nor should we be taken in by all the talk of America's productivity miracle. Japan's productivity in the 1980s was impressive, and over the past two decades it has grown 15 per cent faster than America's. But productivity is not the same as profitability, and in both cases what happened was that the expansion in productive capacity meant that

▶

supply exceeded demand. Low inflation, seen in Japan in the late 1980s and the US in the late 1990s as evidence that the good times would last for ever, was in fact a warning sign that companies were unable to raise prices in a highly competitive business climate.

Edited extract from The Guardian – *United Kingdom; 23 June, 2003*

Cash management and the financial markets

Cash management involves the firm in three interlinked markets. The money market is the market for short-term finance. It is in this market that the firm will find the best terms for depositing cash or for borrowing money. It is in this market, usually via the firm's bank, that finance can be found to support its trading activities.

The foreign exchange (FOREX) market is the international market for buying or selling international currencies. In the next chapter we describe the operation of this market and the factors that determine the rate of exchange between one market and another.

The derivatives market is a specialist market where firms can trade in a variety of derivatives to manage their exposure to risk. Derivatives such as forward contracts, interest rate swap agreements and options are all designed to allow financial managers to vary the terms and conditions upon which they have deposited or borrowed money without having to withdraw from the original agreement. A swap, for example, can allow a company to change from a variable rate to a fixed rate of interest on its borrowing without renegotiating the underlying loan agreement.

Managing the holding of cash

As we have noted above, firms must hold a certain level of cash in order to finance their expected levels of trade. Normally this cash will be forthcoming from customers for goods sold.

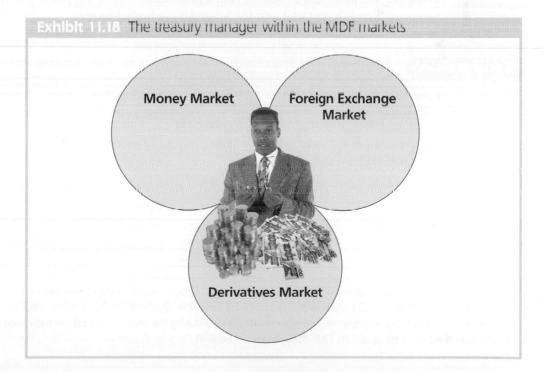

Exhibit 11.18 The treasury manager within the MDF markets

However, as we have outlined above, the firm will require cash for other purposes. Using the motives for holding cash we can state that the amount of cash a firm should have on hand or on short-term deposit is given by:

Exhibit 11.19 Determining the immediate cash requirement

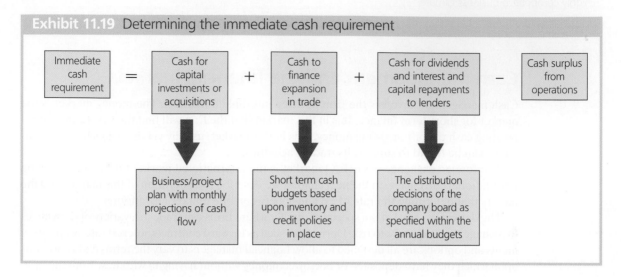

Given that the requirement for cash is expected to be in excess of that provided by the operating cash cycle of the business, the objective is to set that level of cash which minimises the transactions cost of borrowing on the money market (as with physical inventories these costs will rise overall the more frequently the firm has recourse to the money market) and the opportunity cost of the average amount of cash held (this will decline the smaller the average cash holding). There is a simple formula called the **Baumol model** shown in Exhibit 11.20, for estimating the maximum amount of cash a firm should hold at any point in time on the assumption there is a zero **lead time** for drawing down further finance.

Financial realities Sid is reviewing the amount of cash that his firm currently holds on current account and call. His business needs £3.6 million over the next twelve months to finance its trade and other investment requirement. DialaSid's cost of capital is 8 per cent per annum. Inflows from customers are expected to be £2.4 million. The cost of drawing down finance from the money market is approximately £250 per transaction. What is the maximum level of short-term cash holding for DialaSid plc which minimises his cash holding costs?

On the basis of this information DialaSid will have a funding gap of £1.2 million over the twelve-month period. Inputting the information into the cash model gives:

$$ECH = \sqrt{\frac{2Ct}{i}}$$

$$= \sqrt{\frac{2 \times 1\,200\,000 \times 250}{0.08}}$$

$$= £86\,600$$

This model, given the information put into it, suggests that Sid should raise finance in tranches of £86 600. If his annual demand for cash is £1.2 million over and above the cash flow generated by his trading activities this entails that he will need to make approximately fourteen withdrawals during the year (i.e. his annual cash requirement of £1.2 million divided by his optimum cash draw down of £86 600).

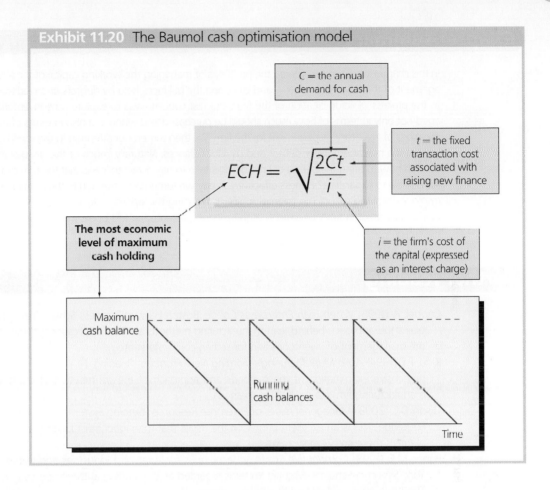

Exhibit 11.20 The Baumol cash optimisation model

Review activity 11.8

Your annual average cash spending is £5000. Your bank charges you 65p for a withdrawal and your cost of finance is 5 per cent per annum. What is the maximum you should draw from the bank and how frequently would you have to do so?

✓ Check the answer to this Review activity at the back of the book (see page 518).

The problem with this cash model is that it depends upon a number of highly restrictive assumptions. It assumes that the use of cash is constant throughout the year, that the annual demand for cash is known for certain and that the cost of capital and the cost of transacting are also fixed for the next twelve months. These are strong assumptions and are unlikely to be met in practice. The strategy that a treasury manager might follow is to establish the total annual cash requirement after trading flows have been accounted for, calculate the maximum cash holding predicted by the model and then budget the firm's actual cash expenditures throughout the year.

Chapter summary

In this chapter we have considered the problems of managing the working capital of the firm. The management of the flows of inventory and cash, and the balances held by debtors and creditors are central to the process of value creation of the firm. Our first concern was to explore how inventories are managed not only in terms of how much should be purchased and when, but also in terms of the wider implications of inventory management for the firm. We then turned our attention to the world of credit policy and the management of debtor and creditor balances. Naturally, much of the discussion was taken up with how to bring the period of time debtors take to pay down to levels that the firm can sustain and still be able to expand its business effectively. Finally, we turned our attention to the management of cash resources and the use of the Baumol model in planning the optimum levels of cash that firms should hold at any point in time. Like many of the models presented in this book, the Baumol model is based upon highly restrictive assumptions but it can be a useful tool in the hands of management.

Further reading

Cooper, R. (1995) *When Lean Enterprises Collide*, Boston Harvard Business School Press. This book explains the approach behind lean manufacturing methods and the implications of the approach for the management of inventories and for setting corporate strategy.

Kidd, P.T. (1994) *Agile Manufacturing – Forging New Frontiers*, Reading, MA: Addison-Wesley. A comprehensive examination of the methods and approach of the contribution of the best Japanese manufacturing firms to production methods.

Olson, D.L. (2003) *Managerial Issues of Enterprise Resource Planning Systems*, New York: McGraw-Hill Education. This is an excellent primer on the issues that managers must face when deciding to implement these software systems.

Porter, M.E. (1998) *Competitive Strategy: Techniques for Analyzing Industries and Competitors*, New York: Simon & Schuster. Michael Porter is regarded as the leading authority on corporate strategy. This book offers a clear insight into his thinking.

Progress check

1. Detail step by step the process whereby raw materials are purchased, converted and sold to customers. (p. 361)

2. What three cycles define the operating cycle of the business? (p. 363)

3. What does it imply about a firm's credit management policy if it can sustain a current asset ratio of significantly less than 1.0. (p. 365)

4. What two categories of cost determine the total cost of stock holding and how do they vary with the order quantity? (p. 366)

5. Write out the economic order quantity formula, defining each of its variables. (p. 366)

6. What is Just-in-Time stock management and what cost condition needs to be in place for it to be justified? (p. 370)

7. What are the two components of the reorder level and how are they determined? (p. 367)

8. List six actions you could take to determine the creditworthiness of a potential customer. (pp. 373–374)

9. What are the benefits of a negotiated reduction in the credit period offered to customers for a firm that is growing its sales? (p. 374)

10. What steps can be taken to mitigate the effects of late payments? (pp. 376–378)

11. How is the 'liquidity gap' measured? (p. 380)

12. List the three economic motives for holding cash. (pp. 381–382)

13. After a firm has met its trading cash requirements what other factors might determine its immediate cash requirement? (pp. 381–382)

14. Write out the Baumol cash model, defining each of its variables. (p. 385)

Questions

The answers to the questions followed by ✓ can be found at the back of the book, the answers to the remaining questions can be found on the website accompanying this book, **www.cengage.co.uk/ryan2**.

1. The following figures have been extracted from the accounts of a manufacturer.

Exhibit 11.21

	2007 £'000	2006 £'000
Sales	1500	1454
Cost of sales	880	900
Purchases	580	550
Finished goods	120	105
Work in progress	12	14
Raw materials	55	33
Trade debtors	170	160
Trade creditors	55	68

You are required to:
(i) Calculate the liquidity gap for this company.
(ii) Comment upon the reasons for the changes. ✓

2. A petrochemical company uses 2.5 million barrels of crude oil a year at an average price of £40 a barrel. Each shipment costs £300 000 and each tanker's capacity is 750 000 barrels. The company's cost of capital is 10 per cent per annum and it needs to be assured of 8 days' supply to account for fluctuations in delivery. The normal delivery lead time is 15 days. What is the firm's optimal reorder quantity and at what level should it reorder its crude oil stock?

3. A wholesale food import company with a £4.8 million turnover has been forced in recent years to write off up to five per cent of its debtor balances because of non-payment. It currently services a client list of 4 large retail chains accounting for 40 per cent of its annual turnover and 180 smaller owner-managed shops. The four retailers have been on its books for over 5 years; they make payment within 45 days of agreed invoice and demand a 2.5 per cent discount on supplies. The smaller shops take on average 4 weeks to pay. The managing director has asked you to write a report outlining ways that they could improve the management of their customer accounts so as to avoid the bad debt write-off.

4. Ruskin plc has implemented a programme for the reduction of its outstanding debtor balances and the time that they are outstanding. As a result of this they have achieved a reduction in the amount of debt lost through defaults from 3 per cent of receivables each year to 1.5 per cent. The average outstanding period has been reduced from 2 months to 1 month and the outstanding balance from £1.45 million to £0.943 million. The company has a cost of funds of 10 per cent.

   You are required to outline the likely benefits to the company of this debtor reduction programme. ✓

5. The monthly projections for a small electronics components manufacturer are as follows:

   Sales revenue currently stands at £78 000 per month and is expected to expand at 1 per cent per month into the indefinite future. This is the average rate of expansion that the firm has enjoyed over the previous six months. The firm's debtors pay up as follows: one-third within one month, half within two months and the remainder within three months. The company has enjoyed a gross profit margin of 25 per cent on monthly sales over the past year and has tried to keep its inventory constant at a very low level. The company's suppliers require payment within one month. They can enforce this condition of trade because of the high demand for microelectronic components. The company's management is considering a 1.5 per cent discount on the invoice value of goods if payment is received within one month. It believes that this will ensure that 50 per cent of the firm's debtors pay within the month and that half the remainder will pay at the end of the second month and the rest at the end of the third month.

   Assume all cash receipts and payments occur on the last day of the month and the company's cost of capital is 0.8 per cent per month.

   (i) Create a projected cash budget for sales less purchases over the next six months, and show the effect on that cash budget if the change in credit policy is implemented.

   (ii) Discuss the problems of maintaining liquidity in a situation of expanding trade. ✓

6. A company disburses about £15 000 from petty cash annually. The cost of drawing down cash replenishments is estimated to be £35 per transaction (to cover the cost to the security firm of each delivery from the bank). The company's cost of funds is 12 per cent. What is the maximum economic drawdown of petty cash for the firm and how many times during the year would it be undertaken? State the assumptions required for your analysis to be effective.

Case exercise

The following high street retailers are all quoted on the London Stock Exchange and their accounts can be obtained from the web sites listed.

www.jjbsports.com
www.monsoon.co.uk
www.next.co.uk

You are required to undertake a comparative analysis of each retailer's inventory and credit management policy. Your report should contain the following:

(i) comparative ratios showing each company's receivables, payables and inventory ages and how they have changed over the last financial year

(ii) an assessment of the annual cost of holding inventory for each company on the assumption that all the companies listed have a cost of capital of 8 per cent per annum

(iii) an assessment of the extent to which each company uses its terms of trade to support the long-term financing of the business.

Chapter 12

Investment appraisal

Introduction

This chapter is designed to give a comprehensive introduction to investment appraisal. Investment is an activity pursued by all firms and organisations when they acquire, at a cost, the long-run capability to create products and services. Investment entails the commitment of cash resources in the acquisition of buildings, physical 'plant' and human resources in order to earn cash return in the future. The fact that such returns can arise far into the future introduces the problem of time and how cash flows arising at different points can be brought to a common base for comparison purposes. In this chapter we explore both the financial and managerial issues in investment appraisal. We consider the problems of projecting cash flows for appraisal purposes drawing upon the insights in Chapters 13 and 14. We then review ways of correcting the cash flows for differences in the time when they arise. Because future flows are intrinsically uncertain we will examine how the risk inherent in investment can be accommodated within our analysis and finally we address some of the more managerial issues in this area of finance.

Learning objectives

In this chapter our learning objectives are as follows:

Matching cash flows over time

- Be able to match cash revenues and expenditures to capital decisions and calculate the net present value of those cash flows.

- Understand the concept of the time value of money and its application to personal and company decision-making.

- Be able to identify the stages of corporate investment decision-making and the principles that need to be applied in practice.

The net present value model

- Be able to identify the relevant cash flows for NPV analysis.

Part 4

Finance and financial markets

● Be able to determine the net present value, to understand its significance and the limitations of its use.

● Be able to modify the application of the net present value model under conditions of capital rationing, tax, inflation and risk.

Other methods of investment appraisal

● Understand the scope and limitations of other methods of investment appraisal.

● Be able to calculate the internal rate of return, payback and accounting rate of return.

Matching cash flows over time

Investment appraisal relies upon the concept of matching. In investment appraisal we use decision matching in two ways:

1. by matching cash revenues and cash expenditures to the decision involved, and
2. by correcting future cash flows to a common time base (usually the point in time the decision is being made) so that they can be compared.

In this section we will deal with the underlying mechanics for doing this cash flow matching over time.

Compounding

If an individual has a cash sum he or she may wish to know how much it will be worth to them to invest that cash rather than spend it immediately. To make this judgement they must choose a 'rate of return' or interest rate that will compensate them for the delay in spending and enjoying their cash. They will then 'roll up' the balance to the end of the bond as follows:

Financial realities   An individual is offered a rate of 5 per cent per annum on a three year savings bond. They have £1000 to invest and interest accrues annually and will be reinvested each year to form part of the accumulating total upon which the subsequent year's interest will be calculated.

At the end of year 1 the balance will have accumulated to the original investment plus the interest on that original investment. Putting the sequence of interest payments and the accumulating balances on a spreadsheet we get the following:

Exhibit 12.1

Year	1	2	3
Opening year balance	£1000.00	£1050.00	£1102.50
Add interest at 5 per cent	£50.00	£52.50	£55.13
Closing year balance	£1050.00	£1102.50	£1157.63

Now this is one of those occasions where a formula is very useful. You will notice that each year we are multiplying the opening balance by (1 + interest rate) to get the closing year balance:

End-of-year balance, year 1 = Investment × (1 + interest rate)

And at the end of year 2:

End-of-year balance, year 2 = End-of-year balance, year 1 × (1 + interest rate)
$$= \text{Investment} \times (1 + \text{interest rate}) \times (1 + \text{interest rate})$$
$$= \text{Investment} \times (1 + \text{interest rate})^2$$

And, by a similar logic, at the end of year 3:

End-of-year balance, year 3 = Investment × (1 + interest rate)^3

To check the example above:

End-of-year balance, year 3 = Investment × (1.05)^3 = £1157.63

In order to do these calculations you will need a calculator that allows you to calculate a power term. If your calculator has a y^x, x^y or $\wedge$ key then it will be able to do this type of calculation. Most calculators go through these steps. First clear the display and then press:

1000 + 1.05 y^x 3 = 1157.6

Your calculator may require you to press a 2nd function or shift key if the y^x is not on the face of a key but is shown as an alternative function on the face of the calculator. Some calculators require a different sequence, placing the 3 before the y^x key and the 1.05 after. A little experimentation should get you to the answer.

This process is known as **compounding**, the current investment we generally refer to as the 'present value' and the final end-of-year balance is the 'future value'. The general formula for compounding is as follows where 'n' is the number of periods of compounding and 'i' is the interest rate per period. In most cases i and n will be the annual rate of interest and the number of years, respectively, but not always. Here is the general formula:

Future value (n) = Present value × $(1 + i)^n$

or

$FV_n = PV \times (1 + i)^n$

Review activity 12.1 (i) An investor has £1000 to invest for 10 years at 5 per cent annual interest. What would be the accumulated value at the end of the tenth year?

(ii) An investor has £10 000 to invest for three months at a monthly rate of interest of 1 per cent per month. What would be the accumulated value at the end of the 3 months?

Do both exercises on a spreadsheet and by using a calculator.

✓ Check the answer to this Review activity at the back of the book (see page 519).

Discounting

Discounting is the reverse of the above logic, where an investor is faced with a future value and wishes to discover its present value when a given rate of interest is applied. The formula shown above can be rearranged as follows:

$$\text{Present value} = \frac{\text{Future value } (n)}{(1 + i)^n}$$

or

$$PV = \frac{FV_n}{(1 + i)^n}$$

Financial realities

An investor expects to receive £3000 in 3 years' time on an investment bond which has an assured rate of return of 6 per cent. What is the present value of the bond to the investor?

Exhibit 12.2

Year	0	1	2	3
Future value of investment				3 000
				$(1.06)^3$
Present value of investment	£2 518.86			

The formula here is = 3 000/1.06^3

Note that the column headed zero means the current point in time, '1' twelve months later, '2' two years later and so on. Using a calculator the steps are as follows:

$$3000 \div 1.06 \; y^x \; 3 = 2518.86$$

How can we interpret the value of £2518.86? There are two answers here:

1. If the rate of interest is being offered by the bank (say) then £2518.86 is the amount you would have to invest now in order to accumulate to £3000 in three years' time at a 6 per cent rate of interest. The table below illustrates this:

Year	1	2	3
Opening year balance	£2 518.86	£2 669.99	£2 830.19
Add interest at 6 per cent	£151.13	£160.20	£169.81
Closing year balance	£2 669.99	£2 830.19	£3 000.00

2. If the rate of interest of 6 per cent is the minimum rate of return that the investor requires for forgoing the consumption that the cash represents currently then £2518.86 and £3000 are identical sums of money to that investor except that the latter sum is delayed by three years.

This second interpretation leads us into an examination of an important concept, 'the time value of money'.

The time value of money

The concept of the time value of money arises because individuals and firms regard cash flows in future time periods to be of less value than cash available today. In Exhibit 12.3, we show the present value of £1000 receivable up to 20 years in the future assuming different rates of discount. For example, £1000 receivable in 10 years' time would be worth just £321.97 today if the investor requires a minimum rate of 12 per cent. Assuming a constant discount rate the present value of a future cash sum decreases the further into the future it is received or paid. Assuming a given number of years into the future the present value also decreases the greater the rate of discount applied. The important point to note here is that the present value of a future cash sum diminishes sharply with increasing time until that cash sum is realised and with the magnitude of the rate of interest applied as the discount factor.

In calculating the present value of future cash flows (as either receipts or payments) the individual or firm needs to know that rate of interest which will just make investment worthwhile. In other words, what rate of interest would just induce the individual or the firm to invest rather than retain a given cash sum? This minimum required rate of return, once identified, allows the investor to equate future cash flows with their present-value equivalents. In economist-speak this minimum rate of return is known as the individual's **marginal rate of time preference** or in the case of a firm its **cost of capital**.

There are broadly three factors which influence the magnitude of this rate for the individual:

● Liquidity preference. Generally, the less well off an individual happens to be the less their willingness to invest and hence the greater the rate of return they will require to induce them to do so. Someone who is very wealthy will presumably be more willing to see at least

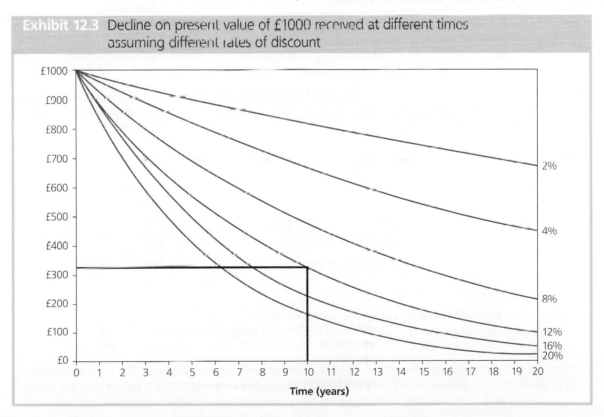

Exhibit 12.3 Decline on present value of £1000 received at different times assuming different rates of discount

a small amount of their fortune go into investment than the pauper at the gate. However, even in a risk-free and inflation-free world the individual, no matter what their current wealth, will put some premium on current liquidity and will have a positive marginal rate of time preference as a result.

● The level of inflation. Generally individuals require a return that will compensate them for the falling purchasing power of the currency. Thus the higher the rate of inflation, the higher the rate of time preference.

● Risk. The greater the uncertainty that attaches to a future return the greater the reward the individual will require and hence the greater the rate of return they will demand before giving up current for future cash.

It is possible to demonstrate under ideal conditions, where everyone can borrow or lend unlimited amounts at a single rate of interest with no transaction costs and no risk, that all individuals will have an identical rate of time preference which will be the money market rate. How does this rather odd result come about? If an individual faced the following situation what would be the most sensible thing to do if an investment opportunity arose that required an investment of £20 000?

Clearly the rate of return on the new investment is not sufficient to compensate the investor for the 8 per cent they require to satisfy their preference for current versus future spending. Given a perfect money market and no uncertainty about future outcomes they could borrow £20 000 at 4 per cent, invest that money at 6 per cent, earning a risk-free profit of 2 per cent per annum (Exhibit 12.4). Their personal rate of time preference has not come into the decision about whether to accept the new investment opportunity or not. This important idea is known as the **Fisher-Hirshleifer separation theorem** and it states that under perfect money market conditions:

● any investment that has a rate of return greater than the ruling money market rate should be accepted

● the individual's need for liquidity is financed by either borrowing or lending money on the market at the ruling rate of interest.

Thus investment decisions are separated from the means by which the investor finances them. This result underpins the validity of many of the basic techniques of investment appraisal and can be extended to firm as well as individual investment decision-making.

Exhibit 12.4

	Rates of Return (annual)
Money market rate of interest	4%
Personal rate of time preference	8%
Rate of return on new investment	6%

 Annuities, terminal values and equivalent rates of return
There are three additional tools to add to the discounting and compounding locker.

Annuities

Sometimes we need to calculate the present value of a stream of identical future cash flows. This can arise if (say) an individual wants to calculate the present value of a constant pension, or perhaps calculate the present value of a stream of future rental receipts on a property. To show the structure of this calculation, consider the following example.

A pensioner is 65 and after a lifetime of good living has an expected lifespan of five years. The rate of return on investments is currently 6 per cent and he wants to know how much he would have to pay for a pension of £20 000 per annum. The structure of the calculation is as follows:

$$PV = \frac{20\ 000}{1.06^1} + \frac{20\ 000}{1.06^2} + \frac{20\ 000}{1.06^3} + \frac{20\ 000}{1.06^4} + \frac{20\ 000}{1.06^5}$$

Mathematically we can extract the £20 000 as a common factor to give:

$$PV = 20\ 000 \times \left[\frac{1}{1.06^1} + \frac{1}{1.06^2} + \frac{1}{1.06^3} + \frac{1}{1.06^4} + \frac{1}{1.06^5}\right]$$

The series in the square brackets is the present value of £1 discounted at 6 per cent over five years. This present value is termed an annuity. There is a useful formula for solving this expression to give a single annuity factor which when multiplied by the £20 000 gives the present value of the original cash flow:

$$\overline{A}|_5^{0.06} = \frac{1 - \dfrac{1}{(1+i)^n}}{i}$$

$$\frac{1 - \dfrac{1}{(1.06)^5}}{.06}$$

$$= 4.212$$

If we multiply £20 000 by 4.212 we get £84 240 which is the present value of the original cash flow. The annuity formula may look cumbersome but think how difficult it would be if he had 20 years to live. The annuity formula makes it easy:

$$\overline{A}|_{20}^{0.06} = \frac{1 - \dfrac{1}{(1.06)^{20}}}{.06}$$

$$= 11.470$$

This when multiplied by £20 000 tells us that a 20-year pension of this amount would be worth £229 400 in present-day terms.

Terminal values

Sometimes it is useful to be able to calculate the future value of a constant cash sum invested each year at a set rate of interest. Assume that an investor wished to put £10 000 away for six years at an assured rate of return of 8 per cent per annum. The structure of the calculation to find the terminal value, assuming the first cash amount is invested immediately, is as follows:

$$FV_6 = 10\ 000 \times 1.08^6 + 10\ 000 \times 1.08^5 + 10\ 000 \times 1.08^4 + 10\ 000 \times 1.08^3 + 10\ 000 \times 1.08^2 + 10\ 000 \times 1.08^1$$

The logic of this calculation is that the first payment of £10 000 will be compounded over six years, the second over five years and so on until the last payment is made at the start of the final year. Again we can factor out the £10 000 as a common sum to give:

$$FV_6 = 10\ 000 \times [1.08^6 + 1.08^5 + 1.08^4 + 1.08^3 + 1.08^2 + 1.08^1]$$

The contents of the square brackets is what is known as the terminal value of £1 invested at 8 per cent over six years. The formula is not much more complicated than before:

$$\overline{S}|_6^{0.08} = \frac{(1 + i)^{n+1} - (1 + i)}{i}$$

$$= \frac{(1.08)^7 - (1.08)}{.08}$$

$$= 7.923$$

If we multiply this figure by the annual sum invested we get £79 230, being the accumulated sum at the end of six years.

Note that the $\overline{A}|_5^{0.06}$ and the $\overline{S}|_6^{0.08}$ are in the standard notation used by actuaries for annuities and terminal values respectively.

Equivalent rates of return

In many situations we are presented with a rate of return assuming compounding over a set period (say a year) and wish to find the equivalent rate for a shorter period (say a month) or vice-versa. The procedure is straightforward: if an annual rate of return is given we can calculate, for example, the equivalent monthly rate by finding the rate, which compounded by the number of time intervals involved, gives the specified annual rate. So, if the annual rate (i_a) is 12 per cent, the equivalent monthly rate (i_m) is found as follows:

$$(1 + i_m)^{12} = (1 + i_a)$$

Therefore:

$$(1 + i_m)^{12} = (1.12)$$

Therefore:

$$i_m = \sqrt[12]{1.12} - 1$$

$$= 0.949 \text{ per cent}$$

Similarly we can go from a shorter-term rate to a longer-term rate. If the weekly rate of interest (i_w) is 0.25 per cent, the annual equivalent rate of return can be calculated as follows:

$$(1 + i_w)^{52} = (1 + i_a)$$

Therefore:

$$i_a = 1.0025^{52} - 1$$

$$= 13.86 \text{ per cent}$$

Using this technique it is possible to convert rates from one compounding interval to another with relative ease.

The net present value model

We assume as a general rule that all individuals attempt to maximise their own cash wealth in all their financial decision-making. Similarly, when firms make investment decisions we assume that they will seek to maximise the cash wealth of their investors. Under perfect money market conditions, the present value of the future cash flows that arise from an investment when discounted at the current money market rate, less the capital invested at commencement represents the increase in the individual investor's cash wealth irrespective of their personal rate of time preference, or, in the case of a firm, the rates of time preference of its shareholders. The method for calculating the net present value of an investment is shown in the example below.

Financial realities   Sid is deciding whether or not to invest in a new 60-seat, air-conditioned executive coach. The cost of the coach is £115 000, and the net cash contribution from the coach in each year over the three years of its useful life is as follows: year 1, £50 000; year 2, £50 000; year 3, £30 000. At the end of the third year it would be scrapped and auctioned and would realise £40 000. The returns are certain and, given the perfection of the Watford money market, Sid can borrow or lend at 5 per cent per annum.

In analysing this exercise we will proceed step by step:

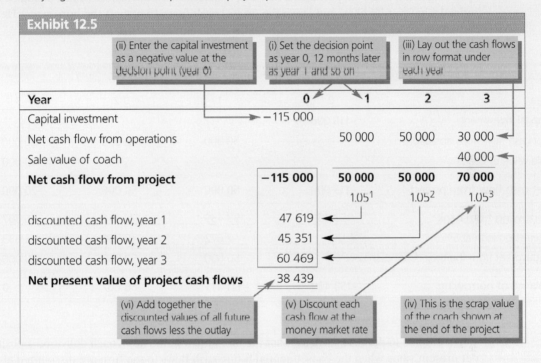

Exhibit 12.5

1. We recommend that you lay out this type of planning exercise in row format with the start of the investment project, the decision point, as time 0, and twelve months later as 1, and so on.

2. Enter the capital investment starting at time zero. In this case the capital investment is deemed to be at the decision point, in practice capital investment outlays may be spread over a number of years – in which case lay them out in the relevant time periods.

3. Lay out the net cash contribution each year from the operation of the coach over its useful life. Note here that these figures will represent the cash receipts less the cash payments that can be uniquely attributable to this decision and this decision alone. The general rules for calculating decision relevant costs and revenues are discussed in Chapter 8.

4. Show the scrap value of the coach in year 3 as a positive cash inflow.

5. After totalling each cash flow to get the annual net cash flow attributable to the project discount each of the future cash flows at 5 per cent using the formula for the present value given above.

$$PV = \frac{FV_n}{(1 + i)^n}$$

6. Add together all of the present values and net of the outlay to get the net present value of the investment project overall.

Sid's example suggests that the net present value of the project is worth £38 439, and under the perfect money market assumptions upon which the example is based this represents the immediate increase in Sid's (or his firm's wealth) as a result of the investment. To prove this we could see what happened if Sid were to finance this project not out of his own cash resources but by borrowing from the bank at 5 per cent. If the conditions hold and the future outcomes are certain, Sid could borrow £153 439, invest £115 000 in the project, enjoy spending the £38 439 on, perhaps, a new BMW Series 3.30 Convertible (black of course), or indeed whatever he likes, and leave the project cash flows to pay off the borrowing. Here's the proof:

Exhibit 12.6

Year	0	1	2	3
Capital investment	−115 000			
Net cash flow from operations		50 000	50 000	30 000
Sale value of coach				40 000
Net cash flow from project	−115 000	50 000	50 000	70 000
Borrowing from Bank	−153 439	−153 439	−111 111	−66 667
Interest on loan at 5%		−7 672	−5 556	−3 333
Repayment from the project net cash flow		50 000	50 000	70 000
Balance of borrowing	−153 439	−111 111	−66 667	0

All Sid had to do was make sure that the investment in the new coach delivered a positive net present value when the consequential future cash flows to the firm are discounted at the money market rate of 5 per cent. Note also that Sid gets his boost in value as soon as he makes his decision to invest. At that point he can borrow against the future cash flows and take the net present value as an immediate cash gain.

To summarise, under conditions of perfect money markets and certainty about the future cash flows from investment:

● Only investments which offer a positive net present value when discounted at the money market rate should be undertaken.

● The net present value of an investment represents the increase in the cash value of the investor.

● This increase in value to the investor can be realised as soon as the opportunity is recognised and the decision to invest made.

However, in the real world money markets are not perfect and, more importantly, the future is uncertain. So how do we proceed? It is to this that we now turn our attention.

The nature of investment decisions

Every firm has a different approach to capital investment decision-making. Generally, the investment decision is made at the end of a development process which, depending on the industry, can take many years from invention to exploitation. In the pharmaceutical industry

Exhibit 12.7 Process review in capital investment appraisal

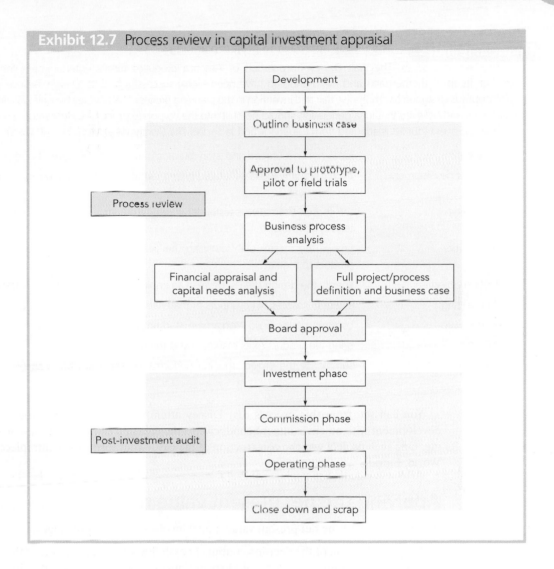

it takes an average of 5.9 years to take a drug from molecular design through approval to clinical release. The idea of a tunnel to link England and France was first proposed in 1802 by a French mining engineer, Albert Mathieu, but it was only in 1986 after many design proposals and false starts that the project received the support of the two governments. It was finally opened in 1994.

However, even with small businesses significant capital expenditure can take many months before a final decision is made to proceed. Part of the reason for this is that a firm, during this stage of the project, is constructing its knowledge base. The question is not so much 'what to buy' but 'how to use it'. In general it is not the acquisition of the new physical resources which adds value to the firm but the integration of the new capability into the firm's existing portfolio of activity. In Exhibit 12.7 we show the various stages of typical project development which will in large organisations proceed through a number of planning steps similar to those outlined in Chapter 9. During the development stage a firm will usually engage in a process of review to ensure that the resources being devoted to the new project are spent to best effect. Many organisations are also keen to ensure that inventiveness and innovation are encouraged during the development stages.

The Disney approach to project planning

The Walt Disney Corporation of America produces family entertainment for a global market. Its films, theme parks and merchandising have been highly successful and its 'Dream, Believe, Dare, Do' philosophy is designed to emphasise flair and invention in the planning process. Walt Disney himself was highly cost-conscious and believed that idea generation should be built into the corporate processes. He instituted a nine-step planning process (our list is adapted from Capadagli and Jackson's *The Disney Way*, McGraw-Hill, 1998):

Blue sky:	ideas are encouraged and 'story building' and fantasy are given full reign
Concept development:	from the many ideas generated one is identified as having the most potential for development
Feasibility:	the chosen alternative is tested for feasibility; this may include building and market testing a prototype
Schematic:	finalise the master plan, outlining the business processes required to bring the product to market
Design objectives:	specify the design details; develop an implementation and budget strategy
Contracting:	establish sources of key inputs of materials and services
Production:	commission the build programme, start production
Install:	bring the product to its market, 'install the show'
Close out:	summarise the project, monitor performance and celebrate a successful launch.

You can see from this process that Disney attempted to marry the process of project development with an environment conducive to the creation of new ideas and problem solving. One such project was the construction of the castle that forms the centrepiece of Disney World, Florida.

Applying the net present value model

The application of the net present value model involves a number of stages:

1. The identification of the decision contingent cash flows over the lifetime of the investment taking into account the effects of changing prices as well as market developments. The principles for doing this were discussed in Chapters 8 and 9 but in outline the following should be rigorously excluded from the analysis:

   a. Sunk costs – being costs incurred prior to the decision point and which the firm cannot avoid.

   b. Decision indirect costs – these are sometimes called 'decision fixed costs' – which the firm will incur irrespective of the outcome of the decision.

   c. Non-cash costs – these are costs such as depreciation, accruals and prepayments, and transfers to and from capital reserves. All of these are bookkeeping entries which are not represented by cash receipts or payments in the period in question.

   d. Interest and other capital charges – these are accounted for in the discount rate which, as we shall see in Chapter 13, is designed to cover the minimum rates of return required by all classes of investor.

   e. Capital receipts from either lenders or borrowers are not included even if they are solely committed to financing the project concerned. The outlay on the project represents

Cinderella's Castle, Disney World (Florida) (© A.B.J. Price)

their capital investment and the net present value shows the value to the investors over and above their investment.

f. Capital repayments are not included. Remember that the net present value takes into account the cost of the capital acquired in the discount rate and the full values of the assets acquired are shown as negative cash flows to the firm when the expenditure is made.

2. Discounting the cash flows using an appropriate discount rate.

3. The evaluation of the result.

In Exhibit 12.8 we show a good standard layout of a capital investment project entailing an immediate capital outlay and directly attributable revenues including the scrap value of the original assets at the end of their lives. We then show the directly relevant costs using the opportunity costing principles discussed in Chapter 8. Finally, the bottom line shows the incremental cash flow to the firm as a whole each year that arises because of the decision to invest.

The process of discounting can be conducted in three ways:

1. Each annual cash flow can be divided by one plus the interest rate raised to the power of the number of the year concerned.

2. Alternatively each annual cash flow can be multiplied by its discount factor. Discount tables are given in the back of the book. The discount factor is simply:

$$\text{Factor} = \frac{1}{(1 + i)^n}$$

Exhibit 12.8 Standard layout for a project cash flow analysis

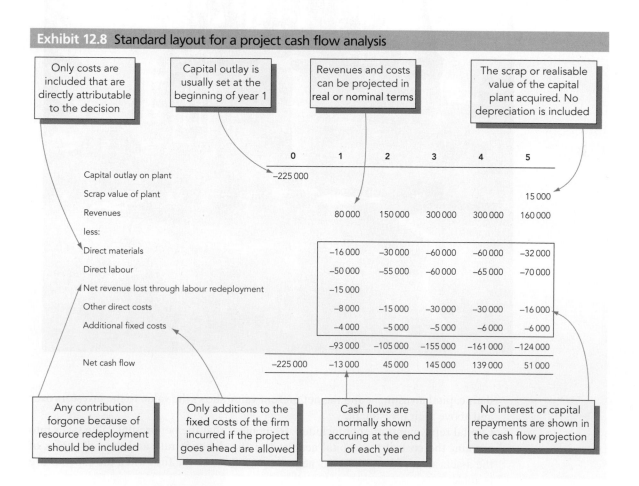

In Exhibit 12.9 we show the application of discount factors for 10 per cent to each of the annual cash flows. The discount factor for year 1, for example is:

$$\text{Factor} = \frac{1}{(1+i)^n} = \frac{1}{(1.1)^1} = 0.909$$

3. By using Excel or another spreadsheet package with the NPV financial function. Do note, however, that the programmers of Excel and other spreadsheet software assume that the investment cash flow is made at the end of the first year and not at the beginning of the investment process. In Exhibit 12.9 we show the NPV function applied to the row of discounted cash flows but excluding the original outlay. This is added (as it is a negative figure) to the NPV function:

$$\text{NPV(function)} = \text{NPV(percentage,value range)} + \text{outlay}$$

to give the correct answer.

Exhibit 12.9

		0	1	2	3	4	5
Net cash flow (NCF)	(i)	−225 000	−13 000	45 000	145 000	139 000	51 000
Discount factor (10 per cent)	(ii)	1.000	0.909	0.826	0.751	0.683	0.621
Discounted cash flow (DCF)	(i) × (ii)	225 000	−11 818	37 190	108 941	94 939	31 667
Net present value = sum (NCF)			35 918				
Net present value Excel = NPV (0.1, NCF yr 1: NCF yr 5) + outlay				35 918			

Finally, we note that the net present value of this investment is positive and therefore offers an increase in value to the owner.

Review activity 12.2 There is a perfect money market where individuals and firms can borrow or lend any amount at 10 per cent interest per annum. The business normally distributes all of its annual earnings to its owner. It has a new investment opportunity as described in Exhibits 12.8 and 12.9, and is looking at two options:

1. Current earnings of £225 000 are retained to finance the project and the owner borrows the capital outlay and the net present value of the investment.

2. The firm makes a full distribution to the owner and borrows sufficient funds to finance this investment. The owner borrows the net present value of the project.

Demonstrate that under conditions of certainty about the future cash flows from this project that options (i) and (ii) are equally attractive to the owner.

✓ Check the answer to this Review activity at the back of the book (see page 520).

Net present value and inflation

From the previous chapter you may remember that 'inflation' is the term given to the increase in the prices of goods across the economy as a whole as measured by the retail price index. There are two approaches to the projection of cash flows:

1. where the cash flows are projected in nominal or money terms, that is taking account of rising price levels for all of the revenues and costs attributable to the decision

2. where the cash flows are projected in real terms, that is with general price increases excluded from the analysis.

Financial realities Taking the cash flow example shown in Exhibit 12.8 above where the projections are in nominal terms it is possible to convert the projection to real terms by first deflating the revenue and cost projections by the rate of inflation. If we assume an inflation rate of 4 per cent per annum our scrap and revenue projections can be converted to current price (real) terms by discounting each value by the rate of inflation.

Exhibit 12.10

	0	1	2	3	4	5
Capital outlay on plant	−225 000					
Scrap value of plant (nominal)						$\dfrac{15\,000}{(1.04)^5}$
Scrap value of plant (real)						12 329
Revenues (nominal)		$\dfrac{80\,000}{(1.04)^1}$	$\dfrac{150\,000}{(1.04)^2}$	$\dfrac{300\,000}{(1.04)^3}$	$\dfrac{300\,000}{(1.04)^4}$	$\dfrac{160\,000}{(1.04)^5}$
Revenues (real)		= 76 923	= 138 683	= 266 699	= 256 441	= 131 508

Repeating this for all of the cost elements we can produce a projection of real cash flows as follows:

Exhibit 12.11

	0	1	2	3	4	5
Capital outlay on plant	225 000					
Scrap value of plant						12 329
Revenues		76 923	138 683	266 699	256 441	131 508
less:						
Direct materials		−15 385	−27 737	−53 340	−51 288	−26 302
Direct labour		−48 077	−50 850	−53 340	−55 562	−57 535
Net revenue lost through labour redeployment		−14 423	0	0	0	0
Other direct costs		−7 692	−13 868	−26 670	−25 644	−13 151
Additional fixed costs		−3 846	−4 623	−4 445	−5 129	−4 932
		−89 423	−97 078	−137 795	−137 623	−101 920
Net cash flow (real)	−225 000	−12 500	41 605	128 904	118 818	41 918

You will note of course that with the effect of inflation eliminated, each of the future net cash flow figures are reduced in value by the rate of inflation over the intervening years. We could have deflated just the net cash flow line to achieve the same result.

We now have to discount the net cash flows projected in real terms but this time using the minimum required rate of return with inflation removed. The real discount rate is calculated using the Fisher formula:

$$(1 + \textbf{Nominal Rate}) = (1 + \textbf{Real Rate}) \times (1 + \textbf{Inflation Rate})$$

Given a nominal discount rate of 10 per cent, and an inflation rate of 4 per cent we can rearrange the above equation as follows:

$$(1 + \text{Real Rate}) = \frac{(1 + \text{Nominal Rate})}{(1 + \text{Inflation Rate})} = \frac{(1.10)}{(1.04)} = (1.05769)$$

The real rate of discount is, therefore, 5.77 per cent. Using this rate to discount the nominal cash flows:

Exhibit 12.12

		0	1	2	3	4	5
Net cash flow (real)	(i)	−225 000	−12 500	41 605	128 904	118 818	41 918
Discount factor (5.769 per cent)	(ii)	1.000	0.945	0.894	0.845	0.799	0.755
Discounted cash flow (DCF)	(i) × (ii)	−225 000	−11 818	37 190	108 941	94 939	31 667
Net present value = sum (NCF)		35 918					

You may by now have detected a large financial rat. both methods of discounting cash flows give exactly the same answer. If we deflate the nominal cash flows by the inflation rate and discount the resultant real cash flows by the real rate of discount we get exactly the same result as before. The conclusions to draw from this are straightforward:

1. Inflation *per se* should not have any impact on the outcome of the investment decision if its effects are accounted for properly.

2. With inflation there are two choices: (a) project nominal cash flows and discount them directly using the nominal rate of discount or (b) deflate the nominal projection by the inflation rate and discount the resulting real cash flow using a real rate of discount.

3. It is wrong to discount real cash flows using a nominal rate (which will understate the resulting net present value) or to discount nominal cash flows using a real rate (which has the opposite effect). Exhibit 12.13 may help you to remember this important point.

4. It is also incorrect to ignore price changes altogether. Because different cost and revenue projections will be subject to their own specific price increases it is important to project a statement of nominal cash flows before either discounting directly at the nominal rate or deflating and discounting at the real rate.

Why bother, given all of this, to deflate nominal figures to real terms and then discount at the real rate? The answer is that many firms assume that it is perfectly valid to project future cash flows using current day prices and then discount at a rate which may or may not be properly corrected for inflation. We have described the correct procedure to ensure that real analysis and nominal analysis give exactly the same result. In practice the nominal procedure is to be preferred because it avoids the two stage discounting process.

> **Exhibit 12.13** Two ways to go wrong and two ways to do it right in investment appraisal

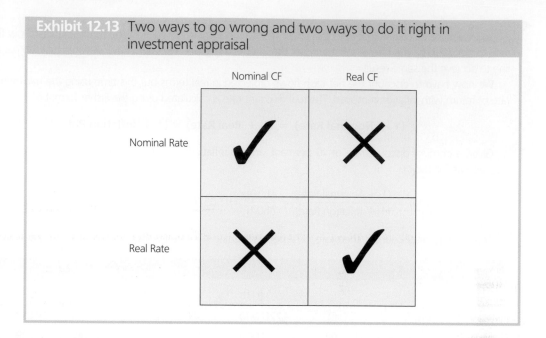

Review activity 12.3 A company had the following projection of net cash flows in nominal terms for a four-year investment. The company's cost of capital is 10 per cent and the rate of inflation is 4 per cent:

> **Exhibit 12.14**

	0	1	2	3	4
Cash flow (nominal)	−145 000	10 000	50 000	60 000	80 000

1. Calculate the net present value by discounting the nominal cash flow by 10 per cent.
2. Deflate the nominal cash flow to obtain the equivalent real cash flow.
3. Discount the real cash flow at the real cost of capital.

Net present value and tax

Taxation impacts upon investment projects in a number of different ways:

- through the incidence of value-added taxes (VAT)
- through profit taxes which are subject to personal tax or corporation tax depending upon the status of the business.

Value-added tax

This is a tax that is levied on sales of goods and services in one form or other throughout the European Union. The large bulk of goods and services sold in the UK carry VAT at the standard rate which is payable by the end-user. A business registered for VAT is normally allowed to offset the tax it pays on its bought-in goods and services against the VAT collected on its sales. Only the difference is paid to, or reclaimed from, Her Majesty's Revenue and Customs which is, in the UK, the government department responsible for the collection of the tax. Because VAT is 'self-clearing', a business engaged in its normal trade does not bear a tax liability unless the goods it sells in its turn are exempt. In that case neither the VAT on capital expenditure nor that on bought-in materials and other supplies can be recovered. This means that the cost projections which entail 'VATable' supplies must be stated with the VAT included. The recoverability of what is referred to as the 'input tax' can be crucial in determining the viability of a given investment project.

Corporation tax

This is the profits tax to which all incorporated businesses are subject. This tax can have a significant impact upon the viability of investment projects. In outline the tax works as follows:

- Taxable profit is calculated as the difference between revenue and allowable costs. Not all business costs are allowable and in particular depreciation on capital plant and equipment must be excluded for tax purposes. Depreciation is replaced by capital allowances of two types:
  1. first-year allowances which allow a set proportion of the initial investment to be offset for tax purposes in the year in question
  2. writing-down allowances which allow the balance of the investment to be written off on a reducing balance basis at a specified rate.
- Any unclaimed capital allowances can be offset against the receipts from the disposal of plant and equipment at the end of its economic life. Any surplus from the proceeds of the sale will then be treated as an addition to taxable profits and any deficit can be claimed as an expense.
- If a firm makes a loss in a given year that loss can be offset against future-year profits and in certain circumstances tax paid on prior-year profits can be reclaimed.
- Interest charges on debt are tax-deductible.
- Taxable profits after capital allowances are taxed on a sliding scale.
- Dividends are paid out of post-tax profits and carry a 'tax credit' which is available to the shareholder to offset against their personal liability for income tax. Normally the tax credit discharges the shareholder's liability for personal tax at the basic rate.
- A firm's corporation tax liability incurred in one year is normally settled in the year following, creating a 'timing difference' between the incidence of the tax and the discharge of its liability.

You will note that we have used the word 'normally' a number of times above. This is because taxes change from year to year and the details of what is an allowed expense for tax purposes are complex. This is one area where any business engaged in large-scale capital investment will need the tax implications to be worked through by its professional advisers.

Financial realities   DialaSid Ltd can claim a first-year allowance on the purchase of its new coach as described in the first case in this chapter. A first-year allowance is available at 100 per cent on the capital equipment and corporation tax is charged or can be offset at the rate of 40 per cent per annum. Tax is paid in the year following the year in which the liability is incurred. The company has other profits available for offset of any capital allowances on this project.

▶

Exhibit 12.15

The first year allowance is available on the capital investment giving a tax saving of 100 per cent = 40 per cent × £115 000

The cash flow is extended by one year because of the lag in tax payment

Year	0	1	2	3	4
Capital investment	−115 000				
Net cash flow from operations		50 000	50 000	30 000	
Sale value of coach				40 000	
Net cash flow from project	**−115 000**	**50 000**	**50 000**	**70 000**	**0**
First year allowance (100%)		46 000			
Tax on increase in taxable profit (40%)			−20 000	−20 000	−28 000
Post tax cash flow from project	**−115 000**	**96 000**	**30 000**	**50 000**	**−28 000**
Discount factor (5%)	1.000	0.952	0.907	0.864	0.823
Discounted cash flow	−115 000	91 429	27 211	43 192	−23 036
Net present value	23 796				

The cash flows are discounted in the normal way

The cash flows from the project are assumed to be a net addition to the firm's taxable profit

Note how the tax benefit from the first-year allowance is calculated. DialaSid Ltd can set off the capital allowance against its other company profits so it will save tax at the rate of 40 per cent on 100 per cent of its expenditure. However, the reduction in tax will only produce the consequential cash change one year later because that is when the tax on the company's profits would have been paid in any event. The net cash flows over the life of the project do not contain any depreciation charges and so we can assume that they represent a net increase in the taxable profits of the firm. As a result they will therefore attract corporation tax at 40 per cent, payable one year following the point at which the liability is incurred.

Review activity 12.4   Using Sid's example draw up a post-tax cash flow projection for each of the following:

(i) on the assumption that tax is paid as it is incurred rather than one year following

(ii) on the assumption that a 50 per cent first-year allowance is available followed by a 30 per cent writing down allowance on the reducing balance.

What general inferences can you draw about the impact of corporation tax on the viability of projects from your answer to (i)?

✓ Check the answer to this Review activity at the back of the book (see page 520)

Net present value in a risky world

The principal difficulty in all forms of capital investment appraisal is handling the issue of risk. If you look back at the Fisher–Hirshleifer separation theorem the obvious question is to what extent the NPV model retains its validity once we admit uncertainty into the analysis.

Two Nobel prize-winning economists, Franco Modigliani and Merton Miller, demonstrated in 1958 that the separation theorem does hold even when there is uncertainty about the future cash flows from investment. Once uncertainty is admitted into the analysis different classes of investor will demand different returns from the firm depending on the burden of risk that they are required to bear. In a world of perfect certainty there would be no distinction between equity and debt. Equity is sometimes known as 'risk capital' because the owners accept the business risk that the firm faces.

Modigliani and Miller, or M&M as they are universally known in the field of finance, made their arguments in terms of the value of the firm, but given the firm is simply the sum of all its investment projects their arguments still apply when considering individual projects. They demonstrated that even under conditions of risk and where the rate of return required by equity investors is different from that required by lenders (debt holders) the value of the firm, and hence the value of all its investment projects, is independent of the way those projects are financed. The average rate of return required by equity and debt investors is, they established, independent of the proportions of equity and debt in a firm's capital structure.

In a second but related piece of work, M&M went on to prove that dividend policy is also irrelevant. They argued that it is irrelevant whether a firm finances its investment through retention of dividends or through a new capital issue; its value (i.e. the NPV of all its constituent investments) would be unchanged. All that mattered, they argued, is that a firm must invest in all projects that have a positive net present value and in a world where it is cheaper from a transaction-cost point of view, to retain profits rather than raise capital, then it should not pay a dividend. Only if there are no further investment opportunities available can a firm make dividend payments to its investors.

There has been considerable debate about the credibility of M&M's arguments and although few doubt that technically they are correct there may be more subtle forces at play that undermine the theoretical structure that supports the NPV model. However, many of the issues which were once thought to be problematic have been at least partly resolved through advances in topics such as the theory of risk. M&M undertook their analysis on the assumption that firms could be categorised into identical risk classes. Later work demonstrated that their results were still valid even when this assumption is removed.

M&M demonstrated that the value of the firm, and by direct analogy the individual capital investments which make it up, is independent of the way it is financed and of the policies management may pursue in paying dividends. Following the M&M line of argument, all that influences the value of a project is the degree of business risk to which it is exposed. There are three strategies for dealing with this risk:

1. By adjusting the investment cash flows to reflect the uncertainty that the firm faces. This can be achieved by 'flexing' the cash flow projections to see how sensitive the net present value is to changes in each of the variables in the analysis.

2. By modelling the distribution of future revenues and cash flows and conducting a 'simulation' of the net present value.

3. By assuming that the cash flow projections are certain, but adjusting the discount rate by adding in a premium to account for the risk to which the firm is exposed.

Using a risk-adjusted discount rate is the most straightforward method of handling risk in investment appraisal. Clearly, the larger the discount rate, the lower the NPV, so a large discount rate will reduce the reported NPV for high-risk projects. In the next chapter we address explicitly how the risk premium can be deduced. We also discuss in more detail the procedures that can be used by a firm in estimating the appropriate discount rate to be used by a firm in its capital investment appraisal.

Here are some of the alternative names given to the discount rate:

- the cost of capital
- the discount rate
- the expected rate of return
- the minimum required rate of return
- the opportunity cost of capital
- the risk-adjusted discount rate.

At this stage we should just regard it as the rate of interest used in discounting future cash flows in order to estimate a firm's net present value.

Net present value when capital is in short supply

The net present value model assumes a perfect money market where money can be borrowed or deposited at a common market rate of interest in any amount. This is often not the case in that a firm may have adequate reserves in its balance sheet but be relatively illiquid in the short run. Going to the capital market (which is the market for long-term finance) can be a lengthy and expensive process. As a result the firm can find itself with a temporary shortage of finance for investment. The firm faced with a list of projects with positive net present values will need to sort them into an order of priority for investment given its limited availability of funds. From a financial point of view the ordering should be on the basis of each project's ability to convert investment capital into net present value. The most value-efficient solution for the firm is to rank its portfolio of projects by NPV per £ of capital invested. The ratio of net present value to capital outlay is known as the **profitability index** or 'NPV index'.

| **Financial realities** | In Exhibit 12.16 we show a situation of four projects where a firm only has £500 000 of free funds to invest. The projects cannot be scaled up but they can be scaled down if necessary. |

Exhibit 12.16

Ranking ratio

	0	1	2	3	4	5	NPV	NPV/£ outlay
Project 1	−225 000	2 000	45 000	145 000	139 000	51 000	49 555	0.2202
Project 2	−140 000	130 000	60 000				27 769	0.1983
Project 3	−25 000	−100 000	30 000	80 000	65 000		13 385	0.5354
Project 4	−720 000	−500 000	800 000	600 000	200 000		74 003	0.1028

Ranked order of projects								**NPV/£ outlay**
	0	1	2	3	4	5	NPV	
Project 3	−25 000	−100 000	30 000	80 000	65 000	13 385		0.5354
Project 1	−225 000	2 000	45 000	145 000	139 000	51 000	49 555	0.2202
Project 2	−140 000	130 000	60 000				27 769	0.1983
Project 4	−720 000	−500 000	800 000	600 000	200 000		74 003	0.1028

When we rank the projects by NPV/£ of outlay we discover that the order they should be accepted is project 3, project 1, project 2. This will use up £390 000 of the available funds. The balance (£110 000) could be used to

Exhibit 12.17

Ranked order of projects

	0	1	2	3	4	5	NPV	NPV/£ outlay
Project 3	−25 000	−100 000	30 000	80 000	65 000		13 385	**0.5354**
Project 1	−225 000	2 000	45 000	145 000	139 000	51 000	49 555	**0.2202**
Project 2	−140 000	130 000	60 000				27 769	**0.1983**
Project 4 (scaled down)	−110 000	−76 389	122 222	91 667	30 556		11 306	**0.1028**
Total investment	**500 000**				**Total Net Present Value**		102 015	

Each cash flow is scaled in the ratio = CF × 110 000/720 000

invest in a scaled-down version of project 4. Assuming that all the cash flows associated with project 4 can be scaled directly then the net present value of the scaled-down project is £11 306.

This ordering of projects gives the highest NPV that can be extracted from this investment plan (indeed you may attempt any rearrangement you like of the ordering of the projects and discover that none offers an NPV overall greater than £102 015).

Project 4 is known in the context of this plan as the 'marginal project'. Given access to further funds, this is the project in which the firm should invest additional cash resources. The NPV/£ of outlay on project 4 is 0.1028 or 10.28 per cent. If you refer back to Chapter 8 you will remember that when a resource is in short supply its opportunity cost consists of two parts: the cost of the resource assuming its free availability and a scarcity premium. That is exactly the case here: the opportunity cost of capital assuming free availability is the discount rate of 10 per cent that the firm has used to obtain the net present values shown above. The scarcity premium is the marginal increase in net present value that would accrue to the firm if it could expand its available capital by £1. The profitability index shows that project 4 will offer an additional £0.1028 for each additional pound the firm can invest over and above the current limit of £500 000. This percentage is therefore the internal scarcity premium which gives a total opportunity cost of capital in the first year of 20.28 per cent (including the 10 per cent discount rate).

Managerial issues and net present value

In theory, if management is solely committed to the maximisation of shareholder value then the NPV technique, if correctly applied, should give the best estimate of the increase in the value of the firm arising from a given investment decision. Given a free availability of capital, any project with a positive net present value will increase the market value of the firm. In practice, there are some real difficulties with the NPV model:

1. Management is unlikely to act solely in the interests of the shareholders. Managers exhibit varying degrees of self-interest that may find expression in ways that conflict with the interests of the equity investors. One way around this is for the equity investors to offer compensation packages that seek to reward management for their efforts on the shareholders' behalf. Bonus schemes, performance-related pay and share-options are just some of the methods that are applied. However, all of these systems entail monitoring costs and present potential problems of moral hazard. Managers have access to information not readily available to the shareholders and may use that information to improve the perception of performance as opposed to its reality

Economists have developed theories of how rational wealth-maximising individuals will act in a situation where one (the 'principal') directs the work of another (the 'agent'). Agency theory predicts that under conditions of uncertainty and in the absence of complete information available to both parties equally the agent will attempt to maximise his or her position to the detriment of the principal by expanding the perks that he or she takes from the contract between them. This agency 'loss' is brought about because the agent invariably has more knowledge of what is going on than the principal. A complete description of agency theory is beyond the scope of this book but readings are given at the end of the chapter which can help enlarge your knowledge of this technical but fascinating branch of economics.

2. Although the NPV model captures the principal cash flow effects upon the firm there are measurement problems in the implementation of the technique at the project level. It is an unstated assumption of the model that the cash flows to the firm as a whole, contingent upon a specific investment decision, can be separated from those generated by other activities. When a company like Disney decides to build a new attraction at one of its theme parks it may be able to distinguish the incremental expenditures that will arise to the business as a whole, but it will not be able to distinguish the incremental revenues. This is an example of what we term an 'entangled asset'. The most important entangled assets are also intangible and it is often impossible to measure with any precision the cash flow implications of investment in assets of this type. So, in practice, although the model is valid theoretically, it often proves impossible to apply in practice.

3. Because there is uncertainty about future states of the world, the cash flow outcomes from an investment are contingent upon what may happen at different stages in the future. Investment in assets that have more generalised application offer future options to the firm compared with those that are more specific. One major road-builder in the UK invested in a tarmac spreader that in one pass could lay down a coat of tarmac at the required thickness along a single lane of motorway. The year after its acquisition, the government altered the standard specification for lane width. The spreader was immediately useless as its width of spread could not be altered. If the firm had recognised this issue it could have purchased a (possibly) more costly spreader that would have given it the option to change the width of spread. The analysis and valuation of such **real options** is now a developing area of research in the theory of corporate finance.

4. It can be argued that what gives value to the owner of an asset is knowledge in how to use it. Whether the asset is an employee or a tarmac spreader, value is only created because the firm knows ways in which the potential within that asset can be realised. 'Knowledge in use', as it is termed, falls into two broad classes: public knowledge and private knowledge. If Virgin Atlantic purchases a new Boeing 767, there is a pool of publicly available knowledge it must have before it can use it: flying aeroplanes is public knowledge, servicing them is mostly public knowledge as well. If all that a firm possesses is public knowledge then the best that it can hope to achieve in a competitive market is a zero net present value. Positive NPVs become available through the accumulation of private knowledge, but how does the firm know the value of private knowledge, until it knows it? In the airline business, Virgin has a considerable stock of private knowledge about how to get added value out of a new jumbo jet. A new airline company, or a company acquiring an asset that is one of its kind (like a new employee), will not be in that situation. In summary, therefore, the positive net present value available to a firm may be invisible at the point the investment is made.

5. Finally, managers may not have confidence that the assumptions required to underpin the validity of the net present value model are realistic. The equity shareholders may not appreciate that an investment has taken place and so are not in a position to bid up the value of the firm in recognition of the positive net present value that has been generated.

Managers will almost certainly wish to see the impact of a new investment on the firm's reported return performance. There may be short-term liquidity problems and managers will be keen to understand the impact of a new investment on the liquidity of a business. To cope with these problems other investment techniques can help round off the picture and assist management in their decision-making.

Real options

The net present value model is the dominant approach to the theory of valuation and capital investment appraisal. However, it is difficult to value the inherent flexibility in an investment project using this technique. The net present value model requires the projection of the most likely or expected future cash outcomes and then to discount them using a rate of return which accommodates the degree of risk involved. The tarmac spreader example above illustrates the problem: presumably it was management expectations that the current road width specifications would remain unchanged. The net present value of the alternative chosen was almost certainly larger than the net present value of the more flexible machine. However, what the net present value calculation for the more flexible machine missed was that the option to change lane width in the future had value because it reduced the risk to which the firm was exposed. This type of option to change course within a capital investment project is called a 'real option'. Typically real options arise when a firm can build into a project or where a project naturally presents:

- An option to defer the whole or a significant part of the investment. If Sid, for example, bought a lease on a plot of land with the intention of holding it until a future use (perhaps as a garage or a new head office) became apparent, then he would have a real option on the future cash flows from his investment.

- An option to stage investment gives the firm the opportunity to abandon if circumstances change against it.

- An option to vary the scale of operations. The acquisition of a garage space with room for extension would offer Sid an option to expand his new car servicing business if the opportunity arose.

- An option to abandon. When Virgin Atlantic or easyJet purchase new jets they will necessarily consider the exit options if new markets fail to materialise and the planes have to be sold. Some aeroplanes are easier to sell on the second-hand market than others, thus opening up the abandonment option to the airline.

- An option to switch output. This was in essence the real option which came with the more general tarmac spreader.

- A growth option. This is where research investment, or the commitment of resources to exploration by a mining or oil company opens up the potential for future growth into new business areas.

- Compound options. Sometimes a project offers more than one of the above options to the decision maker. For example, if Virgin Atlantic invests in a particular class of jumbo jet it may create (i) an abandonment option, (ii) a scale option and (iii) an option to switch output.

The theory of real option valuation is a new and promising area for development in investment appraisal although its appeal lies more in the description of the issues the wise manager should consider when reviewing investment opportunities than in formal methods for attaching values to alternative courses of action. Further references to the real options literature are given at the end of this chapter.

Other methods of investment appraisal

We assume that the principal objective of management is to maximise the shareholders' value. The principal method of investment appraisal is designed to show this increase in shareholder value, which is the value added to the investors attributable to the decision to undertake the investment concerned.

The net present value is the primary performance measure for appraisal purposes and any project that does not promise a positive net present value should be rejected. To cope with short-run capital rationing the NPV index discussed above allows management to maximise the net present value of the portfolio of investments being considered.

Other techniques are designed to measure the return that an investment offers. The **internal rate of return** should show the economic return of a capital investment in percentage terms whilst the **accounting rate of return** and the differential ROCE models are designed to show the impact of an investment on the reported return performance as measured through a company's financial accounts.

A third group of techniques are designed to measure the likely impact of capital investment upon the liquidity of the firm. In an ideal world this problem should not arise because a firm can always go to the capital or the money markets to get finance if it needs it. In the real world it isn't quite like that and managers are often concerned about the speed with which they can recover their capital investment. Fast **payback** opens up future options for further investment especially if a firm is tightly managed and does not run significant monetary surpluses as a matter of course.

Internal rate of return

In many respects the internal rate of return method of investment appraisal is similar to the net present value model. However, instead of calculating the net present value at a defined

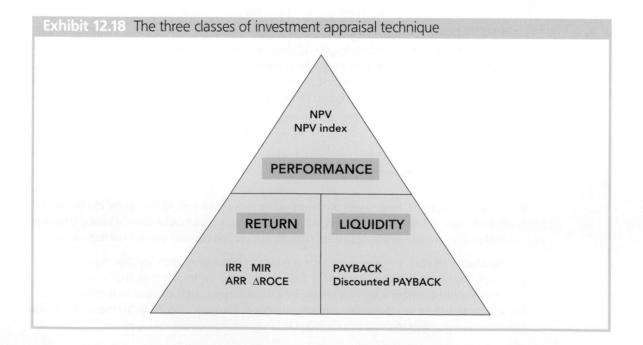

Exhibit 12.18 The three classes of investment appraisal technique

cost of capital, the internal rate of return gives the rate of discount which results in a zero net present value. The internal rate of return is, therefore, a percentage return measure giving the economic yield on the capital investment to the investor. If the internal rate of return is greater than the firm's minimum required rate of return then the capital investment is worthwhile. Anything less and the investment opportunity should be discarded. There are two ways of estimating the internal rate of return: a hard way and an easy way. We do the hard way first.

Financial realities Sid is interested to know what the internal rate of return is on his investment in a new coach. Here are the cash flows again:

Exhibit 12.19

Year	0	1	2	3
Capital investment	−115 000			
Net cash flow from operations		50 000	50 000	30 000
Sale value of coach				40 000
Net cash flow from project	−115 000	50 000	50 000	70 000

Internal rate of return by linear interpolation

Step 1: Calculate the net present value for the investment at a range of different discount rates until two rates are discovered that straddle the zero point (i.e. the lower rate gives a positive NPV and the higher rate a negative NPV):

Exhibit 12.20

Year		0	1	2	3	NPV
Discounted cash flow at	0 per cent	−115 000	50 000	50 000	70 000	55 000
Discounted cash flow at	5 per cent	−115 000	47 619	45 351	60 469	38 439
Discounted cash flow at	10 per cent	−115 000	45 455	41 322	52 592	24 369
Discounted cash flow at	15 per cent	−115 000	43 478	37 807	46 026	12 312
Discounted cash flow at	20 per cent	−115 000	41 667	34 722	40 509	1 898
Discounted cash flow at	25 per cent	−115 000	40 000	32 000	35 840	−7 160

We now know that the internal rate of return lies somewhere between 20 per cent and 25 per cent.

Step 2: Graph the NPV of this investment against increasing discount rate:

If your graphing skills are good enough this may be sufficient to obtain the internal rate of return to the nearest percentage. If not, a further step is required.

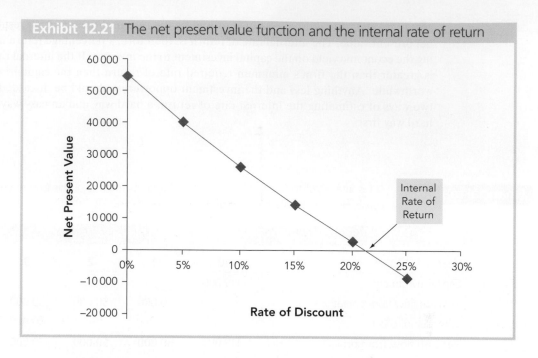

Exhibit 12.21 The net present value function and the internal rate of return

Step 3: Interpolate between the two percentage points to estimate the internal rate of return. As you will notice the NPV shows a curving function against discount rate. If we assume the relationship is linear between 20 per cent and 25 per cent we can estimate the IRR using simple ratios:

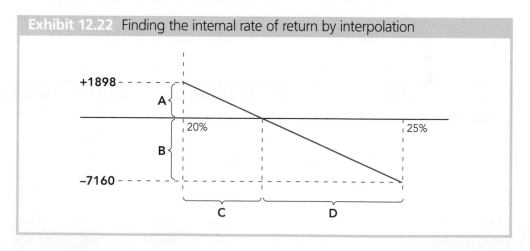

Exhibit 12.22 Finding the internal rate of return by interpolation

Because distance *A* to distance *B* is in the same ratio as distance *C* to *D* it is also true that:

$$\frac{A}{A + B} = \frac{C}{C + D}$$

Substituting in the values from the graph,

$$\frac{1898}{1898 + 7160} = \frac{C}{5\%}$$

$$\therefore C = 1.04\%$$

The internal rate of return is therefore 1.04 per cent above 20 per cent, i.e. 21.04 per cent.

Internal rate of return by spreadsheet

Most spreadsheet packages have an inbuilt function that returns the internal rate of return on an investment. The function in Excel is

= IRR(Values, [Guess])

The 'guess' is a specimen percentage which gives the algorithm which solves for the IRR a starting point and is not absolutely necessary. However, if we use this function putting the range of cash flows from the project into the function and guessing a starting point of 15 per cent the function returns 20.99 per cent. This is obviously much quicker, and once you have understood the mechanics of the calculation as shown by the interpolation method, is the way to estimate the internal rate of return in practice.

The problems with the internal rate of return

The internal rate of return is a well-established technique used by many companies in investment appraisal. Normally, if a project has a positive net present value it will have an internal rate of return in excess of the company's minimum required rate of return. It is possible with projects whose net cash flows veer from positive to negative over the life of the project to obtain multiple internal rates of return. In practice this problem rarely occurs. However, IRR measures can conflict with the net present value rule where investment opportunities are being considered that are mutually exclusive.

Financial realities   Sid is having second thoughts about his coach acquisition. He wonders whether to go ahead with a coach designed for the long-haul holiday market or to buy a somewhat cheaper vehicle with a higher seat density suitable for the school trade. He only has the space to accommodate one further bus within his fleet at the moment. On comparing the net cash flows from the two opportunities Sid is pleased to see that both would be worthwhile but that the school trade prospect appears to have a much higher internal rate of return than its net present value would suggest.

Exhibit 12.23

Year	0	1	2	3	NPV (5%)	IRR
Option 1 – Executive coach						
Capital investment	−115 000					
Net cash flow from operations		50 000	50 000	30 000		
Sale value of coach				40 000		
Net cash flow from option 1	**−115 000**	**50 000**	**50 000**	**70 000**	**£38 439.15**	**21.0%**
Option 2 – School Bus						
Capital investment	−60 000					
Net cash flow from operations		20 000	25 000	40 000		
Sale value of coach				15 000		
Net cash flow from option 2	**−60 000**	**20 000**	**25 000**	**55 000**	**£29 234.42**	**25.2%**

Review activity 12.5 Draw a graph of net present value versus discount rate for this second project and superimpose it on the graph for option 1. What do you notice?

✓ Check the answer to this Review activity at the back of the book (see page 521).

As you can see, the executive coach option does entail a greater outlay than Sid's second option. The net present value of the executive coach option suggests that of the two alternatives this is the option that will maximise Sid's, or his company's, wealth. However, the internal rate of return, whilst being in excess of 5 per cent in both cases suggests that the second option is the better of the two. There are two serious problems with the internal rate of return for making this type of decision:

1. Internal rate of return is dependent on the magnitude of the outlay. As a general rule, the higher the outlay, generally the lower the internal rate of return. Thus, from the point of view of the capital investment involved, smaller projects will tend to be favoured. In a situation where capital funds are in short supply the internal rate of return will favour the project which involves the least capital outlay. However, there are, as we will discuss later, better ways of dealing with the problem of capital shortages that are consistent with the objective of value maximisation.

2. With IRR, it is assumed that project cash flows are being reinvested within the firm at the internal rate of return rather than the cost of capital, as is the case with the net present value method. Given that the discount rate in the net present value calculation should be the firm's minimum required rate of return the assumption of a higher rate is unlikely to be realistic (a lower rate and the project would not be accepted under the IRR rule in any event).

As we can see, therefore, the internal rate of return does have problems but it is popular with managers who are attempting to measure the relative performance of different areas of activity within the business.

Modified internal rate of return (MIRR)

The **modified internal rate of return** is designed to get around the second technical difficulty mentioned above. The principle behind MIRR is that all project cash flows (except the outlay) are assumed to be reinvested until the end of the project at the firm's minimum required rate of return. The internal rate of return for the investment is then calculated using the 'terminal value' representing the sum of the project cash flows compounded to the end of the project's life.

The MIRR calculation for the two opportunities facing Sid is shown in Exhibit 12.24. Taking option 1, the first step is to compound each of the project net cash flows to year 3 using Sid's minimum required rate of 5 per cent. The £50 000 received in year 1 will be compounded over two years to give £55 125 and the £50 000 received in year 2 will be compounded at the same rate for one year to give £52 500. The £70 000 is a year 3 cash flow. Adding the terminal values together we get £177 625 and this value when discounted at 5 per cent gives the same net present value as we had originally. This demonstrates that the modified cash flow and the original cash flow have identical net present values and are equivalent as far as the firm is concerned. All that remains is to calculate the modified internal rate of return. This is much easier than the standard IRR and the following formula will do the trick:

$$\text{MIRR} = \sqrt[n]{\frac{\text{FV}}{\text{Outlay}}} - 1$$

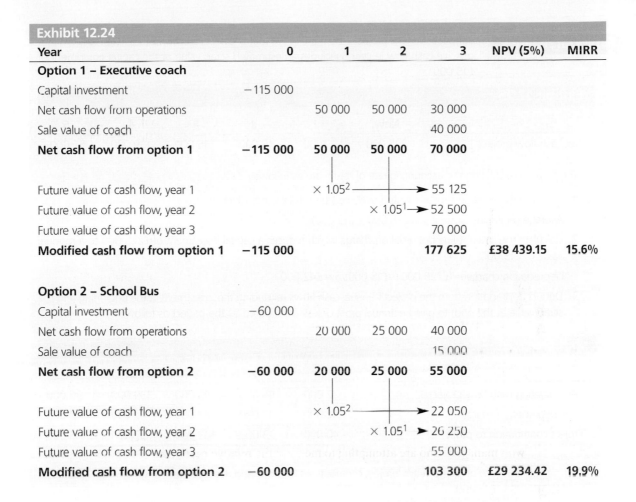

Exhibit 12.24

Year	0	1	2	3	NPV (5%)	MIRR
Option 1 – Executive coach						
Capital investment	−115 000					
Net cash flow from operations		50 000	50 000	30 000		
Sale value of coach				40 000		
Net cash flow from option 1	**−115 000**	**50 000**	**50 000**	**70 000**		
Future value of cash flow, year 1		× 1.05² ──────→		55 125		
Future value of cash flow, year 2			× 1.05¹──→	52 500		
Future value of cash flow, year 3				70 000		
Modified cash flow from option 1	**−115 000**			**177 625**	**£38 439.15**	**15.6%**
Option 2 – School Bus						
Capital investment	−60 000					
Net cash flow from operations		20 000	25 000	40 000		
Sale value of coach				15 000		
Net cash flow from option 2	**−60 000**	**20 000**	**25 000**	**55 000**		
Future value of cash flow, year 1		× 1.05² ──────→		22 050		
Future value of cash flow, year 2			× 1.05¹ ──→	26 250		
Future value of cash flow, year 3				55 000		
Modified cash flow from option 2	**−60 000**			**103 300**	**£29 234.42**	**19.9%**

So, with a future value of the project cash flows (FV) of £177 625 for project 1 and an investment outlay of £115 000 the project has a modified internal rate of return of 15.6 per cent.

Review activity 12.6 Calculate the modified internal rate of return for the second option.

Although technically superior to the standard IRR calculation this method is not well known in practice. However, like the IRR, it is biased towards smaller-outlay projects, which bias management might well wish to inject into their routine investment decision-making.

Accounting rate of return

Accounting rate of return is designed to show the impact upon a firm's reported performance of a new investment project. The accounting rate of return calculates the average annual profitability of an investment as a proportion of the average capital employed over the project's life.

Financial realities Suppose we take project 1 from the set of four shown in Exhibit 12.16. We are told that the positive cash flow in year 5 includes an estimated scrap value of the capital equipment of £15 000.

Exhibit 12.25

	Now	1	2	3	4	5
Net cash flow project 1	−225 000	2000	45 000	145 000	139 000	51 000

The steps in calculating the accounting rate of return are as follows:

1. Calculate the average capital invested over the life of the project which is:

   Average capital investment = (£225 000 + £15 000)/2 = £120 000

2. Calculate the straight-line depreciation charge which reduces a capital investment of £225 000 to a residual value of £15 000:

   Depreciation charge = (£225 000 − £15 000)/5 = £42 000

3. Deduct depreciation from the project's annual cash flows (excluding the investment at the beginning and the scrap value at the end) to give an annual profit or loss contributed by the project as follows:

Exhibit 12.26

	0	1	2	3	4	5
Net operating cash flow project 1		2 000	45 000	145 000	139 000	36 000
Less: depreciation charge		42 000	42 000	42 000	42 000	42 000
Project contribution to profit		−40 000	3 000	103 000	97 000	−6 000

4. Calculate the sum of all the year's 'project contributions to profit' and average them to give £157 000/5 = £31 400.

5. Calculate the accounting rate of return

   Accounting rate of return = 31 400/120 000 × 100 = 26.17 per cent

In practice this figure, although widely used, tells managers very little because presumably what they would like to know is how this project will impact upon the reported return on capital employed in the firm. To do this we turn to another technique which interprets the project's return in terms of the primary return measure when interpreting the company's accounts.

Differential return on capital employed (ΔROCE)

With **differential return on capital employed** we calculate the average return on capital employed on the project. The capital employed is given by the capital investment plus the accumulated cash flow, which equals the capital claim on the original investment plus the accumulated profit or loss. The steps in producing the differential return on capital employed are as follows:

1. project the cumulative cash flows, the net book value of fixed assets and the cumulative project profit or loss as shown in the first part of Exhibit 12.27

2. create 'mini balance sheets' for the project for each year of its life.

Exhibit 12.27

	0	1	2	3	4	5
Net operating cash flow project 1		2 000	45 000	145 000	139 000	36 000
Cumulative cash flow		2 000	47 000	192 000	331 000	367 000
Noncurrent assets	225 000	225 000	225 000	225 000	225 000	225 000
less accumulating depreciation		42 000	84 000	126 000	168 000	210 000
Net book value of noncurrent assets	225 000	183 000	141 000	99 000	57 000	15 000
Accumulated profit (Exhibit 12.28)		−40 000	37 000	66 000	163 000	157 000

	0	1	2	3	4	5
Net book value of noncurrent assets	225 000	183 000	141 000	99 000	57 000	15 000
Cumulative cash flow		2 000	47 000	192 000	331 000	367 000
Net assets employed	225 000	185 000	188 000	291 000	388 000	382 000
Capital invested	225 000	225 000	225 000	225 000	225 000	225 000
Accumulated profit	0	−40 000	−37 000	66 000	163 000	157 000
Capital employed	225 000	185 000	188 000	291 000	388 000	382 000

Average capital employed = (£225 000 + £382 000)/2 = £303 500

Given that the average profit contributed by the project is £31 400 (calculated as part of the accounting rate of return) then:

Differential return on capital employed = £31 400/£303 500 × 100

= 10.35 per cent.

Note that this is the average ROCE for the project and not the change in ROCE for the firm as a whole. However, if we were in a position to measure the firm's current ROCE we would be able to deduce the following:

If ROCE (project) > ROCE (firm) then the project will tend to increase the firm's reported performance over the life of the project, and
If ROCE (project) < ROCE (firm) then the project will tend to decrease the firm's reported performance over the life of the project.

We can create a project's ROCE profile to give an even clearer indication to management of how the new investment will affect the reported accounts each year. To create the profile, calculate the average capital employed in each year as before year 1: (225 000 + 185 000)/2 = £205 000:

Exhibit 12.28

	0	1	2	3	4	5
Average capital employed		205 000	186 500	239 500	339 500	385 000
Profit/loss for the year		−40 000	3 000	103 000	97 000	−6 000
ROCE		−19.51	1.61	43.01	28.57	−1.56

Because of the different way it has been calculated, using annual rather than the five-year change in capital employed, we get a slightly different figure for the average ROCE of 10.42 per cent. Management now has a clear idea of the impact of a project on the firm's reported return on capital employed as each year passes. With this particular example, management may well be concerned that the project could have a significant negative impact on the reported performance of the business in all but two years of the project's life.

Payback and discounted payback

Payback focuses on how quickly a firm can recover its original investment or, in the case of **discounted payback**, recover its original investment plus the opportunity cost of the capital employed. Payback is a highly favoured technique in practice because it is simple to calculate and it does give a measure of a project's ability to refinance the firm.

Financial realities   Take project 1 from the set of four shown in Exhibit 12.16. We are told that the positive cash flow in year 5 includes an estimated scrap value of the capital equipment of £15 000. Now calculate the cumulative cashflow:

Exhibit 12.29

	0	1	2	3	4	5
Project 1 cash flow	−225 000	2 000	45 000	145 000	139 000	51 000
Cum cash flow	−225 000	−223 000	−178 000	−33 000	106 000	157 000

As you can see, the cumulative cash flow turns positive between years 3 and 4 and we can be even more precise by taking the negative value at year 3 (−33 000) and, calculating the proportion change to the cash flow over that year, arrive at the number of days beyond year 3 to payback:

Payback = 3 years + 33 000/(33 000 + 106 000) × 365
       = 3 years, 87 days

One objection to this simple procedure is that it fails to recognise the time value of money. This we can do by taking the discounted cash flow rather than the money flow as follows:

Exhibit 12.30

	0	1	2	3	4	5
Project 1 discounted cash flow	−225 000	1 818	37 190	108 941	94 939	31 667
Cum cash flow	−225 000	−223 182	−185 992	−77 051	17 888	49 555

Following the same technique again we note that breakeven falls between the 3rd and 4th year, and the number of years and days is as follows:

Payback = 3 years + 77 051/(77 051 + 17 888) × 365
       = 3 years, 296 days

One of the most common objections to payback (and discounted payback) is that the technique fails to recognise cash flows beyond the payback period. A project may have large cash returns beyond the payback period and offer a positive net present value. However, it may be that a far less satisfactory project would be given the go-ahead because of a shorter payback period even though it has a much smaller net present value and offers a lower return in later years. But, in an important sense, this criticism is misplaced because it fails to recognise what the technique is trying to do. The technique is attempting to show the time a project will take to recover its investment, and in fully invested firms the recovery of operating cash flows (remember them from Chapter 4) is vital for opening up future opportunities. Payback therefore exposes the real option value of an investment project. Short-payback projects give more options to the firm than projects with long-drawn-out payback periods.

Chapter summary

If managers acted purely on their shareholders' behalf and the shareholders had the same access to information as the managers then NPV would be the method of choice. In the real world managers know more than investors and a firm's financial reports do not perfectly reflect managements' investment intentions or their expectations. As a result the net present value of a project is unlikely to be realised in the value of the firm at least in the short run. Furthermore, many of the technical conditions required for the net present value rule to be valid are not met in the real world. For this reason managers turn to other techniques to amplify their understanding of the financial implications of the investments they seek to undertake. Some of these techniques highlight the significance of the investment choices made by the firm on its reported performance measure. Others test the liquidity implications of the proposal. On top of this managers have their own agenda – no manager has been sacked for an investment decision which boosted his or her firm's reported return on capital employed and offered a short payback. This chapter has provided an overview of all these topics and, taken together with the material in the remaining two chapters of this book, it will build your understanding of the reality of capital investment appraisal in firms.

Further reading

Archer, S. and D'Ambrosio, C.A. (1976) *The Theory of Business Finance – A Book of Readings*, New York: Macmillan. This book of readings is worth the trouble of scouring the libraries or second-hand book-shops to obtain a copy. The classic readings by Markowitz, Sharpe, Gordon, Modigliani and Miller are all here.

Howell, S., Stark, A., Newton, D., Paxson, D., Cavus, M. and Pereira, J. (2001) *Real Options: Evaluating Corporate Investment Opportunities in a Dynamic World*, Harlow: Financial Times Prentice Hall. This is a first class book that is accessible to the non-mathematical reader. Although many fingers were in the writing pie, it is coherent and well written.

Pike, R. and Neale, B. (2006) *Corporate Finance and Investment: Decisions and Strategies*, Harlow: Financial Times Prentice Hall. This book is an excellent text in the area of corporate finance. Most of the methods and techniques discussed in this chapter are extended and the theory behind them is explained in detail. The best book to develop your understanding of the material in this chapter.

Pratt, J.W., and Zeckhauser, R.J. (1991) *Principles and Agents: the structure of business*, Boston MA: Harvard Business School Press. A straightforward set of readings on this difficult area within economic theory.

Ryan, R.J. (2006) *Corporate Finance and Valuation*, London: Cengage Learning, without risk of under statement – a true masterpiece in what is a very tricky area.

Progress check

1. What is the fundamental difference between compounding and discounting? (pp. 394–396)

2. What three factors influence the time value of money? (pp. 397–398)

3. State the assumptions behind and the conclusion of the Fisher–Hirshleifer separation theorem. (p. 398)

4. Write out the formulas for an annuity and a terminal value. (p. 399)

5. What should be excluded from the cash flow projections as part of a net present value analysis? (pp. 404–405)

6. How are real and nominal rates of interest linked? (p. 409)

7. What three approaches can be used to incorporate risk in net present value analysis? (p. 413)

8. What ratio should be used to select projects for investment when capital is in short supply? (p. 414)

9. What are the two principal problems with the internal rate of return criterion and which of these does the modified internal rate of return overcome? (p. 422)

10. How does the differential return on capital employed differ from the accounting rate of return? (p. 424)

11. How is the payback on a project calculated? (p. 426)

Questions

The answers to the questions followed by ✓ can be found at the back of the book, the answers to the remaining questions can be found on the website accompanying this book (**www.cengage.co.uk/ryan2**).

1. A project has a cash flow as follows:

year	0	1	2	3	4	5	6
Net cash flow	−350 000	98 000	245 000	95 000	45 000	30 000	−15 000

Calculate the NPV at 10 per cent, the IRR, MIRR, payback, discounted payback and ARR for this project. ✓

2. A 45-year-old director of a company wishes to build a projected fund for retirement on the basis of an annual payment of £10 000. His planned retirement age is 60. Current projection rates are 6 per cent. What will be the projected fund? ✓

3. The director's fund from (question 2) will be used to purchase an annuity. The annuity rate is 4 per cent. The director's life expectancy is 15 years. What will be his annual pension? ✓

4. Bonderama Leisure Ltd has an investment opportunity worth £60 000 per annum for three years. Its cost of capital for the project is 15 per cent per annum. The investment required is £130 000. Is the investment worthwhile (use the annuity formula)?

5. Melchor plc is considering two mutually exclusive projects.

	0	1	2	3
Project 1	−4 000	3 000	2 000	2 000
Project 2	−140 000	70 000	30 000	80 000

The company has a cost of capital of 10 per cent per annum.

You are required to:

(i) Calculate the net present value and internal rate of return for each project and state, giving reasons, which one the firm should accept if it wishes to maximise its shareholders' value.

(ii) Estimate to the nearest month the payback and the discounted payback for each project.

(iii) Comment upon the validity of each of the techniques you have used.

....

6. A small equity-financed company is considering a range of opportunities that would have a significant impact upon the value of the firm. It has filtered each of these projects according to their net present value and internal rate of return as shown below and is considering which project to accept given the availability of new equity of £300 000 at the company's current cost of capital of 8 per cent per annum. Funding above this limit would incur a significant increase in the rates of return required by investors. Generally, all projects can be scaled down but not up.

The projects are as follows:

Exhibit 12.31

	01-Jan	31-Dec-01	31-Dec-02	31-Dec-03	31-Dec-04	31-Dec-05	NPV	IRR
alpha	−130 000	0	0	0	0	220 000	19 728.30	11%
beta	−9 000	3 000	3 000	3 000	3 000	3 000	2 978.13	20%
gamma	−199 000	200 000	80 000	0	0	0	54 772.29	31%
delta	−44 000	−22 000	70 000	10 000	12 000	0	12 402.03	18%
epsilon	−97 000	20 000	38 000	50 000	25 000	10 000	18 970.58	16%

The company has projected its accounting figures (before the investments proposed above) for the next five years as follows:

	01-Jan	31-Dec-01	31-Dec-02	31-Dec-03	31-Dec-04	31-Dec-05
Turnover		780 500	820 000	861 000	904 000	949 200
Gross profit		172 000	180 400	190 000	199 000	208 500
Capital employed	1 021 250	1 075 000	1 127 500	1 187 500	1 243 750	1 303 125

The company calculates depreciation on all new investments at 10 per cent of the acquisition value of any fixed capital investment incurred within the year concerned.

You are required to:

(i) Advise the company as to which of the above projects the available capital should be allocated and the increase in the equity value of the firm which can be expected following that investment.

(ii) Given your advice above, advise management on the maximum rate of return it should be prepared to pay on the additional funds required to complete this portfolio of investments.

(iii) Calculate the increase in the expected gross annual rate of return on capital employed for this business if your project investment plan is accepted.

(iv) Comment upon the assumptions that you have made in formulating your advice to management. ✓

....

7. East Ham plc, a football club, is considering investing in Burcolene, an Argentinian midfield player whose best years are behind him. The club expects to be able to hold the player for five years. The

transfer fee is £1.25 million in the first year and the net cash flows from gate receipts, merchandising etc. would be £0.4 million per annum over the remainder of his playing life. At the end of the fifth year the player would be put on a plane back to Argentina.

The club pays tax on its net cash flows (less tax allowances) at an average rate of 45 per cent per annum. The company is allowed to deduct from its cash flows an allowance for its expenditure in players of one-fifth of the transfer fee in each of the five years the player stays with the club. The tax payment is made one year after the liability for tax is incurred.

(i) Determine whether the above transfer is worthwhile, assuming an opportunity cost of capital of 10 per cent per annum.

(ii) Calculate the payback period and the discounted payback period for the investment.

(iii) Outline some of the difficulties which managers face in making such long-term investments in players.

8. Bellvue (Chemicals) plc is considering the construction of a chemical plant to produce a staple product used widely in the chemical industry, called alpha-nievene. The production process is continuous and the expected life of the plant is five years. The plant capacity will be 65 000 tons in the first year, but this will rise by 10 per cent per annum over the following two years before levelling off at a constant capacity for the remainder of the plant's life.

The selling price of alpha-nievene is currently £100 per ton, and this is expected to rise by 8 per cent per annum over the plant's life. The total market for the product currently stands at 550 000 tons per annum, which is rising by 5 per cent per annum. Bellvue expects to hold its market share of 10 per cent into the indefinite future. The raw material cost is £30 per ton bought-in, and the expected conversion ratio is 0.7 tons of finished chemical for every ton of raw material input. Raw material costs are expected to rise at a rate of 12 per cent per annum over the life of the project.

While output is rising, labour costs are expected to be directly related to output. The wage rate is currently £25 per ton of finished product and this rate is expected to increase by 6 per cent per annum. Half of the labour force committed to this project are on the permanent establishment and will have to be replaced by direct recruitment. Half of these permanent staff have special skills and their redeployment from other activities within the firm will bring about a loss of £75 000 contribution in the first year. The newly recruited staff should have acquired the necessary skills after their first year of employment. The remainder of the staff necessary for this project will be recruited on short-term contracts.

Current energy costs for the chemical process are £6 per ton produced and are expected to rise by 5 per cent per annum.

The firm depreciates its plant and equipment on a straight line basis over its expected life. Development and pilot plant experimentation have already incurred costs of £80 000. The capital cost of the plant is £6 250 000 which will be spent immediately and the plant will be commissioned and fully operational for the current production year. The plant will be scrapped and dismantled at the end of its life at a net cost of £30 000. All cash flows, except the immediate capital outlay, can be assumed to be incurred at the end of the year in question.

Bellvue would like to plan on the basis of full-capacity operation each year with any final stock balances being sold in the sixth year. Bellvue has an opportunity cost of capital of 10 per cent per annum. The retail price index is expected to continue growing at 4 per cent per annum over the indefinite future.

You are required to:

(i) draw up a cash flow forecast for this project in nominal terms

(ii) project the net cash flow in real terms

(iii) discount the nominal and the real cash flows at the appropriate rate of discount

(iv) calculate the internal rate of return and the modified internal rate of return for this project

9. A company operates in an economic environment characterised by changing price and labour costs. Its current forecasts based upon both internal and governmental data is as follows:

Exhibit 12.32

	0	1	2	3	4	5
Labour rate		4%	4%	4%	4%	4%
Specific price changes (sales)		4%	4%	2%	2%	2%
Specific price changes (raw materials)		5%	5%	5%	3%	3%
General price inflation		2%	4%	4%	2%	2%
Real cost of capital		5%	5%	5%	5%	5%
Units sold		5%	5%	5%	5%	5%

It is considering an investment project that has a five-year life.

Capital plant and equipment are to be purchased immediately for $550 000. This plant and equipment are expected to lose value at a rate of 30 per cent per annum on its reducing balance. The plant would come on line immediately and would be scrapped for its written-down value at the end of the fifth year of operation.

Sales of 10 000 units would be produced at a current price of $40 per unit. The first year's sales are expected to yield this price adjusted for the specific price change shown in Exhibit 12.32.

Labour costs currently are $25 per labour hour and one labour hour produces two units of output. During the first two years the deployment of labour on this project must be found internally and the contribution forgone on other activities is expected to be approximately $76 000 and $56 000 in the first and second year respectively.

Material costs are $10 per unit at current prices.

Project-specific overheads in current prices are $45 000 and these are expected to rise in line with general price inflation.

You are required:

(i) to project a statement of money (nominal) cash flows taking into account stated price changes for the five years of this project and to include capital expenditure and eventual sale proceeds of the plant and equipment for scrap

(ii) to evaluate this project using the net present value criterion *plus* one other investment appraisal technique of your choosing

(iii) to advise management on the acceptability of this project. ✓

Case exercise

MUCAS Electronics

Introduction

Peter Smithfield is one of three contract managers within MUCAS Electronics whose responsibility is to manage special assignments within the digital instruments division. His first day in the office after two weeks in Greece held a rather unpleasant surprise. A contract tender letter had arrived and lain on his desk for ten days and had not been intercepted by his secretary nor by his number two, John Scape. His first reaction was to point the fan in the other direction and call an emergency meeting between himself, John Scape, the firm's divisional financial controller, Margaret Best, and one of his best design engineers, Richard (Dick) Enzian.

The four of them met that afternoon and assessed the situation. The contract required the fabrication and delivery of 450 digital electronic control units over a three-year period. The units themselves appeared to be of a straightforward design and construction consisting of a simple two-pass control unit on a board (the motherboard) hard-wired into a case/control unit. The contract required the delivery of 150 units in single annual instalments for each of the following three years. Peter Smithfield identified three principal items of information that would be necessary before they could make a decision whether to tender: first, the maximum price that they could charge per unit on a fixed basis and still win the contract, second, the resources which would be required to secure the necessary level of production and third, the capital cost of establishing the production system. They decided to meet forty-eight hours later to see if they had enough information to make a decision.

The next meeting

At their next meeting, Scape was adamant that competitive pricing from the other likely bidders would be fierce. In his opinion, the highest fixed price that could be bid with any chance of success would be £200 per unit.

'Well, if you want my opinion – at that price we should give up now', said Margaret Best. 'I doubt that we would even be able to recover our costs, never mind make a profit.'

Undaunted by this, Scape turned to Enzian and asked if he could give any estimate of the likely costs of production over the next three years. Enzian started riffling through a sheaf of notes and computer printouts. Within seconds the table in front of him was covered in paper.

Finding a particular sheet of scribbled notes Enzian said: 'The motherboards are easy – if we fabricate them from components the quantity surveyor reckons we should be looking at £85 per unit for the first year with costs rising at four per cent each year.'

Margaret Best nodded her approval. 'Yes', she said. 'I agree with that level of cost inflation on these items although it does assume that the exchange rate remains steady over the next three years. That's a big assumption given the state of the Far Eastern financial markets. Don't forget we now source most of this stuff from South Korea', she added.

'That's all very well', interjected Scape, 'but don't we already have some of those boards in stock?'

Enzian looked puzzled for a moment and then laughed: 'No, we have a hundred boards of a very similar design, although, as you may remember (glancing at Peter Smithfield), we have already decided to scrap them. They were part of a production run which was rejected because of defects in the control mechanisms. But, it might be possible to rescue the motherboards although we had planned to use some of the board components for other things.'

'Have you any idea of the value of the components you would have saved?' interrupted Best.

'No', Enzian replied, 'but the value of the components we would have had to buy in is approximately £2100. If we were to use the motherboards on this contract we would have to spend about £20 per board to bring its gain up to spec. However, the components stripped off these 100 boards would be worth about £1800 as scrap.'

'So, let me get this right', said Scape, 'we have 100 boards which were scrap although pillaging them for another use would save us £2100 – correct?'

'Yes – that's it.'

'And the cost of converting each one would be £20 a unit and there would be some units left over worth about £1800 – OK?'

'OK', confirmed Scape, 'and perhaps I can make a suggestion about the cases and controls? You remember the MOD contract that went sour in October?' Smithfield nodded. 'Well, 150 cases were purchased for that contract which would fit this specification. In fact, they have already been purchased, although we haven't paid for them yet. Each one cost £45 although we were considering modifying them at £16.50 each for another job which would save us buying in special boxes at £63 each! If we had to buy these original units now they would be paying £48 rather than £45.'

'What would be their scrap value, Dick?', queried Smithfield.

Enzian shrugged non-committally. 'Well, I'm not sure it matters anyway but about £30 a unit I guess. These are useful units and the cost of the rare metals in them is pushing their price up rapidly. We expect at least 12 per cent price increases on these each year.'

'OK', interrupted Smith, 'I think we have gone as far as we can go on the materials side for today. Now what about labour costs?'

Margaret Best produced her notes and said: 'a skilled technician would take two working months to produce the annual quota and, remember, to avoid deterioration, they should be shipped as soon as they are assembled – we can't stockpile. Two working months is about 240 hours and we would need to pull someone off central assembly for the period just before our year-end to meet the annual delivery dates. The salary of a skilled technician runs at about £17 500 gross although we could fill in with some temporaries at about £6 per hour. I suppose we could, at a pinch, do the same thing in future years although we must account for the fact that all staff salary costs and part-time rates are rising at 14 per cent a year. Also, don't forget that we must also charge overheads at £25 per technician hour. Our labour costs are going to be very expensive!'

At this point Smithfield closed the meeting, but asked John Scape to let him have a memorandum of the equipment and tooling costs by the following day. He was beginning, however, to feel rather pessimistic about the contract at the £200 tender price. The job would entail some capital outlay and with interest rates at ten per cent per annum things were not looking good. He also mused on the fact that there was rarely enough information to make a decision of this type and what there was tended to be guesswork.

Memorandum

To: Peter Smithfield
From: John Scape
cc. Margaret Best, Richard Enzian

Subject: Contract 0878 – Equipment Costs

I have looked into the issue of the special tools we would need for this contract and I estimate that they would cost £18 000 and should be purchased immediately. I also think that we should expect them to have zero scrap value after use. A laser assembly tool produced for sale in one of the firm's other divisions is also required. The direct cost of producing this tool is £6 800. From the production records each tool requires 50 technician hours in production and we would normally sell them with a 35 per cent markup on total cost. We keep stocks of the laser assembly tool and so there would be no difficulties meeting current orders if one was used on this contract. Alternatively, we could buy an equivalent tool which could be purchased at a price of £10 900. The second hand market value of this type of machine depreciates at approximately ten per cent per year (reducing balance).

PS Back on my hobby-horse but we have already spent £1500 in meeting time so far on this contract! We must recover this in our costings.

How would you advise Peter Smithfield in this case?

Chapter 13

The nature of the financial markets

Introduction

The money and capital markets are at the economic centre of the industrial and commercial world. Both firms and individuals rely upon the efficient operation of these markets for obtaining capital for investment purposes or money to meet their short-term financial needs. Over the last fifty years the operation of the money and capital markets has been progressively 'globalised' both to finance international trade but also to support multinational business and governments finance their activities. This globalisation has been facilitated by a number of political, economic and technological developments. In this chapter, we explore the financial markets with an outline of their history and their development in modern globalised economies. We devote some time to the concept of a security as a negotiable claim and the phenomenon of securitisation. We outline the structure of the financial markets and, in particular, how the money and capital markets interact. We then turn to the equity market as the primary risk market and discuss the role of information in the pricing of securities and the concept of information efficiency. Although we take a bias towards market efficiency, some anomalous evidence will also be described. Risk and return are then defined and an intuitive appreciation given of the concept of diversification and risk partitioning. The risk–return trade-off is then discussed, leading to an informal discussion of the capital asset pricing model. Finally, topics in the fixed interest market are then discussed before closing with a section on the sources of long- and short-term finance.

Learning objectives

Securities and the financial markets

- To understand the characteristics of a financial market security.

- To understand the nature of the financial markets and the different motives of traders.

- To understand the money markets and the determinants of exchange rates.

The capital markets

- To be able to distinguish between the roles of the primary and secondary capital markets.
- To understand the distinguishing features of equity and debt capital.
- Io have an understanding of the concept of market efficiency.
- To understand the nature of risk and return and the concept of portfolio risk.

The cost of capital

- To be able to use the capital asset pricing model to measure the expected return on equity.
- To be able to estimate the rate of return required by debt investors.
- To be able to calculate the weighted average cost of capital and understand its significance.

Securities and the financial markets

A financial security is a negotiable claim upon the value of some underlying asset. 'Negotiability' is the legal term applied when a claim is 'tradeable' in an open market. The claim will be evidenced by some form of certificate or **bond,** or in the modern era of computerised record systems as a record of entitlement maintained within a database attached to the relevant security trading system. The asset can be either real or intangible, it can be a company or indeed it can be another security. Securities backed by other securities are known as **derivatives.**

The key features of a security are:

- the asset that backs it which will have value
- its 'negotiability' in that it can be traded in a securities market
- the 'entitlement' which it gives to the holder.

The security derives its 'fundamental value' from the asset that backs it. It may well be that the value of the underlying asset is uncertain. This uncertainty imparts 'risk' to the financial return that the holder can expect to get through holding the security concerned.

The financial markets

There is evidence that early financial markets developed to support trade in the ancient world as merchants bought and sold goods and needed investors to provide the money to provision their ships and to purchase commodities to buy and sell. The first financial market of the modern era appears to have arisen at the fairs in the medieval cities of Lagny, Troyes, Provins and Bar-sur-Aube in the Champagne region of France. These fairs were well-regulated events where travelling merchants from across Europe would buy and sell their goods, settle claims with debtors and creditors, and make use of the first banks. One of the innovations of these banks was the creation of letters of credit that were negotiable throughout Christendom. A letter of credit is simply a statement that a certain amount of money is owed to the original holder. The Champagne Fairs had declined in importance by 1250, but the banking system which they started developed rapidly first in Italy and later across Europe and in particular in Britain. The new banks represented the 'retail' end of the money business and the money market emerged as banks traded with one another and with the royal and noble houses forming the 'wholesale' end of the business.

Today the financial markets are divided into two:

- The money markets, which are markets for cash itself and for financial securities of less than one year's duration. Money is the most liquid and immediately negotiable security, underpinned by the strength of the economy of the country that issues it. Other money market securities include government and company **bills** that have less than one year to maturity, negotiable certificates of deposit (i.e. tradeable receipts issued by banks when money is deposited with them) and various bills of exchange which are 'IOUs' issued by companies or by banks as a means of financing their business transactions.

- The capital markets, which are markets for securities of greater than one year's duration. Equity shares, preference shares and company and government bonds are all examples of capital market securities.

Traders in markets

Traders in financial markets (and many other markets as well for that matter) fall into three broad categories defined by the method by which they seek to maximise the return on their trading. Trading methods vary in their success and some can expose the trader in financial securities to exceptionally high levels of risk. We assume that all traders in the financial markets are averse to risk.

Risk can be regarded as the degree of uncertainty that attaches to the future returns on investment in terms of both dividend or interest payments and capital gains and losses. When put this way it is easy to see why risk-aversion should be regarded as a near-universal trait in human behaviour. Technically what risk-aversion means is that if two alternatives are open to the investor, both of which promise identical average levels of return in the future, then the one which has the lower uncertainty about those future levels of return will be the one that will be preferred. Likewise, if two alternatives have identical levels of uncertainty attached to them, the one that offers the greater average level of return will be the one that is preferred. Given risk-aversion we can categorise traders into three distinct classes: fundamental investors, speculators and arbitrageurs.

Fundamental investors

These investors look for value in trading financial securities by examining the future prospects of the company concerned and, in particular, assessing the cash value which will be added by the business over its lifetime. Such investors seek out information about the businesses concerned and on the basis of that information form expectations about the company's future performance in order to decide whether the investment is a 'buy', a 'hold' or a 'sell'. Fundamental investors employ a wide range of research tools when searching for value and when such investors are in the ascendancy in a particular market for a share then the market is said to be driven by 'rational expectations'.

Speculators

These investors are looking for short-term value gain by trying to outguess how the market is likely to react to changing events in the near term. If the speculator believes that the market is going to rise then they will 'buy long', that is buy securities with the intention of selling once their profit materialises. In these circumstances they may also purchase a call option, that is an option to buy the security, at a specified future date at a currently agreed price. If the market rises above that agreed price they will exercise their option and take their profit. If the price remains unchanged or falls they will discard their option, losing only the premium they paid to purchase the option.

If the speculator believes that the market is due to fall they can 'sell short', that is they sell securities they do not own and buy them back at a later date. Because settlement occurs on a daily basis, short-sold positions either have to be closed within the day or the securities must be 'borrowed' from a broker or some other source to support the transaction. A short seller in the market can also use what are called 'put options', that is options to sell at a future date at a currently agreed price. If the market moves in the speculator's favour he or she can buy the securities concerned at the lower market price and use the securities realised by the purchase to exercise the put option and thus make a profit. Because speculators are acting upon their expectations of market movements and the behaviour of the fundamental investors, they are said to be driven by 'adaptive' as opposed to rational expectations.

Arbitrageurs

An arbitrageur is a trader who seeks to exploit the law of one price. This law states that at any given point in time identical assets should command identical prices. If, for example, a market trader notices that at the current rate of exchange, IBM stock is at a different price in London compared with New York, then a simultaneous buy/sell order should achieve a profit at zero risk. By buying in the market where the price is low the action of arbitrageurs will increase demand and the price will rise and by selling in the market where the price is relatively high arbitrageurs will increase supply and force the price down. In their search for zero-risk profits through such contemporaneous transacting, arbitrageurs ensure that mispricing between securities is only transitory. In perfectly competitive markets **arbitrage** opportunities do not exist, but in real markets, providing transaction costs are low, arbitrage is an important mechanism for eliminating mispricing. It is an important presumption when understanding how markets operate and securities are valued that there is an absence of arbitrage opportunities in the pricing process.

Review activity 13.1   Read this extract from an article by business columnist Angus McCrone in the London Evening Standard (16 April 2003).

There are two opinions about arbitrageurs (arbs). The unflattering one is that they are the ticket touts of the financial markets – shadowy and publicity-shy people contributing nothing to the wider economy.

The kinder one is that ever since the fall of self-styled Wall Street arb Ivan Boesky in the late 1980s, they have been given a bad press. The defence case is that arbitrage is a necessary lubricant in the markets, providing liquidity and eliminating anomalies. It is certainly a very common pursuit.

Investment house Schroders has two classes of stock quoted in London – the ordinary shares, and the non voting shares. Dominic Connolly, chief strategist at trading house GNI, says: 'Sometimes, when the stock market roars ahead, the ordinaries shoot up and the non-voters get left behind.' In theory, investors may be able to make money on these occasions by going short of the former and long of the latter, until the two come back into line, but the potential profit margin is very narrow. It is so narrow, in fact, that buying and selling the shares in the conventional way is not an option. The 0.5 per cent stamp duty payable on share purchases would blast a hole in any profit. The only hope is to use contracts for difference (CFDs), a type of derivative that enables investors to go long or short of a share without incurring stamp duty.

Traders also target companies that have share quotes in more than one country such as Royal Dutch/Shell and Unilever, which is also quoted in both London and Amsterdam. The arbitrage is even more difficult with these, because movements in the sterling–euro exchange rate will affect the relative prices. Brian Griffin, chief dealer at CMC/deal4free, says: 'We have seen people trading Shell against Royal Dutch. There may from time to time be a divergence trade available, but you have to get your maths right.' And even if you do, you are likely to find that there is only a very small amount of meat on the bone.

Connolly says: 'There are no risk-free money making schemes available. The market may be inefficient, but it is not that inefficient.'

What do you think is the advantage of arbitrage activity in the examples quoted?

Money and the money markets

Money is the most fundamental security of all. Traditionally, the paper-based currencies of the UK and other western currencies were backed by gold but now the 'asset' which underpins them is the strength of the national economy that issues the currency concerned. The history of money is as long as civilisation. From Roman times the money in circulation in Europe was, until the advent of paper currencies in the late eighteenth century, largely bullion-based, which means it was made from silver or gold. In the UK, the basic unit of currency was the penny introduced by King Offa in around AD 794. The 'pound' was the name given to a bag of 240 silver pennies and it was in 1498 in the reign of Henry VII that the first gold sovereign was struck which had the same bullion value as a 'pound' of pennies. Because gold and silver were uniformly acceptable, currency exchange across Europe was determined purely by the weight of precious metal involved.

Following the emergence of paper money, a system of convertibility into gold was developed which was called the 'gold standard' and formed the basis of international currency exchange until 1913 and again for a short period in the UK between the world wars it was possible to exchange sterling for gold. Since that time, the statement by the Bank of England on UK currency notes that it 'promises to pay the bearer on demand the sum of . . .' has only been worth the paper it is printed on or, to be more precise, the word of the British government that the notes can be exchanged freely within the sterling area of the UK and colonies for that value of goods and services.

How exchange rates are determined

Currencies that are freely tradeable on the foreign exchange (FOREX) markets command a price which changes with the supply and demand for the currency concerned. For example, the ruling rate for converting euros into sterling is 1.4033. What this means is that every pound sterling will buy 1.4033 euros. As this is a sterling exchange rate, the pound is the 'base currency' and the euro the 'counter currency'. Exchange rates can be quoted using the direct method (sometimes called the European method), or by the American or indirect method. The indirect rate is simply the reciprocal of the direct rate.

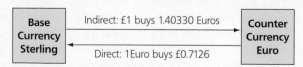

This shows immediate exchange of sterling and euros and is known as the 'spot' rate. It is possible to agree to buy or sell currency at some future date. This is known as a 'forward' contract, and a forward rate will be quoted for delivery of a specified foreign currency on a specified date. The ability to buy or sell foreign currencies on the forward market is very important for companies that need to settle their transactions with overseas suppliers on a particular date and want to avoid the risk of an adverse movement in the currency in the interim period. There are therefore two currency markets:

1. the spot market which is the rate for current transactions in a foreign currency
2. the forward market which is for settlement at a currently agreed rate (the forward rate) usually one month or two months ahead.

When a currency is traded at an exchange rate which is higher in the forward market than in the spot market it is said to be trading at a forward 'premium' and if it is trading at a lower rate it is said to be trading at a forward 'discount'.

There are a number of mechanisms that determine the given exchange rates for a particular currency and the relationship that exists between a given currency's spot rate and its forward rate. The most important factors driving a given country's exchange rate are the strength of its economy, the available supply and demand for capital, and the interest rate policies of its central bank. Two of the most important influences on exchange rates are relative inflation and interest rates.

The law of one price implies that the price of goods in one country should be the same as their price in another. If two economies have identical rates of inflation in prices then, everything else being equal, the exchange rates should be at equilibrium. If the prices in one country go up relative to the other then clearly the law of one price will be broken as it would make sense for producers in the low-inflation economy to sell their goods in the high-inflation economy at what would be a very competitive price. The idea that changes in price levels impact upon the purchasing power of currencies and hence exchange rates forms the basis of the 'purchasing power parity' or PPP theory of exchange rate determination. The evidence suggests that purchasing power parity is an important explanation of interest rates over the longer term.

The second important driver of exchange rates is the relative level of interest rates in the two economies concerned. Generally speaking, high interest rates attract money into an economy, pushing up the exchange rate, whilst low interest rates make that economy less attractive to foreign investors.

There are numerous mechanisms by which the exchange rate adjusts to these factors. Five important mechanisms are known as the 'arbitrage conditions'. Understanding how these mechanisms interrelate allows us to predict how interest rates, inflation rates and currency exchange rates all influence one another in a world where arbitrageurs have eliminated any riskless profits by trading between the economies concerned.

The five arbitrage conditions

1. Purchasing power parity (PPP)

PPP links relative inflation rates to changes in exchange rates. If for example a McDonald's Big Mac burger sells for €1 in Dublin and £1 in the UK this should imply a 1:1 exchange rate or parity. Let us assume for the moment that this is the current rate of exchange. If Irish inflation is expected to rise by 10 per cent and UK inflation by 3 per cent then the price of a Big Mac in one year's time should be €1.10 in Dublin and £1.03 in London. By using the formula we can work out what the spot rate in twelve months time (if using an annual inflation rate) should be:

$$\text{Spot rate (in 12 months)} = \frac{1 + \text{inflation (Counter)}}{1 + \text{inflation (Base)}} \times \text{Spot Rate (current)}$$

The exchange rate against sterling $= 1.1/1.03 \times 1 = €1.068$

Note that this formula uses the indirect rate and reflects the increase in the value of sterling (the low inflation currency) against the euro (the high-inflation currency).

2. Interest rate parity

It is possible to deduce that if one currency has a higher interest rate than another, exchange rates will equilibrate to reflect the relative attractiveness of the currencies. If two currencies are at parity (i.e. a 1: 1 exchange rate) and one of the countries raised its interest rate to a higher rate than the other then arbitrageurs would move in to make a risk-free profit by borrowing at the lower rate of interest in one country and lending at the higher rate in the other. Indeed, it would be possible for the arbitrageur to 'lock in' their profit by selling the currency proceeds of their lending at the higher rate of interest on the forward market in what is known as a 'covered interest arbitrage'.

Interest rate parity is achieved when the premium of the forward exchange rate to the spot rate equals the interest rate differential between the two countries concerned. Because current interest rates are known for borrowing or lending over the forthcoming period of time then interest rate parity gives an exchange rate for a forward contract which does not allow any covered interest arbitrage to occur.

$$\frac{\textbf{Forward Rate (in 12 Months)}}{\textbf{Spot Rate (current)}} = \frac{\textbf{1 + interest rate (counter)}}{\textbf{1 + interest rate (base)}}$$

If the rate of exchange of euros into sterling is 1.4078 euros to the pound and interest rates in the UK are 3.5 per cent compared with 5 per cent in the Eurozone then we would expect to sell at a 'forward premium'. The forward rate is given by the above formula:

Forward rate (12 months) = 1.05/1.035 × 1.4078 = 1.4282 euros/pound

3. Fisher effect

You have already met the idea that if you want to convert a **real rate** of interest to a **nominal rate** then the following formula is what is required (see Chapter 5):

1 + Nominal interest rate = (1 + Real interest rate) × (1 + Inflation rate)

If we assume that the real rate of interest is the same in different countries then

$$\frac{\textbf{1 + Nominal interest rate (counter)}}{\textbf{1 + Nominal interest rate (base)}} = \frac{\textbf{1 + Real interest rate}}{\textbf{1 + Real interest rate}} \times \frac{\textbf{1 + Inflation rate (counter)}}{\textbf{1 + Inflation rate (base)}}$$

Cancelling the effect of the real rate of interest this formula simplifies to:

$$\frac{\textbf{1 + Nominal interest rate (counter)}}{\textbf{1 + Nominal interest rate (base)}} = \frac{\textbf{1 + Inflation rate (counter)}}{\textbf{1 + Inflation rate (base)}}$$

This says that high inflation is associated with high interest rates. So, if US inflation is 10 per cent and Irish inflation 3 per cent, and Irish interest rates are also 3 per cent then US interest rates should also be 10 per cent.

4. The international Fisher effect

If we put the interest rate parity and the Fisher effect formulas together we get a third formula that links nominal interest rates and inflation rates.

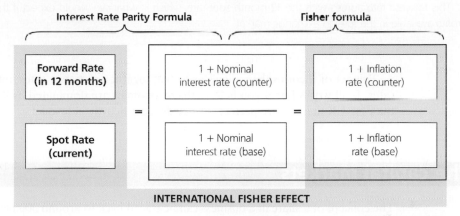

5. The equivalence between expected spot rate and forward rate

This is intuitively straightforward. If the FOREX markets are efficient in the way that currencies are priced then the forward rate should be an unbiased predictor of the expected spot rate. We get this by combining the results of the purchasing power parity and the international Fisher effect. The ratio of the forward to the current spot rate is equal to the ratio of the 12-month spot rate to the current spot rate.

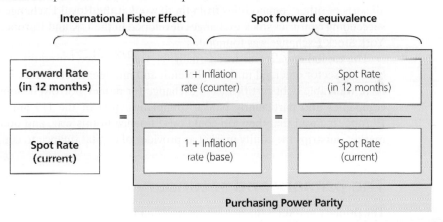

Financial realities The current dollar exchange rate with the pound is 1.5 dollars to the pound. Inflation in the US is 4 per cent and 2.5 per cent in the UK. Interest rates in the UK are 3.5 per cent. What is the predicted spot rate in 12 months, the current US interest rate, and the 12-month forward rate?

Note that throughout we use the indirect rate of exchange which gives the number of dollars that can be purchased with one pound

- Spot rates and inflation rates are linked by the PPP formula.

  Spot rate (in 12 months) = 1.04/1.025 × 1.5 = $1.5220 to the pound

- The current US interest rate is given by the Fisher formula:

  US interest rate = (1.04/1.025 × 1.035) − 1 = 5.01 per cent

● The 12-month forward exchange rate is given by the International Fisher effect formula:

Forward rate = 1.04/1.025 × 1.5 = $1.5220 to the pound

This forward rate agrees with the 12-month spot rate, which is what we would expect if there is no arbitrage profits available in the foreign exchange market.

This set of theories then allows us to link together exchange rates, inflation and interest rates. It all works fine if you believe that economies are dominated by tradeable goods and the FOREX markets are perfect. The evidence is heavily in favour!

The capital markets

The concept of a share in a business can be traced back to around 3000 BC when contracts of property ownership were commonplace. The Assyrians (*c.* 2000 BC) used written partnership agreements that in one case lasted for up to four years and where there was a profit-sharing agreement. The concept of the company was established in Roman times, but the modern idea of formally tradeable shares did not arise in England until the formation of the merchant companies in the Elizabethan era. One such company, the Muscovy, was established under a Royal Charter in 1555 to exploit the trade routes to Russia. The financing of the ventures of the Muscovy was arranged through the issue of shares that were freely tradeable along with all sorts of other commodities from tin to wool at the Royal Exchange in London. Over the succeeding centuries stock exchanges developed in the UK and Europe, and in 1772 the New York Stock Exchange was founded.

The capital market was traditionally the trading place for equity shares. However, as the banking sector emerged in the eighteenth and nineteenth centuries, governments started to issue tradeable debt certificates in exchange for money borrowed from wealthy individuals, companies and particularly banks. Companies, first in the US and then in the UK and Europe, realised that they too could raise finance in this way, and now the corporate bond market outstrips the equity market as provider of capital finance to companies.

The primary and secondary capital markets

The primary market is the market for new finance. If a company with an existing listing wishes to raise new equity, for example, it will seek the assistance of a financial institution (a bank, merchant bank or other finance house) that will arrange and underwrite the new issue. The primary markets consist therefore of three 'players' – the firms that are seeking new finance, investors who will ultimately provide it, and a financial institution that acts as an intermediary.

Secondary markets came into existence because of the conflict of interest between investors who may wish to liquidate their investment and firms that need finance for the longer term. The secondary capital and money markets give investors the opportunity to buy and sell securities, thus being able to liquidate their holdings as necessary and without recourse to the company that originally made the issue. The secondary markets are characterised by:

● a regulated exchange, such as the London Stock Exchange, which governs the way deals are done, provides a mechanism for matching together buyers and sellers of securities and arranges settlement of the transactions when they are complete

Exhibit 13.1 The primary and secondary capital markets

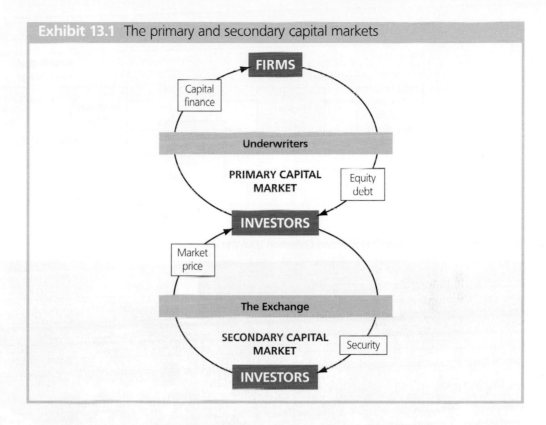

- market makers who are individuals licensed to trade on the exchange buying and selling the securities concerned
- a trading system.

Prior to 1986, the London Stock Market consisted of a trading floor with 'booths' run by a stock jobber whose job was to buy and sell shares and other corporate stock at the request of stock brokers who placed orders on behalf of their clients.

In 1986 the system was changed in what is known as the 'Big Bang' and the London Exchange converted to a computer/telephone system. In Exhibit 13.2 we show the sequence of actions that will occur if an investor wishes to buy or sell shares. First, the investor contacts their stock broker who will for an established client accept telephone or Internet orders. The broker will normally have access to a trading system which either does the trade automatically if the buy or sell order is for one of the top 350 companies using SETS – (Stock Exchange Automated Trading Service), or through the Stock Exchange Automated Quotations System (SEAQ) if the services are required of a market maker. SETS matches buy and sell orders at specified prices automatically whilst SEAQ reports the prices put in by the market makers for buy or sell orders. Once the transaction has been accepted by SETS or the market maker the broker is notified and the details of the trade reported to the Stock Exchange.

 Financial market securities are traded in one of two ways:

- 'over the counter' (OTC), which means that securities are bought and sold between individuals directly or via a broker
- market-traded, where securities are bought and sold through a recognised exchange.

Exhibit 13.2 Trading equities in the UK market

The London Stock Exchange © Hoberman Collection UK/Alamy

Equity capital

Equity capital is the most familiar form of capital with prices of shares and their movements featuring on daily news bulletins. The fortunes of the equity market are tracked moment by moment by a range of indices such as the FT 100 in the UK or the Dow Jones Index in the US. As discussed in Chapter 6, equity shareholders have certain rights which can be summarised as follows:

● the right to appoint directors and an auditor at their company annual general meeting
● the right to receive a dividend if they are declared by their directors as payable

- the right, if sufficient agree, to put the business into liquidation
- the right to receive all information made publicly available and in particular to receive the annual report and accounts
- the right to the residue of the firm's assets after all claims have been paid in the event of a liquidation.

Companies raise equity capital through a variety of mechanisms: they can raise capital through a new issue direct to the public, or via a placement with a financial institution. Alternatively they may go to their existing shareholders and make a rights issue where the shares are offered at a discount on their existing market price. To raise a rights issue a company must first get the agreement of its members. It then issues a Letter of Allotment telling each investor how many shares they have been allotted, the price they will have to pay to take them and the date by which they must sign and return the letter to the company if they wish to take up the offer.

Individuals can hold shares in a variety of ways and indeed few individuals realise the extent to which their personal wealth is held in the form of equity investments:

- Direct share ownership where the individual has purchased shares in companies to form a personal portfolio. Later we will describe the way in which the risk in this simplest form of equity holding is measured.
- Indirect share ownership through unit trust (UK) or mutual fund (US) investment. A unit trust is a fund consisting of many shares managed by a large institution. The unit trust may be 'actively managed', where the intention is to earn better-than-average performance by specialising in particular industrial sectors, countries or sections of the market (value funds, growth funds, etc.). Other unit trusts are 'passively managed' in that they are designed to replicate the performance of a particular index. Whether actively or passively managed both types of fund are designed to give the investor the benefit of holding a large portfolio of shares without the problems of stock selection.
- Equity by proxy. Many financial products, such as endowment policies that many individuals use to finance their house purchase and pension funds, have substantial parts of their available funds invested in the equity market.

Debt capital

Originally, the simplest way for a company to raise debt finance was to borrow money from a bank. However, following the Wall Street Crash in the United States in 1929, many companies decided to circumvent the then discredited banking system and instead raise debt finance from individuals and institutions through the issue of debt certificates. This method of raising finance had been used by governments through the issue of treasury stock and other types of bonds.

FYI   Bills and bonds

Very short-dated debt, that is debt with a term to maturity of less than twelve months, is known as 'bills'. Bills are money-market instruments; they may be coupon-bearing, that is they carry a fixed rate of interest, but more usually they are issued at a 'discount'. That means that the bill is issued at a price which is lower than the value at which it will be redeemed. The difference between the issue price and the redemption value is the return to the holder. A bond is a debt instrument that has a term to maturity of greater than one year and is regarded as a capital-market security.

Companies followed suit, however, the principal difference between their issues and those of governments being one of risk. Debt issued by the governments of the major world economies is free of 'default risk'; this is not the case with company debt. To deal with this problem a number of rating agencies have been established that assess the creditworthiness of individual companies. So when a company seeks to make a debt issue it will pay a rating agency such as Standard and Poors or Moody's, which are the two best known, to rate its financial health on a scale:

Exhibit 13.3

Standard and Poors	Moody's	
Investment Grade Bonds		
AAA; AA+; AAA−	Aaa; Aaa1; Aaa2; Aaa3	Best quality: virtually zero default risk
AA; AA−; A+	Aa; Aa1; Aa2; Aa3	Excellent quality: very little default risk
A; A−; BBB+	A; A1; A2; A3	Rated 'good': minimal risk
BBB; BBB−; BB+	Baa; Baa1; Baa2; Baa3	Medium rating: low but clear risk
Speculative or 'Junk Bonds'		
BB; BB−; B+	Ba; Ba1; Ba2; Ba3	Marginal grade
B; B−; CCC+	B; B1; B2; B3	Significant exposure to default risk
CCC; CCC−; CC+	Caa; Caa1; Caa2; Caa3	Considerable exposure to default risk
CC; CC−; C+	Ca; Ca1; Ca2; Ca3	Very high risk
C	C	Very high likelihood of failure

It is very unusual for Standard and Poors or Moody's to disagree on the credit status of a company.

Once the status of the company is established it can then proceed to offer its bonds on the market. The issue will normally be organised by one of the large finance houses (called a 'lead manager') such as Merrill Lynch, Morgan Stanley or Nomura Securities.

Government debt

Governments finance shortfalls between their revenues from taxes and their spending by borrowing. The commonest way for them to do this is through a regular auction of debt where they invite the financial institutions to bid a price that they are prepared to pay for the security being offered. In the UK, government securities are normally issued at a set 'par' or nominal value of £100 or multiples of £100 and a set rate of interest, the 'coupon rate', with a promised redemption date when the holder will be repaid the par value. UK government bonds are known as 'gilts' because of the gold edging which used to be placed around the certificate in times past. In the US, government bonds are known as 'Govies' by traders.

The common titles of British gilt-edged securities are 'Treasury', 'Conversion', and 'Exchequer'. Thus a Treasury quote of '5 per cent 2020' would therefore be a gilt-edged contract with an interest payment of 5 per cent maturing in 2020.

Exhibit 13.4 UK Gilts: cash market

May 20	Price £	Red Yield	Day	Change in Yield Week	Change in Yield Month	Change in Yield Year	52 week High	52 week Low	Amount £m
Tr 6½pc '03	101.68	3.37	–	−.05	–	−.30	103.51	101.68	8 095
Tr 5pc '04	101.77	3.26	−.01	−.12	−.11	−.38	102.48	100.21	7 504
Tr 8½pc '05	112.16	3.47	–	−.13	−.23	−.49	113.51	110.51	10 486
Tr 7½pc '06	112.85	3.61	–	−.14	.27	.47	114.02	108.93	11 807
Tr 7¼pc '07	114.62	3.72	−.01	.14	−.30	−.45	115.70	109.25	11 103
Tr 5pc '08	105.42	3.75	−.01	−.14	−.30	−.44	106.11	99.48	14 221
Tr 5¾pc '09	110.61	3.90	−.02	−.13	−.31	−.37	111.39	102.62	8 937
Tr 6¼pc '10	114.65	3.98	−.02	−.13	−.30	−.34	115.44	106.21	4 958
Cn 9pc Ln '11	134.37	4.01	−.02	−.13	−.32	−.36	135.43	126.43	5 396
Tr 5pc '12	106.88	4.06	.03	−.14	−.33	−.31	107.31	97.79	13 346
Tr 5pc '14	107.37	4.17	−.03	−.14	−.32	−.24	107.92	100.70	8 050
Tr 8pc '15	136.88	4.19	−.03	−.14	−.32	−.24	137.70	125.69	7 377
Tr 8pc '21	145.79	4.32	.04	−.16	−.29	−.16	146.78	132.78	16 741
Tr 5pc '25	108.96	4.36	−.04	−.15	−.27	−.12	110.16	97.49	10 422
Tr 6pc '28	125.14	4.36	.04	−.16	−.26	−.10	127.04	112.19	11 756
Tr 4¼pc '32	98.36	4.35	−.04	−.16	−.26	−.09	100.11	87.12	13 829
War Ln 3½pc	78.98	–	–	–	–	–	80.60	65.74	1 939
TR 2½pc	55.75	–	–	–	–	–	56.01	45.82	493

Gilts are:

- commonly issued at a par value in units of £100 nominal but sometimes in higher denominations.
- with a fixed coupon rate of interest, and
- redeemed at their par value at any time between two stated dates.

Gilts are described as follows:

- 'shorts' with terms to redemption of less than 5 years
- 'mediums' with terms to redemption of between 5 years and 15 years, and
- 'longs' with terms in excess of 15 years.

Exhibit 13.4 is a list of the prices of gilts of different terms to maturity.

The efficient markets hypothesis

Since their emergence in the 18th century, the major stock markets of the world have grown in sophistication and in the volume and value of shares that they trade. Regulation over the centuries has developed to prevent abuse within the market. It is impossible for any single trader to 'corner the market' in any given company's shares by buying such a large volume of any stock that they can control its price. It is also illegal for any investor to take advantage of insider information.

Such regulation is designed to prevent too much market power falling into one person or institution's hands. Publicly available information is also very cheap to acquire. Companies must make full disclosure of their financial information at regular intervals and are obliged to release information impartially. There is also an army of analysts, newspaper reporters and other market experts waiting to explain every nuance of information flooding into the market from the news media and from companies themselves. Finally, the transactions costs on trading in equities are low. In economic terms the barriers to entry and exit from the market for traders in capital market securities are also low.

What all this means in practice is that the stock market in most securities, most of the time, is as close to the economic ideal of a perfectly competitive market where all investors are price takers and where no one can trade a sufficiently large volume of shares to control the price. This, coupled with the free availability of information means that such a market is likely to be highly efficient in the way that it responds to new information. As soon as an item of news impacting upon a particular company is made public we would expect at least some traders to realise its significance for a given security and trade on the basis of that information. There will be some who will regard the information as more important than it is, and some who regard it as less, but given that there are a sufficiently large number of traders the 'mispricers' will cancel one another out on the average and the core of traders making a rational price judgement will determine the size and speed of the corresponding price movement.

Efficient capital markets are vital for the efficient operation of a capital based economy. If it were the case that the market for (say) equities did not fully reflect all information relevant to the companies concerned then share prices would not fairly reflect the intrinsic value of the companies. Companies that are undervalued by the market will have to issue more shares than would otherwise be necessary in order to raise new capital and companies that are overvalued raise less. As we will see later, the cost of capital as revealed by market prices would not reflect the true cost of capital given the firm's risk and as a result misallocation of capital resources would occur on a grand scale. The potential for economic damage would be high and so ensuring efficiency through a variety of mechanisms is of primary concern to governments and regulators.

There is substantial evidence that price adjustments following new information being released to the market are extremely rapid, which is not surprising given the very low transactions costs involved in trading. However, because price adjustments are accomplished within moments of a new release of information the overwhelming majority of investors will react too slowly to take advantage of that information.

What we have described here is a process whereby the expectations of traders (i.e. their beliefs about the value of new information) are being formed rationally. The market is being driven by what are termed 'rational expectations'. If this is true, and the market is absorbing information into prices as soon as it is released, then we would expect the current price of a share to be a fair value of what is known in the market relevant to the company concerned.

In the absence of any new information price movements are likely to be driven purely by random effects. The best prediction of the future share price will be the current share price and the price movement will follow what is termed a 'random walk'. All the information contained in past share prices must be represented in the current price, so it is not possible by looking at charts of past share prices to predict the movement of prices in the future. This is what is known as 'the **efficient markets hypothesis** in its weak form'. The evidence that has been collected on the statistical properties of the major stock markets and on the ability of technical analysts (i.e. those who use charts to attempt to predict future price movements) to make excess returns over the longer run all leads to the conclusion that the market is highly weak-form-efficient.

But what about new information coming to the market? Again the evidence is that share prices adjust extremely rapidly and that analysts who rely on publicly available information cannot earn a rate of return higher than one would predict on average for holding a randomly selected portfolio of investments of equivalent risk. Reaction studies investigating the price impact of news events point to the fact that the market is highly efficient at processing publicly available information. The stock market is therefore believed to be efficient in the 'semi-strong' form.

The final question we might ask is how efficient the market is in pricing insider information, that is information that is not generally publicly available. There are obvious problems in researching this issue, as few investors will willingly admit to insider trading. However, there have been a number of studies of the performance of fund managers. These individuals try to win superior performance for their investors through specialising in particular markets and we would expect this group of traders to have systematic access to better information than the average market investor. In general, fund managers do not appear to be able to win consistently better returns than one would expect for the risk they are carrying. Indeed, the evidence suggests that they tend to under-perform and that their propensity to buy and sell shares in the search for value leads them into much higher transactions and other management costs than would be the case if they simply adopted a buy-and-hold strategy. The gradual realisation amongst regulators and professional fund managers that they do not perform in picking shares as well as a monkey throwing a dart at the *Financial Times* or *Wall Street Journal* has undermined confidence in this industry. As a result, there has been a large movement to what are called 'index or tracker funds', which are simply designed to replicate average market performance as represented by a specific market index such as the FTSE 100 or FTSE All Shares Index (ASI).

The performance of fund managers

In 1997 Mark Carhart at the University of Southern California published a study of mutual fund performance of some 300 funds over the period 1962 to 1996. This study confirmed early empirical work by Michael Jensen in 1969 that came to an almost identical conclusion. Fund managers do not on average perform as well as one would expect from a simple random stock-selection process. These studies have taken care to eliminate 'survivor bias' from the analysis. Survivor bias creates the illusion that funds are more successful than they actually are – only when the performance of the failures are also included does the true picture emerge.

This research into the efficient markets hypothesis in its 'strong form' has demonstrated a number of interesting facts:

- It is not obvious that exceptional market expertise leads to superior market performance.
- Simple buy-and-hold strategies are likely to be just as effective as more sophisticated investment techniques.
- This says nothing about the use of secret information by the unscrupulous – but that is insider dealing and the penalties if the perpetrators are caught are very high and quite likely to outweigh any gains that may be made.

Are the markets really efficient?

Over many years a number of 'anomalies' have been observed in the market which appear to be contrary to the predictions of the efficient markets hypothesis. The 'January effect', day-of-the-week effects and so on have all been shown at one time or other to offer a higher-than-expected return. The January effect, for example, showed that in most years if investors had bought into the market at the end of December and sold at the end of January they would have made most of the return to be earned over the year as a whole. Similarly smaller high-growth stocks appear to do better than we would expect, and then there is the problem of 'bubbles' and 'crashes' which many argue are incompatible with an efficient market.

In October 1987, over one third of market values were lost in a crash in prices where the market went into free-fall over a period of three days. This has led some researchers to abandon the idea that market traders act rationally and instead they have turned their attention to what is termed 'behavioural finance', i.e. trying to explain market behaviour by appeals to theoretical work in human decision-making. The problem with this type of research is twofold: first, the large majority of anomalies reported in the literature are caused by weaknesses in the research design or statistical problems in the analysis of the results. Others are transitory and yet others, whilst appearing to persist over time, do not offer sufficient return advantage to overcome the transactions costs in exploiting them. However, the biggest problem is that behavioural approaches, whilst useful at explaining individual behaviour, miss the fact that markets, and the prices that result, represent an averaging process, where one person's exuberant beliefs are balanced by another's pessimism. Overall, the 'idiosyncratic' beliefs of investors are balanced out and a core of informed, well justified beliefs emerges to dominate the pricing mechanism. Mark Rubinstein, an eminent finance academic from the University of California quotes a famous case to make the above point (Rubinstein, 2000):

The securities market is not the only example for which the aggregation of information across different individuals leads to the truth. At 3.15 p.m. on May 27, 1968, the submarine USS *Scorpion* was officially declared missing with all 99 men aboard. She was somewhere within a 20-mile-wide circle in the Atlantic, far below implosion depth. Five months later, after extensive search efforts, her location within that circle was still undetermined. John Craven, the Navy's top deep-water scientist, had all but given up. As a last gasp, he asked a group of submarine and salvage experts to bet on the probabilities of different scenarios that could have occurred. Averaging their responses, he pinpointed the exact location (within 220 yards) where the missing sub was found.

But, you might argue, 'if the efficient markets hypothesis is true how did Warren Buffet, Jim Slater and others make fortunes on the stock market?' The most compelling answer is the simplest one: luck. To explain how this comes about here is the tale of the lucky monkey, a story which originated at the University of Manchester in the late 1970s:

There were sixteen monkeys invited to play the stock market. All they had to do was predict whether the price would go up or down the following day. A modest investment and they were off. At the end of the first day eight had won and eight had lost. The next day the eight winners played again, and then there were four. By the end of the fourth day there was just one lucky monkey who had won every time he played. 'How did you do it?', the market pundits asked. 'Did you use the best theories and evidence about how firms and the capital markets operate?', they enquired. 'No', said the lucky monkey. 'I don't believe in all that nonsense – I did it my way.' Before long that lucky monkey was being feted and celebrated as the greatest investor of our generation. Books were written and shops filled with such titles as *The Lucky Monkey Way* and *The Lucky Monkey Guide to Investment*. But how had he done it? How could any investor do it? The answer is: luck. When there are hundreds of thousands of trades occurring on a daily basis across the market there will be some lucky individuals who have always won the game and they will be fabulously rich and influential as a result. It doesn't alter the fact that their opinions on the stock market or their views on the cost of capital are about as relevant as reading *The Lucky Monkey Way*. Understanding the risks involved and the return that can as a result be expected is, for the overwhelming majority of investors, the best route to a more modest fortune.

Return and risk

Throughout our discussion so far we have talked about return and risk without defining what we mean. Return is often talked about in terms of the dividend yield on a share. However, return should also include the capital gain to give a fuller definition of the return on equity:

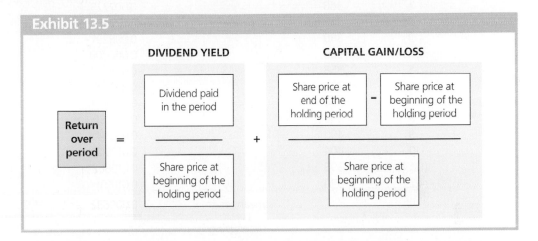

Exhibit 13.5

We can measure return over any time interval we wish: a year, a month, a week or indeed a day.

Exhibit 13.6 shows twelve-month end prices for a particular share. Each month-end we apply the above formula to get the return over the previous month, noting that months 5 and 12 also include a dividend payment. So, for month 5 the return would be given as:

$$\text{Return} = \frac{5}{380} + \frac{358 - 380}{380} = -4.473 \text{ per cent}$$

At the end of the series we can record the mean or average return, which turns out to be 0.9632 per cent (Exhibit 13.6).

To annualise that percentage we recognise that the rate for a year equals the monthly rate compounded 12 times (as each month's return is based upon the previous month). Therefore the annual equivalent rate is:

$$\text{AER} = (1 + \text{average monthly return})^{12} - 1 = (1 + 0.009632)^{12} - 1 = 0.121911$$
or 12.1911 per cent

The equivalent annual rate formula is rather useful and well worth remembering:

$$\textbf{Equivalent annual rate} = (1 + \textbf{monthly rate})^{12} - 1$$

So, for example, you are quoted 1.8 per cent per month for borrowing on your credit card bill. It doesn't sound very much. But, if we apply the formula the shocking truth is revealed:

$$\text{AER} = 1.018^{12} - 1$$
$$= .2387$$
$$\equiv 23.87\%$$

Of course, you can use the same formula for finding the AER from daily or weekly returns by substituting the daily or monthly rate and powering up by 365 or 52 as the case may be. You

Exhibit 13.6 Calculating the average return

	month end price	dividend	return decimal	return percentage
0	367			
1	366		−0.002725	−0.2725
2	378		0.032787	3.2787
3	380		0.005291	0.5291
4	380		0.000000	0.0000
5	358	5	−0.044737	−4.4737
6	325		−0.092179	−9.2179
7	350		0.076923	7.6923
8	390		0.114286	11.4286
9	400		0.025641	2.5641
10	404		0.010000	1.0000
11	396		−0.019802	−1.9802
12	390	10	0.010101	1.0101
		mean return =	0.009632	0.9632
		annualised		12.1911

can also reverse the formula to get the equivalent monthly, weekly or daily rate from an annual rate. For a monthly rate the formula above rearranges to:

$$\text{Equivalent monthly rate} = \sqrt[12]{(1 + \text{annual rate})} - 1$$

The riskiness of this share's returns is given by the standard deviation of its returns, which on the basis of monthly returns = 5.2851 per cent (use your spreadsheet to calculate this). Given a monthly standard deviation we can obtain the annual equivalent by multiplying by the square root of the number of periods in a year (12 in this case):

$$\text{Standard deviation} = \text{monthly standard deviation} \times \sqrt{12}$$

$$= 0.052851 \times \sqrt{12} = 0.18308 = 18.308\%$$

The proof of this is given in Ryan (2006), *Corporate Finance and Valuation*. Risk, therefore is the standard deviation of a share's returns. Standard deviation is a standard measure of the spread of a distribution and, to a good degree of approximation, share returns, using long runs of data over 30 years or more, are normally distributed. A normal distribution is the uniform bell-shaped curve that describes many social and natural processes.

A walkthrough of portfolio theory

Early portfolio theory using a statistical concept of risk was first developed by Harry Markowitz in the 1950s. **Markowitz portfolio theory** won him the Nobel Prize for his work in 1990 and he is regarded as one of the originators of the modern theory of finance. His work was highly mathematical but his theoretical insights formed the basis for modern investment theory and the management of risk. Here are six intuitive steps that will take you to his insight:

1. If share returns are normally distributed then the average return (return) and standard deviation (risk) are all we need to know in order to describe the market performance of

the security concerned. Remember also that investors are rational and risk-averse: for a given level of risk they will choose the investment that gives the maximum average return and for a given level of average return they will look for the investment that gives the lower level of risk.

2. If we locate two securities (say British Airways and easyJet) on the risk–return graph we can choose to invest in one or the other or indeed a combination. The risk and return of any particular combination will not always lie directly between the two securities concerned but may well lie on a curve the shape of which will be dictated by how the two share returns correlate with one another. Where the changing levels of return are negatively correlated the risk of a combination could be considerably less than either share depending on the degree to which fluctuations in one security's return, over time, 'cancel out' fluctuations in the other.

3. If instead of looking at just two shares we look at all shares and other risky securities in the capital market, and every portfolio that can be constructed from any of those shares, a set will emerge which describes the limits of investment possibility in the capital market.

4. The rational investor will try to move to the extreme edge of this 'global set of investment opportunities', as shown at 4 in the exhibit, by choosing a portfolio of investments that gives them the optimum level of return for a given level of risk. Where exactly the investor

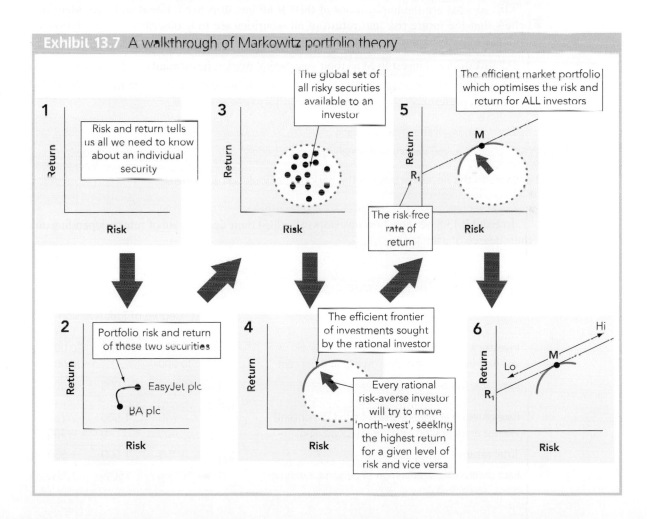

Exhibit 13.7 A walkthrough of Markowitz portfolio theory

will position themself on the 'efficient frontier' is dependent upon the degree of risk they are prepared to accept.

5. If the investor can also borrow or lend money at a risk-free rate of interest one portfolio will dominate all others. In (5) this portfolio lies on the line extended from the risk-free rate of interest (R_f) and just touching the efficient frontier at 'M'. The portfolio at that point M is termed the **efficient market portfolio**.

6. If an investor is happy to take exactly the level of risk at M then he or she can simply invest in that portfolio. If the investor would prefer less risk they can put part of their investment into M and the balance on a deposit account at the risk-free rate of interest (R). This is termed a 'lending portfolio' and represents the most efficient way of investing for low (Lo) risk. If on the other hand the investor is willing to take more risk than that of M, he or she can borrow money at the risk free rate and put all of borrowing plus their own capital into M. This is the most efficient strategy for achieving a high-risk (Hi), high-return portfolio.

The effect of either strategy is that the rational risk-averse investor need not concern themselves with trying to 'cherry-pick' individual shares or indeed custom-building portfolios to suit their risk preferences. Rather, they invest in just one portfolio (M) and adjust to their optimum risk/return position by borrowing or lending at the risk-free rate of return.

OK, so what are the implications of this? If all investors are rational and have identical beliefs that the future risk and return of all securities are fully described by the statistical evidence of past risk and return then:

1. All investors will invest in M as their sole capital market investment.

2. They will use the money market, borrowing or lending at a risk-free rate to optimise their own risk preferences.

Review activity 13.2   Can you identify all the assumptions embedded in the Markowitz portfolio model?

✓ Check the answers to this Review activity at the back of the book (see page 525).

In Exhibit 13.8 we show how investors can adjust their desired rate of return depending on their degree of aversion to risk:

Exhibit 13.8 The Markowitz approach to capital allocation

	Degree of Risk Aversion		
	High	Neutral	Low
Investor's private funds	20 000	20 000	20 000
less Risk-free Deposit or (Borrowing) at 4 per cent	10 000		− 10 000
Investable funds	10 000	20 000	30 000
Rate of return at average market rate (7.5 per cent)	750	1 500	2 250
Interest on deposited funds or on (borrowing)	400	0	−400
Total return	1 150	1 500	1 850
Rate of return as a proportion of personal investment	5.75%	7.50%	9.25%

This 'separation' of the problem of which portfolio to choose from the problem of how to satisfy individual risk preferences is known as 'the Markowitz separation theorem'.

Finally, M will be a portfolio which is owned by all investors. It must by definition contain a mix of all securities in the market because if any security is not included it would not have a market price.

You may argue that the assumptions implicit in Markowitz portfolio theory are unlikely to be perfectly realised in practice. Not all investors will behave rationally, the market is not perfectly efficient at pricing information and there undoubtedly are transactions costs and taxes! However, what matters is not whether a theory's assumptions are realistic but whether, for all its abstraction, it points to some important implications. The proof of the pudding is in the eating, so let us see how this particular pudding tastes in practice.

The capital asset pricing model

One outcome of this theoretical development was the **capital asset pricing model** (CAPM). This model is based upon Markowitz portfolio theory, but instead of measuring portfolio risk in terms of combinations of individual securities this model measures risk relative to a single benchmark of performance. Because all rational investors choose M, then this is the obvious candidate for such a benchmark. The capital asset pricing model allows us to measure the average return we can expect for holding any individual security as part of our investment in the efficient market portfolio. It is a simple model. Indeed, some would say simple enough to win a Nobel Prize for its originator, William Sharpe. However, for all its simplicity it offers an extremely useful theoretical tool for calculating the return required by investors and hence the rate of return that management should use in discounting capital investment projects for businesses financed purely by equity capital.

When looking at the individual security from the point of view of Markowitz portfolio theory we can see that there are two 'risk drivers' at work. In other words the volatility of a share's returns is derived from two sources:

- **Market (or systematic) risk** This is the risk which is caused by market-wide phenomena such as varying interest rates, exchange rates, inflation, taxes and regulations. All securities will be influenced by these factors to some extent or other, and if an investor holds the efficient market portfolio M alone, they will be carrying a standard load of this risk. It is impossible to get rid of this risk by increasing diversification. All that happens as new shares are added to the portfolio is that its market risk approaches the average level.

- **Firm-specific (or unsystematic) risk** This is the component of a security's risk which is unique to that firm: it may be because the management is exceptionally good or exceptionally bad, or because it loses a customer through bankruptcy or indeed for any one of the legion of reasons that cause returns to depart from the average and cannot be explained by market-wide effects. Generally, investing in a well-diversified portfolio of different shares should eliminate the majority of this type of risk through the 'swings and roundabouts' effect. Indeed, a risk-averse investor who efficiently diversifies as Markowitz portfolio theory suggests should not carry any of this risk. Consequently, the returns on shares in an efficient market will not compensate the investor for holding this type of risk.

In Exhibit 13.9 we show how the firm-specific, non-systematic risk declines in importance in a portfolio as the number of shares in the portfolio is increased. The average exposure to market risk soon stabilises as portfolio size is increased, tending towards the average we would expect if we held the market portfolio overall.

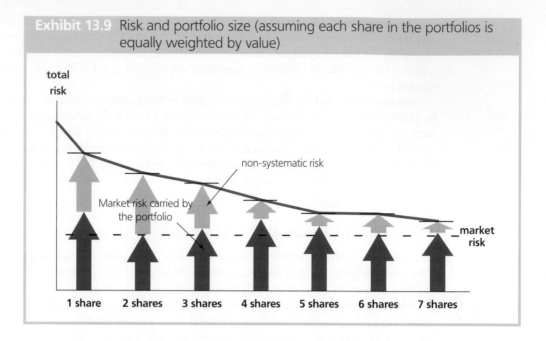

Exhibit 13.9 Risk and portfolio size (assuming each share in the portfolios is equally weighted by value)

If efficient markets do not offer any additional reward to the investor for holding firm-specific risk then the average return on holding any additional security will consist of the following:

The risk-free rate of return (R_f)

This must logically be the minimum level of expected average return obtained or no sensible investor would choose to invest in the security concerned but would put all their investment into a risk-free deposit account or, more likely, purchase risk-free government bonds.

An equity risk premium

This is the premium offered by the market for the degree of market risk to which the security is exposed. If an investor chooses to invest solely in the efficient market portfolio then the premium they will get is the difference between the average rate of return on that portfolio (R_M) and the risk-free rate (R_f):

$$\text{Equity risk premium} = \text{Expected return from holding the efficient market portfolio (M)} - \text{Risk-free rate of return } (R_f)$$

In the next section we discuss how to measure these values but, assuming for the moment that the risk-free rate is 4 per cent per annum and the expected return on holding the market is 7.5 per cent, this would mean that there is a 3.5 per cent equity risk premium.

Overall, therefore, the expected return for holding the efficient market portfolio or any security which had identical exposure to market risk is given by:

This you may think is obvious – and it is. However, the next step is to generalise this to any security which has an exposure to market-driven risk which is different from that of the efficient market portfolio. This was accomplished by William Sharpe following considerable mathematical analysis and is as follows:

The factor β (**beta**) measures the degree of exposure of a given share to market risk. Three situations can hold for an individual security:

- $\beta = 1$. This is the situation already discussed, where the degree of exposure of the security and the efficient market portfolio are the same.
- $\beta > 1$. This is where the security is more exposed than the market (a beta value of 1.2, for example, would indicate that the security concerned is exposed to 20 per cent more market-driven risk than the efficient market portfolio).
- $\beta < 1$. This is where the security is less exposed than the market (a beta value of 0.8, for example, would indicate that the security concerned is exposed to 20 per cent less market-driven risk than the efficient market portfolio).

Using symbols for convenience, we show this relationship formally as follows:

$$E(R_i) = R_f + \beta_i(E(R_M) - R_f)$$

$E(R_i)$ and $E(R_M)$ are the average returns investors expect on an individual security (labelled with a subscript 'i') and the market respectively.

This formula is the capital asset pricing model or CAPM for short. CAPM has proven to be one of the most powerful models in the theory of finance and, although it does not perfectly predict the relationship between the actual returns on a security and its exposure to market risk as measured by beta, it is a reasonable approximation for most applications.

An important implication of the capital asset pricing model is that it predicts that there will be a *linear relationship* between the expected return on an individual share ($E(R_i)$) and its market risk factor.

In Exhibit 13.10 we show the security market line, which is the line drawn from the capital asset pricing model equating the expected return on the individual security with its market risk as measured by beta. The cross-over point with the expected return axis is the risk-free rate and the slope is the equity risk premium. We have shown four cases:

- Case a is a security which carries 20 per cent more risk than the market but is producing a return predicted by CAPM. This security is correctly priced in the model's terms.
- Case b is a security with 20 per cent less risk than the market but again is producing a return in line with that predicted by the CAPM. Again this security is correctly priced.

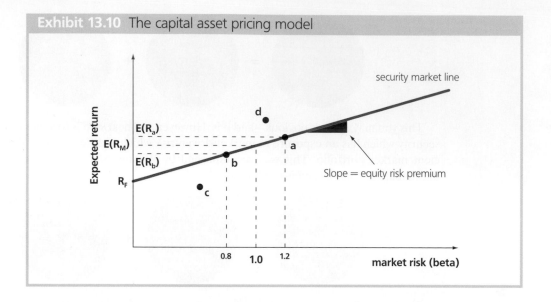

Exhibit 13.10 The capital asset pricing model

- Case c has a lower-than-expected return than would be predicted by CAPM. Given that return and current price are inversely related, CAPM reveals that this security is overpriced.
- Case d has a higher-than-expected return and so is underpriced.

Estimating the inputs to the CAPM

With the capital asset pricing model, as with all models, there are two difficult problems to overcome:

1. Does the model fully specify the 'reality' it is attempting to describe? The CAPM has been subjected to numerous tests of its empirical validity. Studies show that although the risk–return trade-off is linear, the slope of the relationship is not as the model predicts. In practical application the misspecification error is within the bounds of 'usability', and competing models either ignore the problem of risk altogether or are too complex.

2. Finding the appropriate data to input into the model.

The CAPM requires three data elements, two of which can be readily derived or estimated and one of which is more problematic:

The risk-free rate of return

In theory this is the rate of return where all uncertainty has been removed. In practice the best approximation is the rate of return on a very short dated government security. In the UK, the one month Treasury Bill rate is 5.75 per cent. Some sources argue that the long-term bond rate should be used as this is more representative of the investment duration of firms. The problem with long-term rates is that the real return on the bond will be dependent upon rates of future inflation which have considerable uncertainty attached to them. Short-term rates do not have this inflation risk and are therefore closer to the theoretical ideal that the model's assumptions demand. In practice, very short term rates can be difficult to discover so we have used the most up to date yield curve and looked for the rate of return at the zero point on the time axis (see Exhibit 13.11).

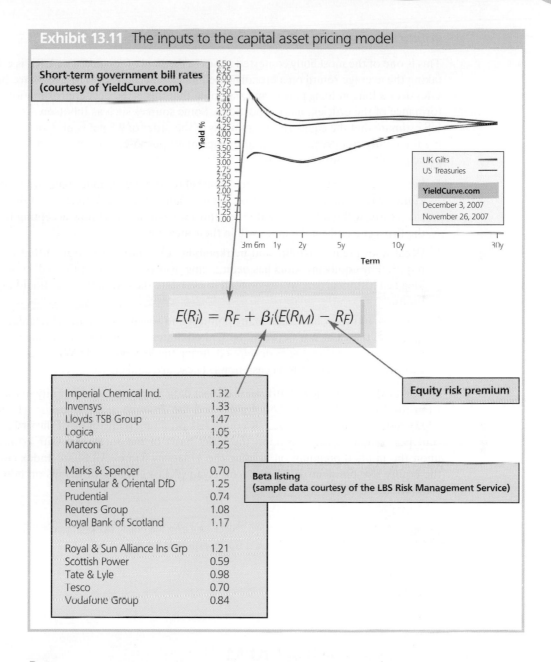

Exhibit 13.11 The inputs to the capital asset pricing model

Beta

A company's beta value is available from a variety of sources. The share price fundamentals as shown by *Investors Chronicle* in the UK, for example, publish beta values. However, the most reliable source of beta values is produced by the London Business School Risk Management Service. The Risk Management Service estimates beta by the use of linear regression between the monthly returns on the share concerned and the corresponding monthly returns on the FTSE All Share Index. The slope of the regression gives the beta value. There are many statistical issues in beta estimation and the Risk Management Service uses a number of procedures to 'clean the data' and remove biases. Beta values for individual companies are unstable and in particular they have a tendency over time to revert towards the average value for the market as a whole. The Risk Management Service corrects for this 'mean reversion bias'.

Equity risk premium (ERP)

This is one of the most hotly contested issues in the field of finance. The ERP is estimated by taking the average return on a broadly based index (such as the FTSE All Share Index in the UK) over a long holding period and assuming that this is the best approximation to the performance of the efficient market portfolio. Some sources such as Ibbotson Associates in the US estimate that the equity risk premium is of the order of 9.5 per cent. However, in predicting the equity risk premium for future investment purposes it is important to eliminate the principal biases in using past data:

1. Survivor bias: using past data of stock market returns will include some firms that featured at the start of the estimation period but had failed by the end. Because of this the historical returns will tend to overstate the return we would expect now accepting that some of the firms currently in the index will in their turn fail.

2. Because of greater stability and marketability of equities it is argued that the premium required by equity investors has been falling over time and that this will continue. Using long run historical data will again tend to overstate the return that we should expect in the future.

3. The past 100 years have seen many political and social disturbances including two World Wars and the Cold War between the United States and the Soviet Union. The periods of recovery as the technologies developed during the Second World War, in particular, led to exceptionally high corporate cash flows. These are unlikely to be repeated.

In an exhaustive study of 101 years of past data across the world equity markets, a team from the London Business School published the *Triumph of the Optimists* (Dimson *et al.*, 2002) and they suggest that the UK equity risk premium is currently of the order of 3–4 per cent per annum depending upon the exact basis of measurement. Our estimates based upon the implied premium on holding the Financial Times All Share Index currently put the equity risk premium at 2.8 per cent. Ryan (2006) gives more details on how to do this estimation.

Financial realities The risk-free rate of return is 5.75 per cent and the equity risk premium is 2.8 per cent. The beta of Marks & Spencer plc is 0.7. Its expected return is as follows:

$$E(R_{M\&S}) = R_F + \beta_{M\&S}(R_M - R_f)$$
$$= 5.75\% + 0.7 \times 2.8\%$$
$$= 7.71\%$$

Two uses for the CAPM

The CAPM, with all its inaccuracies and measurement problems, is a simple and straightforward model for predicting share returns. It has two important uses:

1. To enable estimation of the equity cost of capital. This is the rate of return required by investors in a company with a given exposure to market risk. It gives the discount rate that a company should use in calculating the net present value of new internal investment in capital projects providing it is financed wholly through equity.

2. It gives the rate of return that should be used in valuing the future cash earnings from a company accruing to the equity investors. This is an important part of the process of valuing the equity stake in a business. It is a topic to which we return in the next chapter.

The cost of capital

We have now achieved an important goal in our study of finance in that we have a model which although imperfect allows us to put a 'price' on the risk that the investor carries through holding the equity in a given company. The theory upon which the capital asset pricing model is based predicts that the price of risk in the market will not compensate the investor for all of the risk attaching to the returns on their investment. It will only compensate for risk that cannot be diversified away, that is the component of the total variability of the returns that is driven by market-wide forces and by which all firms are, to differing extents, affected. This price of risk, as given by the capital asset pricing model, is an estimate of the cost of equity capital to the firm. It is an estimate of the minimum rate of return that the firm must deliver, by dividends and/or capital gain, to its equity investors as compensation for the market risk to which they are exposed through their share holding.

However, overall a firm also needs to know the rate of return that other types of investors apart from its equity shareholders require in order to calculate the average rate that it should achieve on its own internal investment in new ventures and projects. It is to this issue that we now turn.

Estimating the required rate of return on debt

As with investment in gilt-edged securities described earlier, debt investors receive two cash flows from the company concerned:

- Interest payments over the life of the bond (usually payable in annual or semi-annual) instalments. This interest payment is calculated at the 'coupon rate' declared on the bond at the date of issue times the bond's nominal value.
- Repayment of capital is made at the date of redemption and will normally be at the nominal or par value of the bond at issue.

As company bonds are traded on the market, the price that investors will pay for the promise of these future cash payments will vary depending on the rate of return they require. This rate of return is governed by three factors:

1. the default risk that they perceive in terms of receipt of their interest payments and the eventual repayment of their capital
2. the level of inflation that they expect over the lifetime of the debt until repayment
3. their loss of liquidity through holding a fixed-interest loan.

In practice there are two methods of calculating the required rate of return or 'yield' on a corporate bond:

Internal rate of return method

The rate of return required on a corporate bond is the discount rate that investors use to equate the market value of the bond (per unit) with the coupon rate payments and the redemption value of the bond. So, for a bond redeemable in three years with annual coupon payments the market value will be given by:

$$\text{Market value of Bond} = \frac{\text{Coupon Interest Year 1}}{(1 + R_d)} + \frac{\text{Coupon Interest Year 2}}{(1 + R_d)^2} + \frac{\text{Coupon Interest Year 3}}{(1 + R_d)^3} + \frac{\text{Per value at redemption}}{(1 + R_d)^4}$$

The rate of return we require is shown as R_d in the equation above. As you will remember from the previous chapter, calculating the discount rate for this type of expression can be done by trial and error using specimen values of the discount rate until the right-hand side of the formula equates to the left-hand side. Alternatively, most spreadsheet packages permit the calculation of the internal rate of return on a bond such as this automatically. That is the method we recommend and is shown in the example below.

Financial realities

A three-year bond has a coupon rate of 8 per cent per annum and is due for repayment at its par value of £100 per unit. The bond currently trades at £104 per unit.

Putting the data into the formula gives the market value of the bond:

$$MV = \frac{I}{(1 + R_d)} + \frac{I}{(1 + R_d)^2} + \frac{I}{(1 + R_d)^3} + \frac{PAR}{(1 + R_d)^3}$$

$$104 = \frac{8}{(1 + R_d)} + \frac{8}{(1 + R_d)^2} + \frac{8}{(1 + R_d)^3} + \frac{100}{(1 + R_d)^3}$$

This formula simplifies and rearranges to what you may recognise as the internal rate of return from the previous chapter:

$$-104 + \frac{8}{(1 + R_d)} + \frac{8}{(1 + R_d)^2} + \frac{108}{(1 + R_d)^3} = 0$$

The entries in a spreadsheet would then appear as follows:

Exhibit 13.12

Year	0	1	2	3
Cash receipt/(payment)	−104	8	8	108
Internal Rate of Return (IRR) =	6.49%			

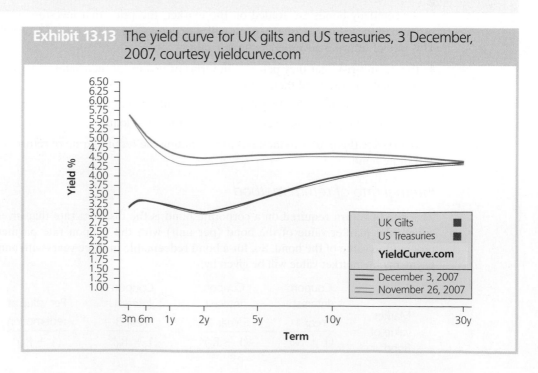

Exhibit 13.13 The yield curve for UK gilts and US treasuries, 3 December, 2007, courtesy yieldcurve.com

The yield curve method

Companies often issue debt, or undertake borrowing at fixed rates from banks and other finance houses, that is not traded on the bond market and for which there is no market value. In such circumstances it is necessary to estimate the current rate for the firm concerned using a current yield curve. The **yield curve** shows the expected rate of return on fixed-interest bonds of different maturities.

There are numerous sources of yield curves in the UK including the Bank of England and **YieldCurve.com**. The shape of the yield curve depends on a number of factors and can from time to time vary. The yield curve in Exhibit 13.13 shows the yield that could be expected on government bonds with different terms to maturity. The yields are given in both nominal and real terms. For our purposes the nominal yield curve is required.

If one has a yield curve for a bond of a specific risk then with a known maturity it would be straightforward to work out the return required by investors in that type of security. However, the published yield curves are derived from government bonds that are essentially risk-free. When using published yield curves a premium would have to be added for the particular credit rating of the bond concerned:

The bond risk premium is dependent upon the credit risk of the firm, although research studies show that the rating given by agencies does not wholly explain the level of the premium observed in practice. Indeed, the bond risk premium appears to be most highly associated with the non-market or unsystematic risk described earlier in this chapter.

Financial realities   A UK company had an 8 per cent debenture redeemable at par in five years' time. The nominal value at issue was £100 per unit. Interest has just been paid. The company believes that its current credit rating would add a risk premium of 1.6 per cent to the required rate of return. The debenture is not traded.

The term to maturity is five years and so from the yield curve of Exhibit 13.13 we can estimate the required rate of return on an equivalent government bond as 4.6 per cent. Adding the risk premium this implies that the current required rate of return on this debt is 6.2 per cent. If the company were solely financed by this type of debt it would need to generate a rate of return on all its internal investment of 6.2 per cent. So this is our best estimate of the company's cost of debt capital. The equivalent market value of a bond of this risk if it were traded can be calculated by discounting the cash flows to the investor at this risk-adjusted rate of return:

Exhibit 13.14

Year	1	2	3	4	5
Cash flow to bond holder	8	8	8	8	108
Discount factor	0.94	0.89	0.83	0.79	0.74
Discounted cash flow to the bond holder	7.53	7.09	6.68	6.29	79.95
Present value of bond	£107.54				

The present value of the bond (£107.54) is our best estimate of the current market value of each unit.

Estimating the cost of capital

Finally, we draw a number of threads together to answer a question posed in the previous chapter: what rate of discount should be used by a firm when evaluating new capital investment programmes? The rate of discount should in principle be the 'opportunity cost of capital' which, as the name implies, is the rate we would have to pay the market to 'replace' the capital 'used up' by the firm in plant, equipment and all the other assets it requires when undertaking a new project. This replacement cost of capital is directly analogous to the opportunity cost concept described in Chapter 8 except this time we ask: what would be the 'price' of acquiring new capital to directly replace what we have used? Because the firm draws capital from its total capital employed, its opportunity cost is the current return the firm would have to pay the market to refinance itself in the same ratio of debt and equity as existed prior to the investment taking place.

In a pure equity firm, the equity cost of capital is the replacement rate and can be most effectively estimated by the capital asset pricing model. In a firm wholly financed by debt, we have already described how to estimate the cost of refinancing the firm's borrowing. In a geared firm, which has both equity and debt, we must calculate the current proportions of equity and debt and calculate a weighted rate. This is known as the 'weighted average cost of capital' or WACC. The only tricky bit is to recognise that we must use the current gearing ratio that reflects the actual investment of equity and debt from the market's point of view. Therefore we need to calculate market value weights.

Financial realities   DialaSid plc is now one of the largest taxi and vehicle rental businesses in the south-east of England. The business is currently financed by 20 million 25p equity shares trading at £2.25 per share and a bond issue of 500 000 units currently trading at £97.50 per £100 nominal unit. Sid's wife (who has now been able to retire from her job as a finance professor) has estimated the firm's equity cost of capital as 8 per cent and the required rate of return on its debt at 6 per cent. What is the firm's weighted average cost of capital?

The proportion of equity in the firm's capital structure is given by the ratio of the total market value of its equity divided by the total market value of its debt plus equity. Likewise, the proportion of debt (which is also referred to as the firm's 'market gearing' ratio) is given by the ratio of the total market value of debt to the total market value of both sources of capital:

$$\text{Proportion of equity in capital structure} = \frac{\overset{\text{Total market value of equity}}{= 20\ 000\ 000 \times £2.25}}{\underset{= 20\ 000\ 000 \times £2.25}{\text{Total market value of equity}} + \underset{= 500\ 000 \times £97.5}{\text{Total market value of debt}}}$$

$$= 48\%$$

Likewise we can calculate the proportion of debt, giving us the market gearing ratio:

$$\text{Proportion of debt in capital structure} = \frac{\overset{\text{Total market value of debt}}{= 500\ 000 \times £97.5}}{\underset{= 20\ 000\ 000 \times £2.25}{\text{Total market value of equity}} + \underset{= 500\ 000 \times £97.5}{\text{Total market value of debt}}}$$

$$= 52\%$$

▶

Finally, we can weight together the expected equity and debt returns to calculate the weighted average cost of capital:

$$WACC = W_e \times E(R_e) + W_d \times E(R_d)$$
$$= 48\% \times 8\% + 52\% \times 6\%$$
$$= 6.96\%$$

Where W_e and W_d are the weights and $E(R_e)$ and $E(R_d)$ are the expected market returns on equity and debt respectively.

Note that the weights in the WACC formula must total to 100 per cent. It is possible to extend this formula if, for example, the company were also financed by a third capital source such as preference shares, in which case the formula would become:

$$WACC = W_e \times E(R_e) + W_p \times E(R_p) + W_d \times E(R_d)$$

Where W_p and $E(R_p)$ are respectively the weight and the expected return on preference capital in the total capital structure of the firm.

The weighted average cost of capital is the best approximation to a firm's opportunity cost of capital. However, in practice there are some problems to beware of:

1. The weighted average cost of capital assumes that any new use of capital will not disturb the pre-existing capital structure of the firm. The firm may be considering a new capital programme or an acquisition which would necessarily entail an alteration in the capital structure of the firm. Because the weighted average cost does not include the transactions costs of raising new capital it may be unsafe to assume that the firm will maintain its existing gearing when refinancing.

2. The firm's new capital investment programme may well distort the firm's exposure to market risk (and hence its equity cost of capital) or its exposure to non-market risk (and hence its debt cost of capital) or, indeed, both! Changing the risk exposure of the firm will necessarily alter the WACC.

3. The returns required by the market may not be the same as the effective returns paid by the firm. This occurs when interest payments on debt are tax deductible whilst dividend payments are made from post-tax profits. This is easily corrected by replacing the expected rate of return on debt by the effective rate after tax.

Financial realities

DialaSid plc pays corporation tax at an effective rate of 25 per cent per (T) annum and debt interest is all allowed as a pretax expense. What is the firm's adjusted weighted average costs of capital?

$$AWACC = W_e \times E(R_e) + W_d \times E(R_d) \times (1 - T)$$
$$= 48\% \times 8\% + 52\% \times 6\% \times 0.75$$
$$= 6.18\%$$

Gearing and the weighted average cost of capital

If the return required by debt holders is usually lower than that required by equity would it not make sense to increase the proportion of debt in the firm's capital structure, reducing the weighted average cost of capital overall? The answer to this question may appear obvious.

Unfortunately it is not so clear-cut. Increasing the gearing of a firm increases the equity shareholders' exposure to 'financial risk'. Financial risk is the additional variability on the earnings of shareholders caused by increases in the level of fixed interest charged to the income statement. We know that if we have a heavy fixed charge of, say, mortgage interest deducted from our pay that any minor alteration in our salary level will have a much more significant impact on what is left over. This additional variability in what is left over after fixed interest is deducted is called financial risk. This increase in exposure to financial risk will result in the equity investors in their turn demanding a higher rate of return to compensate. Two famous finance academics, Franco Modigliani and Merton Miller, won the Nobel Prize in Economics partly for their work in demonstrating that under assumptions of perfect markets any change in the WACC flowing from alterations in the level of debt will be exactly compensated by changes in the required rate of return required by the equity investors. Modigliani and Miller's 1958 study therefore showed that the weighted average cost of capital will not change as gearing changes providing the underlying risk of the firm remains unchanged. Altering the level of gearing only alters the extent to which different classes of investor share that risk. In summary, the ultimate driver of the weighted average cost of capital is not the firm's gearing ratio but rather the overall level of business risk to which it is exposed.

Chapter summary

In this chapter we have explored a wide range of issues to do with the money and capital markets. We have argued that these markets should be and almost certainly are very efficient social systems, permitting the free trading of financial securities and cash. Although no human system is perfect these markets are a close approximation to the ideal of a perfect market where large numbers of buyers and sellers with ready access to information ensure that prices reflect the fair or intrinsic values of securities. Given that, we have then been able to develop simple models that allow us to calculate the required rates of return on different types of finance taking into account, albeit imperfectly, the underlying risk to which investors are exposed. The capital asset pricing model in particular is a very simple and elegant means of establishing the rate of return required by equity investors, and this model forms the basis for calculating the cost of refinancing a firm as capital is used up in investment in new projects. The weighted average cost of capital is, we argue, the best approximation a firm can achieve to the overall cost of financing new investment where different capital sources are involved. This all helps to answer a question posed in the previous chapter: how do we calculate the discount rate to use when valuing a firm's investment in new projects?

Further reading

Dimson, E., Marsh, P. and Staunton, M. (2002) *The Triumph of the Optimists*, Princeton, NJ: Princeton University Press. At £80 a copy this book is not cheap. It's brimming full of detailed research from the UK's leading empirical research team examining the performance of the stock markets over the last 100 years. The main output is their estimate of the equity risk premium for different countries. The book is also replete with clear diagrams and descriptions of the leading empirical research in finance.

Howells, P. and Bain, K. (2007) *Financial Markets and Institutions*, Harlow: Financial Times/Prentice Hall. A very good overview of the modern financial markets. Chapter 6 is excellent on the equity and bond markets.

Malkiel, B.G. (2003) *A Random Walk down Wall Street*, New York: W. W. Norton. This latest update of a classic is a 'must read' for anyone interested in the stock market. It argues the case and gives all the references you will need for the efficient markets hypothesis. For those who like to believe that they can beat the market, this is the book they ought to read before putting their money where their mouth is.

Mishkin, S.G. and Eakins, S.G. (2006) *Financial Markets and Institutions*, Reading, MA: Addison-Wesley. An excellent book that covers much that you need to know about the operation of US and global markets.

Reuters Financial Training Series (1999) *An Introduction to Bond Markets*, Chichester: Wiley. This is an attractive book which is very good at describing the technical details of how the markets work and the trading mechanisms. It does work better as a reference source than as a teaching book.

Reuters Financial Training Series (1999) *An Introduction to Foreign Exchange and the Money Markets*, Chichester: Wiley.

Reuters Financial Training Series (1999) *An Introduction to Equity Markets*, Chichester: Wiley.

Ryan, B. (2006) *Corporate Finance and Valuation*, London: Cengage, London.

Progress check

1. What are the three principal features of a financial market security? (p. 435)

2. What characterises fundamental, speculative and arbitrage traders? (pp. 436–437)

3. What is the difference between the money and capital markets? (p. 436)

4. List the five arbitrage conditions that influence exchange rates and outline their effect. (pp. 439–441)

5. What characterises the difference between the primary and the secondary capital market? (p. 442)

6. What is the difference between investment grade and junk bonds? (p. 446)

7. What is a 'govie'? (p. 446)

8. List the three forms of the efficient markets hypothesis and outline what each implies for the investor. (pp. 447–449)

9. How are return and risk defined? (pp. 451–452)

10. What does the Markowitz separation theorem imply for investors and upon what assumptions is it based? (pp. 454–455)

11. What happens to the risk of a portfolio as diversification is increased? (p. 456)

12. Write out the capital asset pricing model and state how its variables could be determined in practice. (p. 459)

13. What financial measure is used to calculate the cost of debt capital given the firm's debt is traded and you know the coupon rate and redemption value? (pp. 461–462)

14. What does the yield curve tell you? (p. 463)

15. Define the weighted average cost of capital (p. 465).

Questions

The answers to the questions followed by ✓ can be found at the back of the book, the answers to the remaining questions can be found on the website accompanying this book, **www.cengage.co.uk/ ryan2**.

1. An annual rate of discount is 6 per cent per annum. What is the equivalent monthly rate?   ✓

2. A monthly rate is 1 per cent – what is the equivalent annual rate?   ✓

3. A £100 nominal bond pays a coupon rate of six per cent per annum in two equal instalments per year. It is due for redemption in 3 years. What is its present value if the required rate of return on a bond of this type is 8 per cent?   ✓

4. The risk-free rate of return is 5 per cent per annum and the rate of return on a well-diversified portfolio 12 per cent per annum. Borrowing and lending can be undertaken at the risk-free rate in any amount without transaction costs. An investor has £10 000 to invest. How much would she have to borrow/lend at the risk-free rate and how much would have to be invested in the diversified portfolio in order to earn a rate of return overall of 15 per cent?   ✓

5. The return and betas for four securities have been estimated as below:

Exhibit 13.15

Security	1	2	3	4
beta	0.87	1.21	1.05	0.98
average return	10.09	12.47	11.35	10.86

You are required to:

(i) Sketch the security market line implied by these four securities

(ii) Either from your sketch or by calculation estimate the risk-free rate of return and the expected rate of return on the market from these data.

(iii) Calculate the beta and expected return for a portfolio of these four shares equally weighted by value.

(iv) Discuss the role which the capital asset pricing model can play in both personal and corporate investment decisions. ✓

6. Your company is funded by two principal capital sources:

- Equity finance consisting of 1 million issued and fully paid up 25p ordinary shares. The current market value of these shares is £2.20. The rate of return on 90-day government stock is 4.5 per cent and the average return on the FTSE all-share index is 7.5 per cent. It is believed that the firm's equity carries 20 per cent more risk than the market.

- Debt finance consisting of a 3-year redeemable bond at par with a coupon rate of 6 per cent per annum. The current debt in issue is 1 million sterling nominal and its market value is £98 per cent.

You are required to:

(i) Estimate the weighted average cost of capital using the capital asset pricing model.

(ii) Note the assumptions upon which the models you have used are based. ✓

7. A company is attempting to evaluate its cost of capital. You are provided with the following information:

(i) The rate of return on a 1-month government bond is 4 per cent per annum.

(ii) The long-term equity risk premium in the UK equity market is 3.5 per cent.

(iii) The firm's beta is 0.72.

(iv) The market price of a riskless government bond of the same type and average duration as the company's outstanding fixed-interest loan stock is £110 per £100 nominal. The company's debt has a duration of 4 years before redemption at par. The company pays 7 per cent per annum on its loan stock and its credit rating suggests that it should carry a 1 per cent risk premium over and above an equivalent risk-free government bond.

(v) Fixed interest is tax-deductible at the corporation tax rate of 30 per cent per annum.

(vi) The firm's market gearing is 0.65.

You are required to:

(i) Calculate the firm's cost of equity capital, debt capital and weighted average cost of capital.

(ii) Discuss the issues that the firm needs to consider before using the weighted average cost of capital in the appraisal of significant capital investment projects.

8. A newly formed company is looking to expand its markets both domestically and overseas. It is currently financed privately. The directors have ambitious plans and would like your comments on how they could finance their expansion over the next five to ten years. Discuss the pros and cons of the various sources of finance available to a highly capital-intensive firm such as this and the likely requirements that will be imposed by the capital markets on the company and its directors. The company is proceeding to a small capital issue through the alternative investment market.

Case exercise

Using the most up to date accounts for Cobham plc estimate its weighted average cost of capital. You can assume that its debt carries a 1.5 per cent risk premium over the current equivalent U.K. gilt rate. A link to the Cobham site is provided on **www.cobham.com**.

Chapter 14

Market measures of performance and value

Introduction

In this chapter, we round off our introductory treatment of accounting and finance with a look at a range of tools for evaluating accounting information in a market context and in particular the types and significance of the 'investor ratios'. We will apply these ratios to Marks & Spencer plc, measuring the performance of this company both internally and in the market. An important issue discussed in this chapter is why markets often value firms at many times their book value. Part of the explanation for this is that book values do not represent the current market value of all the assets listed in the balance sheet. However, this explanation is a bit too glib given that some firms are valued by the market at up to ten times their book value. We will explore some of the reasons for this discrepancy in value. Building upon the investor ratios we then develop a straightforward method for the valuation of the equity shares in companies. This is useful for testing the prices of shares in the market as well as for estimating the value of target companies for acquisition. A key component of the measurement of value is the expected growth rate of the firm. This we explore using two broad approaches for estimating growth: an exogenous approach using external market forces and an endogenous approach using internal measures of management's reinvestment of earnings.

Learning objectives

Investor ratios

● To understand the nature and significance of the investor ratios.

....

● To be able to retrieve the relevant and most up-to-date information required to calculate the investor ratios.

....

● To be able to calculate the investor ratios.

....

Valuing the firm

● To be able to value the firm using the dividend growth model.

....

● To be able to value the equity market using the dividend valuation models.

....

Measuring the performance of firms

● To be able to summarise the concepts of value management and shareholder value-added.

● To be able to calculate the shareholder value added for a company.

Investor ratios

There are a number of important ratios that are used to help the investor. Some are mixed ratios in that they require access to figures both in the accounts and from market sources. The income statement and the current quoted price per share for the company provide most of the information that is required. To illustrate these ratios we return to Marks & Spencer's accounts, previously discussed in Chapter 7. For the purposes of this chapter we have used the accounts for the year-end 31 March 2007. The income statement, balance sheet and cash flow statement is shown as an appendix to this chapter.

Dividend per share

Dividend per share is the dividends (both paid and declared) during the year divided by the number of ordinary shares in issue and entitled to receive a dividend in the year in question. Most companies declare both an interim and a final dividend in order to smooth the impact of the distribution on cash flow.

Dividend yield

$$\text{Dividend yield} = \frac{\text{Dividend per share}}{\text{Market price per share}} \times 100$$

Dividend yield is the ratio of dividend to current share price and gives the percentage return that an investor can expect from distributions by the company. The current share price of Marks & Spencer is 583.50p per share and the dividend is 16.60p per share. The dividend yield is:

Dividend yield = 16.60/583.50 × 100 = 2.84 per cent

This means that currently Marks & Spencer's shares offer an annual cash return to the investor just in excess of 2.8 per cent. However, in order to obtain the full return we need to add to this yield the capital gain or loss in holding this company's shares. You should also note that

Exhibit 14.1 Marks & Spencer plc – statement of earnings

	52 weeks ended 31 March 2007 £m	52 weeks ended 1 April 2006 £m
Profit for the year attributable to shareholders	**659.9**	523.1
Basic earnings per share	**39.1p**	31.4p
Diluted earnings per share	**38.5p**	31.1p
Basic earnings per share from continuing operations	**39.1p**	31.3p
Diluted earnings per share from continuing operations	**38.5p**	31.0p

Exhibit 14.2 Marks & Spencer plc price and dividend quotation (*Financial Times*, 3 December 2007)

Notes	Price	W'k % Chng	Div	Div cov.	MCap £m	Last xd	City line
Mallett	189	–	9.20	0	26.1	22.8	3 274
Mrchpole	47.75	−16.2	3.35	4.1	13.0	15.8	2 765
Marks&Sp	**†583.50**	−4.5	16.60	2.8	9 844.4	14.11	3 292
Morrison	308.50	+3.7	4.05	3.0	8 283.5	10.10	3 422
MossBros	40	−5.3	1.80	0.5	37.8	17.10	3 424
Mthrcare	350	−4.9	10.40	1.5	305.3	6.6	4 125
Next	£17.40	−4	51.50	3.2	3 558.5	28.11	3 499
NordAng	257.50	−1	–	–	103.1	1'05	1 952

dividends are risky, companies will vary their payouts as circumstances change and so this yield may not be as attractive to an investor as an equivalent yield on a government bond or a savings account. A figure for dividend yield is quoted in the *Financial Times* (Tuesday–Saturday) as 'Yld'. You will find slight rounding errors when comparing the calculation using the published accounts and the figures reported in the newspaper.

Dividend payout ratio

During 2007 Marks & Spencer paid dividends of £260.6 million (£204.1 million in 2006).

$$\text{Dividend payout ratio} = \frac{\text{Dividends declared during the year}}{\text{Distributable earnings}} \times 100$$

The dividend payout ratio is the proportion of dividends to distributable earnings. This ratio is the principal measure of the company's dividend payout policy. Some companies attempt to maintain a constant or growing dividend irrespective of their level of profitability whilst other companies may only make a payout when they have met all their internal investment needs. Marks & Spencer falls into the first category. Its dividend payout ratio is:

Dividend payout ratio (2007) = 260.6/659.9 × 100 = 39.5 per cent
Dividend payout ratio (2006) = 204.1/523.1 × 100 = 39.0 per cent

Retention ratio

The retention ratio is closely related to the dividend payout ratio as follows:

Retention ratio = 1 − (Dividend payout ratio) × 100

In 2007 the retention ratio is 60.5 per cent. As we review this ratio it is worth bearing in mind that this represents a retention of accounting earnings serving to increase the profit and loss reserve in the balance sheet. However, the extent to which the company can invest the capital represented by this increase in its reserves depends upon the extent to which it has or can release cash from its operating cycle. If we assume that Marks & Spencer can reinvest all of this retention we would expect the company to earn its current return on equity of 40.04 per cent (2006: 43.46 per cent). From this we can predict the following year's earnings figure for Marks & Spencer (Exhibit 14.3):

Exhibit 14.3

	2007	2006
Earnings	659.90	523.10
Earnings retained	399.30	319.00
Rate of return on equity	0.4004	0.4346
Forecast addition to earnings	159.88	138.64
Forecast earnings =	**819.78**	**661.74**

Review activity 14.1   Update the above figures using the return on equity from the latest Marks & Spencer financial report and the reinvested earnings of the company. Repeat these calculations for Cobham plc.

As we will see later, the retention ratio, when combined with the rate of return on equity capital, gives an estimate of the potential growth rate of the company.

Earnings per share

A company is required to declare its earnings-per-share (EPS) figure. This ratio is always shown at the foot of the income statement and is provided in three forms:

1. Basic earnings per share: this ratio is simply the distributable profit available to shareholders divided by the number of shares in issue.

2. Diluted earnings per share: this measures the earnings per share after taking into account all shares which could be issued if any shares under a company stock option scheme were to be 'exercised'.

3. Adjusted earnings per share: this figure excludes any exceptional items in the income statement that would be likely to cause an anomalous result.

The purpose behind these adjustments is an attempt to provide a meaningful earnings-per-share figure from which any anomalous events have been removed and any claims upon the shares that could possibly be exercised have been accounted for. The calculation of 'true' earnings-per-share is tricky especially when shares are issued and redeemed during the course of the year in question.

Price earnings (P/E) ratio

$$\text{Price/earnings ratio} = \frac{\text{Market price per share}}{\text{Earnings per share}} \times 100$$

The price/earnings ratio is frequently used by analysts when valuing the firm. It is at one level quite simply stated as the price per share divided by the earnings-per-share. The question is whether to use the basic, diluted or adjusted earnings-per-share figure. If we take the basic EPS as provided by Marks & Spencer, and a current share price of 583.50p:

Price/earnings ratio = 583.50/39.1 = 14.92

This is the price/earnings ratio as defined by the *Financial Times* and as reported by other market information services. In practice, whichever is used, the key is to be consistent when making comparisons between companies.

The P/E ratio gives the market price per pound of reported earnings. For successful, low-risk companies we would expect the P/E ratio to be high. The current average P/E ratio for all companies listed in the Financial Times All Share Index is 12.19, which suggests that the market places Marks & Spencer a little above average. However the P/E ratio for the industrial group – general retailers – to which Marks & Spencer belongs is 13.06, which puts the company just a little below the average for the sector. Later in this chapter we consider the implications of this ratio for the stock market investors in much more detail.

The market to book ratio

As you now realise from your study of accounting in the previous chapters of this book, the book value of a company as revealed by its balance sheet is usually less than the market value of its shares in issue. In those situations where this is not the case and the market value is less than the book value, the company concerned will be ripe for takeover or for liquidation, providing, of course, that the financial accounts reflect the likely disposal value of the firm's net assets.

In the majority of situations, market values will be greater than book values. Part of the difference can be explained by the fact that book values, even if restated to fair value in the balance sheet, are unlikely to be up-to-date, especially in fast-moving markets. The remainder will be explained by the value that the market places upon all of the intangible assets owned by the company: its brands, human resource skills, market networks and the way that it organises its real assets to create value-added.

For Marks & Spencer we note that the book value of the business attributable to the equity shareholders, from the balance sheet, is 1648.2 million and the number of shares in issue is 1699.8 million, giving a book value per share of 97p per share.

$$\text{Market to book ratio} = \frac{\text{market value per share}}{\text{equity capital employed per share}} \times 100$$
$$= 583.50/97.0$$
$$= 6.02$$

This ratio suggests that the market values Marks & Spencer 6.02 times greater than the company accountants.

The principal source of the difference is the range of 'intangible' assets within the company not disclosed in the balance sheet. One very important 'asset' is the way the company has put its assets together. This is the 'entanglement phenomenon'. The axiom of separability, outlined in Chapter 3 and first articulated by Cronhelm, is an implicit assumption within accounting. However, assets in isolation do not create value, nor for that matter do assets bundled together into portfolios. Value is created through 'asset nets', that is combinations of individual assets which enhance one another and create a whole that is greater than the sum of the parts. In other words, value creation is not simply a statistical 'portfolio effect' as described in the last chapter, nor is it just synergy in operation. Value is created by the intelligent coordination of different assets so that they work together.

Knowledge is one such asset and is an important driver of the 'entanglement premium'. Value is also created by firms as they build trust both within and without the firm. Trust is a complex form of 'social capital' which is created by individuals and by firms. Like reputation it takes a long time to acquire and like reputation it is easy to lose. Individuals and firms create trust because they are willing to engage in and honour mutual agreements, on a reciprocal basis and without recourse to law or the establishment of formal contracts.

Valuing the firm

As far as the investor is concerned their decision to purchase shares in a company offers them just two sources of financial return:

1. the dividend payments that the firm will pay over the duration of their holding, and
2. the eventual sale value of the shares, whether sold through the market or via a company repurchase scheme.

However, the only return investors receive from the company is the dividends declared and paid by the directors. In a fair and competitive market the market price of a company's share must equal the present value of future dividends when discounted by the investors' minimum required rate of return for an investment of that risk. But what about the capital gain? The answer is that any future share price must, in its turn, be the discounted value of expected dividends from that date forward. We therefore can reduce the current price to the present value of all future dividends to create what is known as the dividend valuation model (DVM):

$$P_0 = \frac{\text{div}_1}{(1 + E(R_e))^1} + \frac{\text{div}_2}{(1 + E(R_e))^2} + \frac{\text{div}_3}{(1 + E(R_e))^3} + \cdots \infty$$

where P_0 is the current share price, div_1, div_2, etc., are the future dividends per share paid in year 1, 2, etc. through to perpetuity (which reflects the assumption that the firm is a 'going concern' and that we cannot foresee any end point to the dividend series). Note that we have discounted the dividend using the expected return required by the firm's equity investors ($E(R_e)$). This can be estimated using the capital asset pricing model.

Is it possible for a firm that never paid a dividend but reinvested all of its earnings to have a value? The DVM would appear to say not, but that is incorrect. Indeed if div_1, div_2, etc. were zero and all earnings were reinvested, earning the minimum expected rate of return, then the present value of the firm would be infinitely high. We will return to the reason why shortly.

The problem with the valuation model given above is that it is too general. Estimating the future dividend series is virtually impossible without some restricting assumption. One straightforward assumption is to assume that future dividends will grow at a constant rate (g) which means that the first year's dividend in the series will equal the dividend most recently declared plus a percentage growth rate.

Financial realities If a firm paid a dividend of 12p per share in the last financial year then assuming a constant growth rate of 5 per cent the future dividends will be as follows:

$\text{Div}_0 = 12.00\text{p}$

$\text{Div}_1 = \text{Div}_0 \times (1 + g) = 12\text{p} \times (1.05) = 12.60\text{p}$

$\text{Div}_2 = \text{Div}_0 \times (1 + g)^2 = 12\text{p} \times (1.05)^2 = 13.23\text{p}$

and so forth.

We can substitute for future dividends in the valuation model an expression in terms of the last dividend and the expected growth rate:

$$P_0 = \frac{\text{div}_0 (1 + g)}{(1 + E(R_e))^1} + \frac{\text{div}_0 (1 + g)^2}{(1 + E(R_e))^2} + \frac{\text{div}_0 (1 + g)^3}{(1 + E(R_e))^3} + \cdots \infty$$

This formula is what is known technically as a 'geometric progression' and can be solved (see the note that follows) to give:

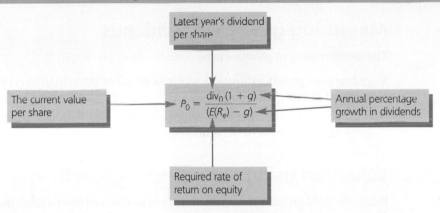

Exhibit 14.4 The dividend growth model

Latest year's dividend per share

The current value per share

$$P_0 = \frac{div_0 \, (1 + g)}{(E(R_e) - g)}$$

Annual percentage growth in dividends

Required rate of return on equity

The general dividend valuation model is as follows:

$$P_0 = \frac{div_0(1 + g)^1}{(1 + E(R_e))^1} + \frac{div_0(1 + g)^2}{(1 + E(R_e))^2} + \frac{div_0(1 + g)^3}{(1 + E(R_e))^3} + \cdots \, \infty$$

To sum this series go through the following steps:

1. Multiply both sides of the equation by $(1 + E(R_e))/(1 + g)$:

$$P_0 \frac{(1 + E(R_e))}{(1 + g)} = div_0 + \frac{div_0(1 + g)^1}{(1 + E(R_e))^1} + \frac{div_0(1 + g)^2}{(1 + E(R_e))^2} + \cdots \, \infty$$

2. Substitute the first formula into the second to give:

$$P_0 \frac{(1 + E(R_e))}{(1 + g)} = div_0 + P_0$$

3. Which on rearrangement gives:

$$P_0 = \frac{div_0(1 + g)}{(E(R_e) - g)}$$

This model is known as the **dividend growth model** or DGM and is the basic 'workhorse' in the valuation of equities. The DGM focuses attention on two key variables:

● The required rate of return on equity. This can be estimated, as noted above, using the capital asset pricing model. CAPM makes some strong assumptions about the efficiency of the capital market and the extent to which investors make rational investment decisions based on their knowledge of the risk and the return of the share concerned.

● The rate of growth in dividends. Assuming a constant dividend payout policy, the rate of growth of dividends will equal the rate of growth of earnings. The rate of growth of earnings is constrained by either (i) the ability of the firm to reinvest in positive net present value projects, discounted by its opportunity cost of capital, or (ii) by external market conditions of which the most important will be the rate of growth of the economy. In the long run a firm cannot continue to exceed the growth rate of its host economy for the simple reason that eventually it would take a progressively larger share of GDP (gross domestic product) until eventually it took over the economy as a whole.

Measuring growth in dividends

The measurement of growth can be done in one of two ways:

- endogenous growth estimation, which looks at the internal drivers of earnings and hence dividend growth
- exogenous growth estimation, which considers the external drivers of growth and in particular the growth of the economy.

Valuation using endogenous growth estimation

Future dividend growth from reinvestment can be deduced from a firm's most recent accounting information and the required rate of return on the firm's equity. However, we do have to make some fairly strong assumptions:

1. Accounting earnings as reported in the income statement represent the true economic earnings of the firm. Our discussion in Chapters 1–7 of the ways in which accounting earnings are created demonstrates the limits of this assumption.

2. That the rate of reinvestment, i.e. the retention ratio (b) is constant and the firm's rate of return on reinvestment ($E(R_e)$) is constant.

3. In the absence of new capital, growth in the value of the firm is driven by the reinvestment of its earnings. This reinvestment should earn a rate of return which is in excess of the firm's cost of capital. The excess between the rate of return a firm earns on its reinvestment and its equity cost of capital is known as the 'rate of return spread' or the 'abnormal return'. However, if the firm is in a competitive market and the conditions for the capital asset pricing model hold, then the actual reinvestment rate should equal the expected rate of return required by the equity investors as predicted by the capital asset pricing model. Over the longer run we can assume that if the firm earns less than this required rate of return it will be overvalued relative to market expectations and the share price will fall until the required rate of return is achieved. If the return is in excess of the required rate then the firm will be perceived as undervalued and the price will correct upwards.

4. Finally, this model assumes that there is no unrealised growth in the existing assets of the firm. This will only be true for a firm which is operating at full capacity in the most efficient way possible.

Given assumption (i), the proportion of the firm's earning that is reinvested depends on the payment of dividends. If a firm pays out all of its earnings to investors then its growth through reinvestment will be zero. If a firm retains all of its earnings then the increase in annual earnings that will result is given by the earnings reinvested. Formally these extreme conditions are:

- If all distributable earnings (E_0) are paid as dividends then the following year's earnings (E_1) will be:

$$E_1 = E_0; g = 0$$

- And if all distributable earnings are retained:

$E_1 = E_0 + E(R_e) \times E_0; g = 100$ per cent

So where will the normal firm sit? The answer depends upon its rate of retentions. The retention ratio (b) was defined earlier in this chapter. So, if the firm maintains the same payout ratio next year as it did last year, the prediction of next year's earnings will be:

$$E_1 = E_0 + b \times E(R_e) \times E_0$$
$$E_0(1 + b \times E(R_e))$$

Financial realities A firm retains all of its earnings for reinvestment. The rate of return required by its investors is 8 per cent and the most recent accounts showed a basic earnings-per-share of 42p. What are next year's earnings predicted to be?

$E_1 = 42p + 8$ per cent $\times 42p$

$= 45.36p$ per share

From this it should be clear that the growth rate of earnings is given by:

$g = b \times E(R_e)$

Financial realities A firm retains 60 per cent of its earnings. The rate of return required by its investors is 8 per cent and the most recent accounts showed a basic earnings-per-share of 42p. What are next year's earnings predicted to be?

$E_1 = 42p + 60$ per cent $\times 8$ per cent $\times 42p$

$= 44.016p$ per share

If we expect a firm to maintain a constant dividend payout then the growth in dividends will equal the growth rate of earnings, which in its turn equals the growth of the value of the firm. Growth in dividends can therefore be expected to be:

$$g = b \times E(R_e)$$

and the share valuation formula can be rewritten as:

$$P_0 = \frac{div_0(1 + b \times E(R_e))}{E(R_e) - b \times E(R_e)}$$

Given that dividends are paid out of earnings then the immediate past dividend can be replaced by the following:

$$div_0 = E_0 \times (1 - b)$$

where E_0 is the earnings-per-share for the previous financial year.

Substituting back into the valuation model and simplifying gives this very important relationship:

$$P_0 = \frac{E_0(1 + b \times E(R_e))}{E(R_e)}$$

Financial reality The risk-free rate of return is 5.75 per cent per annum and the equity risk premium is 2.8 per cent. The current share price for Marks & Spencer is 583.50p. The company has a beta value of 0.7.

The rate of return on equity for Marks & Spencer plc is given by:

$$E(R_e) = 5.75 \text{ per cent} + 0.7 \times 2.8 \text{ per cent} = 7.71 \text{ per cent}$$

On the basis of the earnings per share of 39.1p and a retention ratio of 60.5%:

$$P_0 = \frac{E_0(1 + b \times E(R_e))}{E(R_e)}$$

$$= \frac{39.1 \times (1 + 0.605 \times 0.0771)}{0.0771}$$

$$= 530.79p$$

As you can see from the share price the model is accurate to within 10 per cent of the actual share price.

Valuation using exogenous growth estimation

Many companies are more likely to be constrained by the growth rate of the domestic economy rather than by their ability to reinvest. Companies in the utility industries such as Scottish Power or retailers like Marks & Spencer or Tesco are constrained by the level of general activity in the economy or by the long-term growth in consumer spending. Exogenous growth estimation involves the measurement of economic constraints on a company's growth.

Financial realities If UK GDP is currently 2.70 per cent per annum and the rate of inflation is 2.5 per cent we can recalculate the predicted value for Marks and Spencer plc. With this method of growth estimation we return to the original dividend growth model:

$$P_0 = \frac{div_0(1 + g)}{(E(R_e) - g)}$$

Calculating the last twelve-month dividend for the company from the published yield (28.44p per share) and using the GDP and inflation data to get the nominal growth in GDP:

$$GDP_{nominal} = (1 + inflation) \times (1 + GDP_{real}) - 1$$

$$= 1.025 \times 1.027 - 1$$

$$= 5.26 \text{ per cent}$$

We can then calculate the price per share using the model and setting the growth in dividends equal to the growth in nominal GDP:

$$P_0 = \frac{div_0(1 + g)}{(E(R_e) - g)}$$

$$= \frac{16.60 \times 1.0526}{0.0771 - 0.0526}$$

$$= 713p$$

This suggests that at 583.50p per share that Marks & Spencer is undervalued. It may, however, be alerting us to the fact that the market does not expect the company to grow at the same rate as the economy. That, if true, would be a worrying sign for the future of this business.

Valuing the market

The dividend valuation growth can allow us to check whether the market as a whole fairly reflects anticipated growth in the economy. Given that the corporate sector is unlikely to expand at a rate over the longer run that is greater than the expected growth in gross domestic product we can 'test the index' to see if it is at a level we would expect given the economic conditions.

From the data we can use the actual yield to calculate the 'dividend' paid on the index assuming that the index level of 3280.87 is the average 'price' that would have to be paid in pence for a unit of the index. Therefore:

$$Div_0 = \text{index} \times \text{yield} = 3.02 \text{ per cent} \times 3280.87 = 99.08$$

Substituting the nominal growth in GDP used in the previous example of 5.26 per cent and assuming a risk-free rate is 5.75 per cent, an equity risk premium of 2.8 per cent, and given that beta is 1 by definition, the value of the index is given by:

$$P_0 = \frac{99.08 \times 1.0526}{0.0855 - 0.0526} = 3169.96$$

Exhibit 14.5 The share indices from FTSE ™

FTSE Actuaries Share Indices   **UK Series**
Produced in conjunction with the Faculty and Institute of Actuaries   www.ft.com/equities

	£ Stlg Nov 30	Day's chge%	Euro Index	£ Stlg Nov 29	£ Stlg Nov 28	Year ago	Actual yield%	Cover	P/E ratio	Xd. adj. yld	Total Return
FTSE 100 (100)	6 432.5	+1.3	7 018.7	6 349.1	6 306.2	6 021.5	3.17	2.70	11.70	209.89	3 733.64
FTSE 250 (250)	10 748.8	+0.8	11 728.4	10 664.7	10 591.5	10 698.9	2.28	3.07	14.32	243.11	5 952.88
FTSE 250 ex Inv Co (222)	11 130.1	+0.8	12 144.5	11 047.1	10 973.8	11 223.4	2.36	3.20	13.25	260.61	6 241.41
FTSE 350 (350)	3 349.1	+1.2	3 654.3	3 308.1	3 285.7	3 162.5	3.04	2.74	12.01	104.48	3 956.83
FTSE 350 ex Inv Co (322)	3 336.1	+1.2	3 640.2	3 295.2	3 273.0	3 153.0	3.07	2.75	11.88	104.86	2 025.20
FTSE 350 Higher Yield (77)	3 838.9	+1.2	4 188.8	3 792.1	3 786.0	3 836.6	4.19	2.25	10.62	162.64	4 211.81
FTSE 350 Lower Yield (273)	2 717.7	+1.2	2 965.4	2 684.4	2 652.2	2 417.8	1.89	3.83	13.82	54.92	2 390.54
FTSE SmallCap (329)	3 447.51	+0.2	3 761.70	3 440.72	3 408.62	3 683.90	2.25	1.86	23.96	76.88	3 781.36
FTSE SmallCap ex Inv Co (227)	3 132.29	+0.2	3 417.76	3 126.42	3 105.42	3 583.42	2.76	2.00	18.13	83.47	3 526.08
FTSE All-Share (679)	3 280.87	+1.2	3 579.88	3 241.73	3 219.53	3 110.26	3.02	2.72	12.19	101.49	3 928.05
FTSE All-Share ex Inv Co (549)	3 263.57	+1.2	3 561.00	3 224.21	3 202.49	3 097.09	3.06	2.73	11.96	102.28	2 015.40
FTSE All-Share ex Multinationals (616)	1 136.90	+1.3	1 028.15	1 122.54	1 121.93	1 204.72	3.36	2.72	10.93	38.37	1 470.24
FTSE Fledgling (218)	4 072.92	+0.4	4 444.11	4 055.44	4 032.66	4 191.17	2.16	0.77	60.32	83.09	5 795.78
FTSE Fledgling ex Inv Co (123)	4 705.69	+0.1	5 134.55	4 701.71	4 687.52	5 150.34	2.53	0.48	80.00†	110.22	6 618.44
FTSE All-Small (547)	2 304.96	+0.2	2 515.03	2 299.78	2 279.36	2 451.41	2.24	1.73	25.84	50.84	3 240.06
FTSE All-Small ex Inv Co (350)	2 215.01	+0.2	2 416.88	2 211.05	2 196.90	2 523.60	2.74	1.88	19.41	58.37	3 165.73
FTSE AIM All-Share (1210)	1 053.4	+1.1	1 149.4	1 042.4	1 039.4	1 023.0	0.56	2.57	69.39	12.39	1 037.55
FTSE Actuaries Industry Sectors											
Consumer Services (108)	3 736.66	–	4 077.21	3 738.47	3 745.84	3 842.81	2.65	2.50	15.12	96.28	2 621.18
Food & Drug Retailers (5)	5 646.40	+0.2	6 161.00	5 633.12	5 655.89	4 566.99	1.95	2.60	19.71	100.45	4 907.35
General Retailers (37)	2 064.85	−0.8	2 253.04	2 081.33	2 112.40	2 606.25	4.05	1.89	13.06	86.44	1 726.05
Media (33)	3 997.30	−0.2	4 361.60	4 004.10	3 949.89	4 144.66	2.69	2.08	17.82	110.16	1 826.23
Travel & Leisure (33)	5 446.78	+0.3	5 943.19	5 429.48	5 472.67	6 029.56	2.35	3.68	11.58	115.68	3 967.66

This is a reasonable approximation which leads us to the conclusion that the index is fairly valued given expected growth rates in the economy.

Review activity 14.2   Using the data published in the *Financial Times* extract above, estimate the following:

● the index level for the FTSE 100 given that it has a beta value of 1.05
● the index level for the FTSE All Share Index and the FTSE 100 assuming endogenous growth.

✓ **Check the answer to this Review activity at the back of the book (see page 527).**

Problems with the dividend growth model

The difficulties with the growth model arise from the assumptions upon which the model is based. In its general form, the dividend valuation model is a complete specification of the present value of a firm's future dividends, discounted at the equity investors' rate of return. The use of the capital asset pricing model for predicting the investors' minimum required rate of return is liable to cause some inaccuracies given the limitations of the assumptions upon which it is based. However, problems arise when we simplify the general model to create the dividend growth model. Here are some of the criticisms of the dividend growth model.

It is very unlikely that the growth of dividends will be constant over the lifetime of the company. However, what is important here is not whether the growth in dividends is actually constant but whether investors, and especially professional fund managers, believe that future growth will be constant. Remember that the share price is realised from the consensus of investor beliefs and if all investors make their investment decisions presupposing constant future dividend growth then that is exactly what the share price will reflect. This is an example of what we call 'the market pricing paradox'. If a particular valuation model begins to become influential in shaping the way investors make their own investment decisions then actual prices will tend towards those predicted by the model concerned.

The model imposes a limit on the growth of the firm to the rate of return on equity capital. As the assumed growth rate is increased towards the expected rate of return on equity, the denominator of the DGM approaches zero. When growth equals the equity rate of return the value predicted by the model goes to infinity. However, this is exactly what we would expect in practice. As we have pointed out above, a business that consistently reinvested all of its earnings at the equity rate of return and never paid a dividend would ultimately grow very large indeed.

Some firms engage in 'buy-back' arrangements where they buy back and then cancel a proportion of their equity capital. This, it is argued, invalidates a central assumption of the dividend valuation model that the only return investors receive from their company is their annual dividend. If the buy-back is fairly priced then, from the investor's point of view, a buy-back is just the same as selling the shares concerned on the open market. Complications arise, however, because a buy-back will tend to increase the earnings-per-share of the remaining shareholders and increase gearing. As we have already pointed out, the open-market price for any share should equal the discounted value of future dividends at the date of sale. If the company is buying back and cancelling its equity at a significant premium then this will be to the detriment of the existing shareholders and we would therefore expect the model to misspecify the fundamental value of the shares by the lost premium. Buy-backs do cause other difficulties for the estimation of share value because of the alteration in the firm's gearing and the increase in the return on equity which are implied if the earnings remain constant or continue with their existing pattern of growth. The references at the end of this chapter will give you the necessary techniques to adapt the models.

For further reading on equity valuation see Ryan (2006) where the dividend growth model and a number of other methods are discussed in detail.

Measuring the performance of firms

In recent years there has been growing interest in what is sometimes referred to as value management. The cornerstone of value management is the measurement of the period-by-period value creation by firms. The idea behind value measurement is that firms are measured by how effectively they increase the net present value of the firms for the shareholders. However, firms are unlikely to be able to forecast their future cash flows and to make routine business decisions on the basis of the incremental impact of those decisions to the net present value of the firm. This may be feasible for large investment projects but is quite impractical for the evaluation of the day-to-day decision making by management. Accounting academics and practitioners have for a number of years been looking for a 'proxy' measure of performance. This 'proxy' had to be such that if managers maximised their performance against that measure then they would in effect be working to maximise the value of the firm. The definition of such a proxy measure takes us back to an issue we discussed earlier.

In the valuation examples above, we measured growth assuming that the firm earned the equity rate of return (its equity cost of capital) on the capital invested. We noted that in the short run a firm could earn an actual return which was greater than the equilibrium rate predicted for the given level of market risk. For the firm as a whole, which employs both equity and debt capital, abnormal returns occur when the actual rate of return on capital employed is greater than the weighted average cost of capital. This abnormal or 'economic' profit is therefore defined as:

$$\text{Economic profit} = \frac{\text{Return on capital}}{\text{employed}} \times \frac{\text{Capital}}{\text{invested}} - \frac{\text{Cost of}}{\text{Capital}} \times \frac{\text{Capital}}{\text{invested}}$$

However, the accounting measurement of return on capital employed (net of tax) is given by the ratio:

$$\text{Return on capital employed (net)} = \frac{\text{Operating profit before interest} - \text{tax}}{\text{Capital invested}}$$

Bringing these two equations together the economic profit is given by:

$$\text{Economic profit} = \frac{\text{Operating profit}}{\text{before interest and after tax}} - \frac{\text{Cost of}}{\text{capital}} \times \frac{\text{Capital}}{\text{invested}}$$

Strictly, economic profit is defined as the difference between revenues and the opportunity costs of all the resources used in production. However, in an imperfect world, accounting measures of profit are all that are readily available. As discussed in Chapter 7, profit measures can be manipulated by a variety of techniques and to surmount this problem a variety of corrections have been proposed to create more economically relevant figures. Economic value-added or (EVA®) is a procedure developed and marketed by US management consultants Stern Stewart and Co. Economic value-added is defined as:

$$\text{Economic Value Added} = \frac{\text{Adjusted operating profit before interest and after tax}}{} - \frac{\text{Cost of}}{\text{capital}} \times \frac{\text{Adjusted Capital invested}}{}$$

Open shout trading on the financial markets

The key word in this definition is 'adjusted'. Indeed, Stern Stewart employs over 250 adjustments to the income statement and balance sheet to arrive at a figure upon which the estimation of EVA can be based.

The advantage of such measures of economic performance is that they give a measure of the increase or decrease in the value of the firm over the year. If correctly calculated the economic profit should closely approximate to the net present value of the firm at the end of the year less the net present value at the beginning. In Chapter 5 we gave an overview of this method of measuring the true profit of a business – and so we have come full circle in our discussion. All that remains for the astute manager is to be able to identify the sources of that true profit or value-added within the business and to exploit them.

Financial realities The operating profit for Marks & Spencer plc was £1045.9 million for the financial year ending 31 March 2007. The firm's weighted average cost of capital is 7.4 per cent and the effective tax rate is 30 per cent.

$$
\begin{aligned}
\text{Economic value-added} &= \text{net operating profit after tax} - \text{weighted average cost of capital} \times (\text{total equity} + \\
&\quad \text{total debt}) \\
&= £1045.9 \text{ million} \times 0.7 - 0.074 \times (£1648.2 \text{ million} + £1234.5 \text{ million}) \\
&= £518.8 \text{ million}
\end{aligned}
$$

Chapter summary

In this chapter we have brought together a number of concepts and, indeed, a number of loose ends. Our discussion of financial ratios in Chapter 7 was not quite complete because a number of ratios require an understanding of the workings of the capital market before their significance can be appreciated. We have reviewed those ratios and built your toolkit of accounting techniques for the analysis of accounts. Throughout the book we have also discussed the concept of value and how it is measured. This started with a discussion of the means by which firms create value in Chapter 5, was considerably developed in Chapter 10 with the application of the net present value rule, and in this chapter we have brought it all together into a discussion of how to value the firm. A significant thread within our story of accounting and finance has been the incompleteness of accounting information and in this chapter we have explored the reasons why markets may value firms at many multiples of their book value. Finally, we have reviewed the concept of performance measurement and devised a crude but useful approximation to the economic profit of a firm using cash flow statements and adjustments for the opportunity cost of capital employed.

Throughout it all we have reviewed three companies: DialaSid Ltd which rumour has it is still developing its taxi-cum-transport business in Watford, Cobham plc which has provided a number of good examples of a well-managed growing business, and Marks & Spencer. Marks & Spencer continues its recovery from the low point of 2003. It, like any other company, has no right to survive except by virtue of its own success in delivering superior goods and services to its customers and superior financial performance to its investors. If we have demonstrated the role that finance and accounting can play in helping a business to achieve that then we are content.

Further reading

Barker, R. (2001) *Determining Value – Valuation Models and Financial Statements*, Harlow: Financial Times Prentice Hall. This is an excellent book, not so strong on the practical examples but the writing is very clear and straightforward. Chapters 9 and 10 look at the problem of economic and shareholder value-added, although, given the book's narrative style you will need to read the rest to get the best from those chapters.

Bodie, Z. and Merton, R.C. (2000) *Finance*, Upper Saddle River, NJ: Prentice-Hall. Probably the best book available on finance for readers wishing to go beyond the level in the present book.

Damodaran, A. (2002) *Tools and Techniques for Determining the Value of any Asset*, 2nd edn, New York: Wiley. Probably the best book on valuation currently available. Extremely clear text, well grounded in the theory of finance and with a huge number of examples.

Kettell, B. (2001) *Financial Economics*, Harlow: Financial Times Prentice Hall. An extremely readable review of the operation of the financial markets and their implications for the valuation of equities.

Ryan, B. (2006) *Corporate Finance and Valuation*. London: Cengage.

Stewart, T.A. (2001) *The Wealth of Knowledge*, London: Nicholas Brearley. An easily read overview of the problems of valuing the human capital in organisations.

Vaitilingam, R. (2001) *The Financial Times Guide to Using the Financial Pages*, Harlow: Financial Times Prentice Hall. An indispensable guide to anyone opening the 'markets' section of the FT for the first time.

Progress check

1. Define 'dividend per share', 'dividend yield' and 'dividend payout ratio'. (pp. 472–473)

2. How are the dividend payout ratio and the retention ratio related? (p. 473)

3. How does basis earnings per share differ from undiluted earnings per share? (p. 474)

4. Define the P/E ratio and the market to book ratio and explain why high multiples of the latter are observed in practice. (p. 474)

5. How does the 'entanglement phenomenon' arise? (p. 475)

6. What two sources of financial return to the shareholders drive the value of their equity? (p. 476)

7. Write out the dividend growth model. (p. 477)

8. What are the two broad methods by which growth in dividends can be estimated? (p. 478)

9. How is growth related to the retention ratio? (p. 479)

10. What is the basic formula for measuring the economic value-added by a firm? (p. 483)

Questions

The answers to the questions followed by ✓ can be found at the back of the book, the answers to the remaining questions can be found on the website associated with this book, **www.cengage.co.uk/ryan2**

1. Although world equity markets have lost between 40 and 60 per cent of their value since the peak in spring 2000 many firms are still trading at many multiples of their book value. Discuss the reasons why this is the case and the extent to which the inclusion of brand values, unrealised holding gains and internally generated goodwill would bridge the gap.

2. Below (Exhibit 14.6) is a statement of the current and expected balance sheet and profit and loss account for a limited company. The company accounts are expressed in £000. The company has 1 million £1 ordinary shares in issue at a current share price of £3.80 per share. The company's management expects the firm to grow at 5 per cent into the indefinite future. The rate of return required by its equity investors is 8 per cent.

   You are required to:

   (i) Calculate the firm's current EPS, and its P/E ratio.

   (ii) On the basis that the share price remains unchanged how do you expect the performance of this company to change as measured by a range of no more than five investor ratios?

   (iii) On the basis of the information given, value the firm's equity using the growth figures suggested by the company's management and its own retention policies. ✓

3. The FTSE 100 index currently stands at 5900 and its reported dividend yield is 2.6 per cent. The real growth of the UK domestic economy is forecast at 2.8 per cent and inflation is currently 2.4 per cent. The long-run rate of return on the All Share Index is 10.4 per cent and the beta coefficient of the FTSE 100 index is 1.13. The short-term Treasury bill rate is 5.2 per cent. Press reports suggest that company profitability is expected to slow to 6.0 per cent and recent profit warnings appear to confirm this expectation.

Exhibit 14.6

Balance sheet			year+1	Income statement			year+1
Non-current assets		2500	2944	Revenue		2500	2750
Accum Depreciation		1000	1294	cost of good sold		1250	1375
		1500	1650	Gross profit		1250	1375
Inventories	104		115				
Receivables	208		301	Administrative expenses	400		440
Cash	0		−32	Depreciation	250		294
	312		384			650	734
Payables	52		58	Earnings before interest and tax		600	641
		260	326	interest paid		88	99
		1760	1976			512	542
Long term borrowing		880	988	Tax at 50 per cent		256	271
		880	988	Net profit for distribution		256	271
Owners capital		100	100	Dividends		154	163
Profit reserves		780	888	Profit retained		102	108
		880	988			256	271

You are required to:

(i) Using the data above draw a graph of index value against dividend growth rate.

(ii) On the graph show the likely index range on the assumption that the corporate profitability slows to the level suggested.

(iii) Calculate the proportion of index value which is implied by general growth in the economy.

Discuss the significance of the assumptions implicit in the above valuation process and comment upon their applicability for valuing individual securities as well as an index. ✓

··

4. Attached are the simplified accounts of a high-street retailer which is a public limited company in the UK.

The publicly quoted beta for this company is 0.192 and the average market return is 8.4 per cent. However, there is considerable doubt about the validity of this beta estimate and a figure much closer to the market average is regarded as more likely by the directors of the company. The return on short-dated government stock is 4.8 per cent. The current price per share is 99.5p. Retail sales are expected to continue their strong growth of 6 per cent per annum for the next twelve months before reverting to the growth in GDP which is currently 1.8 per cent per annum. Inflation is currently 1.9 per cent.

The directors of this company are convinced that the current market value is substantially understating the fundamental value of the business. This has been substantiated by a number of analysts' 'buy' recommendations in the financial press.

You are required to:

(i) Make two estimates of the likely dividend growth figures for this company using (a) the economic fundamentals and (b) projected dividends from the accounting information.

(ii) Calculate the value per share as at 28 May 2000 on the basis of the dividend projections estimated in (i) above and comment on the reasons for any difference you obtain.

(iii) Comment on the directors' assertion that the market has understated this company's value in the light of the figures you have obtained and in the light of the efficient markets hypothesis.

Exhibit 14.7 Retailer PLC accounts

Consolidated income statement

For the 52 weeks ended 27 May 2007	2007 £000	2006 £000
Turnover	154 511	132 030
Cost of sales	(59 794)	(51 550)
Gross profit	94 717	80 480
Administrative expenses	(72 816)	(60 880)
Other operating income	518	346
Operating profit		
Before exceptional operating charges	22 927	20 776
Exceptional operating charges	(508)	(830)
Total operating profit	22 419	19 946
Interest receivable and similar income	642	511
Interest payable and similar charges	(69)	(31)
Profit on ordinary activities before taxation	22 992	20 426
Tax on profit on ordinary activities	(7 711)	(7 317)
Profit on ordinary activities after taxation	15 281	13 109
Dividends	(7 998)	(7 998)
Retained profit for the year	7 283	5 111
Earnings per share – basic and diluted	8.60p	7.38p
Earnings per share – adjusted	8.88p	7.84p

Consolidated balance sheet

At 27 May 2007	2007 £000	2006 £000
Non-current assets		
Intangible assets	437	1 199
Tangible assets	28 793	25 348
Investments	–	9
	29 230	26 556
Current assets		
Inventories	16 075	12 901
Receivables	3 864	3 019
Cash at bank and in hand	17 797	10 169
	37 736	26 089
Current liabilities	(30 970)	(23 968)
Net current assets	6 766	2 121
Total assets less current liabilities	35 996	28 677
Non-current liabilities	(2 337)	(2 778)
Net assets	33 659	25 899

	Group 2000 £000	Group 1999 £000
Capital and reserves		
Called up share capital	17 774	17 774
17 742 080 ordinary shares, fully paid		
Merger reserve	5 271	5 271
Profit and loss account	10 614	2 854
Equity shareholders' funds	33 659	25 899

Notes to the accounts

Inventories
Finished goods for resale	16 075	12 091

Debtors
Receivables	847	917

Creditors, amounts falling due within one year
Trade creditors	5 699	5 448

Five year financial record

	2000 £000	1999 £000	1998 £000	1997 £000	1996 £000
Turnover	154 511	132 030	123 406	107 930	79 560
Gross Profit	94 717	80 480	77 010	67 580	49 985
Administrative expenses	(72 816)	(60 880)	(50 704)	(44 047)	(32 729)
Other operating income	518	346	510	961	322
Operating Profit					
Before exceptional items	22 927	20 776	27 745	24 494	17 578
Exceptional Items	(508)	(830)	(929)		
	22 419	19 946	26 816	24 494	17 578
Net interest receivable	573	480	884	868	1 012
Net profit before tax	22 992	20 426	27 700	25 362	18 590
Taxation	(7 711)	(7 317)	(8 930)	(9 883)	(6 194)
Profit after tax	15 281	13 109	18 770	15 479	12 396
Dividends	(7 998)	(7 998)	(15 280)	(10 010)	(11 974)
Retained profits	7 283	5 111	3 490	5 469	422
Earnings per share before exceptional items	8.88p	7.84p	11.03p	8.62p	6.90p
Earnings per share	8.60p	7.38p	10.50p	8.62p	6.90p

Appendix Financial tables

Present Value: The Present Value of £1 discounted at the stated percentage rate over the given number of years

	1	2	3	4	5	6	7	8	9	10	11	12	13	14	15	16	17	18	19	20
0%	1.0000	1.0000	1.0000	1.0000	1.0000	1.0000	1.0000	1.0000	1.0000	1.0000	1.0000	1.0000	1.0000	1.0000	1.0000	1.0000	1.0000	1.0000	1.0000	1.0000
1%	0.9901	0.9803	0.9706	0.9610	0.9515	0.9420	0.9327	0.9235	0.9143	0.9053	0.8963	0.8874	0.8787	0.8700	0.8613	0.8528	0.8444	0.8360	0.8277	0.8195
2%	0.9804	0.9612	0.9423	0.9238	0.9057	0.8880	0.8706	0.8535	0.8368	0.8203	0.8043	0.7885	0.7730	0.7579	0.7430	0.7284	0.7142	0.7002	0.6864	0.6730
3%	0.9709	0.9426	0.9151	0.8885	0.8626	0.8375	0.8131	0.7894	0.7664	0.7441	0.7224	0.7014	0.6810	0.6611	0.6419	0.6232	0.6050	0.5874	0.5703	0.5537
4%	0.9615	0.9246	0.8890	0.8548	0.8219	0.7903	0.7599	0.7307	0.7026	0.6756	0.6496	0.6246	0.6006	0.5775	0.5553	0.5339	0.5134	0.4936	0.4746	0.4564
5%	0.9524	0.9070	0.8638	0.8227	0.7835	0.7462	0.7107	0.6768	0.6446	0.6139	0.5847	0.5568	0.5303	0.5051	0.4810	0.4581	0.4363	0.4155	0.3957	0.3769
6%	0.9434	0.8900	0.8396	0.7921	0.7473	0.7050	0.6651	0.6274	0.5919	0.5584	0.5268	0.4970	0.4688	0.4423	0.4173	0.3936	0.3714	0.3503	0.3305	0.3118
7%	0.9346	0.8734	0.8163	0.7629	0.7130	0.6663	0.6227	0.5820	0.5439	0.5083	0.4751	0.4440	0.4150	0.3878	0.3624	0.3387	0.3166	0.2959	0.2765	0.2584
8%	0.9259	0.8573	0.7938	0.7350	0.6806	0.6302	0.5835	0.5403	0.5002	0.4632	0.4289	0.3971	0.3677	0.3405	0.3152	0.2919	0.2703	0.2502	0.2317	0.2145
9%	0.9174	0.8417	0.7722	0.7084	0.6499	0.5963	0.5470	0.5019	0.4604	0.4224	0.3875	0.3555	0.3262	0.2992	0.2745	0.2519	0.2311	0.2120	0.1945	0.1784
10%	0.9091	0.8264	0.7513	0.6830	0.6209	0.5645	0.5132	0.4665	0.4241	0.3855	0.3505	0.3186	0.2897	0.2633	0.2394	0.2176	0.1978	0.1799	0.1635	0.1486
11%	0.9009	0.8116	0.7312	0.6587	0.5935	0.5346	0.4817	0.4339	0.3909	0.3522	0.3173	0.2858	0.2575	0.2320	0.2090	0.1883	0.1696	0.1528	0.1377	0.1240
12%	0.8929	0.7972	0.7118	0.6355	0.5674	0.5066	0.4523	0.4039	0.3606	0.3220	0.2875	0.2567	0.2292	0.2046	0.1827	0.1631	0.1456	0.1300	0.1161	0.1037
13%	0.8850	0.7831	0.6931	0.6133	0.5428	0.4803	0.4251	0.3762	0.3329	0.2946	0.2607	0.2307	0.2042	0.1807	0.1599	0.1415	0.1252	0.1108	0.0981	0.0868
14%	0.8772	0.7695	0.6750	0.5921	0.5194	0.4556	0.3996	0.3506	0.3075	0.2697	0.2366	0.2076	0.1821	0.1597	0.1401	0.1229	0.1078	0.0946	0.0829	0.0728
15%	0.8696	0.7561	0.6575	0.5718	0.4972	0.4323	0.3759	0.3269	0.2843	0.2472	0.2149	0.1869	0.1625	0.1413	0.1229	0.1069	0.0929	0.0808	0.0703	0.0611
16%	0.8621	0.7432	0.6407	0.5523	0.4761	0.4104	0.3538	0.3050	0.2630	0.2267	0.1954	0.1685	0.1452	0.1252	0.1079	0.0930	0.0802	0.0691	0.0596	0.0514
17%	0.8547	0.7305	0.6244	0.5337	0.4561	0.3898	0.3332	0.2848	0.2434	0.2080	0.1778	0.1520	0.1299	0.1110	0.0949	0.0811	0.0693	0.0592	0.0506	0.0433
18%	0.8475	0.7182	0.6086	0.5158	0.4371	0.3704	0.3139	0.2660	0.2255	0.1911	0.1619	0.1372	0.1163	0.0985	0.0835	0.0708	0.0600	0.0508	0.0431	0.0365
19%	0.8403	0.7062	0.5934	0.4987	0.4190	0.3521	0.2959	0.2487	0.2090	0.1756	0.1476	0.1240	0.1042	0.0876	0.0736	0.0618	0.0520	0.0437	0.0367	0.0308
20%	0.8333	0.6944	0.5787	0.4823	0.4019	0.3349	0.2791	0.2326	0.1938	0.1615	0.1346	0.1122	0.0935	0.0779	0.0649	0.0541	0.0451	0.0376	0.0313	0.0261
21%	0.8264	0.6830	0.5645	0.4665	0.3855	0.3186	0.2633	0.2176	0.1799	0.1486	0.1228	0.1015	0.0839	0.0693	0.0573	0.0474	0.0391	0.0323	0.0267	0.0221
22%	0.8197	0.6719	0.5507	0.4514	0.3700	0.3033	0.2486	0.2038	0.1670	0.1369	0.1122	0.0920	0.0754	0.0618	0.0507	0.0415	0.0340	0.0279	0.0229	0.0187
23%	0.8130	0.6610	0.5374	0.4369	0.3552	0.2888	0.2348	0.1909	0.1552	0.1262	0.1026	0.0834	0.0678	0.0551	0.0448	0.0364	0.0296	0.0241	0.0196	0.0159
24%	0.8065	0.6504	0.5245	0.4230	0.3411	0.2751	0.2218	0.1789	0.1443	0.1164	0.0938	0.0757	0.0610	0.0492	0.0397	0.0320	0.0258	0.0208	0.0168	0.0135
25%	0.8000	0.6400	0.5120	0.4096	0.3277	0.2621	0.2097	0.1678	0.1342	0.1074	0.0859	0.0687	0.0550	0.0440	0.0352	0.0281	0.0225	0.0180	0.0144	0.0115

Annuity: The sum of the Present Value of £1 discounted at the stated percentage for each of a given number of years

	1	2	3	4	5	6	7	8	9	10	11	12	13	14	15	16	17	18	19	20
0%	1.000	2.000	3.000	4.000	5.000	6.000	7.000	8.000	9.000	10.000	11.000	12.000	13.000	14.000	15.000	16.000	17.000	18.000	19.000	20.000
1%	0.990	1.970	2.941	3.902	4.853	5.795	6.728	7.652	8.566	9.471	10.368	11.255	12.134	13.004	13.865	14.718	15.562	16.398	17.226	18.046
2%	0.980	1.942	2.884	3.808	4.713	5.601	6.472	7.325	8.162	8.983	9.787	10.575	11.348	12.106	12.849	13.578	14.292	14.992	15.578	16.351
3%	0.971	1.913	2.829	3.717	4.580	5.417	6.230	7.020	7.786	8.530	9.253	9.954	10.635	11.296	11.938	12.561	13.166	13.754	14.324	14.877
4%	0.962	1.886	2.775	3.630	4.452	5.242	6.002	6.733	7.435	8.111	8.760	9.385	9.986	10.563	11.118	11.652	12.166	12.659	13.134	13.590
5%	0.952	1.859	2.723	3.546	4.329	5.076	5.786	6.463	7.108	7.722	8.306	8.863	9.394	9.899	10.380	10.838	11.274	11.690	12.085	12.462
6%	0.943	1.833	2.673	3.465	4.212	4.917	5.582	6.210	6.802	7.360	7.887	8.384	8.853	9.295	9.712	10.106	10.477	10.828	11.158	11.470
7%	0.935	1.808	2.624	3.387	4.100	4.767	5.389	5.971	6.515	7.024	7.499	7.943	8.358	8.745	9.108	9.447	9.763	10.059	10.336	10.594
8%	0.926	1.783	2.577	3.312	3.993	4.623	5.206	5.747	6.247	6.710	7.139	7.536	7.904	8.244	8.559	8.851	9.122	9.372	9.604	9.818
9%	0.917	1.759	2.531	3.240	3.890	4.486	5.033	5.535	5.995	6.418	6.805	7.161	7.487	7.786	8.061	8.313	8.544	8.756	8.950	9.129
10%	0.909	1.736	2.487	3.170	3.791	4.355	4.868	5.335	5.759	6.145	6.495	6.814	7.103	7.367	7.606	7.824	8.022	8.201	8.365	8.514
11%	0.901	1.713	2.444	3.102	3.696	4.231	4.712	5.146	5.537	5.889	6.207	6.492	6.750	6.982	7.191	7.379	7.549	7.702	7.839	7.963
12%	0.893	1.690	2.402	3.037	3.605	4.111	4.564	4.968	5.328	5.650	5.938	6.194	6.424	6.628	6.811	6.974	7.120	7.250	7.366	7.469
13%	0.885	1.668	2.361	2.974	3.517	3.998	4.423	4.799	5.132	5.426	5.687	5.918	6.122	6.302	6.462	6.604	6.729	6.840	6.938	7.025
14%	0.877	1.647	2.322	2.914	3.433	3.889	4.288	4.639	4.946	5.216	5.453	5.660	5.842	6.002	6.142	6.265	6.373	6.467	6.550	6.623
15%	0.870	1.626	2.283	2.855	3.352	3.784	4.160	4.487	4.772	5.019	5.234	5.421	5.583	5.724	5.847	5.954	6.047	6.128	6.198	6.259
16%	0.862	1.605	2.245	2.798	3.274	3.685	4.039	4.344	4.607	4.833	5.029	5.197	5.342	5.468	5.575	5.668	5.749	5.818	5.877	5.929
17%	0.855	1.585	2.210	2.743	3.199	3.589	3.922	4.207	4.451	4.659	4.836	4.988	5.118	5.229	5.324	5.405	5.475	5.534	5.584	5.628
18%	0.847	1.566	2.174	2.690	3.127	3.498	3.812	4.078	4.303	4.494	4.656	4.793	4.910	5.008	5.092	5.162	5.222	5.273	5.316	5.353
19%	0.840	1.547	2.140	2.639	3.058	3.410	3.706	3.954	4.163	4.339	4.486	4.611	4.715	4.802	4.876	4.933	4.990	5.033	5.070	5.101
20%	0.833	1.528	2.106	2.589	2.991	3.326	3.605	3.837	4.031	4.192	4.327	4.439	4.533	4.611	4.675	4.730	4.775	4.812	4.843	4.870
21%	0.826	1.509	2.074	2.540	2.926	3.245	3.508	3.726	3.905	4.054	4.177	4.278	4.362	4.432	4.489	4.536	4.576	4.608	4.635	4.657
22%	0.820	1.492	2.042	2.494	2.864	3.167	3.416	3.619	3.786	3.923	4.035	4.127	4.203	4.265	4.315	4.357	4.391	4.419	4.442	4.460
23%	0.813	1.474	2.011	2.448	2.803	3.092	3.327	3.518	3.673	3.799	3.902	3.985	4.053	4.108	4.153	4.189	4.219	4.243	4.263	4.279
24%	0.806	1.457	1.981	2.404	2.745	3.020	3.242	3.421	3.566	3.682	3.776	3.851	3.912	3.962	4.001	4.033	4.059	4.080	4.097	4.110
25%	0.800	1.440	1.952	2.362	2.689	2.951	3.161	3.329	3.463	3.571	3.656	3.725	3.780	3.824	3.859	3.887	3.910	3.928	3.942	3.954

Terminal Value: The future value of £1 invested at the stated percentage at the beginning of each of a given number of years

	1	2	3	4	5	6	7	8	9	10	11	12	13	14	15	16	17	18	19	20
0%	1.000	2.000	3.000	4.000	5.000	6.000	7.000	8.000	9.000	10.000	11.000	12.000	13.000	14.000	15.000	16.000	17.000	18.000	19.000	20.000
1%	1.010	2.030	3.060	4.101	5.152	6.214	7.286	8.369	9.462	10.567	11.683	12.809	13.947	15.097	16.258	17.430	18.615	19.811	21.019	22.239
2%	1.020	2.060	3.122	4.204	5.308	6.434	7.583	8.755	9.950	11.169	12.412	13.680	14.974	16.293	17.639	19.012	20.412	21.841	23.297	24.783
3%	1.030	2.091	3.184	4.309	5.468	6.662	7.892	9.159	10.464	11.808	13.192	14.618	16.086	17.599	19.157	20.762	22.414	24.117	25.870	27.676
4%	1.040	2.122	3.246	4.416	5.633	6.898	8.214	9.583	11.006	12.486	14.026	15.627	17.292	19.024	20.825	22.698	24.645	26.671	28.778	30.969
5%	1.050	2.153	3.310	4.526	5.802	7.142	8.549	10.027	11.578	13.207	14.917	16.713	18.599	20.579	22.657	24.840	27.132	29.539	32.066	34.719
6%	1.060	2.184	3.375	4.637	5.975	7.394	8.897	10.491	12.181	13.972	15.870	17.882	20.015	22.276	24.673	27.213	29.906	32.760	35.786	38.993
7%	1.070	2.215	3.440	4.751	6.153	7.654	9.260	10.978	12.816	14.784	16.888	19.141	21.550	24.129	26.888	29.840	32.999	36.379	39.995	43.865
8%	1.080	2.246	3.506	4.867	6.336	7.923	9.637	11.488	13.487	15.645	17.977	20.495	23.215	26.152	29.324	32.750	36.450	40.446	44.762	49.423
9%	1.090	2.278	3.573	4.985	6.523	8.200	10.028	12.021	14.193	16.560	19.141	21.953	25.019	28.361	32.003	35.974	40.301	45.018	50.160	55.765
10%	1.100	2.310	3.641	5.105	6.716	8.487	10.436	12.579	14.937	17.531	20.384	23.523	26.975	30.772	34.950	39.545	44.599	50.159	56.275	63.002
11%	1.110	2.342	3.710	5.228	6.913	8.783	10.859	13.164	15.722	18.561	21.713	25.212	29.095	33.405	38.190	43.501	49.396	55.939	63.203	71.265
12%	1.120	2.374	3.779	5.353	7.115	9.089	11.300	13.776	16.549	19.655	23.133	27.029	31.393	36.280	41.753	47.884	54.750	62.440	71.052	80.699
13%	1.130	2.407	3.850	5.480	7.323	9.405	11.757	14.416	17.420	20.814	24.650	28.985	33.883	39.417	45.672	52.739	60.725	69.749	79.947	91.470
14%	1.140	2.440	3.921	5.610	7.536	9.730	12.233	15.085	18.337	22.045	26.271	31.089	36.581	42.842	49.980	58.118	67.394	77.969	90.025	103.768
15%	1.150	2.473	3.993	5.742	7.754	10.067	12.727	15.786	19.304	23.349	28.002	33.352	39.505	46.580	54.717	64.075	74.836	87.212	101.444	117.810
16%	1.160	2.506	4.066	5.877	7.977	10.414	13.240	16.519	20.321	24.733	29.850	35.786	42.672	50.660	59.925	70.673	83.141	97.603	114.380	133.841
17%	1.170	2.539	4.141	6.014	8.207	10.772	13.773	17.285	21.393	26.200	31.824	38.404	46.103	55.110	65.649	77.979	92.406	109.285	129.033	152.139
18%	1.180	2.572	4.215	6.154	8.442	11.142	14.327	18.086	22.521	27.755	33.931	41.219	49.818	59.965	71.939	86.068	102.740	122.414	145.628	173.021
19%	1.190	2.606	4.291	6.297	8.683	11.523	14.902	18.923	23.709	29.404	36.180	44.244	53.841	65.261	78.850	95.022	114.266	137.166	164.418	196.847
20%	1.200	2.640	4.368	6.442	8.930	11.916	15.499	19.799	24.959	31.150	38.581	47.497	58.196	71.035	86.442	104.931	127.117	153.740	185.688	224.026
21%	1.210	2.674	4.446	6.589	9.183	12.321	16.119	20.714	26.274	33.001	41.142	50.991	62.909	77.330	94.780	115.894	141.441	172.354	209.758	255.018
22%	1.220	2.708	4.524	6.740	9.442	12.740	16.762	21.670	27.657	34.962	43.874	54.746	68.010	84.192	103.935	128.020	157.405	193.254	236.989	290.347
23%	1.230	2.743	4.604	6.893	9.708	13.171	17.430	22.669	29.113	37.039	46.788	58.779	73.528	91.669	113.983	141.430	175.188	216.712	267.785	330.606
24%	1.240	2.778	4.684	7.048	9.980	13.615	18.123	23.712	30.643	39.238	49.895	63.110	79.496	99.815	125.011	156.253	194.994	243.033	302.601	376.465
25%	1.250	2.813	4.766	7.207	10.259	14.073	18.842	24.802	32.253	41.566	53.208	67.760	85.949	108.687	137.109	172.636	217.045	272.556	341.945	428.681

Answers to selected review activities and end-of-chapter questions

Further answers are available on the website at **www.cengage.co.uk/ryan2**

Chapter 1: The role of accounting and finance in business

Review activity 1.1

Monsoon plc is a retailer. Rolls-Royce plc is a manufacturer, British Airways is a service company based upon the utilisation of real assets and Manchester United plc a service company based upon the utilisation of human assets. With each, different modes of value generation play a part. Manchester United is also a retailer, selling goods in its sports shops and food and drink in its club cafeteria and bars. It also exploits real assets such as the Old Trafford ground and its other physical facilities. Its principal value generation is, however, through its players and other staff.

Chapter 2: Introduction to financial accounting

Review activity 2.3

Exhibit Answers 1

	FA +	St +	Db +	C −	STL +	LTL +	OF +	R −	E
Opening balance sheet	30 000	45	50	5 490	0	20 000	15 585		
Purchase of diesel		200		−200					
Diesel used in month		−210							210
Service bill			160	−240					80
Purchase of GPS	560			−560					
Rental charge to month			−10						10
Interest on loan					50				50
Interest paid				−50	−50				
Cash from fares				1 450				1 450	
								1 450	350
Profit for the period							1 100		1 100
Closing balance sheet	30 560	35	200	5 890	0	20 000	16 685	1 450	1 450

Exhibit Answers 2

Revenue (value adding transactions)

Fares		1450
Less expenditures (value reducing transactions):		
Cost of diesel used	210	
Service charge	80	
Proportion of garage rent used	10	
Interest paid	50	
		350
		1100

Exhibit Answers 3

	2 month	1 month	opening
Total value of Assets			
Value of the taxi at cost	30 000	30 000	30 000
Value of the GPS at cost	560		
Diesel in tank	35	45	
Prepayments to garage	40	50	
Prepaid servicing	160		
Cash in hand	5 890	5 490	5 000
	36 685	35 585	35 000
Less Independent claim			
Bank Loan	20 000	20 000	20 000
	16 685	15 585	15 000
Equals the Owner's Claim			
Sid's investment	15 000	15 000	15 000
Net value added to Sid's claim	1 685	1 585	–
	16 685	16 585	15 000

Question 1

	NCA	Inv	Rec	Cash	=	CL	NCL	OE	R	−E
(i) Purchase of non-current (fixed) assets	500 000					500 000				
(i) Cash settlement of purchase				−500 000		−500 000				
(ii) Depreciation of a non-current asset	−80 000									80 000
(iii) A customer fails to settle an account			−2 000							2 000
(iv) Stock write-off		−20 000								20 000
(v) Goods returned		−50 000				−50 000				
(v) Cash returned				50 000		50 000				

Question 2

Ernie Buckle's Balance Sheet

Non-current assets	60 000
Current Assets	
inventories	10 000
receivables	18 000
cash	19 000
	47 000
less current liabilities	− 16 000
less non-current liabilities	− 30 000
	61 000
Subscribed capital	30 500
Retained earnings	
at the beginning of the year	20 000
added during the year	10 500
	30 500
Owner's Equity	61 000

The cash balance of 19 000 is the missing figure

Chapter 3: Building the accounts

Questions

2. (i) The balance sheet and income statement for Mr Sloppy are as follows:

Exhibit Answers 4

Balance Sheet			Income statement		
Fixed Assets		240 000	Sales turnover		316 500
Accumulated depreciation		80 000	less cost of sales		144 000
		160 000	Gross profit		172 500
Current assets			Selling and distribution costs	76 700	
Stocks	45 000		Administrative expenses	43 000	
Debtors	67 000				119 700
Cash	8 400		Operating profit		52 800
	120 400		Interest paid		5 700
less: current liabilities	97 600		Profit before tax		47 100
		22 800	Corporation tax payable		18 840
		182 800	Distributable profit		28 260
Less long-term liabilities		73 500	Dividends paid		11 560
Net assets		109 300	Profit retained for the year		16 700
Owner's equity		50 000			
Accumulated profits		59 300			
Equity capital employed		109 300			

(ii) The principal relationships between the income statement and the balance sheet are as follows:

- The profit retained for the year in the income statement should reconcile to the increase in accumulated profit in the balance sheet.
- The depreciation charge in the income statement should equal the change in accumulated depreciation in the balance sheet unless there have been disposals of fixed assets during the year.

The first is the defining relationship, however, in that the income statement shows the change in the value added to the equity (owner's) account in the balance sheet.

Chapter 4: Cash flow statements

Questions

1. (i) Mr Sloppy's cash flow statement is as follows:

Exhibit Answers 5	
Statement of Cash Flow	
Operating cash flow	66 000
less interest paid	5 700
	60 300
less taxation	16 500
	43 800
Acquisition of fixed assets	35 000
	8 800
less dividend paid	11 560
Net cash outflow during the year	2 760

(ii) The operating profit for a company shows the change in the balance sheet value of equity during the course of the year (excluding any additions or withdrawals of capital). To obtain the income statement the transactions are matched to the year in question. The cash flow statement simply records the cash changes during the year, and these are not matched in a transactional sense as are revenues and expenses in the income statement. The most significant difference is that the income statement will show the matching of capital expenditure via a depreciation charge, whereas a cash flow statement does not include depreciation.

3. Grundy's Breakers Ltd

(i) Projected income statement and balance sheet for the coming year.

Income statement for the year ended 31 December

	2006		2007
Turnover	8 945 000	1.05	9 392 250
Cost of sales	2 100 400		2 017 575
Gross profit	6 844 600	76.52	7 374 675
Other operating costs	4 350 100	0.98	4 263 098
Operating profit	2 494 500		3 111 577
Interest payable	65 000	0.07	35 000
Profit before tax	2 429 500		3 076 577
Tax	1 093 275	0.50	1 538 289
Distributable profit	1 336 225		1 538 289
Dividend's paid and payable	240 000	0.15	300 000
Profit retained	1 096 225		1 238 289
	1 336 225		1 538 289

Balance sheet as at 31 December 2006

Fixed assets at cost	5 018 000	2 200 000	7 218 000
Accumulated depreciation	1 104 569	0.10	1 715 912
	3 913 431		5 502 088
Current assets			
Stocks	60 422	8.00	44 221
Debtors	1 102 808	40.00	1 029 288
Cash	99 747		803 810
	1 262 977		1 877 318
less current liabilities	1 479 683	40.00	1 944 393
	−216 706		−67 074
	3 696 725		5 435 014
less long-term liabilities	1 000 000		500 000
	2 696 725		4 935 014
Shareholder funds			
25p ordinary shares	500 000	500 000	1 000 000
Share premium account	354 500		854 500
Profit and loss reserve	1 842 225		3 080 514
	2 696 725		4 935 014

(ii) Projected statement of cash flow

		Operating cash flow	Interest paid/received	Taxation	Capex Disposals	Dividends Paid	Financing
Operating profit	3 111 577	3 111 577					
less interest payable	−35 000		−35 000				
less tax payable	−1 538 289			−1 538 289			
less dividends paid/payable	−300 000					−300 000	
	1 238 289						
short-term liabilities							
increase trade creditors	19 696	19 696					
decrease interest payable	−30 000		−30 000				
increase tax	445 014			445 014			
increase dividend	30 000					30 000	
	464 709						
long-term liabilities							
decrease loan	−500 000						−500 000
	−500 000						
owner's capital							
share issue	500 000						500 000
share premium	500 000						500 000
	1 000 000						
	2 202 998	3 131 273	−65 000	−1 093 275	0	−270 000	500 000
Fixed assets							
assets acquired	2 200 000				2 200 000		
depreciation for year	−611 343	−611 343					
	1 588 657						
Stocks	−16 202	−16 202					
Debtors	−73 521	−73 521					
	1 498 935	−701 065	0	0	2 200 000	0	0
	704 063	3 832 338	−65 000	−1 093 275	−2 200 000	−270 000	500 000

Statement of cash flow for the year ended 31 December 2007

Operating cash flow	3 832 338
less interest paid	−65 000
	3 767 338
less taxation	−1 093 275
	2 674 063
CAPEX	−2 200 000
	474 063
dividends paid	−270 000
	204 063

financing

decrease loan	−500 000	
equity issue	1 000 000	
		500 000
Increase in cash		704 063

Chapter 5: Principles of financial accounting

Questions

2. In answer to parts (i) and (ii) of the question, the note for depreciation in the accounts is as follows:

Exhibit Answers 6

Accumulated depreciation	Balance 31-Dec-02 £'000	Depreciation for the year £'000	Disposals £'000	Balance 31-Dec-03 £'000
Buildings	1660	218	0	1878
Plant	338	176	0	514
Equipment	144	70	−20	194
Fixed assets at cost	2142	464	−20	2586

(iii) If the buildings were found to be of substantially greater value than that shown in the accounts then there would be a case for their revaluation. The revalued figure would be shown in the balance sheet and the surplus shown within the revaluation reserve. If a company decides to revalue an asset all assets of the same class should be similarly revalued.

If the plant and equipment were shown to be substantially overvalued then they are said to be 'impaired' and should be shown at the higher of net realisable value and value in use. On the presumption that the assets have not been previously revalued upwards then the loss on impairment is charged directly to the income statement.

4. Bernard Ltd

The first step is to lay out the opening balance sheet across the accounting equation. We then proceed to analyse the transactions for the current year:

1. The tax and the dividend paid are settled by a cash payment to clear the short-term liability established at the end of the previous year.

2. Revenue was received of £270 000 and cash paid of £330 000, leaving outstanding customer accounts of £24 000.

3. The stock sold during the year was £140 000. Given that there was £38 000 of inventory on hand at the year-end we can work out that the new purchases were made of £113 000.

Exhibit Answers 7

	FA	+	St	+	Db	+	C	=	STL	+	LTL	+	OE	+	R	−	E
	240 000												50 000				
	196 000		65 000		84 000		9 100		60 400		38 000		53 700				
Opening balance sheet	44 000		65 000		84 000		9 100		60 400		38 000		103 700				
1 Tax paid							−12 300		−12 300								
Dividend paid							−5 000		−5 000								
2 Revenue					270 000										270 000		
Receipts from customers					−330 000		330 000										
3 Stock sold during the year			−140 000														140 000
Stock purchased			113 000						113 000								
4 Other operating expenditures									82 000								82 000
Cash to suppliers							−168 000		−168 000								
5 Depreciation for the year (straight line) − existing assets	−24 000																24 000
6 Purchase of new van	32 000						−32 000										
Depreciation on new van	−5 000																5 000
7 Purchase of management system	18 000						−18 000										
Depreciation	−6 000																6 000
Operating profit															270 000		257 000
8 Sale of van																	
gain on sale of van	2 500														2 500		
proceeds of sale	−10 500						10 500										
9 Interest on the loan									3 040								3 040
Interest paid							−3 040		−3 040								
Profit before tax															272 500		260 040
10 Tax provision									3 115								3 115
															272 500		263 155
Net profit retained														9 345			9 345
															272 500		272 500
Closing balance sheet	51 000		38 000		24 000		111 260		73 215		38 000		113 045				

4. Other operating expenditures were £82 000. As the stock purchases and other operating expenses were £113 000 and £82 000 respectively we can calculate how much was paid for in cash and how much was financed by the increase in the balance of trade creditors. The opening trade creditors were £43 100 (i.e. £60 400 less the tax and dividend liabilities) and the closing trade creditors were £70 100, giving an increase of £27 000. You may re-member from the previous chapter that an increase in short-term liabilities is a source of cash to the business, so in this case the combined value of the stock purchases and the operating expenses (£113 000 + £82 000 = £195 000) were partly financed by this in-crease in trade creditors, leaving £168 000 that must therefore have been paid in cash.

5. Bernard calculated his annual depreciation at £28 000. However, he had included the depreciation on his old van which needs to be removed. Given that the van had been purchased for £24 000 and was being written down to £4000 over five years, this gives a depreciation charge of £4000 per annum:

Depreciation = (£24 000 − £4000) × 1/5 = £4000

The depreciation on the existing fixed assets is therefore £24 000.

6. The purchase of the new van was for cash and, given that Bernard plans to write the ve-hicle down to £7000 over five years, that implies an annual depreciation charge of £5000.

7. The purchase of the software is written down to zero over 3 years, giving a charge of £6000 per annum.

At this stage we rule off the revenue and expenditure columns to denote the operating profit.

8. In order to work out the gain or loss on the sale of the van we need to calculate its net book value in the opening balance sheet:

Net book value (end year 4) = £24 000 − (£24 000 − £4000) × 4/5
= £8000

Given that the sale of the van raised £10 500 we can immediately revalue it, recognising the gain of £2500 as shown.

9. The interest charge is calculated at 38 per cent of £38 000 as £3040. This is shown as creating a short-term liability which is discharged by a cash payment during the year.

10. Finally, before ruling off the revenue and expense columns to calculate the profit retained we deduct a tax provision of £3115 as 25 per cent of the profit before tax (£272 500 − £260 040 = £12 460).

Bernard's accounts are as follows:

Exhibit Answers 8

Bernard's Balance Sheet at the year end

Non current assets	£
Opening balance	240 000
Disposals	−24 000
	216 000
Acquisitions	50 000
Original cost of non-current assets	266 000
Accumulated depreciation	
Opening balance	196 000
disposals	−16 000
	180 000
charge for the year	35 000
	215 000
Net book value	51 000
Current Assets	
Inventories	38 000
Receivables	24 000
Cash	111 260
	173 260
Less current liabilities	−73 215
Less non-current liabilities	−38 000
	113 045
Owner's Equity	
Capital subscribed	50 000
Profit and loss account	63 045
	113 045

Bernard's Income Statement for the year

	£
Sales Revenue	270 000
less operating costs	257 000
Operating profit	13 000
Gain on sale of fixed assets	2 500
Profit after exceptional items	15 500
less interest paid	3 040
Profit before tax	12 460
Tax	3 115
Profit available for distribution	9 345
Profit retained	9 345

Bernard's Statement of Cash Flow

	£
Cash flow from operations	162 000
Interest paid	−3 040
Taxation paid	12 300
Acquisition of fixed assets	−50 000
Disposal of fixed assets	10 500
Dividends paid	−5 000
Increase in cash during the year	102 160

Note that we have shown the calculation of the net book value for fixed assets in some detail. Normally this would be shown as a note to the balance sheet.

A change to a reducing balance for calculating depreciation would entail a depreciation charge to the income statement as follows:

Exhibit Answers 9

Opening balance of fixed assets at net book value	36 000	
(excluding the vehicle sold)		
Depreciation at 35% reducing balance		12 600
Acquisitions during the year	50 000	
Depreciation at 35% reducing balance		17 500
Depreciation charge for year		30 100

From the accounting equation we note that the straight-line depreciation charge for the year is £35 000. This gives an increase in operating profit of £4900. However, as Bernard provides for tax at 25 per cent this increase will be reduced by this increased tax provision as follows:

Exhibit Answers 10

Net increase in operating profit	4900
Increased tax provision	−1715
Increase in retained profit	3185

Chapter 6: Accounting for companies

Review activity 6.4

In this option Sid is introducing a small loan and then purchasing 90 per cent of the equity in Ron's Vans Ltd. In Exhibit 11 we show the balance sheet equation followed by a brief description of the steps involved.

The first step is to correct the DialaSid balance sheet. A company loan has been introduced which we assume is of a short-term nature. If it were for a longer term then it would be introduced as a long-term liability. We then show the issue of the shares and the creation of the share premium as a merger reserve. The total of £45 000 is posted to the 'Inv' or Investment Account along with a further £45 000 in cash. The consolidated account is straightforward with 10 per cent of the equity and preacquisition profits in Ron's Vans Ltd being transferred to the minority interest account. The opening consolidated balance sheet can then be drawn up from the final row of the balance sheet equation above.

Exhibit Answers 11

Review Activity purchase of 90 per cent of the equity for £90 000, half in cash, half in shares

	FA +	Inv +	St +	Db +	C =	STL +	LTL +	OSC +	SPA -	MR +	P&L
									Owner's Equity		
DialaSid Ltd Balance Sheet	1 280 000		5 400	94 500	36 500	92 000	256 000	77 000	924 000		67 400
Introduction of the loan					25 000	25 000					
Acquisition of 90 per cent of Ron's Vans Ltd – shares issued		45 000						2 813		42 188	
Acquisition of 90 per cent of Ron's Vans Ltd – Cash Paid		45 000			-45 000						
	1 280 000	90 000	5 400	94 500	16 500	117 000	256 000	79 813	924 000	42 188	67 400

	FA +	GW +	St +	Db +	C =	STL +	LTL +	OSC +	SPA -	MR +	P&L +	MI
									Owner's Equity			
DialaSid Ltd Consolidated Balance Sheet												
DialaSid's Balance Sheet	1 280 000	90 000	5 400	94 500	16 500	117 000	256 000	79 813	924 000	42 188	67 400	
Ron's Vans Ltd Balance Sheet	64 000		2 000	18 600	600	28 000		20 000			37 200	
Share capital acquired by DialaSid Ltd (90 per cent)		-18 000						-18 000				
Balance to minority interest								-2 000				2 000
Preacquisition profits acquired by DialaSid Ltd (80 per cent)		-33 480									-33 480	
Balance to minority interest account											-3 720	3 720
	1 344 000	72 000	7 400	113 100	17 100	145 000	256 000	79 813	924 000	42 188	104 600	5 720

Questions

5. (i) The share capital account in the Belling Ltd balance sheet is as follows:

Exhibit Answers 12

	£
Share Capital	
120 000 25p Ordinary Shares issued and fully paid	30 000
Share Premium Account	90 000
Profit and Loss Reserve	36 000
Equity Capital Employed	156 000

(ii) The profit and loss reserve is a distributable reserve in that the directors can use the balance on this account to write off future losses, issue fully paid shares, make a future dividend payment and so forth. The share premium account is not distributable and may be used only for the following:

- issue of fully paid bonus shares
- writing off any formation expenses incurred when the company was established
- writing off any expenses incurred in the issue of debenture stock.

6. (i) The balance sheet of Knitpika assuming that a bank loan is transferred:

Exhibit Answers 13

Knitpika Ltd		
Balance sheet as at 1 April		
Freehold land and buildings		850 000
Other fixed assets		154 000
		1 004 000
Current assets		
stocks	18 000	
debtors	53 000	
cash	25 000	
	96 000	
Liabilities due within one year	165 000	
		−69 000
Net assets		935 000
Unsecured bank loan		350 000
		585 000
25p Ordinary shares		150 000
Share premium account		435 000
		585 000

(ii) The cost of repaying the loan is £350 000 less £15 000 from the company's cash account, leaving £10 000 of cash as working capital. Half of the £335 000 required would be financed by a director's loan of £167 500 and the balance as an increase in the premium paid for their shares.

Exhibit Answers 14

Knitpika Ltd
Balance sheet as at 1 April

Freehold land and buildings		850 000
Other fixed assets		154 000
		1 004 000
Current assets		
stocks	18 000	
debtors	53 000	
cash	10 000	
	81 000	
Liabilities due within one year	165 000	
		−84 000
Net assets		920 000
Unsecured director's loan		167 500
		752 500
25p Ordinary shares		150 000
Share premium account		602 500
		752 500

7. The balance sheet equation consolidating the balance sheets of Parent Ltd and Daughter Ltd is as follows:

Exhibit Answers 15

	FA	+ GW	+ St	+ Db	I C	= STL	+ LTL	+ OSC	Owner's Equity + SPA	+ P&L	+ MI
Parent Ltd Balance Sheet	200 000	70 000	80 000	45 000	3 000	80 000	40 000	45 000	90 000	143 000	
Daughter Ltd Balance Sheet	100 000		25 000	10 000	8 000	25 000	10 000	10 000	60 000	38 000	
Eliminate inter company loan				−10 000			−10 000				
Purchase 70% equity		−7 000						−7 000			
Minority equity								−3 000			3 000
Purchase of share premium		−42 000							−42 000		
Minority share premium									−18 000		18 000
Purchase of preacquisition profit		−12 600								−12 600	
Minority preacquisition profit										−5 400	5 400
Minority share of post acquisition profit										−6 000	6 000
Consolidated balance sheet	300 000	8 400	105 000	45 000	11 000	105 000	40 000	45 000	90 000	157 000	32 400

The consolidated balance sheet and income statement is as follows:

Exhibit Answers 16

Parent Ltd
Consolidated Balance Sheet as at 31 December

Fixed Assets		300 000
Goodwill on acquisition		8 400
Current assets:		
Stocks	105 000	
Debtors	45 000	
Cash	11 000	
	161 000	
Less short term liabilities	105 000	
		56 000
		364 400
Borrowing		40 000
		324 400
Owners Equity		
Share capital		45 000
Share premium account		90 000
Profit and loss reserve		157 000
		292 000
Minority interest		32 400
		324 400

Exhibit Answers 17

Consolidated Income statement

	Parent	Daughter	Consol.
Sales turnover	100 000	51 750	151 750
Cost of sales	20 000	10 000	30 000
Gross profit	80 000	41 750	121 750
Other operating costs	39 700	28 000	67 700
Operating profit	40 300	13 750	54 050
Add dividend from Daughter Ltd	0	0	0
Profit before interest and tax	40 300	13 750	54 050
less interest payable	1 000		1 000
	39 300	13 750	53 050
Corporation tax	7 860	2 750	10 610
Profit available for distribution	31 440	11 000	42 440
Minority interest		−3 300	3 300
Dividends declared and paid	5 000	1 000	5 000
Profit retained	26 440	7 700	34 140
	31 440	11 000	42 440

Chapter 7: The analysis of accounting information

Review activity 7.7

The details of this analysis have been given earlier in the chapter.

Exhibit Answers 18

			Trade Receivables	Trade Payables	Inventories
Sales turnover	2006	7797.7	42.0		
	2007	8588.1	67.9		
Cost of Sales	2006	4812.1		242.6	374.3
	2007	5249.9		259.7	416.3
Receivables age	2006		2		
Receivables age	2007		3		
Payables age	2006			18	
Payables age	2007			18	
Inventory holding period	2006				28
Inventory holding period	2007				29

The age analysis in 2006 suggests that the combined receivables age and inventory holding period for Marks & Spencer plc in 2006 was 30 days, against which can be set the creditor age of 18 days, to give 12 days as the adverse liquidity gap. Correcting the creditor age for the volume of turnover to cost of sales:

Corrected creditor age = 18 × 7797.7/4812.1 = 29 days

Thus in 2006 the company had an average of 11 days uncovered.

The short-term liquidity requirement = 1/365 × 4812.1 = £13.2 million from 2006 to 2007 the company reduced its liquidity requirement by £15.5 million.

Questions

6. (i) Ten ratios are as follows:

Exhibit Answers 19

Performance	Return on Capital Employed	0.32
	Net Profit Margin	0.10
	Return on Fixed Capital Employed	0.22
Efficiency	Fixed Asset Turnover	0.93
	Debtor Age	39.95
	Creditor Age	15.13
	Stock holding period	30.53
Liquidity	Current Asset Ratio	6.74
	Acid Test Ratio	4.72
	Cash Exhaustion Ratio	−6.95
Risk	Gearing	0.50
	Interest Cover	6.47

The performance ratios all look healthy although much depends on the type of business involved. However, the very long debtor age and stock holding period as compared with the creditor age suggests a business that may have trouble when expanding its sales. That appears to be confirmed by the very weak cash exhaustion ratio which suggests that this company needs rapid access to an injection of cash to survive. The healthy cover ratio indicates that the business can finance more debt but lenders may be worried by the current high gearing ratio.

(ii) The analysis of the projected cash flow statement is as follows:

Exhibit Answers 20

		OpCF	Int+divs	Tax	CAPEX	Fin
ΔAccVE						
Op Prof	641	641				
Int	−99		−99			
Tax	−271			−271		
Divs	−163		−163			
	108					
ΔSTL	6	6				
ΔLTL	108					108
ΔOC						
Sources	222	647	−262	−271	0	108
ΔFA	444				444	
−Acc Dep	−294	−294				
ΔSt	11	11				
ΔDb	93	93				
Uses	254	−190	0	0	444	0
Net cash flow	−32	837	−262	−271	−444	108

The bottom row, when laid out in vertical format, provides the appropriate cash flow statement:

Exhibit Answers 21

Cash flow from operations	837
Interest and dividends paid	−262
Taxation	−271
Capital Expenditure	−444
Financing	108
	−32

(iii) Financial reports are designed to service the information of a variety of user groups: investors, managers, creditors, customers, employees and the tax authorities. The extent to which a single set of accounts can satisfy all of these diverse information needs is questionable. As far as management is concerned, the accounts should be a summary of information available from other sources. However, the final accounts will have use in making comparisons between the business plans established by management and the actual outcomes during the financial year concerned. As far as equity investors are concerned the delivery of the final accounts is probably too late for them to be able to act upon the information content in buying and selling shares as the stock markets react very rapidly indeed to new information. The accounts should be useful in helping them build their knowledge base to support their judgements in the future.

7. In Exhibit 22 is the income statement and balance sheet. The trick is to start with long-term borrowings and using the gearing ratio obtain the total of owner's equity. The fact that 25p shares were issued at 75p implies that there was a 50p share premium giving a total of £200 000 on that account. The balance of the owner's equity is profit and loss reserve.

Knowing the EPS figure and the number of shares in issue (400 000) the distributable profit can be calculated and the retention ratio will give you the dividend paid. The tax rate, the net profit margin, the gross margin and the interest rate allow you to build up the income statement. With all that in place, given the debtor age, the creditor age, the current asset ratio and the FAT ratio, it is a straightforward job to produce the balance sheet.

Exhibit Answers 22

Income statement		Balance sheet	
Sales revenue	800 000	Fixed Assets	600 000
Cost of sales	480 000	Current assets	
Gross profit	320 000	inventories	60 000
Operating costs	108 000	receivables	100 000
Operating profit	212 000	cash	30 000
Interest payable	12 000		190 000
Profit before tax	200 000	Current liabilities	−40 000
Tax	80 000	Non-current liabilities	−150 000
Distributable profit	120 000		600 000
less dividends	24 000		
	96 000	Owners Equity:	
		Ordinary share capital	100 000
Earnings per share	30p	Share premium account	200 000
		Profit and loss reserve	300 000
			600 000

Chapter 8: The principles of cost and revenue measurement

Review activity 8.2

Before contemplating closure a company may wish to consider the following:

(i) Can it reduce the direct costs of production by (a) more efficient working or (b) negotiating lower input prices particularly in the cost of materials from suppliers?

(ii) Can it increase the selling price without affecting the level of sales?

Finally, the company may wish to consider whether production of this item is independent of its other product lines or will closure influence the perception of the market that (a) it is no longer offering a comprehensive product line or (b) that it is not prepared to offer long-term support for its products.

Questions

3. Below is a spreadsheet showing the difference to Alfred Cookers Ltd of accepting as opposed to rejecting the contract:

Exhibit Answers 23

Alfred Cookers Ltd

	Contract choices		Net cost of
	Accept	Reject	acceptance
Lost business = 50*1200 + 50*2*150	−75 000		−75 000
Installation costs = 50*2*150	−15 000	−15 000	0
Person days reviewing the contract = 10*280	−2 800	−2 800	0
Materials			
original purchase price = 1750*40	−70 000	−70 000	0
foundry scrap = 40*100		4 000	−4 000
salvaged parts = 40*(350−50)		12 000	−12 000
purchase of materials for 10 units	−19 500		−19 500
Labour costs			
Labour cost of engineer if not on the contract		−12 000	12 000
Labour cost if engaged on the contract	−24 000		−24 000
Redundancy	−6 000	−6 000	0
Firm overheads = 50*1500	−75 000	−75 000	0
Scrap value of plant	2 500	4 000	−1 500
Decision relevant cost (opportunity cost)			−124 000
per unit			−2 480
Possible contract price			2 800
Cash contribution per unit			320

5. (i) The flexible budget is as follows:

Exhibit Answers 24

Output	0	10 000	20 000	30 000	40 000	40 001
Variable cost	0	250 000	500 000	750 000	1 000 000	1 000 025
Plant cost	60 000	60 000	60 000	60 000	60 000	350 000
Fixed cost	550 000	550 000	550 000	550 000	550 000	550 000
Total cost	610 000	860 000	1 110 000	1 360 000	1 610 000	1 900 025
Revenue	0	450 000	900 000	1 350 000	1 800 000	1 800 045
profit	−610 000	−410 000	−210 000	−10 000	190 000	−99 980

Output	50 000	60 000	70 000	80 000	90 000	100 000
Variable cost	1 250 000	1 500 000	1 750 000	2 000 000	2 250 000	2 500 000
Transport cost	350 000	350 000	350 000	350 000	350 000	350 000
Fixed cost	550 000	550 000	550 000	550 000	550 000	550 000
Total cost	2 150 000	2 400 000	2 650 000	2 900 000	3 150 000	3 400 000
Revenue	2 250 000	2 700 000	3 150 000	3 600 000	4 050 000	4 500 000
profit	100 000	300 000	500 000	700 000	900 000	1 100 000

(ii) The graph of process is as follows:

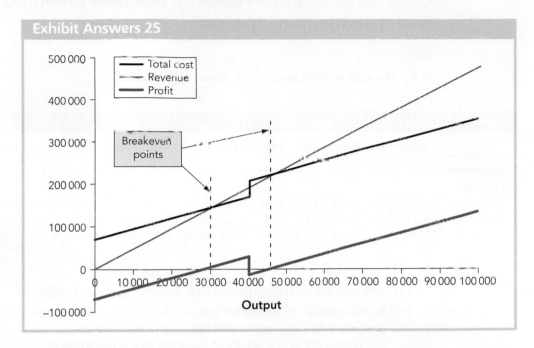

Exhibit Answers 25

(iii) The graph shows a breakeven at 30 000 units of production although the process falls into loss at 40 000 units and re-emerges into profit at 45 000 units.

(iv) At 40 000 units the marginal cost is the difference in total cost between production at that level and 40 001 units, i.e., £290 025.

(v) This suggests that the firm should regard its capacity as being 40 000 units, at which point it will have made £190 000 profit.

6. Because profit equals sales revenue less total cost then:

Profit $= pQ - vQ - F$

As p is £35, v is £20 and F is £100 000 we can rearrange to solve both problems:

(i)

Profit $= pQ - vQ - F$
$0 = 35Q - 20Q - 100\,000$
$Q = 6667$ units

(ii)

Profit $= pQ - vQ - F$
$60\,000 = 35Q - 20Q - 100\,000$
$Q = 10\,667$ units

Chapter 9: Cash forecasting, business planning and management control

Questions

1. (i) The sales revenue projection is shown in Exhibit 26.

Exhibit Answers 26

	Jan	Feb	March	April	May	June	July	Aug	Sept	Oct	Nov	Dec	Total
Sales Revenue	30 000	30 000	30 075	30 150	30 226	30 301	30 377	30 453	30 529	30 605	30 911	31 220	364 848
Cash flow:													
Cash receipts	15 000	15 000	15 038	15 075	15 113	15 151	15 188	15 226	15 264	15 303	15 456	15 610	182 424
Credit receipts	14 925	15 000	15 000	15 038	15 075	15 113	15 151	15 188	15 226	15 264	15 303	15 456	181 739
	29 925	30 000	30 038	30 113	30 188	30 263	30 339	30 415	30 491	30 567	30 758	31 066	364 162

(ii) The cash inflows from these revenues are projected as in Exhibit 26.

(iii) In this exercise the difference between the matched sales revenue and the cash inflow is tiny, as shown by the total figures. Cash sales match the revenue flows and the credit sales are at one month, so the difference is due to the delay in the receipt of cash from the growth in credit sales.

2. Note: only the analysis for part (i) of this question is provided.

The analysis for the balance sheet, income and cash flow statements for each year is as follows:

Exhibit Answers 27

	Year 1 Cash flows	Outstanding	P&L
Revenues	904 500	150 750	1 055 250
Operating Costs	−701 400	−58 450	−759 850
Admin costs	−35 800		−35 800
Property costs	−48 000		−48 000
Initial stock purchase	−28 800	28 800	0
Capital equipment	−450 000	405 000	−45 000
Equity	400 000	−400 000	0
Withdrawals	−30 000	30 000	0
Cash	10 500	10 500	
Profit for the year		−166 600	166 600
Net balance on balance sheet		0	

	Year 2 Cash flows	Outstanding (start)	Outstanding (end)	P&L
Revenues	1 265 900	−150 750	223 030	1 338 180
Operating Costs	−949 425	58 450	−80 998	−971 973
Admin costs	−85 000	0		−85 000
Property costs	−48 000	0		−48 000
Initial stock purchase		−28 800	28 800	0
Capital equipment	−105 000	−405 000	459 000	−51 000
Equity		400 000	−400 000	0
Withdrawals	−60 000	−30 000	90 000	0
Cash	18 475	−10 500	28 975	
Profit for the year		166 600	−348 807	182 207
Net balance on balance sheet			0	

	Year 3 Cash flows	Outstanding (start)	Outstanding (end)	P&L
Revenues	1 548 000	−223 030	264 994	1 589 964
Operating Costs	−1 269 360	80 998	−108 033	−1 296 395
Admin costs	−90 345	0		−90 345
Property costs	−48 000	0		−48 000
Initial stock purchase		−28 800	28 800	0
Capital equipment		−459 000	413 100	45 900
Equity		400 000	−400 000	0
Withdrawals	−80 000	−90 000	90 000	−80 000
Cash	60 295	−28 975	89 270	
Profit for the year		348 807	−378 131	29 324
Net balance on balance sheet			0	

Note that the outstanding column at the end of the year in each case provides the input for the balance sheet and the final column for the P&L. The year-end outstanding for sales is calculated on the basis of the number of months to which the cash sales relates. So, in year 2, the outstanding debtors of £223 030 have been calculated by deducting the opening outstanding from the cash flow for sales (1 265 900−150 750) which represents 10 months of sales matchable to year 2. Two months of this ten months of sales is then outstanding at the year-end. Note also how the signs change, the starting outstandings having their signs changed from the position they were at the end of the previous year.

6. (i) The gross, price and volume variances for sales, labour, materials and contribution are as follows (note that + and − signs have been used):

Exhibit Answers 28

	Actual	Budget	Gross	Price	Vol
Sales					
XP199	2 299 000	2 310 000	−11 000	0	−11 000
XS200	3 542 400	3 800 000	−257 600	−393 600	136 000
XX880	2 863 500	2 970 000	−106 500	124 500	−231 000
	8 704 900	9 080 000	−375 100	−269 100	−106 000
Labour					
XP199	50 283	47 250	3 033	1 359	1 674
XS200	72 581	68 400	4 181	401	3 780
XX880	59 826	60 750	−924	−1 014	90
	182 690	176 400	6 290	746	5 544
Materials					
XP199	585 200	577 500	7 700	10 450	−2 750
XS200	944 640	855 000	89 640	59 040	30 600
XX880	734 550	810 000	−75 450	−12 450	−63 000
	2 264 390	2 242 500	21 890	57 040	−35 150
Contribution					
XP199	1 663 517	1 685 250	−21 733	−11 809	−9 924
XS200	2 525 179	2 876 600	−351 421	−453 041	101 620
XX880	2 069 124	2 099 250	−30 126	137 964	−168 090
	6 257 820	6 661 100	−403 280	−326 886	−76 394

(ii) The activity and efficiency variances for labour are as follows

(AU actual units, BU budget units, FU flexible units):

Exhibit Answers 29

Labour	AU	BU	FU	Activity	Efficiency	Vol
XP199	2718	2625	2612.5	−225	1899	1674
XS200	4010	3800	3936	2448	1332	3780
XX880	3380	3375	3112.5	−4725	4815	90

The flexible units have been calculated by rebasing the original budget for labour to the actual level of output.

Thus, for XP199:

FU = 10450/10500 × 2625 = 2612.50

This is then compared with the actual units to obtain the efficiency variance and with the original budget to obtain the activity variance.

(iii) This type of analysis raises a number of problems:

● Are the cost and revenue functions all linearly related?

● How are the control parameters to be set for identifying variances that are in range or out of range? This can be done by setting arbitrary limits or by establishing acceptable ranges on the basis of previous statistical control performance.

● Once control limits have been set, are there appropriate managerial control systems in place to require staff at the appropriate levels of accountability to explain the variances that have arisen?

Chapter 10: Cost management and pricing

Review activity 10.1

We would classify the costs described in this review activity as follows:

● The first item of cost is mostly value-adding, but note that there is an element of change cost here. The firm is not optimally organised, and the cost of using a more expensive supplier is not transferable to the customer in a competitive market.

● The costs of moving goods around are 'logistic costs' and will only be recoverable in a competitive market in so far as those costs are an irreducible part of the production of the goods concerned.

● This is a change cost; the market cannot be expected to reward a firm for reconfiguring its means of production.

● This is a service cost and will generally be rewarded by the market by a better price than would otherwise be obtainable.

● The customer complaints department is part of the control costs of the firm and not value-adding in the sense that the market will not reward the firm for being in a position of needing to have one!

Questions

1. The problem here is to decide how to charge the capital employed to each unit. We are told that the factory carries a capital employed of £4.62 million and that a 15 per cent recovery is required. This gives a charge of £693 000 per annum. Given no other information such as the capital employed in this area of production there are two ways in which this cost can be allocated: by labour time or by machine hours.

Exhibit Answers 30

Factory charge for capital employed	693 000	693 000	693 000
Allocation basis	labour hrs	machine hrs	mixed
Direct	16.8	16.8	16.8
Allocation of factory costs	21.3	16.0	21.3
Allocation of capital employed	2.3	1.7	1.7
Total price per unit	40.4	34.5	39.9

(i) The analysis of Exhibit 30 shows a price on the basis of the labour hours and the machine hours employed. A price of £40.4 per unit offers complete recovery on the basis of labour time employed, £34.5 on the basis of machine hours in production.

    (ii) The mixed price assumes management requires that labour recovery is used for the indirect factory costs and machine hours for the capital employed in the business.

    (iii) It is impossible from this type of analysis to identify which price is likely to be acceptable to the market given the level of output that the firm wishes to achieve. A more coherent pricing strategy is one where the maximum price the market can bear for the firm's level of output is chosen and this is compared with the direct cost of production to obtain a contribution per unit. The rationale for this type of costing can only be explained in terms of a firm's own mechanisms of internal control through constraining labour time, machine time or, in the case of the mixed method, both.

3. A cost analysis for the theatre on the basis of the current direct costs of production and the indirect costs of operation is as follows:

Exhibit Answers 31

The Bell Theatre, Cold Ashton

Direct cost		<u>80 000</u>
Number of performance		
daily	12	
matinees	<u>4</u>	
	16	
Direct cost per performance		5 000
Number of productions		
weeks	40	
weekly performances	8	
Number of performances per annum	320	
Indirect costs		1 890 000
less Arts Council grant		− 350 000
less Bequest income		− 163 000
Total indirect costs less offset		<u>1 377 000</u>
Total indirect cost per performance		4 303
Total cost per performance		9 303

    The direct costs of each production have been allocated over the number of performances per production and the indirect costs over the total number of performances per annum. A profit and loss for each performance has been calculated using the existing and the proposed pricing structure:

Exhibit Answers 32

Pricing	Current		Revised (10 per cent cut)	
	seats	revenue	seats	revenue
Upper circle	90	1080	120	1296
Circle	132	2376	154	2495
Stalls	162	3564	162	3564
Boxes	18	990	18	900
	402	8010	454	8255
Contribution from merchandising		1000		1129
Revenue per performance		9010		9384
Less total cost per performance		9303		9303
Profit/(loss) per performance		−293		81

The total revenue per performance includes the merchandising revenue which we assume is directly related to the theatre attendance. The revised pricing strategy appears to offer a modest surplus per performance compared with the existing prices.

If the increase in occupancy created by the decrease in prices does occur that would strongly indicate a general position with respect to the ticket pricing for the cheaper seats.

Chapter 11: The management of working capital

Review activity 11.3

(i) Using the EOQ formula and substituting:

$$EOQ = \sqrt{\frac{2dt}{iv}}$$

$$= \sqrt{\frac{2 \times 4500 \times 2}{0.04 \times 2}}$$

$$= 474 \text{ items}$$

Therefore the value of each shopping bill is £949 which implies shopping 9.5 times per annum on average. The model assumes that the functions are all smooth with no 'steps' in the cost curves. It assumes that price levels remain constant and that the level of demand does not change.

Review activity 11.5

(i)

Exhibit Answers 33

Month	−3	−2	−1	0	1	2	3	4	5
Sales	97 000	98 000	99 000	100 000	101 000	102 000	103 000	104 000	105 000
Cash received (existing terms)				97 000	98 000	99 000	100 000	101 000	102 000
Debtors receivable (revised terms)				97 000	98 000	99 000	0	100 000	101 000
change to cash flow				0	0	0	−100 000	−1 000	−1 000

Note the disastrous loss of cash that this change in policy would bring about.

(ii)

Exhibit Answers 34

Month	−3	−2	−1	0	1	2	3	4	5
Sales	103 000	102 000	101 000	100 000	99 000	98 000	97 000	96 000	95 000
Cash received (existing terms)				103 000	102 000	101 000	100 000	99 000	98 000
Debtors receivable (revised terms)				103 000	102 000	201 000	99 000	98 000	97 000
change to cash flow				0	0	100 000	−1 000	−1 000	−1 000

In a situation of falling sales a reduction in credit period will bring forward cash, but at the cost of reduced cash in subsequent months as the impact of the decline is accelerated.

Review activity 11.8

The answer is £360 every 13 days.

Questions

1. (i) The liquidity gap for this company is as shown in Exhibit 35.

Exhibit Answers 35

Ages	2004 days	2003 days
Finished goods holding period	49.77	42.58
Work in progress holding period	6.00	7.05
Raw materials holding period	34.61	21.90
Debtor age	41.37	40.17
	131.75	111.70
Creditor age	40.91	45.13
Liquidity gap	90.85	66.57

(ii) The most significant problem appears to be an increase in the average inventory holding period with the debtor and creditor ages showing small changes against the company. Attention should be paid to the reasons for the increase in the holding period for both raw materials and finished goods which is indicative of a surprise slowing down in the market for the company's goods.

4. The benefit of changing credit policy can be summarised as follows:

(i) The cash flow from the current month's sales will be brought forward, creating a one-off boost in cash flow of £0.943 million less 1.5 per cent defaults.

(ii) The company will make a net saving on defaults (currently £43 500 per month) to £14 145 per month.

(iii) The reduction in the monthly outstanding balance will result in the company saving 10 per cent of the reduction in debtor balances in the cost of financing its debtors.

5. (i) The projected cash budget is as follows.

Exhibit Answers 36

	−3	−2	−1	0	1	2	3	4	5	6
Current sales	75 706	76 463	77 228	78 000	78 780	79 568	80 363	81 167	81 979	82 799
Cost of Sales	56 780	57 347	57 921	58 500	59 085	59 676	60 273	60 875	61 484	62 099
Gross profit	18 927	19 116	19 307	19 500	19 695	19 892	20 091	20 292	20 495	20 700
Current policy										
Sales Cash Flow										
month 1				25 743	26 000	26 260	26 523	26 788	27 056	27 326
month 2				38 232	38 614	39 000	39 390	39 784	40 182	40 584
month 3				12 618	12 744	12 871	13 000	13 130	13 261	13 394
Sales receipts				76 592	77 358	78 131	78 913	79 702	80 499	81 304
Supplier payments				57 921	58 500	59 085	59 676	60 273	60 875	61 484
Net cash flow				18 671	18 858	19 046	19 237	19 429	19 623	19 820
New Policy										
Sales Cash Flow										
month 1				25 743	38 415	38 799	39 187	39 579	39 975	40 375
month 2				38 232	38 614	19 500	19 695	19 892	20 091	20 292
month 3				12 618	12 744	12 871	19 500	19 695	19 892	20 091
Sales receipts				76 592	89 773	71 170	78 382	79 166	79 958	80 757
Supplier payments				57 921	58 500	59 085	59 676	60 273	60 875	61 484
Net cash flow				18 671	31 273	12 085	18 706	18 893	19 082	19 273
Net cash flow benefit										
(New − Current)				0	12 415	−6 961	−530	−536	−541	−547

(ii) Expanding trade impacts upon different businesses in different ways. A company with small debtor balances such as a retailer will normally become cash-rich as business expands. Its problems are ones of converting that cash into useful assets as quickly as possible. A manufacturer on the other hand is likely to have large outstanding debtor balances and will tend to go 'cash-dry' as business expands. For this type of business maintaining liquidity is critical and external sources of financing working capital may be necessary. Such a company may find it useful to have recourse to a debt factor or to some other source of short-term finance. It will also need to maintain a strict control of its debtor balances, asking for prompt payment and chasing up slow debts.

Chapter 12: Investment appraisal

Review activity 12.1

(i)

Exhibit Answers 37

	1	2	3	4	5	6	7	8	9	10
Opening balance	10 000	10 500	11 025	11 576	12 155	12 763	13 401	14 071	14 775	15 513
Add interest (5 per cent)	500	525	551	579	608	638	670	704	739	776
Carried Forward	10 500	11 025	11 576	12 155	12 763	13 401	14 071	14 775	15 513	16 289

The future value is £16 289. Alternatively, to obtain the same result by calculation use the formula for the future value as given in the chapter:

$$FV_{10} = 10\ 000 \times 1.05^{10} = £16\ 289$$

(ii)

Exhibit Answers 38

	1	2	3
Opening balance	10 000	10 100	10 201
Add interest (1 per cent)	100	101	102
Carried Forward	10 100	10 201	10 303

The future value is £10 303. Alternatively, to obtain the same result by calculation use the formula for the future value as given in the chapter:

$$FV_3 = 10\ 000 \times 1.01^3 = £10\ 303$$

Review activity 12.2

Exhibit Answers 39

Net Present Value of the project	0	1	2	3	4	5
Net cash flow	−225 000	−13 000	45 000	145 000	139 000	51 000
Discounted Cash Flow	−225 000	−11 818	37 190	108 941	94 939	31 667
Net Present Value	35 918					
Option 1 Balance Retained						
Borrowing brought forward		260 918	300 010	285 011	168 512	46 364
Interest at 10 per cent		26 092	30 001	28 501	16 851	4 636
Repayment (additional borrowing) from project		13 000	−45 000	−145 000	−139 000	−51 000
Balance carried forward		300 010	285 011	168 512	46 364	0
Option 2 Firm borrows £225 000, owner borrows the net present value						
Firm's borrowing brought forward		225 000	260 500	241 550	120 705	0
Interest at 10 per cent		22 500	26 050	24 155	12 071	0
Repayment (additional borrowing) from project		13 000	−45 000	−145 000	−132 776	0
Balance carried forward		260 500	241 550	120 705	0	0
Owner's borrowing		35 918	39 510	43 461	47 807	46 364
Interest at 10 per cent		3 592	3 951	4 346	4 781	4 636
Repayment from project		0	0	0	−6 225	−51 000
Balance carried forward		39 510	43 461	47 807	46 364	0

Both options yield a zero balance at the end of the project.

Review activity 12.4

Note that the option (i) NPV is 23 063, being exactly 60 per cent of the NPV of the original project cash flows before tax was included in the analysis. This tax regime with a 100 per cent first-year allowance and tax paid in the year in which it is incurred is neutral upon the project in the sense that if a project is acceptable with tax it will be acceptable without. All that happens is that the project value is scaled down by the tax rate.

Exhibit Answers 40

Year	0	1	2	3	4
Capital investment	−115 000				
Net cash flow from operations		50 000	50 000	30 000	
Sale value of coach				40 000	
Net cash flow from project	−115 000	50 000	50 000	70 000	
Discount factor (5 per cent)	1.000	0.952	0.907	0.864	
Discounted cash flow	−115 000	47 619	45 351	60 469	
Net present value	38 439				
Option (i) Tax is paid in the year it is incurred					
Net cash flow from the Project	−115 000	50 000	50 000	70 000	
First year allowance (100 per cent)	46 000				
Tax on increase in taxable profit (40 per cent)		−20 000	−20 000	−28 000	
Post tax cash flow from project	−69 000	30 000	30 000	42 000	
Discount factor (5 per cent)	1.000	0.9524	0.9070	0.8638	
Discounted cash flow	−69 000	28 571	27 211	36 281	
Net present value	23 063				

Option (ii) There is a 50 per cent first year allowance and a 30 per cent writing down allowance

	0	1	2	3	4
First year allowance (50 per cent first year)	57 500				
Writing down allowance (30 per cent first year)		17 250	12 075	8 453	
Unclaimed allowance				19 723	
Net cash flow from the Project	−115 000	50 000	50 000	70 000	
First year allowance (tax benefit at 40 per cent)		23 000			
Writing down allowance (tax benefit at 40 per cent)			6 900	4 830	3 381
Unclaimed allowance (tax benefit at 40 per cent)					7 889
Tax on increase in taxable profit			−20 000	−20 000	−28 000
Post tax cash flow	−115 000	73 000	36 900	54 830	−16 730
Discount factor (5 per cent)	1.000	0.9524	0.9070	0.8638	0.823
Discounted cash flow	−115 000	69 524	33 469	47 364	−13 764
Net present value	21 594				

Note in option (ii) that the 30 per cent writing-down allowance is deducted on a reducing balance basis. We have assumed that in the year in which the project is terminated the balance of the unclaimed writing-down allowance is allowed as final allowance to be offset against the tax which will be charged on the scrap value of the coach.

Review activity 12.5

Notice that at a cost of capital of 5 per cent the net present value of project 2 is less than project 1 whilst the internal rate of return of project 2 is greater than project 1. The internal rate of return is giving a conflicting result with the net present value method. This commonly occurs when projects of dissimilar size present themselves as mutually exclusive alternatives.

Exhibit Answers 41

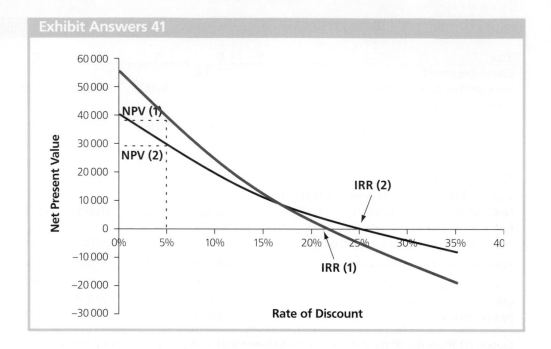

Questions

1. Exhibit 42 shows the analysis of the financial details.

Exhibit Answers 42

Year	0	1	2	3	4	5	6
Net cash flow	−350 000	98 000	245 000	95 000	45 000	30 000	−15 000
Discounted cash flow	−350 000	89 091	202 479	71 375	30 736	18 628	−8 467
Cumulative cash flow	−350 000	−252 000	−7 000	88 000	133 000	163 000	148 000
Cumulative discounted cash flow	−350 000	−260 909	−58 430	12 945	43 681	62 308	53 841
Depreciation		−58 333	−58 333	−58 333	−58 333	−58 333	−58 333
Annual Profit		39 667	186 667	36 667	−13 333	−28 333	−73 333
Future value		157 830	358 704.5	126 445	54 450	33 000	−15 000

NPV=	£53 841
IRR=	17.62 per cent
MIRR=	12.65 per cent
Payback=	2.074 yrs
Disc Payback=	2.819 yrs
ARR=	14.10 per cent

Note that the accounting rate of return has been calculated by averaging the profits (project net cash flow less depreciation) over the six years of the project and dividing by the average capital employed. The opening capital employed is £350 000, the closing is zero, the average point is halfway between.

2. This uses the terminal value formula. In Excel format this formula is:
$$=10\,000* (1.06 \wedge 26 - 1.06)/0.06,$$ to give an answer of £581 564.

3. This uses the terminal value formula =[cell reference for terminal value]/((1 − 1/(1.04) ^ 15)/0.04), to give an answer of £52 306.

6. Here is the full analysis for this question in Excel format:

Exhibit Answers 43

	01-Jan	31 Dec 01	31-Dec 02	31-Dec 03	31-Dec 04	31-Dec 05	NPV	IRR	NPV/£
alpha	−130 000	0	0	0	0	220 000	£19 728	11%	£0.152
beta	−9 000	3 000	3 000	3 000	3 000	3 000	£2 978	20%	£0.331
gamma	−199 000	200 000	80 000	0	0	0	£54 772	31%	£0.275
delta	−44 000	−22 000	70 000	10 000	12 000	0	£12 402	18%	£0.282
epsilon	−97 000	20 000	38 000	50 000	25 000	10 000	£18 971	16%	£0.196
	−479 000	201 000	191 000	63 000	40 000	233 000			

	01-Jan	31-Dec 01	31-Dec 02	31-Dec 03	31-Dec 04	31-Dec -05	NPV	NPV/£	IRR	Investment	CumCash	Project (NPV)
beta	−9 000	3 000	3 000	3 000	3 000	3 000	£2 978	£0.331	20%	9 000	9 000	2 978
delta	−44 000	−22 000	70 000	10 000	12 000	0	£12 402	£0.282	18%	44 000	53 000	12 402
gamma	−199 000	200 000	80 000	0	0	0	£54 772	£0.275	31%	199 000	252 000	54 772
epsilon	−48 000	9 897	18 804	24 742	12 371	4 948	£9 388	£0.196	16%	48 000	300 000	9 388
alpha	0	0	0	0	0	0	£0					
	−300 000	190 897	171 804	37 742	27 371	7 948						79 540

	01-Jan	31-Dec 01	31-Dec 02	31-Dec 03	31-Dec 04	31-Dec 05
Turnover		780 500	820 000	861 000	904 000	949 200
Gross profit		172 000	180 400	190 000	199 000	208 500
Capital employed	1 021 250	1 075 000	1 127 500	1 187 500	1 243 750	1 303 125
ROCE (original)		16.40%	16.40%	16.40%	16.40%	16.40%
Gross profit + NCF		362 897	352 204	277 742	226 371	216 448
Depreciation		32 200	32 200	32 200	32 200	32 200
Accumulated depreciation		32 200	64 400	96 600	128 800	161 000
Gross profit		330 697	320 004	195 542	194 171	184 248
Capital employed	1 321 250	1 364 800	1 385 100	1 412 900	1 436 950	1 464 125
Average capital employed		1 343 025	1 374 950	1 399 000	1 424 925	1 450 538
ROCE (after)		24.62%	23.27%	13.98%	13.63%	12.70%

(i) The projects are ranked according to their profitability index (the ratio of NPV/£ outlay) in the order shown above. The net present value that exhausts the outlay of £300 000 is £79 450, which is the maximum that can be generated from this plan.

(ii) The marginal project is Epsilon which yields 19.6p of NPV for every additional £1 invested. Given that the projects are already discounted at 8 per cent this suggests that the maximum return the firm should be prepared to pay for additional year 1 borrowing only is 27.6 per cent.

(iii) The differential rate of return on capital employed is calculated in stages.

   a. The firm's rate of return on capital employed is calculated first, without the project. The return is approximately 16.4 per cent per annum. Note that we have used the midyear capital employed as the denominator by taking the opening-year and closing-year figures and averaging them.

b. The gross profit is increased by the net cash flow from the project before additional depreciation on the additional capital invested is calculated. In year 1 note that some of the capital on project Delta is not incurred until later in the year. This will not be included as part of the capital spend in arriving at the £300 000 as by this time cash inflows have arrived to alleviate the capital shortage.

c. Accumulated depreciation and the revised gross profit line are calculated.

d. The revised capital employed is calculated, being the original capital employed plus the new capital investment less the accumulated depreciation in each year.

e. The average capital employed is calculated from the opening and the closing figures in each year.

f. The revised ROCE is calculated.

9. The analysis to answer parts (i) and (ii) are shown in Exhibit 44.

Exhibit Answers 44

		0	1	2	3	4	5
Sales revenue	40		436 800	476 986	510 852	547 122	585 968
Labour	0.5		−136 500	−149 058	−162 771	−177 746	−194 099
Shadow price			−76 000	−56 000			
Materials	10		−110 250	−121 551	−134 010	−144 931	−156 743
Project specific overheads	45 000		−45 900	−47 736	−49 645	−50 638	−51 651
Operating cash flows			68 150	102 641	164 425	173 806	183 474
Plant and equipment		−550 000					92 439
NCF		−550 000	68 150	102 641	164 425	173 806	275 913
Money cost of capital			1.0710	1.0920	1.0920	1.0710	1.0710
Compound factor			1.0710	1.1695	1.2771	1.3678	1.4649
Discount factor			0.9337	0.8550	0.7830	0.7311	0.6826
Discounted cash flow		−550 000	63 632	87 762	128 746	127 069	188 347
NPV		45 557					
Cum cash flow		−550 000	−481 850	−379 209	−214 784	−40 978	234 935
Cum disc cash flow		−550 000	−486 368	−394 088	−250 463	−87 714	147 369
Internal rate of return	10.60%						
NPV/£ outlay	0.0828						
Payback	4.1485						
Discounted payback	4.3731						

(iii) Against the net present value criteria this project is acceptable, although the relatively modest value-added and the uncertainty attached to the cash flows would place a question mark against this project. The cash flows have been projected forward at the assumed rates of price changes. Sensitivity analysis could help identify the critical variables in the project.

Chapter 13: The nature of the financial markets

Review activity 13.2

The assumptions of the Markowitz portfolio model are as follows:

- Investors are rational, seeking to maximise their return given their preference for risk.
- Investors are risk averse in that given a choice between two alternatives of identical return they will choose the one with the lower risk, or with two alternatives of identical risk they will choose the one with the higher return.
- Share returns are 'normally' distributed and therefore fully described by their average return and the standard deviation (risk) of those returns.
- There are no transactions costs or taxes inhibiting investors from adjusting their portfolio M as circumstances in the market change.
- All investors have free access to the information required to draw up the efficient set, and prices, from which returns are derived, perfectly reflect that information (i.e. the efficient markets hypothesis holds in its strong form).
- There is a risk-free borrowing or lending opportunity, where any amount of cash can be deposited or borrowed at a single risk-free rate of interest.

Questions

1. Take the twelfth root as follows to obtain the monthly rate:

$$i = \sqrt[12]{1.06} - 1 = 0.487\%$$

2. The annual equivalent rate is:

$$i = 1.01^{12} - 1 = 12.68\%$$

3. Calculate the 6-monthly discount rate:

$$i = \sqrt{1.08} - 1 = 3.92\%$$

Discount the bond as follows:

$$PV\ (bond) = \frac{3}{1.0392} + \frac{3}{1.0392^2} + \frac{3}{1.0392^3} + \frac{3}{1.0392^4} + \frac{3}{1.0392^5} + \frac{103}{1.0392^6}$$
$$= £95.15$$

4. Returns are weighted according to this formula:

$$r_p = w_a r_a + w_b r_b$$

and the weights or proportions of each security must sum to 100%. Because $w_a = 1 - W_b$

$$0.15 = w_a \times 0.05 + w_b \times 0.12$$
$$= w_a \times 0.05 + (1 - w_a) \times 0.12$$

Therefore the weight of the risk-free security (w_a) is, on rearrangement, -42.86%, and the weight of investment in the broadly diversified security is 142.86%. This implies that the investor should borrow £4286 at the risk-free rate and invest £14 286 in the diversified portfolio. To prove: £14 286 invested at 12% yields £1714. Deduct the cost of the borrowed funds at 5% (£214) to give £1500 overall, being 15% of the sum invested of £10 000.

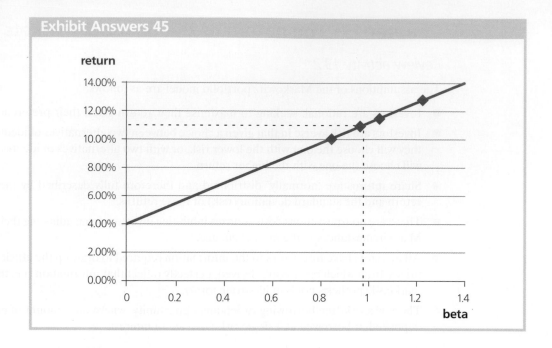

Exhibit Answers 45

5. (i) The security market line is as follows:

   (ii) From the graph in Exhibit 45 the risk-free rate is 4% and the market rate of return 11 per cent. By calculation, assuming that all points lie on the line, the following pair of simultaneous equations can be solved:

   $$10.09\% = R_f + 0.87\,(R_m - R_f)$$
   $$12.47\% = R_f + 1.21\,(R_m - R_f)$$

   (Note that any pair of securities can be solved.)

   (iii) The portfolio beta is given by the weighted average of the betas of the individual components. However, as they are equally weighted we can take a simple arithmetic average, to give 1.0275.

   (iv) The CAPM provides the minimum rate of return required by investors for a security or a portfolio of a given exposure to market risk as measured by beta. For personal investors this allows them to evaluate whether a given income stream from an equity investment is fairly priced in the market. The model also allows them to configure the risk of a portfolio to any level of exposure they require. For the firm the model predicts the rate of return that firm must be able to generate on any new investment to satisfy the requirements of its equity investors. The CAPM is a first approximation to the opportunity cost of equity capital.

6. (i) The equity cost of capital is derived from the capital asset pricing model. The rate of return on 90-day government stock is 4.5 per cent. We can assume that this is an annual rate given the magnitude of the market rate. The market rate is 7.5 per cent and the beta is set at a level 20 per cent greater than the market, i.e. 1.2. Therefore:

$E(R_e) = 4.5\% + 1.2(7.5 - 4.5) = 8.1\%$

The debt cost of capital is found by solving the following by trial and error:

$$98 = \frac{3}{(1 + r_d)} + \frac{3}{(1 + r_d)^2} + \frac{3}{(1 + r_d)^3} + \frac{3}{(1 + r_d)^4} + \frac{3}{(1 + r_d)^5} + \frac{3}{(1 + r_d)^6}$$

At 5% the value of the right hand side is $-£8.15$ and at 3% is $+£2$. Using interpolation the value for the cost of debt is 3.37% (six monthly) or an annual equivalent of: $r_d = 1.0337^2 - 1 = 0.0685$ ($= 6.85$ per cent).

The weights of equity and debt are as follows:

Total equity value of the firm $= 1$ million $\times$ £2.20 $= $ £2.2 million
Total debt value of the firm $= $ £1 million $\times$ £98/£100 $= $ £0.98 million

This gives:

Weight of equity $= 2.2/(2.2 + .98) = 0.692$
Weight of debt $= .98/(2.2 + .98) = 0.308$

Substituting in the formula for the weighted average cost of capital:

WACC $= .692 \times 8.1\% + .308 \times 6.85\% = 7.71\%$

Therefore the weighted average cost of capital is 7.71 per cent.

(ii) The capital asset pricing model is based upon the assumptions of the Markowitz model (see the outline to Review activity 11.3 above) and the assumption that all investors have identical beliefs about the future returns and risk of all securities in the market. The debt model assumes that investors price debt using a constant rate of discount over time. The weighted average cost of capital assumes that in use the gearing and the risk of the firm remain constant.

Chapter 14: Market measures of performance and value

Review activity 14.2

The FTSE 100 data show a yield of 3.52% on an index value of 3971.6 or a dividend of 139.8. Using the data in the text for the growth of the economy we can predict an index level as follows:

$$P_0 = \frac{139.8 \times 1.03781}{(0.07275 - 0.03781)}$$

$$= 4152$$

The endogenous growth model assumes that the growth in dividends equals the multiple of the retention rate and the firm's rate of return on equity capital. Using the equilibrium rate of return in the text and a retention ratio calculated from the FT data as follows for the FTSE ASI:

$$b(ASI) = 1 - \frac{1}{1.64} = .3902$$

$$b(100) = 1 - \frac{1}{1.68} = .4048$$

Using the valuation model:

$$P_0(\text{ASI}) = \frac{67.6 \times (1 + .3902 \times .071)}{(0.071 - .3902 \times .071)}$$

$$= 1604$$

$$P_0(100) = \frac{139.8 \times (1 + .4048 \times .07275)}{(0.07275 - .4048 \times .07275)}$$

$$= 3323$$

You will note that the endogenous method understates the index whilst the exogenous method gives a figure that is too high. One strategy is to take the average result, reflecting the fact that only some companies in the index are likely to be exclusively driven by the UK economy whilst others tend to be governed by their performance internationally.

Questions

2. (i) EPS (current) = net distributable profit/shares in issue

$$= 256/1000$$

$$= 25.6\text{p per share}$$

Efficiency P/E ratio:

Retention ratio (current) $= 102/256$

$$= .3984$$

The efficiency P/E ratio $= 12.9$

Actual P/E ratio $= 380/25.6$

$$= 14.85$$

(ii)

Exhibit Answers 46

Investor ratios	Current	+1
Cover	1.66	1.66
Dividend yield	4.05	4.29
Earnings yield	6.74	7.13
Market to book	4.32	3.85
Payout ratio	0.60	0.60
Retention ratio	0.40	0.40

(iii) Growth (management) = 5%

Growth (retention based) $= 0.4 \times 0.08 = 3.2\%$

$$P_0 = \frac{15.4 \times (1.05)}{(.08 - .05)} = 539\text{p (management)}$$

$$P_0 = \frac{15.4 \times (1.032)}{(.08 - .032)} = 331\text{p (retention)}$$

3. (i) Graph of index level against different growth rates in dividends. Note that the dividend yield and the current level of 5900 imply a dividend per unit of the index of 153.4p and the capital asset pricing model gives a rate of return of 11.076 per cent.

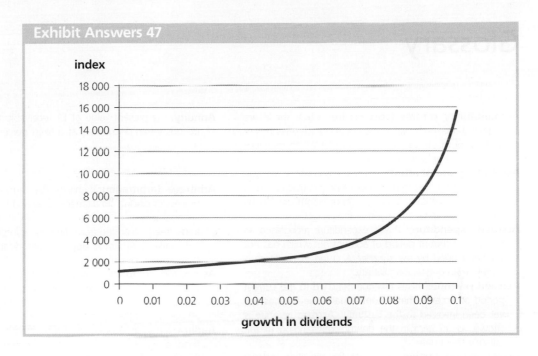

Exhibit Answers 47

(ii)

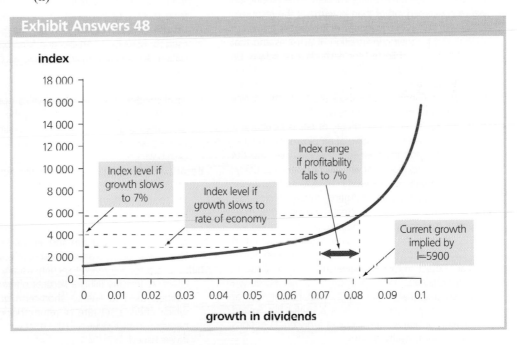

Exhibit Answers 48

(iii) The index if it was set at the growth in economy would be at 2780. Given a current index value of 5900 then 47 per cent of the index is explained by economic growth.

Glossary

Accountability centres (cost centres etc.): these are organisational units within the firm to which revenues or costs or both can be attributed and for which management can be held accountable.

Accounting rate of return: this is the ratio of the average annual contribution to profit from a project (measured as average annual cash flow less depreciation) divided by the average capital employed of the project.

Accrued expenditure: this is expenditure recognised as due to the current period of account but which has not yet been billed by the supplier. Accrued expenditure is therefore an outstanding liability.

Accrued revenue: this is revenue matched to the current period of account that is contractually due but has not yet been invoiced to the customer. Accrued revenue is shown as an item in the debtors outstanding at the balance sheet date.

Activity-based costing: a system for allocating indirect costs based upon the activities involved in the production system concerned rather than in terms of the resources consumed. The system requires that business processes be analysed for their consumption of activities and that the indirect costs collected for each class of activity be allocated to the product concerned using a 'cost driver'. The cost driver is the allocation ratio for the proportionate charging of the indirect costs associated with the activity to the individual product or process.

Agency theory: an economic theory of rational-behaviour contractually based relationship of employment. The theory is based upon the idea that the 'principal' and the 'agent' in such relationships are rational, personal utility-maximisers operating in a world characterised by uncertainty and costly information. Agency theory predicts that the two parties will seek to create contracts that maximise their personal wealth. The principal, it is argued, will seek to minimise the agency loss whereas the agent uses their superior knowledge to maximise the perks he or she can extract from the relationship or to engage in shirking behaviour. The agent, on the other hand, will seek a contract that maximises their financial reward at minimum effort. Agency theory is a useful but limited explanation of human behaviour as it discounts notions such as altruism, loyalty and trust.

Amortisation: this is the term given to the writing down of goodwill and other intangible assets. The mechanics for calculating amortisation are the same as for depreciation except that no residual value is carried in the balance sheet. Amortisation is usually calculated using the straight-line method.

Annuity: the present value of £1 receivable for each of n periods when discounted at a fixed percentage rate (i).

The formula for an annuity is given as: $\overline{A}\big|_n^i = \dfrac{1 - \dfrac{1}{(1+i)^n}}{i}$

Arbitrage (arbitrageur): this is the term given to the process of placing simultaneous buy and sell orders for a financial security or tradable commodity in order to make a risk-free gain arising from differences in prices in different markets. Arbitrage opportunities disappear in perfectly competitive markets.

Associated company: this is a partly owned business where the company holding the shares in the other does not have a controlling interest but does own more than 20 per cent of the equity.

Auditor: a person recognised as competent to examine the financial reports of a business and determine whether they have been truthfully prepared in accordance with the underlying financial transactions of the business and fairly apply current accounting principles and standards.

Authorised share capital: ordinary shares that are authorised for issue by its Articles and Memorandum of Association. A company may not issue all of its authorised shares at any given time.

Baumol model: this is a model which optimises the total cost of holding cash by balancing the interest charges associated with holding large cash balances against the transaction costs of more frequently refreshing smaller cash balances.

Beta: this financial statistic measures the exposure of a given security's returns to market risk. A beta of one implies that the security's returns carry the same exposure to risk and hence the same volatility as a perfectly diversified market portfolio. In practice beta is measured relative to a broadly based stock market index such as the Financial Times All Share Index or the Standard and Poor's 500 Index.

Bill: this is a money market security usually issued at a discount. A Treasury Bill is a security offered to the money markets used to finance short-term government debt which offers a set rate of return, being the difference between its face value and the discounted value at which it was issued.

Bond: this is a financial market security offered by government or companies offering the holder a set rate of interest (the coupon rate) on its face value (its par value) and redemption of the par value at a specified date (maturity).

Breakeven: this is the point at which total revenue equals total cost.

Budgetary slack: this is the term given to the difference between the budget that optimises the organisation's performance and the budget requested by the responsible manager. Where bonuses and other rewards are tied to performance the creation of budgetary slack gives the manager some protection against the perceived risk of not performing to the standard specified or where there is inherent uncertainty in the monitoring systems.

Buffer stock: this is a contingency stock which will be held to reduce the risk of stockout occurring because of variability in demand for the item concerned and/or variability in the lead time between order and supply.

Bygones principle: this is the idea that in decision making only future outcomes matter. Past actions are part of the state of the world as it is and should not be used to evaluate the merits of future alternatives. In decision costing the bygones principle leads to the idea that past expenditures (sunk costs) are irrelevant and should not be included in the analysis of future choices.

Capital asset pricing model: this model defines the linear trade-off between the expected return on a security and its exposure to market risk as measured by its beta. It assumes that the capital markets are perfectly competitive and information-efficient, that share returns are normally distributed and that a risk-free borrowing and lending opportunity exists. The formula for expected return on a given security (i) is as follows: $E(r_i) = R_f + \beta_i(E(r_m) - R_f)$ where $(E(r_m) - R_f)$, the difference between the expected return on the market and the risk-free rate of return, is called the equity risk premium.

Comparability: this is the requirement that accounting information should be comparable in terms of the principles and policies by which it is produced from one accounting period to the next.

Compounding: the process of calculating a future value where an initial principal sum is reinvested at the end of each compounding period along with the accrued interest.

Consolidation: the process of combining together the accounts of a parent company with its subsidiaries to create a combined 'group' profit and loss account, balance sheet and cash flow statement.

Contribution: technically contribution is related to a decision or cost object and is the difference between the directly attributable revenue and directly attributable cost. In a production system where choices can be made about the output, contribution is defined as the revenue less the variable cost of production.

Contribution margin: the ratio of contribution to directly attributable sales revenue arising from the business decision or object.

Correlation coefficient: the correlation coefficient measures the extent to which two variables are related. A correlation coefficient of +1 indicates that changes in one variable will be directly matched by proportionate changes in the other. A coefficient of −1 indicates that the relationship is inverse in that changes in one variable will be perfectly matched by corresponding but opposite changes in the other. A coefficient of zero means that there is no statistical relationship between one variable and the other. High statistical correlation does not imply that there is a causal relationship between the variables concerned. Two shares may have highly correlated returns but not be related to one another.

Cost hierarchy: this denotes the relationship of costs to the level of the business decision incurred. The hierarchy extends from strategic costs, which are those associated with the long-term business decisions of the firm, to the short-term operational and production costs associated with the day-to-day operation of the business or the production of specific goods and services.

Cost object: this is any business object to which costs can be attached. A cost object can be a centre of accountability such as a department or project, or it can be an individual unit of production or a specified activity. Informally, a cost object is literally anything you wish to cost.

Cost of capital: this is the rate of return required by a firm's capital investors in order to maintain the current market valuation of their claim upon the business. This rate of return may be delivered to the investors by distribution in the form of dividends or interest payments or in the form of capital gain. The cost of capital can be regarded as the rate of return that the firm must promise the market in order to attract new capital funds. It is therefore the opportunity cost of capital.

Creative accounting: this is a pejorative term for the process of presenting financial reports in ways which present the view that management wishes to convey rather than the fair representation of the underlying financial reality of the business.

Credit policy: this is the set of policies made by management concerning the extension of credit to customers and the agreement of terms of payment with suppliers.

Credit rating: this is a rating of the creditworthiness of bonds issued by governments and corporations prepared by credit-rating agencies.

Credit risk: this is the risk associated with the failure of a customer or other debtor to honour the debt outstanding. Credit risk covers not only the risk of default on the debtor's part but also the loss associated with late payment.

Current liabilities: these are the financial claims of external stakeholders other than the owner's, where the claim is due for settlement within one year. An important class of such claims is those of suppliers from whom goods and services have been purchased on credit.

Debt factors: financial houses such as banks and other specialised institutions that make payments against good-quality business debts for a fee or on commission. Normally a percentage of the invoiced value of the debt is paid at the point the sale is made and the balance less charges when the debt is discharged.

Deferred revenue: this is income from the sale of goods or services which is matched to a subsequent period of account and will be carried forward in the balance sheet as an outstanding (short-term) liability.

Deflation: this is the economic phenomenon where price levels, as measured in relation to a standard basket of goods and services, are falling. Deflation tends to encourage individuals to defer consumption and will therefore result in falling output within the economy concerned.

Depreciation: the term given for the writing down of tangible fixed assets over their economic life. Depreciation requires an estimate of the life of the asset, its original cost of acquisition and installation, and its residual value. The charge for depreciation can be calculated on any number of bases: straight-line, reducing balance and sum of the year digits are three methods discussed in this book. Depreciation is not a measure of the reduction of value of the asset but is the process of matching the cost of the asset concerned to the revenues generated in a given period.

Derivative: this is a security based upon the underlying value of some other security such as a share, bond, contract of credit or foreign currency. The most common derivatives are (i) options, which give the holder the right to buy or sell the underlying security at or before a set date and at a set price; (ii) futures, which impose the obligation to buy or sell the underlying security; and (iii) swaps, which allow the parties involved to exchange obligations such as the liability to pay either variable or fixed rates of interest on loans.

Differential return on capital employed: this is the financial estimate of the impact of a given investment project upon the reported return on capital employed in the business as a whole. It is important where management regards ROCE as a primary performance measure.

Direct cost: this is a cost that can be unambiguously attributed to a given cost object and would not have been incurred if the cost object did not exist.

Directors' guarantees: a requirement laid down by banks and other lenders that the directors guarantee the sum borrowed, often through the creation of a second charge upon their home or other assets.

Discounted payback: this is payback in terms of the time taken by a capital investment to recover its initial capital outlay accounting for the cost of capital employed. In practice this means that the payback measure uses the discounted cash flows from the investment rather than the nominal cash flow.

Discounting: the process of converting a future cash sum (FV) to its present value equivalent (PV) by removing the implied return on reinvestment of that initial sum at the specified rate of interest (i) over the period of time involved (n). It is often described as the reversal of the compounding process and is achieved by application of the following formula: $PV = \dfrac{FV_n}{(1 + i)^n}$

Dividend growth model: this model expresses the value of firm's equity as a function of its future dividends assuming a constant rate of dividend growth discounted at the investor's required rate of return. The formula for the model is: $P_o = \dfrac{D_0(1 + g)}{(i - g)}$ where D_0 is the latest dividend paid, g is the assumed rate of growth of dividends and i is the minimum required rate of return.

Economic order quantity: this is the reorder batch size that minimises the overall cost of holding the stock concerned.

Efficiency P/E ratio: this is the ratio of a company's share price to its earnings per share assuming that the share is priced in an efficient capital market, and that the firm is able to earn its long-run required rate of return on internal reinvestment. The formula for the efficiency PE is: $EPE = \dfrac{1}{E(r_i)} + b$ where $E(r_i)$ is the expected rate of return required by the market and b is the reinvestment ratio of the firm's earnings.

Efficient market hypothesis: this is the hypothesis that stock market prices are an unbiased estimate of the intrinsic value of the security concerned. In practice the EMH is tested in three forms: (i) weak form which asserts that securities are fairly priced relative to past share price information and future prices are therefore random with respect to past prices, (ii) semi-strong form where shares are fairly priced relative to all publicly available information, and (iii) strong form where shares are fairly priced with respect to both public and private information. By fair pricing we mean that it is impossible to earn an excess return over and above the equilibrium rate of return given the security's risk by access to the information concerned.

Efficient market portfolio: this is the portfolio that is implied by Markowitz portfolio theory as the single vehicle for risky investment by all investors in the capital market. As it is predicted to be the only portfolio which all investors will hold, it contains therefore all risky securities that are traded in the global capital market in some proportion or other. As a perfect representation of the performance of the global capital market the efficient market portfolio is approximated by the performance of broadly based stock market indices.

Enterprise resource planning (ERP) systems: these are integrated software systems based around a data 'warehouse' which is a single database containing all of the business transactions of the firm. The database will cover the financial, production, human resource and physical resource systems of the firm and allows the generation of information reports at various degrees of refinement often based around defined 'business processes'.

Fisher–Hirshleifer separation theorem: this theorem states that under assumptions of a perfect money market the evaluation of a given investment decision can be separated from any consideration about the way that investment will be financed. A perfect money market allows the free switching of cash flows through time by permitting borrowing or lending in any amount at a single market rate of interest. In the presence of such a market all individual marginal rates of time preference will equal the market interest rate as they can satisfy their liquidity preferences by borrowing or lending against their investment opportunities. An implication of the theorem is that under a perfect money market which assumes zero risk, the net present value of an investment when discounted at the market rate of interest will equal the change in the cash wealth of the decision maker at the point the opportunity is recognised.

Fixed cost: any cost attributable to a production system that is not a variable cost.

Flexible budget: this is a production budget that is varied according to different levels of assumed output. A breakeven graph is a representation in graphical form of a flexible budget.

Goodwill: this is a term that expresses the value placed on a business over and above the value of the company as expressed by its balance sheet. If a company is acquired by another, the surplus of the price paid over its book value is termed the goodwill on consolidation.

Indirect cost: this is a cost that cannot be directly attributed to a given cost object and where some basis of allocation is chosen in order to achieve an appropriate cost matching.

Intangible assets: these are assets represented by accumulations of knowledge, reputation or trust. Intangible assets are normally only included in the balance sheet if they are externally generated, that is they have arisen by the purchase of goodwill on the acquisition of another business. The surplus of market value over the fair value or book value of the assets acquired (less liabilities) is the value of the goodwill carried to the balance sheet. Internally generated goodwill, brand values and other intangibles are not normally reported in the balance sheet.

Internal rate of return: this is the discount rate which gives a zero net present value from a series of investment cash flows. It is sometimes referred to as the 'investment yield' or the 'economic yield'.

Journal: this is one of the books of 'prime' or first entry in a double entry book system. It was originally the book in which transactions were noted for later entry into the ledger. In more recent times it has been the name given to the process of recording the closing adjustments in a set of accounts. Two specialised journals, the purchases and sales 'day' books, are commonly used for totalling the respective transactions with suppliers and customers into different classes for posting into the purchases and sales accounts in the nominal ledger.

Just-in-Time: a production management approach that is demand-led. Production to final goods is matched to a customer's demand, and intermediate stages in production are only activated as final goods are required to meet that demand. Goods are called on a continuous basis from suppliers, as they are required by production. Just-in-Time or JIT systems are characterised by very low inventory at all stages of the production sequence and demand consistently high quality to avoid reworking and the consequent buildup of work-in-progress.

Kanban: this is the Japanese term for the 'job card' which would be raised in a Just-in-Time production system and would be passed back down the production line and eventually to the supplier before starting its route back up through the production system married to the item of production concerned.

Lead time: is the term given to the difference between an order requirement being given and the goods delivered or the service discharged by the supplier.

Lean manufacturing: this is an approach to manufacturing where change costs are vigorously minimised, allowing rapid adaptation of the production system to changes in the demands placed upon it. The ultimate goal of the lean manufacturer is to achieve such high levels of adaptability that the batch size in production can be reduced to the single unit.

Ledger: a word from Middle English meaning a large book. Ledgers are heavy (often steel-backed) books of account which contain the financial transactions of a business under the double entry accounting system. More generally, individual accounts are categorised within a small number of 'ledger accounts': the 'bought ledger' which contains the accounts of suppliers, the 'sales ledger' which contains the accounts of customers, the 'nominal ledger' which contains the accounts from which the trial balance is extracted and the 'private ledger' which contains the share transactions of the owners.

Limited liability: a right granted by law to the equity investors of limited companies or the guarantors of a company limited by guarantee that protects them from the claims of creditors in the event of a winding-up. Their liability to the company's debts are limited to the extent of the nominal value of their subscribed share capital.

Linear regression: this is a statistical technique for estimating the straight-line relationship that best fits a series of data points. The technique generates a value for the intercept with the y axis (a), and the slope of the best fit line (b). If the variables being regressed are the returns on an individual share (y) against the returns on a broadly based stock market index (x), the slope coefficient (b) is a measure of the equity's beta value.

Marginal cost: this is the change in a firm's total costs caused by the decision to increase production by one unit.

Marginal rate of time preference: this is the rate of return required by an investor for delaying the consumption of £1 for one time period. The marginal rate of time preference will be a function of three partly interdependent factors: the individual's liquidity preference, the rate of inflation and risk.

Marginal revenue: this is the revenue that accrues to a firm if one extra unit is produced and sold.

Marginality rule: at maximum profit marginal revenue equals marginal cost.

Markowitz portfolio theory: this theory predicts that all investors will hold a single infinitely diversified portfolio of risky securities and will seek their optimum risk preferences by gearing their holding of this portfolio by borrowing or lending at a risk-free rate of interest. The theory assumes that investors are risk-averse, two-parameter utility-maximisers who have perfect knowledge of the expected returns and risk of all securities in the global market place, can trade free of transactions costs or taxes and have access to borrowing or lending at a risk-free rate of return.

Matching principle: this is the principle whereby revenues and expenditures are matched to a period of time, a decision alternative or a business object. The business object may be a centre of accountability such as a department, a division or a project; or it may be an individual product or service. The primary purpose of matching is to determine the surplus attributable to the period of time (profit) or to the decision or the business object concerned (contribution).

Materiality: tone of the five quality criteria set by the Accounting Standards Board for accounting information. For information to be material it must be of sufficient significance to alter the beliefs of the individual decision maker.

Materials requirement planning (MRP) systems: these are software systems that are designed to synchronise and automate the procurement of inventory from suppliers to planned production requirements.

Minority interest: this is the interest in the equity and the profits of a subsidiary company that is separately identified when the consolidated accounts of the group are prepared.

Modified internal rate of return: this is the internal rate of return of the terminal value of an investment's future cash flows reinvested at the cost of capital to the end of the project's expected life.

Net present value: this is the surplus value offered by an investment opportunity when the required capital investment is deducted from the present value of its future cash flows, discounted at the firm's opportunity cost of capital.

Nominal rate of return: the nominal rate of return is that required to reward the investor for the loss of their original investment brought about by changing price levels. It is informally the rate of return accounting for the impact of inflation.

Nominal value: this is the original value placed on a share or other financial security. It is sometimes referred to as the par value. In the case of shares nominal values of 25p,

50p and £1 are the most usual values at which the shares are carried in the ordinary share capital account within the balance sheet. The nominal value on a share defines the maximum liability the holder faces in the event of their company being wound up. In the case of fixed-interest bonds the nominal value is the amount that is repaid to the holder on redemption.

Non-current liabilities: these are non-ownership financial claims that have a duration of longer than one year.

Operating cash flow: this is the cash flow analogue of accounting profit except that all cash receipts and payments are recorded without the application of the matching principle.

Operating cycle: this is the cycle from initial order of materials or service from supplier to the receipt of final payment from the end customer. It thus encompasses the full cycle of procurement, production, delivery and settlement of debt.

Operating profit: this is the profit from the day-to-day operations of the business. It excludes exceptional items, interest paid and received, and taxation.

Opportunity cost: is the decrement in wealth to a decision maker as a result of the decision to adopt one course of action rather than the next best alternative. For an opportunity cost to arise, the decision choice must entail the consumption of scarce resources. Under the conventional interpretation, all resources have scarcity value and normally that scarcity value will be equal to their market price. Where there is no market available then the opportunity cost will be the economic value of the resource to the decision maker in its next best alternative use.

Overtrading: this is the phenomenon where a firm expands its order book at a rate faster than its access to working capital will sustain. The normal symptoms are increasing debtor balances, low cash exhaustion ratio and the withholding of payments to suppliers. If short-term finance is unavailable then overtrading, if sustained, will lead to a catastrophic failure of liquidity and the firm becoming insolvent.

Payback: this is a measure of the period that is required for an investment to return the initial capital outlay. It is a primary measure of the liquidity option attributable to a given capital investment in that it measures the ability of the project to return its capital finance and hence reopen the possibility of reinvestment in situations where access to further funds in the capital market carries substantial cost.

Prepayment: this is expenditure incurred in a given period but which is properly matched against the activities of later accounting periods. This prepaid expenditure will be shown as an outstanding balance within debtors in the balance sheet.

Profitability index: this is the net present value of a project per pound of initial investment. This ratio is useful for ranking projects where there is a limitation on the availability of capital in the short run. The value of this index for the marginal project represents the maximum the firm should be prepared to pay over and above its current cost of capital to relieve a short-term capital shortage.

Provision: this is an accounting claim created by an appropriation from profit against a future liability that is reasonably certain to arise. A common example is a provision created to cover the tax charge calculated against accounting profit and shown in the income statement and that which will actually arise given the current tax legislation.

Rationality principle: this is the principle that individuals act rationally in their own self-interest. To be rational implies that the individual can order the choices with which they are presented according to their preferences in a consistent and non-contradictory way. If I say that I prefer Heineken to Stella to Budweiser it would be inconsistent to say that I also prefer Budweiser to Heineken.

Real option: a real option is the relative advantage that arises if a given investment opportunity allows the firm to delay, accelerate or otherwise alter its future financial commitments. An investment which offers more future flexibility has greater value than one which whilst having the same expected net present value does not offer the same degree of choice.

Real rate of return: this is the rate of return required by the investor discounting the effect of future inflation. Informally, it is the rate of return ignoring the effect of future price changes.

Relevance: this is the idea that accounting information, to be useful, must be relevant to the decision-making needs of the user concerned.

Relevant cost: the net change in the cash wealth of the individual or firm that can be uniquely attributed to the decision to adopt a given course of action to procure or redeploy a resource. The net cash change is always assessed relative to the next best alternative available to the decision maker. Decision-relevant cost is the financial interpretation of the opportunity cost concept.

Relevant range: this is the practical range of output over which the firm can produce and where revenues and costs can be estimated.

Reliability: this is the idea that accounting information should be reliable, that is the user should have confidence that the information has been prepared in accordance with the underlying financial reality of the business concerned using principles and policies the significance of which he or she understands

Reorder level: this is the point of stock depletion at which an order for replenishment should be placed in order to ensure delivery on or before going out of stock.

Share premium: the surplus that investors, subscribing to a new issue of shares, are required to subscribe over and above their stated nominal value. For example, shares with a nominal value of 25p per share, offered to the market at 220p, would carry a share premium of 195p per share. This surplus is credited to the share premium account in the balance sheet and is not generally available for distribution at a later stage.

Stakeholder: a broadly defined term for anyone who has an interest in the activities or performance of a business. The term is normally used in the context of 'stakeholder groups' such as shareholders, managers, lenders, suppliers, creditors, employees and government. Stakeholder value maximisation is often defined as an objective whereby the firm seeks to maximise the value of all stakeholders that have a claim upon the performance of the business and will include employees and government.

Standard costing: a costing system where resource costs are estimated according to known production relationships and yields.

Standard deviation: this is a standard statistical measure of the spread of a distribution. In essence it is the measure of the average deviation of a variable from its mean. However, to avoid the problem that deviations from the mean are both positive and negative, the average of the squared values of the deviations are taken to give what is termed the 'variance' and the square root of the result obtained to give the 'standard deviation'. The formula for the standard deviation of a population is given by:

$$\sigma = \sqrt{\frac{\sum_{i=1}^{i=n}(x_i - \bar{x})^2}{n}}$$

. So for the five values ($n = 5$): 8, 6, 9, 5, 7, the average ($\bar{x}$) equals 7 and the deviations: +1, −1, +2, −2, 0. The summation sign (Σ) means that the squared deviations are added and divided by the number of variables counted to give the average. The squared deviations are therefore: 1, 1, 4, 4, 0 and their average is 2. The square root of the result is taken to give the standard deviation of 1.414. Showing this calculation as mathematical expressions gives:

$$\sigma = \sqrt{\frac{(8-7)^2 + (6-7)^2 + (9-7)^2 + (5-7)^2 + (7-7)^2}{5}}$$

For a normal distribution, the standard deviation encloses 68 per cent of the distribution. This statistic is important in measuring the variability of financial values and is a primary indicator of the riskiness of the variable concerned.

Subsidiary company: this is a company which is controlled by another (the parent) through a shareholding of greater than 50 per cent of the equity. There are conditions under which control may be effective even though 50 per cent is not owned by the parent. In this case there is still a requirement for the accounts of the subsidiary to be consolidated.

Tangible assets: these are physical assets that have a real and verifiable existence. Tangible or 'real' assets include fixed assets such as land, buildings, equipment, vehicles and industrial plant.

Terminal value: The future value of a fund created by the periodic investment of a constant cash sum. Each of the cash sums is reinvested in each subsequent period at a specified rate of interest until the fund comes to maturity. The formula for the terminal value of such a fund at the end of n years at a rate of interest (i) is given by:

$$\overline{S}|_n^i = \frac{(+i)^{n+1} - (1+i)}{i}.$$

Traditional overhead costing methods: this system assumes that indirect costs are allocated to products or processes in proportion to the consumption of some specified resource. The chosen overhead 'cost driver' may be the amount of labour used, machine time employed or space utilised.

Transaction costs: these are the 'side costs' of engaging in either market-based or firm-based transactions. In a market setting, transaction costs include the search costs of finding the right product at the right price, specifying and drawing up the purchase contract and the costs of ensuring completion by the other party. In a firm-based setting the transaction costs will be the managerial overheads associated with ensuring that the job is done effectively, to the standard required and on time.

Transaction cost economics: this is the branch of economics that is concerned with identifying the relative advantage of undertaking certain transactions in an open market versus a firm-based setting. Transactions that are frequent, of uncertain outcome or require highly specialised skills or other assets are usually best 'brought in-house' and conducted within the firm rather than bought in from outside.

Treasury management: this is the branch of financial management concerned with the management of the cash resources of a business. Treasury management involves the active management of funds on deposit as well as the optimal financing of the firm's trade through the use of bills of exchange, letters of credit and similar.

True and fair view: the term used in the auditor's report to describe a set of accounts that truthfully reflect the underlying financial transactions undertaken by the business and fairly reflect the application of generally accepted accounting principles.

Understandability: this is the principle that accounting reports, to be useful, must be understandable to the reasonably knowledgeable user. The test of reasonableness is important in determining the degree of technical sophistication with which financial information should be provided.

Variable cost: this is a cost that directly varies with the level of output of the product or service concerned. Variable costs are therefore direct costs where the cost object is the output of the product or service concerned.

Variance analysis: a systematic process for the separation of differences between actual and budgeted costs into price and volume effects. Volume variances, on the assumption that there is a linear relationship between cost and output, can be separated into an activity variance and an efficiency variance.

Work-in-progress: this is the name given to partly finished goods or an incomplete provision of a service at the balance sheet date.

Working capital: this is a business's net investment in current assets which include: debtors (receivables), inventories, work-in-progress, finished goods, cash and short-term deposits and investments. From the current assets, the firm's current liabilities are deducted to obtain the working capital invested in the firm.

Yield curve (term structure of interest rates): this gives the yield expected on risk-free bonds of different terms to maturity.

Zero-based budgeting (ZBB): a budgeting strategy which assumes that the accountability centre starts with zero activity and must justify its planned levels of expenditures from the bottom up.

Bibliography

Accounting Standards Board (1999) Statement of Principles for Financial Reporting, London: ASB Publications.

Alexander, D. and Britton, A. (2001) *Financial Reporting*, London: Cengage Learning.

Archer, S. and D'Ambrosio, C.A. (1976) *The Theory of Business Finance – a Book of Readings*, New York: Macmillan.

Argenti, J. (1980) *Practical Corporate Planning*, London: Unwin.

Arnold, J. (1973) *Pricing and Output Decisions*, London: Haymarket.

Arnold, J. and Turley, S. (1995) *Accounting for Management Decisions*, Harlow: Financial Times Prentice Hall.

Arnold, J., Hope, A., Southworth, A. and Kirkham, L. (1994) *Financial Accounting*, London: Prentice Hall.

Atkinson, A.A., Kaplan, R.S., Matsumura, E.M. and Young, S.M. (2007) *Management Accounting*, Upper Saddle River, NJ: Prentice-Hall.

Atrill, P. and McLaney, E. (2002) *Financial Accounting for Non-specialists*, 3rd edn, Harlow: Financial Times Prentice Hall.

Barker, R. (2001) *Determining Value – Valuation Models and Financial Statements*, Harlow: Financial Times Prentice Hall.

Baxter, W. (1978) *Depreciation*, London: Sweet and Maxwell.

Biggs, W.W. and Perrins, R.E.G. (1908) *Spicer and Pegler's Bookkeeping and Accounts*, London: HFL Publishers.

Bodie, Z. and Merton, R.C. (2000) *Finance*, NJ: Prentice-Hall.

Capodagli, B. and Jackson, L. (1999) *The Disney Way: Harnessing the Management Secrets of Disney in Your Company*, New York: McGraw-Hill.

Carhart, M.M. (1997) On persistence in mutual fund performance, *Journal of Finance*, March: 57–82.

Cooper, R. (1994) *Citizen Watch Company Ltd: Cost Reduction for Mature Products*, Case Study 9–194–033, Boston Harvard Business School Press.

Cooper, R. (1995) *When Lean Enterprises Collide*, Boston: Harvard Business School Press.

Cronhelm, F.W. (1818) *Double Entry by Single*, London: Longmans, Green.

Damodaran, A. (2002) *Tools and Techniques for Determining the Value of any Asset*, 2nd edn, New York: Wiley.

Davies, M., Paterson, R. and Wilson, A. (2001) *Ernst and Young's UK and International GAAP*, 7th edn, London: Butterworths Tolley.

Dimson, E., Marsh, P. and Staunton, M. (2002) *The Triumph of the Optimists*, Princeton, NJ: Princeton University Press.

Drury, C. (1992) *Standard Costing*, London: Academic Press.

Drury, C. (2006) *Cost and Management Accounting: An Introduction*, London: Cengage Learning.

Edwards, J.R. (1989) *A History of Financial Accounting*, London and New York: Routledge.

Elliot, B. and Elliot, J. (2002) *Financial Accounting and Reporting*, Harlow: Financial Times Prentice Hall.

Emmanuel, C. and Otley, D. (1992) *Readings in Accounting for Management Control*, London: Chapman and Hall.

Epstein, B. (2006) *IFRS 2006 – Interpretation and Application of Financial Reporting Standards*, Chichester: Wiley.

Francis, J. and Schipper, K. (1999) Have financial statements lost their relevance?, *Journal of Accounting Research*, 37(2): 319.

Fusaro, P.C. and Miller, R.M. (2002) *What Went Wrong at Enron*, New Jersey: John Wiley and Co.

Glad, E. and Becker, H. (1996) *Activity Based Costing and Management*, Chichester: Wiley.

Gupta, U. (2000) *Done Deals: Venture Capitalists Tell Their Stories*, Boston: Harvard Business School Press.

Hay, M. and Peters, J. (1999) *The Venture Capital Handbook: Strategies for Successful Private Equity Investment*, Harlow: Financial Times Prentice Hall.

Hennessy, E. (2001) *Coffee House to Cyber Market: 200 Years of the London Stock Exchange*, London: Ebury Press.

Higson, A. (2002) *Corporate Financial Reporting: Theory and Practice*, London: Sage.

Horngren, C., Bhimani, A., Datar, S. and Foster, G. (2008) *Management and Cost Accounting*, Harlow: Financial Times Prentice Hall.

Howells, P. and Bain, K. (2000) *Financial Markets and Institutions*, Harlow: Financial Times Prentice Hall.

Howells, S., Stark, A., Newton, D., Paxson, D., Cavus, M. and Pereira, J. (2001) *Real Options: Evaluating Corporate Investment Opportunities in a Dynamic World*, Harlow: Financial Times Prentice Hall.

Jensen, M.C. (1968) The performance of mutual funds in the period 1945–1964, *Journal of Finance*, 23(2): 389–416.

John, B. and Healas, S. (2000) Financial Reporting Standard for smaller entities – a fundamental or cosmetic change,

ACCA Occasional Research Paper No 30, Certified Accountants Educational Trust, London.

Johnson, H.T. and Kaplan, R.S. (1987) *Relevance Lost – the Rise and Fall of Management Accounting*, Boston: Harvard Business School Press.

Kettell, B. (2001) *Financial Economics*, Harlow: Financial Times Prentice Hall.

Kidd, P.T. (1994) *Agile Manufacturing – Forging New Frontiers*, Reading, MA: Addison-Wesley.

KPMG (1998) *The Companies Act 1985 and 1989*, London: Accounting Books.

Malkiel, B.G. (2003) *A Random Walk Down Wall Street*, New York: W.W. Norton.

Micklethwaite, J. and Woolridge, A. (2003) *The Company: A Short History of a Revolutionary Idea*, New York: Random House.

Modigliani, F. and Miller, M. (1958) The cost of capital, corporation finance and the theory of investment, *American Economic Review*, XLVIII, No. 3.

O'Brien, P. (1988) Analysts' forecasts as earnings expectations, *Journal of Accounting and Economics*, 10: 53–83.

Olson, D.L. (2003) *Managerial Issues of Enterprise Resource Planning Systems*, New York: McGraw-Hill Education.

Parker, R.H. (1999) *Understanding Company Financial Statements*, London: Penguin.

Penman, S. (2000) *Financial Statement Analysis and Security Valuation*, Singapore: McGraw-Hill.

Pike, R. and Neale, B. (2002) *Corporate Finance and Investment: Decisions and Strategies*, Harlow: Financial Times Prentice Hall.

Porter, M.E. (1998) *Competitive Strategy: Techniques for Analyzing Industries and Competitors*, New York: Simon & Schuster.

Pratt, J.W. and Zeckhauser, R.J. (1991) Principals and Agents: the structure of Business, Boston MA: Harvard Business School Press.

Reuters Financial Training Series (1999) *An Introduction to Bond Markets*, Chichester: Wiley.

Reuters Financial Training Series (1999) *An Introduction to Equity Markets*, Chichester: Wiley.

Reuters Financial Training Series (1999) *An Introduction to Foreign Exchange and the Money Markets*, Chichester: Wiley.

Rice, A. (2002) *Accounts Demystified: How to Understand Financial Accounting and Analysis*, London: Prentice Hall.

Rubinstein, M. (2000) Rational markets: yes or no? The affirmative case, Research Program in Finance, Working Paper RPF-294, Haas School of Business, University of California, Berkeley and available at www.haas.berkeley.edu/finance/WP/rpf294.pdf

Ryan, B. (2006) Corporate *Finance and Valuation*. London: Cengage.

Ryan, B. (1995) *Strategic Accounting for Management*, London: Cengage.

Ryan, B., Scapens, B., Theobald, M. and Beattie, V. (2002) *Research Method and Methodology in Finance and Accounting*, London: Cengage Learning.

Schilt, H. (2002) *Financial Shenanigans: How to Detect Accounting Gimmicks and Fraud in Financial Reports*. New York: McGraw-Hill Education.

Smith, T. (1996) *Accounting for Growth, Stripping the Camouflage from Company Accounts*, London: Random House Business Books.

Stewart, T.A. (2001) *The Wealth of Knowledge*, London: Nicholas Brearley.

Stutley, R. (2002) *The Definitive Business Plan*, Harlow: Financial Times Prentice Hall.

Underdown, B. and Taylor, P. (1985) *Accounting Theory and Policy Making*, Oxford: Butterworth-Heinemann.

Vaitilingam, R. (2001) *The Financial Times Guide to Using the Financial Pages,* Harlow: Financial Times Prentice Hall.

Walsh, C. (1996) *Key Management Ratios*, London: Financial Times Prentice Hall.

Zimmerman, J. (1979) The costs and benefits of cost allocation, *The Accounting Review*, 54.

Index

ABC *see* activity based costing
absorption costing 334
account analysis
    objectives 177–8
    questions 184
    strategic 181–4
    strategic pre-evaluation 178–81
    value driver 178
accountability centres 241–2, 530
accountability, cost allocation 328
accountants versus economists 341–4
accounting information
    analysis 174–212
    characteristics 19–23
    nature of 20–3
    purpose 19–23
accounting rate of return 423–4, 530
accounting ratios 188–9
accounting, second and subsequent
    years 61–6
accounting/finance
    context 4–9
    control 5–6
    information 6
    origins 7–9
    planning 6
    roles 4–6
    stewardship 5
accounts, limited company 153–4
accruals 104–8, 126
accrued expenditure 107–8, 530
accrued revenue 107, 530
acid test ratio 206–7
acquisitions 154–67
    cash 157–8
    exchange of equity 158–60
    less than 100 per cent of the
        equity 161–2
activity variance 314–16
activity-based costing (ABC) 346–8, 530
additivity principle 48–9
agency theory 18, 530
Alternative Investment Market
    (AIM) 168
amortisation 107, 530
annuities, investment appraisal
    398–9, 530
appraisal
    assumptions of capability 302
    assumptions of fact 303
    assumptions of state 302
    business planning 301–3
    see also investment appraisal

arbitrage 530
arbitrage conditions
    equivalence between spot rate and
        forward rate 441–2
    financial markets 439–42
    Fisher effect 440
    interest rate parity 440
    international Fisher effect 441
    purchasing power parity 439–40
arbitrageurs 437
asset valuation 127–9
assets
    classification 34–7
    cost of 110
    current 35–7
    definition 34–5
    non-current 35
associated company 154, 530
auditor 141, 530
    role 144–5
authorised share capital 149, 530
AVCO *see* average cost
average cost (AVCO) 121–2

balance sheet
    consolidated 163–5
    constructing 56–9
    creating 43–7
    horizontal format (traditional) 56–7
    limited company 143
    preparation 40–3
    vertical format (UK/IFRS) 57, 58
    vertical format (US) 57–9
    working capital 362–3
Baumol model 384, 530
Beaver failure ratio 204–6
beta 457, 459, 530
bills, capital market 436, 445, 530
bonds, capital market 445, 530
borrowings 39
breakeven 265, 268–9, 530
breakeven analysis *see* cost/volume/
    profit analysis
brokers 10
budget time horizon 303–4
budgetary slack 310, 531
budgeting
    conflict resolution 310
    flexible 267–8
    and forecasting 308
    incremental 311
    management by exception 311–13
    methodologies 311–16

    motivation 308–9
    organisational control 308
    organisational structure 309
    planned 311
    and planning 305–7
    revenue variances 312–16
    role 304–5
    slack 310
    zero-based 311
buffer stock 367, 531
business model 284–5
business objectives 17–18
business organization
    directors of limited companies 15–16
    firm size 11–12
    legal form 13–15
    shareholders 16
    types 9–11
business planning 281–316
    appraisal 301–3
    budgeting 305–7
    business model 284–5
    calculate total cash flow position
        291–5
    cash flow forecast 286–95
    combine revenue/expenditure
        models 291–5
    continuing business 303–10
    expenditure model 285, 291
    finance model 285
    financial statements projection
        295–301
    horizon 304
    lending decision 284
    in practice 286–310
    product/project description 284
    revenue model 284–5, 289–91
    structure 282–5
business start-up, case study 55–60, 70–3
buy-back arrangements 482
bygones principle 243, 531

capital asset pricing model (CAPM)
    455–60, 531
    beta value 459
    equity risk premium 456–8, 460
    estimating inputs 458–60
    firm-specific (unsystematic) risk 455
    market (systematic) risk 455
    risk-free rate of return 456, 458
    uses for 460
capital, cost of 461–6
capital maintenance 129–31

capital markets 436
  anomalies 449–50
  bills 445
  bonds 445
  capital asset pricing model 453–60
  debt capital 445–6
  efficient market hypothesis 447–50
  equity capital 444–5
  government debt 446–7
  origins 442
  portfolio theory 452–5
  primary 167
  primary market 442–4
  return and risk 451–2
  secondary 167
  secondary market 442–4
CAPM *see* capital asset pricing model
CAR *see* current asset ratio
case study, business start-up 55–60, 70–3
cash 36–7
  acquisitions 157–8
cash difference principle 244
cash exhaustion ratio 207
cash flow
  business planning calculation 291–5
  constructing statement of 59–60
  limited company 143
  matching over time 394–400
  measurement of 82–4
  reconciling 91–2
cash flow statements 82–95
  preparing 84–92
cash management 381–2
  financial markets 383
  holding of cash 383–5
certainty, cost/volume/profit analysis 269
change costs 326
claims, classification 37–43
classification
  assets 34–7
  claims 37–43
closing accounts 74–6
Combined Code of Practice 146–7
comparability, accounting information
  22, 531
compounding, investment appraisal
  394–5, 531
conflict resolution, budgeting 310
consistency concept 126
consolidated accounts
  balance sheet 163–5
  group companies 162–7
  income statement 165–7
consolidation 154, 531
contribution 238–41, 531
contribution margin 238–41, 531
control
  accounting/finance 5–6
  costs 326
  and ownership 18
Conversion gilts 446

corporate governance 146–7
corporation tax 39–40, 411–12
correlation coefficient 262, 531
cost
  directly traceable 346
  indirectly traceable 346
  untraceable 346
cost allocation
  accountability 328
  activity-based costing 346–8
  cost driver analysis 334–41
  decision making 329
  economists versus accountants 341–4
  estimating full cost 328
  model 329–30
  more than one cost object 335–41
  overhead method 344–6
  pricing 328
  purpose 328–9
  rationing 329
  single-product/service business 330–4
cost of asset 110
cost behaviour 254–70
cost of capital 397, 461–6, 531
  estimating 464–5
  gearing 465–6
  required rate of return on debt 461–3
  weighted average cost of capital
    465–6
cost centres 241–2, 530
cost driver analysis
  cost allocation 334–41
  criteria 335
cost efficiency ratio 195–6
cost gearing 203–4
cost of goods sold 122
cost hierarchy 238, 531
cost impact 324–8
cost management 324–48
cost object 236, 239, 336, 531
cost pools 337
cost of sales 122
cost variation 255–8
  estimating 258–63
cost-plus pricing 351–3
cost-relevance trade-off, accounting
  information 23
cost/volume/profit analysis 265–70
  certainty 269
  creating flexible budget 267–8
  formal analysis of breakeven point
    268–9
  multiple products 269
  non-linear cost 269–70
  problems 269–70
  relevant range 265
  revenue functions 269–70
  stepped costs 269
costing
  methodology 336
  principles 236–42

creative accounting 125, 531
credit policy 373–81, 531
  credit risk 373–4
  debtor age 374–6
  factoring debts 379
  late payment 376–8
  overtrading 379–81
  receivables management 379–81
  risk assessment 373–4
  setting 374
credit rating 446, 531
credit risk 373–4, 531
creditors *see* payables
credits and debits, double entry
  bookkeeping 66–8
cross-sectional analysis 209–10
current asset ratio (CAR) 206–7
current assets 35–7
current liabilities 39, 531
curvilinear costs 258

debits and credits, double entry
  bookkeeping 66–8
debt capital, capital markets 445–6
debt factoring 379–81, 531
debt investors, required rate of
  return on 461–3
debt recovery 377
debtor age 374–6
  benefits of reducing 374–6
debtors *see* receivables
decision making
  cost allocation 329
  identify choices available 246–7
  lending 284
  make-or-buy 254
  relevant costing 242–54
decision-oriented approach 17–18, 19–20
deferred revenue 107, 532
deflation 382, 532
Dell 370
depreciable amount 110
depreciation 108–19, 532
  cost of asset 110
  definition 108–9
  economic life 109
  methods 110–16
  non-current assets 116–18
  reducing-balance 112–14
  residual value 110
  straight-line 111
  sum of the year digits 114–16
derivatives 40, 383, 435, 532
DGM *see* dividend growth model
difference analysis 185–6
differential return on capital employed
  (ΔROCE) 424–6, 532
direct cost 237–8, 532
direct cost variances 313–14
direct share ownership, capital
  markets 445

directors
  duties 142–6
  freedom of action 168
  public limited company 168
  roles 15–16
directors' guarantees 532
directors' report 143
discontinued business 190
discounted payback 426, 532
discounting, investment appraisal 396, 532
discounts, late payment 378
Disney Corporation, project planning 404
dividend growth model (DGM) 478–81,
      479, 532
  endogenous estimation 478–80
  exogenous estimation 480–1
  market valuation 481–2
  problems 482–3
dividend payout ratio, investor ratio 473
dividend per share, investor ratio 472
dividend valuation model (DVM) 478
dividend yield, investor ratio 472–3
dividends, showing as deduction from
      retained earnings 64–5
double-entry bookkeeping 66–76
  books of prime entry 68–9
  business start-up 70–3
  closing the accounts 74–6
  debits and credits 66–8
  foolproof 76
  ledgers 69
  striking a balance 73–4
DVM see dividend valuation model

earnings before interest, tax,
      depreciation and amortisation
      (EBITDA) 82–3, 91
earnings per share (EPS), investor ratio 474
easyJet
  authorised share capital 149
  Markowitz portfolio theory 453
  NPV 437
EBITDA see earnings before interest, tax,
      depreciation and amortisation
economic context analysis 179–81
economic life 109
economic order quantity (EOQ)
      365–6, 532
economic value-added (EVAR[]) 483–4
economists versus accountants 341–4
efficiency (conversion) ratio 196
efficiency, financial ratios 195–7
efficiency P/E ratio 532
efficiency variance 314–16
efficiency (working capital) ratios 198–201
efficient market hypothesis 447–50, 532
  behavioural approach 450
  bubbles and crashes 449–50
  January effect 449
  luck 450
  pricing 448–9

efficient market portfolio 454, 532
endogenous growth estimation, valuing
      firms 478–80
Enron 147
enterprise resource planning, inventory
      management 372–3, 532
EOQ see economic order quantity
EPS see earnings per share
equity by proxy, capital markets 445
equity capital, capital markets 444–5
equity, exchange of 158–62
equity risk premium (ERP) 456–8, 460
equivalent rates of return, investment
      appraisal 400
ERP see equity risk premium
exchange rates 181
  determining 438–42
  forward market 439
  inflation 439
  interest rates 439
  spot market 439
Exchequer gilts 446
executive summary, business planning 282
exogenous growth estimation, valuing
      firms 480–1
expenditure model 285, 291
  combine with revenue model 291–5
expenditures
  accruals 107–8
  prepayments 107–8
extended trial balance (ETB) 47–8
  closing 50
  using 49–50
extractive enterprise 10

factoring debts 379
finance, raising 149
financial accounting
  cf. management accounting 25–6
  principles 34–43, 48–9, 102–31, 126–31
financial analysis 184–212
  difference analysis 185–6
  margin analysis 186–8
  ratios 188–212
  reading accounts and notes 184–5
financial information analysis 175–210
financial markets
  capital markets 442–60
  cash management 383
  cost of capital 461–6
  exchange rates 438–42
  money 438
  nature of 435–66
  origins 6–7, 435–6
  role 6–7
  securities 435
  traders 436–8
financial objectives 17–18
financial ratios 188–212
  accounting 188–9
  Beaver failure 204–6

cash exhaustion 207
current asset 206–7
efficiency 195–7
gearing 202–4
interest cover 203
investment 189
labour asset turnover 197–202
labour productivity 197–202
limitations 210–12
operating cash flow to maturing
      obligations 208–9
performance 190–5
PERL framework 190
significance of 209–10
financial statements 44–7
business planning projection 295–301
financing model 285
firm-specific (unsystematic) risk
      201–2, 455
firms
  legal forms 13–15
  performance measurement 483–4
  size 11–12
  valuing 478–83
  see also business organization
first-in first-out (FIFO) 121
Fisher effect, exchange rates 440
Fisher-Hirshleifer separation
      theorem 532–3
fixed asset turnover (FAT) ratio 196–7
fixed assets see non-current assets
fixed cost 258, 533
flexible budget 267–8, 533
forecasting
  budgeting 308
  cash flow 286–95
  cash forecasting 281–316
foreign exchange (FOREX) market 383,
      438, 441
forward market, financial exchange
      rates 439
forward rate, equivalence with spot
      rate 441–2
fraud 211–12
free cash flow to equity (FCFE) 82
full cost, estimating 328
full-cost pricing
  boom 353
  recession 353
fund managers 168
  capital markets 449
fundamental investors 436

gearing 465–6
gearing ratio 202–3
gilts, government securities 446–7
going concern 126
goodness of fit, measuring 262–3
goodwill 157, 533
governance, corporate 146–7
government debt 446–7

group companies
    acquisitions and mergers 154–67
    consolidated accounts 162–7
growth of firms, measuring 478–83

history
    accounting/finance 7–9
    capital markets 442
    financial markets 435–6
horizontal cost vector 325
hostile takeovers 168

identity principle 34
income 24–5
income statement
    charging for tax 64
    consolidated 165–7
    constructing 59
    creating 43–7
    limited company 143
incorporation 149
incremental budgeting 311
independent claims 39–40
indirect cost 238, 533
indirect share ownership, capital
        markets 445
inflation 382
    financial exchange rates 439
    investment appraisal 398
    net present value (NPV) 408–10
information
    accounting/finance 6
    see also accounting information;
        financial information
intangible assets 10, 533
interest cover 203
interest gearing 203
interest rate parity, exchange rates 440
interest rates 180
    financial exchange rates 439
internal rate of return 418–23, 461–2, 533
    linear interpolation 419–21
    modified 422–3
    problems 421–2
    spreadsheet 421
international Fisher effect 441
inventories 36
    accounting for 119–26
    buffer 367, 531
    valuation 123–6, 334
inventory management 364–73
    stock levels 364–9
investment appraisal 394–426
    accounting rate of return 423–4
    compounding 394–5
    differential return on capital
        employed 424–6
    discounted payback 426
    discounting 396
    internal rate of return 418–23

matching cash flows 394–400
    net present value 400–17
    other methods 418–26
    payback 426
    time value of money 397–9
    see also appraisal
investment ratios 189
investor ratios 472–5
    dividend payout ratio 473
    dividend per share 472
    dividend yield 472–3
    earnings per share 474
    market to book ratio 475
    price earnings (P/E) ratio 474–5
    retention ratio 473–4
investors, financial markets 436
invisible hand 324

Japanese approach
    JIT 369–72
    lean manufacturing 327–8, 371–2
    risk of deflation 382–3
journal 68–9, 533
just-in-time (JIT) 369–72, 533

kanban 369–70, 533
Kaplan, Robert 370–1

labour asset turnover 197–202
labour, opportunity cost 252–3
labour productivity 197–202
large firm 12
last-in first-out (LIFO) 121
late payment
    credit policy 376–8
    discounts 378
    persuasion 377
laundering accounts 92–5
lead time 384, 533
lean manufacturing 327–8, 371–2, 533
ledger 69, 533
legal forms of firms 13–15
legal framework, limited companies 141
lending decision 284
limitations of financial ratios 210–12
    fraudulent manipulation 211–12
    price changes 212
    timing problems 210–11
    underlying accounting principles 210
    window dressing 211–12
limited companies 140–54
    accounts 153–4
    characteristics 140–7
    corporate governance 146–7
    creation of 147–54
    directors 142–6
    legal framework 141
    provisions 153
    reserves 152–3
    shareholders 148

shares 148–9
    starting up 149–51
limited liability 9, 533
limited-liability companies 13–14
limited-liability partnerships 14–15
linear regression 419–21, 533
liquidity measurement 206
liquidity preference, investment
        appraisal 397–8
logistic costs 326
London Stock Exchange 167–8
London Stock market 442–3

make-or-buy decisions 254
management accounting, cf. financial
        accounting 25–6
management by exception 311–13
managerial issues, net present value
        (NPV) 415–17
manufacturing enterprise 10
margin analysis 186–8
margin ratio 190–1
marginal analysis 270–3
marginal cost 533
marginal rate of time preference 533–4
marginal revenue 270, 534
marginality rule 271, 534
market cost vector 325
market measures
    investor ratios 472–5
    performance 491–4
    value 476–91
market (systematic) risk 201, 455
market to book ratio, investor ratio 475
market valuation 481–2
marketing pricing paradox 482
Markowitz portfolio theory 452–5, 534
Markowitz separation theorem 455
Marks & Spencer plc
    account analysis 177–8, 184
    financial analysis 184–212
    investor ratios 472–5
matching, accruals 104–8
matching cash flows, investment appraisal
        394–400
matching principle 48, 534
materiality 534
    accounting information 21
materials requirement planning (MRP)
        systems 372–3, 534
maturing obligations, operating cash flow
        to 208–9
measurement
    cash flow 82–4
    firm performance 483–4
    liquidity 206
    markets 472–94
    profit 24–5, 46–7, 105–7
    risk 201–2
medium-sized firm 12

merchant enterprise 10
mergers 154–67
micro business 11
Miller, M. 413
minority interest 157, 534
MIRR *see* modified internal rate of return
modified internal rate of return (MIRR)
    422–3, 534
Modigliani, F. 413
monetary driver, value creation 104
money
    financial markets 438
    investment appraisal 397–9
    time value of 397–9
money markets 383, 436, 438
motivation, budgeting 308–9
multi-objective/multi-driver analysis 335
multiple products, cost/volume/profit
    analysis 269

net present value (NPV) 400–17, 534
    applying 404–7
    calculating 400–2
    capital in short supply 414–15
    inflation 408–10
    investment decisions 402–4
    managerial issues 415–17
    real options 416, 417
    risk 412–14
    tax 410–12
net realisable value rule 123
nominal rate of return 534
nominal value 148, 534
non-current asset
    keeping track of 117
    pool of 118–19
    selling 116–17
non-current assets 35
non-current liabilities 39, 534
non-linear cost, cost/volume/profit
    analysis 269–70
NPV *see* net present value

off the shelf company 147
operating cash flow 60, 534
operating cash flow to maturing
    obligations 208–9
operating cycle 362, 534
    analysis 208–9
operating profit 59, 534
    reconciling with cash flow 91–2
operational gearing 203–4
opportunity cost 534
    estimating 245–53
    labour 252–3
    resources 247–53
opportunity forgone principle 243–4
ordinary shares 148–9
organisational control, budgeting 308
organisational cost vector 324–5

organisational structure, budgeting 309
overhead cost allocation 344–6
overtrading 379–81, 534
owner's equity (claim) 37–9
ownership
    and control 18
    resources 247

P/E ratio *see* price earnings (P/E) ratio
partnerships 13
payback 426, 534
perfect competition 348
performance
    financial ratios 190–5
    Marks & Spencer plc 472–5
    measuring 483–4
PERL framework 178, 190
planned budgeting 311
planning
    accounting/finance 6
    enterprise resource 372–3
    materials requirement 372–3
    see also business planning
pooling of non-current assets 118–19
Porter, Michael, cost allocation 346–8
portfolio theory
    capital markets 452–60
    CAPM 455–60
pre-evaluation 178–81
preference shares 148
prepayment 107–8, 534
price changes 212
price earnings (P/E) ratio, investor
    ratio 474–5
price levels, changing 382
pricing 348–54
    cost allocation 328
    cost-based 351–4
    cost-plus 351–3
    full-cost 353
    market-based 349–51
    rate of return 354
    shares 448–9
    target 354
prime entry books 68–9
principles
    costing 236–42
    financial accounting 34–43, 48–9,
        102–31
process cost vector 325
product/project description, business
    planning 284
profit
    measurement of 24–5, 46–7, 105–7
    operating 91–2
profit and loss account *see* income
    statement
profit reserve 152
profitability 534–5
profitability index (NPV index) 414

provision 40, 153, 535
prudence concept 127
public limited company, listing 167–9
purchasing power parity (PPP), exchange
    rates 439–40

quick asset ratio 206–7

rate of return
    debt 461–3
    internal method 461–2
    yield curve method 463
rate of return pricing 354
rationality principle 243, 535
rationing, cost allocation 329
ratios *see* financial ratios; investor ratios
real assets
    accounting for 108–26
    depreciation 108–19
    inventories 119–26
real option 416, 417, 535
real rate of return 440, 535
receivables 36
receivables management 379–81
reducing-balance depreciation 112–14
relevance, accounting information
    21–2, 535
relevant cost 250, 535
relevant range 265, 535
reliability, accounting information 22, 535
reorder level 367, 535
required rate of return on debt 461–3
reserves 152–3
residual value 110
resources
    identify 247
    opportunity costs 247–50
    ownership 247
    short supply 250–3
retained earnings, showing dividends as
    deduction from 64–5
retention ratio, investor ratio 473–4
return on equity capital employed
    (ROE) 192
return on fixed capital employed
    (ROFCE) 192–4
return and risk, capital markets 451–2
return on total assets (ROTA) 194–5
return on total capital employed
    (ROCE) 191–2
revaluation reserve 152
revenue
    accrued 107
    allocation 238
    attribution 238
    recognition 105–7
    variances 312–13
    variation 263–5
revenue functions, cost/volume/profit
    analysis 269–70

revenue model 284–5, 289–91
  combine with expenditure model
    291–5
Rf *see* risk-free rate of return
risk
  credit assessment 373–4
  financial markets 436
  firm-specific 201–2
  firm-specific (unsystematic) 455
  investment appraisal 398
  market 201
  market (systematic) 455
  measurement 201–2
  net present value (NPV) 412–14
  protection 149
risk and return, capital markets 451–2
risk-free rate of return (Rf) 456, 458
ΔROCE *see* differential return on capital
    employed
ROCE *see* return on total capital
    employed
ROE *see* return on equity capital
    employed
ROFCE *see* return on fixed capital
    employed
ROTA *see* return on total assets

sales revenue variances 313–16
SEAQ *see* Stock Exchange Automated
    Quotations System
securities 435
semi-variable cost 258
service costs 326
service enterprise 10
SETS *see* Stock Exchange Automated
    Trading Service
share premium 152, 535
share price, capital markets 448–9
shareholders
  direct share ownership 445
  equity by proxy 445
  equity rights 444–5
  indirect share ownership 445
  ordinary 148
  preference 148
  rights 16
  share premium 148
shares
  direct ownership 445
  indirect ownership 445
  ordinary 148–9
  preference 148
short-term liability *see* current liability
simple accounts, producing 49–50
single-owner-managed business 11
single-product/service business, cost
    allocation 330–4

size of firms 11–12
small-owner-managed firm 11–12
Smith, Adam 324
sole trader 11, 13
speculators 436–7
spot market, financial exchange rates 439
spot rate, equivalence with forward rate
    441–2
spreadsheet, internal rate of return 421
stakeholder 17, 535
standard analysis 209
standard costing 535
standard deviation 535
statistical cost estimation 259–62
step fixed cost 258
stepped cost, cost/volume/profit
    analysis 269
stewardship, accounting/finance 5
sticky costs 258
stock *see* inventories
Stock Exchange Automated Quotations
    System (SEAQ) 443
Stock Exchange Automated Trading
    Service (SETS) 443
stock market 167–8
straight-line depreciation 111
strategic analysis 181–4
strategic planning horizon 304
strategic summary, business planning 282–4
structural cost vector 324–5
subsequent years, accounts for 61–6
subsidiary company 154, 155, 535
sum of the year digits 114–16
SWOT analysis 181–2, 183
systematic (market) risk 455

tangible assets 535
target costing 354
target pricing 354
tax 181
  charging income statement 64
  corporation 149, 411–12
  net present value (NPV) 410–12
  VAT 410–11
technical cost analysis 258–9
terminal values, investment appraisal
    399–400, 536
time series analysis 209
time value of money 397–9
trade payables 39
traders
  financial markets 436–8
  rational expectations 448
traditional accounting, versus value-based
    accounting 131
traditional overhead costing methods 536
transaction cost economics 310, 536

transaction costs 117, 536
transactional driver, value creation 103
transformational driver, value creation 103
Treasury gilts 446
treasury management 381, 536
true and fair view 144, 536

understandability, accounting information
    22–3, 536
unsystematic (firm-specific) risk 455

valuation, stock 123–6
value adding 326
value chain 346–8
value creation 102–8
  accruals 104–8
  market driver 103
  monetary driver 104
  transactional driver 103
  transformational driver 103
value driver analysis 178
value-added tax (VAT) 410–11
value-based accounting
  financial accounting 127–31
  versus traditional accounting 131
valuing firms 478–83
  endogenous growth estimation 478–80
  exogenous growth estimation 480–1
  growth model problems 482–3
valuing markets 481–2
variable cost 258, 536
variable cost with discount 258
variable cost with scale effects 258
variance analysis 311–13, 536
  activity 314–16
  direct cost 313–14
  efficiency 314–16
  revenue 312–13
Virgin Atlantic, NPV 437
virtual firm 328

WACC *see* weighted average cost
    of capital
weighted average cost of capital (WACC)
    464–6
window dressing 211–12
work-in-progress 108, 536
working capital 360–85, 536
  balance sheet 362–3
  cash management 381–5
  credit policy 373–81
  inventory management 364–73
  role 360–2

yield curve 463, 536

zero-based budgeting (ZBB) 311, 536

FINANCE AND ACCOUNTING FOR BUSINESS

SECOND EDITION

Bob Ryan

Finance and Accounting for Business gives managers on executive or general MBA courses an overview of the role of accounting and finance in business, and is also suitable for undergraduate courses where students need an appreciation of accounting and finance. The book is illustrated with vivid cases, real-world examples and worked-through exercises, placing the theory of the subject in a practical context. It incorporates a wealth of question and exercise material using real company cases. Solutions are also provided in the text and on an extensive website full of further resources to support the text. Additional questions are also provided for tutors to use with their students, taking them through complex issues step by step.

Following the success of the first edition with both tutors and students the thoroughly revised and updated second edition includes:

→ IFRS and international accounting presentation and terminology
→ An updated version of the popular running case study of Marks & Spencer plc
→ An introduction to the language and methods of double-entry bookkeeping in Chapter 3
→ A new Chapter 4 on cash flow statements illustrating simple methods for detecting earnings manipulation in practice
→ A completely rewritten and updated Chapter 7 based on the financial analysis of Marks & Spencer plc published accounts.

Bob Ryan started his teaching career at the University of Manchester. He then established the Division of Business at the Hatfield Polytechnic (now the University of Hertfordshire), was the founding director of the Southampton University Management School and then Director of the School of Management, Royal Holloway, University of London. He has extensive consultancy experience both in the UK and internationally and currently holds the chair of financial management at the University of Gloucestershire and a visiting fellowship at the Manchester Business School. He is also examiner in Advanced Financial Management for the Association of Chartered Certified Accountants. Apart from all that, Bob Ryan has an international reputation as one of the world's most outstanding educators of business managers, students and executives. It is this quality as a teacher that informs every page of *Finance and Accounting for Business*.

Also by Bob Ryan:

Corporate Finance and Valuation 184480271X

Research Method and Methodology in Finance and Accounting
(with Robert Scapens, Mike Theobald and Vivien Beattie) 1861528817

Visit the Finance and Accounting for Business companion website at:
www.cengage.co.uk/ryan2

SOUTH-WESTERN
CENGAGE Learning™

For your lifelong learning solutions, visit **www.cengage.co.uk**
Purchase e-books or e-chapters at **http://estore.bized.co.uk**

ISBN 978184480897-7

9 781844 808977